THE
GREAT BOOK
OF WINE

This entirely revised edition of
THE GREAT BOOK OF WINE
has been updated throughout and much enlarged,
incorporating over 240 new illustrations

WITH CONTRIBUTIONS BY

Leon D. Adams
Pierre Andrieu
Jean Arnaboldi
Helmut Arntz
Jean Bertin-Roulleau
Géo-H. Blanc
Denis Bouvier
Philippe Cherix
Raymond Cogniat
Giovanni Dalmasso
Gérard Debuigne
Joseph Dreyer
Pierre Forgeot

Alexandre Fresneau
Bernard Grenouilleau
Serguei Kasko
Gaston Marchou
Kenneth Maxwell
Flavien Monod
Boris Pogrmilovic
Suzanne Chantal Dos Santos
John Stanford
Walter Tobler
Eladio Asensio Villa
Jean Vogel

EDITED BY JOSEPH JOBÉ

THE GREAT BOOK OF WINE

REVISED AND ENLARGED EDITION INCLUDING
OVER 240 NEW ILLUSTRATIONS

CHARTWELL
BOOKS, INC.

CONTENTS

THE WAYS OF WINE AND MAN

FOREWORD

The fact that millions of human beings have from earliest times regarded wine as a noble drink is due to an unusual sequence of events. When a comparison is made with other crafts and customs that have not survived the rough passage of history, the story of wine is remarkable. Without such a fortuitous succession of events, neither vine nor wine would ever have become so widely and so highly esteemed throughout the world.

In the beginning, the only grape capable of producing a pleasant-tasting drink grew wild all over the Middle Eastern countries. It was precisely here that men first began to cultivate the soil, select plants, and live in organized communities. Had the vine been just an ordinary plant, it would probably have shared the same fate as the Middle Eastern and Egyptian civilizations. It was the wine that saved the vine. This subtle beverage was found to possess extraordinary virtues; the intoxication it produced was attributed to divine powers. Consequently, the vine was held to be a gift from the heavens and wine a drink associated with the worship of the gods and the celebration of those favourites of the gods: heroes, poets and artists. Men offered wine in homage to the deities; in their turn, through wine, the gods endowed men with strength, inspiration and a liberating sense of well-being. Wine was at that time as much appreciated as it was rare.

Carried on the tide of the expansion of the Roman Empire, the vine spread and flourished far beyond the boundaries of its native land. Leather bottles, amphoras and butts, all filled with wine, found their way back to Rome from the heart of Gaul, Germania, Africa and the Iberian Peninsula. This wide-flung empire finally crumbled before the onslaught of the Barbarians, who knew nothing of wine, but the art of viniculture had been already handed on and the succeeding chapter in wine's history ensured not only its survival but its spectacular revival. Indeed, since the evening when Jesus Christ shared the bread and wine of the Lord's Supper with his disciples, wine has been an indispensable part in the cult of the new religion which was destined to spread throughout the world. Wherever Christianity was adopted, men endeavoured to cultivate vines and, either by indigenous production or importation, to obtain wine. Monks, bishops and missionaries promoted and encouraged viticulture. Nor were the nobility by any means indifferent to the prestige of a drink so closely associated with holy rites and one, moreover, that promoted gaiety and enthusiasm. Wine became their chosen drink for ceremonial occasions and victory celebrations.

Through the centuries, wine became more popular, and more democratic too. Industrial revolutions, social changes, the gradual breakdown of class barriers and the increasing economic power of the bourgeoisie were all responsible for this development. The luxury of a private cellar was no longer the prerogative of lords, spiritual or temporal. Improvements in vine cultivation and vinification methods helped further this new turn of events.

This new edition of *The Great Book of Wine* has been enlarged and updated. The chapters on Italian and German wines have been recast to conform with the new wine laws of those countries, and the chapters on America and Australia and New Zealand have been entirely rewritten in view of the vast increase in winegrowing since the appearance of the first edition. Finally, all production figures have been brought up to date on the basis of the latest figures available for 1982.

What is the best way to cultivate a palate for wine? How and when should different wines be served? What are the finer points of wine? The answers to these and many other questions will be found in this book which provides a comprehensive range of information to put you at your ease whenever conversation turns to vine and wine. And never forget that you do not really taste a wine unless you look at it, nose it and talk about it.

Joseph Jobé

The names of wines are printed in SMALL CAPITALS and the names of wines in *italics*. British weights and measure are used throughout except in the chapter on North American wines. The publishers have selected the illustrations in this book without being influenced in any way by commercial considerations. The same holds true for the some 6,500 wines in the lists.

WINE
AND CIVILISATION

HISTORICAL OUTLINE

"And Noah began to be an husbandman, and he planted a vineyard: and he drank of the wine, and was drunken." This is the first biblical mention of that illustrious plant to which Old and New Testaments continually allude in countless allegories, parables, symbolic references and stories.

The history of the vine in actual fact, however, goes back much farther. From the very earliest times, it has figured strongly in Eastern mythology and particularly with the legend of Dionysus which spread from Asia to Egypt, through Thrace and the Mediterranean lands.

The worship of Dionysus, or Bacchus, by his initiates went far beyond mere veneration for the creator and patron of the vine. In the earliest Orphic concept, Dionysus was considered a supreme deity. Soon, however, his character was defined more sharply: the cult of Dionysus developed into the celebration of vine and wine. In Athens, it furnished occasions for large-scale festivities, called the Dionysia, with processions, carousing and plays. In Rome, one day every year was dedicated to Bacchus. As for the Bacchanalia, in which more limited numbers indulged, they probably originated in Egypt. Thence they spread to Greece and finally to Rome where they degenerated into outrageous displays of debauchery and disorder. The public authorities finally banned the Bacchanalia, not without stormy arguments, in 186 B.C.

Thus wine, quite literally, had its own god. As a result, it enjoyed an almost sacred reputation, was featured in many religious ceremonies and other rituals even before the dawn of Christianity, and continued to play a prominent part in biblical writings. It is hardly surpris-

ing, therefore, that wine has inspired a wealth of pictorial representation, a symbolism of real documentary value. An Assyrian bas-relief shows two figures drinking against a setting of vine branches and grapes, while an Egyptian tomb decoration accurately depicts the order of viticultural tasks, the grape harvest and the cellar work in the presence of the scribe responsible for keeping the books. Writing tablets uncovered in Carthage, Tunis and Morocco supply us with similar information, and innumerable other relics and traces, whether buried underground or on the sea bed, are constantly coming to light. All these discoveries swell the already great volume of records with which museums, palaces, ancient temples, cathedrals, monasteries and castles are so plentifully stocked, so that archaeological remains alone could provide virtually all the information necessary to trace the history of wine cultivation back to remotest antiquity.

Wine occupies a regal place in the literature of every age. Centuries before Christ, Homer refers to the most famous vineyards in ancient Greece. He gives details concerning cellaring and drinking customs. Innumerable poets throughout the centuries have drawn on wine for their inspiration and some of them, notably Virgil, have made a valuable contribution to its history. On the other hand, accurate and comprehensive information can also be found in treatises on agriculture such as the *De re rustica* by Columella, a Latin agronomist born in Cadiz during the first century. He describes all the viticultural practices which are still applied today, such as tilling, planting, fertilizing, propagation by cuttings, grafting, layering, dressing, as well as winemaking.

◁ Almost always trained upwards, the Egyptian vine, claimed by the Greek historian Diodorus, to have been imported by the god Osiris, served to embellish gardens. At this period, no royal or princely domain nor temple was without its vine-arbour and, accordingly, its wine.

The vine was also cultivated from a very early date in the basin of Mesopotamia and is frequently featured in Assyrian decoration during the time of the Sargonides. In this bas-relief from the seventh century B.C., King Assurbanipal enjoys a cup of wine under a vine-bower.

This fresco, found in a house in the ruins of Herculanium, which was destroyed by the famous erruption of Vesuvius in 79 AD, shows a couple who appear to be enjoying drinking one of the excellent wines which were grown on the very slopes of the volcano.

Thanks to the works of such writers as the poet Hesiod, the historians Herodotus and Xenophon and the geographer Strabo, we know exactly where the vineyards were located in ancient times. In Asia, they flourished on the shores of the Persian Gulf, in Babylonia, in Assyria, on the shores of the Caspian, the Black Sea and the Aegean, in Syria and Phoenicia. Palestine, the homeland of the legendary Canaan grape, possessed a whole range of renowned wines. These wines were produced from plants that were selected and cultivated with the utmost care and in accordance with the methods prescribed by Hebrew law.

Flourishing in Egypt and Asia, the cultivation of the vine reached the heights of glory in Europe. It gained a foothold in Greece, particularly in those islands with the evocative names of Lemnos, Lesbos, Chios, Samos, Kos, Tenos and Naxos. On the latter the magnificent ruins of a huge portico, the last remains of the temple of Dionysus, still rise majestically above the sea. The chain of vineyards stretches on through Rhodes, Crete, Cythera, Leucadia and Corcyra. Suspended, as it were, between the two azure seas, these vines yielded wines which were shipped to the Mediterranean cities, chiefly to Rome, where good Greek wines, sometimes fetching exorbitant prices, long enjoyed unrivalled prestige. Meanwhile, the Italian vintage wines of Mamertine, Falernian and many others soon began to acquire comparable esteem. These were left to age for ten, twenty, thirty years, and sometimes even longer.

Great wine-drinkers as they were, the imbibing of the ancients frequently developed into inveterate drunkenness. The example was set at the highest social levels. The imperial orgies of Nero, Caracalla and Tiberius, to mention only a few, have remained famous. It was solely due to their bacchic exploits that many individuals won favour with Tiberius or other emperors and were thus invested with important offices. In Rome, for a very long time, women were forbidden to drink wine, yet certain Egyptian bas-reliefs depict women of high society clearly in a state of inebriation.

So it seems that drunkenness was not unknown in ancient times, but there were also those enlightened drinkers who knew how to appreciate, respect and to recognize wine as one of the finest gifts of nature and the gods. Wine was and remains one of the basic elements, even one of the motivating forces, of Mediterranean civilizations.

A Greek amphora, preserved in the National Museum of Naples, is decorated with a vintage scene in which the Loves are gathering the grapes. What better way to depict joy and plenty?

A strange stone boat, laden with four immense winebarrels, now in the Trier Museum, on the Moselle. The crew are bearded Gauls, and the ship is one of the oldest witnesses to winegrowing in the region.

Reaching Gaul in the wake of the Roman armies, viticulture spread up the banks of the Rhône as far as Lyons, swept beyond to Burgundy, and on to the Rhine which it also reached via Helvetia. (Wine was known already in these regions. As soon as they had tasted it, the Gauls, the Cimbri and the Germans had begun to import it in large quantities.) At the same time, travelling along the banks of the Garonne, the vine reached Bordeaux. In the third century it occupied the same areas in Europe as it does today, including the districts around the Danube, thanks to the Emperor Probus who willingly converted his legionaries into vinegrowers when there was no fighting to be done.

But Rome suffered the repercussions of this expansion. The overproduction of Italian vintages and the competition of wines from the Empire resulted in falling prices. The slump led the Emperor Domitian to order vines to be pulled up in some regions, particularly those that produced only mediocre wines. Such measures were not dissimilar to those put into practice much later, in the Middle Ages and even in modern times. For the same reason there developed laws, regulations and prohibitions regarding winemaking, trading and shipping, and even the economics of viticulture itself. Cato the Elder is known to have calculated the depreciation over a certain period of his slaves, who were to him no more than the machines of his time.

In spite of these crises and hazards, viticulture prospered, reaping the benefit of the Pax Romana, nor was it unduly affected by the fall of the Roman Empire and the disturbed period that ensued. The Church had taken affairs in hand. The bishop, master of the city, was its vinegrower and cellarman. Not only must enough wine be produced for Holy Communion but also to pay homage to the monarchs and high-ranking dignitaries who broke their journeys at the town. Most important of all, there were the episcopal funds to be kept supplied. This secular viticulture, flourishing throughout the Middle Ages, ran parallel to another branch of viticulture practised by the monks, with the abbeys serving as hostelries. Situated on the main highways, they welcomed men of power—who, in their turn, showed their generosity—as well as the poor and pilgrims. Both monks and travellers appreciated wine.

Kings, dukes and feudal lords were not long in following the example set by the monks and the Princes of the Church. Vines bordered the castle as they did the monastery. Wine retained all its former prestige.

With the growth of the bourgeoisie, many of the vineyards around the towns passed into the hands of rich citizens. The wine trade benefited from an ever increasing clientele in northern countries, particularly Holland, Flanders and England, to which there flowed a steady stream of ports, Madeiras, sherries and certain Mediterranean wines, wines from Bordeaux and Burgundy and, later, from Champagne. Bordeaux belonged to England from the twelfth to the fifteenth century and quite a number of Lord Mayors of London were natives

The Greeks used this striking high-handled jug, which was called a *cyathos*, to draw wine from the mixing-bowls and pour it into the drinkers' cups.

In ancient times, the wine jugs used in Mediterranean countries assumed a great variety of shapes. This Etruscan *olpe* with its round mouth and high handle is reminiscent of the Greek jug *oinochoe*.

This Roman amphora, fashioned in a lustrous polychrome glaze, bears testimony to the great progress achieved in the workmanship and styling of wine vessels by the time of Alexander the Great.

of Bordeaux. Flanders, however, recognized the Duke of Burgundy as its sovereign lord.

A great deal of wine was drunk in the countries to the north. In fact, their inhabitants proved far more intemperate than the natives of winegrowing countries, where the taster of ancient times, like his counterpart today, preserved an almost sacerdotal sobriety.

In 1579, the Dutch acquired independence and began concentrating all their efforts on commerce. They boasted a large and superlatively well organized navy, warehouses and stores. Systematically they applied themselves to a study of the market and succeeded in creating demand and controlling consumption. At the time of Louis XIV, they were buying vast quantities of "small" wines which they proceeded to blend, adulterate and resell at a large profit, openly defying the wine-exporting countries where the integrity of the vintages was scrupulously observed and where the wine trade was subjected to the close surveillance of the guilds and the authorities. It was also the Dutch who, initially for purely lucrative purposes, instigated the production and heavy consumption of spirits.

From the early Middle Ages, especially in France but also in Italy and the regions bordering on the Rhine, viticulture and the wine business played an important part in the extensive development of the communities, the sovereign granting various rights, franchises and privileges to the wineproducers and hence to the municipal authorities. This explains why the pages of

the history of wine are often turned by political events. For instance, among the leaders of the Paris uprising in July 1789, when the Bastille was destroyed, were certain wine merchants who hoped to capitalize on the riots and bring about the abolition of the very unpopular taxes levied on wines imported into the capital.

As early as the Renaissance, the map of European vineyards corresponded very closely to today's. Colonization and the spread of Christianity brought viticulture to countries overseas, such as Latin-America, Mexico, California, South Africa; or gave it new impetus, as in Algeria. There, as in all other Moslem countries, viticulture had been curbed by the teachings of the Koran which forbade the use of alcohol. Nonetheless, twelve centuries after Mohammed Algeria was among the leading wineproducing countries.

Among the many vicissitudes in the history of the vine and wine, the cryptogamic diseases and the parasites brought from America in the middle of the last century were the most deadly. But man's ingenuity and perseverance invariably found a way to overcome all such calamities. During the nineteenth century, winemaking methods were greatly improved, and today they have reached an almost scientific degree of perfection. In this age of space flights and nuclear science, wine has retained all its former prestige. Closely linked with the origin of our civilization, it represents one of its proudest and most pacific achievements. Wine is still the most gracious and the noblest drink of all.

13

THE VINE SPECIES

"Plant your vineyard from good stock." The old French adage proclaims a fundamental truth and underscores the all-important part played by the species of vine in determining the success of the end result, whether this be the wine glinting in our glass, the unfermented grape juice faithfully echoing the original flavour of the fruit, or the ripe young cluster of grapes decorating the dining-table.

The knowledge of the countless varieties of vine, their distant origins, their types, and their history, linked to the history of civilization itself, is a many-sided science, embracing botany, biology, anthropological geography, and even paleontology. The layman, however, has barely ever heard such words as *Merlot, Gamay* or *Riesling*. Little does he care if the northern vineyards are descended from wild vines, as some specialists would have us believe, or if these vineyards were planted with vines brought from southern climes by those migrating north. The true wine-lover, on the other hand, is well informed in such matters.

Among the species yielding red wine that are cultivated in France, he will award the palm to the *Pinot Noir* from Burgundy, the *Gamay* from Beaujolais, the *Cabernet-Sauvignon* from Bordeaux, and the *Grenache* which thrives along the banks of the Rhône, in Provence, Languedoc and Roussillon. He will also award honourable mentions to the *Malbec* and the *Merlot*, grapes which are often blended with *Cabernet*, as well as to *Cinsaut, Mourvèdre, Carignan, Savagnin* from the Jura, the *Black Muscat* from Frontignan, the Savoyard *Mondeuse* and the *Tannat* grow in the Hautes-Pyrénées.

The range of white grapes is equally wide. There is the *Chardonnay*, responsible for the excellence of the wines from Champagne and the vintage wines from Burgundy, the *Sauvignon Blanc* and *Chenin* which produce the wines from the Loire and Anjou, *Semillon* from the famous vineyards in the Gironde, *Muscadet, Clairette*, the *White Muscats* and, finally, the *Chasselas* with which most of the vineyards in the French-speaking cantons of Switzerland are planted.

All these species of grape yield a great variety of different wines, alternately full-bodied, fruity, robust or rich, but this is not the place to start a glossary of the subtle and innumerable nuances so readily distinguished by the professional palate.

Several French grape species have been introduced into other wineproducing countries, such as Spain, Italy, Russia and California, whilst the *Sylvaner, Riesling* and *Traminer* which yield the Rhine and Moselle wines can also be found as far afield as Hungary and Czechoslovakia, and notably in Alsace and Switzerland.

In Italy, a variety of *White Muscat* yields the ASTI. *Barbera* originates in Piedmont, *Nerello* in Sicily. *Soave* prospers from Verona to the Adriatic. Spanish sherry, Portuguese port and Madeira also have their own species of grape while California, a large wineproducer, has adopted the wines from Europe.

Sometimes a wineproducer will content himself with one particular species of grape; but then again, after due consideration, he may decide to combine two or more different varieties. Thus, the wine from Médoc owes its scent and spiciness to the *Cabernet*, its well-balanced richness to the *Merlot*. Similarly, the grape species *Grenache, Mourvèdre, Syrah* and *Clairette* blend their different virtues and temperaments in the opulent CHÂTEAUNEUF-DU-PAPE, the leading CÔTES DU RHÔNE.

Apart from the vines cultivated for wine grapes, there are all those that yield dessert grapes: the French *Gros-Vert* and *Chasselas*, the Italian *Regina* and *Ignea*, the Spanish *Almeria* and *Malaga*, the *Rish Baba* from Persia, the *Emperor* from California, and many more besides, without forgetting the widely cultivated *Zante* and *Muscat* and other varieties whose grapes are usually dried and eaten in the form of raisins.

This brief summary has only skimmed the surface of a major chapter in the study and lore of wine. Albeit rudimentary, its aim has been to evoke the wondrous riches and diversity of this complex and universally famous plant which seems truly to have been, together with corn, one of the earliest and most ancient products of cultivation.

The botanist Linné conferred the name of *Vitis vinifera* on the vine which provides us with both dessert grapes and wine grapes. Its origin can be traced back to the Tertiary period, some forty-five million years ago. Today, several thousand species of this plant are known to man.

14

Dessiné d'après Nature par Apolline De Montesune.

15

The *Chardonnay* (below) is also called *Pinot Blanc Chardonnay*. Widely grown in Champagne and particularly in the famous "Côte des Blancs" region, this grape endows Champagne with all its piquant freshness and delicacy, and also accounts for the fame of the great white wines of Burgundy. Californian wine-growers use it to produce a light, white table wine.

For a long time, the *Pinot Blanc* (above) was confused with the *Chardonnay* (right). *Pinot Blanc* is found in Burgundy, Champagne, Alsace and in Germany, where it is known by the name of *Weissburgunder*. It is also grown in Hungary, Yugoslavia and California. This is one of the great species.

The *Harslevelü* (lime leaf) is of Hungarian origin and has never left its native soil. Blended with another grape, the *Furmint*, it produces the famous Tokay wine which, incidentally, has no connection with the *Tokay* from Alsace, a wine made from the *Pinot Gris*.

The *Grenache* appears to have originated in Spain where it is known as *Garnacha* or *Alicantina*. After having been somewhat spurned, it has now acquired great popularity on both sides of the eastern Pyrenees and as far as the lower Rhône valley.

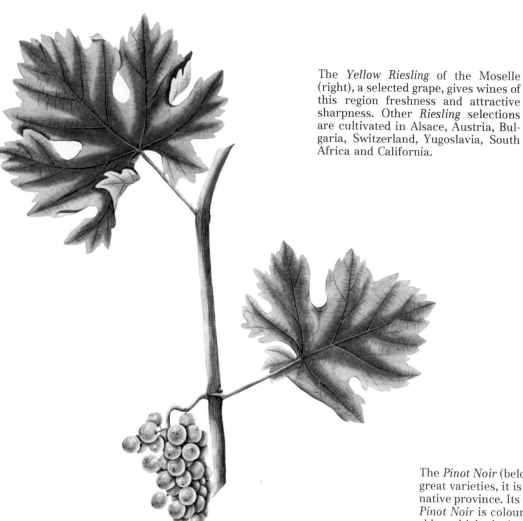

The *Yellow Riesling* of the Moselle (right), a selected grape, gives wines of this region freshness and attractive sharpness. Other *Riesling* selections are cultivated in Alsace, Austria, Bulgaria, Switzerland, Yugoslavia, South Africa and California.

The *Pinot Noir* (below) probably originated in Burgundy. One of the great varieties, it is found in regions having the same climate as its native province. Its German name is *Blauburgunder*. The juice of the *Pinot Noir* is colourless and it is the colouring matter in the grape skins which, during fermentation in the vat, brings to the wine the brilliant ruby hue so extolled by the poets.

The *Riesling* (above) is pre-eminently a species originating on the banks of the Rhine and the Moselle, but it adapts perfectly to various other regions. The *Riesling* from Rheingau has its own very positive character and should on no account be confused with the *Riesling Italico* which yields an altogether different type of wine.

The *Chenin Noir* (left) was the original vine of Anjou. A hardy and fertile species when young, it yields a delicate, clear wine of a fine red colour. Its cultivation is confined exclusively to the valley of the Loire.

17

ous auons dit
plusieurs choses
des plantes des
vignes par de
uant quant nous traitios
de la commune nature des
plantes. Et a present en ce
quart liure nous voulons
parler de la nature ¬ou la
bourache des vignes et de
toutes manieres de vignes
et de tou le prousfit du fruit
en particulier.

De la naticture ¬e la vig

ne en soy et de la vertu des
fueilles ¬des cendres et d
sa larme.

Xascun a congnois
sance des vignes que
cest fors que es froides con
trees ou le fruit ne puet
aoistre Si conclus que cest
vne humble et plorante
arbreillon moult tortue ¬
noeuse et rongneuse qui
a larges conduis ¬pertuz
et pores grant moelle ¬lar
ges et entretrenchees fueilles

VINES, WINE AND WORK

My grandfather was a vinegrower. I remember seeing him using the sulphur spray which was carried on one's back and worked by means of a pump. In those days he wore an old straw hat, old jacket, old trousers and ancient laced boots, all tinged with the blue of the Bordeaux mixture which also stained his moustache and his heavy eyebrows. I remember, too, the wine harvests. In those days, they used to press the grapes, in the vineyards, into containers which were then emptied into a large barrel securely fixed on to a cart. It was quite a long journey to the wine-press. There, in the open, waited an enormous vat. The barrel was rolled on to two stout planks and spewed the grapes into the vat whose contents were subsequently transferred to the wine-press.

The wine-press was worked by an enormous wooden beam called a yoke. At one end there was a rope whose other end was wound round a second vertical beam, turned on its own axis by means of meshed cogs and driven by a crank which was operated by hand. All night long, the creaking of the beams, the groaning of the stretched ropes and the metallic rhythm of the ratchets could be heard, while the must, in its natural state, free from additives and rich in its own yeasts, trickled through pipes into the cellar. And two or three days later the fantastic work of the fermentation began.

This is not ancient history; it happened less than fifty years ago. Yet in those days, men still seemed to take real pleasure in performing these humble and manual tasks, in practising this craft which perpetuated the time-honoured traditions to which the vinegrower was profoundly attached but which, frequently, were very localized and accepted as routine. Then, too, almost everything depended on the efforts and the skill of man, that highly developed, intelligent machine, that very inexpensive source of power.

Today, my grandfather's vines are cultivated in much the same way as they were fifty years ago. They still occupy terraces laid out on steep slopes, are still planted in relatively close rows. This is the custom in nearly all northern vineyards planted on the sides of hills. Elsewhere, in the plains, where the vine can spread out at its ease and where it is encouraged to stretch to medium or full height, machines have long since made their appearance. Subsoil ploughs break up the ground and turn it over, work that can also be carried out with explosives.

Tractors now clatter along between the well-spaced rows, pulling machines behind them that clean the soil and lay the second dressing. Lightening the labours of today's vinegrower are improved sprays, usually machine-driven, atomizers and other accessories, sometimes airborne on airplanes or helicopters, which spread insecticides, fungicides and other substances.

If the cultivator of vines in the days of yore could be compared to a foot-soldier, he now belongs to the ranks of a motorized army of far greater efficiency. As for the production of wine, it has increasingly become the business of oenologists, scientifically trained, who spend much of their time bent over test-tubes, microscopes and other equipment, converting the mysteries of wine into chemical formulae. However, they do not disdain the vinicultural experience handed down through countless generations nor neglect visits to the cellars to inspect the wine in its own habitat, tasting it critically, guiding its progress and nurturing it to maturity as has been done from time immemorial.

Indeed, even if methods have been modernized and the vinegrower, in order to secure his livelihood, has resorted to technical advances and to rationalization of work, the responsible tasks involved in the cultivation of vines and production of wines have remained essentially the same.

Naturally, practices may vary, depending on the region, climate and species of grape. But, by and large, the vinegrower in France performs the same tasks and goes through very much the same motions as his counterpart in Bessarabia or California, experiencing the same hopes and anxieties, the same satisfactions and disappointments. Dependent on his vines he is, himself, subject to the eternal rhythm of the seasons. While today machines have taken over so many viticultural and vinicultural processes, there are numerous tasks, such as dressing the vines, that still require, and will always require, the experience and unique manual dexterity of men.

This illuminated design from the fifteenth century, taken from the *Livre des profits champêtres* by Pierre de Crescens, illustrates the stages in vine cultivation during the Middle Ages: hoeing, weeding, training on trellises, grape-gathering, pressing by foot and broaching the cask.

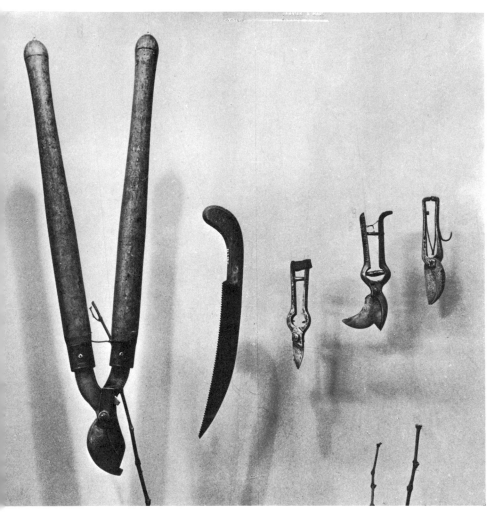

The new year for the vines begins in November when, the grapes all gathered in, the vinegrower thoroughly sluices and scrubs his wine-press, utensils, appliances, vats and casks, not forgetting to use the sulphured wick to prevent mildew. The last leaves drop away from the vine stems after a final glorious display of rich autumnal colours: every shade of gold and yellow in the case of the white grape plants, the resplendent spectrum of crimsons and purples for those which bear the black grape. Thus stripped of its working apparel, the vine obtains to all outward appearances a brief respite.

But if the vine may sleep, the vinegrower can take no rest. This is the time of year when, not so very long ago, the women and children pulled out the vine-props, laying them in orderly groups of six, well spread out between the rows of vines. Today, it is increasingly the practice to leave the vine-props in position as metal vine stakes have long since come into use. Moreover, vines trained into the shape of a goblet, the stem supported by a central prop, seem gradually to be ceding ground to vines trained on wire.

Under the obliging sun of an Indian summer, earth that has gradually slipped downhill is transported by the vinegrower back to the top of his sloping vineyard. This arduous task was performed with the aid of a basket harnessed on the back in times gone by, so that after a few years of this work the same man could truthfully claim to have carried the entire vineyard on his back. Nowadays, this burden and other heavy work has been taken over by power-driven machines, whose

The tools shown above all come from Burgundy. From left to right, they are root-cutting secateurs, a hand saw, secateurs (Côte de Beaune), billhook-secateurs, and secateurs (Côte Châlonnaise). Below, from top to bottom, a sickle and two billhooks.

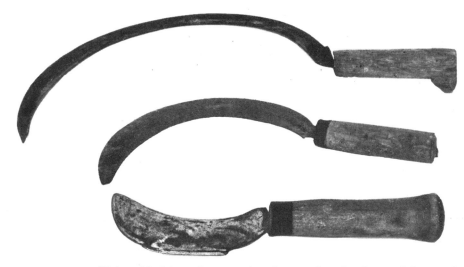

Right: Machines have replaced men for the heavy labour of tending the vines, especially when it is necessary to work the soil. Nevertheless, there are many vineyards that slope so steeply that mechanical implements are impossible to use, as in the Moselle (Germany), the Douro (Portugal), and the Lavaux (Switzerland).

VIGNERON

Vinegrowers of every age were strenuous workers. In 1351, the King of France required that they perform "their day's work loyally, from sunrise to sunset", which left little time for drinking the product.

Today, many of the essential jobs in the vineyards are done by machines. Above: A machine for cutting the vine shoots. The rows of vines are more spaced out than they used to be, in order that machines may pass between them.

Before grafting his vines, the winegrower prepares the cuttings. It was thanks to a systematic grafting that the European vineyards were reconstituted after the ravages of phylloxera at the end of the nineteenth century. Nowadays, grafting enables vines to better adapt to different soils and climates.

sputtering fills the air. But first of all, the digging had had to be done, trenches to be made at the base of the vines all along the walls. And if the walls had shown signs of wear or damage, the vinegrower had to take up his trowel and perform a mason's work, repairing and repointing. "Mortar of winter, mortar of iron", so runs an old French saying.

Earth to carry uphill, walls to reinforce: these are jobs to be done in terraced vineyards spread over the hillsides, not in vineyards on the plains. However, whether on the hills or plains, autumn is the time for tilling and ridging, worked by ploughs which lift and turn over the earth all along between the rows. The old vine-plants must also be grubbed out and their gnarled, blackened and twisted stumps sometimes feed their owner's fire.

Naturally, all this time, down in the cellar, the new wine requires care and constant attention. At ground level, the vinegrower takes shelter from the cold and inclement weather, repairs his tools, puts his equipment in order, cuts new vine-props, sharpening them into points and impregnating them with tar or sulphur. It is also in winter that he prepares the straw used for tying the vine shoots, although this is being replaced more by metal or plastic fasteners.

Once Christmas is past, time rushes by. At the end of January, with the days stretching out, the vinegrower feels a compulsive urge to take up his pruning shears. "If we would drink," runs an old French proverb, "we must dress the vine before St. Gregory's day", St. Gregory's day falling on March 12th.

Dressing the vine necessitates long experience and the greatest care. The plant must be trained and the root stock kept to a reasonable size. Most important of all, production must be controlled, next year's fruit growing on the young shoots that sprout from last year's vine stock. Therefore, these root stocks must be judiciously dressed and, following the example of Janus, the god whose two faces looked in opposite directions and who gave his name to the year's first month, the future judged while paying due consideration to the past.

The vinegrower knows that an overly sturdy vine stock yields fewer fruit than one of less strength that produces a generous quantity but runs the risk of becoming spent. He also knows that the young shoots farthest from the stock bear the most. All his knowledge is behind the apparently casual wielding of his pruning shears. Every cut displays experience and foresight, guiding the development of each branch. If he cuts short, leaving only two or three buds, he wishes to husband the vine stock and not force it to an immoderate yield. If he cuts long, leaving three or four buds to a branch, he aims at a more plentiful harvest. It is up to the vinegrower to decide whether the vine is capable of such output. A wise master, he decides nothing without due consideration and as a result the vine, originally a highly fertile plant, is made to comply obediently with the prescribed directions. These directions vary accord-

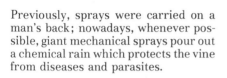

Previously, sprays were carried on a man's back; nowadays, whenever possible, giant mechanical sprays pour out a chemical rain which protects the vine from diseases and parasites.

The artists of the Middle Ages, who were so fond of depicting the various crafts, have bequeathed us faithful pictorial representations in richly illustrated prayer books. The cooper's art was not forgotten. Here are vat-makers, jug-makers, shook-makers, and hogshead binders busy before the approaching wine harvest. After chamfering and turning over the staves, they fit and bind them together with wooden hoops.

ing to region, species of grape, soil and climate whether the vine must have low, medium or tall growths, single stem, lattice-work or "goblet" shaped branches. Dressing vines may be a highly specialized technique but it is also an art and involves a kind of complicity between the man and the plant.

When winter is over, the dressed shoots weep, each horn bearing its glittering pearl. The buds, still muffled in their fleecy down, are ready to open. The vinegrower experiences his first qualms. At any moment, the frost can cut down the young shoots. If this happens, the vines will have to be faithfully tended throughout the year without hope of a satisfactory yield. In northern vineyards, this threat hangs over the vinegrower's head until the end of April, and sometimes even into May, the beginning of which month is notorious for its treacherous weather.

Before dressing, the vinegrower has been attending to grafting, essential since the arrival of the phylloxera, a minute plant louse which found its way to Europe from America in the middle of the last century. This terrible little creature attacked the roots and wrought the most appalling havoc; it would have brought about the annihilation of European vineyards had not the appropriate remedy been found and applied. It was discovered that the roots of the American vines were immune to phylloxera and so now almost every European vine is grafted on to an American root. When this has been done the vinegrower lays out the grafts in boxes full of damp sawdust, which are then stacked in some overheated place. In May, they will be planted in nurseries. Since this job requires considerable care and skill, the vinegrower sometimes prefers to entrust it to the nurseryman.

With winter well and truly behind, and a warm haze rising in the morning sun, the first small flowers venture timidly along the foot of the wall while machines resume their humming and all nature begins to stir. The spring ploughings leave behind a clean and tidy vineyard, a joy to behold with its tautened and refurbished wires stretching out as far as the eye can see, or with its vine props standing to attention like the pikes of a vast army of footsoldiers drawn up in battle array. The soil, as yet free of weeds, conceals the ploughed-in manure, unless dried manure or mineral fertilizers have been spread, as is now often done.

From now until the end of summer, unless the vinegrower relies entirely on weed-killers, the motorized hoe will regularly travel between the rows of vines, replacing men who, not long since, still raked away the weeds with pathetic doggedness from spring to autumn. Each vinegrower's descendants emancipate themselves more and more from this drudgery, acquiring machines that do the job just as well and much more quickly.

In the spring, the grafts in the nursery must be lifted, their roots trimmed and paraffin wax applied. They are then put in sand in a cool place, to prevent them shooting before they are planted in their permanent vineyard. It is also in the spring, as soon as the buds open, that the vinegrower begins the treatments against parasites, insects and cryptogams. This battle with disease continues without respite until a few weeks before the grape harvest.

The red spider is first on the scene, followed shortly afterwards by the first batch of caterpillars and the first fluttering swarms of dancing butterflies. The mushrooms and other fungi are not far behind. The drama

24

The year's labours are rewarded. This scene from the mid-fifteenth century comes from the prayer book which belonged to the Duchess of Burgundy. The seasonal grape pickers, hired in market-places, are paid in cash or in kind by the owner of the vines. It has been a good harvest and everybody, well content, goes off to the wine-press, which is the property of the local lord of the manor or of the local council.

has begun, and the vinegrower is all too grimly familiar with the plot and the leading players with their outlandish names, although he is never sure about what will happen in the last act.

Among the animal parasites, of which the phylloxera is the most deadly, there is a large cast of coleoptera. The larvae of the leaf-hopper devour the undersides of leaves. The common vinegrub is also dubbed "the writer" because it busies itself cutting out fine strips on the leaves, resembling writing, while its larvae attack the vine roots. The leaf-roller, which rolls up the leaves into cigar shape, inside which its grubs snugly nest, joins with weevils of various kinds to complete this unwelcome throng.

The pyralis, the two annual generations of cochylis or vine-moth, the four generations of leaf-roller moths or endemis are very attractive fly-by-nights, waking at dusk or dancing in the moonlight, but their caterpillars, commonly known as vine-worms, ravage the leaves or bunches of grapes before, during and after flowering.

The fungoid growths are equally destructive. The oidium's fibres spread over leaves and branches, their sinister suckers infiltrating everywhere. Mildew is the enemy of leaf, branch and grape, which it withers, darkens and dries out. Black rot, also from America, and the fungi causing white rot or excoriose, which sets in after hail, are allies of those fungi causing root rot and grey rot, a disease of the grape; and finally there is apoplexy, the ultimate and fatal phenomenon of a stock disease. These pests could claim their right to exist as being granted by the Creator but, if allowed to proliferate, they could quickly put an end to the vine.

The vinegrower, once again enlisting the aid of the scientist, relies on his laboratory to produce all kinds of washes and powders for spraying, and on the technolo-

Even within the same region, winegrowers of earlier times invented a variety of baskets to transport the grape harvest from the vines to a cart. Above: a 'bénatou'; below, a basket carried on the back.

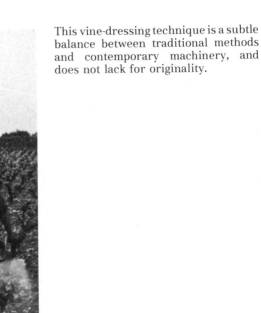

This vine-dressing technique is a subtle balance between traditional methods and contemporary machinery, and does not lack for originality.

gist to devise all manner of machines, from the humble bellows and the old hand-operated spray, carried on the back, to self-propelled sulphurators, powered diffusers and atomizers. The arsenal includes flowers of sulphur, liquid sulphur, copper sulphate, lime, carbonate of soda, acids, perchlorides, oxides, hydrates, dioxides, arsenic and nicotine. Finally, there are multi-purpose concentrated products called synthetic fungicides, each combining several remedies to simplify the vinegrower's work. All these chemicals are administered to the vines, with the same care and foresight as a mother tends her child, in order to ensure their satisfactory growth and development.

Great precision, perseverance and endless patience are required. There can be no clock-watching when the work is pressing; during these long summer days the time for sleep is all too short. Arduous work indeed, spurred on by the hope of due rewards, but also accompanied by the philosophical acceptance of possible frustration. Then, patience and hope give way to resignation which is neither weakness nor despair but courageous wisdom, for the vinegrower can always hope for better fortune next year; the vine is a perennial and will live on through many years, be they good, bad or indifferent.

The battle against parasites, launched in the spring, is waged alongside the other viticultural tasks, particularly those concerned with the leaves. Called "thinning out" in certain regions, this is the first dressing carried out on the young shoots at the time the dry branches are pruned. First of all, as soon as the vine has flowered, the leaves are thinned out and the unwanted buds cut away. The shoots appearing at the foot of the vine, and others which do not contribute to the growth of the plant, sprouting elsewhere than on the dressed branches—all such parasite growth is removed. This delicate task, requiring almost specialist skill, prepares for and facilitates the next winter's dressing. The strength of each plant is taken into account. Carried out early in the season in vineyards to the south, this operation is left until later in those regions subject to frost. But the vine will not wait so this work must be done quickly and perhaps extra labour employed.

Next the tips of the herbaceous shoots are removed, thus controlling future growth. Later and up until August, new toppings or clippings are carried out, although the usefulness of this practice seems questionable. Completing this stage of the work the vine shoots are attached to their props or guide-wires with straw or raffia ties, or rings.

For ten to fifteen days or more the buds in each cluster flower one by one and an exquisite perfume floats over the vineyard, reminiscent of mignonette or incense. Sunny, warm weather gives the vines the chance to blossom and set quickly and in the best conditions. Rain and cold retard the flowering and hamper fertilization. Under these conditions, the pollen may be washed away or the crop may fail because of

26

This miniature from the *Tacuinum sanitatis*, a medical book translated from the Arabic in the fourteenth century, portrays in the most natural and unaffected manner grape-picking as it was carried out during that time in Italy. Worthy of note is the grape-treading, a primitive method of pressing now abandoned; and the use of composite crops, still widely practised in some parts of Italy even to this day.

On examining the details of this spraying machine it is easy to see how efficient a spray can be that has ten or twenty nozzles that allow a fine mist of chemical spray to be forced out under high pressure.

wheeling flocks of starlings appear, avid for the ripe grapes, only momentarily frightened off by the fire-crackers exploded by alert vintners among the vines. High time now for the harvest!

First comes a thorough clean-up of all the implements to be used, which are subsequently left to dry in the sun. As soon as the grapes are ripe, the pickers spread out across the vines. The grapes are heaped in crates and loaded on lorries which are quickly driven to the press. Bearing little resemblance to a wine-press of my grand-father's day on its stone pedestal, with its beam and huge vertical screw, the modern version is a horizontal cylinder into which the harvested grapes are poured after first being crushed in another machine. In fact, especially in large enterprises such as the wine co-operatives, the press has become a kind of small factory where everything is carried out faster and more reliably and where there is very much less manual work than in the past. Knobs and levers are pressed to bring electric, hydraulic and pneumatic forces into play; the chemists, physicists and technologists have done their work.

In some enterprises, the red grapes are no longer vatted, the process which gives the wine its colour. This operation, extending over several days, necessitates considerable equipment which obviously takes up far more space than the cylinder where the grapes are simply heated to achieve the same result.

This progress and these new methods have in no way altered or detracted from the extraordinary phenomenon of fermentation which the ancients attributed to some superhuman spirit and whose mystery was at last explained by Louis Pasteur.

degenerative phenomena or even excessive vigour.

If everything goes according to plan, the buds come out well, the plant has flowers in good weather, there is no loss of pollen and all the parasites are eradicated. The small, hard grapes that the young bunch proudly held out towards the sun now droop towards the ground. Gradually, they become translucent. They are beginning to ripen. About this time, the shoots begin to turn brown and lignify. The owner walks round his vines, carrying brush and pot of paint, marking the stocks from which, in a few months time, he will take grafts for future nurseries.

While the vine, now ripening, passes through its third phase, the vinegrower can at last obtain a brief respite. However, right up to harvest time, a danger hangs over his head. One sudden shower of hail may crash down with a storm, despite all the artillery the vinegrowers can muster in the shape of rockets that explode into the very heart of the clouds—the result is ruthless destruction of leaves, shoots and bunches of grapes.

Whatever the summer may have been, there comes at last a time when in the wide autumnal skies vast,

Grape harvesting with the 'Pelican' demonstrates the new look of contemporary grape-picking. Each grape-picker empties his container into the large concave arm, which rises to slide the grapes into the trailer pulled by the tractor (Hérault).

28

Above: The refractometer is an optical instrument used to determine the index of refraction (or density of colour) of the fermenting juice, and thus to discover the sugar content of the must.

Opposite page: In this Beaujolais vineyard, the vatting of the wine is done in closed vats. During the operation, the colouring matter contained in the grape stalks gives the white juice of the *Gamay* grapes its red wine colour.

Left and below: The grape harvest at Clos-Vougeot still has a traditional aspect. By contrast, in the Moldavian Republic (USSR), the grapes pass from the hopper of an elevator into the trailer tanker.

The yeasts responsible for fermentation are present on the grapes, carried by the winds and insects—supplied, in fact, by nature. But once again that dispenser of the good as well as the bad has been tamed and harnessed to suit man's requirements. Careful observation, selection and judicious training have resulted finally in the production of fine, good yeasts, free from such bacterial maladies as the *tourne*, acescence and other vine diseases. Strong, healthy, honest yeasts prevent sluggish, incomplete fermentation. They are incorporated in the must after being rendered aseptic.

When fermentation is finally complete, the yeasts have finished their work and fall to the bottom of the vat where they form the wine lees. After depositing its lees, the young and troubled milky new wine, saturated with carbonic gas, will clear of its own accord, but usually man lends a helping hand. Clarifying the wine, by adding gelatine-based products, white of egg or separated milk which draw the lees and other impurities down to the bottom of the vat is a long-established craft, now replaced by the more efficient and less hazardous filtering process which also rids the wine of any doubtful germs it may still contain. Among these are the germs which, needing air, proliferate on the surface:

the bacteria of acescence which can change the wine into vinegar, and the surface fungoid growths which spread a thin, whitish film over the wine, reducing its alcoholic strength and value.

To avoid such dangers, the cellarman shields his wine from contact with the air by filling his vats right up to the top, or by burning a sulphured wick to use up any oxygen left in the empty space over the liquid.

Even more dangerous are the germs breeding in the depths of the wine and not requiring air. The *tourne* readily attacks badly fermented wine, making it extremely unpalatable, while the dreaded grease disease makes the wine ropy, oily and insipid. Red wines, poor in tannin and acids, are vulnerable to another disease that turns them bitter.

So much for the bacteria. But there are still various chemical reactions to deal with. Brown casse yellows and sweetens new wines and gives them an artificial taste of age. Black casse gives the wine an unpleasant, leaden colour while white casse makes it cloudy and milky. Again, the wine may acquire musty, earthy smells and stagnant, mouldy tangs, reminiscent of iron or bad egg: these are nearly always the result of faults or negligence, carelessly picked grapes, badly maintained

This ink and wash sketch by Leonar Bramer of Delft, entitled "Halt before the Inn", deftly portrays a pastoral scene of the seventeenth century. The wine shop of those days was often no more than a casually converted farmhouse where, in summer months, passers-by stopped for a few refreshing moments. A barrel serves as a table. Who cares? Life is for living, there is music and companionship and the wine is cool.

vats or cellars, and are seldom met with in the cellar of the conscientious and enlightened vinegrower.

Such mishaps and diseases can generally be prevented by ensuring the utmost cleanliness from the grape harvest to the time of bottling. A good cellarman should also keep his eye on the thermometer. Wine appreciates warmth while it is coming up to its second fermentation, during which it loses its excess acidity, but it needs cool surroundings to clarify itself. Unless these conditions are fulfilled, the wine becomes capricious and unpredictable. In actual fact, the producer could confine himself to certain essential tasks: thorough preparation of his casks, the judicious management of yeasts, careful cellaring and the intelligent use of the sulphurated wick; ensuring that his vats are constantly full; heating, cooling and airing the cellars when the wine demands it and, finally, filtering and decanting at the right moment. Given these and good weather, and if the wine has the right elements and is balanced, all should be well.

However, within the limits of statutory regulations, which clearly stipulate that wine is pure, fermented grape juice, oenology prescribes various methods to remedy various deficiencies, defects or lack of balance, to accelerate or retard various vinicultural processes.

The vinegrower's cellar is a hallowed place, jealously guarded, secret and reserved for the initiated who form a kind of fraternity. Highest in rank is the wine-taster.

Often the diplomatic envoy from some customer, he takes his responsibilities seriously. On other occasions, he may be just a favoured guest. At all times, he is an artist, endowed with enviable physical attributes, the first being excellent sight in order to detect anything that may dim or cloud the crystal transparency of the wine. His nose is a finely-tuned instrument, capable of capturing and analysing every nuance of the bouquet. His taste buds are particularly acute. Having examined and critically sniffed the wine, he rolls it round his mouth, chops it up and down against his palate, rests it on his tongue and contemplates, allowing his senses to appeal to his memory. And at last he lets the noble liquid slip gently down inside him, feels the warm glow, savours its strength and flavour and then, and only then, pronounces judgement.

This elaborate ritual in honour of the wine is perfectly understandable. When the glass is raised in the cellar, the wine gleams as though it held captive the fugitive summer long past, bequeathing us some of its lingering light and splendour.

At this moment, the vinegrower reaps the full recompense for his efforts. He now finds justification for the pride that never leaves him throughout the long seasons and his entire working life which he has dedicated to this hard and unremitting task, constantly renewing his confidence in nature and his faith in what the future holds in store.

CRIEUR DE VIN . 1586.

Sworn public officials, the wine criers were commissioned to promote the sale of wine on behalf of the innkeepers. Jug and glass in hand, they vaunted their wares round the streets or outside the inns. Patronized by the King of France, their guild grew to great power in the thirteenth and fourteenth centuries.

WINE AND THE ARTS

Throughout the viticultural regions of Europe, vine and wine have always provided sources of inspiration for popular art. For centuries, craftsmen have embellished all kinds of workaday articles which play a part in the making and selling of wine, ranging from the wine-press itself to the sign above the tavern. In the Middle Ages, popular art reflected, above all, the vision of a profoundly religious man with a keen sense of symbolism. Christ was frequently represented on or around the wine-press. The wine-press itself is an allegory of Christ's sufferings and a symbol of the prophecy of Isaiah (LXIII,3): "Alone I have trodden at the wine-press and no man from among the peoples was with me. I have trampled them in my wrath, I have crushed them in my fury; their blood has spattered my apparel and all my raiment is stained withal."

All through the Middle Ages the Bible, which mentions vine and wine in more than two hundred passages, proved a virtually inexhaustible source of inspiration. One of the most frequently used themes was that of Joshua and Caleb. The two scouts sent by Moses to explore Palestine brought back a gigantic bunch of Canaan grapes, a sign of the anticipated plenty of the Promised Land. The vine symbolized Christ and life eternal; hence the bunch of grapes held by Jesus, Mary and various saints always alludes to the sacrifice of Christ and the Last Supper. In medieval art, the shape of the vine, symbol of God's people in the Bible, was often borrowed to represent Christ's genealogical tree. Down the centuries, vinegrowers naïvely entrusted the destiny of their vines to popular saints. As rough weather, parasites and disease have always menaced the vine, it is not surprising that when a saint performed a miracle that favoured the vines or the wine he was quickly adopted as protector of the vineyard. In Switzerland, for instance, St. Othmar and St. Theodule were both cre-

Left: St. Theodule, represented as the Prince-Bishop of Sion, Switzerland, is above all honoured in the Valais and Swabia. Below: Billhook in hand, St. Vernier patronizes the vineyards of the Rhine and Burgundy. St. Vincent, attired in deacon's vestments, is also a patron of Burgundy wine. St. Urban, confused with the eleventh-century Pope, protected Alsace and many German wineproducing regions from hail.

Joshua and Caleb, sent to Canaan to reconnoitre the country, discovered grapes which grew to an unbelievable size. They hoisted one of the giant bunches on to a pole and carried it back together.

Little figures in painted wood, the *Büttenmännchen* were characteristic of popular Germanic art and were often used for decorations at social gatherings.

dited with increasing the quantity of wine during bad harvests; hence they were accorded, as a symbol, a small wine cask. St. Vernier was always depicted as a vinegrower and was worshipped in the Rhineland, in Burgundy and the Auvergne. The martyrology of the French Church has this to say about St. Urban: "His patronage in the sight of God often protected the vines from bad weather and destruction. More than once, by his prayers, he drove away the rains, scattered the winds, preserved the vines from storms which threatened: it is because of this that vinegrowers invoke his aid against the vagaries of inclement weather and he is always portrayed with a bunch of grapes." This particular St. Urban was Bishop of Langres. His rôle seems to have been confused with that of his namesake, the more famous Pope Urban, so much so that today it is the celebrated Pope who is recognized as the patron saint of vinegrowers. Many saints became protectors of vineyards simply because their feast-days happened to fall during the flowering of the vine or the ripening of the grapes. As for St. Vincent, very popular throughout Burgundy, he was probably adopted by vinegrowers as a result of a play on the French words *sent le vin*, in other words, *Vincent*. An old saying, still quoted in Santenay,

36

maintains that any vinegrower not keeping St. Vincent's day will have his buttocks eaten by ants while he is having tea. St. Vincent is generally shown as a deacon, holding a palm leaf and a bunch of grapes.

From the sixteenth century onwards, almanacs and record books began to appear, containing symbols of the months as well as pictures of the vinegrower's principal tasks, weeding, dressing the vines, harvesting or making wine casks. These printed pictures brought themes hitherto only found in the prestigious prayer books owned by the great feudal lords within reach of a much wider audience.

Again from the same period, and taking into account the increasing skill of contemporary craftsmen, various articles and guild emblems connected with viticulture proliferated. Local customs began to spring up. In addition to their round-topped chests and guild flags, the vinegrowers, like the coopers, had their own domestic figurines. A favourite subject was the vintager, bowed under the weight of the narrow wooden tub full of grapes on his back. In German-speaking countries these figurines were known as *Buttenmännchen* and were often very attractively worked in wood or metal, gracing the table at social gatherings.

Even today at the carnival that marks the end of the grape harvests in Lower Austria, very unusual types of decorative emblems, peculiar to the region, can still be seen in the traditional processions. These are either wheels made from plaited straw, indicating that the vinegrower is selling his new wine on the spot, or painted wooden suns, drawing attention to the fact that the vineyard is being looked after by guardians. Another interesting local custom is the parading of the "vineyard goat", a frame of wood with a carved goat's head, laden with fruit and generally considered as the symbol of fertility. At the end of the festival, it is either sold by auction or presented to the mayor.

In all wineproducing districts, the architecture of the vinegrower's house is a compromise between work requirements and economic necessity. Naturally, the style varies from one region to another, and according to the social and financial status of the individual, but it

A perishable natural decoration, dessert fruit has sometimes been replaced by faïence imitations. This eighteenth-century plate is a good example of rustic art.

This "goat" was a symbol of fertility. Carved in wood and laden with grapes it formerly played a leading rôle in the processions at the wine festivals that ended the grape harvests in Lower Austria.

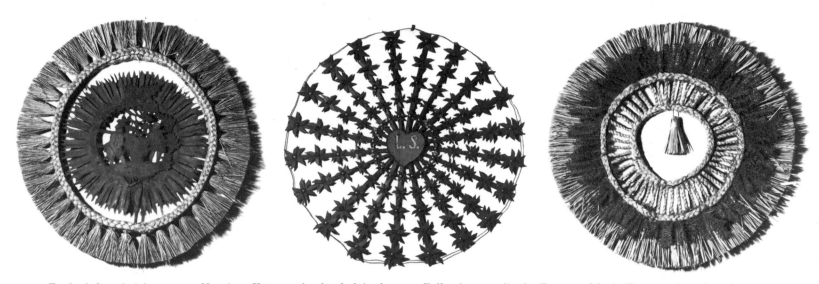

To the left and right are two *Heurigen Kränze*, wheels of plaited straw. Following an edict by Empress Maria Theresa, Austrian vinegrowers have hung these wheels over their doors to show passers-by that there is new wine in their cellar. In the centre is one of the wooden suns which, rising above the vineyards of Wachau, warned that they were guarded against trespassers and helped frighten unwelcome birds.

is always noticeably different from the farmhouses and other country dwellings. The byre and the barn lose ground to the preponderance of vinegrowing over other kinds of cultivation. The cellar, forming the very foundation of the entire building, not only influences the appearance of the house but often indicates the financial circumstances of the owners by its decoration, borrowed from town residences. Sometimes its wide, arched door is the main ornamental feature of the façade. Whatever kind of building it may be, brick or stone, its cellar is always constructed in a similar way. It is made as deep and thick as possible and usually from natural stone. Symbolic grapes and vine-shoots often decorate the doors, beams and even the implements. The same decorative motifs are also seen on crucifixes, particularly at the boundaries of vineyards.

The armorial bearings of many families and municipalities depict the vinegrower's work, with pruning knife and wine-press in evidence as well as the ubiquitous bunch of grapes and twining vines. More than any other activities, the tasks involved in making wine, storing it, carrying and distributing it have encouraged the development of popular art. Everyday articles, traditional in kind and shape, are favourite subjects for decoration. The wooden wine-press is often richly decorated, as it is part of the patrimony, handed down from one generation to the next. Wine casks as well may have their own decoration. Valuable family possessions, these enormous wooden barrels were carved with the names of the vinegrower and his wife for whom they were built, with armorial bearings, monograms and even, like a house, the year of construction, and were often inaugurated at a wedding.

The front of these sometimes richly carved tuns is particularly characteristic of viticultural art. No doubt

these casks, containing special wines from the large vineyards belonging to religious communities or princes, were first carved and ornamented in the wine cellars of monasteries and castles. The great chapters like those of Speyer or Würzburg exercised widespread influence throughout southern Germany, and this custom of decorating the huge casks was revived in the cellars of Austrian monasteries in the baroque period. Clearly, it was the monks who set the fashion for embellishing casks with pictures of saints or the patriarch Noah, considered as the father of viticulture. Occasionally, the abbeys engaged their own woodcarvers, but the work was more usually entrusted to the coopers themselves. During the eighteenth century and into the early part of the nineteenth, a cooper would

Carved into a block of wood 21 inches long, this grape was once the inn sign for an *'Auberge du Raisin'*. It is now replaced by a more modern sign, and is kept in the Swiss National Museum, Zurich.

Corkscrews are rarely reduced to the essentials, a long screw and a handle. While the screw part does not change much, the rest of the corkscrew assumes every possible and imaginable shape; sometimes folding, sometimes with wings, handles with endless screws, amusing or elaborate decorations—they lend themselves to every sort of fancy, whether to be the most beautiful, the smallest, the most valuable, the most efficient, or the most ingenious... or simply, the most ordinary.

39

spend countless, devoted hours carving and painting religious motifs, such as the patron saints of the guild. In the course of the nineteenth century, traditional designs were gradually superseded by simpler or more down-to-earth imagery, carvings of family names or portrayals of everyday scenes. The large casks, fitted with a trapdoor through which a lad could clamber to clean the inside, were particularly well suited to carvings, even on the door itself. Now usually a plain piece of wood, in times gone by this door was often carved in a very special manner. The designs frequently featured fishes, naiads, tritons and other legendary creatures, symbolizing the great volume of liquid contained within the barrel. The richest collections of carved tuns are probably those now in the Wine Museum at Speyer, in the Palatinate, at the Julius Hospice in Würzburg in Bavaria, and in the Wine Museums of Beaune in Burgundy and of Krems in Lower Austria.

Considering their size, so far above average, these giant casks represent significant monuments to the craftsmen of those days. They were constructed as much for the supply of some stronghold as to nourish the vanity of some great personage. Their real function, however, was usually to combine the different wines contributed as tithes into one blend so that all the officials entitled to perquisites in the form of wine received the same quality, thereby eliminating all grounds for complaint.

Most of these giant casks of the baroque period have now disappeared. Among the most richly decorated that of Königstein in Saxony should be mentioned. It was built for King Augustus the Strong. Other notable examples were the second Heidelberg tun, built in 1664 for the Grand Elector Charles-Louis of the Palatinate, and that of Ludwigsburg, built between the years 1717-20 for the Duke Eberhard Louis of Württemberg. The master-cooper Michael Werner of Landau in the Palatinate constructed the first Heidelberg tun for Jean Casimir in 1589; as a result he became famous and was given orders for similar casks from many other potentates. In old engravings, Werner and his helpmates can be seen at work on these enormous casks, proving that even in those days such an undertaking was considered an extraordinary feat and worthy of wide renown. One of these mammoth casks, with a capacity of nearly 53,000 gallons, can be seen to this day by visitors to the cellars of Heidelberg Castle.

Along with the big casks, the coopers produced small barrels for a great variety of purposes. One might be used by the vinegrower to carry his daily ration of wine when he was going to spend all day working in the vines. Another might be presented to the abbot at the time of his election. Still another would be used, year after year, to hold the Midwinter wine. This was a new wine, blessed on December 27th on the occasion of the festival of St. John the Apostle and devoutly treasured, to be drunk only on rare occasions, at a wedding, for instance, or before setting out on a long journey, being credited with beneficial virtues.

Amusing little casks, enabling three different wines to be drawn off by working a disc, are further examples of the cooper's art. They were very much in keeping with the spirit of the baroque age when games and tricks of every kind were much in vogue. After decades of apparent neglect, this craft is now being revived in various regions, notably in Lower Austria, and seems to be in great demand by publicans, wine merchants and affluent private individuals. Created purely for decoration, these casks come almost exclusively from vinegrowing regions: the South Tyrol, Lower Austria, the banks of the Rhine and the Moselle.

The elaborate fronts of many casks have now taken their places in collections. On this tun, which is dated 1880, the carved decoration is still strictly traditional.

Even the bung-hole of a cask provides an excuse for adding an amusing design in carved wood.

America also had its inn signs in the last century. Some were very simple, representing merely a symbolic object such as a bunch of grapes, a bottle or a drinking glass. Others, like this one, are genuine pictorial descriptions of life in days gone by. Errors in perspective were held to be of little consequence, as long as the subject was reasonably well-proportioned and the colours bright enough to attract attention. The wine, served in decanters and prominently displayed, seems to have been in plentiful supply at the "Strangers' Resort". Although vineyards already existed at this time in America, much wine was imported from Europe.

The cultivation of the vine and wine gave rise to a multitude of smaller receptacles. Almost until the end of the eighteenth century, the bottle as a means of preserving wine was still unknown in German-speaking territories. The wine was stored in casks in the cellar, simply drawn off into jugs and then poured into glasses or goblets. The bottle, a French innovation, only appeared in these regions towards the end of the eighteenth century and only with the introduction of sparkling wines. Flasks which slipped easily into the pocket or into saddlebags were used to carry wine when travelling and these first flat, pouch-shaped bottles began to make their appearance around 1820, together with the wood or leather cases which were designed to hold them. This shape of bottle can still be found today in the typical flasks of Franconia called *Bocksbeutel*.

Other longer bottles, also flat and generally fluted, were designed to be carried on the person. All had screw stoppers in pewter or, in the case of gentlemen of rank, even in silver or gold. Humbler versions in wood, earthenware or even fashioned from gourds for use by farm workers have also been discovered. Many such receptacles, fitted with a strap, were intended for

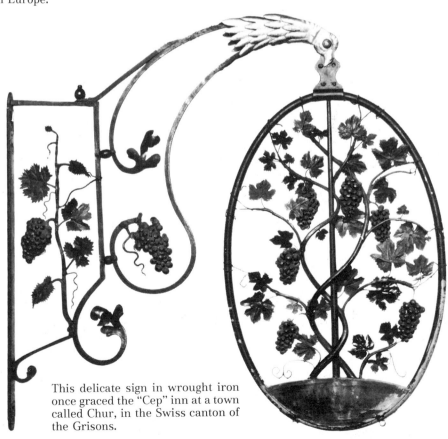

This delicate sign in wrought iron once graced the "Cep" inn at a town called Chur, in the Swiss canton of the Grisons.

41

carrying to work in the fields. Whenever possible, they were left in a spring or stream to keep the wine cool. They might be decorated with proverbial inscriptions, simultaneously bacchic and biblical, such as "Wine gladdens the heart of he who drinks in moderation, but it is harmful to the man who drinks too much", or "What is life without wine?" Innumerable small potteries turned out various types of pitchers, usually with handles, decorated with vine leaves, coats-of-arms and bacchic quotations while elsewhere pewter flagons were popular drinking vessels.

The tavern signs in small towns and in the countryside can also be considered as picturesque and characteristic examples of contemporary art. Those carved in wood have become extremely rare today. Magnificent specimens of hanging signs with their decorative supporting brackets testify to the high standard of wrought-iron work achieved in the eighteenth century. Depicting the vine and a bunch of grapes, as well as a variety of other motifs, these are for the most part the work of long-forgotten village craftsmen.

Our age is one of unceasing change. Like so many other crafts and professions, those associated closely or remotely with vines or wine have developed rapidly over the last few decades. Everywhere, glass or synthetic materials have replaced wood while implements and receptacles whose design seemed to have attained near-perfection are rapidly disappearing from the scene of the cultivation of the vine and are taking their places in museums and auction rooms.

The same tasks engendered the same types of implements all over Europe, but each region endowed them with its own characteristic style. The cooper, the basket-worker and the maker of edged tools all worked to order and to local requirements. In one district, the grape-baskets borne on the back and the harvesting panniers might be made in wicker and, in another, wood. They might be round and deep in one province, oval and shallow in the next. Methods of cultivation, harvesting and wine-making influenced the shape and design of every article. Notwithstanding the fact that their ultimate purpose was the same, they differed from vineyard to vineyard in the same way that their owners differed. Vinegrowers they may all be, but distinguished one from the other by their traditions and working habits. Today, all these tools and implements form part of a common heritage and bear witness to a highly productive art that can be admired in museums devoted to the vine and to wine.

Active promoters of the European vineyards in the Middle Ages, the monks often boasted famous cellars, the forerunners of our inns and public houses. The casks were broached and the wine, mercifully not reserved only for divine service, was drunk on the premises.

The bottle labels of the middle of the nineteenth century, although less precise and less strictly controlled than those of today, sometimes have a charm that is all their own.

Before the use of paper labels became general, people decorated the neck of a bottle brought to the table with a silver collar, which indicated broadly the contents of the bottle. The same thing is sometimes seen today on wines served in decanters.

IN PRAISE OF WINE

THE POETS' HOMAGE

Throughout the history of man, in all the countries where wine is produced or consumed, poets have rallied to praise its merits. Chinese, Persians, Arabs, Greeks, Romans and Germans all gave wine its due homage in their poetry and prose. The same applied to Britain, and the extracts given below show an astonishing unanimity down the ages—from Chaucer to Chesterton, the Bible to Byron—all have swollen the flood of celebration of the joys wine. Perhaps the most notable is Edward Fitzgerald's translation of the Rubaiyat of Omar Khayyam, but the greatest English poets—Keats, Shelley, Shakespeare, Byron and Dryden among others—have contributed memorable lines in praise of wine. For both Horace and Hilaire Belloc were convinced that "no poems can please long, nor live, which are written by water-drinkers".

But that which most doth take my Muse and Me,
Is a pure cup of rich Canary wine,
Which is the Mermaid's now, but shall be mine:
Of which, had Horace or Anacreon tasted,
Their lives, as do their lines, till now had lasted.

Ben Jonson, Epigrams.

And Noah he often said to his wife when he sat down to dine,
"I don't care where the water goes if it doesn't get into the wine."

G.K. Chesterton, Wine and Water.

Meum est propositum in taberna mori,
Uinam sit appositum sitienti ori:
Ut dicant cum uenerint angelorum cori
"Deus sit propitius isti potatori".
(I desire to end my days in a tavern drinking,
May some Christian hold for me the glass when I am shrinking;
That the Cherubim may cry, when they see me sinking,
"God be merciful to a soul of this gentleman's way of thinking."

Archipoeta.

There on the vulgar on the humble bed
I had the body of love, I had the lips,
The sensuous, the rosy lips of wine,
Rosy with such a wine, that even now
Here as I write, after so many years,
In my solitary house, I am drunk again.

C.P. Cavafy, One Night.

The Grape that can with Logic absolute
The Two-and-Seventy jarring Sects confute:

Edward Fitzgerald, Rubaiyat of Omar Khayyam.

Let thy breasts be as clusters of the vine,
And the smell of thy breath like apples;
And thy mouth like the best wine,
That goeth down smoothly for my beloved,
Gliding through the lips of those that are asleep.

Song of Songs, 7, 9.

If all be true that I do think,
There are five reasons we should drink:
Good wine—a friend—or being dry—
Or lest we should be by and by—
Or any other reason why.

Henry Aldrich, Reasons for Drinking

There are two reasons for drinking: one is, when you are thirsty, to cure it; the other, when you are not thirsty, to prevent it... Prevention is better than cure.

Thomas Love Peacock, Melincourt.

Fill a glass of golden wine
And while your lips are wet
Set their perfume unto mine,
And forget,
Every kiss we take and give
Leaves us less of life to live.

W.E. Henley, Fill a Glass of Golden Wine.

Man, being reasonable, must get drunk;
The best of life is but intoxication.

Lord Byron, Don Juan, Canto 2, 179.

And he that will to bed go sober,
Falls with the leaf still in October.

Beaumont and Fletcher, The Bloody Brother.

Ah, my Beloved, fill the Cup that clears
TO-DAY of past regrets and future Fears:
To-morrow!—Why, To-morrow I may be
Myself with Yesterday's Sev'n Thousand Years

Ah make the most of what we yet may spend,
Before we too into the Dust descend;
Dust into Dust, and under Dust, to lie,
Sans Wine, Sans Song, sans Singer and—sans End!

Edward Fitzgerald, Rubaiyat.

Two rather quaint studies of wine-drinkers by Adrien van Ostade (1610-1684).

Good wine is a good familiar creature if it be well us'd.

Shakespeare, Othello.

Drink no longer water, but use a little wine for thy stomach's sake and thine often infirmities.

1 Timothy 5, 23.

Bacchus Blessings are a Treasure;
Drinking is the Soldiers Pleasure;
Rich the Treasure,
Sweet the Pleasure;
Sweet is Pleasure after Pain.

John Dryden, Alexander's Feast

Hans Suess von Kulmbach (1476-1522).
On this rough draft of a joyous banquet, an abundance of wine is of evident delight to ladies and their lords.

Wine is a mocker, strong drink is raging, and whoever is deceived thereby is not wise.

Proverbs, 20, 1.

Prisco si credis, Maecenas docte, Cratino,
Nulla placere diu nec vivere carmina possunt
Quae scribuntur aquae potoribus.
(You know, Maecenas, as well as I, that, if you trust old Cratinus, no poems can please long, nor live, which are written by water-drinkers.)

Horace, Epistles.

Fill ev'ry glass, for wine inspires us,
And fires us
With courage, love and joy.
Women and wine should life employ.
Is there ought else on earth desirous?

John Gay, The Beggar's Opera.

Wel loved he garleek, oynons and eek lekes,
And for to drinken strong wyn, reed as blood.

Chaucer, Canterbury Tales, Prologue.

Wine, true begetter of all arts that be;
Wine, privilege of the completely free;
Wine, the foundation, wine the sagely strong;
Wine, bright avenger of sly-dealing wrong.

Hilaire Belloc, Short Talks with the Dead.

Here with a Loaf of Bread beneath the Bough,
A Flask of Wine, a Book of Verse—and Thou
Beside me singing in the Wilderness—
And Wilderness is Paradise now.

Edward Fitzgerald, Rubaiyat of Omar Khayyam.

Though port should have age,
Yet I don't think it sage
To entomb it, as some of your *connoisseurs* do,
Till it's loosing its flavour, and body, and hue;
—I question if keeping does it much good
After ten years in bottle and three in the wood.

Rev. R.H. Barham, The Wedding Day.

Lily on liquid roses floating—
So floats yon foam o'er pink champagne:
Fain would I join such pleasant boating,
And prove that ruby main,
And float away on wine!

John Kenyon, Champagne Rosée.

When I demanded of my friend what viands he preferred,
He quoth: "A large cold bottle, and a small hot bird!"

Eugene Field, The Bottle and the Bird.

Egbert van Heemskirk (1634-1704).
A public house at the end of the 18th century.

When thirsty grief in wine we steep,
When healths and draughts go free,
Fishes, that tipple in the deep,
Know no such liberty.

Richard Lovelace, To Althea, From Prison.

Fill all the glasses there, for why
Should every creature drink but I,
Why, man of morals, tell me why?

Abraham Cowley, Drinking.

Then sing as Martin Luther sang,
As Doctor Martin Luther sang,
"Who loves not wine, women and song,
He is a fool his whole life long."

W.M. Thackeray, A Credo.

Bacchus must now his power resign—
I am the only God of Wine!
It is not fit the wretch should be
In competition set with me,
Who can drink ten times more than he.

Make a new world, ye powers divine!
Stock'd with nothing else but wine:
Let Wine its only product be,
Let Wine be earth, and air, and sea—
And let that Wine be all for me!

Henry Carey, A Drinking-Song.

Though wine that seeks the loftiest habitation
Went to the heads of Villon and Verlaine,
Yet Hiram Hopper needs no inspiration
But water on the brain.

G.K. Chesterton, On a Prohibitionist Poem.

Once it was mostly monks who grew vines, and even those who didn't grow their own were viniculture experts. Is it any wonder, then, that a cellar-master, like the monk on this wine label, might be led into accepting his guest's invitation to share some of his own wine?

"Tis here, with boundless pow'r, I reign;
And ev'ry health which I begin
Converts dull port to bright champaigne;
Such freedom crowns it, at an inn.

W. Shenstone, Written at an Inn at Henley.

Let us drink and be merry, dance, joke and rejoice,
With claret and sherry, thearbo and voice!
The changeable world to our joy is unjust,
All treasure's uncertain,
Then down with your dust!
In frolics dispose your pounds, shillings and pence,
For we shall be nothing a hundred years hence.

Thomas Jordan, Coronemus nos Rosis.

O for a beaker full of the warm South,
Full of the true, the blushful Hippocrene,
With beaded bubbles winking at the brim,
And purple-stained mouth;
That I might drink, and leave the world unseen,
And with thee fade away into the forest dim.

John Keats, Ode to a Nightingale.

I cried for madder music and for stronger wine,
But when the feast is finish'd and the lamps expire,
Then falls thy shadow, Cynara! the night is thine;
And I am desolate and sick of an old passion,
Yea, hungry for the lips of my desire:
I have been faithful to thee, Cynara! in my fashion.

Ernest Dowson, Non sum qualis eram bonae sub regno Cynarae.

THE ARTISTS' HOMAGE

There are two museums in France that exist to show the relationship between wine and the arts, and which draw attention to the way that wine has inspired artistic thought. The two museums are very different in style and contents; the one, a sumptuous collection housed in the Château Mouton-Rothschild at Pauillac in the Gironde, gathers together a treasury of precious objects, antique glassware, tapestries, chalices, and rare pictures; the other, at Beaune, is more austere, being devoted to Burgundy wines, and displaying a collection of tools and objects connected with the making, keeping, and selling of wine, and the daily life of the wine maker, the whole set off by Jean Lurçat's superb tapestry: The Vine, Source of Life, Triumphs over Death. Thus the two collections, which show the two opposite extremes, well sum up the universal nature of wine.

"Let us drink wine, the noble wine of Bacchus; when we drink it our troubles sleep." These words of the Greek lyricist Anachreon have been echoed many times over the centuries and convey exactly the spirit of this scene decorating an antique vase.

In every age, and in every civilisation, the vine and wine have occupied an important place in the arts, whether in their symbolic or their realistic aspects. In fact, no other subject adapts itself more exactly to the two essential components of a work of art throughout its innumerable metamorphoses. In other words, no pretext answers better to the material and spiritual preoccupations of mankind.

It is certain that all mythology gave wine a central position, probably because it is the element which essentially drew human thought beyond the normal frontiers, and led man beyond himself, even though sometimes in a state of disarray. But this disarray was, in certain measure, a way of escaping the banality of everyday life, and allowed the spirit to penetrate realms of the imagination to climb to a more marvellous universe.

Religion took account of this phenomenon, and took advantage of its powers to accentuate and promote a sense of other-worldliness. Thus if wine, amongst all the gifts of nature, is the element that beyond all others plays a rôle which might be termed magic, it is evident that artists are unable to neglect the use of the vine and wine in their repertoires. It should not be forgotten that painting is, in itself, a form of magic that can suggest on a flat surface the three-dimensional form of an object by the combination of line and colour.

This fact may explain why for long art was practically exclusively in the service of religion. As a consequence, images related with the vine or wine inevitably had a religious character, generally in a cult strictly associated with representations of life, such as the funerary decorations of the Egyptians. Even in the more profane circumstances of Greek vase decoration, wine was often linked with mythological scenes. However, it should be noted that even in religious depictions, wine was also bound up with everyday life, and that this dual tendency is found in every epoch, confirming the double function attributed to wine by mankind.

The result is that the artists' representations either alternate or harmonise symbolical or religious themes, and that, springing from this, especially when connected with a rite, they always preserve an element of recognisable paganism. The Greeks were not mistaken in awarding a divine function to earthly wine. Dionysos, Bacchus to the Romans, became the object of a cult. On the other hand, a celebrated anecdote confirms the importance the Greeks gave to realism. One of them, the painter Zuexis, so accurately depicted a grape that the birds were deceived and flocked down to the representation to peck at the seeds.

The Middle Ages laid even more emphasis on the dual nature: thus, while in certain cases the foundation of original sin was the grape instead of an apple, we are before a purely symbolic representation; but in other

pictures inspired by the Bible, such as scenes from the lives of Noah and Lot, wine returns to its rôle of euphoric drink. The Middle Ages found many occasions to underline that duality belonging to spiritual and material domains, of which the decoration of cathedrals shows many examples, as do the illuminations of manuscripts. The winegrower and the harvester stand in the forefront of the images chosen to evoke the progression of the months, or the useful arts, just as bread and wine come first in the essential needs of mankind.

During the Gothic period, art began to join the great realistic movement which has lasted until our own time, with increasingly numerous depictions in which wine played an active or a supporting rôle, and in all cases proved by its presence that it belonged to every moment in life. Painters were able to take from the New Testament numerous examples which associated the familiar with the sacred; and the custom of giving Biblical heroes contemporary aspects, and of depicting them living and behaving like the people of the time, constitutes an invaluable record of the history of costume, manners and occupations, and a precious witness of the place then taken by the vine and wine in human activities.

The Renaissance, with its appetite for enjoyment, its taste for display, could not be other than constantly tempted by the miraculous aspect of wine; by the jollity of the vintage celebrations, by the indispensible presence of wine at ostentatious banquets, and the homage rendered to wine was so sincere that artists spared no pains to produce the most beautiful objects with which to gather, to offer, to admire and to taste a drink that diffused so willingly such irreality in a world that had a great need of expansion, of overflowing.

Several great tapestries of the Middle Ages have already accustomed us to see how the representation of the wine harvest lent itself to large compositions, justifying the presence of a large crowd, a mass of vegetation, with a mixture of order and disorder which in itself gives the impression of a celebration. This stage was largely surpassed by the works of the great Venetians: Tintoretto and Veronese multiplied the displays of abundance in the Marriage at Cana, and the Feast at the House of Levi. Even in the Last Supper, despite the solemnity of the event and the relative austerity of the treatment, one still feels that wine, at that moment, has a part to play, is a personality present.

With the Flemings, this generosity borders on truculence: Rubens, in his Kermesse or his Bacchanals and Jordaens in his scenes of junketing entitled "The King Drinks" have pushed to the limits these joyous images of an abandoned paganism, which make a curious contrast with the bacchanals of a Poussin. He knew how to hold on to a sense of order, a classic measure, by which we rediscover in his scenes of orgies a ritual echo of religious feeling.

Probably it was in the seventeenth century that the

painter used this theme most frequently, and in the greatest variety. This stems, no doubt, from the fact that it was in this century that man started to grasp more and more avidly the world around him. This he did with an intensity, an appetite for pleasure in which were intermingled both sensuality and spirituality which, in mutual expansion, enriched their own and their reciprocal discoveries. Thus, to the outpourings of Rubens and Jordaens, we can oppose the austerity of the peasants depicted by the brothers Le Nain, and, despite a certain truculence, the drinking scenes by Caravaggio and Vélasquez, which are characterised by a formal rigor deliberately avoided by the Flemings.

The Flemings were so tempted by a joyous independence that their minor masters enjoyed painting drinking-shop scenes. The more or less caricatured good humour of Teniers, van Ostade, Brower and Steen is completely detached from any religious allusion; man is reduced to himself and his pleasure in drinking. It is

Judging from the paintings discovered on the inner walls of their tombs, the Etruscans were great lovers of banquets to the accompaniment of music and wine. Today some of the area's modern wine labels pay homage to the talent of the old Etruscan artists and the refinement of a people who appreciated the good things in life.

Vintage time on the Loire at the end of the sixteenth century. This tapestry shows us people picking the grapes (on the right), treading them (in the foreground) and pressing them (in the background). The feudal lord is following the process closely while his lady is tasting the grapes with feminine grace. The artist very competently incorporated all the baskets, jugs, barrels and pressing equipment with a finely developed sense of decoration. The tapestry is now in the Musée de Cluny in Paris.

certainly possible to associate these minor masters with Brueghel, but with him there is something that is lacking in them, a participation in a certain mystique. Even when man seems only turned towards his physical instincts, Brueghel's revels form part of a popularly inspired imagery behind which one senses the presence of Faith.

In the seventeenth century there developed a new genre of painting, the still life, which up to that time had only been a part of general composition, but which now found its independence and was treated for itself. There again, certain Flemings, such as Snyders or Seghers, revealed in their pictures of tables overflowing with victuals the joy and sensuality that was natural to them. In these still lifes, the rich colours of the grapes the savoury transparencies of the seafood were a temptation to the painters, who practically expressed physical desire by the virtuosity with which they translated in paint their tactile and savoury sensations.

Even amongst the more sober, there lay in glass, in the reflections that it received, and the warm colour of the wine that filled it, objects of curiosity and temptation. That seduction in still-life pictorial material which we have already seen in the scenes of peasant life by Le Nain as in the virtuosities of Vélasquez and Caravaggio, we find also in Franz Hals, allied with a vitality and a power of expression so intense that it is possible to ask sometimes if, in his great portraits of Guild feasts, he did not take as much pleasure in painting the flagons and glasses as the faces of the company.

It should be noted that the new directions taken by painters in their techniques chimed well with this freedom of sensuality. Compared with what it had now become, previous painting of the end of the Middle Ages had a restrained character, a submission to design, which virtually demonstrated a feeling of modesty, while, on the contrary, the art of the seventeenth century is notable for spontaneity, joy, sensuality, and

52

its novel need to reveal the sensibility and temperament of the artist. This need for freedom of expression is one of the reasons for the success of still lifes, and the theme of wine became an ideal pretext which incarnated the newly-acquired liberty.

The eighteenth century offers a less novel, less rich field, in which the artist was busy exploiting known territory. Amorous scenes were accompanied by elegant meals, truculence was no longer the rule, and excesses were only admitted if they were wrapped up in the refinements of good society. In al fresco meals, in the boudoirs, the lovers' feasts took place before well-laid tables, covered with precious dishes; the glasses and their contents are incorporated in a decorative scheme for which they seem to have been created.

This vision of a worldly and superficial life should not be held too fast if a complete idea of the art of the time is to be formed. If there was—especially at the end of the seventeenth century—a current in painting turned towards exterior life, we have seen that life turned in on itself has furnished many painters with subjects for observation from which still life could develop. It is the moment to recall that as well as drinking-shop scenes, there were among Flemish and Dutch painters those who, attached to visions of intimacy—such as Vermeer, Metsu, and Dou—knew how to create an art of silence. Some of them specialised in the representation of elegant tulips, rare glasses and beautiful arrangements of fruits in which the grape naturally found its place. The taste for such intimate painting was not lost in the eighteenth century, and if the dimensions of certain compositions by Despartes and Oudry overstepped the bounds of intimate painting to become huge mural decorations, there also developed more modest forms of this peaceful style.

Pictures in this category often served to decorate the spaces above doors or chimney-pieces. Perhaps it was thanks to this unpretentious rôle that this style of painting did not come up against the ambitions of well-known artists, and it was thus left to acquire its patent of nobility under workmanlike outsiders. At this period, cunning games of trompe-l'œil triumphed: the grape, wine, had previously incited painters to seek poetry in the perfect imitation of the effects of light, and this tendency had followed a normal development. Chardin brought to it a less mechanical accent, a muted poetry, which enveloped the object and the fruit with a soft transparence; thanks to him, the still life was

In this painting by Lucas van Valckenborgh (1530-1597) peasants gather apples, coopers prepare barrels, some winegrowers harvest the grapes and others trample the vintage. The mildness of these last fine days, the abundance of the earth's gifts and the promise of good wine has incited their masters to pass the day in the country: at midday they assemble to eat lunch to the strains of a violin.

placed on a level of the purest sensibility and the truest emotion.

This is all the more praiseworthy in that the eighteenth century did not recognise in still life the same prestige as had the seventeenth century. Certainly, it had extended its use, but in awarding it, as has been underlined, an accessory function. Nevertheless, in Chardin's works reappears that humble dignity that we have remarked in the primitives, but in his case there is a more sentimental atmosphere, which affects the objects and the fruit represented. It was to be for wine and grapes the last period in which they were to be used in a painting, their last effective presence, at least for great painters, as objects in themselves.

The nineteenth century, in brutal reaction against the spirit and forms of the eighteenth, was unable to give the theme of wine and vine a privileged place. Still life,

in the sense that it had developed in the previous centuries as ornate and elegant compositions for mural decoration in elegant buildings, could not find a place within the framework of middleclass life in the nineteenth century. How could it? There could be no question, in a time of break-up, of reviving these games or these symbols, or finding a religious significance, while everything tended towards the exaltation of reality. There was no question, either, of finding in the new reality, made up of political, economic and social uncertainty, a suitable place for that theme, because the humour created by wine was too joyous to be compatible with the passions of the romantic spirit. It is thus necessary to turn towards popular art, humour and caricature if it is wished to find witnesses that a certain continuity existed.

The traces of still life that are found in the works of

This painting by Velasquez (1595-1660) is entitled the Triumph of Bacchus. A good jug of wine has made these wretched Castilian peasants forget their worst misfortunes and at the culminating point of their joyful drunkenness they render homage to Bacchus and to wine.

Italy, where artists find inspiration in the limpid light, where historians and archaeologists explore ancient ruins and sweethearts admire each other to the sound of love songs and mandolins. But Italy would not of course be Italy without the abundantly flowing wine, uniting young and old, men and women, as in this romantic painting of an Italian wine shop by Pietro Lucatelli (1634-1710).

the great painters, whether in the lines of Delacroix or Ingres, are infrequent and do not count for much in the general construction of the painting. Certainly, an undercurrent did exist, but it was of slight importance, which, following the success of eighteenth-century trompe-l'œil painting (Boilly was the last talented practicioner), was represented by numerous submissions to public exhibitions. This undercurrent was mainly supported by women painters, who exploited the genre for years without really adding much to the history of painting in the nineteenth century.

Wine and the vine did not really reappear in the paintings of the masters until the dawn of impressionism. Even then, they only had an accidental rôle to play, as an accompaniment to a picnic, or on a family table, or by the presence of vineyards in a landscape. Although it was exceptional, that presence had value in reintegarating itself into daily life, which is interesting on the anecdotal side, but which cannot really be taken into account when considering the relationship between wine and art. However, one considerable exception should be made for Cézanne's Drinkers. Otherwise, it is necessary to wait until the beginnings of the twentieth century and the appearance of cubism. Even so, it was not drinking nor the fruit itself, nor the effects on colour or composition, nor their picturesque qualities that attracted artists, for their only interest lay in the wine bottle itself. The bottle took first place in a large number of compositions of the period, to the point where it seemed to become a symbolic object, and to lend itself to demonstrations that justified that particular style and gave weight to cubist theories. Through the desire to push art and composition towards an extreme purity and to reduce every object to its essentials, the bottle became the ideal form, which, without modification, met the need to insert everything into a rigid geometry.

The relationship between the object and the work is so clear, that when in the 1920s, Ozenfant wished to push the theories to the extreme in the interests of purism—which was also done by the young Le Corbusier—he used bottles almost exclusively in an ingeniously interlocking fashion. Even before this piece of intransigence, the bottle and its contents helped cubists, about 1910, to justify and explain the direction of their researches into the representation and the invention of reality. Thus, on the one hand, the container could be represented or suggested in whole or in part without undergoing deformations in perspective, and, on the other, the surface of the contents, that is the plane which constituted the level of the liquid, could be summed up in a disc, conforming to the real-truth, and not to the ellipse-illusion, as imposed by perspective.

We can see that during the whole of this particularly dynamic period, bottles and carafes were used for their intrinsic value, as instruments freely chosen by the painter to explain his ideas. Thus, in a certain measure, and by an unexpected route, they regained, in a novel

"Der Trinker" ("The Drinker", if any translation were needed) is the title of this oil monochrome by Grésly Gaspard. He died in 1756, but apart from the clothing and the somewhat unusual hat of his subject here, it seems that little has changed since then.

During the time of the French Revolution, at the end of the eighteenth century, the Parisians' traditional habits were blown to the four winds. To maintain the public spirit, food and provisions were distributed. This painting by Louis-Léopold Boilly (1761-1845) shows wine being handed out in the parks near the Champs-Elysées. Even the presence of mounted constabulary doesn't seem to dampen the wine lovers' enthusiasm.

"Vin de Rubis" ("Ruby Wine") is a tapestry made by Michel Tourière, a Burgundian. The tapestry-makers of the past celebrated the work on the vineyards and the joyous banquets that followed the harvest; today, Tourlière sings the praises of the wine itself, as one causes it to swirl around the glass to admire the subtle nuances of its "robe" or outward colour and to fully savour all the fragrances of its rich bouquet. This tapestry is currently in the Musée du Vin in Beaune.

form, the central rôle which was theirs in the truculent Flemish still lifes of the seventeenth century, or in the elegant paintings of the eighteenth century, but this time in a more irreplaceable manner than in the previous centuries.

Other than this systematic use, the vine and wine returned to their place in the expansion painting underwent between 1920 and 1940. Painters, often taking Cézanne as their model, showed the relaxed aspect of life as inspired by nature. Already, in the famous Drinkers series of Cézanne, the theme-pretext showed how esthetic research and a suggestion of atmosphere, of sentiment, could be reconciled. Later, according to the painters' temperaments, the direction could be varied at will, whether towards the country scenes of Denoyer de Segonzac, or the more visibly constructed scenes of La Fresnaye, or even towards the majority school of poetic reality.

Raoul Dufy, having had to illustrate catalogues for a wine merchant, produced albums which are jealously preserved today by collectors, initiating a departure which was followed by a number of painters in subsequent years. After the Second World War, Bernard Buffet discovered in his turn that the bottle in a different form from that of the cubists was an ideal form for his rigid asceticism. He showed in his own way that a subject, however limited it may appear, is never outworn, and that a fresh artist can always find a new way of treating it, thus demonstrating the ceaseless currents of sensibility.

THE GREAT
WINE REGIONS OF
THE WORLD

THE VINE
CONQUERS THE WORLD

The great botanical family of Ampelidaceae, to which the vine belongs, is very widely represented in all cultivated regions of the world. All plants belonging to the genus *Vitis* bear grapes but out of the forty-odd known species only one, the European *Vitis vinifera*, produces the edible grapes used to make wine. *Vitis labrusca*, a species of American origin, is sometimes cultivated for wine but produces poor results. *Vitis vinifera* thrives only within the temperate zones of the two hemispheres, between latitudes 50 and 30 degrees North and 30 and 40 degrees South. This vine does not stand up well to excessive heat or rigorous cold, nor does it tolerate overly abundant rains or severe drought. Furthermore, it is difficult to make wine when the ambient temperature is above 15°C (about 60°F).

A rapid look at history shows that the regions where *Vitis vinifera* has developed are also the regions where various civilizations reached the peak of their development. This is scarcely surprising, for of all plants which have been improved and transformed by the genius of man, the vine—even more than wheat or rice—is a silent witness to his patience and his untiring work over many generations.

The original or autochtonous vineyards were in the Caucasus (Georgia and Armenia), on the isles of the Aegean Sea and in Egypt. It was these that gave birth to the present-day vineyards. Other natural vineyards in China, Japan and the eastern and central parts of North America did not benefit from conditions suitable for their development and they have remained more or less in an embryonic state. But starting out from the Eurasian regions, *Vitis vinifera* spread widely, for many and very different reasons.

Some of the vineyards owe their existence to the brutal facts of military conquest: a good many French vineyards began to appear as the Roman legions established themselves in the country. Sometimes it was the political supremacy or ideology which sufficed to propagate the vine cultures—this was the case with the Greek vineyards when, at the dawn of modern history, Continental Greece was under the influence of the Aegean powers. Nearer home, colonial conquests have resulted in the vine being transplanted to Australia, New Zealand, South Africa and South America. The missionary zeal of the Christians has often been reflected in a vine culture derived from their liturgical needs for altar wine: thus it was that the Spanish, after the Islamic interlude in the Iberian Peninsula, reintroduced the cultivation of the vine and the use of wine in southern Spain. Similarly, the first vines in California were planted by Franciscan missionaries. Elsewhere, it was the victims of religious persecution who spread a type of culture with which they were closely connected,

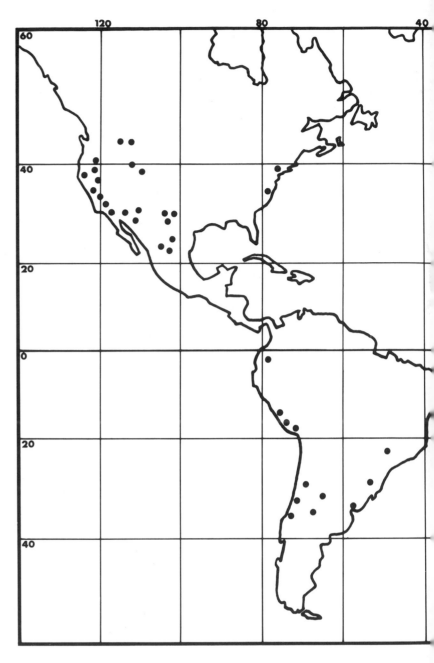

as in South Africa, where the first vinegrowers, well versed in their calling, were the French Protestants who emigrated there after the Repeal of the Edict of Nantes in 1685. Some of the vineyards of southern Russia were created, at the end of the nineteenth century, by the snobbery of an aristocracy which wanted to produce on its own estates wines to which it then gave such famous names as Sauternes or Vougeot. Now Russia is the fifth largest wineproducer in Europe.

The expansion or reduction of the viticultural areas depended also—as is increasingly the case today—on economic fluctuations. In Brazil, following a slump in coffee, plantation owners did not hesitate to lease out part of their lands to vinegrowers of Italian origin. And before the First World War, in the former Austro-Hungarian Empire the areas cultivated to vines varied

60

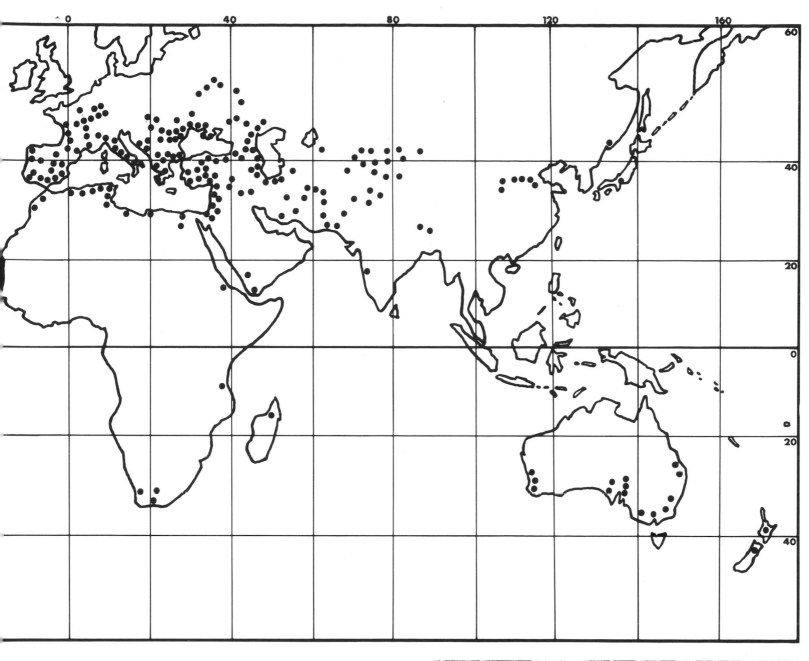

in direct relation to the economic and political situation of the various parts of the Empire.

The *Office International de la Vigne et du Vin* (O.I.V.) (International Office of Vine and Wine) in Paris has been collecting, studying and publishing, for the best part of half a century now, all the information possible on the vine and on wine in the world. The office functions as a centre of co-ordination and also of scientific, technological, economic and legal information for most of the viticultural countries.

The autumn is a bountiful season: the grapes are ripe, it is vintage time. Winegrowers know the same cares, the same work, and the same hopes wherever they are, for the vine grows like a garland all round the world.

61

THE WINES
OF BURGUNDY

PIERRE FORGEOT

The Bible related that the vine was created on the third day with the other plants (Genesis I, 11). But how long did it take to reach Burgundy after Noah and his Ark came to rest on Mount Ararat? No written evidence can possibly tell us. It is generally thought that, long before the Christian era, there were vines, albeit wild, growing in the present Burgundy wine area in the middle of eastern France, north of the Côtes du Rhône region and south-west of Champagne and Alsace. It was only through a slow process of change, doubtless beginning about the third century B.C. and advancing as their skill in the art grew, that our ancestors were able to improve the quality of the grape. Roman rule lasted five centuries and was vital to the development of the vineyards of Burgundy. Many of the Roman legionaries came from the wineproducing areas of Italy, and they brought to the Eduans—as the inhabitants of this region of Gaul were then known—their experience in the cultivation of the vine and in winemaking.

With the clearing of suitable vineyard land and the planting of better selected vine-stock in the first century A.D., it became possible to expand the vineyards and begin to produce the types of wines best suited to the province. The results were spectacular. By the fourth century, Numene was able to report: "The wines of this region are the subject of foreigners' admiration." Somewhat later, in 570, Gregory of Tours proclaimed: "There is no liquor preferable to the wine of these vineyards—it is a noble Falernian." About the year 456, the Burgundians proper arrived on the scene. They may rightly be called a migrant people, having apparently left the distant plains of Asia several millennia before the Christian era. By about 900 B.C., they had reached what is now called Norway and spread through Sweden, Germany and Switzerland before replacing the Romans in the fifth century in south-eastern Gaul, where they created their vast kingdom. In 534 the Burgundians were defeated by the Franks, but though their passage was brief, they had none the less imprinted their personality on the character, habits and customs of the region, and they gave their name to the province.

During this period and through the Middle Ages, Christianity became firmly established. Large religious estates were created through endowments made to churches, convents, abbeys and other institutions, rivalling and soon surpassing those of princes. This state of affairs continued until the French Revolution secularized religious orders and divided their land.

Burgundy was not spared the various disasters of the Middle Ages—invasions (Arab, Norman etc.), civil wars, pillaging, famines, plagues. In his history of Beaune, Rossignol writes: "The archives contain but a few vague words which bear witness to that universal desolation." It is not difficult to imagine that the cultivation of the vine made little progress in those times. Its rise began only in the tenth century with the creation of two monastic orders that were to exert an immense influence in the whole of Europe. The monks cleared the ground, replanted vine-stock and did much for the vineyards of Burgundy, putting them on the road to becoming what they are today. The research carried out first at the Abbey of Cluny and later at Cîteaux led to methods of cultivation and winemaking that, by and large, were the same as those we now employ. The spiritual and physical expanse of these two abbeys was immense—was not one of the abbots, St. Mayeul, called in his own lifetime "the prince of monastic religion and the arbiter of kings"? Cluny possessed two thousand dependencies and Cîteaux more than three thousand. In

The old town of Chablis, which stands on the river Serein, is the centre of a vineyard already known in Roman times. Today, the region produces a dry white wine, made from *Chardonnay* grapes, which goes beautifully with fish and seafood. There are four A.O.C. classifications: CHABLIS GRAND CRU, CHABLIS PREMIER CRU, CHABLIS, and PETIT CHABLIS.

other words, their power was an important factor in the spreading growth both of Burgundy wines and of their fame.

In fact, the quality of Burgundy wines was even the cause of serious diplomatic incidents. Petrarch tell us: "The cardinals [then in Avignon] no longer wish to return to Rome, since there are no Burgundy wines in Italy. Our prelates believe that their lives will not be happy without this liquor—for them, wine is the fifth element." For his part, Pope Urban V said: "I am little concerned to see again those transalpine lands where there is no Beaune wine."

These were the fourteenth and fifteenth centuries, auspicious times for Burgundy, both because of the monastic orders of which we have just spoken and because of the growth of the court of the Grand Dukes of the West, as the dukes of Burgundy then preferred to be called—Philip the Bold, John the Fearless, Philip the Good and Charles the Bold. For over a century, from 1364 to 1477, these four dukes, "the immediate lords of the best wines in Christendom", raised their duchy to such heights of power as to intimidate the kings of France and the princes of Europe. At the death of Charles the Bold, their power extended beyond the duchy of Burgundy (Dijon, Beaune, Mâcon) to the county of Burgundy (Besançon) and across a large part of Holland, Belgium, Luxemburg, Alsace and the counties of Nevers, Artois and Picardie. They cared much for their wines and gifts of them were greatly esteemed, as this letter from Pope Innocent VII testifies: "My son... Greetings... This Beaune wine that you have sent Us has a good and agreeable taste. It is quite pleasing to Our palate and constitution. We have made almost regular use of it as a curative during Our recent illness. Therefore, We call upon your Lordship and request that you send Us more as soon as the possibility arises. We shall be very pleased to receive it and your Lordship will thus be doing Us a very great favour."

Cultivation of the vineyards gradually became more democratic as first the bourgeoisie and then the peasant vintager received greater freedom. The vines were no longer the exclusive property of the nobility and the clergy; the latter, in fact, frequently indulged in such excesses that decent folk were obliged to react. The competence of the monks in the subject of wine and their taste for the beverage caused many a ribald comment. As they said at the time:

Boire en Templier, c'est boire à plein gosier,
Boire en Cordelier, c'est vider le cellier.

To drink like a Templar is to drink heartily,
To drink like a Franciscan is to empty the cellar.

The vineyards were finally and totally democratized in the eighteenth century by the French Revolution. The sale of the property of the clergy and the nobility divided up their immense estates and initiated the process of fragmentation, which subsequently in-creased through successive splits caused, in particular, by inheritances. This fragmentation characterizes the vineyards of Burgundy even today—quite unlike the large estates of Bordeaux. There are twice as many vine-growers in Burgundy as in Bordeaux, in a cultivated area one-third the size, and very few vineyards are wholly owned by a single person. Moreover, towards the end of the last century, the whole area was nearly lost to the notorious pest, phylloxera, an insect from America which attacked the roots and killed off the vine-stock. The whole industry was facing collapse, for no practical and effective remedy could be discovered. In the end, the only way to save the vineyards was to graft old vine-stocks on to American phylloxera-resistant stock. This cure did not affect the quality of the product; quite the contrary, it made possible the creation of improved varieties that were even better suited to the consumers' requirements.

There are certain conditions that must be fulfilled if a really fine wine is to be produced—and we shall only be discussing fine wines here. To the old saying: "The finest gesture a person can make is to fill his neighbour's glass", folk-wisdom will immediately add: "Tell me what you drink and I'll tell you who you are." It being understood, of course, that, as M. de Borose remarked: "good things are made for good people; otherwise we should be obliged to believe that God created them for bad people... which is unthinkable!"

Five specific factors must coincide if a Burgundy is to be able to develop its best qualities:

THE SOIL. Vines are not planted just anywhere but generally on the slopes of hills. The soil on flat country is too rich; the grape absorbs too much water and the wine is diluted. On hilltops the soil is poor; the vine does not grow properly, the grape does not take in all the elements it requires and the wine is incomplete.

In the words of Gaston Roupnel: "Before wine can even be conceived, its chosen soil must be very old and its cradle a tomb replete with the ashes of years and the dust of centuries." One is often surprised to see in this land of great growths so many different names side by side but, nevertheless, possessing significant differences in quality. The mystery of the extremely complex composition of the soil affecting the final result is mentioned by Maurice Constantin-Weyer in his book *L'âme du vin* ("The Soul of Wine"): "A secret alchemy works upon even the least of the soil's riches to produce an elixir beyond compare."

THE VINE. To plant a "hybrid" on the slope of a hill is a little like bandaging a wooden leg. The great wines of Burgundy demand two types of vine-stock: for red wines, the *Pinot*—the finer the grape the better the result—the juice of which is colourless and very sweet; for white wines, the *Chardonnay* grape is used, to which the same applies.

There are two main secondary types that go with the two "greats". One is the *Gamay*, a red grape with white juice which produces the remarkable wines of the

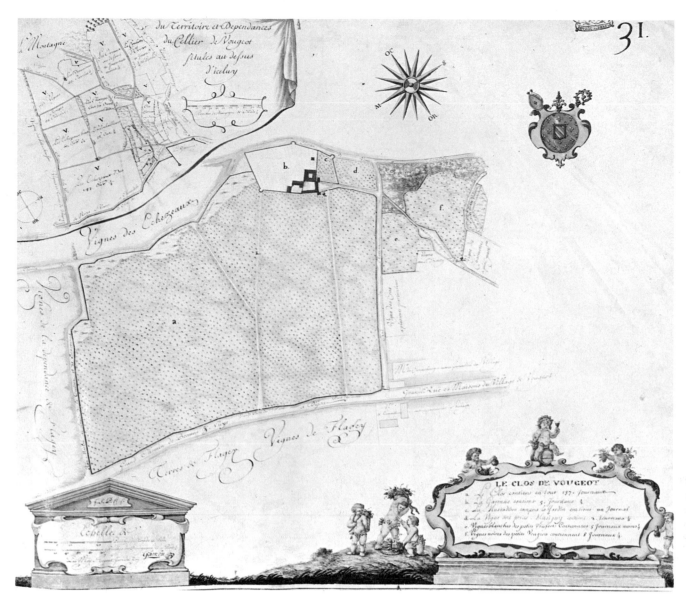

Created in about 1150 by the Bernardine monks of Cîteaux, the Clos-Vougeot estate very soon became a model vineyard. It has quite accurately been called the navel of Burgundy. Despite the many vicissitudes of its early history, it grew steadily until the fourteenth century. Its 128 acres are today divided among 60 different owners.

granite soil of the Beaujolais. As two writers of the region have commented : in order to savour their excellence to the full "you would need a *corniole* [gullet] as long as a swan's to make the pleasure last longer". The other is the *Aligoté*, a white grape, very old, which gives one single wine, the BOURGOGNE ALIGOTÉ.

THE CARE OF THE VINE. Tilling, pruning, looking after the vines, pest control—all these are decisive factors in the proper cultivation of the vine and the production of healthy, promising grapes. The work is done throughout the year, thus justifying an ancient saying: "The vine grows in the vintner's shadow."

The vintage itself is also part of the "care of the vine", for to gather the grapes at the correct stage of ripeness is vital and the date, always chosen with great care, is very important.

Of course, many imponderables can upset the patient vintner's work. Spring frosts, around the beginning of May, may occur in any year, resulting in the loss of up to three-quarters of the crop. *Coulure* (premature dropping of the fruit) is feared when rain or cold in June inhibit fecundation. Hail is a formidable danger to the vine; where it falls, all or most of the crop may be destroyed. The final unforseeable factor beyond man's control is the proper sequence of rain and sun. To produce a great vintage, rain is needed at the right times, and sun is needed in large amounts especially in the two months before harvesting.

VINIFICATION. It is often said that the rules of hygiene are like unattractive women—nobody follows them. To which strong-minded people add without hesitation the following maxim: "Lean heavily on your principles—they'll always give way in the end." Neither of these maxims can be applied to winemaking, especially since Burgundy adopted the shorter vinification method in 1938 in order to produce more flexible wines which matured much earlier while still maintaining their former high standards. And this is where the splitting up of vineyards mentioned above is regrettable since strict rules have to be followed and the vintner often finds it difficult to keep up with the progress made and adopt the new methods.

STORAGE AND TREATMENT. The French word *elevage*, which loosely translated means "upbringing", is much misunderstood when applied to the winegrowing profession. It has been remarkably well explained by two nineteenth-century authors, Danguy and Aubertin: "Once made, red wine must, through constant and unceasing care, be brought to the point at which it possesses all the necessary qualities for it to be tasted with pleasure." In 1885, Dr Lavalle wrote: "Precisely because of all its perfection, the wine of Burgundy demands intelligent care and, like those splendid flowers that must be painstakingly cultivated for several years before they will open their marvellous blooms, full of brightness and perfume, it requires a knowing hand to lead it skilfully and patiently to the point at which it is worthy to be offered to a man of taste."

In Burgundy, it is the buyer-shipper who, over the last few centuries, has lovingly prepared the necessary sanctuaries: cellars vaulted or built so as to maintain a relatively even temperature. The fact is that the vintner, once again because of the fragmentation of property, and the small number of large estates, quite frequently

confines himself to the growing side, and his job ends as soon as the wine is made. Furthermore the investment is considerable—a large amount of space, installations (always interesting to visit), capital to build up large stocks of bottles and barrels for the ageing period and sufficient qualified personnel are all necessary. Finally a sales organization must be set up in France and abroad to dispose of the product. These are circumstances that have made the Burgundian wine shippers, though few in number, very important people. There are two hundred of them, to be found mainly in the large wine centres.

France accounts for about 40 per cent of the buyers of the great wines of Burgundy. They are distributed through three types of buyers—wholesalers from outside the Burgundy area who sell them in their own particular markets and also to a significant number of retailers; hotel, restaurant and café owners, and individual wine merchants; and private individuals, who buy in barrels or assortments of bottles.

In 1980, exports went to 140 different countries throughout the world—18,236,658 gallons of wines with an *appellation contrôlée*, produced in Burgundy. For several years, Burgundy has ranked second among all the production areas of French *appellation contrôlée* wines by value and by volume of wines sold outside France. Quite an achievement, as the official statistics will show. For, again in 1980, Burgundy produced 14 per cent of all French wines entitled to an A.O.C. label (A.O.C. = Appellation d'Origine Contrôlée = Registered Designation of Origin), while its exports accounted for 24 per cent of French A.O.C. wines exported (excluding Champagne and sparkling wines). To be precise, exports were 6,299,942 gallons of wines in casks and 11,936,716 gallons in bottles. These figures do not include non-A.O.C. (but labelled) wines crossing the frontier since the customs statistics do not go into sufficient detail. But here too, Burgundy is at the head of the list by a wide margin.

Among the chief importers of A.O.C. Burgundy (including Beaujolais) wines in terms of volume, Switzerland ranks first. Though a small country in terms of population, it is closely linked to the province and absorbs nearly one-third of its exports. West Germany's position is uncertain because of its present regulations. With the opening of the frontiers, this market, taking 13.9 per cent at present, may be completely transformed. Next comes the United States, which now takes 13.4 per cent of Burgundy's foreign sales, and then Belgium, traditionally a lover of Burgundy wines, with 12.6 per cent. Great Britain follows next with very little concern as to A.O.C.s.; Britons still tend to drink wine *à la tasse*, i.e. by the glass. Imports are, as in the past, piecemeal, and therefore frequently consist of "labelled wines" lacking an A.O.C. but meeting the desired quality requirements. Further principal importers of A.O.C. Burgundy wines are Sweden, Canada, Denmark, and the Netherlands.

The vineyard of Clos de Bèze in the commune of Gevrey-Chambertin lies immediately adjacent to the vineyard which most firmly established this area as a producer of highest quality wine, and whose name the wines and vineyards of the region have nearly all appended to their own: Chambertin. Although Clos de Bèze is a grand cru and an A.O.C. in its own right, and is considered by some experts as being even superior to the production of the Chambertin vineyard, many proprietors take advantage of their legal right to use the famous Chambertin name for commercial reasons. The Abbey of Bèze was founded by Almagaire, Duke of Lower Burgundy, in A.D. 630.

THE WINE AREAS

Over the centuries the kingdom, duchy or province of Burgundy has been like a balloon, swelling and shrinking as circumstances dictated. Its frontiers were always vague, varying largely around a central kernel consisting of a few hundred square miles centring on the cities of Beaune and Dijon. The only definite and undisputable characteristic of Burgundy is that it has always been a crossroads, a fact that throughout its history has brought more trouble than benefits.

No feature in its geographical shape is sufficiently precise for us to be able to describe its shape. Only in the east did the Saône River clearly mark part of the boundary between the duchy (Beaune-Dijon) and the county of Burgundy (Besançon), that is between the present Haute Bourgogne and the Franche-Comté. The very nature of the terrain confirms these differences—the plain of the Saône, the vineyard slopes, the forests of the mountainous Morvan and of the Châtillonnais, a maze of fields, meadows and different crops. The twentieth century has not improved matters much, even though the division of France into departments, often arbitrarily welded together, should have given Burgundy, along with the soul which it has always had, at least a clearly defined territory. But no—and this is true of a number of other French provinces—according to the various civil, military and religious authorities there is not one Burgundy, but several, the land they cover differing quite inexplicably.

When the need arose to define the Burgundy wine area, the official attempt to do so was frankly an innovation. Ignoring history and thankfully taking into account more realistic and practical considerations, the Civil Tribunal of Dijon, in a decree dated April 29th, 1930, defined the production areas authorized to use the title Burgundy as follows: "Local, consistent and time-honoured usage has it that the Burgundy wine area is exclusively composed of the Côte-d'Or, Yonne and Saône-et-Loire departments, plus the Villefranche-sur-Saône *arrondissement* in the Rhône department."

The Burgundy wine area, of which just under half lies in the Beaujolais, consists of 105,000 acres unevenly scattered among four departments. Only the Chablis region in the north between the Yonne and the Armançon seems to hold itself aloof from the natural continuity provided for these glorious vineyards by the river Saône. The other regions on its right bank form an almost continuous belt between Dijon and Villefranche. The Côte de Nuits from Fixin to Corgoloin and the Côte de Beaune from Ladoix-Serrigny to Santanay have shared the benefits of the prestige gained by their vineyards with the whole of Burgundy. The vineyards of Mercurey, more widely scattered than the rest, provide a link with the compact southern group of the Mâconnais and the Beaujolais, linked to the Burgundy area by many geographical and commercial bonds.

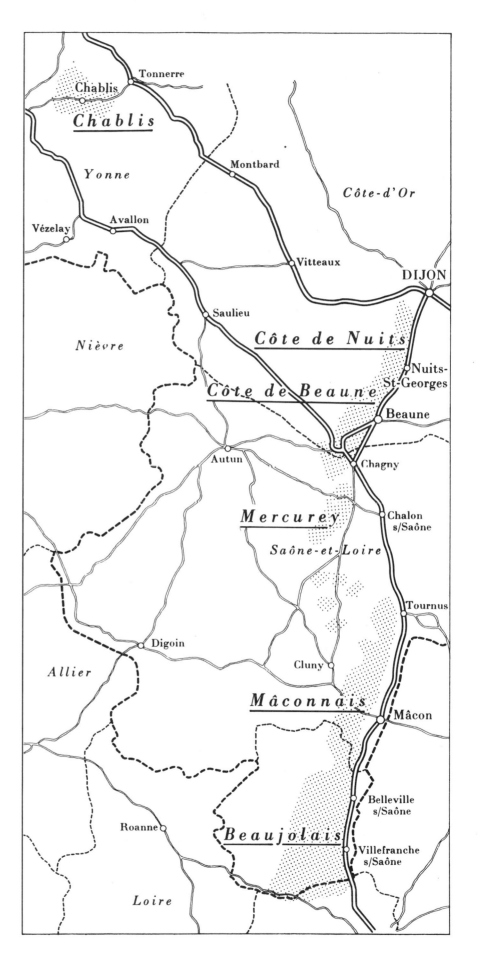

Bygone cellarman's tools: In the background, two candlesticks served to light the cellar, especially during the racking and barrelling; in front, an adze for shaping and cutting the barrel bungs; in front, right, a flat mallet for tapping the barrel to sound out the level of the wine in it.

The Villefranche-sur-Saône district, or to call it by its better-known name, the Beaujolais, has never been politically a part of Burgundy at any time in its history. As the writer, A. Julien said in 1816: "There is cause for astonishment in my joining the Beaujolais and Burgundy, since the first is part of the Rhône department. But my intention is to present and group together wines of the same type, and the wines of the Beaujolais have very little in common with those of the Lyonnais."

It is, therefore, solely on the basis of its geographical situation, the nature of its wines and its commercial traditions that this great wine area has been adopted as an integral part of the Burgundy area. There have never been any complaints about it.

Turning to the north, we find, just above the Beaujolais, the vineyards of the Mâconnais in Saône-et-Loire, quite close to the hills and a little away from the Route Nationale 6 in the south of the department, which narrows towards the north. There it meets the Mercurey region, which lies mainly on the hillside and is sometimes called the Côte Chalonnaise, a comparison with the famous wine areas farther north.

Next we enter the Côte-d'Or and follow Route Nationale 74, a triumphal procession of all the most glorious names in Burgundy. It is a narrow belt of vines, about 200 to 900 yards wide and 30 miles long; the first part is called the Côte de Beaune and the other the Côte de Nuits, after which we reach the administrative capital, Dijon. Finally, right at the top of the map, in the Yonne, we find a small patch of 7,000 acres of vines mainly around the village of Chablis.

Curiously, anyone driving down Route Nationale 6 from Paris to Lyon could remain quite unaware that they had passed through one of the world's most famous viticultural areas. But history provides the reason for this; the roadway was here even before the vine, and horses would of course pick the easiest route through the gentlest valleys. To find the vineyards, one has to leave the main road and set off towards the hills, for the vines grow here on the east or southeast flanks, seeking the greatest amount of sun.

We shall return to discuss in greater detail the structure of the various regions of the Burgundy wine area as officially defined by law.

68

DESIGNATIONS OF ORIGIN

Someone once wrote: "Good wine warms the heart, revives the brain and overhauls the machinery." It should come as no surprise to learn that a beverage with such powers has been strictly controlled since the very earliest times.

We must return to the beginning of the fifteenth century to find a document which, by its very tone, bears a certain similarity to our modern designations of origin. It is the edict of Charles VI, in February 1415, which states that: "the wines of Burgundy shall be those that are produced above the Pont de Sens, whether in the region of Auxerrois or in that of Beaulne". It further divided the wines of Burgundy into two categories—Basse-Bourgogne (Lower Burgundy) for parishes from the Pont de Sens to Cravant, including, in particular, the Auxerrois; and Haute-Bourgogne (Upper Burgundy), which was sub-divided into four regions: the Beaunois, the Mâconnais, the Tournus and the Dijonnais, in that order. The king seems to have had good advisers, since the divisions he established have been respected to this day.

Over two hundred years later, we come to the repression of fraud. On April 27th, 1622, Louis XIII prohibited, with suitable penalties, the sale, "as Burgundies, of wines of the Lyonnais and the Beaujolais".

For many years to come, the *tastevin*, or sampling cup, was to be the sole judge in disputes. "Beaune wine" was, for a very long time, the name given to all the fine wines of the Côte-d'Or and "Auxerre wine" to the wines (then mainly red) of the Yonne.

However, a basic law was enacted on August 1st, 1905 to repress "fraud or attempted fraud as regards the nature, quality, type, origin and denomination of the product". This was supported by the law of May 6th, 1919 which defined the designations and production areas, and the decree-law of July 30th, 1935 which dealt with designations of origin and established the A.O.C. system.

Thus were defined the areas in each wineproducing commune that, according to ancient custom, were entitled to call their produce quality wine, *ceteris paribus*. Thus we now have A.O.C.s. bearing the names of the villages of Fleurie, Pouilly-Fuissé, Meursault, Beaune, Nuits, Chablis, etc.

This region, in fact, is made up of small-holdings, called *climats*, the names of which often refer back to quite ancient title deeds. According to local, consistent and time-honoured usage, a number of these *climats* have been selected in an official document as being most likely to produce the best wines. They are, generally speaking, halfway up the hillside and are called the *Premiers Crus* (First Growths). On labels, price lists and bills, the name of the *climat* or vineyard always comes after the name of the village, as in the cases of BEAUNE-GRÈVES, MEURSAULT-CHARMES and POMMARD-RUGIENS, NUITS-VAUCRAINS, CHAMBOLLE-MUSIGNY AMOUREUSES, to name but a few.

Then, from these First Growths, the law has selected what used to be called *têtes de cuvée* (best of the vintage), which really had to be the best of the best. These are now called the *Grands Crus* (Great Growths) whose names stand out alone on labels and in documents. For exemple—CHAMBERTIN, MONTRACHET, CLOS VOUGEOT, CORTON, CORTON-CHARLEMAGNE, etc.

Bottles stored head to tail in a vaulted cellar. Resting in a dry and even-temperatured place, the bottles may lie for two or three years—the wine constantly improving—before being labelled and then eventually sold.

Within any commune that is not so selected, wines may be produced but they are entitled only to a more general designation—and then under certain conditions, e.g. BOURGOGNE, BOURGOGNE ALIGOTÉ, BOURGOGNE-PASSE-TOUT-GRAINS and BOURGOGNE GRAND ORDINAIRE, or a regional designation such as BEAUJOLAIS, MÂCON, PETIT CHABLIS.

Furthermore, as we have already noted above, the types of vine-stock upon which the right to an A.O.C. depends are also strictly controlled.

Since it is quite difficult to assess quality officially, one way around the problem was thought to be the supervision of two factors—the yield per hectare and the level of alcohol in the wine. The first of these may have a direct bearing on the quality. Nevertheless, it is all quite relative and frequently, if all the necessary conditions have been fulfilled throughout the year, quantity and quality may not be incompatible. This is why the law allows the yield (in the villages of the Côte-d'Or, for example, it is 35 hectolitres per hectare i.e. about 300 gallons per acre) to vary from year to year, according to the quantity and quality of the crop. The procedure is, of course, very complicated and is determined by a decree from the Minister of Agriculture.

The degree of alcohol specified is, in each case, a minimum level and an indifferent standard at that. As Georges Duhamel said during a chapter of the Brotherhood of the Knights of the Tastevin: "Though alcohol is the vital spirit of wine, it is certainly not its soul."

Though perhaps we do not always associate the thought of Burgundy with white wines, Montrachet and its immediate neighbours and cousins produce some of the world's best (and most expensive).

Nobody would dream of buying a great Burgundy wine on the basis of its alcoholic content, as though it were a table wine.

This quite complicated procedure is but a small beginning, since the movement of wine in France is not unrestricted, but governed by a whole series of legal documents as well as all the decrees on wine production. For example, every year before the harvest, the vintner must declare all the wine he possesses. After the harvest, he must declare the amount produced in every one of his vineyards. These two statements are kept by the appropriate services of the indirect taxation authority. If the wine leaves the wineproducer's cellars, whether for sale or as a gift, it must be accompanied by an official document, the excise papers delivered by the above-mentioned authority. Its function is to "release" from bond wines destined for bars, hotels, restaurants, retailers, middlemen and private persons, where the duties must be paid at the outset. If the wine is for a wholesaler or exporter, these papers act as a sort of permit for payment of duties to be deferred in the case of wholesalers or not to be levied at all in the case of exporters.

It is, therefore, easy to check on remaining stocks, which is done by the indirect taxation authority twice a year and also by the fraud and quality control brigade, which may make spot checks at any time.

Further explanation is needed of a number of well known Burgundy A.O.C.s which are difficult to find on any wine map. For example—CÔTE DE BEAUNE-VILLAGES. The fact is that the A.O.C. given by law may, in some cases, be changed, but always downwards. This is called *déclasser* (to downgrade) a wine.

It is often a voluntary process, generally to meet commercial requirements. Thus the wines of many little-known villages are sometimes hard to sell under their own names and are, therefore, downgraded to a more regional A.O.C.—CÔTE DE BEAUNE-VILLAGES or BOURGOGNE, for example. Or a shipper who has created a trade name puts it under a simple regional A.O.C., the highest common denominator of all the wines sold under the name.

Downgrading may, of course, also be compulsory. For example, two or several wines from different A.O.C.s may, for one reason or other, be mixed. In principle, the resulting wine may not use either or any of the original A.O.C.s, but must use one common to them all. Thus, the blending of a CHAMBERTIN with a CHARMES-CHAMBERTIN gives a plain GEVREY-CHAMBERTIN; a BEAUNE and an ALOXE-CORTON gives an ordinary BOURGOGNE. Downgrading is also compulsory if the grower exceeds the allotted maximum yield of any particular A.O.C.

In the Gevrey-Chambertin region, as elsewhere in Burgundy, there are grands crus (in red on the map), premiers crus (in yellow), and village and regional growths (in green).

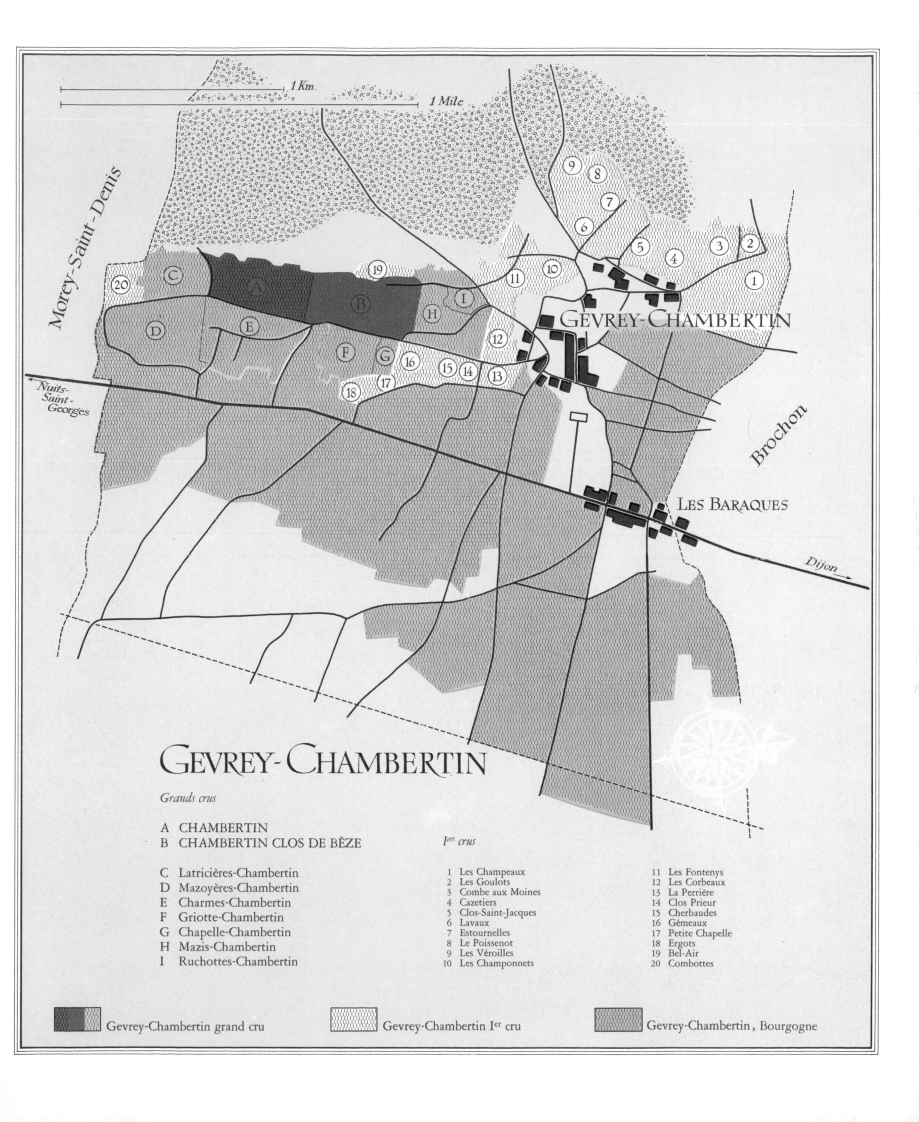

GEVREY-CHAMBERTIN

Grands crus

A CHAMBERTIN
B CHAMBERTIN CLOS DE BÈZE

C Latricières-Chambertin
D Mazoyères-Chambertin
E Charmes-Chambertin
F Griotte-Chambertin
G Chapelle-Chambertin
H Mazis-Chambertin
I Ruchottes-Chambertin

I[ers] crus

1 Les Champeaux
2 Les Goulots
3 Combe aux Moines
4 Cazetiers
5 Clos-Saint-Jacques
6 Lavaux
7 Estournelles
8 Le Poissenot
9 Les Véroilles
10 Les Champonnets

11 Les Fontenys
12 Les Corbeaux
13 La Perrière
14 Clos Prieur
15 Cherbaudes
16 Gémeaux
17 Petite Chapelle
18 Ergots
19 Bel-Air
20 Combottes

Gevrey-Chambertin grand cru   Gevrey-Chambertin Ier cru   Gevrey-Chambertin, Bourgogne

CHAMBERTIN

1. Chambertin – the name of the wine. This simple title should never be confused with the A.O.C. Gevrey-Chambertin (see opposite page). Chambertin is one of the Great Growths of the commune of Gevrey-Chambertin. – 2. The compulsory inclusion of the A.O.C. ensures that the wine is from the 33 acres of the Chambertin *climat* and no other. – 3. The vintage. The fact that it is on the label and not on the neck band is an additional guarantee of authenticity. – 4. The name of the shipper, compulsory in the case of A.O.C. wines. – 5. Bottled by the shipper – another guarantee of authenticity.

CHAMBERTIN – CLOS DE BÈZE

1. Chambertin – the name of the wine. At first glance, no difference between this label and the above. One thing, then, is certain—it is a Chambertin and therefore a great wine. – 1a. Clos de Bèze provides an additional clue. This *climat* is also a Great Growth of the commune of Gevrey-Chambertin (see map on page 71). However, although a Chambertin-Clos de Bèze may be called Chambertin, the reverse is not possible. On some labels, the Clos de Bèze comes immediately below Chambertin in the same type-face. – 2. The compulsory inclusion of the A.O.C. has Chambertin alone; it could equally mention Chambertin-Clos de Bèze. – 3. 4. 5. As above.

CHARMES-CHAMBERTIN

1. Charmes-Chambertin – the name of the wine. In this case, a different name comes before the word Chambertin. It is not the name of the commune but of the *climat* (see map on page 71). Such a label designates a Great Growth, albeit of lesser repute than the two above. Similar labels are used by other *climats*: Chapelle-Chambertin, Griotte-Chambertin, Latricières-Chambertin, Mazis-Chambertin and Ruchottes-Chambertin. All these are Great Growths from the commune of Gevrey-Chambertin. – 2. The A.O.C. may not mention Chambertin alone but must by law cover both – Charmes-Chambertin. – 3. 4. 5. As above.

GEVREY-CHAMBERTIN "LES CAZETIERS"

1. Gevrey-Chambertin – the name of the wine. Here we have the name of the commune; it is therefore not a great wine but a village A.O.C. – 1a. Under the village A.O.C. comes the *climat* concerned – "Les Cazetiers". Since this name is in the list of First Growths (see page 107), the full title, "Gevrey-Chambertin Les Cazetiers" indicates a First Growth from Gevrey-Chambertin. That is to say, a wine whose precise geographical origin guarantees its quality. The name of the vineyard must be mentioned on the label in letters no higher or wider than those of the A.O.C. of the commune. – 2. Note that the A.O.C. mentions Gevrey-Chambertin; it might also have been in full – "Gevrey-Chambertin Les Cazetiers". – 3. 4. 5. As above.

GEVREY-CHAMBERTIN

1. Gevrey-Chambertin – the name of the wine. This label bears only the village A.O.C. It is, therefore, a wine from somewhere in the commune of Gevrey-Chambertin other than a vineyard producing Great of First Growths, except where the latter may have been downgraded to Gevrey-Chambertin. 2. The A.O.C. guarantees that the wine is exclusively from the commune of Gevrey-Chambertin. This is not necessarily a guarantee of quality. – 3. The vintage. – 4. 5. More than in the previous cases, the name of the shipper is the real guarantee of quality. By clearly indicating his name, the shipper stakes his reputation.

BOURGOGNE (BURGUNDY)

1. 1a. Bourgogne – the generic name and "La Vignée", a trade name. This label is very different from the previous ones, firstly because it does not bear the name Chambertin or Gevrey-Chambertin. The generic classification as Burgundy means that the wine is from different places in Burgundy. It may even be Gevrey-Chambertin alone. The shipper is not satisfied with the generic description alone and has added his trade name "La Vignée". This means he attached great importance to the quality of this wine. – 2. The Burgundy A.O.C. only means that the wine was made in Burgundy. In judging its quality, the trade name and the name of the shipper will be decisive factors. – 3. Bottling by the shipper himself also indicates that he attaches a great deal of importance to the quality of the wine. N.B. – It will be seen that the vintage is not mentioned on the label. In this case, it will be on the neck of the bottle or there may be no vintage indicated at all.

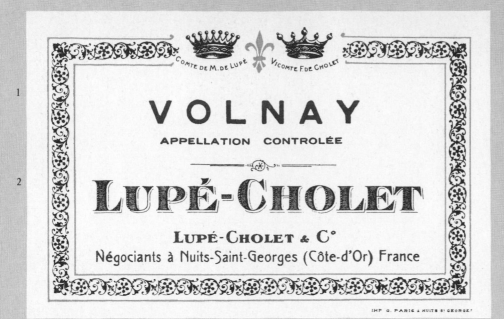

VOLNAY

1. Volnay – the A.O.C. This is a village growth in the Côte de Beaune. A simple A.O.C. guaranteeing quality. – 2. In such cases, the name of the shipper is decisive in any *a priori* judgement of quality.

BEAUNE CLOS DES MOUCHES

1. Beaune – the A.O.C. – 2. The name of the vineyard is "Clos des Mouches". Since it is written in larger type-face than the A.O.C., it must be a First Growth. If it were not, the type-face of the name of the vineyard would have to be no more than half the height and width of that of the A.O.C. – 3. The name of the shipper. His sales monopoly *(monopole de vente)* should be taken as a guarantee of authenticity and quality.

GRANDS ÉCHÉZEAUX

1. Grands Echézeaux – the name of the wine, immediately followed by the A.O.C. At first sight, we see it is not a village A.O.C. It is probably a Great Growth. The connoisseur will then identify it as one of the seven Great Growths of the commune of Vosne-Romanée. – 2. The indication of how many bottles were made and the individual bottle number leave no room for doubt; we have ample proof that this is a very great wine, nicely confirmed by the date of the vintage. – 3. The name of the proprieter is enough to convince even the most cautious. – 4. That it is estate-bottled is a logical conclusion from the fact that the number of bottles made has already been mentioned.

MERCUREY

1. Mercurey – the A.O.C. This is not a great growth or a village A.O.C. but that of a region following the Côte de Beaune (see page 109). Mercurey wines are not unlike the Côte de Beaune wines. – 2. In the case of communal or regional A.O.C.s, the good name of the shipper is the guarantee of quality.

BROUILLY

1. Brouilly – the A.O.C. Only a Beaujolais fan would know that this is a First Growth Beaujolais, for the word Beaujolais is not on the label. Thus a minimum knowledge of the wines of this region is required to tell what wine a Brouilly is. The same type of label is used for the following names: Chénas, Chiroubles, Côte de Brouilly, Fleurie, Juliénas, Morgon, Moulin-à-Vent and Saint-Amour. – 2. Bottling by the shipper is an additional guarantee of authenticity.

BEAUJOLAIS

1. Beaujolais – the A.O.C. This is a regional name. A clear distinction should be made between Beaujolais, Beaujolais Supérieur and Beaujolais-Village, which are three quite separate A.O.C.s. The first is the most common. – 2. The shipper's name here is very important, for there are as many types of Beaujolais as there are producers.

THE CHABLIS REGION

Let us now study the regions of Burgundy in detail, starting in the north and finishing far to the south.

The vines of Chablis go far back in time. They were first widely grown under the Roman occupation. Their home is in the department of Yonne, which takes its name from the river passing through it on its way to Montereau, where it meets the Seine.

The capital of the department is Auxerre, known in the ancient chronicles as Autissiodurum, Autricidurum and Alciodurum, and later Auceure or Aucerre. It is a very ancient town which already existed in the time of the Celts and flourished in Roman times. It was by then a "city"—*civitas Autissiodorum*—and gave its name to a vast region stretching as far as the Loire—the *Pagus Autissodorensis*. Although St. Pilgrim first christianized the inhabitants in the third century, the sixth bishop of the region, St. Germain, who owned vineyards there, contributed equally to the spread of the faith. His youth was eventful and his public life dubious until he was appointed to this important post. At that time he changed suddenly and completely; his conduct became exemplary and he well deserved his eventual canonization. All the while, he carefully tended his extensive vineyards, and though he could not enjoy his wines himself, he unstintingly offered them to his guests who, as an ancient writer records, greatly appreciated them. Together with St. Martin, he was one of the most popular saints.

The wines of the region were then known as the wines of Auxerre. They were red wines and kept their name until the eighteenth century. Meanwhile the wines of Chablis were gaining a reputation of their own. This came through a long-established monastery, founded in 510 by St. Sigismund, and subsequently through a junior branch at the Abbey of Cîteaux, at Pontigny, built in 1114, which created a *clos* (vineyard) like the Clos de Vougeot. Benefiting, as we have seen, from the reputation of the parent branch, it is not surprising that the quality of the wines it produced became known throughout Europe. The vine spread across the whole region and by the twelfth century "the number of presses had to be increased considerably", as the Abbot Leneuf tells us.

It is true that these vineyards had one great advantage; while land transport was difficult because of the vehicles used and the bad condition of the roads, to say nothing of the robbers, brigands and other unsavoury characters so popular at the time, the two waterways of the Yonne and the Saône enabled the wines to reach Paris easily. The capital had "French" wines—that is local wines from the Ile de France—but the better wines were supplied by Auxerre. This enabled produc-

tion to increase so that by the nineteenth century it was the largest in Burgundy. In 1788, 79,487 acres were under vines; by 1866, 93,235 acres were planted and in 1888, when the phylloxera struck, 100,323 acres were producing wine. The bourgeois and the nobility of Paris also contributed: they liked, as they do today, to have a country residence and vineyards in the region. In 1527, there were an estimated 700 or so. By the end of the sixteenth century, Olivier de Serres could write: "One sees the great towns vacated by presidents, councillors, bourgeois and other notables, who retire to their rustic farms for the wines, preferring to take so much trouble to drink well rather than to drink badly and avoid the discomforts of their rustic seats."

The development of the vineyards was abruptly halted by the invasion of phylloxera at the close of the nineteenth century. At the same time, its once so favourable situation was changed for the worse by progress. The birth of the railways opened up new areas to modern transportation. The completion of the Paris-Marseilles line made it possible to ship the wines of the Midi easily to Paris. The vines of the south grew in better conditions and, in particular, were not threatened by frost. Yields were higher and prices lower in spite of transport costs. The winegrowers of the Yonne, faced with this competition and defeated by the ravages of phylloxera, did not believe expensive restocking to be worthwhile. Almost the only area to be restocked was the Chablis, where the great white wines were grown. In 1979, production was 428,714 gallons of red wines, and 3,107,366 gallons of white wines from 5,392 acres under cultivation.

Chablis is a small town that has preserved many facets of the past. It was once a fortified town but the Porte Noël is almost the last vestige of those times. The town is almost exactly halfway between Auxerre (Route Nationale 6) and Tonnerre (Route Nationale 5) and is divided by the river Serein, which is a tributary of the Yonne.

The importance of the Serein is that it has cut a valley at an altitude of about 450 feet through low hills (the average height of which is 900 feet) on which the Chablis vines grow.

On the right hand bank of the Serein, facing Chablis, grow the vines that produce the great wines sold under the name of CHABLIS GRAND CRU, followed sometimes by the name of the vineyard. There are seven of these vineyards: LES BLANCHOTS, exactly opposite the town near the road going up to Fyé: then, to the north, LES CLOS, VALMUR, GRENOUILLES, VAUDÉSIR, LES PREUSES and BOUGROS. Altogether, these Great Growths produce an average of (1974-1978) 98,868 gallons.

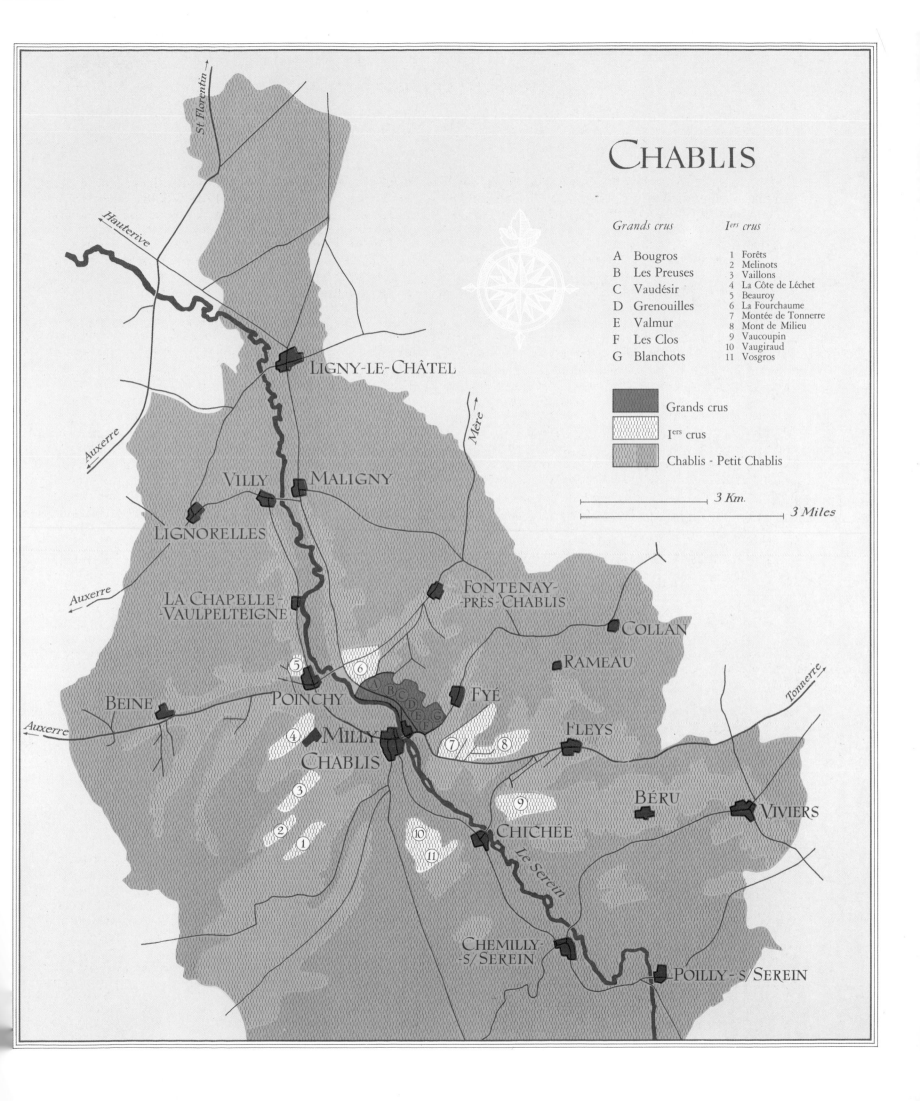

CHABLIS

St Florentin

Hauterive

Auxerre

Mère

Tonnerre

LIGNY-LE-CHÂTEL

VILLY MALIGNY

LIGNORELLES

Auxerre

LA CHAPELLE-
-VAULPELTEIGNE

FONTENAY-
-PRÈS-CHABLIS

COLLAN

RAMEAU

5 6

BEINE

POINCHY

FYÉ

Auxerre

4 MILLY-
CHABLIS

FLEYS

3

9

BÉRU

VIVIERS

2

10 CHICHÉE

1

11

Le Serein

CHEMILLY-
-S/SEREIN

POILLY - S/SEREIN

Grands crus

A   Bougros
B   Les Preuses
C   Vaudésir
D   Grenouilles
E   Valmur
F   Les Clos
G   Blanchots

1ers crus

1   Forêts
2   Melinots
3   Vaillons
4   La Côte de Léchet
5   Beauroy
6   La Fourchaume
7   Montée de Tonnerre
8   Mont de Milieu
9   Vaucoupin
10   Vaugiraud
11   Vosgros

Grands crus

1ers crus

Chablis - Petit Chablis

3 Km.

3 Miles

Other wines produced are the CHABLIS PREMIER CRU, in scattered vineyards on both sides of the river. The main vineyards entitled to this A.O.C. are on the right bank—with MONT DE MILIEU and MONTÉE DE TONNERRE to the south of the Great Growths and to the north FOURCHAUME, with VAUCOUPIN in the commune of Chichée. On the left bank, we find such names as FORÊTS, MONTMAINS, VAILLONS, MÉLINOTS, CÔTES DE LECHET, BEAUROY and others, and in Chichée, VAUGIRARD and VOSGROS. The average yield (1974-1978) of this designation is 444,356 gallons.

The third A.O.C. is CHABLIS, used by various vineyards in the region, still on the same hills as mentioned above. The average production (1974-1978) is 794,530 gallons.

The fourth A.O.C. of the region is PETIT CHABLIS, a name given to white wines grown in a larger area but on quite scattered vines. The average is (1974-1978) 132,594 gallons.

If we add all these figures together we have an average production of 1,470,216 gallons, on a total of some 3,520,000 gallons. The difference is made up by more general types grown throughout the region—BOURGOGNE (red or white), BOURGOGNE GRAND ORDINAIRE (red or white), BOURGOGNE ALIGOTÉ (white). The same occurs in the other wineproducing communes, especially those of the Côte d'Or.

In sum, the least and the most one can say about the white wines of Chablis is that this name is synonymous, throughout the world, with dry white wine, positive proof of their great fame.

In 1759, Canon Gaudin wrote to Madame d'Epinay: "My Chablis wine has body to it. Its fragance caresses the throat and leaves a delicate aftertaste of mushrooms." Under the Restoration, the Chevalier de Piis sang its praises thus:

Qui pourra mettre en oubli
Le limpide et sec CHABLIS
Qui joint à tant d'autres titres,
L'art de faire aimer les huîtres?

Who could ever forget
The clear and dry CHABLIS
Which adds to its many virtues
That of inducing a love for oysters?

In the nineteenth century a wine expert called Jules Guyot passed the following judgement: "The wines of Chablis occupy one of the front ranks of the white wines of France. Spirited without the spirit being felt, they have body, subtlety and a delightful fragrance. They are, above all, outstanding for their cleanness and digestibility as well as the stimulating, warming and clear effect on the intellect. Despite their justly deserved reputation of long standing, their real value is, for me, far higher than their fame."

It is scarcely necessary to add further praise after the passages quoted above. Since the last century the white wines of the Chablis region of Burgundy have been irreproachable. They delight all winelovers when drunk with fish and seafoods during the first part of a well-planned meal.

The slopes of Poinchy are within the Chablis vineyard, and produce famous white wines, particularly the PREMIER CRU BEAUROY.

THE CÔTE DE NUITS

We now leave the region of Chablis and turn west. After 22 miles of many different landscapes, in which there are but a few insignificant vineyards, we reach the Côte d'Or and the administrative capital of Burgundy, Dijon. It is a town with many interesting monuments, such as the former palace of the dukes of Burgundy, La Chartreuse de Champmol, the cathedral of St. Benigne, the churches of St. Michael and Our Lady, old buildings, a magnificent fine arts museum etc., but little to do with the great wines of Burgundy. However, there are large manufacturers of liqueurs—including Crème de Cassis, the famous blackcurrant liqueur and such specialities of the town as mustard and gingerbread. In the past there were many vineyards around Dijon which formed the "Côte Dijonnaise". But first phylloxera and then the growth of the town itself gradually wiped them out.

Dijon was once reputed for its *vins de garde* (wines worth laying down) that took some little time to "settle down" but that aged well and could be kept for many years. Since the short vinification process has been used, these wines are, like all Burgundies, ready earlier. They develop all their qualities much sooner but must also be drunk much sooner.

In order to visit the Côte de Nuits and the Côte de Beaune, we must head due south along Route Nationale 74 which will take us into Saône-et-Loire and on the way show us all the most famous growths of Upper Burgundy. This road is about 720 feet above sea level and to the right of Dijon we can see the small hills that overlook the plain from between 450 and 900 feet. Their summits are almost always denuded or covered with Austrian black pine. On their slopes grow the vines that produce the A.O.C. wines, the Route Nationale almost forming their farthest limit. In the plain that continues to the Saône and the Jura grow scattered vineyards producing a number of ordinary wines but not sufficient to supply the needs of the department. Before beginning our visit of the Côte de Nuits, let us look at a few figures. In all the Côte d'Or there are 19,194 acres of vineyards producing an average 7,480,000 gallons of A.O.C. wines. The number of vineyards of A.O.C. quality amounted, in 1980, to 1,813, with an average surface of 10.5 acres—which once again goes to show how far the land has been split up and the disadvantages this brings.

THE COMMUNE OF CHENÔVE

This is the first of the winemaking villages to come into view, at the foot of a hill 2 ½ miles from Dijon. Here can be visited the great vineyard of the dukes of Burgundy, which contains two magnificent thirteenth-century presses, one of which, used mainly for white wine, was in use until 1926. The names CLOS-DU-ROI and CLOS-DU-CHAPITRE recall their ancient masters. The A.O.C. wines are sold under regional A.O.C.s.

THE COMMUNE OF ·MARSANNAY-LA-CÔTE

Two miles farther on, south of Chenôve, lies this commune, famous for its rosé wines. They have become its speciality, since rosé wines are rare in Burgundy where the preference is for great red or white wines, unless catastrophic weather conditions have wiped them out—fortunately a rare occurrence. Rosé wines, obtained by crushing red grapes without vatting them, can only be sold under a regional A.O.C.—BOURGOGNE, for example, followed in the case of Marsannay by the name of the commune.

THE COMMUNE OF FIXIN

This village gives us our first A.O.C. bearing the local name—Fixin. It is an ancient village and was once attached to the abbey of Bèze. Apart from its wines, it is also famous for a statue by the sculptor Rude, *The Awakening of Napoleon*, set up in a park in 1847 by Noisot, the commander of the grenadier guards.

The vineyards of Fixin produce about 22,000 gallons of red wine. However, other wine is sold under the more general A.O.C.—CÔTE DE NUITS-VILLAGES and other regional A.O.C.s. In the nineteenth century, the wine experts Danguey and Aubertin wrote as follows about the wines of Fixin: "These wines have a spirit, colour and bouquet that develops with age, as well as a great ability to keep a long time." We might mention in passing the classed First Growths of the commune: LA PERRIÈRE, named after a formerly famous quarry, the CLOS-DU-CHAPITRE, near the old buildings of the Chapter of Langres, LES ARVELETS, the name of which derives from *arbelaie* (place where maples grow), AUX CHEUSOTS, today called the CLOS-NAPOLÉON, LES MEIX-BAS and finally LES HERVELETS.

THE COMMUNE OF BROCHON

This village, about half a mile to the south of Fixin, was famous in former times as the home of Dijon's tragic poet, Prosper Jolyot de Crébillon (1674-1762). It now produces wines of which the best are sold as GEVREY-CHAMBERTIN and others as CÔTE-DE-NUITS-VILLAGES or as regional A.O.C.s. Some cheap, non-export wines are also produced from the *Gamay*.

Most of the wines made in the Fixin vineyards (above) are sold under the label 'Vin fin de la Côte de Nuits'; it is rare to see FIXIN and FIXIN PREMIER CRU on winemerchants' shelves.

THE COMMUNE OF GEVREY-CHAMBERTIN

Quite nearby, some eight miles from Dijon, lies the very important wine village of Gevrey, which by royal decree added the name of its best vineyard, Chambertin, to its own in 1847. In the Rue Haute the ruins of a castle belonging to the abbots of Cluny can still be seen. There are a great many vineyards producing a range of very great red wines. Let us consider first of all the Great Growths of which the following first two are the most famous.

CHAMBERTIN-CLOS-DE-BÈZE owes its name to the monks of the abbey of Bèze, who owned this land from the seventh century, through an endowment made by Amalgaire, the Duke of Lower Burgundy. The area under cultivation is 37 acres and the average yield of this designation (1975-1979) 9,614 gallons.

Immediately next to it lies the vineyard of CHAMBERTIN, named after a vinegrower named Bertin who originally owned land adjacent to that of the monks of Bèze, on which he planted the same wine-stock and produced an excellent wine. It became known locally as the *champ de Bertin* (Bertin's field), and has since become one of the most celebrated wines of Burgundy. Its area is 32 acres and it produces an average (1975-1979) of 10,472 gallons. Gaston Roupnel said of this wine: "It blends grace with vigour. It joins firmness to delicacy and subtlety. All these contrary qualities produce in it an admirable synthesis of unique generosity and absolute virtue. It is in itself as great a Burgundy as it is possible to have."

CHARMES-CHAMBERTIN. Part of this vineyard was formerly called Mazoyères-Chambertin. Charmes apparently comes from *chaume* meaning "fallow land". Area—78 acres: Average yield—(1975-1979) 20,900 gallons.

CHAPELLE-CHAMBERTIN. This vineyard once held a chapel dedicated to Our Lady, built in 1155 and razed to the ground in the time of the French Revolution. Area—13 acres: Average yield—(1975-1979) 4,268 gallons.

GRIOTTE-CHAMBERTIN. This name signifies either a place planted with cherries *(griottes)*, or an area of rock called, in the local dialect, *criot*. Area—13½ acres: Average yield—(1975-1979) 1,474 gallons.

LATRICIÈRES-CHAMBERTIN. Area—17 acres: Average yield—(1975-1979) 4,796 gallons.

MAZIS-CHAMBERTIN. Area—31 acres: Average yield (1975-1979) 5,324 gallons.

RUCHOTTES-CHAMBERTIN. Area—8 acres: Average yield—(1975-1979) 1,870 gallons.

The difference in quality among these Great Growths is slight. Gaston Roupnel said of these wines, which all add the name Chambertin to their own: "Nothing is more appropriate than this ancient usage. Between Chambertin on one hand and Latricières and Charmes on the other hand, the difference lies in a toning down of vigour and robustness, often compensated for in good years by a more clearly tangible delicateness that is more sensitive, more mature."

Apart from these Great Growths, there are about 301,136 gallons of great red wines entitled to the A.O.C. GEVREY-CHAMBERTIN. Many vineyards are classified as First Growths. These, too, were praised by Gaston Roupnel, who valued highly "these firm, ruddy wines, of full and flavoured body".

THE COMMUNE OF MOREY-SAINT-DENIS

This village, 2½ miles away from Gevrey-Chambertin, followed somewhat tardily the fashion of the Côte and in 1927 added to its own name that of one of the most famous vineyards. It was, perhaps, commercially a mistake, since Morey is easier to pronounce in every language and therefore a better market prospect.

Its remarkable wines, though relatively little known, were sold as Chambolle-Musigny or Gevrey-Chambertin before the law on A.O.C.s. was passed. Nevertheless, among its vineyards are four Great Growths (red), of which the Burgundy expert Dr Ramain said in the last century that they were "powerful nectars, full-bodied, sappy, with their own special savour and a strong fragrance of strawberries or violets". These Great Growths are four in number, although most of one of them, the vineyard of LES BONNES-MARES, lies in Chambolle-Musigny and will therefore be dealt with under the next heading.

CLOS-SAINT-DENIS. This name was given because the vineyard once belonged to the abbey of St. Denis of Vergy, founded in 1623 by the archdeacon of Autun near Nuits-Saint-Georges. Area—16 acres: Average yield—(1975-1979) 3,542 gallons.

CLOS-DE-LA-ROCHE is the near neighbour of the Great Growths of Gevrey-Chambertin. Area—38 acres: Average yield—(1975-1979) 9,416 gallons.

CLOS-DE-TART. This once belonged to the Bernadine nuns of the convent of Our Lady of Tart, which received it in 1260 from the Chevalier Etienne Dojon. During the Revolution it was sold for 68,000 pounds. Area—18 acres: Average yield—(1975-1979) 3,740 gallons.

Apart from these Great Growths, about 50,776 gallons of MOREY-SAINT-DENIS (including First Growths) are produced, almost all red, of which Danguy and Aubertin gave the following appreciation: "A fine colour, a bouquet developing with age, full-bodied and winy."

THE COMMUNE OF CHAMBOLLE-MUSIGNY

About a mile and a quarter to the south, quite far away from Route Nationale 74 and some three miles from Gevrey-Chambertin, huddled in a coomb, we find the tiny village of Chambolle-Musigny. The name of its most famous vineyard, Musigny, was added to it in 1878. Dr Lavalle, the nineteenth-century writer on Burgundy wines, wrote: "Many people are of the opinion that this commune produces the most delicate wines of the Côte de Nuits". The two best:

MUSIGNY. "The wine of silk and lace, the supreme delicateness of which knows no violence but can veil its vigour", as Gaston Roupnel put it. The name of the vineyard is very ancient; it is already found in an Act of 1110. It produces a few gallons of white wine—quite exceptional in this area and for a Great Growth—about 110 on the average (1975-1979), as against 5,500 for red in a total area of 26 acres.

LES BONNES-MARES. As we have seen, this vineyard lies partly in Morey-Saint-Denis (4½ acres) and partly in Chambolle (34 acres). Its name recalls perhaps the *Maires*, the goddesses who protected the harvests in many ancient nations, or possibly the word *marer*, to plough. An average (1975-1979) of 8,800 gallons is produced here.

Apart from these two Great Growths, Chambolle-Musigny has First Growths entitled to the village A.O.C. Danguy and Aubertin said about them: "They have a fine delicate bouquet and several wine experts have said they are the finest, most perfumed and most delicate in the Côte de Nuits. They are extremely winy, beautifully coloured and pungent." Average yield under the CHAMBOLLE-MUSIGNY A.O.C. (including First Growths) is 96,580 gallons. The following are some of the First Growth vineyards: LES AMOUREUSES, LES CHARMES, LES CRAS, LES BORNIQUES, LES BAUDES, LES HAUTS-DOIX, DERRIÈRE-LA-GRANGE, LES FOUSSELOTTES, LES PLANTES, LES CHATELOTS, LES GRUENCHERS, AUX BEAUX-BRUNS and AUX COMBOTTES.

THE COMMUNE OF VOUGEOT

About half a mile from Chambolle, beside the Route Nationale, lies the smallest village in the Côte but certainly one of the best known throughout the world, especially since the brotherhood of the Knights of the Tastevin began inviting wine-lovers from every country to its "Chapters" held in the château on the property. Apart from these and official guests, representatives of the press, radio, television and cinema—the modern means of communication—are particularly fond of the place. It is not surprising that its name is on everybody's lips. The CLOS-DE-VOUGEOT is "a solemn and beautiful thing, powerful yet not overpowering", said Gaston Roupnel.

The property was first developed by the monks of Cîteaux, early in the twelfth century. There followed a patient task of regrouping, since, apart from endowments, several parcels of land had to be incorporated before it reached its present size of 124 acres.

At first, the monks built a modest chapel, a shelter for their presses and a cellar for their new wines. The wines, when ready, were taken to a safer refuge and better cellars in the Château of Gilly-les-Vougeot, a few miles away in the plain. During the Renaissance, in 1551, the 48th abbot, Dom Jean Loisir, had the château built. It remained the property of Cîteaux until the Revolution, when it was sold as a "national asset". Thus began the subdivisions that only stopped when 65 owners shared the vines and the Brotherhood owned the building.

The wine produced at the Clos-Vougeot, classified as a Great Growth, has always enjoyed the very best of reputations and even received military honours. Stendhal tells us how Colonel Bisson, while passing on his way to join the army on the Rhine, halted his troops and made them present arms before the Clos to the sound of bugles and drums. The Duke of Aumale apparently did the same.

An average (1975-1979) of 28,600 gallons of wine with the A.O.C. CLOS-VOUGEOT or, to give it its modern form, CLOS-DE-VOUGEOT A.O.C., is produced yearly.

Grands crus

1 La Tache
2 Romanée
3 Romanée-Conti
4 Romanée-Saint-Vivant
5 Richebourg
6 Echezeaux
  Grands-Echezeaux   7 Clos-de-Vou

Appellations de commune   NUITS-SAINT-GEORGES   VOSNE-ROMANÉE   VOUGEOT

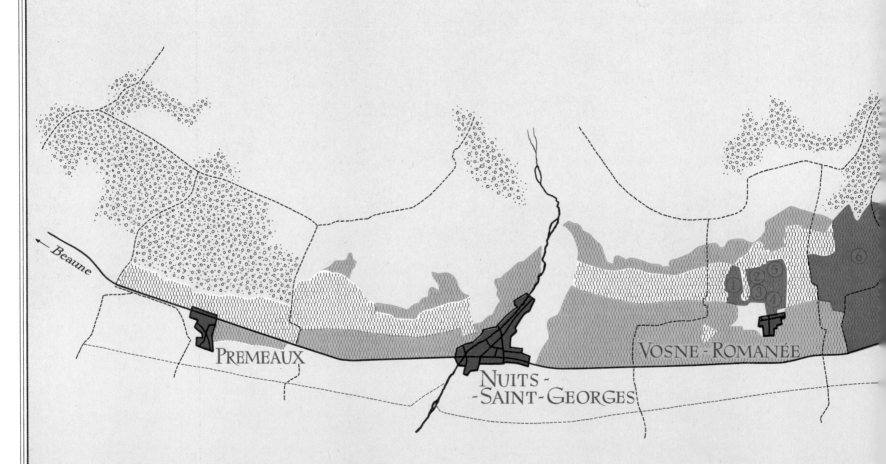

LA CÔTE DE NUITS

14 Mazoyères-Chambertin
15 Latricières-Chambertin
16 Charmes-Chambertin
17 Chambertin
18 Chambertin-Clos-de-Bèze
10 Bonnes-Mares   19 Griotte-Chambertin
11 Clos-de-Tart   20 Chapelle-Chambertin
8 Musigny   12 Clos-Saint-Denis   21 Mazis-Chambertin
9 Bonnes-Mares   13 Clos-de-la-Roche   22 Ruchottes-Chambertin

CHAMBOLLE-MUSIGNY   MOREY-SAINT-DENIS   GEVREY-CHAMBERTIN   FIXIN

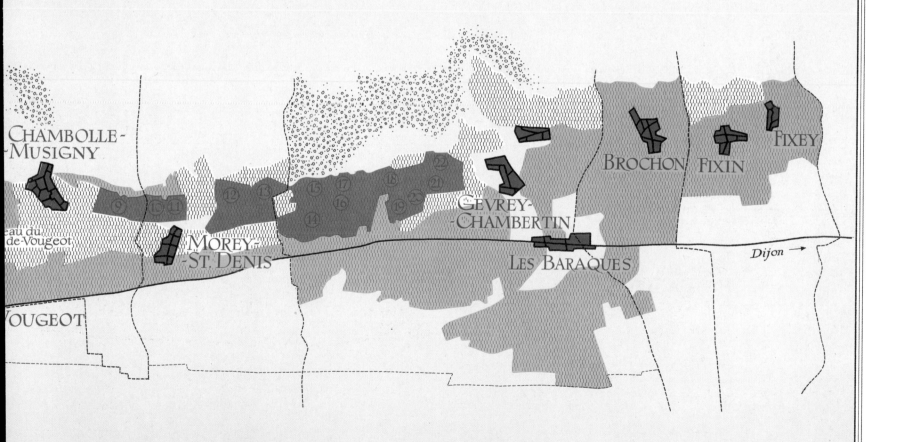

CHAMBOLLE-
-MUSIGNY

FIXEY

BROCHON   FIXIN

eau du
de-Vougeot

MOREY-
-ST. DENIS

GEVREY-
-CHAMBERTIN

VOUGEOT

LES BARAQUES

Dijon →

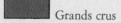 Grands crus   I^{ers} crus   Appellations de commune

Another nineteenth-century wine-lover, Dr Morelot, defined it as follows: "With ROMANÉE and CHAMBERTIN and a few others, it shares the first position among the wines of the Côte d'Or and even the whole of France."

The commune of Vougeot yields various other red wines entitled to the VOUGEOT A.O.C., but not to be confused with the Great Growth. The First Growth vineyards are: the CLOS-DE-LA-PERRIÈRE, LES CRAS, LES PETITS-VOUGEOTS and the CLOS-BLANC.

THE COMMUNE OF VOSNE-ROMANÉE

Courtépée wrote in the eighteenth century: "There are no common wines in Vosne." This little village, two miles from Vougeot, has no fewer than seven Great Growths, of which two are produced in the neighbouring commune of Flagey-Echézeaux but are legally linked with Vosne-Romanée.

The name ROMANÉE recalls ancient deeds and perhaps the beginnings of these vineyards during the Roman occupation. Three different wines carry this name:

LA ROMANÉE. About (1975-1979) 572 gallons produced from just over two acres of land.

The appellation of Vosne-Romanée is curious in that not all the vineyards entitled to use the A.O.C. actually lie in the commune of that name. Many of the wines in fact come from the adjacent and much larger vineyards of Flagey-Echezeaux, which may take their own A.O.C.s if they wish: Grands-Echezeaux and Echezeaux, for example. Part of the reason for using the more general Vosne-Romanée A.O.C. stems from the difficulty non-French speakers find in pronouncing and remembering the more specific names. All wines sold as Vosne-Romanée are red and the best of them owe their fame to a velvety softness and finesse.

ROMANÉE-CONTI. This vineyard became the property of the princes of Conti in 1760. So generously did they spread the fame of their "velvet and satin" wine, as Mgr. de Juigné described it, that their name became forever linked to the property. On 4¼ acres, an average of 1,100 gallons (just over 6,500 bottles) are produced of this wine, which Ramain called "magnificent, with a penetrating bouquet of violets, mingling with a perfume of cherries, the colour of sparkling rubies and an extremely delicate softness". This vineyard was also the last to resist phylloxera. During the last war, however, the shortage of carbon disulphide led to the vine's destruction. New grafted vine-stock had to be planted and the first vintage took place in 1952.

ROMANÉE-SAINT-VIVANT, another vineyard to bear the Romanée name, harks back to the monastery of St. Vivant, founded at the beginning of the tenth century a few miles from Nuits-Saint-Georges (24 acres producing an average [1975-1979] 5,016 gallons).

RICHEBOURG is a wine of which Camille Rodier once said: "This splendid growth with its incomparable velvetiness and wealth of bouquet is one of the most sumptuous of Burgundy." Part of its 20 acres belonged to the monks of Cîteaux before the Revolution. Average yield—(1975-1979) 4,862 gallons.

LA TACHE. With an area of 15 acres this vineyard produces an average (1975-1979) 3,520 gallons.

LES GRANDS ECHÉZEAUX and LES ECHÉZEAUX. These vineyards, the south-east neighbours of the Clos-Vougeot, are in the commune of Flagey-Echézeaux. The first—Area 23 acres: Average yield (1975-1979) 5,368 gallons. The second—76 acres and 21,230 gallons.

A final appreciation: "Burgundy has produced nothing better than this little corner, which epitomizes its enchantments and whose wines express the tender generosity of its spirit."

THE COMMUNES OF NUITS-SAINT-GEORGES AND PREMEAUX

Nuits-Saint-Georges (Saint-Georges, the name of its best vineyard, was added in 1892) is the little Burgundian village that gave its name to this part of the Côte. Little remains of its past except the church of St. Symphorien, founded in the thirteenth century. But it was here that the Brotherhood of the Knights of the Tastevin was founded by Georges Faiveley and Camille Rodier. The first chapter was held on November 16th, 1934 in the Caveau Nuiton. This soon became too small as success followed success, and today it is the Château of Clos-Vougeot, a more imposing structure, that shelters the hosts and guests at the numerous events organized by the Brotherhood.

Many important wine shippers are to be found at Nuits, together with firms specialized in the manufacture of sparkling Burgundy, of which more than one million bottles are made each year. In 1882, one of the

The imposing château of the Clos-Vougeot lies in the heart of the famous vineyard. Built in 1551 by the forty-eighth abbot of Cîteaux, Dom Jean Loisir, it vas confiscated by decree on 13 February 1790, passed through many hands, lay uninhabited for a long time, and was finally rejuvenated in 1944 when it was taken over by the illustrious brotherhood of the Knights of the Tastevin of Burgundy.

shippers, a much travelled man and long a student of the wines of the region, had the idea of using the Champagne method. The result was a white, a rosé and a red sparkling wine, the latter of which is in particularly great demand in the Nordic countries, Great Britain, the United States and other English-speaking countries. There are also several liqueur manufacturers and two large fruit juice firms in Nuits-Saint-Georges. This all goes to make the town a thriving commercial centre. As Paul Cazin remarked: "The only thing you don't see in Nuits is water."

The two communes in the title of this section produce wines sold under the A.O.C.s of NUITS or NUITS-SAINT-GEORGES (which is the same thing), and average (1975-1979) 179,498 gallons of red and 374 gallons of white wines.

Dr Lavalle once wrote: "Generally speaking, the wines of Nuits are less firm, less harsh than the wines of Gevrey and mature more quickly. They have more body and colour than those of CHAMBOLLE-MUSIGNY."

Nuits has a civic hospice, founded in 1692. Through the centuries, endowments have led to its possessing considerable property solely in vineyards producing the First Growths of the town. Every year its wines are sold by public auction, usually the Sunday before Palm Sunday.

THE COMMUNES OF PRISSEY, COMBLANCHIEN AND CORGOLOIN

These three communes are the last of the Côte de Nuits. The last two are mainly famous for their large quarries which yield a stone which is easy to polish and used to cover floors. The wines are partly covered by the A.O.C. CÔTE DE NUITS-VILLAGES.

The wines sold under this A.O.C. do not come from all the villages of the Côte de Nuits, but solely from the following five: Brochon and Fixin, mentioned at the beginning of the chapter; Prissey, Comblanchien and Corgoloin. The more famous A.O.C.s—GEVREY-CHAMBERTIN, MOREY-SAINT-DENIS, CHAMBOLLE-MUSIGNY, VOSNE-ROMANÉE and NUITS-SAINT-GEORGES may never be sold as CÔTE DE NUITS-VILLAGES. The average amount declared (1975-1979) under the A.O.C. CÔTE DE NUITS-VILLAGES is 141,570 gallons, all being red wines.

We shall now leave the Côte de Nuits with its very great red wines. Recalling what we said at the beginning of this chapter, our advice is not to let them get too old. René Engel, that reputed wine expert and Grand Cardinal of the Brotherhood of the Knights of the Tastevin, is fond of saying: "Old wines are unfortunately not always the best... To have very old wines in one's cellar is a little like having a centenarian grandmother in the family. She is proudly presented to the guests, but they must be apologized to in advance in case she has a dewdrop on the end of her nose or if she is only half awake."

The most widespread grape variety in Burgundy is the *Pinot Noir*. Once it was harvested in woven baskets (above); today, plastic, which is just as light, has replaced wicker—efficiency has ousted the picturesque.

THE CÔTE DE BEAUNE

The second part of the great vineyards of the Côte d'Or begins after the stone quarries of Comblanchien.

The wines here are more varied and though there is only one Great Growth, CORTON, among the red wines, all the Great Growths in the white wines are in this area. It used to be said that all the wines of the Côte de Beaune were "early" wines *(vins de primeur)* as opposed to the "laying down" wines *(vins de garde)* of the Côte de Nuits. In other words, they could be enjoyed much younger. Today, however, all wines are ready sooner than in the past.

Let us then follow the south-westerly road that leads from Ladoix-Serrigny in the direction of Mâcon as far as Cheilly. Some names are not always well-known, but if one day the wine-lover can spare a few moments to make the acquaintance of these wines he will have some agreeable surprises. As Guy Faiveley, Grand Master of the Brotherhood of the Knights of the Tastevin, once remarked: "There are some wines that are poets, others that are prose-writers. There are those that are performers or lithe acrobats and others that are overpowering boxers."

THE COMMUNE OF LADOIX-SERRIGNY

This winegrowing commune produces red and white wines sold under various A.O.C.s including CORTON. The reds are sold, apart from under the appellation CORTON—which is the only red Great Growth of the Côte de Beaune—mostly as CÔTE DE BEAUNE-VILLAGES. There is an average yield of about 2,156 gallons of white wine and 43,472 gallons of red sold as LADOIX.

THE COMMUNE OF ALOXE-CORTON

Aloxe is a pretty village on a small hill. In 1862, the name of its most famous vineyard was added to it. Throughout the ages, it has been graced by the exalted. The Emperor Charlemagne owned many *ouvrées* (about one-ninth of an acre) of vineyards. The Emperor Otho was also an owner: he seems to have given his name to CORTON—the *curtis* ("estate" or "garden") *Othonis* ("of Otho"). The large abbeys, including Cîteaux, possessed land in this corner of Burgundy. Two Great Growths are produced here. CORTON was mentioned by Voltaire when writing to Gabriel le Bault, president of the Parliament of Burgundy: "The older I become, Sir, the more I value your kindness. Your excellent wine is becoming indispensable to me." Especially as he did not want to pay for it! The dukes of Burgundy and later the kings of France owned 110 *ouvrées* (about 12 acres) of one of the vineyards in this A.O.C. It is still called *Le Clos du Roy*, "the king's vineyard". CORTON produces (1975-1979) about 54,758 gallons of red and 1,012 gallons of white wine. "The CORTONS of good years are perfect wines, worthy of the most delicate gourmet's table," said Dr Lavalle.

The second Great Growth is CORTON-CHARLEMAGNE, a

Standing out against the autumn mists, the 'bénatou' carrier shows how useful this functional basket is to transport the grapes from the vines to the cart on the road.

Aloxe-Corton is 3 miles north of Beaune, and contains a vineyard which gives the only Grand Cru to the Côte de Beaune; Corton has also a white Grand Cru: CORTON-CHARLEMAGNE, which commemorates the Emperor Charlemagne, who owned vineyards in what is now the commune of Aloxe. It is said that the Emperor planted for white wines in order to avoid staining his white beard.

white wine, the name obviously recalling the Emperor Charlemagne. He loved the region and made numerous gifts to the churches in the province, especially those of St. Vincent at Chalon-sur-Saône, Saulieu and other places. The annual yield averages (1975-1979) 25,564 gallons, of which Camille Rodier said: "A white wine of great bearing, rich in alcohol, forceful, golden, sappy, smelling of cinnamon and tasting of gun flint."

Aloxe-Corton produces an average of 84,986 gallons sold under its name, 99 per cent of the yield being red. Dr Lavalle said of them in the last century: "They are the firmest and frankest wines of the Côte de Beaune."

THE COMMUNE OF PERNAND-VERGELESSES

Behind the Aloxe hillock, at the bottom of a coomb in a very pretty setting, the village of Pernand-Vergelesses produces part of the CORTON and CORTON-CHARLEMAGNE

wines. As well as the CORTON, red wines are sold under the village name or as CÔTE DE BEAUNE-VILLAGES. There are 10,362 gallons of white and 54,032 gallons of red wine produced. Danguy and Aubertin wrote: "These wines are a little firmer than those of Savigny: they have fire and strength and are worth laying down."

THE COMMUNE OF SAVIGNY-LÈS-BEAUNE

Away from the Côte and at the mouth of a deep valley lies this ancient village which, for a very long time, was the home of important wine shippers. In more recent times they have tended to pass over Savigny in favour of Beaune and Nuits, but this village is still quite busy, for its wines are famous. Under the SAVIGNY A.O.C., 5,852 gallons of white and 201,586 gallons of red wines are produced. Camille Rodier said of them: "These perfumed, mellow, young and healthy wines are rich in bouquet."

THE COMMUNE OF CHOREY-LÈS-BEAUNE

Facing Savigny from the other side of Route Nationale 74 is Chorey-lès-Beaune. It produces 74,558 gallons of red wine sold under the village name or under the name of Côte de Beaune-Villages. In 1828, Dr Morelot wrote: "The good Chorey wines are used when the best quality wines are passing through a bad period. They improve them and make them agreeable to drink."

THE COMMUNE OF BEAUNE

Beaune, which has given its name to this part of the Côte since the Roman occupation, is the real capital of Burgundy. Its life is centred around the disposal of fine wines. Over sixty shippers use the numerous cellars which through the centuries were dug into its ramparts. Convents, churches and abbeys in the town and surrounding area have also used them to keep their wines well protected. Many lords have had the same idea, not to mention the militant religious orders.

The imposing bastions that rise from the ramparts and are visible from a great distance have been and still are used to store the bottles and barrels in the deep shelter of their seven-yard thick walls. For this very reason, the shippers' installations are extremely interesting to visit, as the tourists know full well. Beaune is, therefore, an extremely ancient town still almost completely surrounded by walls which guard the many historical monuments—the Basilica of Our Lady, the ancient church of St. Nicolas, the palace of the dukes of Burgundy, which has been made into a wine museum that no enthusiast should miss, the belfrey, the old houses etc., and towering above the rest, the *Hôtel-Dieu*, a marvel of the fifteenth century. It was founded in 1443 by Nicolas Rolin, then chancellor to Philip the Good, Duke of Burgundy, and his wife, Guigone de Salins, to aid the destitute. It has managed to continue its ancient role, a rare achievement. The "ladies of charity" still go from room to room caring for and comforting the sick, as they have done uninterruptedly for nearly five and a half centuries. Although the old hospital now has a modern neighbour, it has not

The Hôtel-Dieu in Beaune, founded en 1451, is one of the architectural jewels of Burgundy. This charity institution has been granted many endowments of vineyards, now totalling over 130 acres, including some of the most reputable growths of the Côte de Beaune. The wines are auctioned on the third Sunday in November.

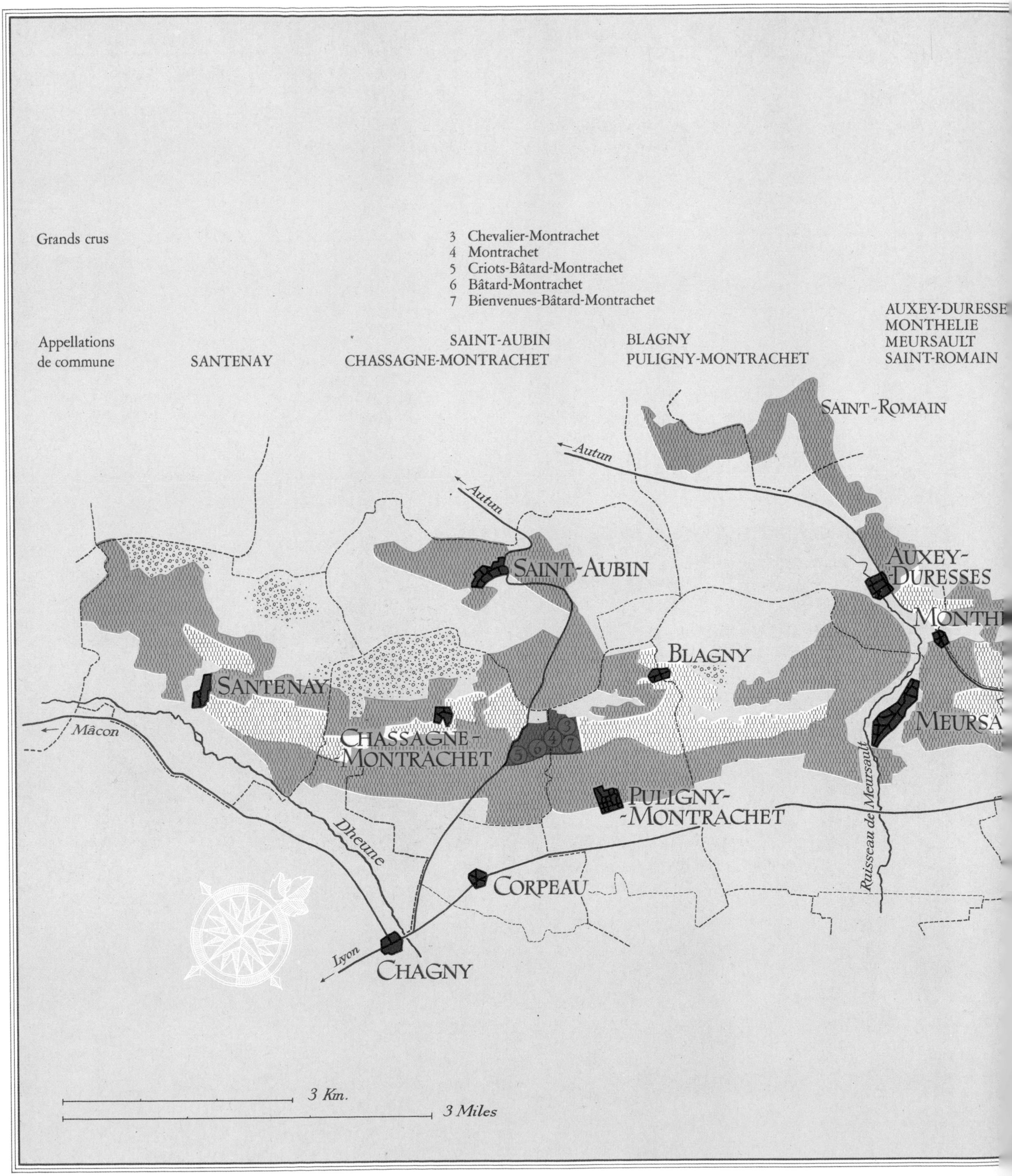

Grands crus
    3 Chevalier-Montrachet
    4 Montrachet
    5 Criots-Bâtard-Montrachet
    6 Bâtard-Montrachet
    7 Bienvenues-Bâtard-Montrachet

Appellations
de commune

SANTENAY

SAINT-AUBIN
CHASSAGNE-MONTRACHET

BLAGNY
PULIGNY-MONTRACHET

AUXEY-DURESSE
MONTHELIE
MEURSAULT
SAINT-ROMAIN

SAINT-ROMAIN

Autun

Autun

SAINT-AUBIN

AUXEY-
DURESSES

MONTH

BLAGNY

Mâcon

SANTENAY

CHASSAGNE-
MONTRACHET

3
4 7
5 6

MEURSA

Dheune

PULIGNY-
MONTRACHET

Ruisseau de Meursault

CORPEAU

Lyon

CHAGNY

3 Km.

3 Miles

La Côte de Beaune

1   Corton (rouge - red)
2   Corton-Charlemagne (blanc - white)

PERNAND-VERGELESSES

SAVIGNY-LÈS-BEAUNE   ALOXE-CORTON

NAY   POMMARD   BEAUNE   CHOREY-LÈS-BEAUNE   LADOIX

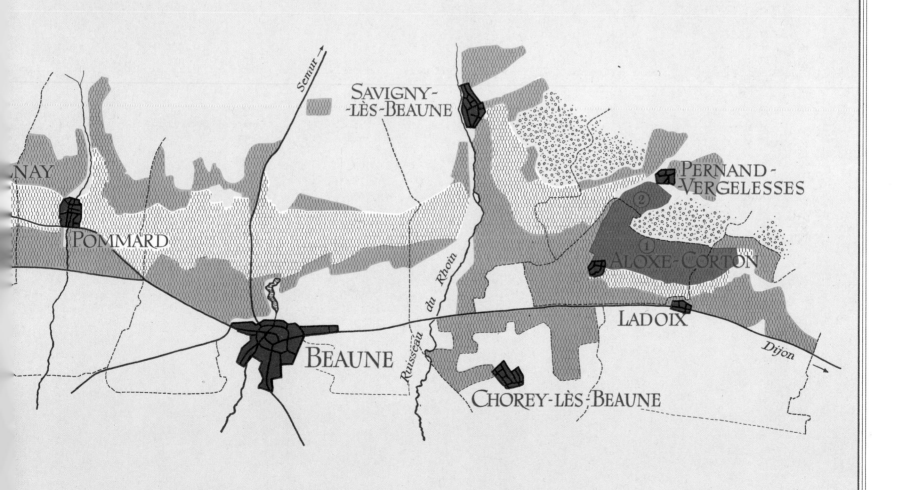

Grands crus   Iers crus   Appellations de commune

Beaune is a very ancient town, lying within a belt of ramparts and bastions. Some of these have been taken over by the wineshippers to use as cellars in which the wine in barrels and bottles can mature safely behind 23-foot walls.

suffered as a result. Its own life flourishes, as can be attested by the tens of thousands of tourists who visit it every year. Over the centuries, many donations have been made to the *Hôtel-Dieu* and the *Hospice de la Charité*, which are kept under joint management. Some 125 acres of vineyards have gradually accumulated to the estate of the Hospice de Beaune: in Corton-Charlemagne and Meursault for white wines and in Aloxe-Corton, Auxey-Duresses, Beaune, Corton, Monthelie, Pommard, Savigny and Volnay for red wines. The auctioning of the Hospice's wines on the third Sunday in November is renowned throughout the world as being "the world's greatest charity sale". And it is a fact that it enables the work of Nicolas Rolin to be continued year after year in support of the old and the needy.

The vineyards of Beaune cover a large area: 1,329 acres are contained within the area allowed to sell wines under this designation. The average yield is 196,900 gallons, of which 95 per cent is red. Dr Lavalle, the famous wine expert of the last century, whom we have already quoted, gave this appreciation of them: "I think that the great wines of Beaune are worthy of the greatest praise. The best vintages, in good years, reach a point at which they cannot be distinguished from the most outstanding wines, except by well-practised experts; and are more often than not they are sold at the highest prices. The second best vintages are the every-day wines of princes."

The vineyards of Beaune that give the best wines are: LES MARCONNETS, LES FÈVES, LES BRESSANDES, LES GRÈVES, LES TEURONS, LE CLOS-DES-MOUCHES, LE CLOS-DU-ROI, LES AVAUX, LES TOUSSAINTS, LES BOUCHEROTTES, LES VIGNES-FRANCHES and LES AIGROTS, to name but a few.

A look around the cellars and a visit to the Hôtel-Dieu is the normal programme of more than 300,000 tourists who visit Beaune every year.

THE COMMUNE OF POMMARD

Who does not know the name of this village two miles south of Beaune? Nevertheless, to reach it you must leave Route Nationale 74 and take Route Nationale 73 towards Autun, passing through many vineyards.

Pommard, a name easy to pronounce in any language, was for this very reason long a synonym for the wines of the Côte de Beaune. The law on A.O.C.s restricted the use of its name to those wines produced on the 838 acres in the commune. Many wines from neighbouring villages were affected by this measure, since they lost a traditional and easy marketing channel. About 217,712 gallons of "firm, ruddy, frank and long-lasting wines", to quote Dr Morelot, are now produced under the POMMARD A.O.C. These wines were steady favourites of the great lords and abbeys.

THE COMMUNE OF VOLNAY

En dépit de Pommard et de Meursault,
C'est toujours Volnay le plus haut.

In spite of Pommard and Meursault,
It's still Volnay that's the highest.

This Burgundy saying does not refer to the relative qualities of the wines but to the geographical situations of these villages, with Volnay on top of the hill above its vineyards and Meursault and Pommard below.

The vineyards produce (1975-1979) an average of 161,502 gallons, all of red wine. The wines of Volnay are qualified by Camille Rodier as being "less ruddy than BEAUNE or POMMARD, noted especially for their elegance, smooth taste, perfect balance and quite delicate bouquet. After MUSIGNY, they are the finest wines in all Burgundy." It should be noted that VOLNAY-CAILLERETS are produced in Meursault.

THE COMMUNE OF MONTHELIE

A mile and a half from Volnay, with its back to the Côte, this village is made picturesque by its ancient

houses that rise like steps up the hill. Its vines grow on a little over 230 acres which produce an average (1975-1979) 1,386 gallons of white wine and 66,132 gallons of red. A technical adviser to the I.N.A.O. (National Institute for Designations of Origin) had expressed the opinion that these wines are not as well known as they ought to be.

THE COMMUNE OF AUXEY-DURESSES

At the foot of Monthelie, deep in a large valley, lies the little village of Auxey-Duresses. The area was much frequented by the Gauls, who built a camp on the mountain overlooking the countryside. On the vineyards under the village name an average (1975-1979) of 22,528 gallons of white wine and 66,242 gallons of red are produced. The red wines are *forts gravains*, meaning not lacking in colour, body or bouquet. Pierre Léon Gauthier wrote: "On the vines of Duresses ripens a wine that was long sold under the VOLNAY and POMMARD labels—this was before A.O.C.s—without any detriment to the good name of those great wines."

THE COMMUNE OF SAINT-ROMAIN

At the foot of the magnificent cliffs that surround the valley of Auxey-Duresses the houses of Saint-Romain climb like stepping stones up the slope. The village once possessed a castle, the ruins of which are still to be seen. It produces an average (1975-1979) 19,954 gallons of white wine and 21,384 gallons of red under the village name. Roland Thévenin, poet and mayor of the village, sang its praises thus:

> O SAINT-ROMAIN *hardi, robuste et si fruité,*
> *Nous aimons ta fraîcheur ainsi que ta finesse.*

> O SAINT-ROMAIN, forthright, robust and so fruity,
> We love your freshness and delicacy.

THE COMMUNE OF MEURSAULT

We now return to the Côte, to the little town of Meursault which covers the entry to the valley leading to Auxerre. It was probably the first place occupied by the Romans when they penetrated this region. The

The Pommard vineyards, 1½ miles south of Beaune, are well-known overseas, for the name is easy to pronounce in most languages. Pommard wines, reds only, have always enjoyed the reputation of being firm, well-coloured wines, full of taste and keeping well.

vineyards of Meursault have always been famous for their white wines. For four miles the soil becomes quite unlike that of Beaune or Volnay, and the *Chardonnay* grape is king. There are some 17,468 gallons of red wine produced here but the 311,718 gallons of white wine are better known by far. Camille Rodier wrote: "MEURSAULT white wines have the following special characteristic—they are both dry and mellow, which is quite unusual. They are rich in alcohol, a beautiful golden green in colour, bright and clear, they keep well and have the frank taste of ripe grapes and a touch of hazelnut. They are among the most famous white wines of France."

Meursault is also famous for its *Paulée*, which takes up the last of the Three Glorious Days devoted to the wines of Burgundy. The *Paulée* was created in 1923 by Count Lafon and is the official dinner closing the vintage. It is given by the vineyard owners for all those who worked in the vintage with them. Nowadays, about four hundred persons attend this joyous banquet, which is not too official, since custom has it that everyone brings a bottle of his greatest and rarest wine to pass around the table—and that does not tend to dampen the celebrations!

THE COMMUNES OF
PULIGNY-MONTRACHET AND
CHASSAGNE-MONTRACHET

At the northern end of the Côte d'Or, in the commune of Gevrey-Chambertin and the neighbouring villages are the Very Great Growths of red wines. In the south, we find the Great Growths of white wines. Puligny-Montrachet, like the Côte de Meursault, produces almost nothing but white wines. There are five Great Growths in this region which we shall describe in descending order of merit.

MONTRACHET sits astride two communes: two-thirds in Puligny and one-third in Chassagne. Both added its name to theirs towards the end of the nineteenth century. In 1878, Bertall wrote: "this admirable white wine is the first among the white wines of Burgundy, as CHÂTEAU-YQUEM is the first among the white wines of Bordeaux. Let us not compare the two, say enthusiasts, let us merely say that they are both the first among the white wines of the world." This goes hand in hand with Dr Lavalle's comment in 1855: "The wine of Montrachet must be considered as one of those marvels whose perfection can only be appreciated by a small number of the elect." Only 4,730 gallons are produced annually. There is very little true Montrachet and the enthusiast must be careful not to confuse it with all the other wines that include the word Montrachet in their A.O.C.s.

CHEVALIER-MONTRACHET is geographically just above MONTRACHET and is about the same size. The wine can be drunk a little earlier than its neighbour, but it rarely attains the same perfection. It is, therefore, classified

just below MONTRACHET. The average (1975-1979) yield is 3,718 gallons.

BÂTARD-MONTRACHET grows just below Montrachet; the two are separated by a path. The vineyard sits astride Puligny and Chassagne and produces an average 8,316 gallons (1975-1979).

BIENVENUE-BÂTARD-MONTRACHET, average yield (1975-1979) 2,728 gallons and CRIOTS-BÂTARD-MONTRACHET, situated in Chassagne, producing an average 1,232 gallons, are the last of the Great Growths of white wines.

The origin of these names is often debated. One story, which we summarize here although we cannot guarantee its authenticity, has it that during the Crusades, the governor of the castle of Montrachet had a son who departed for the Holy Land. Meanwhile, the old lord was bored at the castle and took to passing near the Clos des Pucelles, where the young maidens of the region disported themselves. The Devil tempted him and nine months later a blessed event took place. The Duke of Burgundy, who was not amused, decreed that in the line of the Montrachets, the old lord was henceforth to be known as Montrachet the Elder, the Crusader as the Chevalier Montrachet and the child as the Bâtard Montrachet. The crusader was killed in battle so the bastard inherited and was welcomed at the castle with cries of "welcome to the bastard of Montrachet". But the lord, already an old man, could not bear to hear the baby crying and protested in patois: a *crio l'Bâtard* (the bastard is crying). When the castle was destroyed, these names were given to the vineyards in their memory.

Puligny-Montrachet produces 176,071 gallons of white and 5,213 gallons of red wine under the village name. Camille Rodier says of them: "These fruity, distinguished and sweet-smelling white wines are related to the better MEURSAULTS." And, in fact, LES CAILLERETS, LES COMBETTES, LES PUCELLES, LES FOLATIÈRES etc. are very distinguished wines.

Chassagne-Montrachet produces much more red wine than Puligny, averaging 151,698 gallons (1975-1979). These are among the best on the Côte. Camille Rodier had no hesitation in saying: "The red CHASSAGNES are undeniably like certain good vintages of the Côte de Nuits." There is also a good deal of white wine—100,288 gallons on average (1975-1979), resembling all the others produced on this part of the Côte, relatively dry and extremely subtle.

THE COMMUNE OF SAINT-AUBIN

Just behind Chassagne, towards Paris on Route Nationale 6, we cross this little winegrowing village. Under its name, or more generally under the appellation CÔTE DE BEAUNE-VILLAGES, an average (1975-1979) of 16,784 gallons of white and 48,505 gallons of red wine are produced. The hamlet of Gamay, where the vine of the same name was born, is part of Saint-Aubin.

THE COMMUNE OF SANTENAY

Santenay is the last winegrowing commune of the Côte d'Or. It has been inhabited since time immemorial and its grottoes contain many traces of their neolithic and iron-age inhabitants. Although a wine village, Santenay has distinguished itself further by possessing, of all things, a mineral water spring! The villagers tend to avoid it, however, and leave it to the "city folk" to enjoy. The vines produce, under the SANTENAY label, an average (1975-1979) 233,398 gallons of red and only 3,211 gallons of white wines. Minimum alcohol content for the red wines is 10.5° and for the white wines 11°. Dr Lavalle describes these wines as follows: "They are firm, mellow and always keep well. With age, they acquire a very delicate bouquet." The best are from the *climat* of Les Gravière, the only one in the commune with a *tête de cuvée* classification. Some wines are blended with those of other communes and are accordingly sold under the necessarily rather more general A.O.C. CÔTE DE BEAUNE-VILLAGES.

THE COMMUNES OF CHEILLY, DEZIZE AND SAMPIGNY-LES-MARANGES

After the Côte d'Or, we enter Saône-et-Loire through these villages. As their vineyards are next to Santenay, they are included in the Côte de Beaune, but are sold either under their own names or under the A.O.C., CÔTE DE BEAUNE-VILLAGES. The area under vine is about 300 acres in Cheilly, 100 acres in Dezize and 150 acres in Sampigny-les-Maranges. Very little wine is declared under this appellation and the villages are producing an average of 4,500 gallons, 2,600 gallons and 2,500 gallons of red wine respectively.

THE CÔTE DE BEAUNE-VILLAGES A.O.C.

This is an A.O.C. that is used a great deal and that is well-known to consumers. The preceding tour of the Côte de Beaune villages reveals many names that are not familiar to the wine-buying public. The CÔTE DE BEAUNE-VILLAGES appellation allows these lesser known villages to come together under the same title, thus avoiding any difficulties they might otherwise have in selling their excellent wines. (They nevertheless retain the right to produce wines under their own names if they wish to do so.) CÔTE DE BEAUNE-VILLAGES always indicates a red wine, and comes from the villages or parts of the villages in the following list: Auxey-Duresses, Chassagne-Montrachet, Cheilly-lès-Maranges, Chorey-lès-Beaune, Côte de Beaune, Dezize-lès-Maranges, Ladoix-Serrigny, Meursault rouge, Meursault-Blagny, Monthelie, Pernand-Vergelesses, Puligny-Montrachet, St-Aubin, Sampigny-lès-Maranges, Santenay, Savigny.

Meursault is primarily famous for its white wines, which are both dry and mellow. Every year, the day after the Beaune charity auctions, the *Paulée* is held here, a festival which brings all those who make their living from the vine around one common table.

Chassagne shares with the neighbouring commune of Poligny the celebrated Montrachet growth. The two communes have appended the growth name to become Chassagne-Montrachet and Poligny-Montrachet. MONTRACHET is the greatest white wine of Burgundy just as CHÂTEAU YQUEM is the greatest white wine of Bordeaux.

THE REGION OF MERCUREY

We now leave the Côte d'Or for Saône-et-Loire, but, in a sense, we are still in the Côte de Beaune of which Mercurey is traditionally a continuation through its methods of cultivation and vinification, the character of its wines and its trading customs.

These vineyards were named the Côte Chalonnaise after the town of Chalon-sur-Saône, a busy trading centre in the first few centuries of our era since it was well situated for both land and river transport. At a later date, it became an important wine centre for the region, but this has gradually been eroded by industry, which is now master of the town.

We shall travel from north to south in dealing with the four A.O.C.s in the region—RULLY, MERCUREY, GIVRY and MONTAGNY.

RULLY. This is an ancient village, 14 miles from Beaune, near Chagny and Route Nationale 6. It dates back to Roman times. Its caves were even inhabited in the stone ages. It was originally on the hill, but the plague of 1347 forced the inhabitants to resettle farther down. The village still has a thirteenth-century feudal castle, altered in the fifteenth century.

The vineyards of the RULLY A.O.C. give 20,546 gallons of white wine and 44,721 gallons of red (average 1975-1979). This white wine is very individualistic, heady and perfumed and lends itself to the Champagne method. It was the original reason for the considerable trade in sparkling Burgundy wines which developed in this village.

MERCUREY. The wines permitted to use this A.O.C. are produced in a large vineyard situated within several communes. Mercurey is reminiscent of the Roman occupation through its very name; Saint-Martin-sous-Montagne is one of the many villages named after the most popular saint in Burgundy; and finally, across the Orboise River from Mercurey, there is Bourgneuf-Val-d'Or. These wines are in all respects similar to those of the Côte de Beaune. "They differ from the Santenays only by an imperceptible degree," said Claude Bonvin. A. Jullien wrote: "The red wines of Mercurey are distinguished by their perfume: they are honest and may be kept for a long time." The average yield (1975-1979) is 380,807 gallons of reds and 16,212 of whites. The First Growths take the names of the five following vineyards: CLOS-DU-ROY, CLOS-VOYEN, CLOS-MARCILLY, CLOS-DES-FOURNEAUX, CLOS-DES-MONTAIGUS.

GIVRY. The ancient township of this name goes back to Gallo-Roman times. It produces, in its confines, the wines allowed to use this A.O.C. Once upon a time they were in great demand, but since the law on A.O.C.s, few enthusiasts have heard their name—a great pity. In the nineteenth century, A. Jullien said that the privileged growths of this commune were superior to those of Mercurey. Frank, strong and perfumed, they are the wines of connoisseurs. Nowadays, the average yield under the GIVRY name is 80,952 gallons of red wine and 8,337 gallons of white.

MONTAGNY. The wines sold under this A.O.C. come from the communes of Montagny, Buxy, Saint-Vallerin and Jully-les-Buxy, and produce 65,290 gallons of white wine alone (average 1975-1979). It is said they "keep the mouth clean and the head clear".

THE MÂCONNAIS

This is the most important wine area of the Saône-et-Loire, taking its name from its capital. Mâcon, "the queen of the Saône", is called thus because it lies beside a magnificent stretch of water, which makes it a metropolis for boat lovers as well. Known in Roman times as *Matisco in Aeduis*, the city was part of the Eduens, the same Gallic province as the future Côte d'Or. The town was important in Roman times. It possessed grain stores and a factory producing arrows and javelins "because the wood in the region was excellent for the purpose". At that time, it was built at the foot of the Roman Castrum, but gradually the city slipped down towards the Saône, especially after being devastated by the Barbarians in the fifth century and the Saracens in the eighth. It still possesses many Gothic and Renaissance remains, including a famous wooden house and various aristocratic residences of the eighteenth century.

The Mâconnais is, therefore, a very ancient region, with magnificent vineyards and remarkable Romanesque churches in many of its tiny villages. There were more vineyards before the phylloxera plague than today. In the north of the region, for example, lies Tournus, a very ancient town with the famous Romanesque church of St. Philibert and some very old houses. The vineyards surrounding it were mentioned by the poet Ausonus and were increased in size by the abbey of Cluny. It was even said that "Tournus produced a *Pinot* wine at the end of the sixteenth century as good as the most famous." However, there remain today

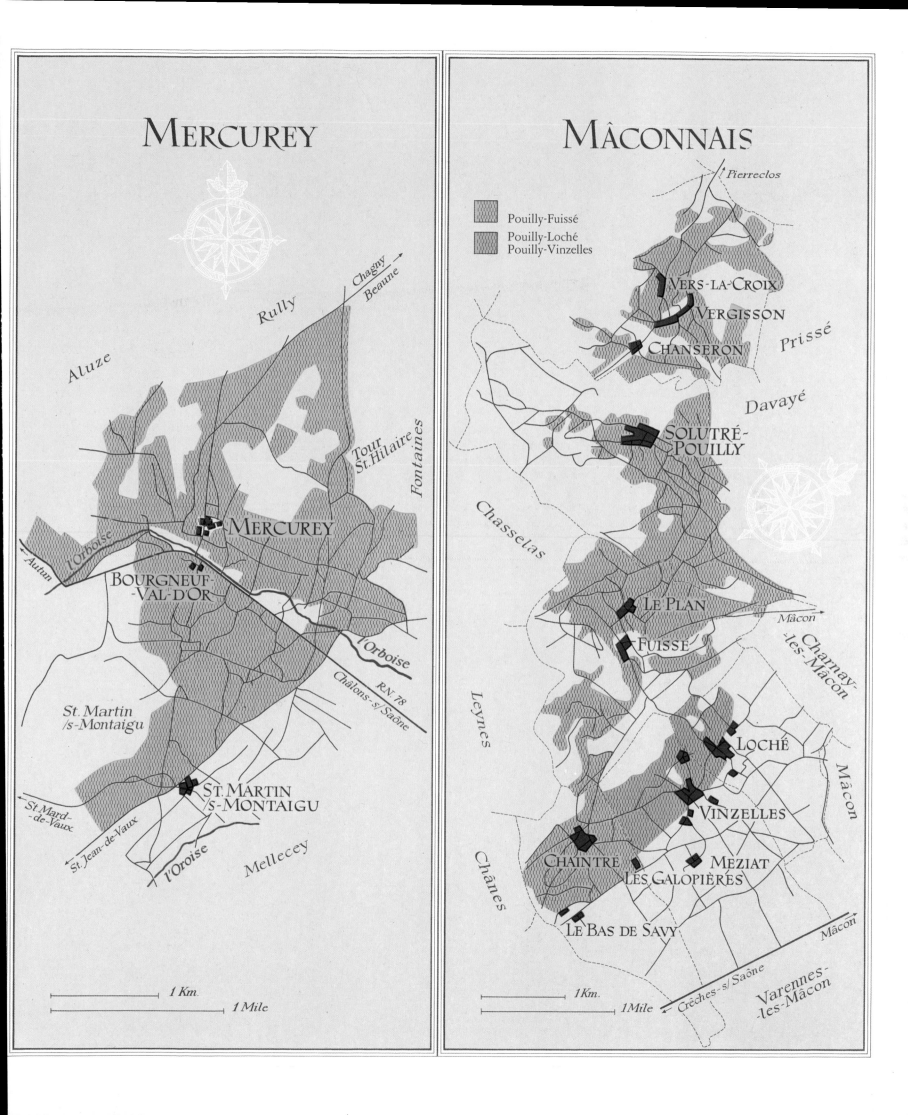

MERCUREY

MÂCONNAIS

Rully
Chagny
Beaune
Aluze
Tour St.Hilaire
Fontaines
l'Orboise
Autun
MERCUREY
BOURGNEUF-VAL-D'OR
l'Orboise
Châlons-s/Saône
RN 78
St. Martin /s-Montaigu
St.Mard--de-Vaux
St. Jean-de-Vaux
ST. MARTIN /s-MONTAIGU
l'Oroise
Mellecey

1 Km.
1 Mile

Pierreclos
Pouilly-Fuissé
Pouilly-Loché Pouilly-Vinzelles
VERS-LA-CROIX
VERGISSON
Prissé
CHANSERON
Davayé
SOLUTRÉ-POUILLY
Chasselas
Mâcon
Le Plan
Charnay--les-Mâcon
FUISSÉ
Leynes
LOCHÉ
Mâcon
VINZELLES
Châtré
MEZIAT
Chânes
LES GALOPIÈRES
LE BAS DE SAVY
Mâcon
Crèches-s/Saône
Varennes--les-Mâcon

1Km.
1Mile

but a few scattered vineyards producing mainly white wines. One must go down to the south of the Mâconnais to find a very important vineyard at the foot of a hill, where, according to Lamartine "the autumn grapes distill their balmy liqueur". Lamartine considered himself "a vintner rather than a poet" and his memory is kept all along the "Circuit Lamartinien", through Milly-Lamartine where he lived as a child, the château of Monceau, one of his favourite residences, and the château of Pierreclos, home of Marguerite, the Laurence of his *Jocelyn*. This area contains the various A.O.C.s discussed more fully below.

The region of Mâcon is remarkable for the diversity of its soils over such a comparatively small area. The soil of Pouilly-Fuissé, south-west of Mâcon itself, is a

The Mâconnais vineyards lie in south Burgundy. The Solutré vineyard (photograph) belongs to the POUILLY-FUISSÉ appellation, and produces a vigorous white wine with a seductive bouquet that caresses the palate.

mixture of limestone and slate and the landscape presents a series of dips and rises, but to the north-west of the town lies a long valley where chalky oolite has created sufficient topsoil for vines. Both these areas are ideal for producing excellent white wines. In the north there is a complete lack of homogeneity, chalk and slate preponderance varying from one point to another, and the wines varying at the same rate.

POUILLY-FUISSÉ. The white wine sold under this A.O.C. is too well known throughout the world to need a lengthy description. It comes from the communes of Pouilly, Fuissé, Solutré, Vergisson and Chaintré. This region is easy to locate because of the two spurs of rock that stick up like saw teeth at Vergisson and Solutré. At the foot of the latter lies the prehistoric site after which the Solutrian epoch of paleology was named. A large number of human skeletons and the bones of thousands of horses have been found there. The view from the top of these rocks is magnificent, with vineyards surrounding them on all sides and stretching, to the east, as far as Mâcon and the Beaujolais on the horizon. POUILLY-FUISSÉ charms the eye before the palate. Its colour is golden shot with emerald: it is as vigorous as the greatest growths of Burgundy; its thoroughbred delicacy is perfumed with a particularly delightful bouquet. An average 660,357 gallons of this wine are produced (1975-1979).

POUILLY-VINZELLES and POUILLY-LOCHÉ. These two A.O.C.s, also applicable to white wines, are different from the previous ones. POUILLY-LOCHÉ may be called POUILLY-VINZELLES but not vice versa. The vineyards are near those of POUILLY-FUISSÉ and the quantity is very similar, but not much is produced under these two A.O.C.s—39,772 gallons of POUILLY-VINZELLES and 24,703 of POUILLY-LOCHÉ.

MÂCON. The vineyards of the Mâconnais are too extensive to permit giving all the details of the various A.O.C.s. Some villages have been singled out and are allowed to append their names to the word Mâcon (these are white wines) or are allowed to sell their wines as MÂCON-VILLAGES.

The difference between MÂCON SUPÉRIEUR and MÂCON white wines is mainly a matter of yield per acre and minimum alcoholic strength. As for the red and rosé wines, usually made from the *Gamay* grape, some villages may append their names to Mâcon, but their wines may never be sold as MÂCON-VILLAGES, which is strictly for white wines. These Mâconnais wines hold an important position in the Burgundy wine selection. White wines that may be sold as MÂCON-VILLAGES or MÂCON SUPÉRIEUR are often sold as BOURGOGNE BLANC and have a worldwide reputation under this general A.O.C. The red wines, without claiming the qualities of the Côte d'Or wines, honourably fulfil their role as the vanguard of the fine wines of Burgundy. They are quite full-bodied and agreeably fruity early wines, to be drunk young but unlikely to turn vinegary even if kept for a long time.

THE BEAUJOLAIS

We are now in the south of Burgundy, in this great and beautiful vineyard of the Rhône department whose northern tip overlaps the Saône-et-Loire department.

The region gets its name from the château of Beaujeu, built in the middle of the ninth century and very important under the first family of the house of Beaujeu until 1265. One of the lords, Humbert III, built a new village in 1110 nearer the Saône, then the major artery of communications. He little realized that the new village, Villefranche, would gradually assume the position and influence of Beaujeu in the management of the affairs of the Beaujolais, becoming, in 1532, the capital of the region.

The province, at first a buffer state between the Mâconnais and the Lyonnais, was later joined to the kingdom of France, where it remained until 1560. Then it fell into the hands of the Bourbon-Montpensiers and still later, in 1626, into the hands of the Orleans family. The revolutions of 1789, 1830 and 1848 passed almost unnoticed in the Beaujolais, which throughout its existence has known events of greater local impact—invasions, pillages, famines and plagues. In 1790, the province was integrated into the newly created departments—first Rhône-Loire, then Rhône from November 1793 when Lyons, its capital, revolted against the Convention.

The present vineyards, 32 miles long and between seven and ten miles wide, have 37,065 acres of fine wines, reaching an altitude of over 1,600 feet towards the Monts-du-Beaujolais that crowd the western horizon. To the east, Route Nationale 6, following the Saône at several hundred yards distance, marks the far boundary of the vineyards. It is necessary for the traveller to leave the main road if he wants to further his acquaintance with this beautiful region. The vineyards of the Beaujolais were not always admired as they are today. Their history and development are quite unlike those of the other regions of Burgundy. Although some names are indubitably Roman in origin—Julié, Juliénas, Romanèche, for example—the first document known to speak of vineyards, the Cartulary of St. Vincent, goes back to the end of the tenth century. The next is of a vineyard at Brulliez, now called Brouilly, mentioned in an endowment made in 1160. Another ancient document referring to the existence of vines tells of a canon of Lyon, Odon Rigaud, who, in 1282, gave his cathedral church a great bell called the "Rigaud" and a vine, the produce of which was to be kept for the persons who rang the bell. This is the origin of the expression, well known throughout Burgundy, "to drink by ringing the Rigaud" or "to drink like a bell-ringer".

The wines of Beaujolais were originally used to quench the thirst of Lyons. Even now there is still a saying that three rivers flow into the town—the Rhône, the Saône and the Beaujolais. They were very often in competition with the vintners of the Mâconnais, who had to pay extremely high duties before their produce was allowed into the town.

Furthermore, since the Beaujolais is not part of the duchy of Burgundy, its wines could not be sold there. An ordinance of 1446 stated that in Dijon "provisions may include the wines of Tournus, the Chalonnais and the Beaunois and this side of the mountains as far as Messigny, but not those of the lowlands such as the Lyonnais, the Viennois, Tournon and other places".

It was purely by chance that the wines of the Beaujolais, towards the seventeenth century, became known outside their own area. Some merchants from the Lorraine, while in Mâcon, tasted some wines unknown to them. They were taken to where they were produced and bought several cellars. The news was heard by two other shippers, this time from Paris, and business rapidly expanded between the Beaujolais and the French capital.

However, when it came to taking the wines to the north the means of transport were found to be all but non-existent. The opening of the Briare canal made it easier to reach Paris via the Monts-du-Beaujolais and the Loire—a very important event for the wines of the Mâconnais as well, since they also benefited.

After the royal edict of 1776, which at Turgot's instigation established unrestricted transport and trade of wines throughout the kingdom, the difficulties of transporting the wines of the Mâconnais and especially those of the Beaujolais diminished and the region really began its rapid development. During the nineteenth century, the Beaujolais became more and more a part of Burgundy and through its constant development the first among the Burgundian vineyards.

The region is traditionally divided into two halves, Lower and Upper Beaujolais, which are no more than geographical terms. Taken as a whole, they look like a great expanse of hills and dales descending from west to east, which offer every variety of exposure to the sun. The region is scattered with a great number of isolated vineyards, often featuring the very beautiful houses of the masters or small châteaux and their outhouses, the historical successors to the Roman *villae*. The tiny villages are also very scattered. The overall effect of the setting, the scattered villages and the variety of exposures of the soil is quite unusual and extremely pleasant.

Lower Burgundy begins about 12 miles from Lyons, just before Saint-Jean-des-Vignes, an evocative name. It continues to the north through the districts of Anse, the Bois-d'Oingt and Villefranche-sur-Saône. It includes

very many villages and a beautiful landscape of vines, fields and woods, varying according to the altitude and exposure. It produces what are called *vins de comptoir*—over the counter wines sold in the bars of the Lyonnais to refresh the thirsty and tired citizens. They are doubtless less delicate and less complete than their northern neighbours, but then they are modest wines and lay no claims to perfection.

Upper Beaujolais consists of the districts of Belleville-sur-Saône and Beaujeu in the Rhône department, and La Chapelle-de-Guinchay canton to the south in the Saône-et-Loire. It would be very much worth the unhurried tourist's while to spend a few hours looking around the area. There are two well-signposted routes—the quick route, marked by red signposts which will take him from Villefranche to Crèches-sur-Saône, almost missing the hills but passing through all the "growths" of the Beaujolais; or the tourist route, mapped out in green, which is very much to be recommended. When you reach Beaujeu, you are well advised to leave it and take departmental road 136 up through spectacular scenery and remarkable views of the whole region. Then come down the Fût-d'Avenas Pass with its panoramic observation platform. On a clear day the view embraces a good deal of the Beaujolais and the Saône plain right up to the Jura and the Alps. We can guarantee that no-one who tries it will regret this detour, which enables the traveller to get a better idea of the size and variety of this district.

The date of the wineharvest, in the Beaujolais as elsewhere in Burgundy, depends on the maturity of the grapes. There are Wine Research Stations which, after sampling and analysis, give helpful guidance to the winegrowers. But in any case, September is the vintage month.

In the Upper and Lower Beaujolais, the wines are permitted to use three A.O.C.s —Beaujolais, Beaujolais-Supérieur and Beaujolais-Villages. There are, further, nine "growths". They are almost entirely red wines, since the 55,000 gallons of white Beaujolais amount to 0.16 per cent of the total average yield and are, in fact, produced in vineyards that border on the white Mâcon area.

Beaujolais is the basic A.O.C. and the difference between it and Beaujolais-Supérieur is the minimum alcoholic content which is a degree higher for the latter. The 1980 average yield for both A.O.C.s, 10,744,175 gallons, is as vast as is the area under production.

Victor Rendu wrote that: "The fine and almost fine Beaujolais wines are delicate, light and sappy. Though they are not so rich in bouquet as the great wines of Upper Burgundy, they do not lack fragrance. They are, in general, not deeply coloured; or, to be more accurate, they settle quickly and come rapidly to maturity. Precociousness is one of their main features."

Let us say, then, that the Beaujolais is a good unpretentious wine to be drunk with friends, their full glasses clinking merrily in the bar or wine cellar but always far from any formal occasion. It fosters sudden friendships because it is a wine that inspires those who appreciate its intrinsic qualities—friendliness, tenderness and generosity.

The wines that may use the A.O.C. Beaujolais-Villages come from 28 wine communes in the Rhône department and eight in the Saône-et-Loire: Juliénas, Jullié, Emeringes, Chénas, Fleurie, Chiroubles, Lancié, Villié-Morgon, Lantigné, Beaujeu, Régnié, Durette, Cercié, Quincié, Saint-Lager, Odenas, Charentay, Saint-Etienne-la-Varenne, Vaux, Le Perréon, Saint-Etienne-des-Oullières, Rivolet, Arbuissonnas, Salles, Saint-Julien, Montmelas, Blacé and Denicé in the Rhône; and Leynes, Saint-Amour-Bellevue, La Chapelle-de-Guinchay, Romanèche, Pruzilly, Chânes, Saint-Vérand and Saint-Symphorien-d'Ancelles in the Saône-et-Loire. These wines may also be sold under their own names, often tacked on to the word Beaujolais.

From this list we should mention Vaux, not so much for its excellent wines as for the reputation it has gained through the second name given it by the writer Gabriel Chevalier—Clochemerle.

The average yield (1980) under this A.O.C. is 10,357,692 gallons. Louis Orizet, the poet of the region, wrote: "Beaujolais-Villages, we love you because you are not quite great. If you were we would have to wait many months to drink you, which would be a pity... A boon to the mistress of every household, a Beaujolais goes with all sauces... It has that rare privilege for a red wine—to be drunk cool..." The late Georges Rozet, historiographer of the Brotherhood of the Knights of the Tastevin, wrote: "They do not overwhelm the drinker and their basic quality is their smoothness. They are soft, fruity, tasty, inviting, etc... There is no end to the list of adjectives used to define them. I should like to see

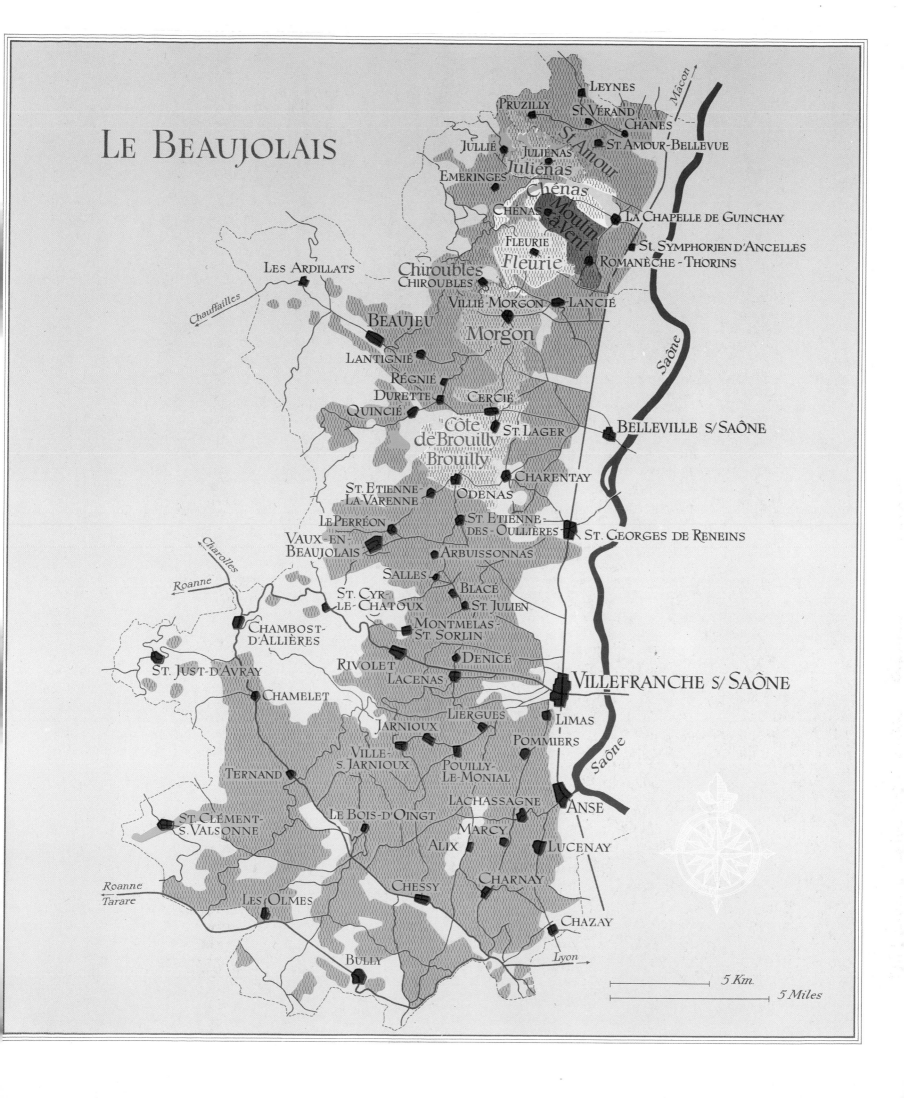

LE BEAUJOLAIS

LEYNES

PRUZILLY

St. VÉRAND
CHÂNES

St. Amour

JULIÉ
JULIÉNAS

St. AMOUR-BELLEVUE

EMERINGES

Juliénas
Chénas

CHÉNAS

Moulin
à Vent

La Chapelle de Guinchay

FLEURIE

St. Symphorien d'Ancelles

Chiroubles

Fleurie

Romanèche - Thorins

LES ARDILLATS

CHIROUBLES

VILLIÉ-MORGON

LANCIÉ

Chauffailles

BEAUJEU

Morgon

LANTIGNIÉ

RÉGNIÉ

DURETTE

CERCIÉ

QUINCIÉ

"Côte
de Brouilly

BELLEVILLE S/ SAÔNE

St. LAGER

Brouilly

CHARENTAY

St. ÉTIENNE-
LA-VARENNE

ODENAS

Le PERRÉON

St. ÉTIENNE-
DES-OULLIÈRES

St. GEORGES DE RENEINS

VAUX-EN-
BEAUJOLAIS

ARBUISSONNAS

Charolles

SALLES

Roanne

BLACE

St. CYR-
LE-CHATOUX

St. JULIEN

CHAMBOST-
D'ALLIÈRES

MONTMELAS-
St. SORLIN

DENICÉ

St. JUST-D'AVRAY

RIVOLET

LACENAS

VILLEFRANCHE S/ SAÔNE

CHAMELET

LIERGUES

LIMAS

JARNIOUX

POMMIERS

VILLE-
S. JARNIOUX

POUILLY-
LE-MONIAL

TERNAND

LACHASSAGNE

Le BOIS-D'OINGT

ANSE

St. CLÉMENT-
S. VALSONNE

MARCY

Roanne
Tarare

ALIX

LUCENAY

CHARNAY

CHESSY

LES OLMES

CHAZAY

Lyon

BULLY

5 Km.

5 Miles

Mâcon

Saône

Saône

them placed in three columns like litanies, like the flowing epithets that poured once upon a time from the inexhaustible pen of the creator of Pantagruel."

BEAUJOLAIS-VILLAGES is an extremely agreeable wine and, at a modest price, will accompany any dish without disappointing. It will not be browbeaten by strong dishes and, in spite of everything, always manages to guard its own flavour intact. It need not be drunk by the thimbleful either. "Let me refill your glass" was the watchword of the inn-keepers of yore when they saw their customers' glasses rapidly emptying. One can do that with this wine and still abide by the rule of Burgundy: Drink well (never let a wine unworthy of you pass your lips) and to your own measure (never drink too much—it is nothing to be proud of).

Since we have to begin somewhere, let us begin our discussion of the nine "growths" of the Beaujolais from the southernmost of these—it would be too difficult to classify them by quality.

BROUILLY and CÔTE-DE-BROUILLY. At about the level of Belleville-sur-Saône, 5 miles towards the hills from this town, the Mont-Brouilly reaches up to an altitude of some 1,300 feet. On top is a chapel, built in 1857, which can be seen from anywhere in the region and is a place of pilgrimage for the winemakers. The wines using the BROUILLY A.O.C. are produced in six communes huddled around the hill. The average production is 792,000 gallons on about 2,000 acres of land. BROUILLY is typical of Beaujolais wines—halfway between the light wines and the Great Growths. It loses nothing by ageing.

CÔTE-DE-BROUILLY comes from vines that cling to the sides of the hill and cover about 500 acres. The 1980 yield was 337,955 gallons.

The above two A.O.C.s are entirely different and should not be confused.

MORGON. A few miles to the north, the little hamlet of Morgon, with its narrow, winding streets, has given its name to the 1,360 acres of vineyards in the Villié-Morgon. It is a very sturdy wine which can be kept for a very long time. 1980 yield—1,208,856 gallons.

CHIROUBLES. The village bearing this name is much nearer the hills, and high up. Thanks to Pulliat, the writer on vines, it was the first to plant the grafted vine after the phylloxera plague.

The area under the CHIROUBLES A.O.C. produced (1980) 360,437 gallons of a distinguished wine, halfway between MORGON and FLEURIE.

Continuing along the road beyond Chiroubles we reach, just before the Fût-d'Avenas Pass, the lookout point mentioned earlier, which offers a fine view of most of the Beaujolais and the Mâconnais.

FLEURIE. The name is aptly chosen for "the queen of Beaujolais", as this scented wine is called. A little more versatile than the rest, it is more delicate and finely perfumed. This commune, its name redolent of spring, lies near Romanèche-Thorins. Its slender clocktower looks down upon the many châteaux and masters' houses, some quite old, scattered around the country-side. The area under the FLEURIE A.O.C. is one of the largest in the Beaujolais producing (1980) an average 879,520 gallons.

MOULIN-À-VENT. This growth, without doubt the best known and most sought after in the Beaujolais, is produced on part of the Chénas (Rhône) and on Romanèche-Thorins (Saône-et-Loire). There are about 1,730 acres of vineyards. Its name comes from an ancient windmill, the only one of its kind in the region, of which only the tower remains. A writer once stated that: "No one has ever contested the excellence of these vines. They are the realm of Bacchus, and Moulin-à-Vent and Thorins form the very heart of it. The soil is so precious to the vine that none is spared for the larger trees." The wine was formerly known as THORINS—Romanèche, the bearer of a Roman name, appended the name of its best vineyard to itself. The 1980 yield was 749,757 gallons of fine, ruddy wine—full-bodied, firm and, after a few years, very much like some of the wines of the Côte d'Or.

CHÉNAS. Once again a vineyard straddling two communes, Chénas (Rhône) and La-Chapelle-de-Guinchay (Saône-et-Loire). It overlooks the Moulin-à-Vent vineyard, with its hillock that was formed, according to legend, by the giant Gargantua unloading his basket.

It is also said that the name of Chénas comes from the oak trees (chênes) that formerly covered the district and indeed most of the Beaujolais.

Morgon is certainly the heartiest of the Beaujolais wines and may even be laid down for several years; two characteristics rather more typical of the Burgundies grown a few miles to the north. This makes the wines from the expansive Morgon vineyards ideal for blending, and so a good deal of them are never sold under this appellation. The wines are a deep ruby red, often intense in colour, and in flavour they are rounded, with much substance, and much character.

Morgon
Appellation Contrôlée

GEORGES DUBŒUF
ROMANÈCHE-THORINS, SAONE-ET-LOIRE

The FLEURIE vineyards, whose very name is an echo of spring, give the Beaujolais one of its premier crus. It has a splendid bouquet, great finesse, and perhaps is more supple than the others. It has often been called the Queen of the Beaujolais. It is made from *Gamay* grapes, which are black and give a white juice. The wine should be drunk fresh, at cellar temperature. It is particularly thirst-quenching.

The area of this A.O.C. produced, in 1980, 277,834 gallons of generous, perfumed wine.

JULIÉNAS. The wine that may use this A.O.C. is produced within the commune of Juliénas—named after Julius Caesar, it is said, as well as in Jullié, Emeringes and Pruzilly. The first grapes of the Beaujolais are said to have ripened along the Roman road, on vines planted in this soil which so resembles the one that Claudel described as: "dry and lumpy like curdled milk and full of tiny pebbles that retain the heat like firebricks so that the plump and sleepy grapes cook through on both sides". It gave (1980) 665,483 gallons of full, fruity, warm wine that matures well.

SAINT-AMOUR. We conclude our trip around the nine growths of the Beaujolais with this A.O.C. produced in the commune of the same name situated in the Saône-et-Loire. If this name did not exist, it would have to be invented—"holy love of the vine, holy love of the wine that flows for the holy love of mankind". This vineyard lies between Juliénas and Pouilly-Vinzelles, 8 miles south of Mâcon. Its vines now belong with the Beaujolais, though for a long time they were one of the gems of the Mâconnais. They used to belong to the Chapter of Saint-Vincent-de-Mâcon. The yield in 1980 was 309,225 gallons of fresh, frank, agreeable wine.

Emile Vuillermoz said that these growths provided "all the chromatic scale, from the velvety notes of the delightful FLEURIE, though the more mysterious sounds of BROUILLY, the resonance of JULIÉNAS, the arpeggios of MOULIN-À-VENT, the frank impact of MORGON and the harmonies of CHÉNAS, to the clear sounds of SAINT-AMOUR and CHIROUBLES".

This ends our journey in this vast area that gives us Beaujolais, the wine that used to be drunk in all the taverns from "pots"—stone jugs painted blue. We have also reached the end of our pilgrimage around the different growths of Burgundy—CHABLIS, CÔTE DE NUITS, CÔTE DE BEAUNE, the regions of Mercurey and the Mâconnais. Henri Béraud's comment would apply to many of them: "This wine is not a *nouveau riche*. It remains and shall remain what it has always been. Its clear flow will bring us a little of the soul of the vintagers who brought it into existence on their hillsides, a soul full of strength, wisdom and joviality."

103

The picker has emptied the contents of another *bénaton* or basket; the grapes are beginning to pile high on the cart that will take them off to the press.

Vintage time in Burgundy. Armed with their shears the vintagers (*layots* in the Burgundian patois) gather the grapes into wicker baskets.

Burgundians have for long had the reputation of living well. These two jovial winegrowers are delighted to find in their wine all the benefits nature has bestowed upon it and all the experience of their forefathers. And then, to drink just a little...

The Chapters of the Brotherhood of the Knights of the Tastevin are held regularly in the ancient cellar of the Château of Clos-Vougeot. When their "wine education" is complete, the new members of the Brotherhood are initiated by a ceremony that combines humour and the picturesque.

LIFE IN BURGUNDY

It has been written of the Burgundians that they are "deep-thinking, even calculating, moderate like their country in all ways, active and energetic but loving logical order and reasoned practicality, greatly preferring life as it is and its material benefits, genial observers, formidable scoffers, often ingenious and witty".

We might add a few touches to this quite realistic portrait as regards their eating and drinking habits. And here everyone agrees with Clément Vautel: "There can be no lasting pleasure nor possible harmony in a house where the lunch is a failure and the dinner bankrupt."

How can one not enjoy good food when it is accompanied by "that divine juice that its lovers drink pure in the morning and unadulterated at night" and which, apart from all its other merits, "is pleasant to wives when their husbands have drunk it"?

But let us finish our portrait by remembering that Burgundy has been called, among other things, "a hospitable land". Why not? One need scarcely ask on seeing the pleasure on the faces of those returning from this region. Nor do they stint their numbers: Beaune, as already noted, has 300,000 visitors a year.

Daily life in Burgundy is quiet and unspectacular. The vintner's work requires a good deal of patience throughout the year and the cellarman remains always underground. From time to time, however, the calm surface

breaks and the sound of laughter, songs and dances fills the air. Harvest time and the Vine and Wine Festival organized every September in Dijon by the Burgundian Committee are two such occasions people come from far and wide to attend.

Life in Burgundy is also punctuated by other events —we have already mentioned the sale of wines at the Hospices of Beaune, the oldest of the three known as *Les Trois Glorieuses*. In connection with this famous sale, which, let us recall, takes place on the third Sunday in November, there are various events in Beaune on the Saturday, such as the general exhibition of the wines of Burgundy and, in the evening, at the Château of the Clos-Vougeot, the "extraordinary" chapter of the Brotherhood of the Knights of the Tastevin. On Sunday, the exhibition continues and the wines of the Hospices of Beaune are sold. The day ends with a dinner by candlelight in one of the bastions of the town belonging to the Hospices. On Monday, the last day, there is the *Paulée* of Meursault, which is the traditional dinner marking the end of the vintage.

In all the regions of Burgundy that we have visited only briefly in this book, there are special celebrations attractive to follow and pleasant to participate in.

In the north, Chablis houses the Brotherhood of the Piliers Chablisiens (Pillars of Chablis), which holds its chapters in the wine-cellar of Vaucorbeil several times a year, usually on St. Vincent's day. This is the occasion for the exhibition and tasting of the wines of the Yonne and for the traditional event in the region—*le repas du cochon* ("the feast of the pig"). The singing and dancing of a chorus lends added charm to these candlelight banquets.

In Dijon, we have the Burgundian Committee which holds its rites in the magnificent thirteenth-century cellar of Clairvaux and organizes the Vine and Wine Festival. The rites are accompanied by folklore groups and recall the dubbing ceremonies of the Middle Ages. New distinctions are conferred in the Order of the Grand Dukes of the West, a reminder of the four great dukes of Burgundy.

Continuing south, we pass by the Clos-de-Vougeot, to greet the institution that is so much admired and copied everywhere—the Brotherhood of the Knights of the Tastevin—who were the first to establish contacts between wine-lovers and the wines of a province. "To invite someone is to assume responsibility for his well-being for as long as he is under your roof", said Brillat-Savarin, and this is the rule of the Brotherhood during its chapters. They have proved so successful that they have had to organize additional chapters, splendid banquets during which the sponsors instill their spirit of gaiety, humour and the wit that is the mark of companionable people. They are assisted by the Cadets of Burgundy, created by the Brotherhood, and they have

attained the necessary skill in folklore throughout the years as well as the much more complex arts of music and diction.

Let us remember, in passing, the Saint-Vincent-Tournant, created by the Brotherhood, which brings together all the winegrowing communes of the Côte in a religious and secular ceremony for the feast of the patron saint of vintagers. There is also the *Tastevinage*, at which good wines are selected for the wine-lover—this has become a famous ceremony. Any wine-producer or shipper wishing to participate must possess a given number of bottles of the same vintage. He then must send in samples—one to be tasted and the others for subsequent checks. In the cellar of the Château of the Clos-Vougeot, the specialists meet the press and, of course, consumer representatives. The tasters are always very severe: between 30 and 35 per cent of the wines are rejected each year, not because they are bad, but because they do not attain the level of distinction required. These two events have been very successful and well attended from the start.

About 12 miles farther south, in the little village of Savigny-lès-Beaune, the *Cousinerie de Bourgogne* (Cousinhood of Burgundy) meets under the sign of hospitality that is legendary in the province. "Bottle on the table and heart in hand" is its guiding principle and "all gentlemen are cousins" is its motto.

The headquarters of the Brotherhood of the Vintagers of Saint-Vincent is in Mâcon, in the Saône-et-Loire. During its chapters, distinguished guests and wine-lovers, if their conduct in wine matters is irreproachable, are received as knights or officers. These chapters are enlivened by a choir which sings all the traditional songs of the region.

Finally there is the Brotherhood of the Companions of the Beaujolais, created in 1947 and now holding its own vattings at Lacenas, after being received into all the most important cellars in the Beaujolais. The Companions swear an oath of wine to promote the wines of the Beaujolais in every way and to love and assist other companions. He who breaks his oath is "for all time unworthy to drink with an honest man".

Burgundy boasts 35 grands crus and premiers grands crus: 7 whites from Chablis, 21 reds from the Côte de Nuits, 1 red and 6 whites from the Côte de Beaune. Here are some bottles chosen from amongst the best: Musigny (Chambolle-Musigny); Corton (Aloxe-Corton), Romanee-Conti (Vosne-Romanée); Clos-Vougeot (Vougeot); and Clos de Tart (Morey-Saint-Denis).

106

WINES OF BURGUNDY

CHABLIS • WHITE WINES

Regional appellation : Chablis, Petit Chablis.

Principal first growths

Chablis-Mont de Milieu, Chablis-Montée de Tonnerre, Chablis-Fourchaume, on the right bank of the Serein.
Chablis-Forêts, Chablis-Vaillons, Chablis-Mélinots, Chablis-Côte de Léchet, Chablis-Beauroy, on the left bank of the Serein.
Chablis-Vaucoupin, Chablis-Vaugros, Chablis-Vaugiraud, in the commune of. Chichée.

Great growths

Chablis-Vaudésir, Chablis-Preuses, Chablis-Les Clos, Chablis-Grenouilles, Chablis-Bougros, Chablis-Valmur, Chablis-Blanchots.

CÔTE DE NUITS • RED WINES

Generic appellation :

a) Bourgogne ordinaire, Bourgogne grand ordinaire • *b)* Bourgogne Passe-tout-grains • *c)* Bourgogne, Bourgogne Marsannay, Bourgogne Hautes Côtes de Nuits • *d)* Vins fins de la Côte de Nuits or Côte de Nuits-Villages (Communes of Fixin, Brochon, Prissey, Comblanchien, Corgoloin).

Appellation of communes	Appellation of first-growth communes	Great growths	First great growths
Fixin (only red wine)	La Perrière, Les Hervelets, Les Meix-Bas, Aux-Cheusots, Le Clos du Chapitre, Les Arvelets.		
Gevrey-Chambertin (only red wine)	Les Véroilles, Village Saint-Jacques called "Le Clos Saint-Jacques", Aux Combottes, Bel-Air, Cazetiers, Combes-aux-Moines, Estournelles, Lavaut, Poissenot, Champeaux, Les Goulots, Issarts, Les Corbeaux, Les Gémeaux, Cherbaudes, La Perrière, Clos-Prieur (only upper part), lé Fonteny, Champonnets, Au Closeau, Craipillot, Champitonnois called "Petite Chapelle", Ergots, Clos-du-Chapitre.	Charmes-Chambertin Chapelle-Chambertin Griotte-Chambertin Latricières-Chambertin Mazis-Chambertin Ruchottes-Chambertin	Chambertin Chambertin-Clos-de-Bèze
Morey-Saint-Denis (red wine and 1·6 % white wine)	Les Larrets or "Clos-des-Lambrays", Les Ruchots, Les Sorbés, Le Clos-Sorbés, Les Millandes, Le Clos-des-Ormes, Meix-Rentiers, Monts-Luisants, Les Bouchots, Clos Bussières, Aux Charmes, Les Charrières, Côte Rôtie, Calouères, Maison Brûlée, Chabiots, Les Mauchamps, Les Froichots, Les Fremières, Les Genévrières, Les Chaffots, Les Chenevery, La Riotte, Le Clos-Baulet, Les Gruenchers, Les Faconnieres.	Clos-de-Tart Clos-St.-Denis Clos-de-la-Roche	Bonnes-Mares
Chambolle-Musigny (only red wine)	Les Bonnes-Mares, Les Amoureuses, Les Charmes, Les Cras, Les Borniques, Les Baudes, Les Plantes, Les Hauts Doix, Les Chatelots, Les Gruenchers, Les Groseilles, Les Fuées, Les Lavrottes, Derrière-la-Grange, Les Noirots, Les Sentiers, Les Fousselottes, Aux Beaux-Bruns, Les Combottes, Aux Combottes.		Musigny (2 % white wine)
Vougeot (only red wine)	Le Clos Blanc, Les Petits-Vougeot, Les Cras, Clos de la Perrière.		Clos-de-Vougeot
Vosne-Romanée (only red wine)	Aux Malconsorts, Les Beaux-Monts, Les Suchots, La Grand'Rue, Les Gaudichots, Aux Brûlées, Les Chaumes, Les Reignots, Le Clos des Réas, Les Petits-Monts.	Romanée Romanée-St-Vivant Grands-Echezeaux Echezeaux	Romanée-Conti Richebourg La Tâche
Nuits-Saint-Georges (red wine; 0·4 % white wine)	Les Saint-Georges, Les Vaucrains, Les Cailles, Les Porets, Les Pruliers, Les Hauts-Pruliers, Aux Murgers, La Richemonrfe, Les Chabœufs, La Perrière, La Roncière, Les Procès, Rue-de-Chaux, Aux Boudots, Aux Cras, Aux Chaignots, Aux Thorey, Aux Vignes-Rondes, Aux Bousselots, Les Poulettes, Aux Crots, Les Vallerots, Aux Champs-Perdrix, Perrière-Noblet, Aux Damodes, Les Argillats, En la Chaîne-Carteau, Aux Argilats, Clos de la Maréchale, Clos-Arlots, Clos des Argillières, Clos des Grandes Vignes, Clos des Corvées, Clos des Forêts, Les Didiers, Aux Perdrix, Les Corvées-Paget, Le Clos-Saint-Marc.		

CÔTE DE BEAUNE • RED WINES

Generic appellation :

a) Bourgogne ordinaire, Bourgogne grand ordinaire • *b)* Bourgogne Passe-tout-grains • *c)* Bourgogne • *d)* Côte de Beaune • *e)* Côte de Beaune-Villages

Appellation of communes	*Appellation of first-growth communes*	*Great growths*
Aloxe-Corton . . . . . . (1 % white wine)	Les Valozières, Les Chaillots, Les Meix, Les Fournières, Les Maréchaudes, En Pauland, Les Vercots, Les Guérets, La Maréchaude, La Toppe-au-Vert, La Coutière, Les Grandes-Lolières, Les Petites-Lolières, Basses-Mourettes.	Corton
Pernand-Vergelesses . . . (11 % white wine)	Ile-des-Vergelesses, Les Basses-Vergelesses, Creux-de-la-Net, Les Fichots, En Caradeux.	Corton
Savigny-lès-Beaune . . . (4 % white wine)	Aux Vergelesses, Aux Vergelesses dit Bataillière, Les Marconnets, La Dominode, Les Jarrons, Basses-Vergelesses, Les Lavières, Aux Gravains, Les Peuillets, Aux Guettes, Les Talmettes, Les Charnières, Aux Fourneaux, Aux Clous, Aux Serpentières, Les Narbantons, Les Hauts-Marconnets, Les Hauts-Jarrons, Redrescuts, Aux Guettes, Les Rouvrettes, Aux Grands-Liards, Aux Petits-Liards, Petits-Godeaux.	
Chorey-lès-Beaune . . .	Chorey-lès-Beaune.	
Beaune. . . . . (5 % white wine)	Les Marconnets, Les Fèves, Les Bressandes, Les Grèves, Les Teurons, Le Clos-des-Mouches, Champs-Pimont, Clos-du-Roi, Aux Coucherias, En l'Orme, En Genêt, Les Perrières, A l'Ecu, Les Cent-Vignes, Les Toussaints, Sur-les-Grèves, Aux Cras, Le Clos-de-la-Mousse, Les Chouacheux, Les Boucherottes, Les Vignes-Franches, Les Aigrots, Pertuisots, Tielandry ou Clos-Landry, Les Sisies, Les Avaux, Les Reversées, Le Bas-des-Teurons, Les Seurey, La Mignotte, Montée-Rouge, Les Montrevenots, Les Blanches-Fleurs, Les Epenottes.	
Pommard	Les Rugiens-Bas, Les Rugiens-Hauts, Les Epenots, Les Petits-Epenots, Clos-de-la-Commaraine, Clos-Blanc, Les Arvelets, Es-Charmots, Les Argillières, Les Pézerolles, Les Boucherottes, Les Sausilles, Les Croix-Noires, Les Chaponnières, Les Fremiers, Les Bertins, Les Garollières ou Jarollières, Les Poutures, Le Clos-Micot, La Refene, Clos-du-Verger, Derrière-Saint-Jean, La Platière, Les Chanlins-Bas, Les Combes-Dessus, La Chanière.	
Volnay	En Caillerets, Caillerets-Dessus, En Champans, En Chevret, Fremiets, Bousse-d'Or, La Barre or Clos-de-la-Barre, Le Clos-des-Chênes, Les Angles, Pointe-d'Angles, Les Mitans, En l'Ormeau, Taille-Pieds, En Verseuil, Carelle-sous-la-Chapelle, Ronceret, Carelle-Dessous, Robardelle, Les Lurets, Les Aussy, Les Brouillards, Le Clos-des-Ducs, Les Pitures-Dessus, Chanlin, Les Santenots, Les Petures, Village-de-Volnay.	
Monthélie . . . . . . (2.5 % white wine)	Sur Lavelle, Les Vignes-Rondes, le Meix-Bataille, Les Riottes, La Taupine, Le Clos-Gauthey, Le Château-Gaillard, Les Champs-Fulliot, Le Cas-Rougeot, Duresse.	
Auxey-Duresses . . . . . (32 % white wine)	Les Duresses, Les Bas-des-Duresses, Reugne, Reugne called La Chapelle, Les Grands-Champs, Climat-du-Val called Clos-du-Val, Les Ecusseaux, Les Bretterins called La Chapelle, Les Bretterins.	
Santenay . . . . (2 % white wine)	Les Gravières, Clos-de-Tavannes, La Comme, Beauregard, Le Passe-Temps, Beaurepaire, La Maladière.	
Cheilly, Dezize, Sampigny- lès-Maranges	Le Clos-des-Rois, La Boutière, Les Maranges, Les Plantes-de-Maranges.	
Chassagne-Montrachet . .	Clos-Saint-Jean, Morgeot, Morgeot called Abbaye-de-Morgeot, La Boudriotte, La Maltroie, Les Chenevottes, Les Champs-Gain, Grandes-Ruchottes, La Romanée, Les Brussolles, Les Vergers, Les Macherelles, En Cailleret.	
Other appellations . . . . *of communes*	Saint-Romain, Meursault-Blagny or Blagny, Puligny-Montrachet, Ladoix, Saint-Aubin.	
Saint-Aubin . . . . . . (4 % white wine)	La Chatenière, Les Murgers-des-Dents-de-Chien, En Remilly, Les Frionnes, Sur-le-Sentier-de-Clou, Sur Gamay, Les Combes, Champlot.	

CÔTE DE BEAUNE • WHITE WINES

Generic appellation: **a)** Bourgogne ordinaire, Bourgogne grand ordinaire • **b)** Bourgogne aligoté • **c)** Bourgogne • **d)** Côte de Beaune.

Appellation of communes	*Appellation of first-growth communes*	*Great growths*	*First great growths*
Aloxe-Corton		Corton-Charlemagne	
Pernand-Vergelesses		Corton-Charlemagne	
Chorey-lès-Beaune . . .	Chorey-lès-Beaune.		
Saint-Romain			
Meursault . . . . (4 % red wine)	Aux Perrières, Les Perrières-Dessus, Les Perrières-Dessous, Les Charmes-Dessus, Les Charmes-Dessous, Les Genevrières-Dessus, Les Genevrières-Dessous, Le Poruzot-Dessus, Le Poruzot-Dessous, Le Poruzot, Les Bouchères, Les Santenots-Blancs, Les Santenots-du-Milieu, Les Caillerets, Les Petures, Les Cras, La Goutte-d'Or, La Jennelotte, La Pièce-sous-le-Bois, Sous-le-Dos-d'Ane.		
Puligny-Montrachet . . . (6·4 % red wine)	Le Cailleret, Les Combettes, Les Pucelles, Les Folatières, Clavoillons, Le Champ-Canet, Les Chalumeaux, Les Referts, Sous-le-Puits, La Garenne, Hameau-de-Blagny.	Chevalier-Montrachet, Bâtard-Montrachet, Bienvenues-Bâtard-Montrachet, Criots-Bâtard-Montrachet.	Montrachet
Chassagne-Montrachet . .	Morgeot, Morgeot called Abbaye-de-Morgeot, La Boudriotte, La Maltroie, Clos-Saint-Jean, Les Chenevottes, Les Champs-Gain, Grandes-Ruchottes, La Romanée, Les Brussoles, Les Vergers, Les Macherelles, Chassagne or Cailleret.	Bâtard-Montrachet Criots-Bâtard-Montrachet	Montrachet
Other appellations . . . . of communes	Ladoix, Meursault-Blagny or Blagny, Saint-Aubin, Cheilly-Dezize-les-Maranges, Sampigny-lès-Maranges.		

MERCUREY REGION

Generic appellation : Bourgogne.

Appellation of communes	*First growths*
Mercurey (red 95 %) . .	Clos-du-Roy, Clos-Voyens or Les Voyens, Clos-Marcilly, Clos-des-Fourneaux, Clos-des-Montaigus.
Givry (red 87 %)	
Rully (white 80 %) . . .	Margotey, Grésigny, Vauvry, Mont-Palais, Meix-Caillet, Les Pierres, La Bressande, Champ-Clou, La Renarde, Pillot, Cloux, Raclot, Raboursay, Ecloseaux, Marissou, La Fosse, Chapitre, Préau, Moulesne.
Montagny (white) . . .	

MÂCONNAIS

Generic appellation : Bourgogne • Mâcon supérieur (red wine 37 % and white) • Mâcon-villages (white wine) • Mâcon (red wine 76 %) Pinot-Chardonnay-Mâcon (white wine).

Appellation of communes   Pouilly-Fuissé (white), Pouilly-Vinzelles (white), Pouilly-Loché (white).

BEAUJOLAIS

Generic appellation: **a)** Bourgogne ordinaire, Bourgogne grand ordinaire • **b)** Bourgogne Passe-tout-grains • **c)** Bourgogne aligoté **d)** Bourgogne • **e)** Beaujolais • **f)** Beaujolais supérieur • **g)** Beaujolais-Villages.

First growths . . . . . . (red wine)   Brouilly, Chenas, Chiroubles, Côte de Brouilly, Fleurie, Juliénas, Morgon, Moulin-à-vent, Saint-Amour.

THE WINES OF THE RHÔNE

PHILIPPE CHERIX and JEAN BERTIN-ROULLEAU

In the course of history, some rivers have divided the land through which they flowed, while others, much more rarely, have united and held together the peoples of each bank. Few rivers have done this to such lasting effect and over such a long period as has the river Rhône. Since time immemorial, it would seem, Nature has drawn man's attention to this vast furrow of fertility so propitious to peaceful relations: and when the vine crept in, right behind the first Greek merchants and the Roman legions, it was at home from the beginning. For close on six hundred years, the plant lingered in the plains of the Lower Rhône, fruitful in what was then Gaul around Narbonne, reaching the town of Lyons only in the first century of our era. From there, part of the vine escaped up the river Saône to conquer Burgundy, and it is surely one of the Rhône's claims to glory that it thus facilitated this bewitching viticultural colonization. Savoy and the Pays Romand saw in their turn this wine of the Rhône, and the vine-shoots of Dionysus reached even farther—as far, indeed, as they could go, until the great Alps stopped them and they reached the river's very source.

What an astonishing destiny for that thin trickle of limpid-clear water that springs from the unending fountain-head of the Furka glacier! Jostled from all sides in the rocks, the infant river drops dizzily to where, some 1,640 feet lower at Visperterminen (altitude 4,260 feet), the vine awaits. From here onwards to the sea, these plants will never leave the river's banks. In this rocky region, the vines must struggle for life under a sun that is often harsh: but the winegrower of the Valais canton, his face dried like parchment by the winds, the burning *fœhn* and the chilling *bise* in turn, is a hard and tenacious man. His task is a veritable gamble, yet the result is admirable: a range of wines, mostly whites and mostly dry, of which some are real works of art. The plants lie on the slopes in asymmetrical plots, giving the landscape a curiously mottled effect. Almost all the planting is on the river's right bank, facing the sun, or in the lateral valleys.

The river continues its flow down towards the plain, its waters more and more cloudy, swollen with the rivers feeding it from north and south. And then suddenly, quite unexpectedly, at Martigny, the Rhône appears to change its mind. It forms a sharp right-hand turn and seems about to betray its southern destiny as it tries to return to a Germanic land. But then the plain opens wide and the river hurls itself forward: laden with mud and silt, it digs its bed deeply between the cantons of Vaud and Valais. The vines thin out on the left bank but spread profusely on the other.

The Rhône is still a grey torrent full of fury when it meets Lake Leman. The soothing lake disciplines, warms and cleans the river in a series of operations that the eye does not even suspect: the Rhône seems to have disappeared completely. Yet it is but hidden, mysteriously, in the waves and the vine has not ceased to follow the river. It spreads in steeply terraced rows along the shores to Lausanne, the Lavaux region where begins that marvellous land of La Côte in which the living seems so easy. The plants, lined up neatly as if on shelves, give every sign of opulence.

Across the lake lies France. On the slopes of the Savoy mountains (Chablais and Faucigny), cultivation is much more sparse, and winters harsh. Here in this hard, tormented countryside, dominated by the forerunners of the mighty Alps, the vineyards produce a vigorous white wine: CRÉPY.

Farther west, the vineyards close up against each other between the lake and the Jura mountains. Geneva is not far away, where the lake is usually called Lake of Geneva. And the river, bursting at the very gates of Calvin's city out of the deep waters, can once again appear between its own banks and run, flirting, through the vineyards of the Mandement and the Upper-Savoy Genevois.

From Seyssel to Vienne, across the frontier now, in France, for about 110 miles the vineyards are scarce, and the Rhône, fortified with the waters of the Saône, rolls on towards Dauphiné, widening as it goes. The vine is not stubborn to the point of trying to grow in soils that do not suit it, but this momentary self-effacement of the Rhône vineyards is already preparing a special awakening. Only a few miles from Vienne, at Ampuis, where the vines are grown in little bow-like arches, with the plants tied together three-by-three, there is a cultivation of CÔTE RÔTIE. This is the threshold of an enormous vineyard stretching for almost 125 miles southward.

111

In the Vispertal, Switzerland, the vines are planted up to nearly 4000 ft above sealevel. A very special wine is produced from them, known as 'Vin des Payens' or 'Heidenwein', made from *Salvagnin blanc* grapes.

The CÔTES DU RHÔNE, which include about one hundred varied communes, form two distinctly different agglomerates: one near Tournon, the other near Orange. The first is concentrated around HERMITAGE, while the second is around that illustrious CHÂTEAUNEUF so loved by the popes.

The whole of this very picturesque region has a wild, tormented surface, with marls, molasse and alluvial deposits forming stony slopes and high dry terraces where the red grape dominates. The river Rhône, here gorged with the waters of the Isère and the Drôme, has on occasion some formidable floods, but fortunately a hot sun makes haste to comfort the unfortunate vinegrower.

This is now the Pays de Vaucluse, that which formerly was the Comtat Venaissin: it is already part of the Provence, that region of extremes *par excellence*, where brutal rains and parching drought, cutting *mistral* wind and northern *tramontane* alternate with each other. Eternal Provence, with its perfume of plants and fruit, its heavy silence scarcely rippled by the chirping of the grasshoppers or the solid swearing of the winegrowers. The flavour of the western language pleases the Rhône and reminds it of other tongues of other folk of the vineyards: the roughness of the Valais and Savoy *patois*, the slowness of the accent of the Leman, the dry rhythm of the man from Lyons and then, from Valence on, the French that the people of Provence sing so well.

The Rhône, now become enormous, is preparing itself majestically to flow into the all-absorbing sea. But the vineyards along its banks will stop near Avignon. From there, taking full advantage of the wonderful richness of the southern soil, yet wishing to avoid the humid Camargue, the vines spread to east and west so that, from Saint-Raphaël to Perpignan, other vineyards are formed: those of the Côtes de Provence, Languedoc and Roussillon. It was in these regions that the Greeks and the Romans first transmitted to France that wondrous heritage of wine which later winegrowers were able to exploit to the fullest.

Thus the river Rhône has given the vineyards, along the almost 500 miles of land traversed, a thousand-year-old birthright to bring man pleasure. True, the winegrowers of Languedoc, Provence, Savoy and Valais must battle with various problems in order to succeed: the sun, so necessary to breathe life into the wine, is not always kindly; the vine-plants do not feed everywhere on the same soils; the geography of the area often brings

The general description *"vins du Rhône"* unites under one term the wines of the Rhône Basin: those of the Valais, the Swiss shores of Lake Leman and Savoy, the wines of Côtes du Rhône from Lyons to the Camargue, and also the wines from neighbouring regions. These are on the one hand the French Jura area whose vineyards join the Rhône plain through the gap at Bresse, and on the other hand the regions of Languedoc-Roussillon and Provence, which join the main axis of the river at Avignon.

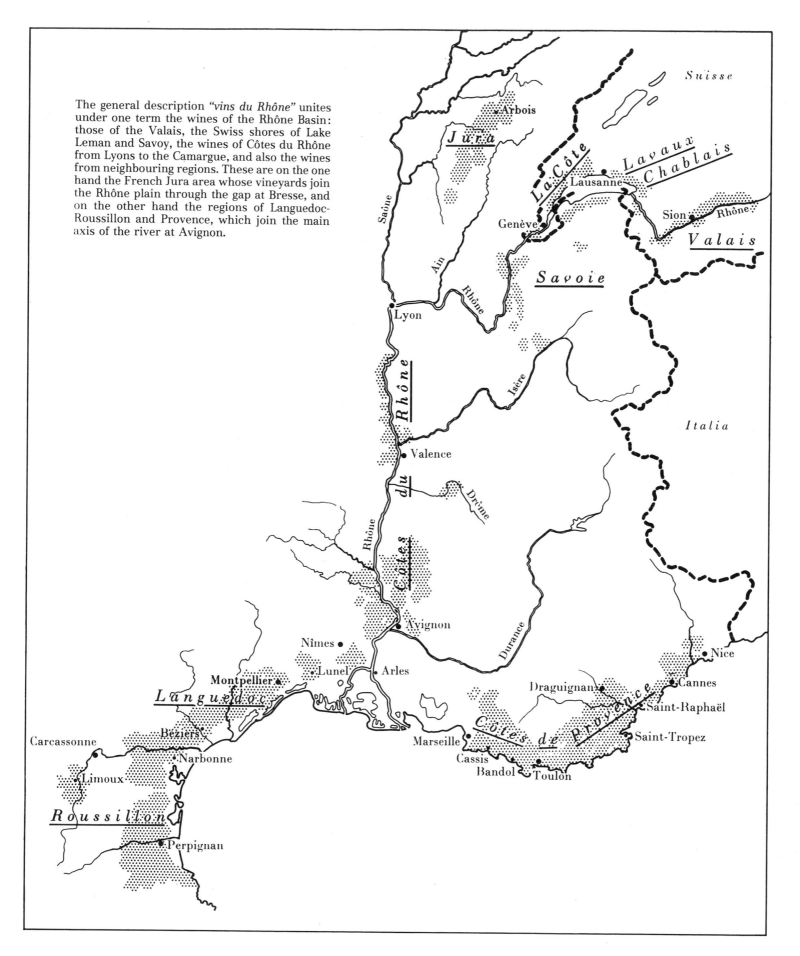

a disordered layout to the winegrower's plans for planting. But the river itself has managed to smooth out many of these diversities of cultivation. Man, guided quite naturally by that flowing water, has been able to bring Mediterranean wine into the heart of Europe. Then, by dint of constant and profitable exchanges with his neighbours, he has striven to increase and improve his wines. The great fraternity of a common language, from Sierre to Marseilles, has joined that other fraternity of the wine to create an authentic Rhône mentality, as sung by Frédéric Mistral and Charles Ferdinand Ramuz.

THE SWISS WINES OF THE RHÔNE VALLEY

French-speaking Switzerland stands out as having the largest production of wine of all Swiss viticultural regions. The vineyards are for the most part planted on the slopes along the Rhône, in the level area of the river plain and on the more or less steep slopes alongside Lake Leman. There is an important production of white wines, while that of red wine, about 25 per cent of its total, is constantly increasing. Geographically, politically, and qualitatively too, three characteristic regions are prominent along the Swiss run of the Rhône: the cantons of Geneva, Valais and Vaud.

The method of cultivation used is generally the low cultivation *en gobelet*, as practised in the Canton of Vaud. A few timid attempts have been made to introduce the semi-high and high methods of cultivation, usually on flat or almost-flat land. But the desire always to bring out the natural richness of the wines generally keeps the winegrowers faithful to techniques, well-tried and cheap, which they have used over the years, both for working the land and for thinning and preparing the vines. This latter is very delicate work, carried out during the month of June, and consists of tying the vine-shoots and stems to the vine-props. In former times, this work was done by the girls of the Aosta Valley (in Italy), Savoy (in France) and Valais (in Switzerland), who used to come into the Canton of Vaud for the occasion, but this custom is dying out now. Dressed in their beautiful local costumes, the girls left their neighbouring regions and, for ten or twelve days, worked the vines *en tâche*, that is, by plots of just over an acre each.

Cultivating *en gobelet* allows the grapes, growing closer to the ground, to benefit from a more complete maturing and an optimal enrichment in natural sugar. Plants trained in this way have a single vertical trunk terminating in several arms following the shape of a goblet. The advantages of such a method are its simplicity and that no vine support is needed.

Canton of Valais

The traveller descending the Rhône valley sees the first vines appear soon after Brig, alongside the river and up in the lateral valleys. The land in Valais used for vine cultivation has usually a poor soil which has been improved over the centuries only by tremendous effort. Patient maintenance work is needed to maintain the little terrace walls which alone hold back the soil clinging to the mountainside. In this valley bordered by mountain peaks with eternal snow, the sun brings its warmth and blessing with great generosity.

The people of Valais are a sturdy race, proud of many traditions, who have known how to get the best results from the almost Mediterranean climate of the Rhône valley. The vine is queen in a canton where excellent fruit orchards produce apricots, asparagus and strawberries. It must have existed there since earliest times, but the vines which were cultivated in those far-off days have been almost completely abandoned in favour of varieties perfectly suited to the valley's soil and climate. The extent of the vineyard in Valais, which is still expanding, is about 12,350 acres. To reap the full benefit of the sun the vines are mostly planted on the right bank of the river; and the vinegrowers cover the soil, or mix gravel or crushed shale into it, to catch and hold the warmth still more. The vinegrower of this land has an endless patience: he has gone close to the great mountain glaciers to seek the water source for the essential irrigation of his plants, and has led the precious liquid down to the vineyards by artificial canals or *bisses* along the mountainside, distributing it by trickling or sprinkling.

This is a deeply religious land, but one that is very realistic too. A famous vinegrower, now dead, liked to tell the following tale: "Back in the days when the Bishop of Sion, today the cantonal capital, was both spiritual and temporal prince of the Valais, an angel of the Lord appeared to him in his prayers and spoke as follows: 'The Lord has been touched by the great troubles of the people of Valais, whose vines dry up in the sun, while the people of Bern [the neighbouring canton, separated from Valais by a chain of mountains] receive a plentiful rain to produce beautiful green and lush grazings. Therefore my Master, in order to distribute better his blessings, will cause it to rain on Valais as on other parts of Helvetia. Its people will be able to abandon their costly and dangerous *bisses* and instead of killing themselves in this work of leading the water to the vines and watering, they will be able to relax and have a good time.' The bishop, deeply moved, thanked the angel profusely but asked leave for eight days before giving his assent to this generous celestial proposition, in order to be able to submit it to his dear brethren. Eight days later the angel, punctual at the rendez-vous, received the following answer: 'My brethren thank the

The fortified church of Valère dominates the vineyards near Sion in the Swiss Valais. Here the white FENDANT is produced from the *Chasselas* grape, and the red DÔLE, made from *Pinot Noir* and *Gamay* grapes.

Lord for all his blessings, but as far as the matter of watering is concerned, they would prefer to look after it themselves, for they know better than anyone else what needs doing.' And since that time the sun shines for everyone, with special care for this canton."

The wines which are harvested in Valais and which have gained it fame carry the name of FENDANT for the white wines produced from *Chasselas* (*Fendant Roux* and *Fendant Vert*), and that of DÔLE for the reds. The latter is a harmonious mixture of wines derived from the *Pinot Noir*, which originates from Burgundy, and the *Gamay*, a typical Beaujolais vine-stock. Each year, some 8,799,200 gallons of FENDANT, DÔLE and other wines from special stock are harvested, to bring to sagacious drinkers fresh strength, a delight to the palate, warmth of heart and a flowering of the spirit.

The white wines of the Valais are very numerous and very different from each other, depending on the stock which produced them. But the best-known and most widely sold is certainly FENDANT; harvested for probably about a century, it comes from vine-stocks which originated in the neighbouring canton of Vaud, where they were already well acclimatized. It is an admirable wine which pleases at all hours by its balance, its restrained strength and even, in hot years, by its hidden violence; it is a dry wine without any residual sugar in suspension. It is chosen as the friend and companion of those evenings for eating the *raclette*, a well-known cheese dish typical of Valais.

It is JOHANNISBERG which occupies the second place of importance among the white wines. Produced from *Sylvaner* or *Plant du Rhin*, whose grape-bunches are

115

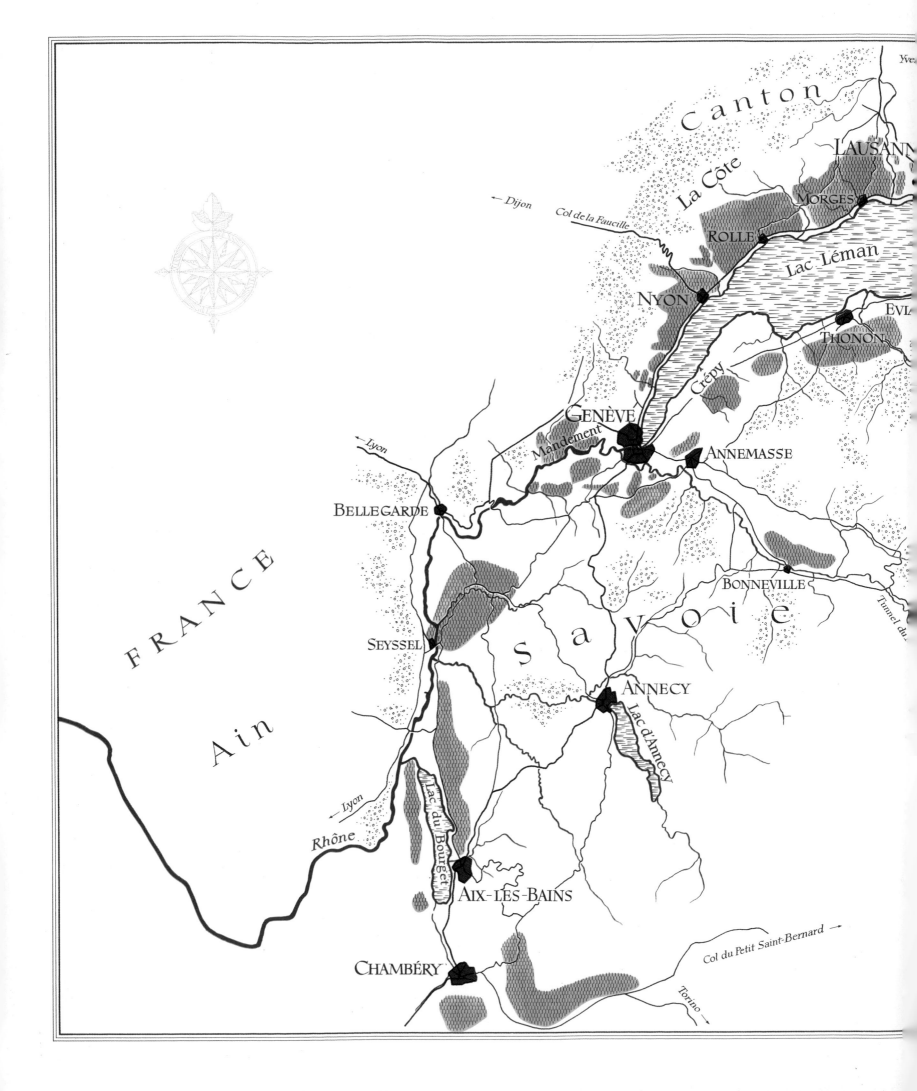

RHÔNE SUISSE · SAVOIE

recognizable by their small size and closely-packed clusters, this wine is warmer than FENDANT. It is selected with special care, is remarkable for its strength, but nevertheless combines a great distinctiveness with an attractive charm. This wine makes a good companion to the locally grown asparagus.

The art of guiding the wine, of leading it to its perfect flowering, is very well-known here, and the concern and respect for the profession of oenologist have brought a wide fame to the wines of Valais. As with FENDANT, one must drink JOHANNISBERG while it is still young; it is not a wine that should be allowed to age too much.

Beside these two well-known wines, one must mention a few other specialities whose quantities are, however, very small, at the most not more than 5 per cent of the entire harvest of Valais.

PINOT GRIS or MALVOISIE (Malmsey) is a heady and strong wine which, in good years, does not manage to change all the natural sugar it contains into alcohol. It is especially a dessert wine, mellow and flavoursome, with its bright colour shining brilliantly in the glass like molten gold. MALVOISIE therefore charms the drinker as much by its beauty as by its taste and its bouquet, bringing a note of agreeable bliss to the conclusion of a meal that was perhaps full of extravagances.

ERMITAGE is a firm, powerful and strongly-alcoholic wine, capable of being kept for a long time and with a bouquet which sings all the beauties of Valais.

Then there are PETITE ARVINE, AMIGNE and HUMAGNE, typical local wines which have not emigrated elsewhere. ARVINE is a virile and lively wine which sometimes has some bite; it resists the ravages of time thanks to its natural liveliness. AMIGNE *(vinum amoenum)* is a more delicate, more pleasant wine with a light bouquet; it holds its own at the beginning of a meal as well as at the end. HUMAGNE *(vinum humanum)*, which is gradually

The château of Aigle, in the region of Vaud known as the Chablais, contains a Wine Museum, founded by the Confrérie du Guillon, which has the same relation to Vaud wines as does the Confrérie du Tastevin to Burgundian wines. The Chablais is known for its harmonious white wines which form a bridge between the wines of the Lavaux, on the shores of Lake Geneva, and the Valaisan FENDANTS.

On the banks of Lake Leman, above the village of Saint-Saphorin, the terraced vines of Lavaux turn towards the south-west to benefit from a triple share of the sun's warmth: that of the heavenly body itself, that received from the lake by reflection and, in the cool of the day, that returned to the soil from the little walls of sun-baked stones. In this vineyard, the most widely grown vine-stock is the *Chasselas*.

disappearing, brings to mind certain old winegrowers of Valais: it has not only their brusqueness and sharpness, but also their frankness and nobility.

Some other wines also deserve mention, notably MUSCAT. Very little is harvested but it is vinified as a dry wine and then fermented to have more savour and bouquet: it is a wine which, if drunk while still young, flatters the most exacting noses and taste-buds by its aroma. Finally, one can mention two local specialities which are not commercialized and which one must be lucky enough to drink on the spot in order to appreciate fully their true qualities: PAYEN, made from a very old vine-stock, *Sauvagnin*, and VIN DU GLACIER, also from an old plant, *Rèze*. All these wines are specialities of Valais which are much discussed but which are unfortunately difficult to find, owing to their extreme rarity.

Among the red wines, DÔLE deserves a special mention: it is a wine which has body and mellowness yet which is nevertheless not heavy nor tiring. A delightful blending of *Pinot Noir* and *Gamay*, DÔLE can only carry this name if it contains a minimum amount of natural sugar, which is very closely checked, and if the entire crop has been supervised by the Cantonal laboratory. If the alcohol content is not high enough, the wine will be named GORON: lighter and very pleasant, this seldom leaves the Valais.

Canton of Vaud

As far as Saint-Maurice, the Rhône valley is relatively narrow, but then it widens suddenly to form the vast Lake Leman, along all of which stretches the Canton of Vaud. In effect, there are three different viticultural regions in this canton; Chablais, Lavaux and La Côte.

Vaud produces chiefly white wines, marketed under the name DORIN, although a production of red wines under the name SALVAGNIN has been increasing over the past ten years. This canton produces about 6,600,000 gallons each year from 8,400 acres of vines. All wines bearing the name DORIN come from the *Chasselas* (*Fendant Roux* and *Fendant Vert*), a vine that has kept its name when commercialized.

DORIN, CHABLAIS, YVORNE and AIGLE have, in particular, built up a big reputation: these dry wines, true-bred, warm and of a great finesse—a major quality in wine—are much sought after. Among them, one must single out for special notice OVAILLES D'YVORNE, one of the best sites in the canton.

119

Lying between Lausanne and Geneva, the La Côte vineyards extend across gentle slopes and peaceful hills, like those around the village of Fechy (photo). It is a region of large holdings. The wine is fuller than that of Lavaux, and it is said locally that it is a bolder wine.

Among the vineyards of La Côte, Vinzel (photo) produces a white wine of quality, fruity, elegant, and agreeably dry. The greater part of the white wines of the Vaud vineyards are made from the *Chasselas* grape, and are sold under the label DORIN.

The landscape of Lavaux, between Lausanne and Montreux, has been transformed by the labours of the winegrowers. The vineyards are small, anchored on the slopes by retaining walls that prevent the soil from slipping down the hillsides.

The Lavaux wines carry the names of communes or the local name of the area they are grown in; thus, there are bottles labelled VILLETTE (commune), EPESSES (commune) and DÉZALEY (area—photo).

121

In the Lavaux region, the Dézaley wines are excellent; coming from vineyards hanging on steep slopes, these wines—aristocratic, rich, full—are dry with all the delicacy and exquisite bitterness needed to assure them a long life, and the slight hint of a flinty taste is a characteristic flavour. These are once more wines from the *Chasselas* grape, which because of its large yield and sturdiness and the earthy taste of the wine is still preferred by the conservative Swiss vinegrowers to the more noble vines that the vineyard would seem to favour. The Dézaley is a big terraced southern slope with glacial moraine overlying the original mollasse. It lies between Vevey and Lausanne and obtains its excellent microclimate mainly because of its proximity to Lake Leman. This vineyard was created around 1100, together with the other famous vineyards mentioned above, thanks to the untiring efforts of Cistercian monks. After the desecularization of the clergy it fell under Bern sovereignty and today belongs to the Wine Estates of the City of Lausanne.

In the canton of Vaud, wines are presented with the name of their commune of origin, so that one has for the region of Lavaux such famous labels as EPESSES, RIVAZ, SAINT-SAPHORIN (usually abbreviated to SAINT-SAPH), among others. The white wines of Vaud are, as a general rule, less tender than those of Valais, but also less lively than the wines of Geneva. These shades of meaning were much clearer in olden times, and winegrowers of Vaud, great ones for picturesque speech, liked to say that the wines of Geneva were *raides et pointus* ("stiff and pointed") like the North Wall of the Eiger, only to hear the Genevese Calvinists reply that the Vaud wines were as flat as the pages of the psalm-book! But progress in oenology has erased all these faults, so that today these wines are delicate, fruity, fresh and pleasant, as much at home during a meal as on any other occasion.

The slopes of La Côte, the most important viticultural region of the Canton of Vaud, are gentler, and if the wines harvested there are also less full-bodied and warm, they are nevertheless also appreciated for their remarkably fresh bouquet.

Large co-operative cellars and big firms have made the wines of this region well known, with such names as the famous VINZEL, MONT, FÉCHY, LUINS, TARTEGNIN and MORGES. There are, in addition, numerous châteaux along La Côte, rich in history and hiding in their cellars the inviting and exhilarating wines from the vineyards which surround them.

The red wines of Vaud carry the name SALVAGNIN (from the name of this old vine-stock); but only reds from noble stock (*Pinot* and *Gamay*) may in fact carry it, for this name is only given after a severe quality test. Elegant, balanced, velvety, flattering, well-bred, these slightly dark-coloured wines are warm enough and rich enough in alcohol to accompany spiced and seasoned foods. The ceaseless search for fresh markets leads some proprietors to offer their wines by separating the vine-stock used; the *Pinot Noir* can then do full justice to all its real magnificence and, as Latin-speaking winegrowers might be tempted to say, *in Pinot veritas*.

Red wines, which do not have the SALVAGNIN name are sold under various trade names. In very great demand, these wines are served cool like Beaujolais wines and should also be drunk while young, unlike the PINOT which reveals itself, after a few years of ageing, as a wine of high class.

Special vine-stocks are much less cultivated in the Canton of Vaud than in Valais or Geneva; one does, however, find generous JOHANNISBERGS, sweet white PINOT-CHARDONNAYS, and RIESLING-SYLVANERS with a strongly muscat bouquet. But on the whole, these wines are rare as much by their high quality as by their small quantity, although they may well carry to a seventh heaven those who partake of them.

Canton of Geneva

Leaving the Canton of Vaud, the traveller arrives in Geneva, the site not only of a great international city with many attractions but also of a rich and flourishing

Switzerland does not have a uniform system for labelling its wines. The label shown above states that the wine comes from the estate known as La Tour de Marsens, in the Dézaley area. But nothing says that it is a white wine, or that Dézaley has the right to use the area name.

A few miles from the international city of Geneva lies a 2,500 acre vineyard, which has the largest yield per acre in all Switzerland. The vineyards are planted on a gentle, sunbathed slope. White wines, from the *Chasselas* grape, predominate, and are known as PERLAN.

vineyard of about 2,500 acres. One-fifth of this area is planted to red stock, and *Gamay*, which comes especially from Beaujolais, is the most used vine stock; *Pinot Noir*, however, of Burgundian origin, is carving for itself an increasing large share of the canton's wine production. The white wines come from different vine-stocks of which the most important, *Chasselas*, covers an area of 1,235 acres. About 740 acres produce wines which are original and full of personality; they come from special, well-acclimatized vine-stocks: *Riesling-Sylvaner, Sylvaner* and *Aligoté*. Some other plants, such as *Pinot Gris, Chardonnay* or *Pinot Blanc*, in particular, produce exquisite and well-bred wines in, alas, only small quantities. About 500 acres are planted to red vine-stock, producing, in a year and for an average total of 2,640,000 gallons, as much red wine as white.

The winegrowers of Geneva are proud to be the descendants and the worthy successors of very long lines of antecedents. These vineyards, in fact, date back to the time of the Roman conquest, and several emperors have left their mark in various decrees. Domitian, trying to prevent the expansion of the vine, ordered the

uprooting of half of those not belonging to Romans; Probus, on the other hand, favoured its cultivation and kept his soldiers busy in their spare time spreading the noble plant to numerous regions.

The vineyard of Geneva had a very chequered history over the centuries and the vinegrowers needed a firmly rooted faith to persevere in their work. Having survived the pillaging, pilfering and general murdering characteristic of, in particular, the sixteenth and seventeenth centuries, they saw towards the end of the nineteenth century two new pests emerge, as elsewhere in Europe: phylloxera and mildew. Powerless to fight against these two calamities, they suffered the disappearance of half their vineyards; but the vineyards were re-planted and now extend in gentle folds between the Jura mountains and the Salève ridge.

The wines produced from *Chasselas* and called PERLAN have gained for themselves an enviable place over the past few years: generally light, they are usually sold *sur lie*, that is, they have not been decanted. They have kept their natural carbonic acid gas, have a delicate perfume and rejoice the eye of the connoisseur as they

sparkle gently in the glass. It has been said they are much like the Genevese: not very biting at one's first meeting, they turn out to be the most joyous and friendly of companions. These wines can be drunk still milky, before they have finished fermenting, although it is preferable to allow them to reach full maturity. However, they are not rich enough in alcohol to gain much by being kept for several years.

The success of the wines produced from special vine-stocks must be mentioned here. Talented wine-growers in this region offer, for example, RIESLING-SYLVANER with a slightly musky perfume; dry and strong, this is much drunk as an aperitif. SYLVANER or JOHANNIS-BERG take the richness of the vine from which they come and deserve encouragement from the drinker; thanks to the little-known *Muscat* plant, and also to *Aligoté* and *Chardonnay*, which are very high-class stocks, excellent and harmonious wines can be offered to the consumer.

The greater part of the wines of Geneva are very well produced, with modern methods and the large cellars grouped together under a single trade name. A few well-equipped individual proprietors produce, on their own, wines which are becoming better known.

A final mention must be made of the red Geneva wines GAMAY and PINOT NOIR: the former are produced in some quantity and are supple and friendly wines, not heavy, and excellent in company; the PINOT is a richer wine which has already brought joy to a few connoisseurs in good years.

The Bacchic Brotherhoods

Everywhere, be it in Geneva, Valais or Vaud, one sees the marvels and the gifts that wine brings in its train. One must admire not only the wine itself, but also the manner in which the ideas of the land are enriched, the customs strengthened and even the thoughts and way of life of Rhône-side dwellers heightened—wherever wine is present.

Recently, between the years 1950 and 1960, several brotherhoods of wine were formed in these three Swiss cantons, with the sole aim of making the varieties of wealth offered by the Rhône vineyards better known and more appreciated. The Académie du Cep in Geneva, the Channe in Valais and the Confrérie du Guillon in Vaud all organize great gastronomic dinners, usually in the château de Dardagny in Geneva, the château de Chillon (immortalized by the poet Byron) in Vaud, or a number of other famous places in Valais. The dishes and the wines are presented, served and commented upon with love, humour and competence. These well-dressed occasions see the friends of wine come running from just about everywhere, to meet *ce fils sacré du soleil* ("this sacred son of the sun") as Baudelaire put it, in order to prove that this drink mentioned in the Bible is admirably adept at forging faithful friendships, opening hearts, broadening the spirit and giving the final proof that wine throughout the world is the ambassador of civilization.

THE WINES OF SAVOY

Two writers of ancient Rome, Pliny the Younger and Columella, made famous the wines of Allobroge, the Savoy of today. The prince of Roman gourmets, Lucullus, had Savoy wines served at his table and the vinegrowers of Savoy are proud of the title of seniority that history has conferred on them.

With the exception of the local table wines drunk in the region, the wines of Savoy make up that honourable company called *vins délimités de qualité supérieure*, or more simply "V.D.Q.S.". There is no outstanding vintage wine; there are simply good, honest wines which are, none the less, well known outside their place of birth.

The vineyard of Savoy can be divided into three zones:

1. To the north, the southern shores of Lake Leman, from Evian to Annemasse; the right bank of the river Arve from Annemasse to Bonneville, and the area along the Swiss frontier to Saint-Julien-en-Genevois. These make up a relatively homogeneous zone which is chiefly planted, as across the border in Switzerland, with *Chasselas*. The winegrowers produce fresh, light white wines, such as MARIN, RIPAILLE and MARIGNAN. First

place, however, must go to COTEAUX-DE-CRÉPY and PETIT CRÉPY, both of them clear, semi-sparkling wines with a delicate perfume of almond, reputed also to be the most diuretic wines in France.

2. In the centre, the region of the Lake of Bourget, Seyssel and the left bank of the Rhône gives a very characteristic wine called Savoy ROUSSETTE, the principal vintages of which are FRANGY, MARESTEL, MONTHOUX and SEYSSEL. These wines have a good bouquet; fruity and full-bodied, they are the product of *Altesse*, a vine brought back, it is said by the Count of Mareste from a crusade. Seyssel also has a pleasant sparkling wine.

3. To the south, the vineyard encompasses the region of Chambéry, the right bank of the river Isère from Saint-Pierre-d'Albigny to Sainte-Marie-d'Alloix, and the Arc valley up to Saint-Michel.

Apart from the local wines, a few white wines have emerged from anonymity; these are the wines of Monterminod, Apremont, Abymes, Chignin, Cruet, Montmélian and Saint-Jean-de-la-Porte. To these white wines one can add a few reds and rosés, light, easy to drink and which, it is said, do not upset the drinker's temper.

THE WINES OF THE FRENCH JURA

The Roman naturalist Pliny, who also served in the armies of Germania, recalled "this grape needing no special preparations which produces the pitch-flavoured wine recently bringing pleasure to Sequani the area of the river Seine". If one is to believe this statement, the vine was established on the western edge of the Jura mountains right at the beginning of our historic age. The resulting VIN D'ARBOIS gained wide renown.

In the year 1885 occurred the first attack of phylloxera, which within the next ten years was to destroy the entire vineyard. The pre-phylloxera vines were cultivated with the aid of props and with no particular order or symmetry. The new vines were planted in lines and trained on to wire supports, a method allowing the use of a plough to work the land wherever it does not slope too much and an arrangement which also enables the grapes to soak up the maximum warmth of the sun. The first harvests of the twentieth century bear witness to the rebirth of this vineyard.

Today, the vineyard of the Jura, well situated and with a cold, humid climate in winter, extends from Salins in the north to Saint-Amour in the south, a stretch of some 50 miles in length by 8 miles at its widest part. It is planted to *Ploussard* or *Poulsard*, *Trousseau* and *Gros Noirin* for the red wines, and to *Naturé* or *Savagnin*, *Chardonnay* or *Pinot Blanc* for the white wines. Apart from the local table wines, the Jura produces three well-known wines:

The CÔTES-DU-JURA are full-bodied, heady red wines, earthy rosés, and dry whites which, although lively and fruity, are sometimes a little acid when young.

The VINS D'ARBOIS are finer and more generous than the above-mentioned ones; the reds and rosés come from the *Ploussard* and, to a lesser degree, from the *Trousseau* and *Pinot Noir*. It is interesting to recall, in passing, that it was in Arbois, where he was born and where he owned a vineyard, that the illustrious Louis Pasteur worked on his study of fermentation.

The CHÂTEAU-CHALON is the wine *par excellence* of the Jura vineyards. This amber-coloured wine—hence its name *vin jaune*—is unusual in its production and handling. In the spring of the second year, after a normal vinification, it is transferred to a cask already impregnated with *vin jaune*. There it is left to age, without being touched in any way—not even the skin on its surface is disturbed—and it is bottled only after six years. This *vin jaune* is a truly original wine and one of the best white wines in France. Some of it is also produced under the name CÔTES-DU-JURA or ARBOIS, but it is the CHÂTEAU-CHALON which is the undisputed leader. It is the only white wine which must not be served chilled but slightly *chambré*, nearly at room temperature, in its special bottle, the *clavelin*.

The Jura vinegrowers also produce, apart from a sparkling wine processed by the *méthode champenoise* around Arbois, the so-called *vin de paille*, or straw wine.

Planted on the western flanks of the Jura mountains, the Châton-Châlon vineyards are celebrated for *vin jaune*, made from *Salvagnin* grapes by a special process. The grapes are gathered at the beginning of November, and the unusual vinification makes the wine one of the best white wines of France.

It is a wine of the winter frosts, made from grapes harvested at the end of the autumn which have been stored carefully on trays of straw until February; the grapes are then pressed, and the wine is kept in little oaken barrels. The *vin de paille* is a beautiful burned-topaz colour, a dessert wine with an unctuous bouquet. Among the unusual Jura wines, one should not forget MACVIN, an aperitif produced by cooking the must from white grapes, infusing spices and, after filtering, adding *eau-de-vie de marc* (white brandy).

THE WINES OF THE CÔTES DU RHÔNE

An infinite variety of locations and an infinite variety of wines—such are the characteristic features of the Côtes du Rhône region, stretching 125 miles along the majestic river, from Vienne-la-Romaine to Avignon, city of the Popes. In a few short hours by train or car, one passes from a northern world to a southern world, from forests of chestnuts to forests of olive trees. The wines produced in the various parts of the Rhône valley are different for reasons of variations of climate, of soil and also of vine-stocks.

The Côtes du Rhône region can be divided into two parts, separated by non-viticultural areas: the northern part from Vienne to Valence, and the southern part from Bourg-Saint-Andéol (just opposite Pierrelatte) as far as Avignon.

The cultivation of the vine has developed particularly in the vineyards of the CÔTES-DU-RHÔNE *appellation d'origine contrôlée*, but perhaps principally in the vineyards producing the basic type of wine. Thus, between 1956 and 1967, the area planted to vine increased from 31,085 acres to 60,330 acres, and wine production (including vintage wines) from 8,030,000 gallons to a level of 19,798,200 gallons in 1967. In 1980, production rose to 43,996,000 gallons from 98,840 acres. As for the marketing side of wine production, the domestic demand has followed the increase in production, while exports have leaped ahead, from 3,744,147 in 1968 to about 11,357,171 gallons in 1980.

The basic regional name of the wine, which includes all types, is CÔTES-DU-RHÔNE. Within this vineyard, however, there are the following *appellations d'origine contrôlée* established by special decree of the French authorities: CHÂTEAUNEUF-DU-PAPE, CÔTE-RÔTIE, CONDRIEU, CORNAS, HERMITAGE, SAINT-PÉRAY, TAVEL, CHÂTEAU-GRILLET, CROZES-HERMITAGE, LIRAC and SAINT-JOSEPH.

CÔTE-RÔTIE: The vineyard of CÔTE-RÔTIE lies 22 miles south of Lyons and almost opposite Vienne, on precipitous slopes where the soil must be held in place by small walls. Two vine-stocks, *Viognier* and *Syrah*, produce a wine with a great fragrance and a delicate perfume which recalls violets and raspberries.

This red wine, harvested at Ampuis, develops its qualities to the full after ageing in casks for three or four years; it can be kept in the bottle for more than 20 years. The average production is 65,994 gallons.

CONDRIEU: This white wine comes solely from the white vine *Viognier* and must have an alcohol content of at least 11°. Its area of production includes the three communes of Condrieu (Rhône), Vérin and Saint-Michel (Loire). This gives an average production of about 4,400 gallons from the 17 acres of vineyards that the fifteen or so producers cultivate. Cultivation is carried out solely on small, stone-walled terraces, a type of exploitation of the land that is extremely difficult because it is impossible to employ mechanical aid. This difficulty accounts for the fact that these vineyards are being gradually abandoned.

The fermentation of Condrieu wines is allowed to proceed more or less slowly according to the prevailing temperature; it continues up to the end of the year when the rigorous winter stops the process. Fermentation re-starts in the spring and continues until some time in summer, if dry wines are being produced. To obtain the sweet wines, which contain 15-30 grammes of sugar per litre and represent 80 per cent of the total production here, fermentation is stopped by successive racking, combined with blending.

This wine is not drunk when it is old, because although it stands up to ageing very well, it loses that special fruitiness which has made its name. Bottling is therefore carried out, depending on the type of wine, during the first or the second year.

CHÂTEAU-GRILLET: This vintage wine is not cultivated very extensively and is confined to a few plots of land in the communes of Verin and Saint-Michel-sous-Condrieu (Loire).

The granite hillsides of Château-Grillet, facing south and dominating the Rhône, have a climate which is dry and hot during the summer and mild during the autumn, allowing the vine *Viognier* to attain over-maturity. The character of this tiny vineyard lies in its topography: the whole is made up of small, stepped terraces planted to not more than two rows of plants, and sometimes to only a few individual plants.

Harvested in late October, the must from these white grapes is put in casks and allowed to ferment very slowly over several months. It is racked a number of times to ensure a perfect clarification, and forms a very particular bouquet of violets. After two years of constant care, it is bottled, and it can then be kept for many years. Dry and fairly heady, it has some resemblance to Rhine wine, although it has more body and gives off a better developed perfume.

CROZES-HERMITAGE: This wine is produced in the communes of Serves, Erome, Gervans, Larnage, Crozes-Hermitage, Tain-l'Hermitage, Mercurol, Chanos-Cur-

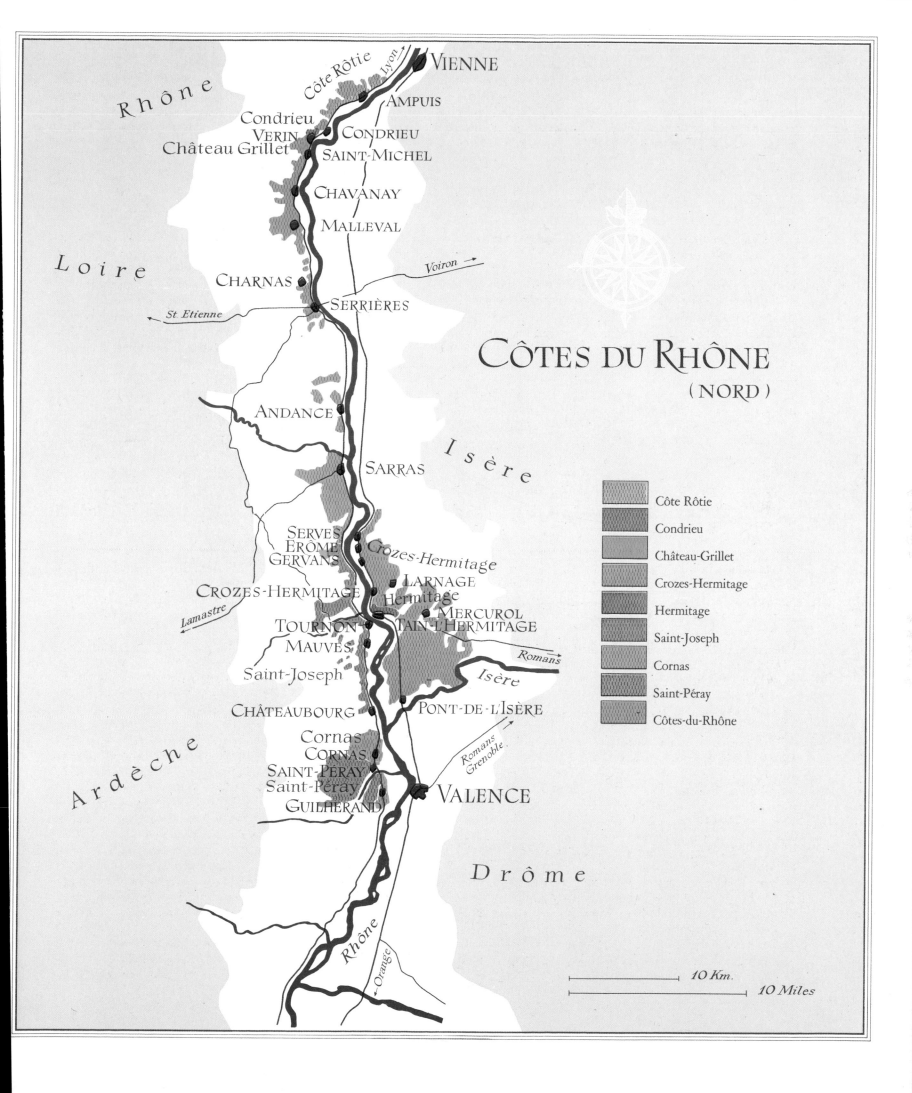

Côtes du Rhône
(Nord)

Rhône

Loire

Ardèche

Drôme

Isère

Isère

Vienne

Côte Rôtie

Lyon

Ampuis

Condrieu

Verin

Château Grillet

Condrieu

Saint-Michel

Chavanay

Malleval

Charnas

Voiron

Serrières

St Etienne

Andance

Sarras

Serves

Erôme

Gervans

Crozes-Hermitage

Crozes-Hermitage

Larnage

Hermitage

Mercurol

Tain-l'Hermitage

Lamastre

Tournon

Mauves

Saint-Joseph

Châteaubourg

Pont-de-l'Isère

Romans

Cornas

Cornas

Saint-Péray

Saint-Péray

Guilherand

Valence

Romans

Grenoble

Rhône

Orange

Côte Rôtie

Condrieu

Château-Grillet

Crozes-Hermitage

Hermitage

Saint-Joseph

Cornas

Saint-Péray

Côtes-du-Rhône

10 Km.

10 Miles

son, Beaumont-Montreux, La Roche-de-Glun and Pont-de-l'Isère.

The red wines are produced solely from the *Syrah* grape; the whites from the *Roussanne* and *Marsanne* varieties. However, the addition of *Marsanne* and *Roussanne* white grapes within the limits of 15 per cent is authorized for the production of red wine.

The hilly nature of the terrain makes cultivation here an extremely arduous affair. On the stepped-up terraces, all work must be done by hand, and fertilizers as well as the entire harvest can be carried only on the backs of men. The average production (1973-1980) is 549,950 gallons.

These red wines are lighter and more purplish than the HERMITAGE wines which follow in these pages, and they retain a tang of the soil, although they are less mellow or fine.

The white wines are very slightly coloured and sometimes lack a certain flavour and strength; they are, however, fine and light, with a perfume of hazelnut.

L'HERMITAGE: The hillside of l'Hermitage, which produces the wine of that name, lies in the northern part of the Côtes du Rhône region, in the department of Dauphiné. It commands the little town of Tain-l'Hermitage, in the department of Drôme, beside the Rhône on Route Nationale 7 between Vienne and Valence.

The earliest vineyards here date back to the tenth century, but legend has it that Henri Gaspart de Sterimberg, a knight returning from the Crusades under Louis VIII and weary of wars, sought from Queen Blanche de Castille a corner of land to which he could retire. This would explain the origin of the name "Hermitage". HERMITAGE obtained its titles to nobility as a wine under Henry IV and Louis XIII and especially under Louis XIV. Up to the time of the phylloxera disaster at the end of the last century, this was universally considered to be one of the foremost wines of France, being the favourite vintage wine of the Tsar's court in Russia. It was also much esteemed in nineteenth-century England.

The HERMITAGE vineyard is blessed with a quite exceptional geographical position: it faces south-west at an altitude of 894 feet above sea-level, only 6¼ miles from the 45° parallel of latitude.

The red wine is produced entirely from the vine *Syrah*, while the white wine comes from *Marsanne* with the addition of a small quantity of *Roussanne*. The wines of Hermitage are no longer the wines of the Lyons region, following on from Burgundy, nor are they wines of Provence; they are strictly Rhône wines.

SAINT-JOSEPH: The name of Saint-Joseph is a relatively recent one, since it was authorized by a decree dated June 15th, 1956. It had had, nonetheless, its "letters patent of nobility" for many years: according to Elie Brault, Louis XII would allow on his table only the wines from his property at Beaune, his land at Tournon or his vineyards at Chenoves.

Six communes in the department of Ardèche are entitled to produce this wine, with the exception of lands which are unsuitable on account of their soil or their position. The communes are: Glunn, Mauves, Tournon, Saint-Jean-de-Muzols, Lemps and Vion.

For the red wines the *Syrah* grape is used while the *Marsanne* and *Roussanne* produce the whites.

The vine is cultivated on the steep slopes overlooking the right bank of the Rhône. Most of the work is done by hand, and the vintage is carried in on the grapepickers' backs. The mean annual production (1973-1980) is 114,389 gallons.

The SAINT-JOSEPH reds are fine wines with a perfumed bouquet although they are, perhaps, rather less full-bodied than the HERMITAGE wines. They have a fine ruby colour and are agreeable to drink after a few years in the bottle. The whites are fruity, supple and mellow; to be drunk young while they retain their full perfume.

CORNAS. Every day throughout the centuries, as the rising sun sheds its rays on the Rhône valley, the first communes to benefit from them have been Château-bourg and Cornas, situated as they are with their backs to the Cévennes. The commune of Cornas has a Provençal type of climate, as witness the olive, fig and almond trees which flourish in many a garden there. This privileged situation has encouraged the cultivation of the vine for more than a thousand years. A document of the time of Charles V reveals that the Great Compagnies halted at Cornas for far longer than was scheduled in their marching programme since they could not resist the good wine in the inns of this countryside.

GRANDE CUVÉE

MARQUE DÉPOSÉE

Chante-Alouette
APPELLATION HERMITAGE CONTRÔLÉE

M. CHAPOUTIER S.A.

NÉGOCIANTS-ÉLEVEURS A TAIN L'HERMITAGE (DROME) FRANCE

The information given by wine labels is not always easy to understand, and sometimes assumes some knowledge on the part of the reader. The name 'Chante-Alouette' is the name of a growth, which the shipper guarantees comes only from the Hermitage appellation region, within the Côtes-du-Rhône. But how to tell that it is a white wine?

Vintage time in the Châteauneuf-du-Pape vineyards, which extend over the communes of Châteauneuf-du-Pape, Orange, Courthezon, Béddarides and Sorgues. The wine is made from a blend of 13 grape varieties, of which the principal seven are: *Grenache, Clairette, Mourvèdre, Picpoul, Ferret, Syrah,* and *Cinsault*; while the 6 others are: *Counoise, Muscadin, Vaccarèse, Picardan, Roussane,* and *Bourboulenc.*

The A.O.C. CORNAS covers the area around the village and the granite slopes; the alluvial soils in the Rhône valley are excluded.

The grapes grown in the vineyard are the *Syrahs.* Since they are not very productive, long shoots are permitted and this means that the shoots must be fastened to the props before the spring. All the work of cultivation on the terraces must be done by hand and the harvest seldom exceeds 44,000 gallons.

The best wine comes from the grapes ripened on the slope. It is richer and fuller bodied, fruitier and heavier with a characteristic taste of the soil due to its richness in tannin. In its first year, CORNAS may be a little sour and astringent; it reaches its peak of quality after three winters in the wood and two years in the bottle.

SAINT-PÉRAY. At the foot of Mount Crussol and in the latitude of Valence, we find the village of Saint-Péray. It would seem that the department of Ardèche has always been a favourite winegrowing country and, with CORNAS and SAINT-JOSEPH, SAINT-PÉRAY forms the trinity of fine Vivarais wines.

The vineyard, which is one of the oldest in the northern Côtes du Rhône area, is quite limited in area. The soil is tilled by hand because of the narrowness of the space between the rows of vines. In the parcels where the slope is less steep it is sometimes possible to use horse-ploughs or hand-ploughs.

The only white grapes permitted are the *Roussette* (or *Roussanne*) and the *Marsanne.* The *Roussette* is a fine grape variety and produces a high-class wine with a strong perfume, but since it is not very productive and is sensitive to disease, it is gradually being abandoned. Because of the soil type lighter wines are produced than on the other side of the Rhône.

Until the beginning of the nineteenth century, the Saint-Péray wines were served *nature*, i.e. as still wines. Attempts by local wine-merchants in 1828 to convert them into sparkling wines produced excellent results, and since then Saint-Péray has been available in that form also. Classical white-wine vinification is used. After pressing and drawing off, the must is fermented in 50-gallon hogsheads called *pièces.* The fermentation must be completed before winter. The dry white wines are usually bottled after two or three years.

The wines produced are marketed, therefore, either as still wines, as dry SAINT-PÉRAY, or as sparkling wines. It is the latter form—SAINT-PÉRAY MOUSSEUX—which is now the better known.

CHÂTEAUNEUF-DU-PAPE. This is the "Pontiff" of the Côtes du Rhône wines. In addition to possessing all the

129

The Gigondas vineyards lie on the left bank of the river Ouvèze, between Vaison-la-Romaine and Avignon. They are mainly planted with *Grenache* grapes, which give a brilliant deep garnet red wine, and which is amongst the best of the Côtes-du-Rhône.

Wines coming from the commune of Sablet, Provence, have a right to the appellation Côtes-du-Rhône. As can be seen from the photograph, not all winegrowers are mechanised. However, it is increasingly rare to see horses working among the vines at vintage time.

warmth of the Provençal sun, this wine is perfumed by the full aroma of that region's sparse soil. Between Orange and Avignon, dominating one of the widest and most breath-taking landscapes of Provence, an abrupt hill bears a picturesque village crowned by an imposing medieval ruin. The place was formerly selected by the popes as their summer residence. Climbing up the sides of the hill, the impressive vineyard of Châteauneuf-du-Pape reveals that the local winegrowers have lost nothing of the traditional renown attached to this soil. The wine produced is still in every way worthy of the pontifical table. The territory entitled to the A.O.C., i.e. the commune of Châteauneuf-du-Pape and parts of the communes of Orange, Courthezon, Beddarides and Sorgues, has been strictly limited since 1923. Incidentally, the national regulations on A.O.C.s, promulgated in December 1936, were inspired by what had been achieved at Châteauneuf-du-Pape.

The methods of cultivation, vinification and conservation have been fixed both by law and by the strong force of local tradition.

CHÂTEAUNEUF-DU-PAPE comes from thirteen grapes, seven of which, *Grenache*, *Clairette*, *Mourvèdre*, *Picpoul*, *Terret*, *Syrah* and *Cinsault*, are regarded as principal grapes, while the other six, *Counoise*, *Muscadin*, *Vaccarèse*, *Picardan*, *Roussanne* and *Bourboulenc*, are regarded as ancillary. Each of these grapes contributes its own special note to the wine produced: the *Grenache* and the *Cinsault* give it warmth, sweetness and mellowness; the *Mourvèdre*, the *Syrah*, the *Muscadin* and the *Vaccarèse* contribute colour, solidity and staying-power; the *Counoise* and the *Picpoul* supply wininess, taste, freshness and a special bouquet, while the *Clairette*, *Bourboulenc*, *Roussanne* and *Picardan* give it elegance, fire and brilliance.

The wines of Châteauneuf-du-Pape are always highly coloured and very warm. They have a powerful bouquet reminiscent of oriental spices. They are very varied in type: the pebbly soils give a great deal of strength while the sandy and sandy-clayey soils produce a wine of great finesse and elegance.

The average production of the vineyard 1973-1980 reached 1,951,222 gallons.

Side by side with the great vineyards we have just mentioned, there is a host of small villages whose names strike no particular chord but which are excellent producers of wine with the A.O.C. CÔTES-DU-RHÔNE and CÔTES-DU-RHÔNE-VILLAGES. This wine comes from no less than 138 communes with an average annual production of 43,996,000 gallons. Some of the areas involved are entitled to a stricter commune regulation, the place-name being granted after compulsory tasting. Three such are Cairanne, Gigondas and Vacqueyras.

Although the *Grenache* and the *Carigan* form the framework of the CÔTES-DU-RHÔNE wines, any or all of the following grape varieties can be used to distinguish one wine from another: *Clairette*, *Syrah*, *Mourvèdre*, *Terret Noir*, *Counoise*, *Picpoule*, *Muscardin*, *Bourbou-*

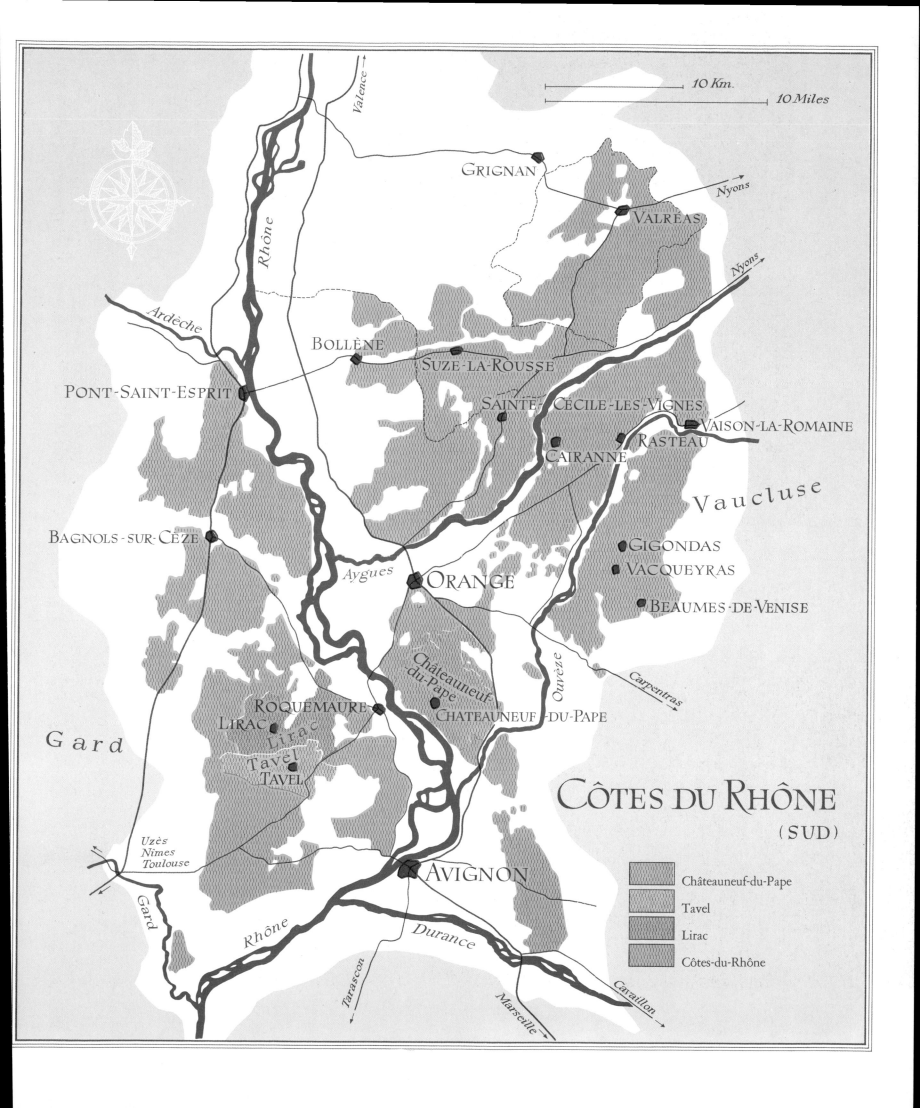

Beaumes-de-Venise is situated at the foot of Mont-Ventoux, and produces a natural sweet wine, rich and velvety, from *Muscat* grapes, which has been praised by the poet Mistral.

lenc, *Ugni Blanc, Roussanne, Marsanne* and *Viognier.* It should be added that there are also variations due to the soil, the exposure, and individual cultivation which give each growth its originality. Everything is carefully regulated: the grape variety, the soil, the pruning of the plant, the degree of alcohol and the yield.

CAIRANNE. This is one of the oldest of winegrowing terrains. Almost all the Clairanne vineyard, which covers 3,000 acres, consists of slopes and terraces facing due south.

VACQUEYRAS and GIGONDAS. The main GIGONDAS grape is the *Grenache* while VACQUEYRAS is still largely based on the *Carignan,* which is gradually being replaced by the *Cinsault* and *Syrah.* The red wines are of great quality and approach those of CHÂTEAUNEUF-DU-PAPE.

LIRAC. The LIRAC wines, whether red, rosé or even white, have each their own special type.

The principal grape, the *Grenache,* must make up at least 40 per cent of the planting for Lirac reds and rosés, the other 60 per cent consisting of *Cinsault* and *Mourvèdre.* Secondary grapes such as *Syrah* and *Picpoul* are permitted. In the case of the whites, 30 per cent of the planting must be the *Clairette* grape.

All these old local grapes, mixed together at harvest, endow the charming Lirac wines with their pronounced bouquet and particular perfume.

TAVEL. A little village 8 miles from Avignon, Tavel, harvests from a particularly arid soil about 637,942 gallons on the average of a light red wine obtained from such old grape varieties as: *Clairette, Cinsault, Grenache,* etc. This wine was very much appreciated by the Popes of Avignon, and by Philippe le Bel who claimed that "the only good wine is that from Tavel". It has an incomparable bouquet and, although strongly alcoholic, is light to the taste. Tavel can be taken as an aperitif or with red meat; it develops its full savour when it is put as an accompaniment to a young partridge or when served with a thrush with juniper berries.

RASTEAU. In this case, a single grape, the *Grenache,* has given birth to an excellent natural sweet wine. The must is vinified according to the classical method of obtaining naturally sweet wines. During fermentation, a certain amount of alcohol is added and this prevents the sugar from being completely transformed into alcohol. The wine thus retains a certain amount of sugar, which is the reason for its sweetness, while at the same time developing a high alcohol content.

BEAUMES-DE-VENISE. This is a natural sweet wine produced from various white *Muscats* with a special taste which are among the finest of their type. These wines are aged in casks or demijohns; when exposed to the sunlight, they develop a beautiful golden colour.

THE WINES OF THE CÔTES DE PROVENCE

The wines of the Côtes de Provence are of very ancient origin; under the name of "Provence wines", they were already known to the Romans. According to a statement by Justinian, it was the Gauls who cultivated the first vines brought from Italy and the near East by the Phocaeans, and they were already honoured during the reign of Caesar, who speaks of them in his Commentaries. The fame of the Provence wines continued through the Middle Ages and into the Renaissance; the Cartulary of Lérins mentions them and lords and abbots began to fix the rules for their production and marketing through such decrees as the Act of King Charles II in 1292, and the authorization by Queen Mary in 1391, both sovereigns of Provence.

In the seventeenth and eighteenth centuries, they were in high repute at the Court of the Sun King, where Madame de Sévigné became their best ambassadress. From this period dates the foundation by Louis de Vauvray, Naval Intendant at Toulon, of one of the first baccanalian orders, that of the "Knights of Medusa". In the nineteenth century and at the beginning of the twentieth, the *appellation contrôlée* and even the fame of the Côtes de Provence wines were in decline; under various names, some of these wines were used for

The winegrowers of the Bouches-du-Rhône and Languedoc produce a very large quantity of wine, which suffers from competition from Italian and Spanish wines. This is a problem that worries the winegrowers and their organisations, and which has given trouble to the national Government and the Common Market authorities.

133

blending and others for making vermouth. Only a few owners, proud of their growths and strong in the markets they had conquered, kept aloft the flag of this A.O.C.: under the auspices of the Syndical Association of the Winegrowing Landowners of the Var, established in 1931, they were to form the basis for the resurrection of the CÔTES-DE-PROVENCE.

The area of production is the result of a delimitation based on the geological, hydrological and climatic study of the land by a commission nominated by ministerial decree and composed of representatives of the National Institute of Place-Name Descriptions of Origin *(appellation d'origine)*, the General Inspectorate of the Ministry of Agriculture and the Science Faculties of the Universities of Marseilles and Montpellier. The area of production is limited to the following zones: the coastal zone of Provence from La Ciotat to Saint-Raphael; the Permian depression which stretches from Sanary through Toulon to Carnoules and Leluc; the triassic plateau of Lorgues-Carces; the terraces of the valley of the Var and the area described by geologists as the Eubeau Basin in the Alpes-Maritimes. A card index has been established for each producing commune and an individual card index per producer. They are all minutely followed.

The delimitation of the area of production, the fixing of a minimum production per acre and the determina-tion of the grapes did not, in the eyes of the producers, constitute a sufficiently strict selection and they conse-quently imposed upon themselves the obligation to submit their produce, which already met the standards laid down, to an organoleptic analysis followed by examination by a tasting commission to decide if the wine were worthy of the *appellation contrôlée* CÔTES-DE-PROVENCE. In 1953 the wines were granted a statue allowing those of a sufficiently high standard to be sold as CÔTES DE PROVENCE V.D.Q.S. *(Vins Délimités de Qualité Supérieure)*, which is a secondary quality guarantee, and some wines are permitted to be sold as Classified Growths.

GRAPES. The varieties making up the CÔTES-DE-PROVENCE are fairly numerous. Some of them, however, play only a secondary part, though everywhere the same basic grape varieties are cultivated.

Among the red grapes, the *Carignan* clearly heads the field, occupying as it does 25 per cent or more of the area of the vineyard. Late in budding, of average productivity but sensitive to oïdium, it gives full-bodied alcoholic wines which are sometimes rather sour in their youth. This bitterness rapidly disappears with age. A certain proportion of this grape is required.

The *Cinsault*, like the *Grenache* elsewhere, contri-butes suppleness, mellowness and bouquet. The same is true of the *Tibouren*, which is cultivated in a substantial area of the Maures mountains.

The *Mourvèdre*, an élite grape, formerly held a much more important place than at present; the irregularity of its production has caused it to lose ground. However, under the impulse of a few progressive winegrowers, it is once again gaining a certain favour and is now definitely extending its sway. If it is included in suitable proportions, it should ensure that the wines age well and should distinctly improve their quality.

Among the white grapes, the *Ugni* and the *Clairette*, together with the *Rolle* in the Alpes-Maritimes, have an almost complete monopoly. To these principal grapes, however, are sometimes added some other high-quality varieties including the *Syrah*, the *Cabernet*, the *Barba-roux*, the *Picpoul*, the *Roussanne* and the *Pecoultour*.

It is by a judicious association of grapes, each contributing its particular characteristics, that the CÔTES-DE-PROVENCE acquire their balance and their spe-cial quality. There is a growing trend toward increasing the proportion of high-quality grapes, and rapid pro-gress is being made. We should mention that the law imposes a minimum alcohol content of 11° for the red and rosé wines and of 11.5° for the white wines.

VINIFICATION. On their arrival in the cellars, whether private or co-operative, the vintages are carefully sel-ected so that only grapes entitled to the A.O.C. will be introduced into the vats. Since the use of the mustimet-er and the refractometer have become generalized, the winegrowers wait until the grapes have reached com-plete maturity so as to have the maximum number of degrees.

36 cl

Clos d'Albizzi

APPELLATION CASSIS CONTROLÉE

F. DUMON
PROPRIÉTAIRE

CASSIS (B.-DU-R.)

The Clos d'Albizzi label clothes a bottle from the A.O.C. region of Cassis, a Côtes-de-Provence appellation. Clos d'Abrizzi is a dry white wine, elegant and full of character, made from *Ugné blanc*, *Clairette* and *Sauvignon* grapes; it is one of the aristocrats of Provence wines.

134

Fermentation usually takes place in concrete vats; some owners of classed growths, however, vinify in wooden vats. On the other hand, wood is always used when storing the wine for any length of time; this is obligatory for producers who sell in the bottle. A frequent practice is to remove the stalks. Vatting is generally quite short: 4 to 5 days for red wines but somewhat longer for the white wines, which ferment for about a fortnight; and only 24 hours for the rosé wines which are the natural result of the first 100 per cent pressing of rosé grapes. The white wine is usually obtained by the so-called "bleeding" method. It consists in leaving open the drainage tap of the vat which contains the trodden vintage and withdrawing a certain proportion of the must.

The environmental conditions and the grapes cultivated make it possible to obtain, by rational vinification and careful storage, wines of the very first quality each and every year.

CLASSED GROWTHS. The commission on Boundaries noted that, among the mass of producers, there were some who were organized to vinify in the best conditions and to store part of their harvest every year which was later sold, after ageing, in bottles. The Commission therefore adopted the idea of Classed Growths for any estate which had formerly practised ageing. It considered whether the fame of the wines from such-and-such a holding was justified on the basis of the environmental conditions, the grapes used, the cultivation methods, the vinification and growing processes used and the quality of the wines obtained. Moreover, it demanded a minimum ageing of 15 months for the red wines and 8 months for the rosé and white wines. Of more than 60 vineyards visited, the Commission decided that only 30 merited selection as CÔTES-DE-PROVENCE Classed Growths.

The fact that Provençal wines adapt easily to almost any dish might have accounted for the expansion of the A.O.C. to the detriment of certain wines.

The rosé, the great speciality of the CÔTES-DE-PROVENCE, is fruity and full-flavoured and has an irridescent robe. A choice companion to all dishes, it adds a note of high quality, which is much appreciated by the epicures, to the festive board.

The white wine is generally dry, sometimes sparkling, but always full of the savour of the Provençal hills and proves a most happy foil to the fish and shellfish of the Mediterranean coast. The dace of the gulf of Saint-Tropez, the crayfish of the Corsican creeks, the red mullet from the rocky depths of the Var coast as well as the Mediterranean shell-fish take on their full gustatory value when set off by the bouquet of a bottle of CÔTES-DE-PROVENCE.

The red wine, which is very full-flavoured, is at its best when accompanying pâtés, pasties, game and roasts. It is the perfect foil to venison and brings out still further the delicate aroma of woodcock flamed in old armagnac.

As in the case of a number of other wines, a special shape of bottle has been created for CÔTES-DE-PROVENCE. It is derived from the original Provençal bottle.

Wine Confraternity

Faithful to their tradition, the winegrowers of the Côtes-de-Provence, like those of many other wine-producing regions, have created a wine society or, more exactly, have revived a very ancient confraternity, founded in 1690, the Confraternity of the Knights of Medusa, from the name of one of the classical gorgons. Its first Grand Master was M. Dantan, its chief founder being the Naval Intendant at Toulon, M. Louis Girardin de Vauvray, who was named a benefactor member of the Order in 1697.

The rituals of the Order unfold in the sumptuous setting of the Château de Sainte-Roseline, at Arcs-de-Provence, in its cloisters and in its park, and they are governed by a President and a Grand Council.

THE WINES OF LANGUEDOC AND ROUSSILLON

In Languedoc-Roussillon we find a very large wine-growing area which flourishes under extremely favourable natural conditions. The cultivation of the wine is at present the dominant activity of the region. In certain districts it is combined with other activities such as market gardening and fruit-growing on the Garde bank of the Rhône, cattle-raising in the region of Garrigues and the lower Montagne Noire, industry in the coalfields of Alès and near the urban centres of Montpelliers, Nîmes and Béziers and fishing along the coast, but it remains the sole activity for most of the communes in spite of the changeover which has begun.

Although 85 per cent of the wines are ordinary wines for current consumption, produced from the best grapes and vinified under first-class conditions, it should not be forgotten that 12 per cent are wines of simple *appellation d'origine* while 3 per cent are wines of *appellation contrôlée*. Over the last five years, wines for current consumption coming from vineyards free of hybrids and obtained from recommended grapes, which

Perched against the eastern Pyrenees on terraces, the Collioure vineyards produce one of the best BANYULS, naturally sweet red or rosé wines. Curnonsky, prince of gastronomes, said of BANYULS that it had 'a Saracen warmth and flexibility'.

have satisfied a series of analyses and been passed by a tasting commission, can use the title of "selected wines" and be sold as such without blending.

These selected wines are beginning to take their places besides the growths of good repute such as SAINT-CHINIAN, COTEAUX-DU-LANGUEDOC, CABRIÈRES, FAUGÈRES, MEJANELLE, MONT-PEYROUX, PICPOUL DE PINET, PIC SAINT-LOUP, SAINT-CHRISTOL, SAINT-DREZERY, SAINT-GEORGES D'ORQUES, SAINT-SATURNIN and VESARGUES, all delimited wines of superior quality (V.D.Q.S.) produced in the department of Hérault. It should not be forgotten that the Hérault plain also produces some very aromatic muscat wines such as FRONTIGNAN, MUSCAT DE LUNEL, MIREVAL and CLAIRETTE DU LANGUEDOC.

In the department of the Gard, as well as the CÔTES-DU-RHÔNE wines with an *appellation d'origine contrôlée*—particularly the ROSÉ DE CHUSCLAN, TAVEL and LIRAC—the V.D.Q.S. COSTIÈRES-DU-GARD are agreeably fruity and palate-pleasing wines.

The second largest French department in terms of wines produced, the Aude produces guaranteed place-name description wines: CORBIÈRES, MINERVOIS. It

should be added that, in the case of wines for ordinary consumption, there is a growing tendency to improve the grapes used (*Grenache* and *Cinsault*). Vinification is also being very appreciably improved. The co-operative cellars in the department vinify between 55 per cent and 56 per cent of the wine production. The winegrowers to an increasing degree are producing wines which are drinkable "as they stand".

In the range of quality wines there are, in addition to CORBIÈRES and MINERVOIS, the names of FITOU, CLAPE, QUATOURZE, BLANQUETTE DE LIMOUX (374,000 gallons) and the natural sweet wines, with a comparable production, which have ensured the winegrowing reputation of the department.

Coming solely from the delimited Limousin slopes in the Upper Valley of the Aude, the BLANQUETTE DE LIMOUX is a sparkling white wine, prepared according to a very ancient method with *Mauzac* and *Clairette* grapes. For many centuries, BLANQUETTE DE LIMOUX has been favoured for its sparkle, elegance and fruitiness. It should be mentioned that the wine was granted an *appellation contrôlée* in 1938.

136

The Corbières vineyard is mainly located in the department of the Aude. The vine is cultivated there according to careful and time-honoured local methods, with a respect for tradition calculated to maintain the specific characteristics of the wines. Judicious regulations have gone far to establish a balance between the necessary progress in technology and the improvement of the quality of the wines. These wines should have a minimum alcohol content of 11° and similar regulations are found in all French areas producing wines entitled to an *appellation* (delimitations of the parcels of land, grapes, degree, yield and viticultural practices). The annual production exceeds 22 million gallons.

The CORBIÈRES are, for the most part, red wines with a few rosé wines. White CORBIÈRES are much rarer.

The reds are substantial, complete wines whose quality improves with age. After a year, they lose a great deal of colour; after the second winter, their quality begins to blossom and they can be bottled. This produces a wine whose bouquet harmonizes well with pork, fowl, roasts, game and cheese.

The rosé wines are distinguished by their fruitiness, their elegance and their nervousness. They form a perfect accompaniment to fish and shell-fish; generally speaking, they have the advantage of being drinkable with all dishes.

As for the natural sweet wines of Roussillon and the Midi, the origin of the titles of nobility of which they are so proud is very ancient. The vineyards from which these wines come are to be found on steep terraces, on sunny slopes that overhang the sea as at Banyuls, or clinging to the last buttresses of the Pyrenees.

It is in the Pyrénées-Orientales, for the most part, that the BANYULS, MAURY, RIVESALTES, CÔTES-D'AGLY and CÔTES-DE-HAUT-ROUSSILLON wines are harvested. The southern winegrowing part of the Corbières of Aude, adjacent to Roussillon, also produces some of them but in much smaller quantities.

At Banyuls, the *Grenache Noir* predominates. It is cultivated under the direct influence of the winds from the sea, on the abrupt flanks of the last foothills of the Albères, in the small amount of arable land left by the

The Roussillon vineyards, such as those of Castelnou (photo) produce table wines (sold under the protection and guarantee of a co-operative label) and natural sweet wines, which are A.O.C. wines.

slow crumbling of a bedrock of primary schists which has a rusty colour and looks like old timber.

In the Fenouillèdes, near Maury, the *Grenache Noir* prevails once again in conjunction with an exceptional soil. The vineyard clings to rounded hillocks of dark flakey marls. Boxed in between two high white cliffs of hard limestone, the vineyard in its arid corridor profits by a particularly favourable concentration and a great intensity of sunshine. The first preoccupation of the purchaser and consumer should be carefully to verify the origin of the bottles he is buying. If it comes from Banyuls of Maury it will be a dark red or brick-coloured wine. Ageing brings reflections of purple and gold; when very old, the BANYULS and the MAURY often acquire the special taste described as *rancio* which is much appreciated by Catalan epicures. The experienced taster will recognize the special bouquet of the *Grenache Noir* in the BANYULS and the MAURY and will appreciate all the warmth and charm of these wines which are vinified by the maceration process. During fermentation, the must remains in more or less prolonged contact with the pulp and skin; macerated in this way, it acquires the most subtle of its qualities.

In the Côtes-d'Agly, as well as a large number of plantations of *Grenache Noir*, we find the *Grenache Gris*

The chapel of Montalba, near Amélie-les-Bains (Pyrénées orientales) stands out above the vineyards, which produce mainly everyday table wines that are warm, solid, and firm.

and the *Grenache Blanc* mixed together and supplemented by the *Maccabéo*. These grapes are planted mostly on secondary soils, but also on prime holdings constituted by the breaking up of primary ferruginous schists and black schists, the later of which are appropriately called "grape schists"—schists which were once used to improve the soil of the vineyards.

At Rivesaltes, besides parcels of land completely planted to *Muscat*, the *Grenache Blanc* and the *Malvoisie* give wines of great elegance; most of the wine is established on terraces of ancient, very pebbly, alluvium soil types between Salses, Rivesaltes and the "Crest" of Pia.

In the Côtes-de-Haut-Roussillon, the Aspres region, the *Grenaches* still have priority but they are giving way more and more to *Muscat* and *Maccabéo*, which contribute their very special bouquet. The ranks of the vines are planted on white gravelly or pebbly alluvial hills, red in colour, which were deposited at the tertiary period and then furrowed by erosion. This area is also very arid, hence its name Aspres.

White wines with a golden tint are also produced at Rivesaltes, the Côtes-d'Agly and the Côtes-de-Haut-Roussillon; in ageing, they often take on a beautiful burnt "topaz" tint. Once vinification is complete, these wines should have a minimum total potential alcohol content of 21.5° and titrate at least 15°.

The consumer should take care to cool his bottles to between 5° and 10°C; these are the ideal temperatures for consuming the natural wines. It should not be forgotten that the *Muscats* are always very sweet and should be ranked with the sweetest of natural sweet wines but that, under the other descriptions, several more or less sweet types can be found. Natural sweet wines based on *Malvoisie* and, particularly, on *Grenache* will, when aged in certain ways, acquire the much sought-after *rancio* taste.

In their country of origin, the wines of Perpignan are regarded as the essential concomitant to various regional gastronomic manifestations. They prepare or conclude the *cargolades* at which the whole menu (snails, sausages, cutlets etc.) is grilled in the embers of a vine-shoot fire; they are used to accompany fruit dishes as well as Catalan pastries such as *bougnettes*, *rousquilles* and aniseed cakes.

The Catalan, settling himself firmly, drinks his wine through open lips from the *porrón*, a glass carafe with a finely drawn out conical spout which is held up at arm's length: a very fine jet of golden amber describes a harmonious and scintillating curve. In this skilful way of drinking *à la régalade*, the wine splashes out over the tongue, the palate and the taste buds. These natural sweet wines can be served as aperitifs. In this case, however, the drier types such as BANYULS and MAURY should be sought out. The wines of Perpignan are also particularly suitable as dessert wines or *digestifs*. Whether white, brick-coloured or of the muscat type, they should all be served very cold but not iced.

138

SWISS WINES OF THE RHÔNE VALLEY

CANTON OF VALAIS

WHITE WINES

Types of wine	Appellation of the growth and commercial appellation
Fendant	Fendant, Les Riverettes, Grand-Schiner Le Père du Valais, Brûlefer, Combe d'Enfer, Trémazières, Sur Plan d'Uvrier, Rives du Bisse, Réserve de Tous-Vents, Vieux Sion, La Guérite, Les Murettes, Etournailles, Vieux Sierre, Clos de Balavaud, Rocailles, Solignon, Montibeux, Grand Baillif, Pierrafeu, Vin des Chanoines, Etoile de Sierre, Ste-Anne, Réserve du Procureur, Fendant du Ravin.
Johannisberg	Johannisberg, Burgrave, Le Grand-Schiner Prince de l'Eglise, Johannisberg de Chamoson, Ravanay, Rives du Bisse, Brûlefer, Novembre, Salgesch, Mont d'Or, St-Théodule, Rhonegold, Grand Bouquet, Johannisberg Balavaud, Johannestrunk, Vin des Chevaliers.
Malvoisie	Malvoisie, Marjolaine, Combe d'Enfer, Malvoisie mi-flétrie, Rives du Bisse, Côte Dorée, Vieux Sierre, Rawyre, Vieux Plants, Brindamour, Malvoisie de la Fiancée, Malvoisie Pinot gris.
Amigne	Belle Valaisanne, Rives du Bisse, Raisin d'Or.
Arvine	Belle Provinciale, Petite Arvine de Chamoson.
Ermitage	Ermitage, Rives du Bisse, Hermitage, Ermitage « Cuvée réservée », Vieux Plants, Ermitage Vétroz, Les Chapelles.
Humagne	Humagne Vétroz.
Païen	Vin du Glacier.
Rèze	Vin du Glacier.
Riesling	Riesling, Goût du Conseil « Mont d'Or », Colline des Planzettes Sierre.

RED WINES

Dôle	Le Grand-Schiner Chapeau Rouge, Clos du Château, Combe d'Enfer, Dôle de Chamoson, Dôle-Pinot noir sur Plan d'Uvrier, Dôle von Salgesch (La Chapelle), Dôle Ravanay, Rives du Bisse, Hurlevent, Les Mazots, Dôle du Mont, Dôle de Salquenen, Vieux Sierre, Soleil de Sierre, Sang de l'Enfer, Clos de Balavaud, Dôle de Balavaud, Girandole, Crêta Plan, Chanteauvieux, Gloire du Rhône, Dôle-Pinot noir, Vieux Villa, Vieux Salquenen, Romane.
Merlot	Colline des Planzettes Sierre.
Pinot noir	Pinot noir de Chamoson, Le Sarrazin, Le Grand Schiner Saint Empire, Pinot noir du Valais, Rives du Bisse, Uvrier, Vendémiaire, Rhoneblut, Römerblut, Oeil-de-Perdrix, Millésime, Beau Velours, Colline des Planzettes Sierre, La Tornale, Ste-Anne, Vieux Cellier, Le Préféré, Chapelle de Salquenen, Johannestrunk, Pinot noir de Salquenen, Vin des Chevaliers, Crête de l'Enfer.
Rosé	Oeil-de-Perdrix, Rosé d'Eros.

CANTON OF VAUD

WHITE WINES • Dorin (Chasselas)

Appellation of communes	Appellation of the growth and commercial appellation
CHABLAIS	
Bex	Chêne.
Ollon	Côtes de Verschiez.
Aigle	Clos de Beauregard, Clos du Paradis, Clos de la Vineuvaz, Les Forteresses, Clos du Cloître, Crosex-Grillé, Aigle Royal, Hospices Cantonaux, Domaine de la Commune, Les Cigales, Merveilles des Roches, Les Murailles, Réserve du Vidôme.
Yvorne	Château Maison blanche, Vieux Collège, Clos de la George, Clos des Rennauds, Clos du Rocher, L'Ovaille, Le Chant des Resses, Les Fornets, Les Portes Rouges, Le Petit Vignoble, Plan d'Essert, Près Roc, Domaine de la Commune.
Villeneuve	Sur la Tour, Clos du Châtelard, De nos Domaines, Caves des Hospices cantonaux, Les Terrasses, Vin de l'Empereur.
Villeneuve (pinot gris)	Ovaille, Jeu du Roy.
LAVAUX	
Montreux	Rossillion, Château de Châtelard, Côtes de Pallens, Coteaux du Haut-Léman.
La Tour-de-Peilz	Clos des Mousquetaires.
Vevey	Caves de l'Hôpital.
Corsier	Cure d'Attalens.
Corseaux	Clos Châtonneyre, Clos sur la Chapelle.
Chardonne	Clos des Berneyses, Château de Chardonne, Cave des Allours, le Chantey, Le Fin de la Pierraz, Burignon, Clos de la Chenalettaz, Petite Combe.
Saint-Saphorin – Rivaz	Faverges, Les Rueyres, Blassinges, Charmus de la Cure, Château de Glérolles, Larchevesque, Les Fosses, Planète, Roches Brûlées, La Riondaz, Roche Ronde, Roc Noir, Pierre Noire, Grand Vigne, Domaine d'Ogoz, Le Grillon, Clos des Plantaz.

Appellation of communes	Appellation of the growth and commercial appellation
Dézaley	Chemin de Fer, L'Evêque, L'Arbalète, Chapotannaz, Clos des Abbayes, Dézaley de la Ville, Embleyres, Clos des Moines, Clos de l'Ermite, Clos du Philosophe, Château Marsens, Sous-Marsens, De la Tour, La Borne, La Gueniettaz, Mousquetaires, Renard, Pertuizet, Sur les Abbayes, La Médinette.
Epesses	Boux d'Epesses, Braise d'Enfer, Calamin, Chanteperdrix, Coup de l'Etrier, Crêt-dessous, Crêt-brûlé, La République, Terre à Boire.
Cully	Les Blonnaises, Chenaux, St-Amour, La Perle.
Riex	Maison Blanche.
Villette-Grandvaux . . .	Bouton-d'Or, Belletaz, Bien-Venu, Clos des Echelettes, Clos des Roches, Daley Villette, Treize Vents, Domaine du Daley, En Genévaz, Côtes de Courseboux, Clos de la Cour.
Lutry	Bolliattaz, Grandchamp, Montagny, Clos de Chamaley, Joli Cœur, Ma Réserve, Boutefeu, Clos des Cloîtres, Châtelard, Clos des Brûlées, Bertholod.

LA CÔTE

Morges	Bravade, Clos des Abbesses, Marcelin, Domaine de la Commune.
Nyon	Château de Crans, Château de Duillier, Banderolle.
Aubonne	Curzille.
Allaman	Clos du Château, Ville de Lausanne.
Féchy	Clos des Bayels, Clos du Martheray, Vieux Coteaux, Mon Pichet, Joli Site.
Bougy	Domaine de Riencourt, Cave de Fischer, Château de Bursinel.
Gilly	Château de Vincy, Coteau de Gilly.
Perroy	Malessert, Clos de la Dame, Clos de la Donery, Abbaye de Mont Ville de Lausanne, Cave du Prieuré, Clos de l'Augmendaz.
Mont	Autecour, Haute-Cour, Crochet, Montbenay, Clos des Truits, Château de Mont, La Viborne, Chatagnéréaz, Mont-Crochet, Les Pierrailles, La Montoise, Beau-Soleil, Domaine de la Bigaire, Famolens, Beauregard.
Tartegnin	Clos du Rousillon, Clos des Panissières.
Vinzel	Domaine de la Bâtie, Château de Vinzel, Clos du Château de Bursins.
Luins	Château de Luins, La Capite, Domaine de Sarraux-dessous, Sarraux.

RED WINES

CHABLAIS	Salvagnin Eminence, Salvagnin Mille pierres, Clos de l'Abbaye, Clos du Châtelard, Clos de la George, Côtes de Verschiez, Bex, Pinot noir Monseigneur, Pinot noir le Notable.
LAVAUX	Salvagnin des Caves de l'Hôpital, Salvagnin de l'Hôpital des Bourgeois de Fribourg, Salvagnin Cep d'Or, Salvagnin Chevron rouge, Salvagnin Coteaux du Haut-Léman, Salvagnin Forban, Salvagnin Grain rouge, Pinot noir Coin des Serpents, Pinot noir Cuvée du Docteur, Pinot noir Grand-Croix, Pinot noir Sept Murs, Pinot-Gamay Montorgueil, Pinot-Gamay Roche rouge, Pinot-Gamay Saint-Saphorin printanier, Pinot-Gamay sous l'Auvent, Pinot-Gamay Burignon, Dôle d'Epesses.
LA CÔTE	Salvagnin Commune de Morges, Salvagnin Château de Saint-Saphorin, Salvagnin Domaine de Valmont, Salvagnin du Baril, Salvagnin Chapeau rouge, Salvagnin Croix du Val, Salvagnin Licorne, Salvagnin Piganot, Clos des Abbesses Clos du Paradis, Pinot noir Clos du Satyre, Pinot noir Grand Brocard.

ROSÉ WINES

Gamay	Bellarosa, Busard, La Caille, Perle Rose, Roussard, St-Martin, Vieux Murs.
Pinot	Oeil-de-Perdrix, Oeil-de-Perdrix - Clos du Terraillex, Oeil-de-Perdrix - Chantemerle.

CANTON OF GENEVA

WHITE WINES

Types of wine	Appellation of the growth and commercial appellation
Chasselas	Les Contamines, Chasselas Genève, Clos des Curiades, Clos de la Donzelle, Perle du Mandement, Coteau de Lully, Bouquet Royal.
Riesling-Sylvaner	Riesling-Sylvaner Satigny, Les Argoulets.
Aligoté	Lully, Clos des Curiades.
Pinot blanc	Les Curiades.

RED WINES

Gamay	Gamay de Gondebaud, Les Clefs d'Or, Gamay-Lully, Domaine des 3 Etoiles.
Gamay rosé	Rose Reine.
Gamay Pinot	Gamay Pinot, Pinogamay.
Pinot noir	Clos des Curiades, Le Damoiseau, Pinot noir Lully.

FRENCH WINES OF THE RHÔNE VALLEY

WINES OF SAVOY

Generic appellation	Appellation of the growth or of the commune
Vins de Savoie	Marin, Ripaille, Marignan, Coteaux de Crépy, Petit Crépy, Monterminod, Apremont, Abymes, Chignin, Cruet Montmelian, Saint-Jean-de-la-Porte
Roussette de Savoie . .	Frangy, Marestel, Monthoux, Seyssel.

WINES OF THE JURA

Generic appellation	Côtes-du-Jura, Château-Chalon, L'Etoile, Arbois.

CÔTES DU RHÔNE

WHITE WINES

Generic appellation	Appellation of the growth or of the commune
Saint-Péray	Amour de Dieu, Arboisset, Château de Beauregard, Bellevue, La Beylesse, Biguet, Biousse, Blaches, Bouzigues, Le Bret, Buissonnet, La Cacharde, Cerisier, La Chaume, Le Chêne, Combette, Coste Claude, La Côte, Coteau-Caillard, Coudiol, La Crozette, Déseret, Fauterie, Fourniers, La Gamone, Le Géant, Grand-Champ, Hongrie, Issartel, Jirane, Lubac, Maison Blanche, Malgazon, Marcale, Mois de Mai, Moulin-à-vent, Pateaud, Perrier, Pinchenas, La Plantier, Prieuré, Putier, Aux Putiers, Rochette, Ruines de Crussol, Sainte Fleurie, Les Sapettes, Soulignasses, Thioulet, Tourtousse, La Venance, Vergomars.
Château-Grillet	
Condrieu	Chéri, La Garenne, Vernon, Boucher, Château-Grillet, Laboye, Le Colombier.

ROSÉ WINES

Tavel	Aqueria, Blaise d'arbres, Bouvettes, Cabanette, Campey, Carcenies, Comeyre, Cravailleu et Alexandre, La Genestière et Fourcadure, Manissy, Montezardes et Trinquevedel, Olivet, Les Patus, Plaine de Vallongue, Plans et Palus, Les Prés, Roc Crispin et Malaven, Romagnac, Tavelet et les Oliviers, Vau et Clos, Vaucroze, Vaucroze et Vacquières, La Vaussière, La Vaute, Vestides, Le Village.
Côte-du-Rhône Chusclans	

WHITE WINES AND RED WINES

Châteauneuf-du-Pape . .	L'Arnesque, Barbe d'Asne, Bas-Serres, Beau Renard, La Bigote, Les Blaquières, Bois de Boursan, Bois de la Vieille, Bois Senescau, Les Bosquets, Le Boucou, Les Bourguignons, Les Brusquières, Cabrières, Cansaud. Castelas, La Cerise, Charbonnières, Chemin de Sorgues, Le Clos, Colombis, Combes d'Arnavel, Combes Masques, Coste-Froide, Coteau de l'Ange, Les Coulets, La Crau, La Croze, Devès d'Estouard, Les Esqueiron, Farguerol, La Font du Loup, La Fortisse, Four à Chaux, Les Galimardes, La Gardine, Grand chemin de Sorgues, Grand Devès, Grand Pierre, Les Grands Galiguières, Grandes Serres, La Grenade, Jaquinotte, Le Lac, Le Limas, Les Marines, Les Mascarrons, Mont de Viès, Montolivet, Mont Pertuis, Mont Redon, Moulin à Vent, La Nerthe, Le Parc, Les Parrans, Pelous, Petite Bastide, Petites Serres, Pied-de-Baud, Pied-Redon, Les Pielons, Pierre-à-Feu, Pignan, Les Plagnes, Les Pradels, Relagnes, Les Revès, La Roquette, Roumiguières, Saint-Joseph, Les Serres, Terres-Blanches, Les Tresquous, Vaudieu, Cabane Saint-Jean, Cansaud, La Chartreuse, Chemin de Châteauneuf, Les Combes, Le Coulaire, Coteau de Saint-Jean, La Crau, Croix de Bois, Duvet, Les Escondures, La Font de Michelle, La Font du Loup, Les Garrigues, Le Grand Plantier, Marron, Patouillet, La Petite Crau, Pied-Redon, Piegeoulet, Ras-Cassa, Reveirores, Sauvines, Terre-Ferme. La Barnuine, Barratin, Les Bédines, Chapouin, Coucoulet, La Crau, Le Cristia, Font du Loup, La Gardiole, Le Grès, Guigasse, La Jamasse, Le Mourre de Gaud, Le Mourre de Vidal, Le Mourre des Perdrix, Palinteau, Pignan, Le Pointu, Le Rayas, Saint-Georges, Saintes-Vierges, Les Saumades, Valori, La Bertaude, Boidauphin, Boilauzon, Cabrières, Maucoil, Palestor, Chafeune, Franquizons, Le Grand Collet, La Lionne.
Crozes-Hermitage	Bourret, Les Habrards, Martinet, Les Mejeans.
Hermitage or Ermitage. .	Beaumes, Les Bessards, La Croix, La Croix de Jamot, Les Diognères, Les Diognères et Torras, Les Greffieux, Les Gros des Vignes, L'Hermite, L'Homme, Maison Blanche, Le Méal, Les Murets, Péléat, La Pierrelle, Les Rocoules, Les Signaux, Varogne.
Lirac	
Saint-Joseph	
Côtes-du-Rhône	Rochegude, Saint-Maurice-sur-Eygues, Vinsobles, Cairanne, Gigondas, Rasteau, Roaix, Séguret, Vacqueras. Valréas, Visan, Laudun.

RED WINES

Côte Rôtie . . . . Les Arches, Basseron, La Blanchonne, Les Bonnevières, La Brocarde, Le Car, Chambre-tout, La Chatillonne, Les Chavaroches, La Chevalière, Chez Gaboulet, Chez Gueraud, Les Clos et Claperonne, Le Cognet, Le Combard, Combe de Calon, Corps des Loups, La Côte Baudnin, Le Crêt, Fontgent, Lefouvier, La Frizonne, Les Gagères, La Garde, Les Germines, La Giroflarie, Grande Plantée et la Garelle, Les Grandes Places, Le Grand Taillé, Grosse Roche et la Balayat, La Guillambaule, Janville, Les Journaries, Lancement, La Landonne, Les Lézardes, Le Mollar, Montmain, Montuclas, Le Moulin, Les Moutonnes, Nève, Le Pavillon Rouge, La Pommière, Les Prunelles, Les Rochains, Rosier, Les Sévenières, Thramon de Gron, Les Triottes, Le Truchet, La Turque, La Viallière, La Viria.

Cornas

PROVENCE AND THE SOUTH-EASTERN REGION

Generic appellation or
appellation of communes

Bandol, Bellet, Clairette de Die, Palette, Coteaux d'Aix-en-Provence, Coteaux des Baux, Côtes du Lubéron, Coteaux de Pierrevert, Côtes-de-Provence, Coteaux du Tricastin, Côtes de Ventoux, Haut-Comtat, Châtillon-en-Diois.

LANGUEDOC AND ROUSSILLON

Generic appellation, appel-
lation of the growth or of the
commune

Corbières, Minervois, Costières du Gard, Coteaux du Languedoc, Coteaux de la Méjanelle, Saint-Saturnin, Montpeyroux, Coteaux de Saint-Christol, Quatourze, La Clape, Saint-Drézéry, Saint-Chinian, Faugères, Cabrières, Coteaux de Verargues, Pic Saint-Loup, Saint-Georges-d'Orques, Picpoul de Pinet, Fitou, Roussillon dels Aspres, Corbières du Roussillon, Corbières Supérieures du Roussillon.

THE WINES
OF THE LOIRE

ALEXANDER FRESNEAU

Long before the invasion of the Gauls the vine existed on the banks of the Loire. The Romans invaded this region 22 years after Christ, and probably found it growing wild. Its first cultivation, according to a popular legend, began in A.D. 380 when St. Martin and his disciples planted vines in the Abbaye de Marmoutier near Tours, which was founded at that time. These events are recounted by the historian Gregory, Bishop of Tours from 573 to 595, in his *Ecclesiastical History of France*, and by Fredegarius in his chronicles of the year 757. The vine flourished and spread rapidly; but in the thirteenth century it was restricted to the hillsides where it produced wines of a superior quality.

The first viticultural region along the Loire is the Massif Central, which contains the vineyards of Auvergne, Saint-Pourçain-sur-Sioule and Chateaumeillant. A little farther on the river crosses the chalky and flinty hills between Pouilly-sur-Loire, Sancerre and Menetou-Salon. Then come the two vineyards of Quincy and Reuilly, situated one near the other with identical soil, then the Val de Loire which one may consider as being on the very edge of the Loiret. This department also harbours the Giennois and Orléanais vineyards which have lost much of their importance in the last fifty years.

It is at Blois, the gateway to the Touraine, that the chalky soil has its beginning. It then stretches for miles and miles, following the course of the Loire and fertilizing the vineyards of Monts-Près-Chambord, Vendômois, Coteaux du Loir, Jasnières, Touraine, Vouvray, Montlouis, Bourgueil, Chinon and Saumurois, as far as the Angevine schists which introduce the Armorican Massif. The Angevine vineyard is the most important, and is responsible for nearly all the wines produced in this region. Aubance and Lyons bring one to the maritime zone of the Loire, and leaving Anjou behind one comes next to the MUSCADET vineyard in Basse-Bretagne. Special mention should be made of the Ancenis vineyard and the *Gros Plant* so sought after by tourists. From Orléanais to the ocean, the Val de Loire presents a soft and gentle spectacle to the traveller, with its sumptuous châteaux and variety of viticultural treasures. Other landscapes may offer fairer sights, but there is none more harmonious nor more compelling than these banks of the Loire.

In order to obtain choice wine, winegrowers have constantly taken pains to improve their vine-plants either through selection, by developing new varieties, or by importing grapes from distant parts.

It is possible that the vine-stocks developed by the monks in Touraine and elsewhere are derived from a particular type of vine which produced black grapes found growing wild in the forests. It is perhaps to this same wild lambrusca that the sixteenth-century poet Ronsard refers in his ode to Aubepin. This red vine was called *Pineau d'Aunis*, Aunis being a small village in Saumur. It deserves our gratitude, for it is thought that on some unknown date it produced, after selection, the white variety, *Chenin Blanc*, or *Pineau de la Loire*, a wonderful plant found in Touraine and Anjou. It is impossible to know exactly when this vine-plant was given the name *Chenin*, but it was already known as such in the early sixteenth century.

The *Sauvignon*, a noble plant found in Pouilly-sur-Loire, Sancerre, Quincy and Reugny is, however, of unknown origin. There is no document to show whether it is a plant indigenous to the region or whether it was imported.

On several occasions, numerous vines taken from foreign or other French viticultural regions were planted in these parts. It is not known exactly how or when the *Muscadet* grape came to the region of Nantes, but it would seem to date from the seventeenth century. When the frozen vines were replanted following the terrible winter of 1709, the *Muscadet* grape was introduced on a wide scale into the region. It would appear to have been brought from Burgundy, where it was known as *Melon*.

143

A ruined windmill stands guard over the widely-spaced rows of vines in Anjou. The wine harvest is here again, and whole families spend their days in the vineyards until the crop is picked.

Spread across some fifteen viticultural departments, from the Massif Central to the Atlantic Ocean, the famous vineyards of the Loire are ranged in tiers on the slopes which dominate the "royal river" and its tributaries. The wines of this charming valley are produced in four major regions: the Centre (around Nevers, Giens, Bourges and Orleans), in Touraine, in Anjou-Saumur and in the region of Nantes.

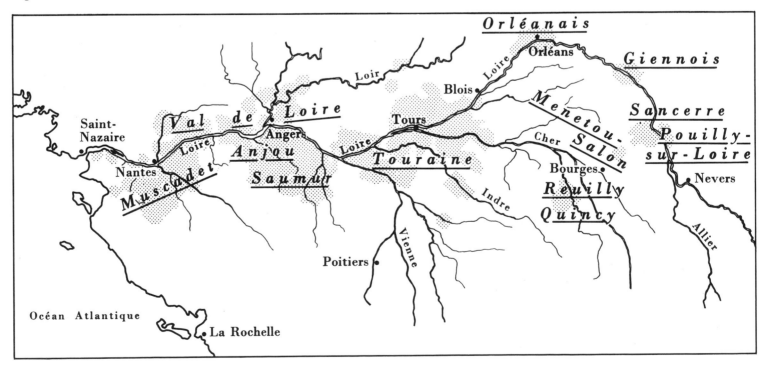

The *Gros Plant*, cultivated in the Atlantic Loire, originally came from Charentes through an exchange with Poitou, an intermediary province. It wine was at first distilled, but today it produces a highly sought-after dry wine. It is of the same grade as the Muscadet.

The *Cabernet Franc*, which is cultivated in Touraine and in the regions of Bourgueil and Chinon as well as in Anjou, has a much disputed origin. According to some, it came from Rhuis, in Bretagne. According to others, and this seems more logical, the Bordelais grape was brought to the Loire valley either by Abbot Breton, an administrator of Richelieu, when he inherited the property of the Abbey of Saint-Nicolas-de-Bourgueil; or even before, if we believe Rabelais when he speaks of "the good Breton wine, which does not grow in Bretagne but in this worthy land of Verron".

The *Côt* grape is cultivated in various places, but it certainly originated in Bordelais. The *Groslot de Cinq-Mars* or *Grolleau* was obtained around 1810 through the selection process in the region of Chinon.

Other grapes, such as the *Pinot Noir, Pinot Beurot*, and *Meunier* are thought to have come from Burgundy.

The vine region which produces the *appellation contrôlée* wines of the Loire Valley is about 140,847 acres in area. However the actual surface under cultivation is in fact bigger as part of the harvest is reserved for making table wines.

The Loire growths, mentioned by Rabelais, have a long history. Above: the fresh-picked grapes are poured into the press in a cellar hewn out of the living rock.

POUILLY-SUR-LOIRE - SANCERRE - QUINCY
REUILLY - MENETOU-SALON

The staple grape of these vineyards is the *Sauvignon*, blended at times with another variety.

POUILLY-SUR-LOIRE. Under this classification come all the wines produced in the communes of Pouilly-sur-Loire, Saint-Andelain, Tracy-sur-Loire, Saint-Laurent, Saint-Martin-sur-Nohain, Garchy and Mesves-sur-Loire.

Depending on what grape variety they are made from, the wines of Pouilly-sur-Loire are known under one or the other of the following two categories: POUILLY FUMÉ (which should not be confused with another white wine, the POUILLY FUISSÉ produced in Burgundy) or BLANC FUMÉ DE POUILLY for those wines made from the *Sauvignon* grape alone; POUILLY-SUR-LOIRE in the case of wines derived from the *Chasselas* grape, whether blended with the *Sauvignon* grape or not. Only the communes of Pouilly-sur-Loire, Saint-Audelain and Tracy are true viticultural regions, although the actual area under cultivation is notably smaller. At present it includes about a thousand acres.

The commune of Saint-Audelain, larger than Pouilly-sur-Loire, has the most important vineyards, more so than those of Pouilly and Tracy. Other communes have a smaller area under cultivation. Since only about a thousand acres are capable of being harvested, it follows that each holding is quite small; there is one of more than 32 acres, but a dozen are in the order of 7½ acres each. The average production figure for POUILLY FUMÉ is about 46,200 gallons; for POUILLY-SUR-LOIRE about 154,000 gallons. POUILLY FUMÉ has a distinct and even sometimes pronounced bouquet; it is musky and smoky at the same time, a long-lived wine which ages well. The POUILLY-SUR-LOIRE, on the other hand, is considered to be best when drunk within the year.

SANCERRE. Thirteen communes come under this heading: Sancerre, Saint-Satur, Bué, Suvry-en-Vaux, Menetou, Ratel, Ménétréol Thauvenay, Vinon, Verdigny, Cresancy and some isolated parcels of land at Bannay and Veaugues.

The area under cultivation is some 1,500 acres, of which 1,300 acres grow the *Sauvignon* grape and the rest the *Pinot Noir*. Production has developed in the last ten years. During this time, the average yield was 143,000 gallons while present production, which is

still increasing, gives an average yield of more than 330,000 gallons annually.

As in Pouilly-sur-Loire, the soil in which the vine grows is a calcerous-clay deposit, or sometimes mass formations of calcium formed on the slopes in the same geological era. The plains that dominate these slopes are clay-like and unsuitable for winegrowing. Each type of soil produces wine of a different character. The blended vines are sometimes of a higher quality than that of the components. SANCERRE is somewhat more mellow than the POUILLY FUMÉ and generally matures sooner than the latter.

These are pleasant, very fruity wines, though they cannot be compared to Burgundies made from the *Pinot Noir* grape. The red and rosé varieties have only recently qualified for the *appellation contrôlée*.

QUINCY. This vineyard is situated about 12 miles to the west of Bourges, along the right bank of the Cher. It is a small vineyard, of about 600 acres, which will probably develop in the next few years. It comprises the communes of Quincy and Brinay. The average wine-harvest is about 110,000 gallons, worked by 250 growers. The average grower cultivates about 2 acres and there are about twenty properties of 5 to 8 acres each and one of about 25 acres. QUINCY, which is nearly always dry, gets its fine quality from the soil which serves as its cradle and makes it an excellent companion to oysters.

REUILLY. This name is given to the wine of four communes, two in the Indre, Reigny and Diou regions, and two in the Cher, Chery and Lazenay. Their vineyards are situated along the banks of the Arnon, 6 miles to the west of Quincy.

The area planted with the *Sauvignon* grape is definitely getting smaller. At present it is about 62 acres, almost entirely in Reigny and Diou. Production is very much lower here: about 1,300 to 1,800 gallons yield a dry and semi-dry wine for local consumption.

MENETOU-SALON. Some 16 miles to the west of Vierzon is Menetou-Salon which has given its name to the youngest of the *appellation d'origine* wines of the Loire, created by decree in 1959. It is cultivated on a very small scale as its vineyard covers only 1,500 acres. It grows two grapes, the *Sauvignon* which produces a wine similar to that of Sancerre, though not nearly as well-balanced or as fine in flavour; and the *Pinot Noir* from Burgundy whose red and rosé wines have a most agreeable taste. The total production of this category varies yearly from 132,000 to 220,000 gallons.

TOURAINE

Touraine, so peaceful and welcoming, has been planted to vines since the fourteenth century, and the fame of its wines has grown with the years. Rabelais and Ronsard sang their praises, Alfred de Vigny and Balzac knew how to appreciate them and the beauties of their birthplace, and Alexander Dumas had the King's Musketeers drink them. According to Jules Romain "they are the very essence of French wit".

Their production is more varied than abundant. The white wines, whether dry, semi-dry or dessert wines, are fresh with full bouquets; the best of them are to be found in the lovely village of Vouvray. The delicate red wines of Bourgueil, Saint-Nicolas and Chinon are followed by a cheerful group of gay companions: red wines and rosés from the Côtes du Cher, white wines made from the *Pineau* or *Sauvignon* grape, which one must taste when visiting the châteaux.

A classic definition of Touraine describes this province as "a rough tweed trimmed with gold". The plains covered with forests, sandy moors and ploughed fields give the land an impression of sadness. There are the forests of Montrichard, Amboise, Chinon, Champeigne between Cher and the Indre, the Richelais and the Gâtine. But cutting across these unproductive regions are smiling valleys whose rich culture, sumptuous castles, white villas, and harmonious landscapes present such an enticing picture as to make a man believe that this is the very place where it would be wonderful to live.

The climate of Touraine is neither unbearably hot in summer nor excessively cold in winter, as the sea breeze modifies the differences in temperature.

Along the border, where the plains meet the valleys, on chalky slopes or terraced embankments pebbled by the Loire and the Vienne—this is where the Touraine winegrowers planted the present vineyards some fifteen centuries ago. The soil which nourishes the vine is often supported by yellow chalk or "Touraine tufa", in which the magnificent Vouvray caves have been carved. This immense blanket of chalk is covered with granitic sand sometimes mixed with silex clay which occurs when the chalk decalcifies.

The soil at the bottom of the slopes contains flinty sand, clay and chalk ; it is the *aubuis* so perfectly suited to the *Pineau de la Loire*. It produces the finest and by far the most full-bodied wines.

On both banks of the Loire and the Vienne, in the Bourgueil and Chinon regions, the gravelly beds, brushed by the waters and mixed with sand clay, offer a soft and fertile soil for the *Cabernet Franc* grape.

The region of the white wines made from the *Pineau* grape extends from Tours to Blois, where the vines are

146

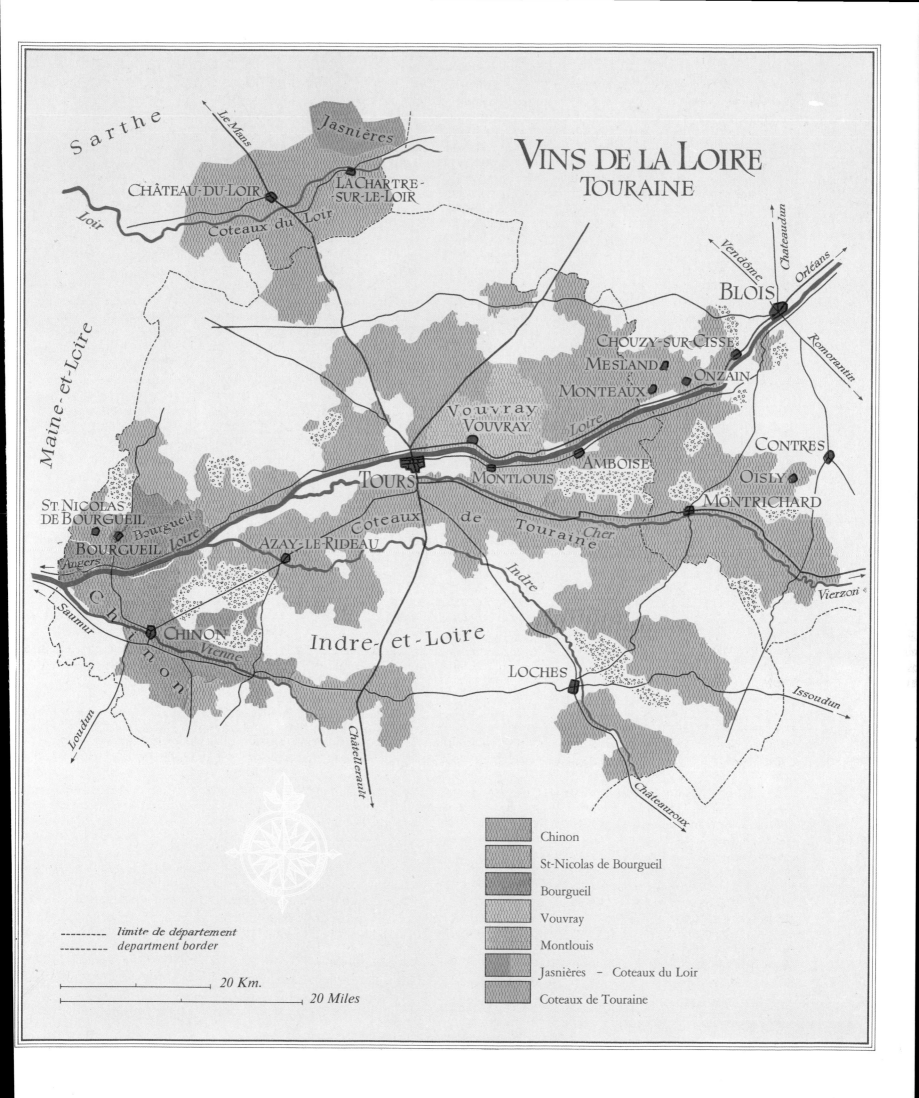

cultivated on chalky slopes covered with the mixture locally known as *aubuis*. The vineyard of Vouvray is situated at the head of this region, near Tours.

In Loir-et-Cher, the Mesland region, with identical soil, offers excellent rosés and red wines produced from the *Gamay* grape, side by side with the clear fruity wines made from the *Pineau* grape. Farther south, along the chalky banks of the Cher and the Oisly plain where the ground is composed of sand over clay, red wines grow in the company of fine white wines made from the *Pineau* and *Sauvignon* grapes. In Touraine, the vine spreads over some 19,768 acres, producing wines of the *appellation contrôlée* category in the amount of 7,303,336 gallons per annum.

THE GREAT WHITE WINES. In Touraine as in Anjou, these are derived almost entirely from a single grape, the *Pineau de la Loire*. It alone is responsible for the reputation of the great wine of Touraine. The *Menu Pineau*, also called *Arbois*, gives more delicate wines and has decreased in quantity in Vouvray and Mont-louis, but it still flourishes in Loir-et-Cher, the Contres plain, and Pontlevoy, as well as along the banks of the Cher. The *Sauvignon* grape in these regions has, in the past ten years, become more and more popular.

There are differences in pruning methods for the *Pineau de la Loire* and the *Sauvignon* which have important implications for their wines.

When pruning the *Pineau de la Loire*, it is desirable to cut well back into the stalk so as to produce wines with rich bouquets. However, this is not always possible, for this single most important operation in vine culture must take into account the strength on the vine-shoot, its stock and the nature of soil in which it is planted. The *Sauvignon*, on the other hand, need not be cut back too far, but should be dressed long, in the *Guyot double* manner with two long spurs and from six to eight buds.

The *Pineau de la Loire* grape is always cultivated close to the ground, at a density of about 2,240 plants per acre. *Sauvignon* vines, being taller (4 feet as against 3) are planted less densely, only 1,800 plants per acre. Attempts to raise the height of cultivation of the vine have proved inconclusive and unsatisfactory. The vine does not mature so well and has a stronger acid content; the wine is less robust and full-bodied.

The *Sauvignon* grape is picked before it reaches full maturity, usually towards the end of September. The *Pineau de la Loire*, however, is harvested according to the destination of its grape. If the wine-harvest is to be made into sparkling wines, the grapes must be picked before they are completely ripe, when their acid content is from seven to eight grams. If the proprietor wishes to produce a natural wine he must wait until the grape has become fully mature and then select his grapes. This can only be done in very good years. But these wines have a particularly fine bouquet, they are very sweet and at the same time fresh, delicate, robust, and of an exceptionally high quality.

GREAT RED WINES. The best of these, from Bourgueil and Chinon, are made from a grape cultivated in Gironde, especially in the Saint-Emilion region: the *Cabernet Franc* which must be pruned so as to leave a long stalk and a branch bearing seven to eight buds. The grower grafts a piece of bark containing sap on to the vine stalk so that the stem can grow. This stock is common but not extensive. It is considered exceptional to produce more than 1,335 gallons from an acre. The soil has a great influence on the wine. It might be difficult for the uninformed to distinguish a BOURGUEIL from a CHINON, but connoisseurs can easily tell the difference between a wine which has been planted in gravelly soil and one from a tufa soil.

The wines from grapes grown in gravelly soil are fine wines with good bouquets. They acquire their full qualities reasonably quickly, while the grapes planted in tufa are harder, do not bear fruit until a year later, and conserve admirably.

The wine of Bourgueil charms with its bouquet, its raspberry flavour and its invigorating freshness. It is a fruity, delicate wine, pleasant when young, but at its best after three or four years in a bottle. Some wines which are hard in the first years lighten with age.

CHINON differs from BOURGUEIL in its bouquet—which invokes violets—and its mellow warmth. It is particularly good when drunk young, full of a delicious sweetness. Demand for these wines seems to be growing. For some ten years the vineyards seem to have been developing, especially in the communes of Cravant and Chinon.

It should be mentioned, moreover, that these wines are made from stalked grapes. This operation was once performed manually in the vineyard. Nowadays, thanks to a lack of labour to undertake the arduous job, winegrowers have had to use machines, known as *égrappoirs*, which remain in the cellars.

Most wineries ferment wine in wooden vats with loose lids. Big wineries, however, ferment their wine in cement vats.

Contrary to the practice of many viticultural regions, the period of fermentation here is long, from 18 to 20 days. For example, in the wooden vats where the storage temperature is more than 17°-18°, the secondary fermentation takes place on the twelfth to thirteenth day, and thus the wine can be marketed quickly without any risk to the buyer afterwards. The alcohol content must not be below 9.5° for the wine to be entitled to the *appellation contrôlée* CHINON.

OTHER WINES OF THE TOURAINE. Aside from VOUVRAY, MONTLOUIS, BOURGUEIL and CHINON, Touraine has some other very charming wines which often equal these famous growths, but they are rarely to be found outside the region. Among these are:

AZAY-LE-RIDEAU. This region is better known for its castle than its wines. The communes around the area—especially Saché, where Balzac wrote *Le Lys dans la Vallée*—have always enjoyed a reputation for dry and

semi-dry white wines, which are fruity and fresh and of which they produce 22,000 to 26,500 gallons. Unfortunately, since the Second World War, production of these wines has decreased, as the producers have replaced a considerable number of vines with apple orchards. They are also trying to orient their production towards sweet wines.

AMBOISE. The canton of Amboise, situated at the eastern tip of the department of Indre-et-Loire, is as famous for its castle as Azay-le-Rideau; however, it also produces fine quality wines which keep well. This is not surprising as both banks of the Loire form an extension of the vineyards of Vouvray and Montlouis. As always in Touraine, the wines are cultivated in a subsoil of calcareous tufa. This region also produces pleasant red and rosé wines made from the *Côt* grape, sometimes from the Beaujolais *Gamay* and less often from the *Cabernet* variety.

MESLAND. The Mesland region in Loir-et-Cher continues the Touraine vineyard along the right bank of the Loire, with Monteaux, Onzain and Chouzy-sur-Cisse. It produces more than 241,978 gallons—half the wine produced as *appellation* TOURAINE in Loir-et-Cher.

All these wines are very agreeable when young, but the rosés made from the *Gamay* grape are the most successful, which perhaps accounts for the fact that more of them are produced. They get their fruitiness, lightness and fine texture from the granite sands which cover the chalky subsoil of Touraine.

JASNIÈRES and COTEAUX DU LOIR. At the far end of the three provinces, Touraine, Maine and Anjou, some 25 miles to the north, the valley of the river Loir offers the same favourable conditions for the vine as can be found in Touraine. The position of this little river, the nature of the soil, as well as the climate, are all the same here as above and below Tours. This region is at the northern tip of the viticultural zone and only in those years when the sun has been particularly generous does the *Pineau de la Loire* produce white wines of quality, and the *Pineau d'Aunis* become sufficiently ripe to give good red wines. This vineyard used to be far more important than it is today, but the wines have retained their reputation. Ronsard sang the praises of the wines of the Loir, and in *Pantagruel* Rabelais informs us joyfully that the little town of La Chartre was full of wine merchants and had at least twenty-seven inn-keepers.

The Brissac vineyards, in Anjou, produce the A.O.C. Coteaux de l'Aubance wines. This label may be completed by the mention Val de Loire. They are dry white wines, fruity, and with a taste of the soil.

SAUMUR AND ANJOU

The Saumur region used to be known as "Haut-Anjou". The Saumur wines at that time were the most prominent of this region. At the end of the eighteenth century, as Dr Maisonneuve tells us in his study of Anjou wines, a large quantity of white wine from Saumur was exported, the red wines being reserved for local consumption.

In those days, the winegrowers neglected natural wines somewhat in favour of sparkling wines, which were highly sought after. There, as in Vouvray, several wine-merchants or companies would produce some 7 million bottles of sparkling wine, 20 per cent of which were for export. In the last twenty years, however, this trade has undergone a slump, and today's figure is barely 3½ million bottles.

Protected from the birds by nets, the grapes ripening in the Coteaux de Layon await the harvest. The wine produced has a delicious taste and a delicate perfume made up of the scent of roses, raspberries and quinces. It is a good wine to lay down.

The sparkling wines made in Saumur have an advantage over those of Vouvray. The latter can only be produced from a single grape, the *Pineau de la Loire*, or *Chenin Blanc*. In Saumur, however, the regulations allow for a certain percentage of white wines made from red grapes to be added—up to as much as 60 per cent. This, as well as refining the froth, adds to the quality of the *cuvée* and reduces the somewhat objectionable tang of the soil. The *Cabernet* and the *Groslot* are the grapes which are used for this purpose. The former is of a higher quality and is sought after for the large vats.

The sparkling wines made in Saumur have distinguished qualities—fine, with agreeable bouquets, and a distinct, even personal character—which they owe to a privileged climate and soil as well as to carefully selected grapes.

Apart from the sparkling wines, there are also some slightly effervescent white and rosé wines which are constantly growing in quantity and importance. The amount produced for commercial purposes has increased within the last fifteen years, and now equals that of sparkling wines. The bottling is similar to that of "still" wines; the cork is held by a thin wire fastener, as there is very little pressure.

Rosés of Cabernet. The Saumur region produces rosé only from the *Cabernet* grape, while elsewhere in Anjou rosés are also made from *Groslot*.

The Saumur rosé made from the *Cabernet* grape is of a very light colour, as it is usually made from a white vinification, that is to say from grape pressings which have not been crushed, but allowed to ferment from their own weight. Their very pale colour means that they can be added without any difficulty to sparkling white wines.

Some rosé wines which have been slightly crushed have a stronger colour and a richer bouquet.

The other centres of production for rosé wines made from the *Cabernet* grape are the regions of Layon and Brissac in Aubance. In these regions the grapes are crushed and allowed to soak for a few hours. The cells of the broken skin of the grapes mix with the fermenting must, a more or less important part of coloration. The skins are broken and added for colour at the same time as the grapes are pressed. This process is carried out rapidly in order to achieve the finest quality wine. The pressure should not be too great, to avoid breaking the stalks, which would make the wine astringent.

Wines which have fermented in a vat where the skins of the *Cabernet* grape were added are light pink; those which are pressed and go through a rapid vinification have a characteristic slightly yellow colour. If they have a strawberry hue, this means that a richly coloured juice was added afterwards.

These wines should only contain small quantities of anhydrous sulphur, to avoid discoloration. They should

150

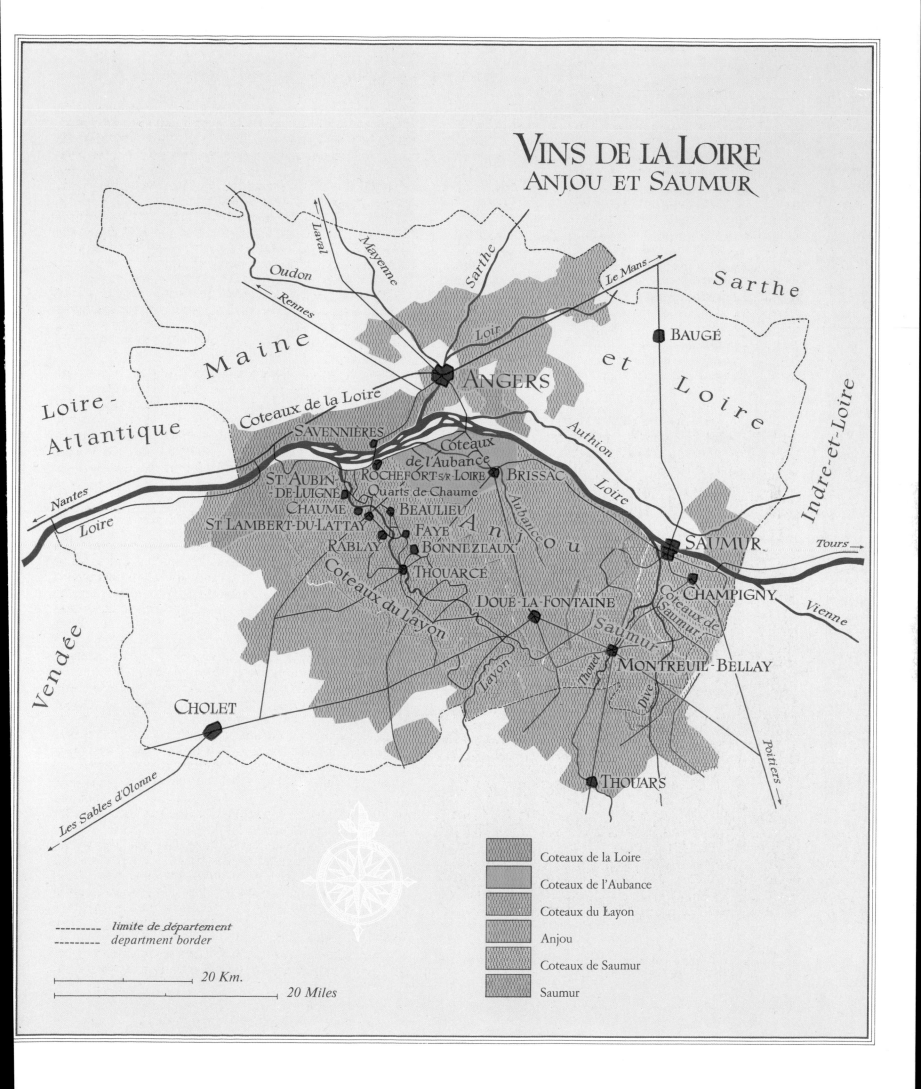

VINS DE LA LOIRE
ANJOU ET SAUMUR

Maine

Loire-Atlantique

Oudon

Laval

Mayenne

Sarthe

Rennes

Loir

Le Mans

Sarthe

BAUGÉ

ANGERS

et

Loire

Coteaux de la Loire

SAVENNIÈRES

Coteaux
de l'Aubance

Authion

Indre-et-Loire

Nantes

St-Aubin-
-de-Luigné

ROCHEFORT s/r LOIRE

BRISSAC

Loire

Loire

Quarts de Chaume

CHAUME

BEAULIEU

A n j o u

Aubance

SAUMUR

Tours

St-Lambert-du-Lattay

FAYE

RABLAY

BONNEZEAUX

THOUARCÉ

Coteaux de
Saumur

CHAMPIGNY

Vienne

Coteaux du Layon

DOUE-LA-FONTAINE

Saumur

Vendée

Layon

Thouet

MONTREUIL-BELLAY

Dive

CHOLET

Poitiers

Les Sables d'Olonne

THOUARS

limite de département
department border

20 Km.

20 Miles

	Coteaux de la Loire
	Coteaux de l'Aubance
	Coteaux du Layon
	Anjou
	Coteaux de Saumur
	Saumur

not have more than 11° to 12° in order to remain fruity and fresh. A drop of sweetening does them no harm and helps to cover slight faults. These wines are best when young, otherwise they lose their fruitiness and life.

ROSÉS OF GROSLOT. Before the war, these were almost the only wines cultivated in the area. They are fresh, light, and should be drunk within the year.

If there is only a little wine made from the *Groslot* grape, say about 350 to 450 gallons to an acre, then the wine is very pleasant with an alcohol content from about 9° to 10.5° or exceptionally 11°. The *Groslot* likes gravelly soils as well as clay or calcareous sands, and produces a special seed. The rosé it makes is much better dry; when sweet the wines tend to be heavy. To produce a very fruity, well-balanced, full-bodied rosé, one should add a small amount of *Gamay*, *Cabernet*, or *Pineau d'Aunis*.

ANJOU. The wines of Anjou have been praised by the poets of the Pléiade and enjoy a reputation which dates back to the sixth century when Apollinius praised the town of Angers as having been blessed by Bacchus. In the thirteenth century these wines gained great fame during the reign of the Plantagenets, who imported them to England. Still later, the Dutch and Belgians were good customers for more than two centuries. Boats laden with wine would travel up the Loire to depots at Chalonnes, Rochefort, and Ponts-de-Cé. The wine was brought to the river either by water (Layon, Thouet) or by land. In *Eugénie Grandet*, Balzac recounts an incident where "Père" Grandet tries to sell his wine-stock.

Boats no longer go up the Loire, but wine has found a new means of transport and has conquered new markets—a tribute to its quality and to the efforts made by winegrowers and wine-merchants. There is an infinite variety of Anjou wines. There are white wines made from the *Chenin* and *Pineau* grapes, reds and rosés from the *Cabernet* grape and rosés from the *Groslot* grape variety. There are also dry wines, semi-dry, sweet and dessert wines, still wines, slightly sparkling and sparkling wines, light or robust wines, which have been harvested in several stages by picking grapes which have attained the *pourriture noble* or "noble rot" category.

The Anjou wines are harvested throughout most of the south-east area of Maine-et-Loire, along the slopes which border the Loire below Angers, as well as from the land of the seventeen communes of Deux-Sèvres, from the area around Bouillé-Loretz, and from eight communes along the Vienne River south of Saumur.

The largest wineproducing cantons are Thouarcé and Rochefort-sur-Loire. Then come the viticultural regions that lie to the south of Saumur: Montreuil, Bellay, Doué-la-Fontaine.

The charm of Anjou lies in its climate—the deep blue sky, softened by a slight haze from the sea, the gentle winters, the early spring. Anjou is not a natural geographical region, but the focal point of several provinces which have widely diverging characteristics: the Vendean and Armorican mountain massifs, the mountain passes of Poitou and Touraine. Owing to this lack of homogeneity in its geographical make-up, Anjou offers a varied soil which reflects almost every geological era: schists, sandstone, primitive calcareous rock, sands, clay, diorite-sand and especially calcareous tufa, chalky sands and a flinty, gravelly soil. To the west of Saumur, in the valley of Layon, the slopes are rich in calcareous sands which nourish a fertile vineyard which produces rosé and white wines. About 40,000 acres are covered in fine quality grapes. The white wines are produced from a single grape, the *Chenin Blanc*. A recent law has permitted, in certain circumstances, a small quantity of *Sauvignon* or *Chardonnay* grapes to be added. The best red grape is, as in Touraine, the *Cabernet Franc*. For about twelve years now, however, it has been either replaced to a certain extent by the *Cabernet Sauvignon* grape, which in the selection procedure produces a higher quality of wine, or else the two varieties are mixed. These two grapes are the ones most frequently used to produce red and rosé wines of superior quality. The other grape varieties are used to produce rosés only. The *Groslot* grape, much cultivated during the reconstruction period, has now been replaced by the *Cabernet Sauvignon*, the *Gamay* and the *Pineau d'Aunis*. The red grapes, which ripen before the *Pineau*, are harvested earlier, usually from September 20th on. To make a rosé wine, the grapes are pressed immediately, without being crushed, in order to obtain a must with a very light colour. The must always ferments without any

Work in tending the vines in Parnay (Coteaux de Saumur) is largely mechanised, hence the vines are planted in widely-spaced rows to enable the machines to pass between them.

152

stalks. The grapes which go to make red Champignys are only pressed when all the stalks have been removed. Fermentation in open vats with unhinged lids or in cement vats lasts from eight to ten days. The wine is then preserved for a year in a large wooden barrel. For some years now, quite a significant amount of red wine has been produced by means of carbonic fermentation, a method yielding light, fruity wines which are most certainly considered to be at their best when young, rather than when aged. The *Pineau de la Loire* and *Chenin* grapes are picked first towards the beginning of October, but only in small quantities, for the grapes are still fresh and ripe. Later, when the *pourriture noble* (noble rot) sets in, they are picked again in larger and larger quantities. Often the harvest continues into the middle of November.

Not long ago, the grapes were carried to the press in vats placed in horse-drawn tumbrils. Today, this is just a memory, and most transport is motorised.

The vines of the Coteaux de Layon are among the best in Anjou. As in the Sauternes region, the harvest is gathered by successive 'selections' when the grapes have reached the stage of 'noble rot'. The liquorish wines are fruity, well cut, and have a perfume of apricots or lime-flowers.

Fermentation takes place in wooden barrels, each of which contains 50 gallons. The temperature of the wine-cellars is from 10° to 35°, which enables these wines, through a slow fermentation, to attain the bouquet and finesse which is characteristic of them. Often the producer is obliged to heat the underground cellars during the first cold spells in order to bring them up to a temperature of 16° to 18°. In Anjou, as in all the other regions of the Loire, the wine benefits from being bottled in the early spring after having been racked, clarified and sometimes even filtered several times. When the wine is bottled later in the year, from May to September, the character of the wine changes, and the freshness and lightness which give it its essential quality are diminished.

Sulphur dioxide is indispensable. It acts both physiologically, since it stops fermentation, and chemically in that its anti-oxygen properties prevent premature ageing, the unwanted sweetness and colouring of maderization, and the spread of oxidasic casse. The anhydride is then eliminated by oxydation which leaves the wine clear and pure but retaining all its freshness and bouquet.

Within Anjou there are two regional *appellations*: ANJOU and SAUMUR. The Saumur region is in fact considered a part of Anjou, according to provisions of legislation passed by the Angers tribunal, and following decrees controlling both *appellations*: a wine made in Saumur may be sold as an ANJOU, but not vice versa. The sub-regional *appellations are*: COTEAUX DU LAYON, COTEAUX DE LA LOIRE, COTEAUX D'AUBANCE, COTEAUX DU LOIR. The *appellations* of individual communes or vineyards are: BONNEZEAUX and QUARTS DE CHAUME, along the slopes of Layon; SAVENNIÈRES, along the Loire, as well as the CULÉE DE SENANT and ROCHE AUX MOINES varieties.

THE MUSCADET REGION

To leave Anjou at Ingrandes is to leave behind all the grape varieties discussed so far and to discover two new ones. Since 1955 a new trend has manifested itself in the Ancenis area: planting and propagating a *Gamay* grape for the production of red and rosé wines. In Basse-Bretagne, the area under vine cultivation at the time of the Romans was for a long time very small. In fact only the grounds belonging to the Abbey and its fortified enclosures were reserved for the vine.

When did the *Muscadet* grape first make its appearance in the Loire-Atlantique? Certain documents in Nantes disclose that in 1639, on numerous small farms, the red grapes were pulled out to be replaced by a good grape-stock from Burgundy. The terrible winter of 1709, however, almost entirely wiped out the vineyards. It was necessary therefore to replant completely, which required great effort. Leases provided that the replanting be in *Muscadet de Bourgogne* grapes. Thus it was in 1735 that the *Muscadet* grape of today was first known.

At the end of the last century, the *Muscadet* grape occupied approximately a third of the land reserved for the vine, the rest being taken up mainly by the *Gros Plant* grape, a variety of the *Folle Blanche* stock, a staple grape of the Cognac region.

When the vineyards were replanted again after the phylloxera epidemic, the *Gros Plant* lost out to the *Muscadet* grape.

The entire vineyard area here is situated on crystalline schists, on layers of gravelly soil, and on rare calcareous islets which in no way alter the lay of the land. The vine is planted on the gravelly slopes facing the south-west. The vineyards are concentrated in the regions to the south of the Loire, Sèvres and Maine. This region produces three-quarters of the MUSCADET stock. It is also cultivated to the north of the Loire, mainly in the area between Nantes and Ancenis and around Grand-Lieu Lake.

The *Muscadet* grape ripens early. It is picked very early in the season, towards the beginning of September. Usually, already towards the 15th of this month, the harvesters are in full swing. The flat countryside offers no natural underground cellars; winecellars in this region consist of small buildings with tile roofs.

The wine is fermented in casks or tuns which hold a maximum of six litres (over 10½ pints). The process of fermentation is slow, in order that it may acquire a fine bouquet and fruity texture. The wine must be bottled in haste, in fact only a few months after the grapes have been picked. When bottled on its lees, with a small amount of carbonic gas, it retains a finesse and charm which make it very agreeable and much sought after as a companion to sea-food.

MUSCADET generally has a slight acid content, is of a pale yellow colour and light character. It is very difficult to define its bouquet and flavour. The niceties are infinite, and vary considerably from commune to commune and even vineyard to vineyard.

It is possible, however, to distinguish other characteristics peculiar to each type of MUSCADET. The wine that comes from the hillsides along the Loire is particularly full-bodied, often with a higher acidity; this is not a fault since a lack of acidity would make this wine spiritless and sharp in character.

The area covered by the vine is nearly 29,652 acres, producing an average of about 10,999,000 gallons per annum.

154

WINES OF THE LOIRE

CENTRAL REGION

Name of the wine	Principal growths		
White wines	**Pouilly Fumé**.	Château du Nozet Coteaux des Loges	La Loge aux Moines	Côteau des Girarmes
	Pouilly-sur-Loire	Les Berthiers Bois-Fleury Boisgibaud Bouchot Le Bouchot-du-Bas	Le Bouchot-du-Haut Les Cassiers Château du Nozet Les Chétives-Maisons Les Girarmes	Le Grand Bouchot Le Grand Puizac Mezières Le Petit Soumard
	Ménetou-Salon			
White, red and rosé wines	**Quincy**	Bourg Les Brosses Bruniers	Les Chavoches Cornancay Le Grand Chaumoux	Les Gravoches Rimonet Villalin
	Sancerre.	Amigny Coteau de Bannon Beauregard Les Belletins Chambraste Champtin Les Chassaignes Château de Sancerre Chavignol Chemarin Chêne Marchand Les Chevillots Les Coinches La Comtesse	La Côte La Côte-de-Verdigny Les Côtelins Les Coudebraults Les Crilles Clos de l'Epée Fricambault La Grande Côte Les Groux Lare Les Montachins Les Monts-Damnés La Moussière Le Paradis	La Perrière Les Plantes La Porte du Clos La Poussie Reigny Les Rochons Saint-Martin Les Terranges Château de Thauvenay Le Thou Côte de la Vallée Les Vicairies Les Vignes-Chatton Les Vignes de Menetou
	Reuilly	Beaumont Les Beauregards Les Bossières Chatillons.	Les Couagnons Le Figuier Les Lignys	Les Marnais Clos des Messieurs Les Varennes

TOURS REGION

Name of the wine	Commune	Principal growths	
White wines	**Touraine — Azav-le-Rideau**	Azay-le-Rideau		
	Montlouis	Montlouis.	Clos de la Barre Clos de la Frelonnerie La Milletière	Clos Renard Les Sicots
		Lussault	Cray	Pintray
		Saint-Martin-le-Beau . . .	Château du Boulay Cange	Clos de Mosny
	Jasnières (in the Sarthe, a fairly rare wine)	Jasnières	L'Aillerie Les Beduaux La Bonatiere Les Côtières Les Fleuries Les Gargouilles La Gidonniere Les Haurieres Les Heridaines	Les Hussières Les Jasnières Les Longues Vignes Les Mollières La Mule Le Paradis Saint-Jacques Sous-le-Bois Les Verboisières

VOUVRAY

	Commune	Principal growths		
White wines	Vouvray	Les Argouges	La Fontainerie	La Muscadelle
		Domaine de l'Auberidière	Les Fouinières	Clos Naudin
		Clos des Barguins	La Gaillardière	Clos de Nouis
		Clos de la Barre	Clos de Gaimont	Perrets de Minuze
		Clos Baudoin	Château Gaudrelle	Clos du Petit-Mont
		Clos Bel-Air	Clos des Girardières	Le Portail
		Clos des Bidaudières	Grand Echeneau	La Renardière
		Clos du Bois-Rideau	Clos des Gues d'Amant	Clos des Roches
		Les Bois Turmeaux	Le Haut-Lieu	Clos Saint-Come
		Clos Le Bouchet	Coteau J.-Jouffroy	Clos Saint-Mathurin
		Clos du Bourg	Clos des Lions	Sauzelles
		Clos de la Brianderie	La Loge	Clos Toulifaut
		Coteaux des Brosses	Clos la Lucassière	Vallée Coquette
		Les Brosses	Clos de Marigny	Clos de Val-Roche
		Les Brûlées	Monaco	Clos Vaufuget
		Coteau Chatrie	Château Montcontour	Clos les Verneries
		Clos Dubois	Clos le Mont	Clos le Vigneau
		L'Epinay		
	Chançay	Clos des Augustins	Croix-de-Vaux	La Pirée
		Clos Baguelin	Clos de la Forêt	Château Valmer
		Coteau de Chancay	Grand Bathes	Clos de Vau
		Clos de Charmigny	Château Gaillard	Coteau de Vaux
		La Croix-de-Bois	Petites Bastes	Veaux
	Noizay	Clos d'Anzou	Le Grand Coteau	La Roche-de-Cestres
		Les Barres	La Grotte	Clos de la Rochère
		Coteau de Beaumont	Les Hauts-Bois	Coteau de la Rochère
		Clos de Beauregard	Clos Hure	Roquefort
		Clos du Bois d'Ouche	Clos Marteau	La Tremblaie
		Bois Guyon	Molaville	Clos de Venise
		Clos de la Bretonnière	Château d'Ouche	Coteau de Venise
		Goguenne	Clos de la Roche	
	Rochecorbon	Clos de l'Alleau	Clos de la Bourdonnerie	Clos de l'Olivier
		Château les Armuseries	Les Chapelles	Clos des Pentes
		Château des Basses- Rivières	Clos de la Chasse-Royale	Clos de Sens
			Clos Château-Chevrier	Clos de la Taisserie
		Clos des Batonnières	Château de la Lanterne	Le Clos Vaufoinard
		Bois-Soleil	Château de Montgouverne	
	Sainte-Radegonde	Clos de l'Archerie	Clos Mon-Baril	Clos Saint-Georges
		Clos de la Hallotière	Clos de Rougemont	
	Vernou-sur-Brenne. . . .	Les Batailleries	Hardilliers	Perrets-de-Fou-Joint
		Bel-Air	Haut-Cousse	Les Pichaudières
		La Carte	L'Hermineau	Poupine
		Le Cassereau	La Joubardière	Clos de Pouvray
		Clos de Chaillemont	Clos des Longs-Reages	Clos Roc-Etoile
		Clos Chauvin	Clos des Madères	Rue Baffert
		Chopet	Clos Mauguin	Clos des Surins
		Le Clos	Clos de la Meslerie	Tabourneau
		La Coudraie	Mialet	Terne
		Les Deronières	Les Morandières	Clos Thenot
		Château de l'Etoile	Le Mortier	Clos des Thierrières
		Le Feau	La Neurie	Tortemains
		La Folie	Noyer-de-Cens	Vau-Louis
		La Follière	Pain-Perdu	Vaux-Barres
		Clos de Fougerai	Pâtureaux	Vignes-Morier
		Clos Franc	Peu-de-Cartes	Clos de Vilmier

	Name of the wine	Commune	Principal growths	
White, red and rosé wines	Chinon	Chinon	Les Aubuis Les Bruneau Les Closeaux Montrobert Clos du Parc Clos du Pin	Repos de Saint-Martin La Rochelle Rochette Saint-Jean Saint-Louand La Vauzelle
		Avoine	Les Lignes	
		Beaumont-en-Veron . . .	Château de Dauzay Les Gresilles Clos du Langon Le Martinet	Les Peuilles Les Picasses Les Pineaux Roche-Honneur
		Cravant-les-Coteaux . . .	Les Battereaux Bel-Air Les Coutures La Gresille	Clos de la Haie-Martel Les Quatre-Ferrures La Semellerie Coteaux de Sonnay
		Rouzilles	Pelivet	
		Huismes	Bauregard La Colline	Clos Marie Le Pin
		La Roche-Clermault . . .	Les Aiguillons Les Bessardières	Les Rosettes Sassay
		Ligré.	Clos de Galonnes La Noblaie Le Paradis	Clos du Saut-du-Loup Saute-aux-Loups Le Vau-Breton
		Panzoult	La Galippe La Haie-Martel	Clos Queron Ronce
		Rivière	La Croix-Marie Les Croulards	Les Harrassons Clos Saint-Hilaire
Red and rosé wines . .	Bourgueil	Bourgueil	Chevrette Les Galuches Clos des Geslets	Clos de l'Oie-qui-casse Les Pins-Les Sablons La Salpetrerie
		Benais	Beauvais La Chanteleuserie	Petit-Mont Les Raguenières
		Chouzé-sur-Loire	Les Goutierreries	Les Grandes Ouches
		Ingrandes-de-Touraine . .	Clos de Blottières Cru des Brunetières	La Gallotière Minière-Château
		Restigné	Les Evois Fougerolles Domaine de la Gaucherie Les Grands-Champs Les Hauts-Champs	Château Louys La Philebernière Clos de la Platerie Les Rosaies Clos du Vendôme
		Saint-Nicolas-de-Bourgueil	Beaupuy La Contrie Clos de l'Epaisse Les Fondis Forcine La Gardière	La Jarnoterie La Martellière Port-Guyet Clos de la Torrillère Clos du Vigneau La Villatte

SAUMUR REGION

	Name of the wine	Commune	Principal growths	
White wines	Coteaux de Saumur	Montsoreau	Clos des Rotissants	Clos des Pères
		Bizay	Clos des Treilles	
		Brézé	Les Clos du Château de Brézé	Château La Ripaille Clos des Carmes
		Parnay	Clos des Murs	Clos des Saints-Pères
		Saint-Cyr	Butte de Saumoussay	
		Turquant	Château Gaillard	
		Dampierre	Clos des Morains	
		Souzay	Champ Chardon	Clos de la Bienboire
		Saumur	Château de la Fuye	

Name of the wine	Commune	Principal growths
Red wines . . . . . . Cabernet de Saumur	Souzay	Champigny-le-Sec
	Saumur	Souzay Varrains
		Parnay Allonnes
		Saumoussay Brain-sur-Allones
Rosé wine . . . . . . Cabernet de Saumur		

ANGERS REGION

White wines

Name of the wine	Commune	
Coteaux de la Loire	Savennières	*Principal growths* . . . . La Coulée de Serrant La Roche-aux-Moines
		Château d'Epire Clos du Papillon
	La Possonnière, La Pommeraye, Ingrandes, Montjean, Bouchemaine, Saint-Barthélemy, Andard, Brain-sur-l'Authion.	
Coteaux du Loir	Huillé	*Principal growths* . . . . Clos des Tertres Clos du Pineau
		Clos Pilate Clos la Patrie
	Lézigné, Durtal, Baugeois.	
Coteaux du Layon	Rochefort-sur-Loire	*Principal growths* . . . . Quart de Chaume Les Guimonières
		Clos de Sainte-Catherine
	Beaulieu-sur-Layon	*Principal growths* . . . . Château du Breuil Les Mullonnières
	Saint-Aubin-de-Luigné	*Principal growths* . . . . La Roulerie Plaisance
		Château La Fresnaye
	Rablay	*Principal growths* . . . . L'Argonette La Touche
		Le Clos de la Roche Les Sablonnettes
		Les Gonnordes Les Celliers
	Faye-sur-Layon	*Principal growths* . . . . Château de Chanze La Saillanderie
		Château de Mongeneau La Pierre-Gauderie
		La Madeleine Les Jouets
		Les Noëls Le Miroir
	Thouarcé	*Principal growth* . . . . . Bonnezeaux
Other vine-growing communes	Saint-Lambert-du-Lattay, Le Champ, Chaudefonds, Martigné-Briand, Chavagnes, Brigné, Concourson.	
Coteaux de l'Aubance	Murs-Erigné, Vauchrétien, Sainte-Melaine-sur Aubance, Quincé, Brissac, Juigné-sur-Loire, Saint-Saturnin-sur-Loire, Saint-Jean-des-Mauvrets.	

Rosé wines

Rosé d'Anjou	Dampierre, Varrains	
Cabernet d'Anjou	Chacé, Bagneux, Martigné-Briand, Tigné, Le Thoureil, Vauchrétien, Murs, Notre-Dame-d'Alençon, Brissac.	

NANTES REGION

White wines . . . . . *Name of the wine*	*Principal growths*	
Muscadet de Sèvre-et-Maine	Vallet La Chapelle-Heulin
	Mouzillon La Regrippière
	Le Pallet Saint-Fiacre-sur-Maine
Muscadet des Coteaux de la Loire	Saint-Herblon Liré
	Ancenis Drain
	Saint-Géréon

THE WINES
OF BORDEAUX

GASTON MARCHOU

Between the first and third centuries of the Christian era, the Bordeaux countryside witnessed the triumph of the medium-sized estate. The large Gallic domain, hitherto indivisible under the authority of the chieftain of the clan, began to break up. In most cases, the chief was anxious to obtain the title of "Roman citizen", which obviously implied an obligation to accept the conqueror's legal system. Since Roman Law did not recognize the right of inalienability, land was bought, sold and sub-divided. It became a matter for speculation, a means of self-enrichment and a way of paying debts. It could be bequeathed by will.

Agrarian reform, though almost imperceptible, was rendered inevitable by the interaction of customs and vested interests. When great landowners reappeared, even before the break-up of the Empire, the large domain was not re-established. Wealth no longer meant the ownership of a single immense territory but of a number of adjoining estates, each having its own economy. In some cases, in fact, there were no means of communication between such land-holdings.

The cultivation of the vine and the preparation of wine were much better suited to this sub-division than to the vast expanses of territory under a single head. Where necessary, in fact, it encouraged the process.

In A.D. 92, Domitian inaugurated a policy which was to continue until the present day, despite successive repulses and the harmful consequences it was to produce. This emperor, who has been harshly judged by history for other reasons, tried to remedy the shortage of wheat by prohibiting the planting of new vines on Italian soil and ordering that half those that existed in the western provinces should be uprooted. Montesquieu, it is true, gives another reason for Domitian's decision: "This weak and timid prince", he said, "caused the vines in the two Gauls to be grubbed up lest the wine should attract the barbarians." Possibly the author of the *Spirit of the Laws* was loath to leave a Roman emperor, even a mediocre one, in the company of the mid-eighteenth-century economists who advocated pull-

ing up vines. Nevertheless, he was wrong to state as a fact that the Gallic vineyards even partly disappeared under Domitian. The governor of the province was obliged to grant official privileges and exemptions. Incidentally, the winegrowers of Bordeaux often dispensed with them both. They simply bribed the officials responsible for applying the edict.

Even in Rome itself, the winegrowing interests of Bordeaux were defended with typically Gascon asperity and irony. By means of clandestinely distributed pamphlets, the vine, condemned to death by Domitian but still very much alive, addressed the Emperor: "Eat me down to the roots," it said, "I shall still bear enough grapes for great libations to be poured on the day that Caesar is slain!"

Domitian was assassinated four years later. One cannot attack the vineyards of Bordeaux with impunity. The great French administrator Tourny was also to discover the fact. Although he sacrificed his fortune for the city and lavished his affection on it, he was disgraced because he forgot that the fame of its wine was more important than his own.

If the vine, which climbs in serried ranks up the slopes of the right bank of the Médoc, drives back the forest from the left bank and rushes through the sands of the delta to the ocean, has succeeded in defending itself against arbitrary central power, this is most clearly explained by the medium- and small-holding system. It would have been much easier for the officials to ensure that the vines were uprooted in the domains covering the area of a canton or several communes, it would have been far more serious for anyone to disobey the Emperor and the landowners would have been more vulnerable.

At the time of Domitian, the vineyards were grouped around the city; but Burdigala, as it was than known, was built on a very simple plan and was still rustic. The proprietor lived on his land, in his Gallo-Roman villa. He preferred the scent of new-mown hay and the strong perfume of his wine-cellar to the frenzied habit of

159

writing verse which he was to contract at the time of Ausonius, when he was completely latinized. This final latinization of Aquitaine, incidentally, in the twilight of the Empire, coincided with a decline of Latin influence in the East.

While awaiting his conversion to poetry, the master of the villa trembled for his flowering vine if the nights of May were clear. In his short hood and gaiters, he would rise early in the morning to go and see it. He would take the fragile corollas delicately between index finger and middle finger and regard them with a paternal eye. He would meet his workmen, unless he was up before them. He would talk to them, ask the advice of the most experienced, look up at the sky, observe the colour of the river, sometimes shining like a silver lake, sometimes restless and yellow if heavy rain was approaching from the uplands. From his garden-neat vineyard, laid out in tasteful and human geometrical patterns, he had banished the fruit trees which were grown elsewhere. He personified the ageless proverb that Olivier de Serres was to borrow from the land of the Gironde:

> The shadow of a good master
> Makes the vine grow much faster

However, this good master was not only a winegrower whose ear was the first to hear the cuckoo heralding the certain arrival of fine summer days. Since the villa had to provide for all its own needs, he was also an artisan or even an engineer. He brought to life the lost dream or self-sufficiency which is still evoked in Olivier de Serres' *Theatre of Agriculture and Field Management*. Every villa possessed a forge, a carpentry shop and a pottery kiln. It manufactured earthenware pottery, tools and instruments. The owner supervised everything, like a paterfamilias who, living close to the land, was well aware of the limits of productive efforts and the precariousness of their results.

He stamped an impression on the soil of the Gironde which successive invasions were unable to efface. It is to the credit of the first Gallo-Roman landowner, to his peasant mentality, and the care he bestowed on his vine which he cherished like a queen, that the region, when the Gallic system of serfdom was renounced, refrained from introducing the despicable Roman custom of slave labour.

The seeds of what the all-embracing goodness of a Younger Pliny had attempted in Italy and what Christianity was to achieve in due course, were already present in the Bordeaux vineyards by the middle of the third century A.D. The Gironde landowner of the fifth century was thus appreciably better off than the debt-ridden Italian farmer of whom Columella tells us. He was a man who lived well from his free labour and harvested the fruits of the earth, at least partly to his own advantage. The famous wine which was drunk from silver cups in the palaces was also drunk by him from his rustic earthenware goblet. He caught the echo of the praises lavished on the "liquor of the Gods" like a father hearing a tribute to his infant prodigy.

The wine of Bordeaux was to become the sole preoccupation of a whole population. Thanks to it, the social classes, so well-marked elsewhere, were intermingled in a common faith. Beyond the narrow compartmentation of feudalism, it opened up new horizons so attractive that archbishop and cobbler, noble and burgher were assembled together in a kind of superior guild. In the centuries to come, a singular wine-born aristocracy was to arise, in the eyes of which all other products of human activity, including politics and war, would be negligible or secondary.

In the first half of the eighth century, Bordeaux found itself briefly under Arab domination, the only régime which could definitely endanger the vine, since the Moors were conquerors who did not drink it. When deliverance came with Charles Martel, the city still had to face twenty years of war during which the dukes of Aquitaine defended their inheritance against the successors of Clovis. Finally, the Bordeaux country became a march of the Carolingian empire. A noble procession now passes by, a glittering interlude in the mediocrity of those remote ages. Charlemagne comes first, mounted upon his battle charger, holding his sword "Joyeuse" with its ruby-encrusted hilt, with which he will touch the sarcophagus of St. Seurin. Four pages on horseback hold a canopy above his head. Next come his three sons, then the bishops, the dukes, the Twelve Peers, the counts and the knights. The Emperor is interested in the winegrower's way of life; he visits the wineries. He forbids the custom of carrying Bordeaux wine in leather bottles and prescribes the use of hooped casks. He discusses vintages with the merchants and orders good years to be aged in jars.

The eternal wine of Bordeaux is a continuous creation; not only as regards winegrowing and viticultural techniques, in which scientific innovations must constantly be controlled by references to tradition, but also at the prestige level, where promotion efforts are ineffective unless constantly renewed. Hence, in the Middle Ages, after the marriage of the beautiful Eleanor of Aquitaine to Henry Plantagenet of England, the *Jurade* or City Council of Bordeaux based the whole of its foreign policy on the need to keep and develop the English market, the sole outlet for claret. After the reunion of Guienne with France, Bordeaux wine could no longer depend exclusively upon exports. Continental consumers had to be found. From the sixteenth century onwards, the city fathers carried out a systematic campaign to find them.

In 1555, the Mayor of Bordeaux visited the French Court, taking with him twenty *tonneaux* (four hogsheads) of wine for presentation to noblemen who were favourably disposed to the city and its trade. A year later, twenty *tonneaux* of Graves were sent to the Cardinal of Lorraine and to Marshal Saint-André for the same reason. In 1559, the Duke of Alba, while passing

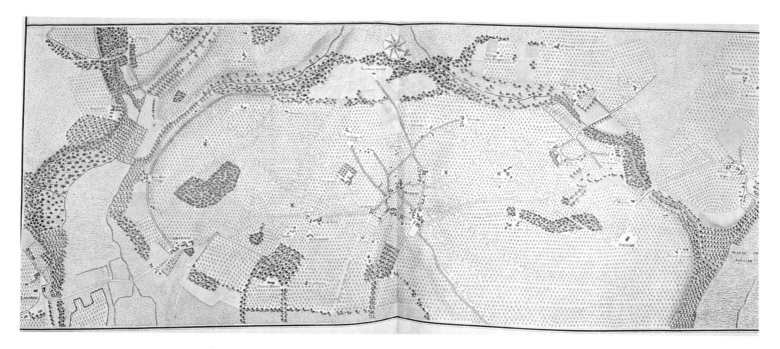

Situated in the Haut-Médoc, on the left bank of the Gironde, the commune of Margaux owes its world-wide renown to Château Margaux, one of the great lords of the Bordeaux wine-country. In the middle of the eighteenth century, Monsieur de Fumel, the military Governor of Bordeaux, planted it with fine, carefully selected vines which quickly made the estate's name. It is shown here on a contemporary plan.

through Bordeaux, was visited by the *Jurats* or aldermen who offered him a present of wine. In 1596, a Bordeaux *Jurat* named Pierre de Brach, on a mission to Paris, was instructed to distribute several *tonneaux* of wine to the best effect. He recounts the difficulty he had in bringing the wine into the capital: "An hundred times I wished the wine back on its vine, for truly I believe it less troublesome to bring a king into Paris than a little wine. There are fifty formalities, routines and prescripts." On June 3rd, 1681, the Muscovite Ambassador arrived in Bordeaux and, having greeted him, the *Jurats* presented him with several dozen bottles of fine wine and some brandy. It is noteworthy that bottled Bordeaux thus made its official appearance at the end of the seventeenth century, even if bottling was not yet the standard commercial practice. It was not until the following century that the establishment of the first industrial glass-works gave birth to the Bordeaux fine-wine business which was to produce the first classification by parishes and then by châteaux or estates.

In 1728, twelve years before Tourny was appointed intendant of Bordeaux, the Duke of Antin was able to write to Robert de Cotte: "The Bordelais prefer to sell their wine rather than to put up fine buildings." The fine buildings were not, in fact, to be put up (as later events were to prove) until the area became closely dependent on the central power. The Bordeaux wine trade, on the other hand, was still to remain for a long time yet the privilege of the people of Bordeaux.

The "Great Privilege" or "Wine Privilege" remained in force until the Revolution, when it was abolished as an unjust feudal institution. In fact, the privilege was perfectly justified. Quite apart from the guarantees it gave of quality production, the beneficiaries were responsible for maintaining the city and its ramparts. This very complex legal monument was the *Jurade's* masterpiece. Its purpose was to restrict access to the port of Bordeaux to wines produced in the seneschalcy.

In addition, everything connected with wine—brokerage, retail sale in the Bordeaux taverns and pothouses, the shape and capacity of the *barrique* (a barrel containing about 50 U.K. gallons, the standard model for which was installed in the City Hall in 1597), everything was regulated and the regulations were scrupulously observed. Every *barrique* had to carry, at both ends, the growth mark, burnt in with a hot iron. This mark was removed once the *barrique* was empty, unless it was returned to the vineyard of origin. Its owner had to obtain a certificate ("stamp") from the local mayor or parish priest that the cask had been duly returned. The text of the "stamp" stipulated that "it is enjoined upon all merchants' masters of the wine-stores to erase immediately, under penalty of a fine of three thousand livres [about £ 600 or $ 1,440] and corporal punishment, the marks on *barriques* which have been broached in their stores whether for consumption, ullaging, fine bottling or cutting down."

This affair of the "stamp" brought the constant conflict between traders and producers to a height of tension. It aroused so many protests among the traders of Chartrons, the trading quarter of Bordeaux, that the regulation was annulled. It should be realized, inciden-

161

At the entrance to Château Mouton-Rothschild, the visitor is welcomed by a statue of Silenus, carrying the infant Bacchus on his head. Perhaps it serves as a reminder that the Bordeaux vineyards were celebrated by the Latin poet Ausonius.

tally, that the chief result of the "stamp" system, as elaborated by the *Jurats*, was not only to prevent the dilution of the wine but also to turn the merchants into habitual lawbreakers, since all normal work in a wine-store became impossible. The sovereign power of the *Jurade*, no longer able to assert itself in grand designs, was degenerating into officiousness.

The quarter of a century between the treaty of 1763, which ended the Seven Years War, and 1789 was, roughly speaking, the period of the "Trade with the Isles". Never had the flame of enterprise burned more brightly in the "Port of the Moon". With a rapidity comparable to the lightning development of the towns of the American West in the nineteenth century, Bordeaux carried out be programme outlined by Tourny. The society which was to die under the knife for the crime of "merchandizing" was certainly the gayest and most

artistic that the City of Montaigne had ever known. It had subtlety, poetry and a very lively taste for nature, though without the dialectic bent so dear to Rousseau. Each year when autumn came the whole of that fashionable society, counsellors of the *Parlement* at its head, left the "Folies" of the suburbs embalmed in the fragrance of the wine-vat; Pomona's sleep began, and the port of Bordeaux awoke. The crescent-shaped roadstead was immense. It stretched from the old Salinières quarter to the more modern quarter of Chartrons, making a semi-circle in front of the classical perspective of the house-fronts.

Breaking the medieval records of which Froissart had spoken, the port was filled with as many as 300 ships, not counting brigs and brigantines. The vessels flew the flags of England, Holland, the Hanseatic towns, Denmark, the Baltic countries, Spain and the distant American republic. At that time, Bordeaux was the greatest distribution centre for colonial goods in all Europe and monopolized a quarter of France's foreign trade.

In fact, if the time of the "Trade with the Isles" is reduced to the period during which it was brilliant and stable, it will be realized that it lasted no longer than fifteen years! Fifteen years during which the *barriques* from those parishes of Médoc and Graves whose growths had, for the first time, been arranged in a hierarchy in 1755, were lined up and modestly concealed behind piles of exotic wealth.

The Jacobin incursion plunged Bordeaux into the same stupor as the arrival of the Barbarians had done. For that happy-go-lucky city, the Napoleonic wars were a long and sombre tunnel. When peace was restored, the port for a long time remained deserted and the "Trade with the Isles" became a shadowy memory. Happily, however, during those fifteen years the wine of Bordeaux had become a "European creation", as Gabriel Delaunay well put it. English, Germans, Dutch, Belgians and Scandinavians could no longer do without it. It was their fidelity to this unique product that saved Bordeaux. Stripping off the white gloves they had worn to handle samples of indigo, the people of Bordeaux had no recourse but to return to their vines and their winestores, and this they did. Since then, whatever the economic climate, however enticing the promise of an industrial future might be, the Bordeaux winegrowers have known where they are going. They will never again depart from their vine-bordered road.

I remember, during the war, a honey-sweet morning draped in a luminous, velvety mist. It was at a spot in that immense Central European plain where the very shape of a vine-stock is unknown. That morning, for the first time in months, I felt my distant birthplace refilling my void. Like many another, I knew that extraordinary, almost painful moment when the wearisome dizziness of captivity suddenly becomes fixed in a blinding revelation. By undreamt-of approaches, our lost France reclaimed her anonymous flock and gave each of us back his provincial identity. With the help of a sign,

expressly given to us, marvellous images of the past rose up under our closed eyelids with a force, a truth, a wealth of detail which the seeing eyes can never achieve.

It needed that dawn in the early Silesian autumn, the melancholy of a desolate grassland on which innumerable rain-puddles reflected clouds driven by the West wind, the misty prospect of the huts and strange quality of the sounds in the atmosphere, to give me back the soft and magnificent "grape-gathering weather" in the middle of Elsterhorst Camp.

This well-known phenomenon of exile turned me into one of those naïve travellers of ancient times who would suddenly discover an unknown city from the brow of a hill. But my discovery was a symbolic one. It gave me a destiny. I realized that the glory of Bordeaux both siezes

upon the senses and obtrudes upon the intellect, for even before encountering the miraculous life of Joan of Arc, translating Voltaire or sending its women to Paris for their frocks, a civilized nation makes the acquaintance of Bordeaux wine.

On the other hand, there is a vine epic in the Bordeaux country. Through wine, the vine presides over the social, moral and political activities of every day; it regulates life, of which it is the essential framework. A child born on the banks of the Garonne cannot conceive of a countryside without vineyards.

Throughout the centuries, the vine has been the friend of man in every country where the grape ripens. But once and once alone, in the history of mankind, it hat been a whole people's reason for living; and that was in Bordeaux.

THE REGIONS OF BORDEAUX

If you look at a map of France, your eye will be caught by the blue indentation of the Gironde estuary. It is a vast gateway to the ocean, the longest and widest along the whole coastline. From Ambès Bill, where the Garonne and the Dordogne meet, to the sea is a distance of some 60 miles and, at that point, the river is 2 miles wide. Downstream, the two banks are more than 6 miles apart. This expanse of water is subject to tidal action. When the ocean rises, its irresistible mass pours into the estuary, hurling back the current. This is the phenomenon known as the "bore" which is more or less violent according to season. The tidal wave moves with the speed of a galloping horse, raising in front of it a wall of seething, yellowish water. The bore does not slacken off before reaching Bordeaux and the violent agitation is still visible well above the city.

In the age of wooden ships, the mouth of the Gironde, although it had not yet achieved its present configuration, was an excellent route for penetrating into the continent. No other European river could carry ships so far inland. If, however, the reader follows the course of the Garonne in an atlas, he will realize that the river is not only the "maryne-lyke waie to the see of Biscaye and the noble and puyssante citie of Bourdeaulx" as the old portulan maps put it. Crossing the Limogne, you reach the Naurouze plateau which connects the basin of the Garonne to that of the Aude. This is the easiest and most agreeable route between the Mediterranean and the Atlantic. Long before the conquest, the Romans of Narbonne used to send their merchants down the Garonne, whence they took ship for the British Isles and the ports of the north.

Although the right bank of the estuary, which is bordered by a succession of cliffs, has been unchanged for thousands of years, this is not true of the left bank. Even as late as the historical period, this was a confused jumble of dunes and marshes through which the waters of the river made their way, depositing silt. Not more than six or seven centuries ago, the river embraced part of the long riparian plain now called the Médoc before losing itself in the Atlantic. The island thus formed was, at high tide, crossed by other arms of the river which, although a true estuary to the east, opened out into a delta in the west.

The department of the Gironde, the limits of which more or less coincide with the frontiers of the ancient Guienne, is the largest in France and covers more than 2½ million acres. It can be divided into two distinct regions. The first, covering about 1,500,000 acres, is bordered by the ocean on the one side and, on the other, by the left banks of the Gironde, the Garonne, the Ciron and the Barthus. It is a well-wooded countryside which belongs to the great Landes forest. Near the river, however, an outcrop of quaternary gravels forms a ridge on which are found the most famous vineyards in the world. The second region consists of a succession of hills and plateaus on the right banks of the Gironde and the Garonne. Their soil varies considerably. Starting from the south, we come to the Réolais, consisting of more or less argillaceous sandstones, the Entre-Deux-Mers and, on the right bank of the Dordogne, the very characteristic sub-regions of the Fronsadais and the Saint-Emilionnais where the gravel becomes more and more clayey and gives birth to several Great Growths.

The Blayais-Bourgeais region, which is opposite the Médoc, across the Gironde, borders the right bank of the estuary, like a predominantly limestone wall.

Even nowadays, despite the vine which reigns on both banks, despite the links forged between all the inhabitants of the Bordeaux country over two millenia, the great river still separates two different worlds. To the west, the impenetrable curtain of coniferous forest shuts off the horizon behind the vineyards. To the east, there rise up hills so steep that the whiteness of limestone outcrops can be seen on their flanks, towering tall on the horizon.

The mild winters of the Gironde are due to the Gulf Stream. The temperate summers with their golden light, which will be entrapped in the liquid prison of the grape, are saved from excessive heat by a protective bank of clouds. The wine of Bordeaux is as much the offspring of a climate as of a soil.

THE "APPELLATIONS CONTRÔLÉES"

These three bottles contain wine classified Premiers Grands Crus of Haut-Médoc in the 1855 classification. From left to right, they are: Château Latour (commune of Pauillac); Château Margaux (commune of Margaux); Château Lafite-Rothschild (commune of Pauillac). A fourth has recently been added to their ranks: Château Mouton-Rothschild (commune of Pauillac).

What is meant by the three words: "Wine of Bordeaux"? Speaking at Nogent-sur-Marne one day, the late-lamented Jean Valmy-Baysse replied to that question with as much elegance as simplicity : "the wine of Bordeaux, gentlemen, is France personified!"

To the foreign consumer, the trademark "Bordeaux" does, in fact, mean the rarest and most sought-after of products, regular consumption of which is a sign of good taste and distinction.

Bordeaux wine is, as someone once put it, "something quite other than merchandise". It is a product which, according to Aristotle's definition, may be classified among the great universals. If, however, the universal makes the unity of the species, the particular makes its number. The legal descriptions of origin BORDEAUX and BORDEAUX SUPÉRIEUR belong to the number.

Here we shall have to indulge in a little more history. These "descriptions of origin" are so loaded with references, they express the idea of collective heritage and ownership so well that, not so long ago, their delimitation gave rise to a hot dispute which was finally settled only by a decree published in the *Official Gazette* of February 19th, 1911.

Before they came to their decision, the legislators were bombarded with more or less justified claims that the description BORDEAUX should be extended to wines which were sometimes far removed from the city that actually bore that name.

The archivist Brutails helped them to decide on the limits by bringing his historical knowledge to bear and making a clear distinction between the wines of the seneschalcy and those of the Uplands (Haut-Pays) in accordance with traditions dating from as far back as the Middle Ages.

In that distant era, the only wines entitled to the description BORDEAUX were those harvested in the immediate vicinity of the city by winegrowers who were freemen of the city and dwelt *intra muros*. To guard the privilege King John had stated on April 15th, 1214: "We desire that all the wines of our citizens of Bordeaux, which come from the vines of their city, should travel

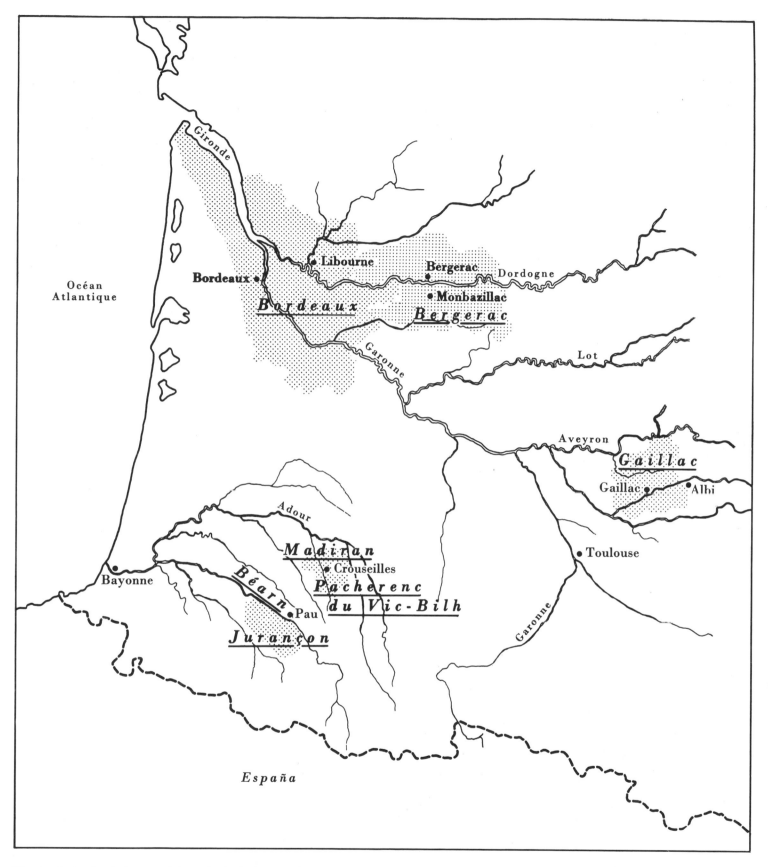

The following labels appear on the map:

Gironde

Océan
Atlantique

Libourne
Bergerac • Dordogne
Bordeaux •
• Monbazillac
Bordeaux
Bergerac
Garonne

Lot

Aveyron
Gaillac
Gaillac • • Albi

Adour
Madiran
• Crouseilles
• Toulouse
Béarn
Pacherenc
du Vic-Bilh
Bayonne
• Pau
Garonne
Jurançon

España

The Aquitaine basin is one of the principal winegrowing regions in France. The vine is mainly cultivated in the department of the Gironde which groups, around the proud name of Bordeaux, a great number of famous designations such as Médoc, Graves, Sauternes, Barsac and St-Emilion. Other vineyards are to be found around Bergerac and Monbazillac, in the middle reaches of the Dordogne; around Gaillac in the Albigeois and, finally, in the former province of Béarn, to the south of the Adour and the Gave de Pau.

freely on the river." In other words, all other wines were subject to a blockade and were discriminated against fiscally.

Like waves spreading out from a stone splashing in water, the description—or, more exactly, the privilege—was then extended to the 350 parishes of the seneschalcy of Guienne. Such was the legal position of the vineyards in 1789. It was not too critical.

The new administrative division of France into departments, on the threshold of the nineteenth century, once again extended the area of the description BORDEAUX. Instead of the 350 parishes of the seneschalcy, it covered almost all the 554 communes of the Gironde. It was only a strike by the Council General that prevented the description being also extended to 63 communes of the Dordogne and Lot-et-Garonne.

After the decree of 1911, the winegrowers of the Lot-et-Garonne tried to call their wines "wines of the Bordeaux Uplands". This attempt was rejected by the courts since the description *Haut-Pays bordelais* was not a traditional one. Quite the contrary, in fact, since the term "Haut-Pays" was used to identify wines other than those known by the trademark BORDEAUX. So much so, indeed, that cutting the city wines with wines from the Haut-Pays had always been prohibited, as is evidenced by numerous fiats of the Bordeaux *parlement* down the centuries. The Act of 1911 was thus perfectly straightforward. Its purpose was to fit the place-of-origin concept into the framework of modern law and to protect the description BORDEAUX from the concept of "provenance" with all the possibilities of generalized fraud it entailed.

At this stage of regulation, however, the name "Bordeaux" covered all the growths of the Bordeaux region without distinction, including the Great Growths which had been the beneficiaries of the 1855 classification and which had made use of all their prestige to obtain the decree.

In early 1919, the problem of descriptions of origin came up again with a new urgency owing to the Peace Conference being held at Versailles. If respect for descriptions of origin was to be imposed upon Germany, internal regulations had to be set up. The Descriptions of Origin Act was promulgated on May 6th, 1919. From then on, legislation proliferated. The most decisive laws were the Capus Act of 1927 and the Decree-Act of 1935. The fact was that the winegrowers were unable to accept geographical origin as the sole criterion entitling to a "description". The 1919 Act was supplemented therefore by others which took account of new factors such as soil, vine species, degree of alcohol and yield per acre. Thus were born the *appellations d'origine contrôlée* (A.O.C.), guaranteed descriptions of origin.

In the case of the Bordeaux region, the result of these provisions was a sort of hierarchy. It may, perhaps, have been a mistake to put the most limited description at the top and gradually descend to more and more general descriptions with an increasingly large production.

Thus, in order of descent, a Pauillac growth was entitled to the descriptions PAUILLAC, MÉDOC and BORDEAUX.

To put it another way, a Pauillac wine which was considered to be unworthy of its name of origin and which lacked the characteristics required of a good Médoc could always be marketed as a BORDEAUX. This use of the description BORDEAUX as a catch-all was to produce great confusion in view of the world-wide renown of the greatest fine-wine producing region in France. However famous some celebrated châteaux or a few restricted descriptions might be, the foreign wine-lover had great difficulty in understanding that the word BORDEAUX standing alone indicated the more modest products of the Bordeaux region. The most recent example of this regrettable confusion was given by the world press when commenting on a speech made by the then French Minister of Agriculture, Mr. Edgard Pisani, during a visit to Bordeaux. He said: "I have been and still am struck by the fact that the 'Bordeaux' flag is fast reaching the stage when it waves over the most mediocre goods and that so much disorder has been created in this winegrowing area that the first care of every winegrower is to put on a château label instead of the Bordeaux one."

Being badly informed about the A.O.C. legislation, all that some journalists gleaned from his statement was the inference that Bordeaux wine was mediocre in general. Nonetheless the Minister's criticism was perfectly justified and the reluctance of some Girondin producers to use the name BORDEAUX was quite understandable. It does not mean, however, that they were entirely in the right. Although the descriptions BORDEAUX and BORDEAUX SUPÉRIEUR were used to denote the more mediocre products, the great mass of BORDEAUX wines in terms of the Capus Act were of excellent quality and widely used to improve growths better placed economically.

It was necessary to escape from that blind alley and take up the challenge to logic. The question was who would take the first step on the way back to a sound tradition. One solution would have been for the Great Growths to meet their historic responsibilities and once more inscribe the name of Bordeaux on the pediment of their fame. In that way, they would have taken up anew their centuries-old mission and, like true nobles, would have returned to the head of their troops and imposed discipline amongst them. The hesitation to sign such a blank cheque, however, was quite understandable. The other solution, more in keeping with the style of our era, was for those involved to take the revaluation of the description BORDEAUX into their own hands and that, in fact, was what they did.

Thanks to Mr. Pierre Perromat, President of the National Institute of Descriptions of Origin but who never abandoned the presidency of the BORDEAUX and BORDEAUX SUPÉRIEUR wine syndicate, these wines have, since 1967, enjoyed full descriptions of origin. They are subject to tasting and analytical tests like most of the

other Gironde descriptions and have recovered their independence. There is no longer a catch-all description. Henceforth, the only refuge for disinherited Bordeaux descriptions is the category: "wines for everyday consumption".

The description BORDEAUX CLAIRET, which derives from the description BORDEAUX, has been highly fashionable in recent years. It is a rosé wine from any red grape already covered by the regional description and is obtained by "bleeding" the vat before the must has taken on its full colour; in fact, the grape skins are left in the vat for no more than two or three days. A fairly small proportion of sulphur is also added to the must at this stage to ensure that fermentation is not jeopardized or slowed down. Final stabilization of the wine is achieved by fining, or sometimes with the addition of some more sulphur. BORDEAUX CLAIRET has nothing in common with the old claret, which was a briefly fermented red wine. It is none the less a charming, fruity wine, both delicate and cheerful.

In the Bordeaux region, as elsewhere, the must is 'weighed'. A simple operation, it consists of filling a test-tube with must, then dipping an araeometer or 'must-weigher' into it, which indicates the density of the must and the quantity of sugar in it. Thus the quality of the vintage can be checked.

Despite the ever-increasing mechanisation in the vineyards, the wine harvest is still mostly performed by hand. There are two excellent reasons for this: the grapes need to be cut with care to avoid bruising or losing them, and it is essential to see that no leaves or twigs are mixed with the must.

Château Cheval Blanc

1964

St. Emilion

1ᵉʳ Grand Cru Classé

HÉRITIERS FOURCAUD-LAUSSAC
PROPRIÉTAIRES

Mis en bouteille au Château (FRANCE)

APPELLATION SAINT-ÉMILION 1ᵉʳ GRAND CRU CLASSÉ CONTROLÉE

Imprimé en France — BERTHON · LIBOURNE

CHÂTEAU CHEVAL BLANC
1. 1a. Trade name "Château Cheval Blanc". This name is well-known to wine-lovers but the merchant-viniculturist gives further details on his label and indicates that the wine is a "first great growth". The vintage is also mentioned on the label. – 2. 2a. Place-name description of origin: Saint-Emilion, which is confirmed by the reference to "Saint-Emilion, first great growth". Nothing could be more explicit, therefore, than this label, and the knowledgable wine-lover will also be aware that the Cheval Blanc is one of the two "first great growths classed as (a)" in the area. – 3. Name of the merchant-viniculturist. – 4. The reference to bottling at the Château is compulsory for the great growths of Bordeaux; it is a guarantee of both quality and authenticity.

CHÂTEAU HAUT-MARBUZET
1. Trade name "Château Haut-Marbuzet". This growth did not appear in the list of growths classified in 1855 but was mentioned in the syndicate merit-list of March 3ʳᵈ, 1966 with the annotation "exceptional great-bourgeois" (see page 158). – 2. Guaranteed descriptive name: Saint-Estèphe. The Saint-Estèphe area is in the Haut-Médoc near the border of the Bas-Médoc.

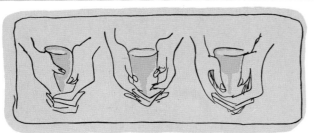

Dessin inédit — de Henry Mevre

1964   1964

Cette récolte a produit :
167.444 Bordelaises et ½ Bˢᵉˢ de 1 à 167.444
2.580 Magnums de M 1 à M 2.580
37 Grands Formats de G F 1 à G F 37
double-magnums, jéroboams, impériales
3.000 "Réserve du Château" marquées R.C.
Ci,

Philippe de Rothschild

Château Mouton Rothschild

BARON PHILIPPE DE ROTHSCHILD PROPRIÉTAIRE A PAUILLAC
APPELLATION PAUILLAC CONTROLÉE
TOUTE LA RÉCOLTE MISE EN BOUTEILLES AU CHÂTEAU

1966

CHATEAU HAUT-MARBUZET

APPELLATION
SAINT-ESTÈPHE
CONTROLÉE

MIS EN BOUTEILLES
H. DUBOSCQ
PROPRIÉTAIRE A SAINT-ESTÈPHE (GIRONDE)
AU CHATEAU

CHÂTEAU MOUTON-ROTHSCHILD
1. Trade name "Château Mouton-Rothschild". This label is laconic and, apart from its more elegant style, nothing distinguishes it from its next-door neighbour. As a great noble, Château Mouton-Rothschild does not mention its rank in the 1855 classification in which it was one of the eminent second growths (see page 158). – 2. Place-name description of origin: Pauillac. Some people will find it difficult to place Pauillac in the Haut-Médoc and to realize, at first glance, that Mouton-Rothschild is a Bordeaux wine. – 3. Name of the merchant-viniculturist. – 4. 4a. Careful details of the château bottling process are given, the bottle being numbered after the word "Ci". Confirmation of this operation is given in 4a.

CHÂTEAU RIEUSSEC

1. Trade name "Château Rieussec". We are immediately informed that it is a first great growth. – 2.-2a. Place-name description of origin: Sauternes. This is a great dessert wine. The year gives the knowledgeable wine-lover and indication of quality. The description of origin is in the prescribed form. – 3. Name of the merchant-viniculturist. – 4. Reference to bottling at the Château.

CHÂTEAU PÉTRUS

1. Trade name "Pétrus". The indication "great wine" is not very explicit. – 2. Place-name description of origin: Pomerol. – 2a. This area has no official classification like those of the Médocs and Saint-Emilions, but Pétrus is regarded as the best of the Pomérols. The description is repeated in the prescribed form. – 3. Reference to bottling at the Château. – 4. Name of the merchant-viniculturist.

CHÂTEAU LA MISSION HAUT BRION

1. Trade name Château la Mission Haut Brion. The reference to "classified great growth" make it immediately clear that this is a great wine; it should not, however, be confused with Château Haut Brion which is a "first classed great growth". – 2. Place-name description of origin: Graves. Since there are both red and white Graves, I should, perhaps, mention that Château la Mission Haut Brion is a red wine. – 3. Reference to bottling at the Château. – 4. Name of the merchant-viniculturist.

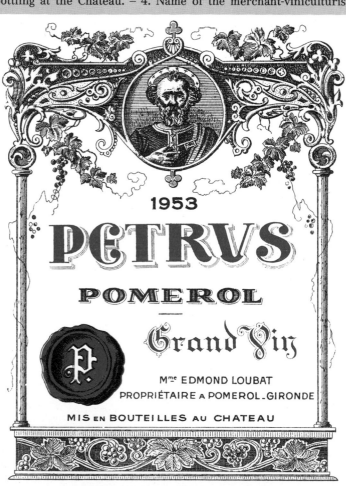

THE WINES OF THE LEFT BANK OF THE GIRONDE
AND THE GARONNE

MÉDOC

In 1855, a patriot of the Médoc, Mr. Saint-Amant, could write: "The Médoc appears rich and sumptuous: yet it both is and it isn't. A great year lavishes abundance there, but such a year arrives but once every three or four years. In other years, it is difficult to meet expenses, which are much greater on the large domains where people talk unceasingly of restricting their size without ever taking any measure to that end. The owner of a great growth of Médoc should not sink all his fortune in it, but half at most, in order to support the costs and be able to await the favourable moment to sell his wines. The revenue from the vines is precarious and unequal. Such a domain should be held as a subsidiary and its owner should glory in it."

A century ago, the great Bordeaux wines had reached their zenith. What would Mr. Saint-Amant write now about the wonderful vocation of an area which is noble among the noblest?

It will be realized that the period in which Mr. Saint-Amant was defining the viticulture of Médoc was also that of the celebrated "classification". The idea of the "parish" (which dated from 1755) gave place to that of the "château", the "manor-house", thereby marking a dual evolution in the vineyard: a technical evolution as the practice of château bottling developed and an economic evolution whereby the exploitation of the Médoc was improved by an injection of business capital. In 1855, Médoc viticulture was beginning to reveal a veritable humanism. A great Médoc winegrower proved it not so long ago by showing us his "book of reason". It was the treasured wealth of a long experience of husbandry. In it we find, indeed, traces of events which shook the world throughout the century: wars, revolutions and massacres; but what our venerable friend noted down was, perhaps, more important. It was the creation of that masterpiece, an eminent bottle of wine. Nothing but short remarks, dates and figures, but these notes have a Homeric quality, the flavour of an epic constantly rolled up and unrolled to the rhythm of the seasons and the rhythm of work. The patriarch had recorded, for future generations, the softness of a morning, the freshness of an evening, the time taken by a wagon to come from the vine to the wine-store, the song of the first cuckoo or the flight of the symbolic blackbirds which formed part of the folklore of the domain.

In Médoc, viticulture is first and foremost an act of faith. If the earth were to explode tomorrow, the justification of our existence would be that we are able to present to our Creator this book of reason in which a wise man questioned the whole of nature to discover the right moment for "pouring", bottling or ploughing.

To the extent that Médoc is unquestionably a work of art, its production, like that of the other great wines of Bordeaux, involves an irreducible minimum of traditional husbandry. This does not mean that, as Paul Valéry put it, the Médoc winegrower "backs into the future". He is by no means filled with nostalgia for the past. He refuses to subject the traditional vineyard to an experimental aspect of technology, but no one is more delighted when technology performs some function which is of service to the vineyard. If, for example, our planners clear away the spider's web of electricity and telephone wires from the Médoc skies, we shall see this "husbandman" immediately adopt the aircraft or the helicopter to spread insecticides or fungicides. If the agricultural machinery industry manages to supply him with a reasonable engine for his ploughing, he will abandon animal traction which, in some places, is still indispensable.

Over a distance of fifty miles in the direction of the river, with a depth inland of six to ten miles, the vineyards of Médoc produce wines which, though different, are all remarkable, even in years which are poor in alcohol content. There are no finer, more thoroughbred, more intellectualized wines. This nobility proceeds from their bouquet and aroma which are unique among the great French wines.

The truth is that a Médoc can hold its peak of perfection for a very long time. When President Albert Lebrun came to Pauillac to open the first of the famous festivals to longevity, it was not only the centenarian winegrowers who were fêted. An 1834 growth was tasted and that, too, was in excellent health.

The northern part of the Médoc Peninsula constitutes the generic place-name description MÉDOC.

This region stretches from Saint-Seurin-de-Cadourne to the Pointe de Grave and skirts the Gironde estuary over a distance of twelve miles, its width being from four to five miles.

At the very edge of the river, vineyards cover a strip of gravelly land, cut by shallow valleys, which is from one to two miles wide. It is this tongue of land which produces the best wines. On the other soils (clayey limestones), the wines produced are more commonplace but are held worthy of the name "Great Ordinary".

In the 1855 classification, Médoc was not allotted any classed or "Superior Bourgeois" growths but only "Bourgeois" growths. There were quite a number of these, however, and they often fetched prices well above

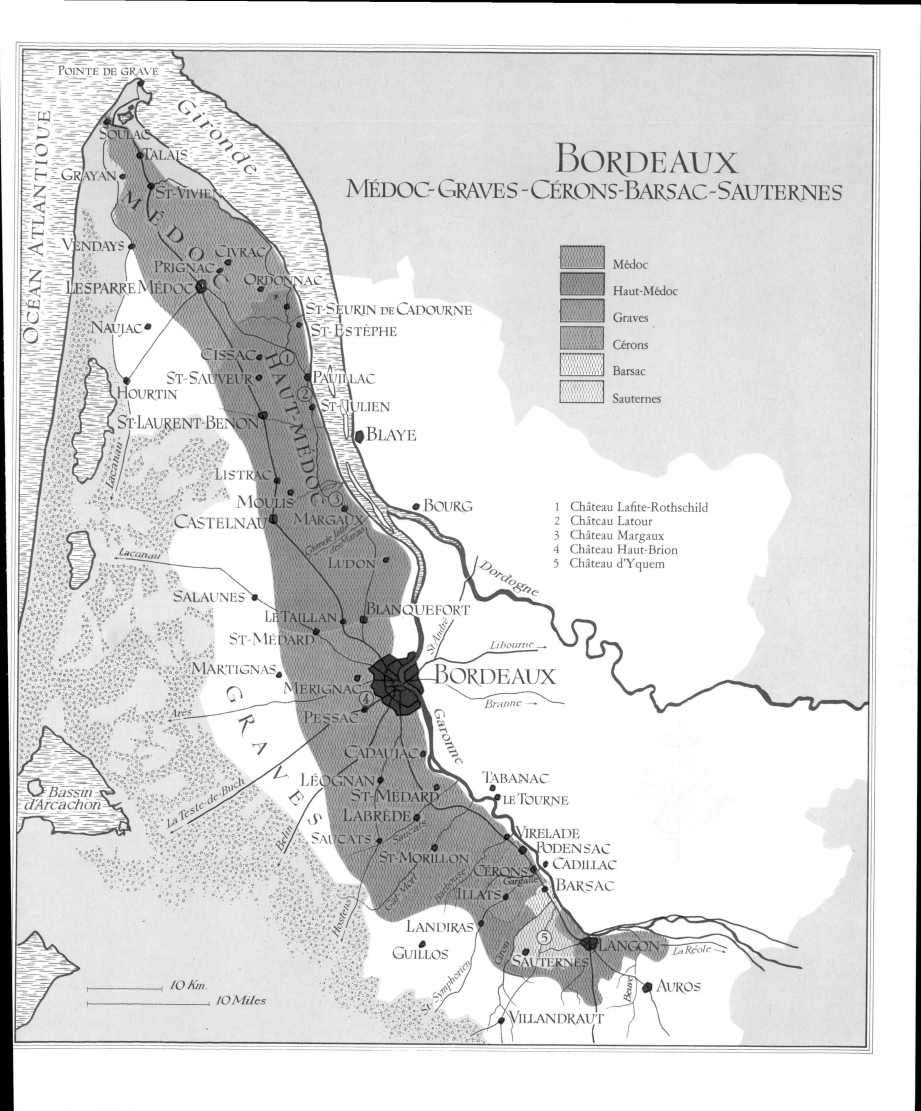

BORDEAUX
MÉDOC·GRAVES·CÉRONS·BARSAC·SAUTERNES

Médoc
Haut-Médoc
Graves
Cérons
Barsac
Sauternes

1 Château Lafite-Rothschild
2 Château Latour
3 Château Margaux
4 Château Haut-Brion
5 Château d'Yquem

OCÉAN ATLANTIQUE

POINTE DE GRAVE

Gironde

SOULAC
TALAIS
GRAYAN
St-VIVIEN
VENDAYS
CIVRAC
PRIGNAC
ORDONNAC
LESPARRE MÉDOC
MÉDOC
NAUJAC
St-SEURIN DE CADOURNE
St-ESTÈPHE
CISSAC
St-SAUVEUR
PAUILLAC
HOURTIN
HAUT-MÉDOC
St-JULIEN
St-LAURENT-BENON
BLAYE
Lacanau
LISTRAC
MOULIS
BOURG
CASTELNAU
MARGAUX
Grande Jalle des Marais
LUDON
Lacanau
SALAUNES
BLANQUEFORT
LE TAILLAN
Dordogne
St-MÉDARD
Libourne
St-André
MARTIGNAS
BORDEAUX
Bassin d'Arcachon
MÉRIGNAC
Ares
Branne
GRAVES
PESSAC
Garonne
La Teste-de-Buch
CADAUJAC
Belin
LÉOGNAN
TABANAC
St-MÉDARD
LE TOURNE
LABRÈDE
Saucats
VIRELADE
SAUCATS
Saucats
PODENSAC
St-MORILLON
CADILLAC
Caf Mort
CÉRONS
Hostens
Barbouse
Gargalle
BARSAC
ILLATS
LANDIRAS
Ciron
GUILLOS
LANGON
La Réole
St-Symphorien
SAUTERNES
Beuve
AUROS
St-Symphorien
VILLANDRAUT

10 Km.

10 Miles

The Mouton-Rothschild *domaine* is one of the largest in France; about 175 acres of vines owned by a single tenant. It has been in the same family since 1853. In one wing of the buildings, the present proprietor, Philippe, has created a splendid museum where one can admire works of art inspired by the vine and wine dating from the third millenium B.C. to the present day.

their position in the Médoc hierarchy. Eleven communes possessed such "Bourgeois" growths: Saint-Germain-d'Esteuil, Ordonac-et-Potensac, Saint-Yzans, Conquèques, Blaignan, Saint-Christoly-de-Médoc, Bégadan, Lesparre, Valeyrac, Civrac and Prignac.

To the south of this region, towards Bordeaux, is the area which has earned the place-name description of origin HAUT-MÉDOC. It covers a number of subdescriptions which are well-known throughout the world and are among the brightest jewels in the Bordeaux crown, MARGAUX glowing in their midst like a royal ruby. Since the dawn of time, several neighbouring parishes have shared in its ancient renown but nowadays four communes, in addition to that of Margaux, are entitled to the description, namely Cantenac, Soussans, Arsac and Labarde. CHÂTEAU MARGAUX, whose nobility is equalled only by the historic memories attached to the domain and the magnificent mansion of the same name, is a *Premier Cru Classé*, or "First Growth". The description MARGAUX as a whole connotes a great, sometimes very great, fine full-bodied and elegant wine with a world-wide reputation.

Moulis is situated in the centre of the Haut-Médoc. At the end of the Hundred Years War, this little area was still more sylvan than viticultural and Pey Berland, the future Archbishop of Bordeaux, used to graze his father's flocks there. Moulis, however, with its good-quality gravel soils, clearly had a winegrowing vocation. Moulis growths are mentioned in the list drawn up by the Intendancy of Guienne in 1767 but, according to the 1855 classification, it contained only "Superior Bourgeois" growths.

The wines of MOULIS, which are very much appreciated in Germany, Belgium and the Netherlands, have the rare advantage that they will keep in perfect safety. In addition to the delicacy, bouquet and elegance of the great Médocs, they have also a balanced constitution which guarantees them a happy old age.

The Listrac vineyards occupy one of the lighest hill-tops in the Haut-Médoc. The growths of this place-name description are reminiscent of the MOULIS in their body and vinosity. For centuries, this parish has also produced white wines, which strongly resemble the best white GRAVES. The 1855 classification gave no classed growths to Listrac but it had several "Superior Bourgeois" growths.

"Passers-by, you are now entering the ancient and celebrated vineyard of Saint-Julien, bow low...". Such is

172

the proud inscription at the boundary of Saint-Julien-Beychevelle. It is now applied to an excellent vineyard, one of the richest dependencies of the Haut-Médoc. It refers, however, to the sailors' custom of striking their sails in salute when passing the Château de Beychevelle, residence of the Duke of Epernon, Grand Admiral of France. SAINT-JULIEN can be distinguished from the other famous wines of the Haut-Médoc by its beautiful purple colour, its great elegance and its mellowness. More full-bodied than MARGAUX, less hearty than PAUILLAC, it can also be recognized by a very personal bouquet that develops quickly.

Encouraged by its winegrowing mayor, Saint-Julien is steadily increasing its fame. There is so much competition among the producers in this commune that several "Superior Bourgeois" or "Bourgeois" growths, which were formerly almost unknown, have become as much valued as a "classified growth".

Situated about thirty miles from Bordeaux, Pauillac is the most important of the winegrowing communes of the Médoc. It has a House of Wine and is the headquarters of the *Commanderie du Bontemps-Médoc.* This fraternity uses the town as a starting point for all its

ceremonies, the most important of which, the Flower Festival, is the occasion for a gathering of lovers of Bordeaux wine from all over the world. The place-name description PAUILLAC also applies to the wines harvested in certain of the lands of Saint-Sauveur, Saint-Estèphe and Cissac. The Lesparre Decree, one of the most detailed instruments of viticultural jurisprudence, lists the vineyards, plot by plot, in which PAUILLAC is grown. In some cases, even the rows of vine-stocks are measured and numbered. This description, the most representative of the Gironde winegrowing region, is the only one which possesses two first growths, three seconds, one fourth, eleven fifths and a whole train of "Superior Bourgeois" and "Bourgeois" growths, the nobility and brilliant qualities of which are often very close to the Great Growths.

PAUILLAC wines, whether they have a great coat of arms or a simple shield, are the most masterful of the wines of the Médoc. The great years give them characteristics which can be rather surprising if they are drunk before the ageing process which develops their incomparable charms. Nevertheless a PAUILLAC, even when it is too young and astringent, charms the exper-

These venerable bottles of Château Lafite-Rothschild (from left to right: 1858, 1865, 1919, 1895, 1887, 1874, 1902, 1903) are just a small selection from an unique collection of bottled wines ranging from 1797 to today, preserved in the cellars of the château. The property has belonged to the Barons Rothschild since 1868, and consists of 300 acres, of which 160 are planted to the vine.

ienced palate. This wine is always promising and has never lied.

The place-name description SAINT-ESTÈPHE is reserved solely for growths from the commune of that name, one of the largest in the Médoc. The SAINT-ESTÈPHE wines have an individual bouquet, and are delicate, mellow and distinguished. The soil, which is gravelly over an iron-pan subsoil, produces five classified growths, two of them being seconds; numerous "Bourgeois" growths, and a whole series of "artisan" and "peasant" growths. This rather byzantine hierarchy is very often pushed aside, however, by the great reputation for quality of all the SAINT-ESTÈPHE wines.

The time has now come to speak of the famous "classification". To what extent did the grandeur and luxury of the Châteaux of Médoc affect the judgement passed on their growths? It would be difficult to say. It is certain, however, that the first Bordeaux labels using a château name were always adorned with the picture of a genuine château. It must also be admitted that great mansions are to be found throughout the Médoc area. For the most part, they reflect the taste of the early nineteenth century when they were built. They are reminiscent of the neo-Gothic style popularized by Sir Walter Scott in 1812, when he built his Abbotsford manor on the south bank of the Tweed.

The main factors taken into account in establishing a hierarchy of quality were, it is true, the taste of the wine, the price it fetched, the more or less cared-for appearance of the vineyard, technical details of wine-making equipment and a few historical references. Nevertheless, since the initiative for classification came from a Chartrons firm of wine merchants, then at the zenith of its power, which either owned or was closely connected with the largest domains in the Médoc, we may well think that the 1855 classification reflected a vague notion of "caste" (at least to the extent that subjectivity inevitably played its part).

Hence, the châteaux of the Médoc have, from the very beginning, been a commercial factor as well as an architectural one. They formed the backbone of the classification system and spread the fame of Bordeaux wine far and wide. Consequently, a château label was desired for every growth of any quality in the Bordeaux area, even if the winegrower lived in the simplest of dwellings. The multiplicity of châteaux in the Gironde is by no means a product of Gascon ostentation, of a rather childish arrogance; it is the result of hard economic facts. It became necessary, therefore, to regulate the legal use of the word château. The Decree of September 30th, 1949 fixed the following conditions for its use:

1. The wine must be entitled to a place-name description of origin.

2. The wine must come from an agricultural holding, designated by the word château or by an equivalent word, which must genuinely exist as an agricultural holding and be already precisely designated by these words and expressions.

3. The name of the château or its equivalent must be restricted to the produce of the agricultural holding designated by the proposed words.

Legal usage, by its interpretation of the word château, had already prepared the way for the evolution implicit in the Decree. A ruling by the Bordeaux Civil Court, May 8th, 1939, had declared that the word château denoted a given agricultural or viticultural holding.

It should not be hastily concluded, however, that the majority of the châteaux in the Bordeaux region are of recent construction or that they exist only in the official register of wine growths. The ancient seneschalcy of Guienne, with its fascinating history and wealth of legend, is a veritable goldmine for the archaeologist and the art-lover. Noble mansions abound, often surrounded by famous vineyards.

Thus we find in the Médoc, for example, the Château d'Angludet which, although rebuilt in the eighteenth century, was the lair of a notorious robber baron during the Hundred Years War. The Château d'Issan at Margaux also dates from the Anglo-Gascon alliance. With its nine pavilions and pyramid-topped towers, it has a fairy-tale appearance. The present buildings have succeeded two or three earlier structures at one time inhabited by famous French families.

Ornamented by its Grecian façade, Château Margaux is rather more than the most famous "label" in the world. It once belonged to King Edward III of England. In the twelfth century, it was known by the name of La Mothe. At that time it was, of course, a fortified castle. It was successively the property of the d'Albret, de Montferrand and de Durfort families. Towards the middle of the eighteenth century, its then owner, Monsieur de Fumel, assisted the Marquis de Lafayette to embark for America, despite the Court. The present owner of Château Margaux is Mr. Pierre Ginestet, Grand Chancellor of the Bordeaux Wine Academy.

A little to the north, at Pauillac, Château Mouton-Rothschild has known four generations of the Barons de Rothschild since 1853. In the more remote past, the great winegrowers of Mouton were the Seigneur de Pons (1350), the Duke of Gloucester (1430), Jean Dunois, Gaston de Foix, the Dukes of Joyeuse and the Dukes of Epernon. Baron Philippe de Rothschild, the present proprietor, has established a superb wine museum adjacent to the wine-sheds of the Château. The objects on display are rich beyond compare but give not the slightest impression of ostentation. They include a Mycenean goblet of the thirteenth century B.C., masterpieces of the German goldsmith's art and paintings by Picasso, Giacometti and Juan Gris.

The labels for Château Mouton-Rothschild are very original and easily recognised. Each year, Baron Philippe commissions an artist to illustrate the upper part of his label, so that it is possible to call a Mouton-Rothschild 1960 a Mouton-Rothschild-Villon.

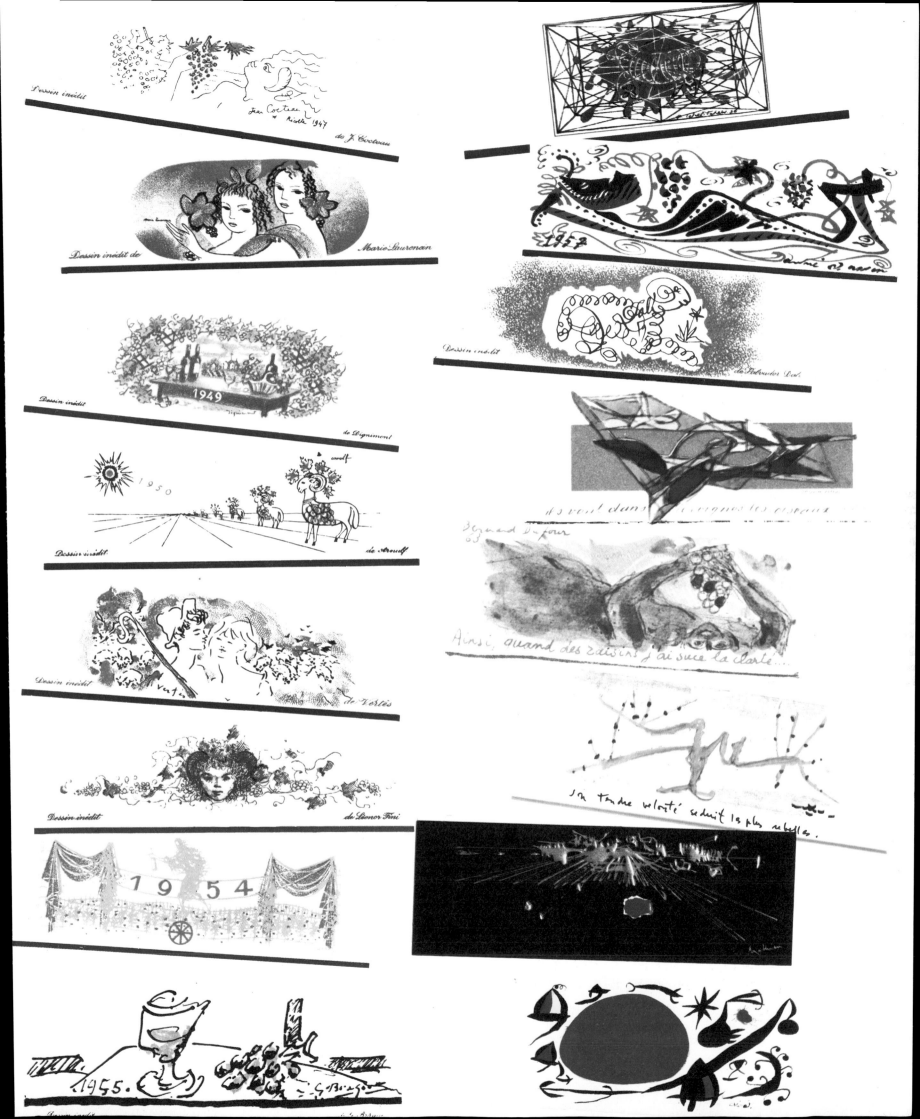

Dessin inédit

Jean Cocteau
* Milly 1947

de J. Cocteau

Dessin inédit de

Marie Laurencin

1957

de André Derain

Dessin inédit

1949

de Dignimont

Dessin inédit

de Salvador Dali

1950

Dessin inédit

de Arnulf

ils vont dans les vignes les oiseaux

Dessin inédit

de Vertès

Bernard Dufour
63

Ainsi, quand des raisins j'ai sucé la clarté....

Dessin inédit

de Leonor Fini

Sa tendre volupté séduit les plus rebelles.

1 9 5 4

1955.

G. Braque

Dessin inédit

de G. Braque

Since time immemorial, the lands of Graves have surrounded Bordeaux, except on the east where the ancient city is bounded by the river. Since the vineyards of Bordeaux are primarily a creation of the city, Graves has always been their focal point. It was not the vineyard which gave birth to the town but the citizens of Bordeaux who, having planted the civilizing grape, lavished the most constant and attentive care upon it and honoured it as a divinity. In the Middle Ages, the grape was still being harvested *intra muros*, in the very centre of Bordeaux. The Gascon terriers (land-holding registers) have revealed the existence of a vineyard entirely within the town, the harvest from which was sufficient to stock the cellars of the *Jurats* and the chapters. By the end of September, baskets were being filled with grapes in the Rue de Saint-Genès, near St. Nicholas' Church, at the Croix-Blanche, at Terre-Nègre, in the Place Dauphine, at the Palais-Gallien and the Rue des Capérans, charming spots which the ravages of urbanization have not spared. Nowadays, the vineyard of Graves begins at the Jalle de Blanquefort, the southern boundary of the Médoc. To the south, it extends as far as Langon, having left the river at Virelade to encircle the Cérons and Sauternes-Barsac areas as, to the north, it once encircled the former Burdigala. Its total length is 38 miles and its average width does not exceed six miles.

It was for the wine of Graves (and not for the others which were then too far from Bordeaux) that the collegiate government of the city proclaimed the edicts forming the basis of the most extraordinary legal monument of all time: the famous *Privilège des Vins*, as evidenced by the highly secret records of the deliberations of the *Jurade*, otherwise called the *Livre des Bouillons* from the copper bosses—*boullons*—which protected its cover.

Halfway through the Middle Ages, with the same eagerness to regulate everything, the *Jurade* of Bordeaux set up the official corps of Taverners. Although this seemed, at first sight, an attempt to introduce a police force into the wineshops and keep them orderly, the main objective of the *Jurats*, in this case, was to control frauds within the municipal jurisdiction. For example, to help sales of nondescript wines, it had been customary to cry "a very drinkable wine of Graves". This commercial misrepresentation now became impossible, and much too dangerous for an official clothed in all the majesty of the municipality.

Moreover, all the control measures applied at both the production and distribution stages and which had such a favourable effect on the reputation of Bordeaux wines, originated from the desire felt by the winegrowing burghers to protect their urban growths, i.e. the place-name description GRAVES. That is why the Bordeaux archives for the sixteenth, seventeenth and eighteenth centuries reveal the names and activities of the inspectors of urban vineyards, an office that was already of very ancient foundation.

Today, in our mind's eye, we can see these velvet-clad burghers jogging on horseback across the vineyards. The warm, juicy bunches are presented to them on white cloths and we see them, having brushed away a greedy wasp with a gloved and beringed hand, tasting a grape thoughtfully and then, raising their heads, gazing wisely and reflectively at the vine.

In permanent session throughout the harvest time, the *Jurade* would listen to the reports of its itinerant experts and, after debate, would fix the day on which the grape pickers, the *laborador de vinhas* could begin picking with the best chance of obtaining a wine of quality. The great bell of the City Hall would then "ring in the wine-harvest".

The period when there was no Bordeaux wine other than Graves was, *par excellence*, the time of CLARET. The English gave the name to the produce of a region much smaller than the Bordeaux region of today but the antiquity of which, as compared with the Bordeaux winegrowing area as a whole, is unquestionable.

Much closer to us, in the middle of the eighteenth century, any red Bordeaux exported to Germany became, for the importing wine merchant, Pontac wine, the name of the then owner of Château Haut-Brion, the uncrowned king of Graves. The future member of the "big four" served as an insignia for the whole vineyard, a century before the 1855 classification.

During the whole nineteenth century the place-name description GRAVES was predominantly "red". Nowadays, in the second half of the twentieth century, the grape distribution has virtually returned to what it was in its hey-day, namely, the era when the harvests of La Brède and Martillac were gathered by Charles Secondat de Montesquieu. This new balance between whites and reds is, perhaps, mainly due to the fact that the city of Bordeaux for the last two hundred years has been extending its limits, intensifying building operations and swallowing up communes which were formerly famous for their production of red wine: Caudéran, Talence, Mérignac etc. Moreover, ten miles to the south of Bordeaux, in centres such as Léognan which had been entirely devoted to red grapes before the phylloxera crisis, whole estates have been replanted with white grapes. At present, the figures for the production of GRAVES are 1,033,906 gallons of white wine and 1,319,880 gallons of red.

However that may be, the white GRAVES have often reflected great glory on the place-name and have been deservedly fashionable, as has once again been the case during the last twenty years. But this fashion has never been the result of a snobbish insistence that white GRAVES should be this or that, that it must be dry or

semi-dry. It is what it has to be, whatever a few professional food-pundits may say. The white GRAVES harvested in the north of the region are naturally dry with a charming touch of acidity. At Martillac, La Brède, Saint-Morillon, Saint-Sèlve, Saint-Médard and Cadaujac, they are still dry but already softened by the suave bouquet characteristic of the soil of Léognan. Speaking of these thoroughbred wines, Rabelais described them as "gay and fluttering". At Portets, Arbanats, Landiras and Budos, they became more unctuous, trickling down the inside of the glass. The brokers distinguish these wines by saying they are fat. Lastly, the nearer we come to Langon, the more the wines are reminiscent of CERONS mellowness. In the Graves country, therefore, some less dry wines are found alongside the more numerous dry wines, all of them being admirable because they are quite natural.

Leaving aside all personal preference, however legitimate it might be, the soul of Bordeaux is undoubtedly to be found in a glass of red GRAVES.

As often happens in the case of the eldest of a large family, GRAVES bears the most striking resemblance to its father. MÉDOC, with its subtle and complex bouquet, or SAINT-EMILION, with its reckless gallantry, need envy their elder brother in nothing except the dominating fragrance which follows a red GRAVES everywhere like an invisible escutcheon. It is the perfume which has been transmitted from stock to stock and from vat to vat for over 2,000 years. One has to experience this privilege of the red GRAVES in order to become convinced.

That is what I must have perceived at a very early age when my grandfather first gave me a small piece of goatsmilk cheese (to clean my palate) and after it a finger of HAUT-BRION 1888. In that already remote period, the growth was not called a red GRAVES, as it is today, but a GRAVES DE BORDEAUX. The memory of that initiation and of that inward resplendence has, once and for all, enabled me to identify a Bordeaux wine, whether noble or artisan, red or white, from the left bank or the right bank of the Garonne.

Of course, one has to be up-to-date. It must be realized that there has been, not a development of taste—taste has not developed since the Parthenon—but a certain depravation of taste. Some will claim that henceforth the general public will be looking for supple, round red wines; in other words, wines stripped of their authentic character. With respect to some products without breeding or which have been badly vinified, the general public may be perfectly right. It may well be that agreeable mediocrity is preferable to decayed and aggressive nobility. This is a valid point of view but for anyone who tasted his first GRAVES three or four years after his last feeding bottle, the criterion could never be that of the wine-canning industry.

A good GRAVES remains "as eternity itself has shaped it". It is food for the body and the soul. It has a luminous robe the colour of those rustic window-panes through which our childhood reveries recreated a summer twilight in the midst of winter. It is as elegant as the solution to a Euclidian theorem. Above all, since it is from Graves, it has that bracing and discreet bitterness that makes it kin to all the savours of the Bordeaux soil.

Direct in its taste, frank in its attack, though full of mysteries and chaste aromas, GRAVES rises from the depths of memory like a promise of happiness and peace, so needful in this anguish-stricken world.

THE CÉRONS REGION

Situated 22 miles to the south-east of Bordeaux, on the left bank of the Garonne, the Cérons region is made up of three communes: Cérons, Illats and Podensac. The boundaries of this place-name description are slightly fictional. There are dry CÉRONS wines which possess the characteristics of the finest GRAVES, the only distinction being a particularly fruity aroma, while other CÉRONS are closely related to SAUTERNES-BARSAC. The sweet CÉRONS are, however, lighter than the growths obtained in the soil of Barsac.

The soil of Cérons, silicious gravel over clayey limestone, is virtually the same as in Sauternes. To obtain sweet CÉRONS, picking is carried out (as in Sauternes) by successive stages and the must, which is comparatively less rich, nevertheless produces wines with a strength of 12° to 15° of alcohol and, in addition, 1° to 3° of *liqueur*. The CÉRONS type is distinguished by its nervousness, elegance and extremely fine bouquet. All these qualities, combined with the ambiguous position of the Cérons region, have caused its produces to be described as a link between the best dry white wines and the most famous of the great sweet wines.

In Cérons more than elsewhere, we thus encounter those imponderables which make white Bordeaux so variable. The place-name description produces annually an average each year of 219,980 gallons.

SAUTERNES-BARSAC

The essential originality of the winemaking process in the Sauternes area consists, first of all, in the method of harvesting.

Normal ripening is insufficient. The winegrower has to wait for the grape to become "overripe" and develop a rot which is so special, so peculiar to the microclimate that it is described as "noble". It is caused by a characteristic mycoderm, which flourishes only in certain winegrowing regions and which is called *botrytis cinerea*, a minute fungus which, in great years, produces the famous "roast" that can be recognized in old bottles.

The Bordelais winegrowing country is not particularly beautiful. But it is the type of soil that counts: on the surface is a layer of 'grave' or gravel which consists mostly of round, light-coloured pebbles, which make up a thin and meagre soil that is not adapted to other plants than the vine. Nevertheless, the vines planted there produce wines of the highest quality.

It is not always easy to turn the *botrytis* to best account. Its effect on a given bunch of grapes is not uniform. Hence the need to harvest by picking individual grapes. If it rains, picking has to be suspended until the grapes dry out. The result is that the harvest has to be staggered over a period of up to two months, and quantity is sacrificed to quality, yields being less than 170 gallons per acre.

Thanks to this process, which is quite unique in viticultural technology (it amounts to a veritable concentration of the vintage on the vine), the musts have a sugar content of between 15° and 20° or even more on leaving the press. In 1929, 25° was found while, in 1959, some musts were recorded which attained 30°.

In an average year, the ideal is to obtain a balance after fermentation between the alcohol content (14°) and the unconverted sugar content (4° of *liqueur*). In a very great vintage year, the divergence can be considerable. The care lavished on the wine-store is mainly aimed at activating alcoholic fermentation. As will be realized, the glory of SAUTERNES-BARSAC is an expensive one. There can never be any question, in this soil, of sacrificing the supreme, the "extravagant" quality to considerations of cost.

The wine of Sauternes-Barsac is still and will always remain one of the few things in this world whose inimitable nobility brushes aside the notion of "productivity", as conceived of by economists dealing in large quantities of ordinary consumer goods rather than rare products.

The Sauternais can best be compared, therefore, to a dream country ruled over by a wizard, the wizard being the most famous wine on earth, the wine of kings and the king of wines. The region must be entered deliberately, but once we are there, time seems to lose its meaning and the ordinary world, humming with cares and duties, drifts far away from our eyes and from our memories. All the enchantments of this magic land weave round us a fairy net which holds us willing prisoners in a life of rarest pleasure.

I can remember a fine afternoon in June. The park of the Château of Suduiraut appeared, under a thrilling sky, to be rising out of the vaporous haze which bathes Fragonard's *Fête de Saint-Cloud* or Jean-Baptiste Pater's *Garden Party*, or was it the slight mist of the *Embarkation for Cythera*? Maurice Chevalier was singing, clutching a jeroboam of CHÂTEAU D'YQUEM to his breast, proving that there are mysterious affinities between the most varied forms of art. The only condition to be fulfilled is that, however appearances may change, artistic creation must remain faithful to the classic standards of quality. What music, painting and song offer us in their highest forms is also to be found in the subtle bouquet of a SAUTERNES-BARSAC. That is why you should make the circuit of the Sauternes country (which is well signposted for the visitor) at a slow speed with the engine barely ticking over, just as you move slowly and appreciatively past the wonderful masterpieces in the Uffizi Gallery.

There are some discoveries that are worthless unless you make them for yourself. In the Palazzo Vecchio in Florence, for example, I came across the most intelligent of guides. He watches visitors coming, going, dreaming, strolling and sometimes retracing their steps (which is so important). Then, smiling, he intervenes, simply because someone has overlooked something he loves. I should like to imitate him and not drag the reader by main force to the entrance of a vineyard if he is attracted by the slate-crowned roof of a tower. Let it suffice that, en route, you do not neglect a growth which, once known, will have a permanent place in your heart and in your memory. Whether you approach the Sauternais circuit from the beginning or from the end, you will find only one road marked "No Entry": the road to mediocrity. It is a magic carpet straight out of a fairy-tale and, if the turnings appear frequent, it could be that your head might be turning round a little.

THE WINES BETWEEN
THE GARONNE AND THE DORDOGNE

PREMIÈRES CÔTES DE BORDEAUX

When the contemporaries of Ausonius visited him, they did so languorously stretched out in boats furnished with carpets and cushions, under canopies of laurel branches and with pennants streaming. This patrician luxury which was shared by winegrowers and poets, men of the world and philosophers in an intimate society marks the zenith of the region now called the Premières Côtes de Bordeaux. This place-name description covers thirty-four communes along the right bank of the Garonne, between Bassens and Saint-Macaire. It is essentially an area of abrupt slopes which dominate the river for 38 miles. The plateaux of Entre-Deux-Mers (Between the Two Seas) forms its hinterland as far as the left bank of the Dordogne.

Despite its exceptional length and the size of its production (1,759,840 gallons), the Premières Côtes region produces growths which head the list at international exhibitions. Although the northern part of the region is almost exclusively devoted to red wines, the southern part, beyond Gambes, covers what are usually called the great white wines of the right bank.

The red PREMIÈRES CÔTES DE BORDEAUX were undoubtedly among the first Bordeaux wines regularly exported. Pey Berland, the last Gascon Archbishop of Bordeaux, possessed an important red vineyard in the Parish of Bouillac. Under the archiepiscopal privileges, therefore, it was a PREMIÈRES CÔTES DE BORDEAUX growth which the English, on their arrival with the "wine fleet", would purchase as a first priority.

When young, these wines are robust, fruity, rich in tannin and very tonic. With age, they acquire considerable delicacy and the bouquet characteristic of the Bordeaux soil. As for the white, semi-dry or sweet PREMIÈRES CÔTES DE BORDEAUX, they sometimes reach such a degree of delicacy and elegance that their nobility requires some specific place-name descriptions in the form of enclaves: such is the case with CADILLAC and GABARNAC.

LOUPIAC AND SAINTE-CROIX-DU-MONT

Loupiac and Sainte-Croix-du-Mont are also enclaves in the PREMIÈRES CÔTES DE BORDEAUX but have no legal connection with the latter place-name description.

Both LOUPIAC and SAINTE-CROIX-DU-MONT belong to the kingdom of the *Semillon, Sauvignon* and *Muscadelle*

grapes. Apart from this triumvirate, no other grape is permitted to enter into the composition of these illustrious sweet growths. On the abrupt and sunny slopes, the bunches of grapes are not picked until they have reached a subtle degree of overripeness. And yet, what delicacy, what tang of the soil is to be found in a LOUPIAC or a SAINTE-CROIX! What gaiety is to be found in one or another of these bottles! Without wearing the sumptuous garb of a SAUTERNES, they too evoke the bronze satin in which Watteau dresses the beauties in his enchanted parks.

The Bordeaux vineyards contain 50 A.O.C.s, several classifications, and more than 3,000 châteaux. 'Château Camarsac' belongs to one of the four general appellations: Bordeaux, Bordeaux supérieur, Bordeaux clairet and Bordeaux mousseux.

179

The sweet warmth of these wines, their bouquet, their topaz robe go beyond the vocabulary of the gourmet; it would need the music of a Verlaine poem to give an adequate impression of so much grace.

The boundary of the place-name description LOUPIAC is a little to the south of Cadillac, whose best growths are in no way inferior to those of the two gems of the PREMIÈRES CÔTES DE BORDEAUX.

HAUT-BENAUGE

The place-name description HAUT-BENAUGE is restricted to white wines produced by the communes of Arbis, Cantois, Escoussans, Ladaux, Soulignac, Saint-Pierre-de-Bat and Targon. This region, although much smaller than the former county of Benauge, has nevertheless retained as its centre the enormous and majestic castle built by the redoubtable Lords of Benauge on the hill of Arbis. In former times, the county was called "Black Benauge" and was darkened by the oak forests from which was obtained the timber for the manufacture of the *barriques*. But the winegrowers cleared the land and, ever since, the serried ranks of vine-stocks have occupied the flanks of the valleys. Black Benauge is one of the world's most beautiful viticultural areas. It produces a white, semi-dry wine which has harvested awards and medals.

CÔTES DE BORDEAUX-SAINT-MACAIRE

The place-name description Côtes de Bordeaux-Saint-Macaire extends the Premières Côtes de Bordeaux towards the south. It covers the communes of Saint-Macaire, Pian, Saint-Pierre-d'Aurillac, Saint-Martin-de-Sescas, Caudrot, Saint-André-du-Bois, Saint-Martial, Saint-Laurent-du-Bois, Saint-Laurent-du-Plan and Sainte-Foy-la-Longue. Few white wines are so adaptable as CÔTES DE BORDEAUX-SAINT-MACAIRE. Robust and fine, they form an agreeable accompaniment to sea-food as well as to desserts and even certain roasts.

GRAVES DE VAYRES

In the vicinity of Libourne, on the ancient road which once linked Burdigala to Lutetia, the communes of Vayres and Arveyres, on the left bank of the Dordogne, constitute the winegrowing territory entitled to the place-name description GRAVES DE VAYRES. This designates a colourful and subtle red wine, of great delicacy, reminiscent of the second growth of POMEROL and endowed with the precious commercial quality of being drinkable at an early age. The white wines from the same soil can be distinguished from the excellent products of Entre-Deux-Mers by their mellowness and their very typical aroma.

SAINTE-FOY-BORDEAUX

The canton of Sainte-Foy-la-Grande comprises only fifteen communes, but the controlled place-name description SAINTE-FOY-BORDEAUX has nineteen. They have been detached from the north-eastern part of the vast Entre-Deux-Mers region to delimit a sweet or semi-dry white wine, the dominant characteristics of which are suppleness and elegance. Coming from the Périgord confines of the Bordeaux country, this white wine is, if dry, a perfect foil for the oysters, shellfish and delicious shad caught in the Dordogne.

ENTRE-DEUX-MERS

Entre-Deux-Mers is a name which really appeals to the imagination. It evokes all kinds of ideas of distant voyages and unknown lands. People who are unfamiliar with the place-names of these great winegrowing regions are generally disappointed to learn that "Between the Two Seas" refers to the territory between the right bank of the Garonne and the left bank of the Dordogne. The place-name description does not, of course, include those which have just been defined but it nevertheless extends over the largest and most productive part of the Bordeaux vineyard, and in fact, covers one-fifth of the area of the department. The spontaneous luxuriance of the vegetation in Entre-Deux-Mers and the survival of large tracts of oak, hornbeam and elm are relics of the ancient forest cleared by the Romans to plant the civilizing vine. After the Barbarian invasions, immense tracts of these woodlands reappeared and, this time, it was the monks who launched a new attack on the hardy forest mass. The Abbey of Saint-Girard, at La Sauve, was founded in 1090. For centuries, this community shared, with the monks of Sainte-Croix, at Bordeaux, the privilege of supervising the winegrowing destiny of Entre-Deux-Mers. In 1547, a wine of the region was selling for 20 to 25 crowns the *tonneau* as against only 18 to 22 crowns for a Libournais-Fronsadais product. The place-name description of origin ENTRE-DEUX-MERS, which has been defined since 1924, became a guaranteed description by the decree of July 31th, 1937. According to this legal instrument, the place-name description can only be applied to white wines made exclusively from the noble grapes : *Sauvignon*, *Semillon*, *Muscadelle*, and *Merlot*, harvested within the area delimited. Red wines of the same origin are called simply BORDEAUX.

In the last few years, spurred on by the youthful officers of its viticultural syndicate, ENTRE-DEUX-MERS has regained its ancient fame. This was achieved through a policy strongly emphasizing quality which is intended to give this dry white wine back its natural characteristics. Fifteen years ago, the persons responsible for the place-name description decided to increase the proportion of *Sauvignon* in the vineyards. As this

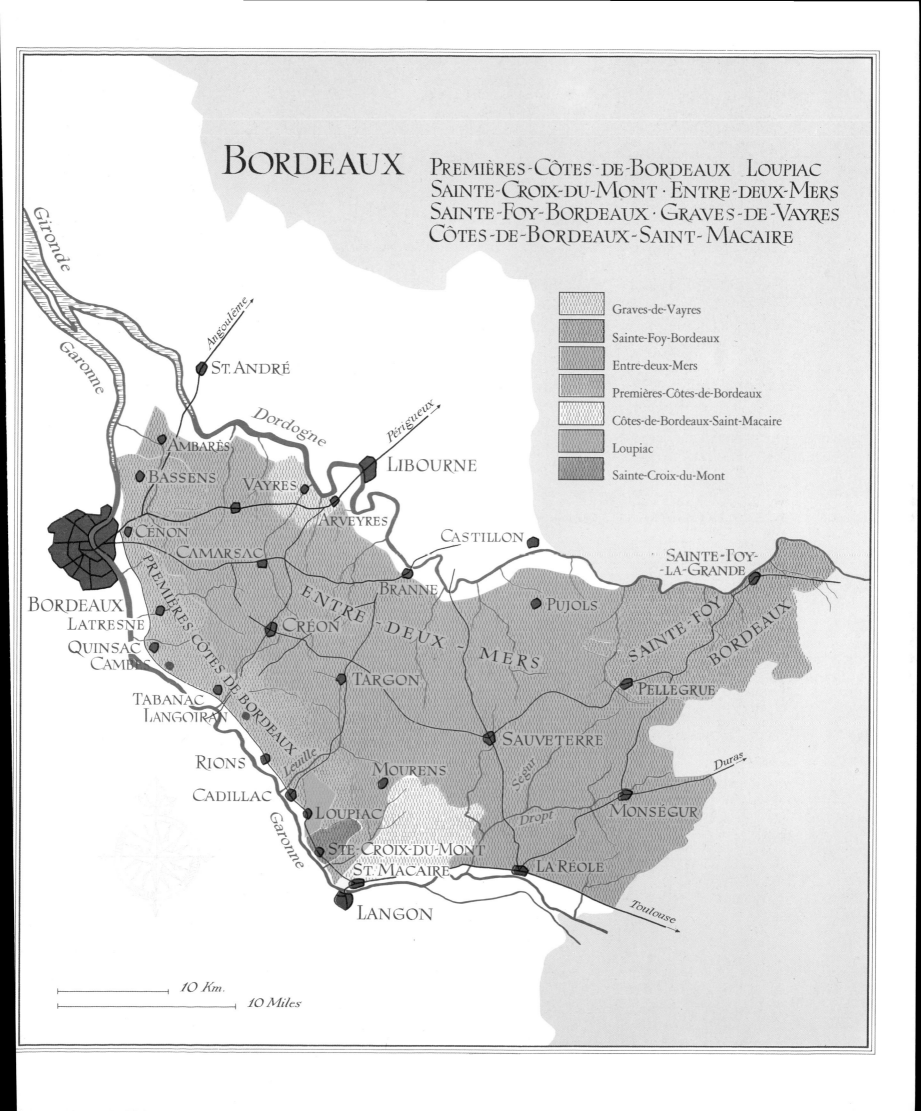

BORDEAUX

PREMIÈRES-CÔTES-DE-BORDEAUX · LOUPIAC
SAINTE-CROIX-DU-MONT · ENTRE-DEUX-MERS
SAINTE-FOY-BORDEAUX · GRAVES-DE-VAYRES
CÔTES-DE-BORDEAUX-SAINT-MACAIRE

- Graves-de-Vayres
- Sainte-Foy-Bordeaux
- Entre-deux-Mers
- Premières-Côtes-de-Bordeaux
- Côtes-de-Bordeaux-Saint-Macaire
- Loupiac
- Sainte-Croix-du-Mont

Gironde

Garonne

Angoulême

ST. ANDRÉ

Dordogne

Périgueux

LIBOURNE

AMBARÈS

BASSENS

VAYRES

ARVEYRES

CÉNON

CAMARSAC

CASTILLON

SAINTE-FOY-LA-GRANDE

BORDEAUX

LATRESNE

BRANNE

PUJOLS

ENTRE-DEUX-MERS

SAINTE-FOY BORDEAUX

QUINSAC
CAMBES

CRÉON

PREMIÈRES CÔTES DE BORDEAUX

TABANAC
LANGOIRAN

TARGON

PELLEGRUE

SAUVETERRE

Duras

RIONS

Leuille

MOURENS

Ségur

CADILLAC

Dropt

MONSÉGUR

LOUPIAC

Garonne

STE-CROIX-DU-MONT

ST. MACAIRE

LA RÉOLE

LANGON

Toulouse

10 Km.

10 Miles

trend has continued ever since whenever new vines were being planted, ENTRE-DEUX-MERS has once again become a very fruity and recognizable wine, both fresh and nervous, which meets the requirements of the consumer of today. It should not be forgotten, however, that ENTRE-DEUX-MERS is a Bordeaux wine. In other words, it is an hygienic wine, a healthy wine, just like the red wines of similar origin. In addition to the incomparable satisfaction to the taste buds, it possesses other important qualities which should be mentioned: its richness in vitamin P and its high bactericidal power which is completely independent of its alcoholic content. Invigorating, tonic and diuretic, it is just the wine for people who have difficulty in taking other white wines. It is an unfailing destroyer of the pathogens which are found in raw vegetables and well-informed doctors do not hesitate to attribute to it therapeutic virtues also. All this has been known empirically for a very long time, but serious studies carried out by learned professors and their pupils in the laboratories and universities on ENTRE-DEUX-MERS have made it possible to formulate it scientifically.

The Entre-Deux-Mers region (here at St Jean-de-Blagnac) extends along the plateau and the slopes lying between the rivers Dordogne and Garonne in the Gironde department. The wines are only white; fresh, with a flinty taste, they are dry or very slightly sweet.

THE WINES OF THE RIGHT BANK OF THE DORDOGNE AND THE GIRONDE

SAINT-EMILION

On the right bank of the Dordogne, Saint-Emilion and its vineyards are high places where the wind of the spirit blows free. The whole of France and a good part of the civilized world can testify to that.

The "great" little city—with apologies for the paradox—has known a cosmopolitan animation every year since very ancient times. In fact, Camille Jullian, in his history of the Gauls, states that Saint-Emilion was one of the ritual stages on the journey to Compostella. A pious and motley crowd always filled the monolithic church. An extraordinary vitality and spirituality overflowed from those narrow streets and corbelled houses, and faith in a world in which men were brothers was proclaimed from all the towers in joyous peals of bells and in solemn fanfares of trumpets.

At Saint-Emilion, the tumultuous heartbeat of French history can be felt. Here and there, as you walk about the town, you suddenly encounter an astonishingly fresh vision of the past, whether it be the Tour du Roi or the Grotte des Girondins. But in this acropolis where all the friends of wine come to worship together in the high traditions of the past, there are other voices than those of stones, vigorous human voices raised in eloquent testimony of the centuries which have passed.

Today as yesterday, the vine and wine are the reason for living, the cause of happiness and, sometimes, suffering for the viticultural peoples of the eight communes which make up the place-name description: Saint-Emilion, Saint-Laurent-des-Combes, Saint-Hippolyte, Saint-Christophe-des-Bardes, Saint-Etienne-de-Lisse, Saint-Sulpice-des-Faleyrens, Saint-Pey-d'Armens and Vignonet. The area of the place-name description amounts to 11,250 acres.

In our days, the poets have glorified the powerful and noble wine of SAINT-EMILION, as did Henri d'Andeli in the eleventh century. Today we may still compare SAINT-EMILION to the nectar of the gods, as Louis XIV did in 1650. It is not only the town of stone which is immutable. As well known in the past as the wines of Graves, the wines of Saint-Emilion continue their royal career without any artificial vinification. When the weight of years has broken down the other wines and has left in the bottles nothing but a tasteless and colourless water, then it is that SAINT-EMILION develops all its wealth and all its perfume. "The wine of Saint-Emilion," wrote Victor Rendu, "has body, a beautiful colour, an agreeable delicacy, generosity and a special bouquet which is found in particular in the best sections of this distinguished vineyard. Good Saint-Emilion wine should, after its early years, have a dark, brilliant and velvety colour and a touch of bitterness which flatters the palate. In addition, it must have body which does not prevent it from becoming very smooth at a later stage. It becomes very much finer after six months in bottle but does not reach its full perfection until it is from 6 to 10 years old."

The most prestigious domains of the place-name description have recently been granted a classification but are still subject to the rigorous quality control exercised by the illustrious *Jurade* and the Saint-Emilion Viticultural and Agricultural Syndicate, which is alone entitled to bestow upon the wine a "certificate of approval" for marketing.

In addition to the communes entitled to the simple place-name description, the following five others have obtained the right to add Saint-Emilion to their own names: SAINT-GEORGES-SAINT-EMILION, MONTAGNE-SAINT-EMILION, LUSSAC-SAINT-EMILION, PUISSEGUIN-SAINT-EMILION, PARSAC-SAINT-EMILION.

As for the special place-name description SABLES-SAINT-EMILION, this refers to a small part of the commune of Libourne, between Saint-Emilion and Pomerol, which produces excellent red wines which are subtle and fragrant and mature quite quickly.

POMEROL AND ITS REGION

The commune of Pomerol, which covers 1,550 acres, is a few miles to the north-east of Libourne. It is bordered by the vineyards of Saint-Emilion to the east and of Fronsac to the west.

As far back as history records, the existence of Pomerol is evidenced by memorials of every kind. This clayey-gravel plateau was crossed by a Roman road which the winegrower poet Ausonius had to take when travalling from the port of Condat, on the Dordogne, to his magnificent villa of Lucaniacus near Saint-Emilion.

In the Middle Ages, the Knights Hospitallers of St. John established their first commandery at Pomerol. From the twelfth century onwards, therefore, the famous borough was endowed with a fortified manor, a hospital and a Romanesque church which has now, unfortunately, disappeared.

With the Knights Hospitallers, as in the time of the Romans, the vine was in high honour in Pomerol. But

the Hundred Years War which, of course, lasted three centuries, was not very kind to this ancient countryside. Time and time again, French and Anglo-Gascons turned the parish into a battlefield. Moreover, as long as Pomerol remained under the fleur-de-lis, its wine could not take the Bordeaux road, i.e. they could not be sold to its good and faithful English customers. However, after the decisive French victory at Castillon in 1453, which entailed the surrender of Guienne, the wines of Pomerol made rapid progress in gaining a reputation and soon became one of the most precious jewels in the Bordeaux crown.

For these are complete wines which gladden both the nose and the palate. These growths have a fine and generous vinosity which comes from grapes such as the *Bouchet* and the *Merlot*. While retaining the delicacy of the SAINT-EMILION wines, they also approach the wines of the Médoc. POMEROL wines go extremely well with red meat, game and cheese.

In certain vineyards, such as Saint-Emilion (photo), there have recently appeared strange harvesting machines which enable the grapes to be gathered more quickly and less expensively. However, this method of harvesting can only be used in large vineyards that are flat and without other obstacles.

184

The guaranteed place-name description LALANDE DE POMEROL, with its soil varying from siliceous clay to clayey gravel, produces fine red wines comparable with those of its famous neighbour. Next door, the commune of Néac, which corresponds exactly to the area of the place-name description, contains a some 740-acre vineyard. The NÉACS are generally supple, velvety, full-bodied and have a strong bouquet. Although it is impossible to establish any absolute rule in this field, it is agreed that the First Growths of NÉAC are roughly comparable with the second First Growths of POMEROL.

CÔTES DE FRONSAC

When crossing the Bordeaux country on his return from Spain, Charlemagne had fortifications built on the knoll of Fronsac which commands the Dordogne. This fortress became the bastion *par excellence* of the strategic region. The enormous castle still existed in the fifteenth century, but it could not survive three days of battering by the artillery of Jean Bureau, Master of Artillery of France under Charles VII. Even genius is powerless to control the future. If Fronsac with its knoll deserves to be called a high place, it is not because of its military history. Fronsac is glorious for its red wines. High-coloured, robust and plump, with age they gain an exquisite distinction. They have never betrayed the attention given them by the flower-bearded emperor and, in more modern times, by the Duke of Richelieu (1706-1788), who was as famous for his knowledge of wine as for his amorous successes. Richelieu, who also held the title of Duke of Fronsac, built on the knoll one of those charming "follies" that the eighteenth century sprinkled throughout the Bordeaux region. In that house, he gave fashionable parties. It was about the same time that Richelieu introduced the wine of Bordeaux to the Court of France.

On the legal plane, the description FRONSAC does not exist. The name forms part of two separate place-name descriptions: CÔTES DE CANON-FRONSAC, which includes the best slopes, particularly that of Canon; and CÔTES DE FRONSAC.

CÔTES DE CASTILLON

The Côtes de Castillon comprise the territory of Castillon-sur-Dordogne (recently rebaptized Castillon-la-Bataille) and of several neighbouring communes. This is not only an ancient winegrowing region but also an historic site. Castillon-sur-Dordogne became Castillon-la-Bataille in 1953 when the commune celebrated the fifth centenary of the last battle of the Hundred Years War. It was at Castillon that Talbot, the English general, fell and Albion's continental ambitions melted away in the smoke of Charles VII's mortars. A dreary plain? No, indeed! The symmetrical rows of the

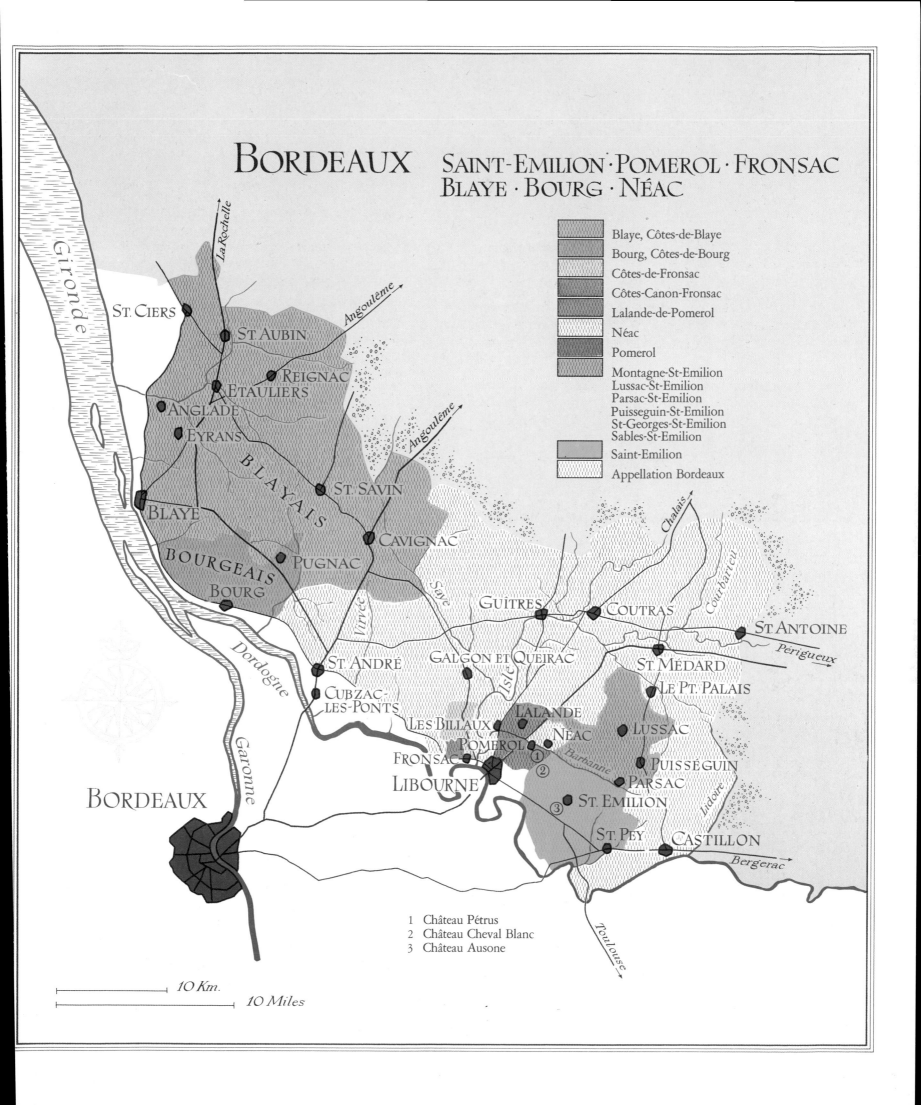

BORDEAUX

SAINT-EMILION · POMEROL · FRONSAC
BLAYE · BOURG · NÉAC

Légende:
- Blaye, Côtes-de-Blaye
- Bourg, Côtes-de-Bourg
- Côtes-de-Fronsac
- Côtes-Canon-Fronsac
- Lalande-de-Pomerol
- Néac
- Pomerol
- Montagne-St-Emilion
  Lussac-St-Emilion
  Parsac-St-Emilion
  Puisseguin-St-Emilion
  St-Georges-St-Emilion
  Sables-St-Emilion
- Saint-Emilion
- Appellation Bordeaux

Gironde

La Rochelle

Angoulême

St. Ciers

St. Aubin

Reignac

Etauliers

Anglade

Eyrans

BLAYAIS

St. Savin

Angoulême

Blaye

Cavignac

BOURGEAIS

Pugnac

Bourg

Saye

Virvée

Chalais

Courbarieu

Guîtres

Coutras

St. Antoine

Périgueux

St. André

Galgon et Queirac

Isle

St. Médard

Cubzac-les-Ponts

Le Pt. Palais

Dordogne

Les Billaux

Lalande

Néac

Lussac

Pomerol

① ②

Barbanne

Fronsac

Libourne

Puisséguin

Parsac

Lidoire

③

St. Emilion

BORDEAUX

Garonne

St. Pey

Castillon

Bergerac

Toulouse

1 Château Pétrus
2 Château Cheval Blanc
3 Château Ausone

10 Km.

10 Miles

vines are interrupted by fields of clover, alfalfa and maize in which tractors and a last few patient oxen carry out their manœuvres. In this fertile countryside, the ghosts of the past are imprisoned in a small circle traced out, from dawn to dusk, by the shadow of the cenotaph erected in memory of the illustrious defeated. Anyone, according to his sense of history, can put whatever he likes into an empty tomb. Filling one's glass is a much more serious procedure. Hence, no one should ever go to Castillon without taking the opportunity of tasting for himself the excellent wines which are entitled to carry this famous name. The red wines (80 per cent of the harvest) have a richly tinted robe, a generous fragrance and a full body which does not prevent them from acquiring great suppleness from at least the third racking onwards. In the spring following the vintage, they deserve a respectable place on the connoisseur's table. The white wines, which represent only a small part of the harvest, come from the north-west part of the area. Fine and delicate, they keep perfectly (The recognition of CÔTES-DE-CASTILLON by I.N.A.O., the National Institute of Descriptions of Origin, is fairly recent.)

Patiently, basket after basket, day after day, a few men carry on their shoulders the entire grape harvest of a château. It should be noted that it takes about 280 to 330 pounds of grapes to make twenty-two gallons of wine.

BOURGEAIS

The general appearance of the town of Bourg-sur-Gironde is that of a small fortified medieval city. It bears some resemblance to Saint-Emilion overhanging the valley of the Dordogne, but its origins may be even more ancient. Discoveries of the greatest interest dating from the palaeolithic and neolithic eras have been made in twenty-eight different spots at Bourg. Thousands of objects and tools have been found, tons of chipped flints and wall-carvings of great beauty. Many caves have yet to be explored. Such are the unquestionable proofs of the presence of prehistoric humanity in this large village.

It is clear that the first inhabitants of Bourg came from the Eyzies region through Rouffignac, the forest of La Double, the Entre-Deux-Mers and the Fronsac region. According to the theory dear to the heart of André Siegfried, they had quite naturally followed the "fall of the waters" and had halted in front of the immense estuary (which they took for the ocean itself), finally settling down to plant the vine on the slopes dominating its bank.

Some time ago, an English archaeological journal published an article on the villa of Ausonius at Bourg. It was situated on the outskirts of the town, towards the present Blaye-du-Bourg, on the slope facing the sea. Very comfortable and luxurious, like the other villas which the poet-consul possessed in Guienne, it was also the centre of an important vineyard. Ausonius himself speaks of it in clear and precise terms when singing the praises of the wine of Bourg. There seems good reason to believe that this vineyard had already been in existence for several centuries, since it takes much longer for a vine to produce a famous wine than for a poet to compose a poem!

From the Gallo-Roman epoch to the Middle Ages and the present day, the history of Bourg has been closely linked with that of Bordeaux. The two cities have the same love for the vine and for freedom. Without a break since 1273, the winegrowers and burghers of Bourg have elected their mayor and corporation. The last *Jurats* (wearing a hood and a livery of red and white damask) were elected two years before the Revolution. This proud commune was never the vassal of any lord apart from the greatest lord of all, the King. When the king was English, Bourg took advantage of his remoteness to stretch its liberties and privileges as far as was considered possible.

Thus the burghers of Bourg, unlike Archbishop Pey Berland, have felt the "wind of history" caress their walls and shiver among the vine shoots. They opposed no resistance to Charles VII. Basically animated by the same municipal passion as Bordeaux but more rural and less torn by Italian-style factions, Bourg was able to keep its unity and follow a single line of conduct while the metropolis of Aquitaine saw its cohesion break up under the pressure of events.

Everywhere the ground and the climate were favourable, monks planted and cultivated the vine, and this was equally true of the Bordeaux region. The Hundred Years War drove out the Dominicans from their monastery close to Saint-Emilion; nowadays, only sections of the walls of their church among the vines mark their passage.

It is hardly possible to say whether the virtues and wisdom of the Bourg vintners were responsible for the fame of the wine of this region, or vice-versa. Anyway, the fact is that this fame, which goes back to the dawn of history, was confirmed once again at the end of the eighteenth century by the chronicler Abbé Baurein: "The wines of Bourg were so esteemed in the last century that private individuals with property in the Bourgeais and in the Médoc would only sell their Bourg wine on condition that the purchaser also agreed to take

the Médoc." This evidence has been much contested in modern times but there are still proprietors with vineyards on both sides of the water.

The red wines of the Bourgeais are rich in vitamins, have a very agreeable bouquet and age excellently. As for the white wines, whether semi-dry or sweet, they are sturdy, nervous and full-bodied. It should be noted that some of the white wines do not have the right to carry the appellation BORDEAUX because of the types of grapes used to produce them.

A former staging point on the way to Compostella, the citadel of Blaye, built by Vauban in 1652 on the remains of a Roman *castrum*, is haunted by the ghost of Jauffré Rudel, the twelfth-century troubadour and poet of the Distant Love, and the more tragic shade of the Duchess of Berry, imprisoned in 1832 for attempting to organize an uprising against Louis Philippe.

The whole countryside is bathed in the poetry of the sea. It was selected as the locale for the film *Moderato Cantabile* with the 2½-mile wide estuary providing the backdrop. But the slopes overhanging the Gironde are covered with vines. "Opulent plains with gentle hillocks, sumptuous hills, abrupt spurs which defended Bordeaux against the Saracen and Norman invasions," so wrote E. Lacroix, "the lands of Blaye, coveted by the conquerors of the north and the south, still remain one of the finest flowers of the soil of France. Since the most ancient times, the vine, under a temperate sky, has occupied this privileged earth in which the limestones reluctantly surrender to the silicas and red clays which already announce the truffle-perfumed slopes of Périgord."

The wineproducing area of the place-name descriptions BLAYE and CÔTES-DE-BLAYE covers the cantons of Blaye, Saint-Savin and Saint-Ciers-sur-Gironde.

The simple description BLAYE deals expressly with both red and white wines. The first must come from the following grapes which, incidentally, are not all to be found elsewhere in the appellation BORDEAUX: *Cabernet, Béquignol* and *Verdot*. The use of any other grape cancels the right to the place-name description.

The white wines must be made from the following grapes: *Semillon, Sauvignon, Muscadelle, Merlot Blanc, Folle Blanche, Colombard, Pineau de la Loire* and *Frontignan*. The last four grapes are not encountered anywhere else in the place-name description BORDEAUX. In the place-name description CÔTES-DE-BLAYE, there is still some tolerance regarding grapes, at least as far as the red wines are concerned. In the case of the whites, only the classic trilogy of *Sauvignon, Semillon* and *Muscadelle* is permitted.

The reds are colourful, fruity and sweet, and gain by early bottling. The tannin and iron they contain recommend them as tonic wines. Of all the wines of the Gironde, they are perhaps the only ones whose savour recalls the good growths of Burgundy. The white wines are nervous and delicate. By one of nature's happy juxtapositions, they make an ideal accompaniment to the delicious oysters of Marennes whose beds are established on the nearby Seudre.

WINES OF THE NEIGHBOURING REGIONS

The basins of the Garonne, Dordogne and Adour are devoted to viticulture. We shall not go back to the problems which arose, at the beginning of the present century, with respect to these "marginal" vineyards when it was a question of marking out the boundaries of the production area of Bordeaux wine. In the long run, the autonomy granted to the "marginal" wines turned out to their advantage in that it made it possible for them to bring out their individuality.

Thus, the wine of Cahors, before being marketed in the "Port of the Moon" under the name of VIN DE HAUT-PAYS, had been sung by Horace and Virgil. Like the wines from the slopes of the Isle and the Lot and from around Bergerac, it is a powerful, highly-coloured red wine which, though rough in its youth, has a remarkable vinosity after a few years in the bottle. Its basic grape is the *Malbec* which gives it a very agreeable bouquet. The slopes of Marmandais, an area of mixed farming with an abundance of fertile orchards, also supply some agreeable red wines from near the great place-name descriptions of the Gironde. The CÔTES DE BUZET, also in Lot-et-Garonne, are V.D.Q.S. red wines (delimited wines of superior quality) which are fruity and light, supple and round. The VILLAUDRIC are red

wines harvested a few miles from Montauban which have the same qualities and also the advantage that they can be drunk young. On the Côte d'Argent and in the Basque country, the *gastronomade* (gourmet) takes pleasure in the growths of IROULEGUY, SAINT-ETIENNE-DE-BAIGORRY and ANHAUX. These are delicately fruity and act as an excellent foil to the local ham. The wines of Béarn are often vinified as rosé and are accommodating enough to go equally well with fish and with white meat. Astride two departments (Landes and Gers), the vineyard of Tursan was formerly quite famous and produces white and red wines as well as a few rosés with a very elegant bouquet. On the borders of Languedoc, Fronton also produces red, white and rosé wines, the principal outlet for which is Toulouse. Elegance and delicacy characterize the LAVILLEDIEU, red and white growths from Tarn-et-Garonne.

The wines of MONBAZILLAC can, in good years, compete with the best of the luscious white wines of Bordeaux, although their aroma is rather less complex. In this soil, which has long been famous, the wine-growers must, as in Sauternes and Barsac, await the "noble rot" before harvesting. In the first two or three years after picking, the MONBAZILLAC wines are very attractive and run like

liquid gold. It would be wrong, however, to yield to temptation. As they age, they acquire a deeper but no less luminous colour and, above all, develop their full character which then differs appreciably from that of a great luscious white wine of Bordeaux of similar age.

Without aspiring to the heights of the MONBAZILLAC, the dry, semi-dry or semi-sweet wines of BERGERAC have charm and a distinguished bouquet which, as André Lamondé wrote, make one celebrate the food-stuffs of that "land of Périgord paved with truffles and heavenly with *foie gras*". However, a type of BERGERAC of higher quality is to be found in the place-name descriptions CÔTES DE SAUSSIGNAC and CÔTES DE BERGERAC.

The Périgord poet Armand Got glorified MONTRAVEL in the following terms:

Montravel! Montravel!
Les sucs fruités, moelleux, d'un bouquet non pareil,
Les vins "de bonne foi" comme un "dict" de
Montaigne,
Qui font "vivre à propos" et sont de bon conseil.

Montravel! Montravel!
Mellow, fruity juices of a fragrance clear and wise,
Doughty wines which savour of a saying of
Montaigne,
Conducive to right living and magnanimous advice.

The simple place-name description MONTRAVEL is reserved for wines harvested in the plain. The place-name descriptions CÔTES DE MONTRAVEL and HAUT-MONTRAVEL cover less fertile soils and produce growths of a greater distinction. They are remarkably fruity and elegant. The best white wines of the Lot-et-Garonne are from the Côtes de Duras: less sweet than the MONTRAVEL wines, but fresh and delicate.

Decked in pale gold, ardent and heady, ROSETTE comes from the white grapes used in the Bordeaux country: *Semillon, Sauvignon* and *Muscadelle.*

The winegrowers of Gaillac were among those who, not so long ago, fought the most bitterly for inclusion in the place-name description BORDEAUX. Their wine is now managing very well on its own, thanks to the Confraternity of Bacchus to which part of their élite belongs. The sweet GAILLAC is a rough wine drunk very soon after the harvest. However, the guaranteed place-name description of origin GAILLAC indicates a dry white wine without excess acidity which is light and very drinkable. GAILLAC PREMIÈRES CÔTES has a fine colour and a great frankness of taste which it keeps in its age and which it owes to its dominant grape, the *Mauzac*, which has the peculiarity of producing a thick-skinned fruit which can ripen fully despite the rains of September. GAILLAC PERLÉ is a perfectly natural sparkling wine, no product other than the grape being used to obtain it. Without acidity or tartness, gushing with savoury cream, it is an exquisite "lady's wine", as the saying went half a century ago, in its lusciousness, deli-

cacy and relatively low alcohol content. The red wines are unequal in quality but the best of them have body, a fine colour and travel well.

Surrounded by a large area which produces only white wines, Madiran has a shrine sheltering a small wooden Virgin of great antiquity named Our Lady of the Vines. The vines in question are red. The chief growths of this Bigorre soil are ANGUIS, LE PARSAN, LES TUILERIES, LES TURCOS and HECHACQ. They are made from the noble grapes: *Cabernet Sauvignon* and *Cabernet Franc* which are used in the best holdings of the Bordeaux country. These wines have an aroma which is reminiscent of that of the grape-flower, a spare, very fluid scent which is obviously due to the *Cabernet.* Unfortunately, more fertile grapes have been introduced into the vineyards on the pretext of productivity. In the context of the new outlets offered by the Common Market, it would no doubt be a wise policy to eliminate these intruders. Tonic and digestive, MADIRAN keeps for a very long time. However, a sediment forms which adheres to the side of the bottle and the wine must be decanted.

Portet is the tiny capital of a winegrowing area which may, perhaps, be more ancient than that of Jurançon. It produces a white wine from a grape called *Pacherenc* with which the *Mansenc*, a Jurançon plant, is sometimes mixed. The harvest is late. Formerly, picking was still being carried out at Christmas. Nowadays, it is just about finished before the end of November. Hence the winegrowers of this countryside have been rather resistant to the benefits of modern oenology. The savours of their wine give themselves without evasion "like the virgins of Béarn" as Paul de Cassagnac, who admired this growth and its countryside, once wrote.

Caring little for fashion, PORTET is luscious, sweet or dry according to the caprices of nature. It maderizes readily but the winegrower is indifferent to this. He does not mind the maderized taste and he produces his wine for himself, not for the wine-merchant.

Some very interesting wines resembling the PORTET have been obtained at Lambeye, Montpezat and Crouzeilles, which are communes of the Vic-Bilh.

Even if there is no historic proof that Henry IV had his lips moistened at birth with Jurançon wine, this legendary episode continues to shed an immortal glory on the slopes in front of which the town of Pau was built. What is more, the scene is part of the spiritual heritage of our civilization. Whether authentic or not, it generally annoys and irritates the enemies of wine in France. It is by no means necessary, however, to resort to this reference to prove the nobility of a growth harvested at the end of autumn in the communes of Jurançon, Gan, Laroin, Saint-Faust, Aubertin and Monein. It owes nothing to anyone. None of the grapes which compose it has been identified in any other viticultural region. Very sensitive to oïdium, the large and small *Mansencs*, the *Cruchen* and the *Courbu* produce tight bunches of juice-heavy grapes which are naturally reduced, dried and candied on the vine, producing a veritable concen-

tration of the must before picking. The richness in sugar of this must is transformed into liquid without altering the delicacy of the final bouquet.

JURANÇON is in the first rank of the most famous sweet wines. It involves both the senses and the spirit and lends itself to that famous "after-taste" of which the great connoisseurs speak.

Around that great queen—a vintage bottle of Bordeaux—we find a host of noble companions and maids of honour which, according to protocol, may be less beautiful but are sometimes so pretty that, in a sense, they become her equal. The wines of the south-west form the retinue without which there could, of course, be no sovereign.

THE LIFE OF THE WINE PEOPLE IN THE BORDEAUX COUNTRY

In the last fifteen years or so, something has changed in the hearts and spirits of the Bordeaux winegrowers. They have not lost sight of the fact that the area of production is of paramount importance as regards the quality of the growth, but they have remembered that the origin of a wine is not enough to make it good, any more than the highest birth and impeccable ancestry will make a gentleman if his education be defective.

The rebirth of the three great pilot-confraternities of the Bordelais (*Jurade de Saint-Emilion, Commanderie du Bon-Temps Médoc et des Graves* and *Connétablie du Guyenne*) is due to this new viticultural psychology, although, in some cases, it has been the cause of it. The confraternities, by bringing together the wine professionals on a more human and humanist level than could be achieved by the trades unions, by reviving ancient handicraft and corporative traditions and by excluding all demagogy and disputes from their meetings, have

restored to a place of honour that comradely mentality which, in the past, was the glory of the guilds, even though the guilds were also syndicates which fought the authorities to retain their "privileges".

The modern Bordeaux confraternities have taken from these old associations only their noblest and most disinterested features and have left for the trades unions the technological and contentious aspects which all modern viticulture must entail, even if it has a thousand years of history behind it.

THE JURADE DE SAINT-EMILION

The development and prosperity of the Jurade de Saint-Emilion date from the twelfth century when Richard the Lionheart accorded it various privileges and freedoms. The most ancient document known

The most illustrious of all the Bordeaux whites comes from the 370 acres of the Château d'Yquem (above).

The first pressing operations often take place on the picking site. The baskets of the wine-pickers are emptied into the *baste*, a little tub of light wood containing about 5 1/2 gallons. The grapes are rammed down in the rudimentary manner shown in the picture.

190

concerning the town of Saint-Emilion is the Charter of Falaise, dated July 8th, 1199, in which on the death of his brother Richard, John Lackland confirmed the privileges granted by his predecessor. The great concessions made by the English kings were, of course, designed to create conditions under which the Bordeaux vintners could provide the best wine possible for the ever-thirsty English market.

This was the origin of the *Jurade*, composed, as the old writings put it, of "honest folk" elected by their fellow-citizens to administer with sovereign power the interests of the commune. As regards the cultivation of the vine and vinification, the *Jurats* displayed a tireless and scrupulous vigilance. They held the "vintner's mark" (a branding iron with the arms of the town), proclaimed the "ringing in" of the harvest, banned the sale of insufficiently "fine" wine and dealt rigorously with abuses and fraud.

From the tunning stage onwards, they watched over the quality of the growths, visited the wine-stores and cellars and checked the *barriques*. After which the "vintner" branded the casks of "good wine" with the coat of arms of the town. "Unworthy" wine was destroyed by fire. Lastly, the *Jurats* issued certificates without which it was forbidden to transport wine. These measures, which may appear excessively authoritarian, ensured the prosperity of the region through the resounding fame of SAINT-EMILION, which the English then called the king of wines.

The men of goodwill who, on September 13th, 1948, with due solemnity and authenticity reconstituted the *Jurade*, did not aspire to the political powers of their ancestors but limited themselves to the immense task of placing the wine of Saint-Emilion once again on the throne of its ancient splendours.

THE COMMANDERIE
DU BON-TEMPS MÉDOC ET DES GRAVES

Likewise, in October 1951, the men of the Médoc desired one thing and one thing only: to establish an organization which, in modern society, could really serve the cause of their wine, irrespective of classification or privilege, great growths and modest artisan growths alike, with the sole proviso that they were the good Médoc wines on which the universal glory of Bordeaux was founded.

Thus, under the distant patronage of a winegrowing religious order formerly active in Médoc, this utterly unique society was formed. It comprises the winegrowers, whether owners of famous châteaux or simple "bourgeois" growers, the wine-brokers (the link between production and trade) and, lastly, the wine-merchants who for centuries have been exporting Médoc throughout the whole world.

The *Commanderie* has taken as its emblem the wooden bowl which was well-known to the image-carvers of

The *Connétablie de Guienne*, here shown being solemnly received in the City Hall of Gouda in the Netherlands, revived in 1952 the title if not the administrative functions of an institution which in the Middle Ages had extensive influence in the Bordeaux country.

the gothic churches. This *bontemps*, or *lou desquet* as it is called in the local dialect, is a tiny piece of winemaking equipment used for beating the whites of eggs which are then "whipped" in the *barrique* of new wine to clarify it. The commanders' hats are shaped like the *desquet* and are topped by a white cover reminiscent of the beaten egg-whites. It is also with *lou desquet* that, in the wine-stores of the Médoc, when summer has come again, the happy marriage between the new harvest and the wine ready for bottling is achieved.

For some years now, the Médoc *Commanderie* has had two offshoots in the white-wine country: the *Commanderie du Bontemps de Sauternes-Barsac* (dressed in golden velvets) and the *Commanderie du Bontemps de Sainte-Croix-du-Mont* (in light-yellow linen).

THE CONNÉTABLIE DE GUIENNE

The *Connétablie de Guienne*, much referred to throughout the Middle Ages in the Bordeaux country, was the link which bound to the great mother-city the small winegrowing daughter towns which are still dotted along the banks of the Garonne and the Gironde. The important administrative functions of the Constable, with his headquarters in the Palais de l'Ombrière, though carefully distinguished from the attributions vested in the *Jurats* of Bordeaux, were inspired by the same concern: to serve the viticultural interest of the

seneschalcy by controlling the origin and the quality of the wines. Memory of those past ages aroused enthusiasm in the hearts of those who founded the contemporary *Connétablie*, in 1952. They were winegrowers from the Premières Côtes de Bordeaux, Entre-Deux-Mers, Benauge and part of Graves who were later joined by those of the Côtes de Bourg, Blaye and Saint-Macaire.

As the *Connétablie* marches by torchlight under the porticos of the quasi-royal Château of Cadillac-sur-Garonne, dressed in majestic black robes stamped with the golden cross, the moving rite of the enthronement unfolds in the barrel-vaulted crypt. While prominent personalities listen to the indictment which will open to them the gates of the Privy Council, the spectators feel themselves enveloped in ten centuries of history.

THE HOSPITALLERS OF POMEROL

It was at the beginning of the twelfth century that the powerful Hospitallers of St. John of Jerusalem chose Pomerol as the site for their first Commandery in Libournais. In the post-Roman era, it was they who, for nearly five centuries, cultivated the vine in that parish. From it they produced a wine regarded as a wonder for the comfort of pilgrims and the cure of the sick. In the spring of 1968, with the permission of the Sovereign

The 'maître de chais' or cellar-master composes his wine by blending musts from various grape varieties.

Order of Malta, the winegrowers of Pomerol reconstituted the Commandery which joined the other confraternities in the Grand Council of Bordeaux.

GRAND COUNCIL OF BORDEAUX

The Grand Council of Bordeaux is not still another confraternity but a high assembly which, during the Middle Ages, presided over the destiny of the city and of the province. At times of crisis, all the corporate bodies of Bordeaux and Guienne met in the Great Council for joint deliberation as to the decisions which should be taken with respect, chiefly, to the production of and trade in wine. That is what still happens today. Although it is true that the city among the vines reigns over a great variety of soils, it has but one soul and one history.

While respecting the personality of each of the viticultural regions of the Bordeaux country, the Grand Council is thus responsible for safeguarding and strengthening the idea of unity contained in the three words: wines of Bordeaux.

It has a dual significance. Within the limits of the Bordeaux country, it makes a reality of the necessary idea of association. Outside, particularly in new markets where the name of Bordeaux takes precedence over the numerous place-name descriptions of the Gironde, it makes it possible to fix the attention on a product whose great variety should not cause one to forget its unique provenance.

When all the confraternities are met together, the Grand Council holds chapters either at Bordeaux, in the House of Wine, headquarters of the Inter-Professional Wine Council of Bordeaux, or in great foreign cities during which, according to an ancient ritual, it awards to some highly privileged persons the title of "Companion of Bordeaux".

THE BORDEAUX WINE ACADEMY

The Bordeaux Wine Academy, which is not a confraternity either, is entitled to a seat in the Grand Council. It is an academy in the full sense of the word. Around a few celebrated writers who are members of the French Academy, it groups in all 40 life members belonging to Letters, Science and the Arts, the owners of Great Growths, winegrower merchants etc. It sits either in the city of Bordeaux itself or in the region's châteaux.

The aims of the Academy are noble in their humanism. The company puts in the forefront of its work the defence and the glorification of Bordeaux wine by the exact observance of refined tasting usage and the study of viticultural and winegrowing dialectics. It publishes annually a code of vintages which is not a simple scale of values applied to Bordeaux growths but a mass of information concerning the development of a number of harvests since 1920.

WINES OF BORDEAUX
LEFT BANK OF THE GARONNE AND OF THE GIRONDE

SAUTERNES AND BARSAC REGIONS • WHITE WINES

CLASSIFICATION OF THE GREAT GROWTHS OF 1855

Superior first growth . . . Château d'Yquem . . . Sauternes

First growths

Château La Tour-Blanche . . .	Bommes	Château Rabaud-Sigalas	Bommes	Château Climens	Barsac
Château Lafaurie-Peyraguey . .	»	Château Rabaud-Promis	»	Château Guiraud	Sauternes
Clos Haut-Peyraguey	»	Château de Suduiraut	Preignac	Château Rieussec	Fargues
Château Rayne-Vigneau	»	Château Coutet	Barsac		

Second growths

Château de Myrat	Barsac	Château Filhot	Sauternes	Château Romer	Preignac
Château Doisy-Daene	»	Château Broustet	Barsac	Château Lamothe	Sauternes
Château Doisy-Védrines	»	Château Caillou	»	Château Nairac	Barsac
Château Doisy	»	Château Suau	»		
Château d'Arche	Sauternes	Château de Malle	Preignac		

OTHER GREAT GROWTHS OF SAUTERNES AND BARSAC

Château Raymond-Lafon . . .	Sauternes	Château du Mayne	Barsac	Château Montjoie	Barsac
Château Lafon	»	Château Camperos.	»	Château Lapeloue	»
Château Lanère	»	Château Saint-Marc	»	Château Moura	»
Domaine du Coy	»	Château Gravas	»	Château des Rochers.	Preignac
Château Comarque	»	Château Latrézotte	»	Château Bastor-Lamontagne . .	»
Château d'Arche-Vimeney . . .	»	Château Villefranche.	»	Château d'Arche-Pugneau . . .	»
Château Haut-Bommes	Bommes	Clos des Princes	»	Château du Pick	»
Château Mauras	»	Clos du Roy	»	Domaine de Lamothe-Vigneau,	
Cru Bel-Air	»	Château Petit-Mayne	»	château des Remparts	»
Château Cameron	»	Château Brassens-Guiteronde . .	»	Domaine de la Forêt	»
Cru Bergeron	»	Château Fleury	»	Château Jonka	»
Château Le Hère	»	Château Simon	»	Château Saint-Amand	»
Château Lamourette	»	Château Jacques-le-Haut . . .	»	Château de Veyres	»
Domaine de Souba	»	Château Bouyot.	»	Château d'Armajan-des-Ormes .	»
Château Cantegril	Barsac	Cru Hournalas	»	Château Guimbalet	»
Château Baulac.	»	Château du Roc	»	Château Monteils	»
Château Piada	»	Château Grand-Mayne Guy-né-		Cru Peyraguey	»
Château Piot	»	Marc	»	Château Laribotte	»
Château Grillon	»	Château Simon Carrety	»	Château Fontebride	»
Château Mathalin	»	Château Menauta	»	Château du Mayne	»
Château Dudon	»	Château Coustet	»	Clos de l'Ecole	»
Château de Carles	»	Cru La Pinesse	»	Château Gilette	»
Château Guiteronde	»	Château Ducasse	»	Château Haut-Bergeron	»
Château La Clotte et Cazalis . .	»	Château Péchon	»	Château de Pleytegeat	»
Château Roumieu	»	Château Saint-Robert	»	Clos du Pape	Fargues
Château Massereau	»	Château Massereau-Lapachere .	»	Château de Fargues	»
Château Rolland	»	Château Mercier.	»	Cru Fillau	»
Château Pernaud	»	Château La Bouade	»	Cru Mothes	»
Château Prost	»	Château Grand Carretey	»	Château Paillon-Claverie	»
Château Luziès	»	Château L'Haouilley	»	Château Portarrieu	»
Château Liot	»	Château Jany	»	Château de Touilla	»
Château Hallet	»	Château Menate	»		

CÉRONS REGION • WHITE WINES

Château de Cérons et de Calvi-mont	Cérons	Château Mayne-Binet	Cérons	Château Haut-Mayne	Cérons
Grand enclos du Château de Cérons	»	Cru Larrouquey.	»	Clos Barail	»
Lalannette-Ferbos	»	Château Sylvain.	»	Domaine des Moulins à Vent . .	»
		Château Lamouroux	»	Cru de Peyroutène.	»

Domaine de Freyron	Cérons	Crus des Grands-Chênes	Cérons	Domaine de Castagnaou	Podensac
Château Beaulieu	»	Crus Ferbos-Lalanette	»	Château du Hau-Rat	Illats.
Château Grand Chemin	»	Cru des Moulins à Vent	»	Château Archambaud	»
Château Barthez	»	Clos des Moulins à Vent	»	Clos du Tauzin	»
Cru du Moulin-à-Vent	»	Domaine de Caillou	»	Château Cantau	»
Château des Bessanes	»	Château Méric	»	Château Beaulac	»
Cru Haut-Mayne	»	Cru du Moulin	»	Château Haut-La-Huntasse	»
Clos Bourgelat	»	Cru Haut-Belloc	»	Château Le Huzet	»
Château de l'Emigré	»	Cru Voltaire	»	Domaine de Calbet	»
Château Balestey	»	Clos Avocat	»	Château Thôme-Brousterot	»
Château du Seuil	»	Cru Larrouquey	»	Domaine de Prouzet	»
Cru de Du Peyrat	»	Cru Majans	»	Château Despeyrères	»
Clos de l'Avocat	»	Cru Cravaillas	»	Château Haut-Gravier	»
Château La Salette	»	Cru du Freyron	»	Domaine de Jaussan	»
Cru Dauphin	»	Cru Le Mayne	Podensac	Clos des Roches	»
Cru La Liste	»	Château d'Anice	»	Cru Navarot	»
Cru des Magens	»	Cru des Cabanes	»	Château Haut-Bourdat	»
Cru Menaut-Larrouquey	»	Château de Madère	»	Château Cazès	»
Cru Chacha	»	Cru Le Bourdieu	»	Clos du Bas Lancon	»
Cru de Pineau	»	Cru Boisson	»	Cru de Brazé	»
Clos Cantemerle	»	Cru Maucouade	»	Cru Haut-Boutoc	»
Cru Cleyrac	»	Cru du Brouillaou	»	Château Tinan	»
Château Lalanette	»	Cru Madérot	»	Cru de Lionne	»
Domaine du Salut, Château Huradin	»	A Mayne d'Imbert	»	Domaine de Gallier	»
		Domaine Le Cossu	»	Domaine de Menjon	

GRAVES REGION • WHITE WINES AND RED WINES

CLASSIFIED GROWTHS • I.N.A.O. classification officially recognized by the decree of February 16, 1959

RED WINES

Château Haut-Brion	Pessac	Château de Fieuzal	Léognan	Château Malartic-Lagravière	Léognan
Château Bouscaut	Cadaujac	Château Haut-Bailly	»	Château Olivier	»
Château Carbonnieux	Léognan	Château La Mission-Haut-Brion	Talence	Château Pape-Clément	Pessac
Domaine de Chevalier	»	Château La Tour-Haut-Brion	»	Château Smith Haut-Lafitte	Martillac
		Château La-Tour-Martillac	Martillac		

WHITE WINES

Château Bouscaut	Cadaujac	Château Couhins	Villenave-d'Ornon	Château Laville Haut-Brion	Talence
Château Carbonnieux	Léognan			Château Malartic-Lagravière	Léognan
Domaine de Chevalier	»	Château La-Tour-Martillac	Martillac	Château Olivier	»

The above classification is in alphabetical order, except for the Château Haut-Brion, classified in 1855

LIST OF THE PRINCIPAL GROWTHS

Château Haut-Brana	Pessac	Château Lespault	Martillac	Château des Fougères	La Brède
Château Haut-Carré	Talence	Château La Solitude	»	Château Guillaumot	»
Château Pique-Caillou	Mérignac	Château Lafargue	St-Médard-Eyrans	Domaine de Lasalle	»
Château Chêne-Vert	»	Château Lamothe		Cru de Magneau	»
Château Baret	Villenave-d'Ornon	Château de La Prade		Cru de Méric	»
Château Cantebau-Couhins	d'Ornon	Château Lusseau	Ayguemorte	Clos du Pape	»
Château Pontac-Monplaisir	»	Château du Méjan	morte	Château Bel-Air	St-Morillon
Château Bardins	Cadaujac	Château Saint-Jérôme	»	Château Belon	»
Château Malleret	»	Château Boiresse	»	Domaine de Gravette	»
Château Lamothe-Bouscaut	»	Château de Beauchêne	Beautiran	Domaine du Jau	»
Château Poumey	Gradignan	Château Grand Bourdieu	»	Château Piron	»
Château de France	Léognan	Château de Tuquet	»	Château du Bonnat	St-Selve
Château Gazin	»	Château Ferrande	Castres	Domaine du Barque	»
Domaine de Grand-Maison	»	Château Foucla	»	Domaine de La Peyrère	»
Château La Louvière	»	Château Bas-Pommarède	»	Château Bernard-Raymond	Portets
Château Larrivet-Haut-Brion	»	Château Pommarède de Haut	»	Château Cabannieux	»
Château Le Pape	»	Château Lognac	»	Château Crabitey	»
Château Chaviran	Martillac	Domaine de Sansaric	»	Château de Doms	»
Château Ferran	»	Château de La Brède	La Brède	Château Jean-Gervais	»
Château Lagarde	»	Cru de Bichon	»	Château des Graves	»
Château Malleprat	»	Château La Blancherie	»	Château Les Gravières	»
Château Haut-Nouchet	»	Château de l'Espérance	»	Domaine de La Girafe	»
Château La Roche	»	Cru d'Eyquem	»	Château de Graveyrion	»

194

Château Lagueloup	Portets	Château de Virelade	Virelade	Domaine d'Ordonnat	Langon
Château Lhospital	»	Château de Gayon	»	Clos Léhoul	»
Château Madelis	»	Château des Tilleuls	»	Château Ludeman	»
Château Millet	»	Château d'Arricaud	Landiras	Château Péran	»
Château Le Mirail	»	Château Batsères	»	Domaine de Toumilot	»
Château Moulin	»	Château Pessille	»	Château Bellefontaine	St-Pierre-
Château Pessan	»	Cru de Baylen	Budos	Clos Cantalot	de-Mons
Château du Pingoy	»	Château de Budos	»	Clos Cazebonne	»
Château de Portets	»	Château des Charmettes	»	Château des Jaubertes	»
Château Rahoul	»	Cru de l'Hermitage	»	Clos La Magine	»
Château La Tour-Bicheau	»	Domaine de Courbon	Toulenne	Château Magence	»
Domaine de Videau	»	Château de la Gravère	»	Clos du Moulin-à-Vent	»
Château Vieille-France	»	Clos Louloumet	»	Château Peydebayle	»
Cru du Bérot	Arbanats	Château Respide	»	Château des Queyrats	»
Château Mamin	»	Château La Tourte	»	Château de Respide	»
Domaine des Places	»	Château Tustoc	»	Château Toumillon	»
Château Tourteau-Chollet	»	Château Chanteloiseau	Langon	Clos d'Uza	»
Domaine de Teychon	»	Domaine des Gluchets	»		

MÉDOC REGION • RED WINES

GREAT GROWTHS OF THE 1855 CLASSIFICATION

First growths

Château Lafite-Rothschild, Pauillac   Château Margaux, Margaux   Château Latour, Pauillac   Château Mouton-Rothschild, Pauillac

Second growths

Château Brane-Cantenac	Cantenac	Château Léoville-Lascases	St-Julien	Château Rausan-Ségla	Margaux
Château Cos-d'Estournel	St-Estèphe	Château Léoville-Poyféré	»	Château Rauzan-Gassies	»
Château Montrose	»	Château Léoville-Barton	»	Château Pichon-Longueville	Pauillac
Château Ducru-Beaucaillou	St-Julien	Château Durfort-Vivens	Margaux	Château Pichon-Longueville-La-	
Château Gruaud-Laroze-Sarget	»	Château Lascombes	»	lande	»

Third growths

Château Kirwan,	Cantenac	Château Palmer	Cantenac	Château La Lagune	Ludon
Château Calon Ségur,	St-Estèphe	Château Desmirail	Margaux	Château Giscours	Labarde
Château Cantenac-Brown	Cantenac	Château Ferrière	»	Château Lagrange	St-Julien
Château Boyd-Cantenac	»	Château Malescot-Saint-Exupéry	»	Château Langoa	»
Château d'Issan	»	Château Marquis-d'Alesme-			
		Becker	»		

Fourth growths

Château Beychevelle	St-Julien	Château Talbot	St-Julien	Château Prieuré-Lichine	Margaux
Château Branaire-Ducru	»	Château Duhart-Milon	Pauillac	Château Pouget	Cantenac
Château Saint-Pierre	»	Château La Tour-Carnet	St-Laurent	Château Marquis-de-Therme	Margaux
				Château Lafon-Rochet	St-Estèphe

Fifth growths

Château Pontet-Canet	Pauillac	Château Haut-Bages-Libéral	Pauillac	Château Pédesclaux	Pauillac
Château Batailley	»	Château Lynch-Bages	»	Château Clerc-Milon	»
Château Haut-Batailley	»	Château Lynch-Moussas	»	Château Belgrave	St-Laurent
Château Croizet-Bages	»	Château Dauzac	Labarde	Château Camensac	»
Château Grand-Puy-Ducasse	»	Château Mouton-Baron-Philippe	Arsac	Château Cantemerle	Macau
Château Grand-Puy-Lacoste	»	Château Le Tertre	Pauillac	Château Cos-Labory	St-Estèphe

EXCEPTIONAL GROWTHS

Château Angludet	Cantenac	Château Bel-Air, Marquis d'Aligre	Sousans	Château Moulin-Riche	St-Julien
Château La Couronne	Pauillac	Château Chasse-Spleen	Moulis	Château Ville-Georges	Avensan

LIST OF THE PRINCIPAL BOURGEOIS GROWTHS ACCORDING TO THE SYNDICAL PRIZE-LIST OF MARCH 3, 1966

EXCEPTIONAL GREAT BOURGEOIS GROWTHS

Château Agassac	Ludon	Château La Closerie	Moulis	Château Houissant	St-Estèphe
Château Andron-Blanquet	St-Estèphe	Château Citran	Avensan	Château Lanessan	Cussac
Château Beausite	»	Château Le Crock	St-Estèphe	Château de Marbuzet	St-Estèphe
Château Le Boscq	»	Château Dutruch-Gd-Poujeaux	Moulis	Château Meyney	»
Château Capbern	»	Château du Glana	St-Julien	Château Phélan-Ségur	»
Château Caronne-Ste-Gemme	St-Laurent	Château Haut-Marbuzet	St-Estèphe	Château Villegeorge	Avensan

GREAT BOURGEOIS GROWTHS

Château	Commune	Château	Commune	Château	Commune
Château Belle-Rose	Pauillac	Château Hanteillan	Cissac	Château Paveil-de-Luze	Soussans
Château Bel-Orme	St-Seurin	Château Labégorce-Zédé	Margaux	Château Pibran	Pauillac
Château Bibian-Darriet	Listrac	Château Lafite-Canteloup	Ludon	Château Pomeys	Moulis
Château Le Bourdieu	Vertheuil	Château Lamarque	Lamarque	Château Potensac	Potensac
Château Le Breuil	Cissac	Château Laujac	Bégadan	Château du Raux	Cussac
Château La Cardonne	Blaignan	Château Lestage	Listrac	Château Rolland	Pauillac
Château Canteloup	St-Estèphe	Château Lestage-Darquier	Moulis	Château Saransot-Dupré	Listrac
Château du Castera	St-Germain	Château Liversan	St-Sauveur	Château Ségur	Parempuyre
Château Coufran	St-Seurin	Château Loudenne	St-Yzans	Château Sénéjac	Le Pian
Château Coutelin-Merville	St-Estèphe	Château Mac-Carthy	St-Estèphe	Châteaux Sociando-Mallet et Pontoise-Cabarrus	St-Seurin
Château Cissac	Cissac	Château Malleret	Le Pian	Château du Taillan	Le Taillan
Château Fonbadet	Pauillac	Château Morin	St-Estèphe	Château La Tour-de-By	Bégadan
Château Fonréaud	Listrac	Château Moulin à Vent	Moulis	Château Verdignan	St-Seurin
Château Fontesteau	St-Sauveur	Château Moulis	»		
Château Fourcas-Dupré	Listrac	Château Patache-d'Aux	Bégadan		
Château Grandis	St-Seurin				

BOURGEOIS GROWTHS

Château	Commune	Château	Commune	Château	Commune
Château Bel-Air-Lagrave	Moulis	Château Haut-Padarnac	Pauillac	Château Romefort	Cussac
Château Bonneau	St-Seurin	Château Larrivaux	Cissac	Château Roquegrave	Valeyrac
Château Bellegrave	Listrac	Cru Lassalle	Potensac	Château La Rose-Anseillan	Pauillac
Château de Come	St-Estèphe	Château Mac-Carthy-Moula	St-Estèphe	Château Saint-Bonnet	St-Christoly
Château Chambert	»	Château Malescasse	Lamarque	Château Saint-Christoly	»
Château Donissan	Listrac	Château Maurac	St-Seurin	Château Tayac et Siamois	Soussans
Château Grand-Duroc-Milon	Pauillac	Château Monthil	Bégadan	Château Les Ormes-Sorbet	Couquèques
Château La Fleur-Saint-Bonnet	St-Christoly	Clos du Moulin	St-Christoly	Château La Tour-Blanche	St-Christoly
Château La Fleur-Milon	Pauillac	Château Moulin-Rouge	Cussac	Château La Tour-des-Termes	St-Estèphe
Château Fonpiqueyre	St-Sauveur	Château Pabeau	St-Seurin	Château La Tour-St-Bonnet	St-Christoly
Château Fort-de-Vauban	Cussac	Château Le Privera	St-Christoly	Château Victoria	Vertheuil
Château Gallais-Bellevue	Potensac	Château Labatisse	St-Sauveur	Château Vieux-Moulin	Cussac
Château Grand-Saint-Julien	St-Julien	Château Renouil-Franquet	Moulis		

SOME OTHER BOURGEOIS GROWTHS

Château	Commune	Château	Commune	Château	Commune
Château Dillon	Blanquefort	Château Barreyre	Arcins	Château La Tour-Milon	Pauillac
Château Fongravey	»	Château Poujeaux	Moulis	Château La Tour-d'Anseillan	»
Château Grand-Clapeau	»	Château Duplessis Hauchecorne	»	Château La Garosse	St-Sauveur
Château de Parempuyre	Parempuyre	Château La Closerie Gd Poujeaux	»	Château Peyrabon	»
Cru Ségur-Fillon-isle-d'Arès	»	Château Robert-Franquet	»	Château La Tour du Mirail	Cissac
Château La Dame-Blanche	Le Taillan	Château Gressier-Grand-Poujeaux	»	Château La Tour Saint-Joseph	»
Domaine de Chalet-de-Germignan	»	Château Duplessis-Fabre	»	Château Le Roc	St-Estèphe
Château Ludon-Pomiès-Agassac	Ludon	Château Ruat-Petit-Poujeaux	»	Château Tronquoy-Lalande	»
Château La Providence	»	Château La Morère	»	Château Fonpetite	»
Château d'Arche	»	Château Médrac	»	Château de Pez	»
Château « Trois-Moulins »	Macau	Château du Testeron	»	Château La Haye	»
Château Maucamps	»	Château l'Ermitage	Listrac	Château Pomys	»
Château Fellonneau	»	Château Semeillan-Mazeau	»	Château Les Ormes de Pez	»
Château Larronde-Desormes	»	Château Semeillan Balleu-Faulat	»	Château Ladouys	»
Château Larrieu-Terrefort	»	Château Lafon	»	Château Saint-Roch	»
Château d'Arsac	Arsac	Château Fourcas-Hosten	»	Château Clauzet	»
Château Montbrison	»	Château Rose-Sainte-Croix	»	Château Grand-Village-Capbern	»
Le Moulin-Avensan	Avensan	Château Granins	»	Château Domeyne	»
Château Rosemont	Labarde	Château La Bécade	»	Château Picard	»
Château Siran	»	Château du Cartillon	Lamarque	Château Mac-Carthy	»
Château Martinens	Cantenac	Château Cap-de-Haut	»	Château Laffitte-Carcasset	»
Château Montbrun	»	Château Moulin-Rose	»	Château Latour de Marbuzet	»
Château Rouge Port-Aubin	»	Château Lanessan	Cussac	Château Faget	»
Château Pontac-Lynch	»	Château Beaumont	»	Domaine de Pez	»
Château de Labegorce	Margaux	Château Lamothe-Bergeron	»	Château Reysson	Vertheuil
Château L'Abbé-Gorsse-de-Gorsse	»	Château Larose-Trintaudon	St-Laurent	Château La Gravière-Couerbe	»
Château La Gurgue	»	Château Larose-Perganson	»	Château Charmail	St-Seurin-Cadourne
Domaine de Clairefont	»	Château Galan	»	Château du Haut-Carmail	»
Château La Tour-de-Mons	Soussans	Château Corconnac	»	Château Livran	St-Germ.-d'Esteuil
Château La Bégorce	»	Château La Tour Marcillanet	»	Château Beaulieu	»
Château Haut-Breton	»	Château Gloria	St-Julien	Château Carcanieux-les-Graves	Queyrac
Château Marsac-Séguineau	»	Château Haut Bages Monpelou	Pauillac	Château La Croix-Landon	Begadan
Château de l'Aiguillette	»	Château Malécot	»	Château Bellegrave	»
Château La Tour-du-Roc	Arcins	Château Balogues	»	Château Bellerive	»
Château d'Arcins	»	Château Latour-L'Aspic	»	Château Les Lesques	Lesparre

196

REGION BETWEEN GARONNE AND DORDOGNE

CÔTES DE BORDEAUX SAINT-MACAIRE • WHITE WINES

Château Cordeliers	St-Macaire	Domaine de Flous	St-Pierre-	Château Machorre	St-Martin-
Domaine de Belle-Croix			d'Aurillac		de-Sescas
Domaine des Charmettes	St-Martial	Château Perrayne	St-André-	Château La Serre	Caudrot
Château Haut-Bardin	»		du-Bois	Domaine de Jacob	St-Laurent-
Cru Terrefort	Le Pian	Château Malromé	»		du-Pian
Château Fayard	»	Château d'Arche-Lassalle	»	Domaine de Beaulieu	Ste-Foy-
Cru Rigal	»				la-Longue

SAINTE-CROIX-DU-MONT • WHITE WINES

Château Loubens	Ste-Croix-	Domaine de Morange	Ste-Croix-	Château Terfort	Ste-Croix-
Château de Tastes	du-Mont	Château La Gravière	du-Mont	Château Les Marcottes	du-Mont
Château Bouchoc	»	Château Labory	»	Domaine de Roustit	»
Château Lafüe	»	Château Coullac	»	Cru des Arroucats	»
Château Laurette	»	Château Loustauvieil	»	Clos Belle-Vue	»
Château Bel-Air	»	Château Roustit	»	Château La Graville	»
Château de L'Escaley	»	Domaine du Tich	»	Cru de La Gravière du Tich	»
Château du Grand-Peyrot	»	Domaine des Sorbiers	»	Château Lapeyreyre	»
Château La Rame	»	Château Jean Lamat	»	Château Copis	»
Château La Mouleyre	»	Château du Pavillon	»	Château La Caussade	»
Château Médouc	»	Château Bertranon	»	Château du Verger	»
Château des Mailles	»	Clos de Verteuil	»		

LOUPIAC • WHITE WINES

Château de Ricaud	Loupiac	Château Lanusse-Couloumet	Loupiac	Château La Yotte	Loupiac
Château Mazarin	»	Château du Vieux-Moulin	»	Cru de Montallier-Lambrot	»
Château Dauphiné-Rondillon	»	Clos Champon-Ségur	»	Domaine du Chay	»
Château du Cros	»	Domaine de Turon-Lanere	»	Domaine de Barbe-Maurin	»
Château de Loupiac-Gaudiet	»	Château des Roches	»	Château Terrefort	»
Château Pontac	»	Domaine de Rouquette	»	Château Le Portail Rouge	»
Château Tarey	»	Château Le Tarey	»	Château de Martillac	»
Domaine de Malendure	»	Cru du Couloumet	»	Cru du Merle	»
Clos Jean	»	Domaine de Pasquet	»	Clos de Giron	»
Château de Rondillon	»	Château Pageot-Couloumet	»	Domaine de Miqueu-Bel-Air	»
Château La Nère	»	Château Peyruchet	»	Château Roustin	»
Domaine du Noble	»	Domaine de Roby	»	Domaine de Guinot	»
Cru de Couloumet-Les Boupeyres	»	Domaine du Rocher	»	Château de Beaupuy	»
				Château Margès-Dusseau	»

PREMIÈRES CÔTES DE BORDEAUX • WHITE WINES

Château Laurétan	Langoiran	Château Terrasson	Langoiran	Château de Plassans	Tabanac
Château Sauvage	»	Cru Baylibelle	»	Château Lucques Bessan	»
Château La Tour Maudan	»	Château Lagareyre	»	Château Lamothe	»
Château Pommarède	»	Domaine du Pin	»	Château Sentour	»
Château Biac	»	Château Barrère	»	Château Renon	»
Château Le Gardera	»	Domaine du Gourdin	»	Château La Providence	»
Château Tanesse	»	Domaine de Côte-Rôtie-Lamothe	»	Domaine d'Armaing	»
Château Faubernet	»	Château Dutoya	»	Château Laroche	Baurech
Château du Vallier	»	Château Chauvin	»	Domaine de Melin	»
Domaine de Bellevue	»	Domaine de Lagaloche	»	Château Puygueraud	»
Château Gourran	»	Château La Ronde	Le Tourne	Château de Lyde	»
Château Lapeyruche	»	Château Pic	»	Château Gaussens	»
Château Langoiran	»	Domaine de Moutons	»	Château Pressac	»
Château de l'Eglise	»	Château Le Mesnil	»	Château de Haux	Haux
Château La Ligassonne	»	Domaine de la Côte Rôtie	Tabanac	Château du Juge	»
Domaine Crassat-Gramman	»	Château Lagarosse	»	Château La Gorce	»

Château Peneau	Haux	Château Mony	Rions	Château Faugas	Gabarnac
Château Gréteau	»	Clos du Monastère du Broussey	»	Domaine de La Cure	»
Château Brigaille	»	Domaine de la Bastide	»	Cru du Bourdieu	Monprim-
Château Lamothe de Haux	»	Château des Remparts	»	Château Beau-Site Monprimblanc	blanc
Château du Grava	»	Château Peironnin	»	Domaine de Lagrange	»
Château de La Bézine	»	Clos de Ricouet	»	Clos La Burthe	»
Domaine de Bernadon	»	Domaine de Carsin	»	Domaine Lambert	»
Château du Courreau	»	Château La Roque	La Roque	Château de Teste	»
Château Jeanganne-Préfontaine	»	Château Peller	»	Cru de Vigneyre	»
Château Bellegarde	Paillet	Clos Dezarneauld	»	Domaine de la Frairie	»
Château Paillet	»	Château Haut-Laroque	»	Domaine de Poncet	Omet
Château l'Ermitage	»	Château Lassalle	»	Domaine des Biscarets	»
Château de Marsan	Estiac-sur-	Château Birot	Béguey	Domaine de Camelon	»
Au Moulin des Graves	Garonne	Domaine du Pin	»	Clos du Boudeur	»
Château du Peyrat	Capian	Château Peyrat	»	Domaine de La Bertrande	»
Château de Caillavet	»	Château Boisson	»	Château Mont-Célestin	Verdelais
Château Suau	»	Domaine de la Marquise	»	Château Pomirol le Pin	»
Château Barakan	»	Château de Garreau	Cadillac	Cru Cantegrit	»
Domaine de Sainte-Anne	»	Château du Juge	»	Domaine de Grava	»
Château de Grand-Mouëys	»	Château des Tourelles	»	Château Gravelines-Semens	»
Château Ramondon	»	Château Arnaud-Jouan	»	Domaine de Joffre	»
Domaine de Potiron	»	Château Fayau	»	Domaine de Lescure	»
Château de Grand-Branet	»	Château de Beaulieu	»	Cru du Haut-Roudey	»
Château Lezongard	Villenave-	Clos des Capucins	»	Cru de Nazareth	»
Château Fauchey	de-Rions	Château Lardiley	»	Domaine de Boustit	»
Domaine de Lamarque	Cardan	Château Côte-Belle	»	Château La Prioulette	St-Maixant
Château Janisson	»	Château Justa	»	Château du Point-de-Vue	»
Château Videau	»	Clos Saint-Cricq	»	Château Chante-l'Oiseau	»
Domaine de Bourgalade	»	Château de la Passonne	»	Château Malagar	»
Domaine de Lhoste	»	Château du Gard	»	Château Montonoir	»
Domaine de Mespley	»	Cru Peytoupin	»	Château Pique-Caillou	»
Château du Payre	»	Cru La Gravette	»	Château Lavison	»
Château Mageot	»	Domaine de Chasse-Pierre	»	Château Saint-Germain	St-Germain-
Château de l'Espinglet	Rions	Domaine de Saint-Cricq	»	Domaine de la Maroutine	de-Graves
Domaine du Broussey	»	Château du Pin	»	Château Génisson	»
Domaine de Hautes-Graves	»	Château Marcelin-Laffitte	Gabarnac	Clos de Millanges	»
Domaine de Cholet	»	Clos Pierre-Jean	»	Domaine de Goursin	»
Château Jourdan	»	Domaine du Moulin de Ballan	»	Château Saint-Germain	»
Domaine de Cardonne	»	Clos du Grand-Bonneau	»	Domaine du Fihl	Donzac
Château Caïla	»	Château Latour Feugas	»	Domaine du Haurin	»
				Domaine de Prentigarde	»

PREMIÈRES CÔTES DE BORDEAUX • RED WINES

Château Bassaler Castanède	Bassens	Château Léon	Carignan	Château La Rigaudière	Camblanes
Château Favols	Carbon-	(Domaine de Camelon)	»	Château de Courtade	»
	Blanc	Château Malherbes	Latresne	Château Damluc	»
Château La Croix	Lormont	Château Gassies	»	Domaine de Cluseau	»
Château de Cypressat	Cenon	Domaine de Pardaillan	»	Château Lestange	Quinsac
Château Costeriou	Bouliac	Domaine du Grand-Parc	»	Château Péconnet	»
Château Montjon-Le-Gravier	Ste-Eulalie	Château Pascot	»	Château de Pranzac	»
Château La Tour-Gueyraud	»	Château Rauzé-Sybil	Cénac	Domaine de Chastelet	»
Château de Chelivette	»	Château Haut-Brignon	»	Domaine de Castagnon	»
L'Abbaye de Bonlieu	»	Château Materre	»	Château Montaigne	»
Château Larose	»	Château Saint-Sève	»	Château Bel-Air	»
Château Malbec	»	Château La Mouline	»	Château Bellevue	»
Château d'Intrans	»	Château Duplessis	»	Château du Peyrat	Cambes
Château du Grand Jour	Yvrac	Château Rauze	»	Château La Navarre	»
Château Bellevue	»	Domaine de Roquebrune	»	Château Maran	»
Domaine de Bouteilley	»	Château Latour	Camblanes	Château Puy-Bardens	»
Château Maillard	»	Château Bel-Air	»	Château Brémontier	»
Château Canteloup	»	Château Brethous	»	Château Lardit	»
Château Labatut	»	Château Courtade Dubuc	»	Château Roubric	»
Château Cayre	»	Château Lafitte	»	Château La Chabanne	»
Château Miraflorès	»	Château Lagarette	»	Clos de Gourgues	St-Caprais-
Château Tertre du Renard	»	Château Tapiau	»	Château Campet	de-
Château de Carignan	Carignan	Château du Tasta	»	Domaine de Luc	Bordeaux
Château Roqueys	»	Clos Haut-Forcade	»	Domaine des Conseillants	»

198

ENTRE-DEUX-MERS • WHITE WINES AND RED WINES

HAUT-BENAUGE

Château du Vert	Arbis	Domaine de Fongrane	Gornac	Domaine de la Grangeotte	Gornac
Domaine de Gouas	»	Château Cazeau	»	Château d'Ories	»
Clos de Terrefort	»	Château Martinon	»	Domaine de Pédebert	»
Château de Benauge	»	Château Pouly	»	Domaine de Troubat	»
Domaine de Meyssau	Cantois	Château d'Hauretz	»	Domaine de Peyrines	Mourens-
Domaine de Fermis	»	Domaine de la Gaborie	»	Domaine de Mondain	Monpezat
Domaine de Talusson	»	Domaine de Terrefort	»	Domaine du Ferron	Soulignac
Domaine de Pasquet	Escoussans	Domaine du Houre	»	Château de Toutigeac	Targon
Domaine de Nicot	»	Château La Mazerolle	»	Domaine de Brufanno	»

CANTONS OF BRANNE, OF PUJOLS, OF SAUVETERRE AND OF PELLEGRUE

Domaine de Fauchey	Branne	Domaine de Vignolles	St-Quentin-	Château de Pressac	Daignac
Château de Blagnac	Cabara	Clos Picard	le-Baron	Château Mauros	Guillac
Château du Grand Puch	St-Germain-Puch	Château de Bellefontaine	Baron	Château de Vidasse-Pessac	Pessac-s.-
Domaine Le Pin	St-Aubin-de-Blaignac	Château Raymond	»	Domaine Le Mayne	Dordogne
		Château Ramonet	»	Domaine de Glayse	»
		Domaine du Grand-Canteloup	Nérigean	Domaine de la Rivière	Pujols
Domaine de la Girolatte	Naujan-et-Postiac	Château Martouret	»	Château de la Salle	Rauzan
Château Beaufresque		Château de Montlau	Moulon	Château Villotte	»
Château de Naujan	»	Château Mouchac	Génissac	Château du Bedat	Blasimon
Domaine de la Rouergue	»	Château Rambaud	»	Château de Roques	Mauriac
Château Bonnet	Grézillac	Château du Burg	»	Château de Courteillac	Ruch
Domaine de Cabirol	Camiac	Château Fantin	St-Jean-de-Blaignac	Château de Grand-Champs	St-Sulpice-de-Pomiers
Domaine de Balestard	St-Quentin-le-Baron				

CANTONS OF CARBON-BLANC AND OF CRÉON

Château du Burk	Ambès	Château La Mothe	Montussan	Clos de Dominge	Camarsac
Château Sainte-Barbe	»	Château La Tour	Sallebœuf	Château Seguin	Lignan
Château Parabelle	Ambarès	Château Grand-Monteil	»	Clos Saint-Jean	»
Château du Tillac	»	Château Pontac-Gasparini	»	Château de Tustal	Sadirac
Château Formont	»	Château de Lesparre	Beychac-et-Cailleau	Domaine de Calamiac	»
Château du Gua	»	Château Quinsac		Château Guillaumet	»
Château du Peychaud	»	Domaine de La Grave	»	Château Lestage	»
Château Lagraula	St-Sulpice-	Château Senailhac	Tresses	Domaine de Landreau	»
Château Beauval	Cameyrac	Château Bel-Air	»	Château de Bergerie	St-Genès-de-Lombaud
Château Quantin	»	Château Lestrilles	Artigues		
Château de Reignac	St-Loubès	Château Lafitte	»		
Château Lescart	»	Château Landeron	Pompignac	Château Beauduc	Créon
Château Labatut	»	Château Rivasseau	»	Château Patrouilleau	La Sauve
Château Chelivette	»	Château des Arrouches	»	Domaine de Castebelle-des-Praud	
Château Les Dauphins	»	Château Beaulé	»		
Château La Tour-Puymirand	Montussan	Domaine des Carmes	»	Château Chateauneuf	»
Château Lavergne	»	Château de Camarsac	Camarsac	Château de Goélane	St-Léon
Château Fonchereau	»	Château Beauséjour	»	Château Le Cugat	»
				Château du Bedat	Blasimon

SAINTE-FOY-BORDEAUX REGION • RED WINES AND WHITE WINES

Château de Courauneau	Ligueux	Château de Langalerie	St-Quentin-de-Caplong	Château de La Tour Beaupoil	Pessac-sur-Dordogne
Château La Roche	Les Lèves	Domaine de Mayne			
Château des Vergnes	»				

GRAVES-DE-VAYRES • RED WINES

Château Bel-Air	Vayres	Château Bussac	Vayres

RIGHT BANK OF THE DORDOGNE AND OF THE GIRONDE

SAINT-ÉMILION REGION • RED WINES

GREAT GROWTHS OF THE 1955 CLASSIFICATION

First great classified growths (a)

Château Ausone	St-Emilion	Château Cheval-Blanc	St-Emilion

First great classified growths (b)

Château Beauséjour	St-Emilion	Clos Fourtet	St-Emilion	Château Magdelaine	St-Emilion
Château Bel-Air	»	Château Figeac	»	Château Pavie	»
Château Canon	»	Château La Gaffelière	»	Château Trottevieille	»

Great classified growths

Château l'Angélus	St-Emilion	Château Le Grand-Corbin-		Château Le Couvent	St-Emilion
Château l'Arrosée	»	Pécresse	St-Emilion	Château Le Prieuré	
Château Balestard-la-Tonnelle .	»	Château Grand-Mayne	»	Saint-Emilion	»
Château Bellevue	»	Château Grand-Pontet	»	Château Mauvezin-La-	
Château Bergat	»	Château Les Grandes-Murailles .	»	Gommerie	»
Le Cadet Bon	»	Château Guadet-Saint-Julien . .	»	Château Moulin du Cadet . . .	»
Château Cadet-Piola	»	Château Jean-Faure	»	Château Pavie-Decesse	»
Château Canon-La-Gaffelière . .	»	Clos des Jacobins	»	Domaine Pavie-Macquin	»
Château Cap de Mourlin	»	Château La Carte	»	Pavillon Cadet	»
Château Chapelle-Madeleine . .	»	Château La Clotte	»	Château Petit-Faurie-de-Soutard	»
Château Chauvin	»	Château La Cluzière	»	Château Ripeau	»
Château Corbin	»	Château La Couspaude.	»	Château Sansonnet	»
Château Corbin-Michotte . . .	»	Château La Dominique	»	Château Saint-Georges-	
Château Coutet	»	Clos La Madeleine	»	Côtes-Pavie	»
Château Croque-Michotte. . . .	»	Château Larcis-Ducasse	»	Clos Saint-Martin	»
Château Curé-Bon-la-Madelaine .	»	Château La Marzelle	»	Château Soutard	»
Château Fonplégade.	«	Château Larmande	»	Château Tertre-Daugay	»
Château Fonroque	»	Château Laroze	»	Château Trimoulet	»
Château Franc-Mayne	»	Château La Serre	»	Château des Trois Moulins . . .	»
Château Grand-Barrail-		Château La Tour-du-Pin-Figeac	»	Château Troplong-Mondot . . .	»
Lamarzelle-Figeac.	»	Château La Tour-Figeac	»	Château Villemaurine	»
Château Grand Corbin Despagne	»	Château Le Châtelet	»	Château Yvon-Figeac	»

Principal other growths

Château Badette	St-Emilion	Château Dassault	St-Emilion	Château Haut-Simard	St-Emilion
Clos Badon	»	Château Daugay	»	Domaine de Haut-Veyrac . . .	»
Domaine de Badon-Patarabet .	»	Domaine De Rey	»	Château Hermitage-Mazerat . .	»
Château Baleau.	»	Château De Rol	»	Château Jacquemeau	»
Château Beau-Mazerat	»	Château Etoile-Pourret	»	Château du Jardin-Saint-Julien .	»
Château Belles-Plantes	»	Château Fongaban-Bellevue . .	»	Château du Jardin-Villemaurine.	»
Château Berliquet	»	Château Fonrazade	»	Château Jaugue-Blanc	»
Château Bézineau	»	Château Franc-Patarabet. . . .	»	Château Jean de Mayne	»
Château Bord-Ramonet	»	Château Franc-Pourret.	»	Château Jean Voisin	»
Château Bragard	»	Clos du Grand-Châtelet	»	Clos Jean-Voisin	»
Château Cadet-Soutard	»	Domaine du Grand-Faurie . . .	»	Château La Clotte-Grande-Côte .	»
Château Cadet-Fonroque	»	Château Grand Mirande	»	Château La Croix-Chantecaille .	»
Château Cantenac	»	Château Guadet-Le-Franc-Grâce-		Château La Fleur-Mérissac . . .	»
Château Cardinal-Villemaurine .	»	Dieu	»	Château La Fleur-Pourret . . .	»
Château Cartau	»	Château Gueyrot	»	Château La Fleur-Vachon . . .	»
Château Cassevert	»	Château Haut-Berthonneau. . .	»	Domaine La Gaffelière	»
Château Cauzin	»	Château Haut-Cadet.	»	Château La Gommerie	»
Château Champion	»	Château Haut-Fonrazade	»	Château La Grâce-Dieu	»
Domaine du Châtelet	»	Château Haut-Grâce-Dieu . . .	»	Château La Madeleine	»
Domaine de Chante-Grive-Badon	»	Château Haut-Grand-Faurie . .	»	Château Le Manoir	»
Château Châtelet-Moléonne . .	»	Château Haut-La Rose	»	Clos La Marzelle	»
Château Cheval-Noir	»	Château Haut-Mazerat	»	Château Laniotte	»
Château du Clocher	»	Domaine Haut-Patarabet . . .	»	Château Laplagnotte-Bellevue .	»
Château Cormey	»	Château Haut-Pontet	»	Château Laporte	»
Château Cormey Figeac	»	Château Haut-Pourret	»	Château La Rose	»
Couvent-des-Jacobins	»	Clos Haut-Pourret	»	Château La Rose Pourret . . .	»
Château Cravignac	»	Château Haut-Sarpe	»	Château La Rose-Rol	»
Château Croix-de-Chantecaille .	»	Château Haut-Segotte	»	Château La Tour-Fonrazade . .	»

Château La Tour-Pourret	St-Emilion
Château La Tour-Saint-Pierre	»
Château Magnan	»
Château Magnan-La-Gaffelière	»
Château Malineau	»
Château Martin	»
Château Matras	»
Château Matras-Côte-Daugay	»
Château Mazerat	»
Château des Menuts	»
Clos des Menuts	»
Côte Mignon-Lagaffelière	»
Château Montlabert	»
Château Moulin-Saint-Georges	»
Château Petit-Figeac	»
Château Mouton-Blanc	»
Château Clos de l'Oratoire	»
Château Le Palat	»
Château Patris	»
Château Petit-Cormey	»
Château Petit-Faurie-Trocard	»
Domaine Petit-Val	»
Château Peyraud	»
Château Peygenestou	»
Clos Picon-Cravignac	»
Château Pindefleurs	»
Château Pontet	»
Château Pontet-Clauzure	»
Château Pontet-Fontlabert	»
Château Puygenestou	»
Château Régent	»
Château Royland	»
Clos Saint-Emilion	»
Château Saint-Julien	»
Domaine de la Salle	»
Château Simard	»
Château Soutard-Cadet	»
Enclos de Soutard	»
Château La Tour-Pourret	»
Château Trianon	»
Cru Troquart	»
Château Truquet	»
Château Vachon	»
Clos Valentin	»
Château de la Vieille-Cloche	»
Château Vieux-Ceps	St-Emilion
Château Villebout	»
Château Vieux-Grand-Faurie	»
Château Vieux-Moulin-du-Cadet	»
Château Vieux-Pourret	»
Domaine de Yon	»
Château Yon-Figeac	»
Château Barde-Haut	St-Christophe
Château Les Basiliques	des-Bardes
Château Brun	»
Château du Cauze	»
Château Coudert	»
Château Fombrauge	St-Emilion
Château Gaubert	»
Château Grangey	»
Château Guillemot	»
Château Haut-Sarpe	»
Château Lapelletrie	»
Château Laroque	»
Château Larquet	»
Château Marrin	»
Château Panet	»
Clos des Moines	»
Château Quentin	»
Château Rol-de-Fombrauge	»
Château Saint-Christophe	»
Château Sarpe-Grand-Jacques	»
Clos de Sarpe	»
Château Sarpe Pelletan	»
Château La-Tour-St-Christophe	»
Château Vieux-Sarpe	»
Château Bel-Air-Ouy	St-Etienne
Domaine du Calvaire	de-Lisse
Château Canterane	»
Château Côte Bernateau	»
Château de Lisse	»
Château La Fagnouse	»
Domaine de Haut-Bruly	»
Château du Haut-Rocher	»
Domaine de Haut-Veyrac	»
Château Jacques-Blanc	»
Château Lamartre	»
Château Mangot	»
Château Mont-Belair	»
Château de Pressac	»
Château Puy-Blanquet	St-Etienne
Château du Rocher	de-Lisse
Château du Vieux-Guinot	»
Château Baladoz	St-Laurent-
Clos La Barde	des-Combes
Château de La Barde	»
Château de Béard	»
Château Bellefont-Belcier	»
Château Belle-Isle-Mondotte	»
Château La Bouygue	»
Château Godeau	»
Château Haute-Nauve	»
Château Pipeau	»
Château du Sable	»
Château Villebout	»
Château Larcis-Ducasse	»
Château Capet	St-Hippo-
Château de Ferrand	lyte
Château Capet-Guillier	»
Château Haut-Plantey	»
Château Lassègue	»
Château Maurens	»
Château Monlot-Capet	»
Château Pailhas	»
Château Pipeau-Ménichot	»
Clos des Sarrazins	»
Château Gros	St-Pey-
Château Fourney	d'Armens
Château Jean-Blanc	»
Château La Chapelle-de-Lescours	»
Cru Peyrouquet	»
Château de Saint-Pey	»
Château Saint-Pierre	»
Château Le Castelot	St-Sulpice-
Château Grand-Pey-Lescours	de-Faleyrens
Château Lande de Gravet	»
Château de Lescours	»
Château Monbousquet	»
Château de Faleyrens	»
Château Saint-Martial	»
Château Trapeau	»
Château Quercy	Vignonet
Château Peyroutas	»
Château Rouchonne-Vignonet	»

SABLES-SAINT-ÉMILION • RED WINES

Château Martinet	Sables-
Clos de la Bordette	St-Emilion
Château de la Capelle	»
Château Garde-Rose	Sable-
Château Doumayne	St-Emilion
Clos Froidefond	»
Château Cruzeau	Sable-
Château Gueyrosse	St-Emilion
Château Quinault	»

MONTAGNE-SAINT-ÉMILION • RED WINES

Château Bayard	Montagne-
Château Beauséjour	St-Emilion
Château Bellevue	»
Château Calon	»
Château Corbin	»
Château Coucy	»
Château de Fontmurée	»
Château Gay-Moulin	»
Château Haut-Goujon	»
Château Les Hautes-Graves	»
Château Haut-Plaisance	Montagne-
Château Jura-Plaisance	St-Emilion
Château La Bastienne	»
Château La Bichaude	»
Château Lafleur	»
Château La Papeterie	»
Château La Picherie	»
Château La Tête-du-Cerf	»
Château La Tour-Calon	»
Château La Tour-Corniaud	»
Château La Tour-Montagne	Montagne-
Château La Tour-Paquillon	St-Emilion
Château Maison-Blanche	»
Château des Moines	»
Château Montaiguillon	»
Château Mouchet-Montagne	»
Château Moulin-Blanc	»
Clos des Moulins-de-Calon	»
Château Négrit	»
Château Paradis	»

Château Petit-Clos	Montagne-	Château Les Tuileries-de-Bayard	Montagne-	Domaine de Faizeau	Montagne-
Château Pierrot-Plaisance	St-Emilion	Château Vieille-Maison	St-Emilion	Domaine de Fontmurée	St-Emilion
Château Plaisance	»	Château Le Vieux-Logis	»	Domaine de Gillet	»
Château Rocher-Corbin	»	Vieux Château Goujon	»	Domaine de La Barde	»
Château Roudier	»	Domaine de Beaudron	»	Domaine de Labatut.	»
Château Saint-André-Corbin	»	Domaine de Cazelon	»	Domaine de La Clotte	»
Château Saint-Jacques-Calon	»	Domaine Croix-de-Mission	»	Domaine de La Vieille	»
Château des Tours	»				

SAINT-GEORGES SAINT-ÉMILION • RED WINES

Château Bellevue	St-Georges-	Château La Tour du Pas-Saint-	St-Georges-	Château Samion.	St-Georges-
Château Calon	de-Montagne	Georges	de-Montagne	Château Tourteau	de-Montagne
Château Bel-Air Haut-Mont-		Château Macquin	»	Château Troquard	»
guillon	»	Château Saint-André-Corbin	»	Château Vieux-Guillou	»
Château du Châtelet	»	Château Saint-Georges	»	Domaine de Maisonneuve	»
Château Guillou	»	Château Saint-Georges Cap-d'Or.	»	Domaine de Grimon	»
Château Haut-Troquard	»	Château Saint-Louis	»		

LUSSAC SAINT-ÉMILION • RED WINES

Château Belair	Lussac	Domaine de Lagrange	Lussac	Château Petit-Refuge	Lussac
Château Bellevue	»	Château La Tour-de-Ségur	»	Château Poitou-Lussac	»
Clos Blanchon	»	Château Lion-Perruchon	»	Château Souchet-Piquat	»
Domaine du Courlat	»	Château de Lussac	»	Château Taveney	»
Château Croix-de-Blanchon	»	Château du Lyonnat	»	Château Terrien	»
Château Haut-Larose	»	Clos du Lyonnat	»	Château Tiffray-Guadey	»
Château Haut-Piquat	»	Domaine de Rambaud	»	Château La Tour-de-Grenet.	»
Château La Fleur-Perruchon	»	Château La Ferrière	»	Château Les Vieux-Chênes	»

PUISSEGUIN SAINT-ÉMILION • RED WINES

Château Beauséjour	Puisseguin	Château Guibot-la-Fourvieille	Puisseguin	Château de Puisseguin	Puissseguin
Cru Belair	»	Château Haut-Bernon	»	Château du Roc de Boissac	»
Château Chêne-Vieux	»	Château La Clotte	»	Clos du Roy	»
Château Durand	»	Château des Laurets	»	Château Teyssier	»
Château Guibaud	»	Château du Mayne	»		

PARSAC SAINT-ÉMILION • RED WINES

Château Langlade	Parsac	Château Malagin	Parsac	Château Piron	Parsac
Château Lestage	»	Château Musset	»		

POMEROL • RED WINES

Château Beauchêne (former Clos		Clos du Clocher	Pomerol	Château Grandchamp	Pomerol
Mazeyres)	Pomerol	Château Conseillante.	»	Domaine des Grands-Champs	»
Château Beauregard	»	Château La Croix-Saint-Georges.	»	Château Grate-Cap	»
Clos Beauregard.	»	Clos l'Eglise	»	Château Guillot	»
Château Belle-Brise	»	Domaine de l'Eglise	»	Clos des Hautes Graves	»
Château Bourgneuf-Vayron	»	Clos l'Eglise-Clinet	»	Domaine de Haut-Pignon	»
Château Brun-Mazeyres	»	Château l'Enclos	»	Château Haut-Plateau	»
Château Le Caillou	»	Château L'Evangile	»	Domaine Haut-Pomerol	»
Château de Cantereau	»	Château Ferrand	»	Château Enclos Haut-Mazeyres	»
Château Carillon	»	Château Feytit-Clinet	»	Château La Cabanne.	»
Château Certan-Demay	»	Château Gazin	»	Château La Croix	»
Château Certan-Marzelle	»	Château Gombaude-Guillot et		Château La Commanderie	»
Château du Chêne-Liège	»	Grandes Vignes Clinet réunis	»	Château Lacroix-de-Gay	»
Château Clinet	»	Château Gouprie	»	Château Lafleur	»

La Fleur du Gazin	Pomerol	Clos Mazeyres	Pomerol	Château Saint-André	Pomerol
Château La Fleur-Petrus	»	Château Monbran	»	Château Saint-Pierre	»
Château La Ganne	»	Château Monregard La Croix	»	Château de Sales	»
Château Lagrange	»	Château Moulinet	»	Château Samson	»
Château La Grave-Trigant-de-Boisset	»	Château Mouton-Mazeyres	»	Château Sudrat-Boussaton	»
Château La Pointe	»	Château Nenin	»	Château du Tailhas	»
Château Latour à Pomerol et Grandes Vignes réunies	»	Cru de La Nouvelle-Eglise	»	Château Taillefer	»
Château La Violette	»	Château Petit-Bocage	»	Clos des Templiers	»
Château La-Vraye-Croix-de-Gay	»	Château Petit-Village	»	Clos Toulifaut	»
Château Le Gabachot	»	Château Petrus	»	Château Tristan	»
Château Le Gay	»	Château Plince	»	Château Trotanoy	»
Château Le Prieuré La Croix	»	Château La Providence	»	Château de Valois	»
Château Mazeyres	»	Clos René	»	Château Vieux-Certan	»
		Clos du Roi	»	Vieux Château Cloquet	»
		Château Rouget	»		

LALANDE-DE-POMEROL • RED WINES

Clos des Arnaud	Lalande-de-Pomerol	Clos l'Etoile	Lalande-de-Pomerol	Château de Musset	Lalande-de-Pomerol
Château de Bel-Air		Domaine de Grand-Moine		Château Perron	
Château Bourseau	»	Château Grand-Ormeau	»	Sabloire du Grand Moine	»
Petit Clos de Brouard	»	Château La Gravière	»	Château Sergant	»
Château de la Commanderie	»	Clos Haut Cavujon	»	Château Templiers	»
Château La Croix-Saint-Jean	»	Château Laborde	»	Château de Viaud	»
Château Les Cruzelles	»	Château des Moines	»	Domaine de Viaud	»
Clos de l'Eglise	»	Clos des Moines	»	Clos de la Vieille-Forge	»

NÉAC LALANDE-DE-POMEROL • RED WINES

Domaine du Bourg	Néac	Château Garraud	Néac	Domaine de Machefer	Néac
Château Canon Chaigneau	»	Château Gachet	»	Château Moulin-à-Vent	»
Clos du Castel	»	Domaine des Grands-Bois-Chagneau	»	Château Moulin-Blanc	»
Château Chaigneau-Guillon	»	Domaine du Grand-Ormeau	»	Château Moncets	»
Château Châtain	»	Château Haut-Ballet	»	Château Nicole	»
Clos du Châtain	»	Château Haut-Chaigneau	»	Domaine du Petit-Bois	»
Domaine du Châtain	»	Château Lacroix	»	Château Saint-André	»
Vieux Château Chevrol	»	Château La Croix-Saint-André	»	Château Siaurac	»
Château Les Chaumes	»	Château Lafaurie	»	Domaine de Surget	»
Château Chevrol-Bel-Air	»	Château Lafleur-Lambaret	»	Château de Teysson	»
Château Drouilleau-Belles-Graves	»	Château Lavinot-la-Chapelle	»	Château Tournefeuille	»
Château Fougeailles	»			Château Yveline	»

CANON FRONSAC • RED WINES

Château Vray-Canon-Boyer	St-Michel-de-Fronsac	Cru Gros-Bonnet	Fronsac	Château Capet-Bégaud	Frousac
Château Canon		Château de Toumalin	»	Clos Lariveau	St-Michel-de-Fronsac
Château Vrai-Canon-Bodet-La Tour	»	Château Barrabaque	»	Château Pey-Labrit	
Château Vrai-Canon-Bouché	»	Domaine de Trepesson	St-Michel-de-Fronsac	Cru La Tour-Ballet	»
Château Canon-Lange	Fronsac	Domaine de Trepesson-Lafontine		Domaine de Roulet	Fronsac
Château Junayme	»	Château Bodet	Fronsac	Domaine de Bourdieu-Panet	»
Château Canon	»	Château Panet	»	Château Toumalin-Jonquet	»
Château Comte	»	Domaine du Haut-Caillou	»	Domaine de Margalis	»
Château Belloy	»	Château Gaby	»	Château Coustolle	»
Château Mazeris-Bellevue	St-Michel-de-Fronsac	Château Moulin-Pey-la-Brie	»	Château Pichelèvre	»
Château La Fleur-Canon		Cru Casi-Devant	St-Michel-de-Fronsac	Cru Combes-Canon	St-Michel-de-Fronsac
Château du Pavillon-Haut-Gros-Bonnet	Fronsac	Domaine du Haut-Mazeris		Clos Nardon	
		Château Cassagne	»	Clos Toumalin	Fronsac
Château Mazeris	St-Michel-de-Fronsac	Château La Marche-Canon	Fronsac	Clos Haut-Cailleau	»
Château des Combes-Canon		Château Vincent	»	Château Canon-Bourret	»
Château Grand-Renouil	»	Château Haut-Ballet	St-Michel-de-Fronsac	Château Canon de Brem	»
Château Maussé	»	Crus Moulin-à-Vent		Château La Tour-Canon	»
Château Lariveau	»	Château du Gazin	»	Château Lamarche-Candelayre	»
Château La Chapelle-Lariveau	»	Château Cassagne	»	Château Roulet	»
		Château Larchevesque	Fronsac		

CÔTES DE FRONSAC • RED WINES

Château des Trois-Croix	Fronsac	Château La Tour Beau-Site . .	Fronsac	Château de Carles	Saillans
Château Gagnard	»	Domaine de la Croix	»	Châteaux de Malgarni et Coutreau	»
Château de Pontus	»	Clos Bellevue	St-Michel-	Château Mayne-Viel	Galgon
Château La Dauphine	»	Château Queyreau-de-Haut . .	de-Fronsac	Cru Vincent	St-Aignan
Château La Valade	»	Château Tasta	St-Aignan	Château Vincent	»
Château La Fontaine	»	Château Tasta-Guillier	»	Domaine de Vincent	»
Château Arnauton	»	Château Jeandeman	»		

BOURGEAIS REGION • RED WINES AND WHITE WINES

Château du Bousquet	Bourg	Château de Blissa	Bayon	Château Mendoce	Villeneuve
Domaine du Boucaud	»	Clos Nodot	»	Château Peychaud	Teuillac
Château du Haut-Gravat . . .	»	Château Rousset	Samona	Château Cottière	»
Château Croûte-Charlus	»	Château Barrieux	»	Domaine de Rivereau	Pugnac
Château Croûte-Mallard	»	Château Macay	»	Domaine de Viaud	»
Château Mille-Secousses	»	Domaine de Bel-Air	»	Château Lamothe	Lansac
Château Lalibarde	»	Domaine de Bouche	»	Château de Taste	»
Château Rider	»	Château de Thau	Gauriac	Château La Barde	Tauriac
Château Cambes-Kermovan . .	»	Château du Domaine de Desca-		Domaine de Guerrit	»
Château de la Grave	»	zeaux	»	Château Nodoz	»
Château Rebeymond-Lalibarde .	»	Château Poyanne	»	Château de Maco	»
Domaine de Paty	»	Domaine de Bujan	»	Château Grand-Jour	Prignac et
Château Rebeymont	»	Domaine de Peyror	»	Château Le Mugron	Gazelles
Château Belleroque	»	Clos du Piat	»	Château de Grissac	»
Domaine de Noriou-Lalibarde .	»	Clos de Seillas	»	Domaine de Christoly	»
Château Gros-Moulin	»	Domaine de Bonne	»	Château Laureusanne	St-Seurin
Château Lagrange	»	Château La Grolet	St-Ciers-	Château Berthou	Comps
Domaine de Lalibarde	»	Château Rousselle	de-Canesse	Domaine des Augiers	»
Château Tayac	Bayon	Château Guiraud	»	Domaine de Fonbonne	Teuillac
Château Eyquem	»	Château La Tour-Seguy	»	Château des Richards	Mombrier
Château Falfas	»	Domaine de Grand-Chemin . . .	»	Château Guienne	Lansac
Château de la Croix (Millorit) . .	»	Château de Barbe	Villeneuve		

BLAYAIS REGION • RED WINES AND WHITE WINES

Château Cazeaux	St-Paul	Château Breuil	St-Martin-	Château Meneau	Mazion
Château Lescadre	Cars	Château La Brousse	Caussade	Château La Cure	Cars
Château Crusquet	»	Château Petit-Trou	»	Château Les Alberts	Mazion
Château Barbet	»	Château La Garde	St-Seurin-	Château Le Virou	St-Girons
Château Bellevue	Plassac		Cursac	Château Chasselauds	Cartelègue
Château Les Chaumes	Fours	Château Clos d'Amières	Cartelègue	Château Le Coudeau	Cars
Domaine du Chai	»	Château Le Cone Moreau . . .	Blaye	Château Dupeyrat	St-Paul
Château Pardaillan	Cars	Château Le Cone Sebilleau . . .	»	Château Guillonnet	Anglade
Château Gontier	Blaye-Plassac	Château Berthenon	St-Paul	Château Gordat	Cars
Château Monconseil	Plassac	Château Perreyre	St-Martin	Château Haut-Cabat	»
Château Le Cone Taillasson . . .	Blaye		Caussade	Château Lagrange Marquis de	
Château Gigault	Mazion	Château Pinet La Roquete . . .	Berson	Luppe	Blaye
Château Le Menaudat	St-Androny	Château Lamothe	St-Paul	Château Puy Beney	Mazion
Château Les Petits-Arnauds . .	Cars	Château Ricadet	Cartelègue	Château La Garde Roland . . .	St-Seurin-
Château Sociondo	»	Château Rebouquet	Berson		Cursac
Château Charron	St-Martin	Château La Girouette	Fours	Château La Hargue	Plassac
Château Saugeron	Blaye	Château Pinet	Berson	Château Gadeau	»
Château Les Moines	»	Château La Bertonnière	Cartelègue	Château Lafont	Cartelègue
Château Le Mayne Gozin . . .	Plassac	Château Peybrune	Plassac	Château Pomard	St-Martin
Château Lassale	St-Genès	Château La Perotte	Eyrans	Château Boisset	Berson
Ancien Manoir de La Valette . .	Mazion	Château Le Mayne Boye	Cars	Château Cantemerle	St-Genès
Château Puy Beney Lafitte . .	»	Château La Cave	Blaye	Château Perrein	Mazion
Château Segonzac	St-Genès-	Château Chaillou	St-Paul	Château Mazerolles	Cars
	de-Blaye	Domaine de Graulet	Plassac	Château Les Bavolliers	St-Christ.-
Château La Cabane	St-Martin-	Château Les Ricards	Cars		de-Blaye
	Caussade	Château La Tour Gayet	St-Androny	Moulin de la Pitance	St-Girons
Château La Taure Sainte-Luce .	Blaye	Château Mayence	Mazion		

THE WINES OF SPAIN

ELADIO ASENSIO VILLA

Legend says the vine was first brought into Spain under some very ancient civilization. Indeed, in some parts of southern Spain it is even said that the Phoenicians came to Spain, in the course of their Mediterranean trading, to buy the wine grown there. Historically, however, it has been proved irrefutably that it was the Romans who introduced winegrowing into Spain under the Empire. Thereafter, it spread over the northeastern provinces, the coast of the Spanish Levante (the east coast from Tarragona to Alicante) and to Andalusia, where it flourished exceedingly, especially under the Arab rulers. Later, the vine began to be cultivated in the temperate zones farther inland. Gradually the large number of varieties of vine which Spain produces today began to be planted in the valleys, on the slopes and on the foothills (up to 3,000 feet) and in the coastal area of the Spanish Levante. The geographical distribution of the vine in Spain is as varied as the character of the regions. Another factor is the widespread existence of small-holdings, since, originally at any rate, winegrowing was particularly suited to one-family farming. There are a number of other special features, notably the fact that winegrowing is carried on side-by-side with the cultivation of the olive, the other great Mediterranean crop, and in some cases vineyards and olive groves are inextricably mingled.

Wine was one of Spain's largest resources in the Middle Ages, as it was in other Mediterranean countries. The trade in Spanish wines really began to flourish in the tenth century, carried by sea and river to the northern European countries and to some areas in eastern Europe. This prosperity continued until the end of the eleventh century. In the twelfth century the economic, and one might even say cultural, renaissance of wine took place. Consumption increased in the wealthiest northern and central European countries as well as in the Mediterranean countries, where it was already the usual beverage and where the wines produced in Spain were well known.

Because of its geographical location, Spain was to some extent outside the main flow of European trade, and this placed it in a very special position. Under these conditions, wine could not be exported, and so it came to be consumed domestically. But once it was possible to establish normal trade from the ports of Barcelona and Valencia, Spain made a great effort to conquer the foreign markets and sell its most typical commodities, especially its wines, which already enjoyed a great reputation.

The Spanish wine trade, however, like the trade in other Spanish commodities, suffered greatly from the repercussions of economic crises in several European countries. This state of affairs was reflected in the measures taken by several of the Spanish kingdoms before the unification of Spain. This continued until 1868, the year in which the great French vineyards were invaded and ruined by the phylloxera, for this opened up new outlets for Spanish wines throughout the world. Spanish winemaking techniques also profited, for a great many French growers settled in the best Spanish winegrowing districts after their own vineyards had been destroyed and introduced their skills and practices. But, as always happens when success comes too suddenly, disorganization prevailed in the Spanish markets abroad and Spain neglected to consolidate the markets it had gained as a result of the disappearance of French wines. Winegrowing in Spain, too, underwent a severe crisis when the phylloxera crossed the Pyrenees and made its appearance there in turn, wiping out numerous vineyards and leading to very serious economic and social consequences which left deep traces on the history of the vine in Spain and indeed on Spanish agriculture in general.

Over the past forty years Spanish wine production has been very unequal in quantity. It has been influenced not only by climate but also by unfavourable natural phenomena occurring in other countries. It may, however, look forward to a more promising future, since the public authorities are taking a greater interest in it and the trade itself is eager for more effective organization. According to the official statistics for 1979, the total area planted to vines was 4,225,410 acres, of which 25 per cent is planted to mixed crops. In area, therefore, the Spanish vineyards are the largest in the world, making up a wine region more extensive even than the French and Italian.

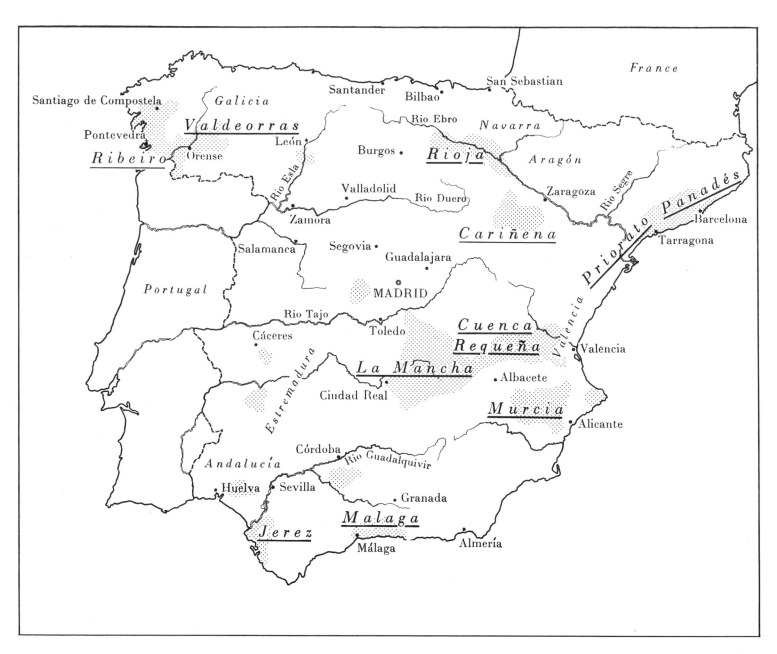

Enjoying as it does a splendid climate, the Spanish winegrowing region is one of the largest in the world and few provinces do not produce wines of their own. The principle wine regions include the Rioja, Navarre, the province of Saragossa, the east coast from Barcelona to Alicante, La Mancha and the southern provinces with Malaga and Jerez de la Frontera, and the Canary and Balearic Islands.

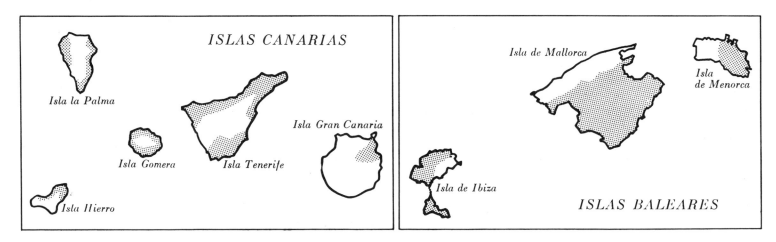

The importance of wine and grape production to Spanish agriculture and the economy of Spain is due to the fact that the area planted to vine accounts for 3.73 per cent of the total cultivated area, and especially to the fact that the area planted to the wine grape accounts for 3.62 per cent of it. A comparison of the winegrowing area with that under other crops shows that it is exceeded only by grain and olives.

Average production in 1973-1979 was 75,387,146 gallons. This is a significant figure which may be taken as representing the potential of Spanish grape production. The 1979 harvest can be considered a record with 111,089,900 gallons; it was due to a combination of favourable climatic conditions in that year.

As we have seen, the Spanish vineyards are distributed all over the Peninsula, since its climatic conditions are everywhere favourable to the vine, which requires above all long periods of unbroken sunshine. The roots remain in the ground for fifty years, sometimes longer, and this is a factor contributing to keeping the population on the land.

A glance at the map of the agricultural regions in Spain shows that every province, including the Balearic and Canary islands, has its winegrowing districts. As to area, La Mancha and the region of Utiel and Requeña (province of Valencia) take first place, followed by Catalonia and the area between Alicante and Jumilla (province of Murcia), where over 30 per cent of the land is planted to vine. Classifying groups of provinces by the area of vineyards, the order is:

Group I (over 250,000 acres per province): Ciudad Real, Toledo, Valencia and Albacete; the four provinces total 1,542,000 acres, or over one-third of the total area planted to vine in Spain.

Group II (from 123,550 to 247,100 acres): Saragossa, Tarragona, Cuenca, Badajoz, Alicante, Barcelona and Murcia; these seven provinces have 1,290,000 acres of vineyards.

Group III (61,775 to 123,550 acres): Zamora, León, Malaga, Navarre, Madrid, Logroño and Valladolid; the vineyards in these seven provinces cover 551,033 acres.

Group IV (24,710 to 61,775 acres): Cadiz and Cordoba, two provinces with wines of a high quality.

Group V (12,355 to 24,710 acres): Pontevedra, Gerona, Granada, Segovia, Seville, Almeria, Álava, Lugo and Guadalajara. The vineyards in these nine provinces cover 170,000 acres. Winegrowing is less important here, but the province of Álava should be mentioned for its wines of exceptionally good quality and the provinces of Gerona and Pontevedra, which produce very acceptable wines.

Lastly, in Group VI (under 13,000 acres) are the provinces in which winegrowing is only of secondary importance: Balearic Islands, Santa Cruz de Tenerife,

The Ausejo vineyards, situated about 18½ miles to the east of Logroño, are part of the Rioja baja; mostly *Garnacha* is grown, and the majority of the wines are red. There are many winegrowing cooperatives in this region.

Jaen, Soria, Las Palmas, Corunna, Oviedo, Santander, Vizcaya and Guipuzcoa.

To sum up, the area of the winegrowing districts varies between a maximum of 646,000 acres in the province of Ciudad Real and a minimum of 64 acres in Guipuzcoa. Average yields and number of plants per acre vary a great deal from region to region in accordance with the climate, the grape varieties and the categories of the wines.

The total area of grape growing in irrigated regions is only 96,430 acres, 66,250 of which only are planted to wine grapes. Planting is forbidden by law nowadays on land that is not irrigated. The vineyards that existed on this land at the time when they became restricted areas are liable to a graduated tax.

Wines are classified according to their colour (red, white). Production (official figures for 1973) is: red

wines 48 per cent, white wines 52 per cent. White wines predominate in New Castile, Andalusia and Catalonia, red wines elsewhere. Comparing the regions by vineyards which bottle in their own cellars, we find that in the north-west (Galicia and Asturias) there is a definite breakdown into very small properties so far as winegrowing is concerned. Western and eastern Andalusia, the Spanish Levante and New Castile have a more rational and consequently more profitable structure. In general, the co-operative movement is continuously expanding, speedily rationalizing the sectors in which reforms are most urgently needed. It promotes the concentration of cellar-bottling, which is essential from the economic point of view, and likewise an improved quality, for the small growers do not possess the skills and technical equipment necessary to guarantee at least a minimum of quality, classification and presentation. Vinification is carried out practically in the vineyard itself, as the grape does not travel well to the vat, even in co-operatives. As a rule, the larger co-operatives are no more than some six miles away from the vineyards. The wines may be classified as, first, the ordinary (corrientes) for immediate national consumption, and, second, the better wines for maturing.

The wines, of course, differ from each other owing to the differences inherent in the climate, nature of the soil, exposure, variety of grape and method of vinification, so that the wines from different regions have from the outset very marked characteristics of their own. Different methods of vinification within the regions produce further variations, as can be seen from the many different types of sherry.

THE WINES OF THE RIOJA

The winegrowing region of the Rioja covers the region of that name comprising the provinces of Logroño and Álava and some communes in Navarre. It is the region of quality wines; they are some of the most sought-after of the wines of guaranteed origin, the Spanish equivalent of the French *appellation d'origine contrôlée*. It stretches from around Haro to Alfaro in the valley of the Ebro and beyond its banks. It may be divided into three main districts: the Lower Rioja between the Yregua and the right bank of the Ebro; the Upper Rioja, a more humid area, the centre being Haro and taking in the north-western part of the province of Logroño on both sides of the Ebro; and the Rioja Alavesa, formed by the valleys of several tributaries of the Ebro, the Oja, Tirón, Najerilla, Leza and Cidacos; it is a transitional land in which the natural characteristics of the Basque provinces, Castile and Navarre all blend together.

In most of the districts in the Rioja winegrowing is extremely important. The region produces a very wide range of wines, all of them differing in strength, taste and bouquet. This is due to the large number of grape varieties and the proportions in which they are used, which differ from district to district. All of them, however, obviously belong to the same family because of the characteristics they have in common.

In the Upper Rioja the red varieties are the *Tempranillo*, *Mazuela*, *Graciano* and *Garnacha* and the white the *Viura* and *Malvasia*. The red wines, mostly from the *Tempranillo*, are very well-balanced, robust, well built, with a good acidity and a prominent bouquet, well suited for maturing. They run from 10.5° to 12° in strength, according to their origin. The white wines are rather lower in alcohol content; they are dry and have a fair bouquet.

The Lower Rioja is the largest district, stretching from the town of Logroño to Alfaro. The *Garnacha* predominates, and so most of the wines are red. They are very full-bodied with an extremely high alcohol content, ranging from 14° to 16°; they are thick, hardly acid at all and rather sweet. Co-operatives are very common in this region.

The Rioja Alavesa, a long narrow strip north of the Ebro, is protected by the Cantabrian Mountains and, owing to its exposure, gets more sun than the Upper Rioja. The wines are typically very well-balanced, very full-bodied, very heavy and excellent for maturing. Their taste and bouquet have a character all their own, and their average strength may be as high as 14°.

Ageing of the wines is considered of great importance in the Rioja: they must be matured within a carefully delimited zone for a period of at least two years, one year of this in oak casks.

RIOJA is aged in fairly small oak Bordeaux casks (225 litres—about 50 gallons) in underground cellars called *calados*. The must and grapes are carefully selected, since not all the wines are suitable for ageing. With some varieties of grape the colour is not stable enough and the wines therefore do not keep. The *Tempranillo* variety ages best.

The first stage (maturing in Bordeaux casks) should last from two to five years, according to the character of the wine and the type of wine desired. The necessary racking is done during this period and slow oxidation occurs in the cellar, which is kept at a constant and cool temperature. This stabilizes the wine.

The second stage consists in reduction. The wine is bottled and kept for a period that depends on the results of the first stage. This is the stage in ageing during which the aroma begins to develop. The red wines acquire a

RIOJA

Provincia de Burgos

Provincia de Alava

Provincia de Navarra

← *Miranda de Este*

Rio Ebro

HARO

Rioja Alta

Rioja Alavesa
LAGUARDIA

STO. DOMINGO
DE LA CALZADA

NAJERA

LOGROÑO

Provincia de Logroño

Rio Oja

Rio Najerilla

Rio Leza

Rio Jubera

CALAHORRA

Rio Ebro

TORRECILLA DE CAMEROS

ARNEDO

Cidacos

Rio

Rioja Baja

ALFARO

Zaragoza →

*Provincia
de
Navarra*

CERVERA DE
RIO ALHAMA

*Provincia
de
Zaragoza*

Provincia de Soria

20 Km.

20 Miles

ruby tint and are quite clear, with an intense and characteristic bouquet.

The Rioja wines most widely sold are usually first-year wines that are shipped by the growers or co-operatives themselves. The wines called *corrientes*, or ordinary light carafe wines, are wines which have been stabilized and bottled during their first year. Stabilized wines bottled and kept for two years are commonly known as harvest wines or second-year wines, and are white, red or rosé. Wines of a light-red colour (darker than rosés, but lighter than reds) are called RIOJA CLARETES. These are the wines that generally reach the foreign market and are served in the better Spanish restaurants.

Lastly, wines aged in oak casks before bottling are designated as third, fourth, etc. year wines, or *viejas reservas* (old reserve). They include reds, claretes, dry whites, sweet whites and rosés. Unfortunately some of these lose much of their charm from being over-aged.

Switzerland imports a great deal of Rioja. The U.S. market is promising and the Cuban market is fairly promising but irregular.

THE WINES OF NAVARRE

In the province of Navarre, adjacent to the Rioja, the valley of the Ebro broadens and the river receives as tributaries the Ega, Arga and Aragón. Navarre stretches along the foothills south of the Pyrenees and the region is one of fertile valleys and slopes with a very good exposure, moderately sunny and sheltered from the prevailing winds, two ideal conditions for winegrowing. The wine district comprises roughly the southern half of the province, hence the name guaranteeing the origin. The principal grape variety is the *Garnacha*; the *Tempranillo* is also used, but to a lesser degree, like the *Viura* and the *Malvasia*. The *Moscatel* is used for making dessert wines.

Climatic conditions, which are quite different in northern and southern Navarre, obviously influence the characteristics of the vineyards and consequently the wines. In the north, where the rainfall ranges from 30 to 40 inches, the wines are not as high in alcohol content as in the Ribera district, where the rainfall is 20 inches at most. Both districts produce very tolerable wines, allowing for their special characteristics.

The wines produced on 8,055 acres of vineyards within the province of Navarre and in the communes adjacent to the province of Logroño are entitled to carry the RIOJA label.

The winegrowing area producing NAVARRA wines may be divided into three quite different regions: the Lower Ribera, made up of the area near the Ebro in the south of the province, which produces very strong red wines, sometimes as high as 18°, and very good fortified wines; the district of Valdizarbe, where the wines are not so strong (from 11° to 15°) and more acid than the Ribera wines; and the district of Montaña, whose wines do not sell as well as those from the other two districts. Some of the better Navarre wines are the light wines of Estella, on the banks of the Ega, the reds and *claretes* of Peralta, Salces and Artajona in the valley of the Arga, the reds of Olite and Tafalla on the banks of the Cidacos and the reds and *claretes* of Murchante, Cintruénigo and Cascante on the banks of the Ebro. Most of the wines are sold for local consumption, although a proportion is exported each year.

Seldom seen outside Spain—or even the region itself—the wines of Navarre have won constant high praise by connoisseurs who have made the journey there to taste them. André L. Simon commented: «The Riojas are the Spanish grandees, and the [Navarre] wine I tasted was rather like his beautiful young bride.»

210

THE WINES OF CARIÑENA

The board of directors in charge of awarding guarantees of origin has recently awarded the label to CARIÑENA, defining its production area as a fairly small one in the province of Saragossa south of the former capital of Aragon. It is made up of the communes of Aguaron, Alfamén, Almonacid de la Sierra, Alpartir, Cariñena, Cosuenda, Encinacorba, Tosos, Langares, Paniza and Villanueva de Huerva. In this area, whose name covers the reputedly best regional vineyards, various types of wine are made, very typical of those harvested all over the province of Saragossa.

The traditional grape varieties are the *Cariñena, Black Garnacha* and *White Garnacha*, which produce very full-bodied, heavily coloured wines with a high degree of dry extract. The first variety produces wines of a strength ranging from 14° to 17°, seldom less than 13° and sometimes rising to as much as 18°. This is the same as the maximum strength obtained experimentally in the laboratory. The dry extract ranges from 20° to 32° according to the type of wine. The wine is fermented in underground wells and in spite of the advent of cooperatives with their modern techniques some treading still goes on. There are red table wines, dry table *claretes* and various other kinds of sweet and fortified dessert wines.

The communes of Alfamén, Alpartir, Almonacid de la Sierra and the lower part of the commune of Sariñena produce wines for blending. The communes of Langares, Cosuenda, Aguaron, Tosos and Villanueva de Huerva produce *corrientes*. The higher parts of these communes and of the communes of Encinacorba and Paniza make wines which, aged by well-tested techniques, display the characteristics of fine table wines: they are very well-balanced, they have an agreeable and delicate flavour and their alcohol content does not run much above 14°.

The whole region produces the classic Aragon *claretes*, which are somewhat like the light-coloured red wines from some other regions. Brilliant in colour, these are highly appreciated table wines; they have a high alcohol content similar to that of the usual red wine. Both the red wines and the *claretes* are very suitable for blending, the reds especially, because of their deeper colour.

THE WINES OF THE EAST COAST

TARRAGONA. The region which produces Tarragona wines, comprising part of the province of that name, is made up of a large number of communes. The most characteristic varieties of grape are the *Cariñena, Garnacha* and *Picapoll* for the reds, and the *Macabeo, Malvasia, Moscatel, White Picapoll* and *Pansa* for the whites. Mixed cultivation is sometimes practised.

The TARRAGONA CAMPO wines should be distinguished from the TARRAGONA CLASICO. They are red and white sweet dessert wines, from 2.5° to 7° Beaumé, with an alcohol content ranging from 14° to 23°. The very typical Tarragona vinification process is rapid oxidation of the must at very high temperatures. The cellars are not underground, but very well-aired and subject to abrupt changes in temperature. The wine is stored in glass containers. With the current trend towards dry wines and spirits the sweet TARRAGONA CAMPOS are not as widely seen as they used to be.

PRIORATO. The name of this region derives from the priory of a fifteenth-century Carthusian monastery, the ruins of which are still to be seen. These wines are produced in an enclave within the region covered by the TARRAGONA guaranteed origin label. The region is made up of several communes and the towns of Reus, Valls and La Secuita where the maturing is done. The permitted grapes are the *Cariñena*, the *Garnachas*, the *Macabeo* and the *Pedro Ximénez*.

The Priorato wines make excellent table wines and are good for blending. They have a high alcohol content, from 14° to 18°, while the fortified and aged dessert wines may run as high as 22°.

PANADÉS. The district which produces the Panadés wines—which are good table wines, mostly white—is made up of parts of the provinces of Barcelona and Tarragona. The wines enjoy the guarantee of origin and are derived from the *Macabeo, Xerel-lo, Parellada, Sumoll, Merseguera, Moscatel, Garnacha* and *Malvasia* grape varieties for the whites; the main varieties for the reds are the *Black Sumoll, Cariñena, Morastrell, Black Garnacha* and *Tempranillo*. The first-year wines have a low dry extract, a moderate alcoholic content (10° to 12° in general), but a high acidity, so that they are very suitable for making sparkling wines.

These cellar-bred wines are matured with the greatest biochemical care. The first-year wine is bottled with the yeast and the racking liquor to produce the second fermentation characteristic of wines made by the Champagne method. The bottles are then laid flat in underground cellars to enable the added sugar to ferment and produce the carbonic acid gas characteristic of wines of this type, which escapes when the bottle is uncorked. The maturing of the sparkling wine really begins after the second fermentation. The quality of the sparkling Panadés wines has been constantly improved.

More and more different varieties of this wine are being produced and the market is continuously expanding.

ALELLA. This small district, with two quite different slopes, the larger with a southern exposure towards the sea, the other facing north, is part of the province of Barcelona. It produces delicate table wines, very pale whites, light reds and rosés. The drier wines run to between 11° and 13°. The grape varieties used are the *Pansa, Garnacha, Picaboll, Macabeo* and *Malvasia* for the whites and the *Black Garnacha, Tempranillo* and *Sumoll* for the reds.

MALVASIA DE SITGES. This wine comes from a very small district planted solely to the *Malvasia* grape. Sweet, very agreeable to the taste, old gold in colour, it is greatly appreciated as a dessert wine but it has the disadvantage of giving only a very small yield.

CONCA DEL BARBARÁ. The winegrowing district of this name is situated in the south of the province of Tarragona below the Priorato; there are some very good table wines similar to those coming from Alella and Panadés. Together with two other East Coast regions, Barcelona and Malvasia de Sitges, Conca del Barbará comes under the official place-name control *(denominacion de origen)* regulations, a programme for which was established some years ago.

ALICANTE. The Alicante winegrowing district may be divided into two parts. The first, running west from Alicante itself, produces wines for blending and some table wines; the second, in the north-east of the province where the soil varies considerably and the main variety of grape is the *Moscatel*, supplies mostly fortified wines. The deeply coloured red wines, which are used for blending, have an alcohol content between 14° and 18° and their dry extract titrates between 25° and 35° Beaumé. The alcohol content of the *clarete* and red table wines does not exceed 14°, while that of the fortified wines varies between 14° and 17°, with a Beaumé measurement ranging from 7° to 10°.

VALENCIA, UTIEL-REQUENA and CHESTE. These three wines of guaranteed origin are regulated by the Board and are divided into three sections corresponding to the three growing districts.

The Utiel-Requena district is in the west of the province of Valencia. The Cheste district is an enclave in the centre, and the Valencia district proper covers the remainder of the province.

The Utiel-Requena district is the highest-lying and most rugged, and so the reds, *claretes* and rosés have a lower alcohol content (10° to 13°). They are very suitable for ageing owing to their high fixed acidity. Grapes used are the *Bobal, Garnacha* and *Crujidera*.

The Cheste wines are made from a wide range of varieties, the *Pedro Ximénez, Planta Fina, Moscatel, Merseguera, Macabeo* and *Planta Nova*. All of them are white wines running between 11° and 15°. The wines in the third district, Valencia, are very varied. The grape varieties are the same as for the Cheste wines, with, in addition, the *Malvasia* for the whites and the *Garnacha Tintorera* and *Monastrell* for the reds. This district produces red table wines, fortified and dessert wines and sweet wines named after the grape from which they are derived: *Malvasia, Pedro Ximénez* or *Moscatel*. The alcohol content of the dessert wines can be as high as 23°.

THE WINES OF THE CENTRE AND THE SOUTH-EAST

The districts that produce the wines of the central and south-eastern part of Spain are part of the provinces of Ciudad Real (the Manzanares and Valdepeñas) and Toledo (the Noblejas), which, with the provinces of Cuenca and Albacete, make up La Mancha. Vines take up the greater part of the arable land in this region. The province of Ciudad Real comes first with 23.6 per cent of the cultivated area; then Toledo with 12.8 per cent, followed by Albacete (12.9 per cent) and Cuenca (12 per cent). The vineyards of these four provinces account for about 35 per cent of the total Spanish winegrowing area. The figures show the vast importance of grape and winegrowing in this part of Castile. Here, as in the Catalan and Andalusian regions, whites predominate, though the few red wines produced are very good.

La Mancha is a broad plain between 1,500 and 2,400 feet above sea-level. The climate is dry and semi-arid, which accounts for the comparatively low yields of the vines. Indeed, La Mancha is a name that has derived from the Moorish word *marzo*, meaning "dry land". The wines from all the communes in La Mancha have certain characteristics in common, due both to identical climatic conditions and to the fact that the processes of vinification used are fairly similar.

Most of the grape varieties are white, like the wines themselves; the *Airen* is by far the most common, the *Pardillo*, *Verdencho*, *Albillo* and *Macabeo* less widely grown. The most characteristic red varieties are the *Cencibel*, with some *Garnacha*. The varieties with the largest yields are the *Airen* among the whites and the

North-east of Alicante, the vineyards that encircle Calpe (our photo) produce mostly *mistelles*, wines derived from the *Moscatel* used primarily for blending, together with light red or rosé wines of high alcohol content (13-14°).

Cencibel among the reds. In the province of Ciudad Real the average yield is about 6 hundredweight per acre, slightly higher in Cuenca. La Mancha is the main region producing *corrientes*, dry wines with an alcohol content of 11.5° to 13°, with a moderate degree of fixed acidity. They are used all over Spain as table wines and aperitifs, especially in the capital, Madrid. Most of the La Mancha wines are vinified in *tinajas*, the large vats of baked clay typical of the region. Although more modern vats are to a certain extent taking over from the *tinajas*, the old-fashioned clay pots are still widely used and are generally preferred by the vintners. Each vessel is made individually by hand and may hold up to as much as 2,500 gallons of wine.

The most characteristic of the La Mancha wines is the VALDEPEÑAS from the *Cencibel* grape. It is ruby-coloured with fine shadings and up to 14° alcohol content. The wines called ALOQUE, from the same district, are pleasant-tasting *claretes* which are almost rosés. The generic guaranteed origin label MANCHA covers growths from a wide area made up of a large number of communes, the principal being Alcazar de San Juan, Campo de Criptana, San Martin de Valdiglesias, Socuellamos, Ciudad Real, Manzanares, Méntrida, Tarancón, Ocaña, Noblejas, El Bonillo and Villarobledo. To be entitled to the label the wines must be at least two years old and have been matured for at least one year in oak casks. The wines of Manchuela and Almansa, which also are entitled to a guaranteed origin label, deserve more than a passing mention here.

By far the majority of the commonest regional white wines are derived from the *Airen* grape. Their alcohol content is 12° to 14°. They are golden, clear, but not very brilliant, and their fixed sulphuric acidity is low (2.40°). They are usually drunk in their first year. The wines made from the *Pardillo* grape at Tarancón and the red wines of Belmonte, the *claretes* of Noblejas and the wines from Yepes, Ocaña and Esquivias are well liked in some parts of the country, especially in the province of Cuenca, and have a strong local following. Excellent local wines are produced in this central region, in the provinces of Toledo and Madrid. Very deep-coloured wines with a high alcohol content and a high dry extract are produced in the districts of Méntrida (province of Toledo) and Navalcarnero (province of Madrid) and in the communes of Arganda and Colmenar. The Méntrida wines are entitled to the guaranteed origin label as laid down in the statutes.

The grape varieties are the Madrid *Red Garnacha* and some *Cencibel* for the reds, and the *Jaen*, *Torrentes* and *Pardillo* for the whites. The red wines of Arganda, Colmenar and San Martin de Valdeiglesias run to 15° and are slightly astringent, low in acid and usually with a good taste. Some dessert wines are made, the most notable of these being the MOSCATEL.

The very reputable wines from the province of Avila, north-west of the province of Madrid, may also be included in this region. The *Garnacha* and *Tempranillo* grapes are most used for the reds and mainly the *Jaen*, *Malvar*, *Torrentes* and *Verdejo* for the whites. The village of Cebreros produces the best known of the Avila wines, red wines without much colour, almost *claretes* in fact, and white wines with a good taste but little body. Quite agreeable dessert wines are made from the reds. The white table wines are golden in colour, light and generally dry.

Cordoba and its surrounding area have a long history of wine production which continued, despite its prohibition in the Koran, throughout the period of Islamic rule that has left its Arabic stamp still on the town. The wines are now known as MONTILLA-MORILES, which bear a remarkable similarity to the much better known wines of Jerez de la Frontera.

214

THE WINES OF JUMILLA (MURCIA)

The province of Murcia is not part of Andalusia, even though it is in southern, or rather south-eastern, Spain. It produces wines which are highly spoken of, mostly from the *Monastrell* grape, with some from the *Garnacha*. They are entitled to the JUMILLA label. The JUMILLA-MONASTRELL wines range from 14.5° to 18° alcohol content, and this strength is wholly natural, since no alcohol is added during fermentation. There are some other types of wine also entitled to the label, running between 12.8° and 15°, made from grape varieties of which the *Monastrell* accounts for at least 50 per cent. This, of course, tends to promote the growing of this variety, for, even though its yield is small, its quality is excellent. The Board is therefore quite right in keeping the wine under control. The reds and *claretes* from this district are greatly liked in Spain and abroad. They have a high dry extract and their deep, rich red colour reflects the amount of tannin in them. They age very well, though they are very often drunk while still quite young as *corrientes*.

THE WINES OF SOUTHERN SPAIN

In the Montilla-Moriles district the first-year wines are rather insipid but are very suitable for maturing, which gives them a remarkable aroma and other fine qualities. They are produced all over the province of Cordoba from the vineyards on the limestone of the Sierra of Montilla and Moriles Altos. Their guaranteed origin labels are MONTILLA ALBERO and MORILES ALBERO. They are matured in a district made up of Montilla, Los Moriles, Aguilar de la Frontera, Lucena, Cabra and Doña Mencia, Puente-Genil and Cordoba.

By far the largest proportion of the wines of the Montilla and Moriles district are made from *Pedro Ximénez* grape; the *Lanren, Baladi, Baladi-Verdejo* and *Moscatel* are also cultivated but in far smaller amounts. The continental climate, the soil and the slopes are very well suited to these varieties. The traditional types of these wines, all of them white, are known as *fino, fino viejo* (or *amontillado*), *oloroso* and *oloroso viejo*. The first-named has an alcohol content of 16° to 16.5°, the *fino viejo* 17° to 17.5°, the *oloroso* 18° to 19° and the *oloroso viejo* 19° to 21°. Although these wines are blended to match the standard sherry grades no alcohol at all is added, whereas in the sherry vinification process grape alcohol is used to stabilize and fortify the wine. The wines are pale greenish-gold in colour, limpid and transparent, with a very prominent bouquet and a special taste which marks them out from the sherries (q.v.) of the same name. Light and dry, they have a delicate bitter-almond flavour.

MALAGA. Wine has been grown in this district from remote ages. The winegrowing district of 89,000 acres of vineyards covers the whole province, with a definite predominance of the *Moscatel* and the *Pedro Ximénez*. The *Moscatel* makes raisins, the *Pedro Ximénez* produces sweet and semi-sweet wines, old gold in colour, with an alcohol content of 14° to 23°. This type is known as the LACHRYMA CHRISTI. With their low acidity, Malaga wines are famous throughout the world for their incomparable bouquet and taste.

HUELVA. This province is in western Andalusia and its winegrowing district was once known as the Condado de Niebla (County of Fog). The main winegrowing districts are Niebla, Bollullos del Condado, Paterna, Almonte, Bonares and Moguer. The main varieties are the *Palomino, Garrido Fino, Mantuo de Sanlucar* and *Listan*. The wines are golden and very fragrant, and they are sweeter in the Moguer district than elsewhere. The wines are something like those of Jerez owing to the similarity of climate, soil and grape, but do not in general have such a delicate flavour.

MONTILLA, which falls under the D.O.C. MONTILLA-MORILES, is a white wine made from the *Pedro Ximénes*. Although in taste it closely resembles SHERRY, it contains no added alcohol.

154

OTHER WINE DISTRICTS

RIBEIRO. There are three separate winegrowing districts in the Galician province of Orense. The largest is Ribeiro in the western part of the province, west of the town of Orense. The *Treixadura* is most used for the white wines, and to a lesser extent the *Albariño*; the *Garnacha*, *Caiño* and *Brancellao* for the reds. The alcohol content of the white wines runs to 10° to 11°, the reds to 10° to 12°. These sharp, clean, light wines with their slight sparkle are appreciated locally. The red wines are deeply coloured and acid.

VALDEORRAS. The second district is Valdeorras, a region of gently sloping hills where the vine is always planted above 2,500 feet and trellised against cryptogamic diseases. White wines are made from the *White Godello* and the red wines from the *Garnacha*, *Alicante* and *Mencia*.

MONTERREY. In the third district, the valley of Monterrey, the vines are grown on gentle slopes, not above 2,500 feet. The rainfall is nearly 40 inches and the vine is usually trellised. The grape varieties are the same as in the other districts. The red wines are rather more full-bodied than elsewhere in the province.

ESTREMADURA. In the provinces of Badajoz and Caceres, which make up Estremadura, *corrientes* are produced among which that from Almendralejo is notable. In the Barros district the vineyards cover 20 per cent of the cultivated area. The wines are drunk locally or taken elsewhere to mature. Most of the whites come from the *Unite Jaen*, but the *Airen* is also grown. The

Garnacha and the *Morisca* are used for the reds. The *Pedro Ximénez*, *Palomino* and *Macabeo* are grown in this area primarily as table grapes.

Many of the red wines produced here have the unusual attribute—for Spanish wines—of producing a crust when sufficiently aged; and while still young, they can sometimes be found to be cloudy. This is no doubt due in large part to their being sold very soon after primary fermentation has finished, and thus one can expect some secondary fermentation to take place in the bottle. For all that, though, they rarely exhibit sparkle, suggesting that their cloudiness may be closely connected with the fact that clarification of the wine while still in the vat is by no means as widespread here as it is throughout France, for example. This argument is offered more solid backing when one considers that the so-called "flower" in certain cheaper bottles of sherry is undoubtedly due to this same circumstance.

The white wines of Almendralejo are light, sweet and golden, not very acid and run to 13°. Those of Villanueva de la Serena are rather more straw-coloured and also rather stronger, about 15°, and are often drunk as aperitifs. The red wines of Guarena are pleasantly fresh and almost purple in colour. Stronger red wines are made in the Salvatierra de los Barros district, and rosés in Fregenal. In the province of Caceres the *Jaen*, *Cayetana* and *Airen* are used for the whites, and the *Garnacha* and *Negra de Almendralejo* for the reds. Both the reds and whites are of very unequal quality. The best are the whites from Cañamero, the *claretes* from Montehermoso and the reds from Montanchez.

RUEDA and TORO. The Castilian province of Valladolid and the provinces of León and Zamora produce a great deal of *corrientes* and a few wines with some character. In the province of Valladolid the best wines come from Rueda, La Nava, Peñafiel, Cigales and La Seca, in León from La Bañeza and in Zamora from Toro. The *White Verdejo* and the *Red Garnacha* are the main varieties in the Rueda district. The climate is dry, the mean rainfall 16 inches. The alcohol content of the Rueda wines is 13°, sometimes higher; they are straw-coloured and are drunk locally. The white wines of La Seca and Nava del Rey are well spoken of. The *clarete* of Cigales and the wines from Mucientes and Fuensaldaña, which enjoy a deserved reputation, are not quite so strong. Very full-bodied, thick, purple red wines are produced around Peñafiel. Besides these *corrientes* there are some special wines which, when matured and bottled, are much sought after in the domestic market. Light, sharp, slightly acid, pleasant-tasting wines are made from the *Red Mencia* and *Prieto Picudo* grapes in the province of León. Lastly, in the north of the province of Zamora, the district known as Tierra del Vino (Wineland) produces the Toro wines, *corrientes* of good quality which, however, unfortunately do not age.

The table wines produced on the Balearic Islands are mostly drunk locally by the islanders and tourists. Below: A Majorcan vineyard near Felantix on the eastern side of the island.

The vines of Lanzarote, in the Canary Isles, are far from ordinary. They grow on a black volcanic soil swept by fierce winds, and so the winegrowers plant each vine in a hollow dug into the ground and surrounded by a little wall of dry stone for protection. The wine, mostly white, is very distinctive and of high alcohol content.

THE WINES OF JEREZ

The town of Jerez de la Frontera (province of Cadiz), situated in the centre of the district which has given its name to sherry, was founded by the Phoenicians. The name Xera, "a town situated close to the Pillars of Hercules", is found in documents dating from the fourth century B.C. Martial (A.D. 40-104) mentions the wines of Ceret in some of his epigrams. When the Moors occupied Andalusia, they called the town Sherisch, from which comes the English "sherry", the name by which the Jerez wines are generally known. In 1894 the phylloxera destroyed almost all the vineyards, but there were luckily enough vine stocks left to re-establish vineyards with qualities similar to those which had been current in pre-phylloxera days.

The wine known as JEREZ or SHERRY, the label of origin being legally protected, is made exclusively from grapes gathered within a restricted area in the north-west of the province of Cadiz comprising the communes of Jerez de la Frontera, Puerto de Santa Maria, Sanlucar de Barrameda, Chiclana, Puerto Real, Chipiona, Rota and Trebujena. The outstanding vineyards are those on the calciferous soils of the communes of Jerez de la Frontera, Puerto de Santa Maria and Sanlucar de Barrameda. These communes, together with the neighbouring communes of Rota and Chipiona, make up the district of Upper Jerez.

GRAPE VARIETIES. The two varieties best suited to sherry-making are the *Palomino* and the *Pedro Ximénez*. The two sub-varieties of the *Palomino*, the *Palomino Fino* and the *Jerez*, are white, and account for more than 70 per cent of the vineyards in the district. The *Palomino* is particularly well suited to the local soil and climate, and its shoots take very well on the stock of the *Berlianderi*, the best American vine for calciferous soil. The *Pedro Ximénez* supplies first-rate 13° to 14° musts, and with enough exposure to sun the grapes can produce wines with an alcohol content running as high as 30° to 32°. When semi-fermented, these musts produce the PEDRO XIMÉNEZ, a natural sweet wine with very special organoleptic charactistics.

217

The cultivation of the vineyards in all its details is far too vast and specialized a subject to go into here, but it may be noted that throughout the district the vines are treated with as much loving care as a stately garden.

HARVESTING and PRESSING. The vintage usually starts in the first two weeks of September, but the date, of course, varies with the weather. The grapes are never gathered until they are fully ripe, for it is only then that they produce the maximum quantity of juice and, as their sugar content is at its height, they give the alcoholic strength desired. The ideal time to begin the vintage is shown by the changes in the grapes' colour from green to a dark tobacco brown and in the stalks, which become woody.

The grapes are picked in stages, since only the fully-ripened bunches are gathered. They are then placed in baskets which hold about 25 pounds each and are transported to the *almijar* with which all large vineyards are equipped.

The *almijar* is a very clean platform of beaten earth on which the bunches of grapes are spread in the sun on woven *esparto* mats and left for varying periods according to the type of wine to be made. The grape throws off any remaining humidity. At night the grapes are all covered with mats to protect them from the dew. This age-old practice causes certain changes in the grape and must which affect the character of the wine. In the first place, the evaporation of the humidity reduces the weight; this brings about a concentration of the juice and consequently gives the must a higher sugar content, an increased total acidity and an increase in the alkaline content of the cinders. It is interesting that despite the increase in overall acidity, part of the malic acid disappears, so that its concentration is halted or even reduced. This should be borne in mind, for this acid affects the wine's aroma and flavour. The grapes are then taken from the *almijar* to the presses. The must is expressed by various methods ranging from the classic grape-treading by men in spiked leather boots to mechanical presses. In every case the juice which exudes naturally from the press before pressure is applied is kept separate from the juice extracted from the mush after pressing. In other words the first juice is expressed by light pressure on the grapes (the weight of the man who treads them, for instance). The presses may either be screw-presses, the oldest and best-known type, or modern variable-pressure machines. The juice from the mush alone will make lower-quality wines, which are generally used for distilling.

Besides exposing the picked grapes to the sun, another very typical process has been used from time immemorial in the Jerez de la Frontera district. This is "plastering", which is the addition of gypsum or calcium sulphate to the musts to induce the necessary degree of acidity. There is a great deal of controversy about this method with regard to the way calcium sulphate acts on the musts. They become brighter, fining is speeded up, the colour brightens too, large deposits are formed and

the alcohol content rises because of the more complete fermentation. The amount of gypsum used in this method is about 26 ounces to 32 ounces in a 110-gallon cask. Plastering, however, is subject to strict regulation, since the limits are fixed by law in many countries, including Spain itself. But broader limits are tolerated for sherry and other fortified wines. The wine-making equipment and containers are normally sterilized with sulphuric acid (sulphur anhydride or sulphur dioxide) or with potassium bisulphite or liquefied pure SO_2. The purpose of this sterilization is to prevent infection by micro-organisms that may damage the musts or wines. Though this method is lethal to micro-organisms if enough sulphur is used, it does not damage the yeasts most suited to vinification.

VINIFICATION AND MATURING. If a wine is to be entitled to bear the label SHERRY with its guarantee of origin, it must undergo a process of maturing and ageing in wood within a district defined by regulation, that is to say, in cellars situated within the communes of Jerez, Puerto de Santa Maria and Sanlucar de Barrameda. It may not be matured in any of the other communes. The maximum permitted production is 700 gallons per acre in the Upper Jerez district and 900 gallons elsewhere. The purpose, of course, is to protect the wine's quality.

Maturing sherry is a delicate affair, for it has to be geared to the musts each year, since owing to the factors set out earlier in this section each vintage produces different musts. The Jerez cellarers are past masters in the art of maturing their wines and are able to coordinate the various factors which continually affect it at this stage of its vinification so as to obtain sherries of such uniform and constant quality that they live up to their brand name.

The must obtained by one of the processes described above is drawn off straight into casks holding 30 *arrobas*—about 110 gallons—which are immediately taken to the cellar.

A few hours after treading and pressing, the first fermentation, called "lively fermentation", begins. It is therefore essential to transport the casks as quickly as possible to the cellars (which are usually close to the towns) since too high a temperature may damage the normal proliferation of the yeasts which are to convert the glucose into alcohol. Disease germs may also develop at this stage, reducing the sugar content which, in turn, would reduce the alcohol content and could even produce acetic acid.

The cellars in the Jerez de la Frontera district are not constructed underground, as in the other winegrowing districts. They are long buildings made up of several cellars some twenty feet high, separated by long galleries. The casks are stacked lengthwise one above the other, in several rows, usually three, on either side of the cellars, leaving access corridors down the middle of each cellar. To get as much fresh air as possible and, above all, ensure a stable temperature, the cellars are built some miles from built-up areas, with thick walls

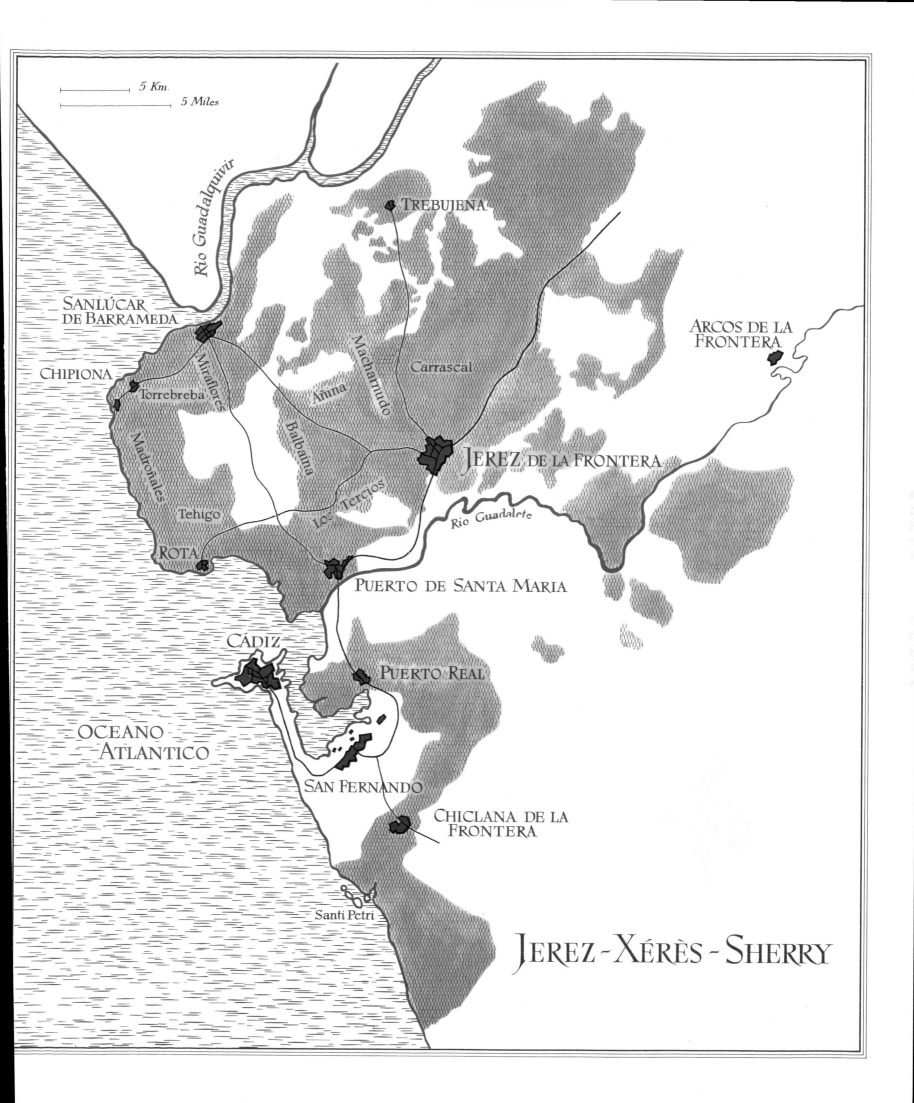

5 Km.

5 Miles

Rio Guadalquivir

TREBUJENA

SANLÚCAR
DE BARRAMEDA

ARCOS DE LA
FRONTERA

CHIPIONA

Miraflores

Carrascal

Añina

Macharnudo

Torrebreba

Balbaina

Madronales

Tehigo

Los Tercios

JEREZ DE LA FRONTERA

Rio Guadalete

ROTA

PUERTO DE SANTA MARIA

CÁDIZ

PUERTO REAL

OCEANO
ATLANTICO

SAN FERNANDO

CHICLANA DE LA
FRONTERA

Santi Petri

JEREZ·XÉRÈS·SHERRY

and in an open space facing south-west or south, where they catch the sea-breeze. Since a great deal of oxygen is needed in maturing sherry, the cellars have small windows some way up the walls and they are always left open in order to set up a constant draught. The floor of the cellar is of beaten earth and is frequently watered to keep the air fresh and the temperature even. It is covered with small oak squares at places where the casks are rolled or any work is to be done.

Since the climate in this region is temperate in September, there is no need to fear any sudden rise in temperature during the fermentation, which might have a harmful effect on the wine, in particular a reduction in the alcohol content. This danger is further mitigated by the fact that the casks hold so little. Nevertheless, a constant strict watch is kept to prevent any accidents. When the lively fermentation is completed, the cellarer inspects the wine-musts (the local name for musts less than a year old) to see whether they have kept dry; if so, the fermentation is completed. He then waits until January, February, or March at the latest, to start the racking in order to separate the wine-musts from the deposits or lees formed at the bottom of the cask. During the racking he engages in one of the most delicate of the operations which are to determine the future wine: an initial classification of the contents of each cask by its special characteristics, such as delicacy of flavour, aroma and colour. A mark is then placed on the bottom of each cask: one or more *palmas* (stylized palms) if the wine is likely to be fit for *finos*; one or more *rayas* (stripes) if it is fuller-bodied; one or more stripes barred diagonally, whence the name *palo cortado* (cut stick) when it is sweeter and sharper, though still fairly full-bodied. After the classification has been made, the next stage, in March, is fortification, consisting in adding a certain amount of alcohol. The casks are then transferred to the ageing cellar where the real sherry process takes place. This process gives the wine the strength it lacks and raises the alcohol content to 15.5°, or slightly more for the wines of the *rayas* and *olorosos* type.

One of the most interesting things in the making of sherry is the action of certain micro-organisms which live in the wine and feed on its components. They cause chemical reactions which liberate aldehydes and free acids; these determine the aroma and taste peculiar to sherry. They are known as *flor*, or flower. The flor is composed of yeasts which form a very thin film on the top of the wine at the beginning of the second stage in their development, and this film gradually thickens if the temperature and humidity are right. While the flor is forming, the casks are examined frequently to watch over the characteristics—consistency, colour and so on—and at the same time to see whether the wine is still in the same class as it was—*palmas*, *rayas* or *palo cortado*—or if its classification has changed. The flor does not act continuously in the maturing of sherry, but only when the temperature and humidity are favourable, i.e. first about April and then in August or Sep-

tember. During these two periods white spots appear on the surface of the wine and spread till they form irregular patches resembling small flowers—hence the name. The patches gradually expand until they form a species of thin white coating which finally attains the thickness and consistency of cream. The chemical and biological transformations of these yeasts which live and grow on the wine combine to make up one of the major characteristics of maturing sherry.

With the type of wine called *finos* (pale dry) of the *amontillados*, the formation and development of the flor is allowed to proceed during the first years of ageing until the wine is bottled. With the *olorosos* (sweet, dark), *paloscortados* (midway between the *finos* and the *amontillados*) and in the final stage of the *amontillados* the development is muted by the addition of a little wine alcohol, which raises their alcoholic content slightly. This and fortifying are the only things added in the course of maturing the wine.

Ageing by the *solera* system works differently. Its purpose is to keep indefinitely a specified type of wine which will always have exactly the same characteristics no matter when it is drunk. Losses either by racking and filtering or from natural causes are made up by adding younger wines. In this method of ageing a number of casks are used, all of them containing wines which may be old or young, but are invariably of the same type and in the same classification while maturing.

In the cellars of Jerez the casks are ranged above each other in three or four rows. The lowest are the casks called *sole*, the row nearest the ground—hence the term *solera*. To avoid confusion, it should be explained that this term is also applied to very old and noble dark wines, since all the dark sherries, whether *finos* (fine), *palidos* (pale) or *añejos* (aged), come from the *sole* casks. Above the row of *sole* casks are ranged two or three rows of casks known as *criaderas* (breeders).

The wines to be marketed are drawn from the *sole* row; they are the oldest. Great care is taken not to draw off more than half the contents of each cask. The *solera* casks are filled up with slightly younger wine from the *criaderas* row. The *criaderas* in turn, are filled up with younger wine from the third row. The number of *criaderas* varies with the types of wine; there are usually more for the *finos* than for the *olorosos* and *amontillados*. In blending care is taken to add a smaller amount of young wine than the amount of old wine left in the cask, so that the older wine may act on the younger, imparting to it its better qualities. The cellarers are very skilled in making these careful blends and in adapting each type of new wine to the wine of previous years and the result is that the oldest casks remain always the same in quality.

The maturing of MANZANILLA must be described separately, as it has features of its own. The general process is similar to that we have just described, but in the Sanlucar de Barrameda district the harvest is brought in fairly early, about the first week in September.

The winegrowers of Jerez have been cultivating the vine for more than two millenia, and during that time have understandably become remarkably experienced viti-viniculturalists. It is impossible to confuse a SHERRY with any other wine, Spanish or otherwise.

Exposure to the sun, which raises the alcohol content of the wine-must to 12°-13°, does not take place, nor are the musts for making MANZANILLA given the *añada* treatment for more than twelve months. The *solera* and *criadera* casks must never be full; a void corresponding to at least 22 gallons is essential. There should be ten or twelve casks in the *sole* row. Too much wine should not be drawn off in the racking, but it should be racked frequently; four or five cellar jugs (capacity about 20 pints) should be drawn off monthly or even every five days. The alcohol content should not exceed 15.5° while the dry MANZANILLA is maturing. If it does, it has to be lowered with young wine; but if it falls below 14.8°, it must be raised by adding wine with a higher alcohol content or an admixture of sherry or alcohol known as *miteado* or *combinado*. The dry MANZANILLAS become MANZANILLAS *pasadas* if the process is prolonged, the alcohol content gradually increasing to 17° or 20°. Owing to this high alcohol content, the flor dies, but the wine already has all the qualities to which it owes its great reputation.

When the wines from the *soleras* are drawn, they are clarified to stabilize them and to keep them perfectly clear and bright. This is done with beaten egg-whites, five to twenty per 500-litre (about 110 gallons) cask.

The regulations for the SHERRY guarantee require four groups of cellars: vinification cellars, production cellars, maturing and storage cellars, and maturing and shipping cellars. This last group is sub-divided into cellars for shipping to Spain and shipping abroad.

The regulations also prescribe that no cellar to which they apply may sell or export more than 40 per cent at the most of its reserves in hand at the beginning of each crop year. No wine may use the guaranteed origin label unless it is at least three years old. A Board exists to see that the regulations are observed.

Export sales of sherry to the United Kingdom in barrel are by far the largest, with some 6,600,000 gallons, increasing fairly regularly each year (by an average of 374,000 gallons). Annual shipments to Denmark and Sweden are also increasing; they are 550,000 and 330,000 gallons respectively. Sherry exports to the United States have doubled since 1961.

The following general characteristics of sherry should be particularly born in mind:
1. There is no such thing as a vintage sherry, that is a sherry produced from the wine harvested in one particular year. The year of bottling is sometimes seen marked on the cork, but since this does not indicate a "vintage" it is of no special interest.
2. An eighty-year-old sherry does not mean a wine that is eighty years old, but a sherry from a cask first filled eighty years ago. It is possible that traces of the original wine are still present in the sherry but the usual

221

MANZANILLA
1. Name of wine: Manzanilla. Manzanilla is a very pale, dry light sherry with a special bouquet and an alcohol content between 15.5 and 17°. – 2. Reminder: Manzanilla comes from the restricted region of Jerez. – 3. Origin. – 4. Grower and shipper's name.

DON ZOILO
(below left)
1. Trade name "Don Zoilo". – 2. "Very Old Dry Sherry" describes the wine; it has no vintage year, so the shipper has to produce a sherry that will be precisely the same year after year. Actually, the real name is Don Zoilo Dry. – 3. Origin. – 4. Grower and shipper's name. The wine's quality is bound up with the shipper's reputation.

PEDRO DOMECQ
1. Trade name "Primero". – 2. Type of sherry: amontillado. The wine has a more pronounced bouquet and taste than Manzanilla and is older. "Medium Dry Nutty" are details of the wine. This is the most typical sherry; alcohol content ranging from 16 to 18°, old amontillados from 22 to 24°. – 3. Origin. – 4. Grower and shipper's name.

By Appointment Wine Merchants

to His Majesty King George VI

S.B. 74- 6909

"BROWN BANG" SHERRY
(GOLDEN OLOROSO)

SANDEMAN BROS. & CO
JEREZ DE LA FRONTERA SPAIN

Sandeman Bros. & Co.

(REGISTERED TRADE MARK)

SANDEMAN

ESTABLISHED IN THE YEAR 1790

BROWN BANG SHERRY
1. Trade name "Brown Bang Sherry". – 2. Oloroso has more body and bouquet than amontillado; this wine is golden, but some olorosos may be slightly lighter in colour (tawny). – 3. Origin. – 4. Grower and shipper's name. – 5. This shows that this wine was served to King George VI.

SOLDADO
1. Trade name "Soldado". – 2. "Old Brown" sherry is sometimes called "Raya"; it is dark brown and sweeter than oloroso and stronger too, 18 to 20°, but with less bouquet. – 3. Origin. – 4. The shipper mentions the "bodega" where the sherry was matured. – 4. Grower and shipper's name.

DIAMOND JUBILEE
1. Trade name "Diamond Jubilee". – 2. This sherry of the "cream" type is sweet, with a very strong flavour and great vigour. – 3. General origin. – 4. Grower and shipper's name. This name should not be confused with the name of the sherry; this is not quite clear from the label.

interpretation is that the particular blend has been maintained unchanged for eighty years.

3. The longevity of sherries in the bottle is very hard to determine and depends on the quality. A good quality sherry from a well-reputed house can be kept in the bottle for many years. Since this wine is fortified it travels much better than fine wines and the consumer can buy it when he needs it.

4. The sherry bouquet is produced by the oxidizing effect of certain varieties of yeast that form a film on top of the wine which "blossoms" into flors twice a year. This flor is carefully watched by the cellar masters and the casks are only part-filled to give the air access.

TYPES OF SHERRY

FINOS. Drier, less full-bodied and not so strong as the *olorosos*. There are two types.

— the *finos* proper, straw-coloured, pale, with a sharp and delicate aroma, which may be compared to that of almonds; they are light, dry and not very acid; the alcohol content is between 15.5° and 17°.

— the *amontillados*, amber-coloured, very dry, with less bite, soft and full in flavour, nutty; alcohol content 16° to 18°.

OLOROSOS. Darker, heavier and stronger than the *finos*. There are several types:

— the *rayas* are lower-class *olorosos*, old gold in colour, fuller-bodied and less delicate in aroma. They sometimes taste somewhat sugary, possibly because fermentation was not completed; strength 18° and over.

— the *olorosos* proper, dry, dark golden, with great aroma, though less bite than the *finos*. Their delicate taste may be compared to that of the walnut. They are called *amorosos* when they are sugary and rather fuller-flavoured. The alcohol content is the same as the above.

— the *paloscortados*, midway between the *amontillados* and *olorosos* proper; they may be called the higher-class *oloroso* type. They have the aroma of *amontillados* and the flavour of *olorosos*; colour and alcohol content similar to the latter.

— the "creams", rather sweet, with the body of *olorosos*. A judicious blend of dry *olorosos* with some PEDRO XIMÉNEZ. The blends are matured in *soleras* before they are sold.

DULCES. These are deep-coloured sweet wines from various grape varieties:

— PEDRO XIMÉNEZ is a natural sweet wine, its sweetness due to the exposure to the sun of *Pedro Ximénez* grapes after they are picked in order to obtain a must at nearly 30° Beaumé which is subjected to partial fermentation. In some cases, the grapes intented for this type of wine are exposed for as long as twenty days, so that complete fermentation is not possible. The wine is dark, with an alcohol content between 10° and 15°.

— MOSCATEL, a natural sweet wine from grapes of this variety, between 10° and 20° Beaumé.

MANZANILLA. A dry wine produced in the Sanlucar de Barrameda district. It comes under the Sherry Regulation Board, but has a different label from SHERRY. The two types of MANZANILLA come from the same district and the same variety of grape. The difference begins at the maturing stage. MANZANILLAS must by law be matured in cellars at Sanlucar de Barrameda. MANZANILLA is a delicate, light, very pale and very aromatic, dry and only slightly acid wine with a slightly bitter taste and an alcohol content between 15.5° and 17°. There are two types: MANZANILLA FINA is smooth and slightly bitter and does not age; MANZANILLA PASADA acquires a special taste by ageing and has a more prominent aroma, somewhat like that of the *olorosos*, but the taste is dry and has the characteristics of MANZANILLA FINA.

The sherries that are produced in California or in the South African Republic are wines produced in the same way as those of the Jerez region. But the differences in soil and climate give wines of the sherry type, wines that are analogous but not identical to the original sherries. To taste and compare for oneself is the only means by which one can form a judgement on this subject. The same comparison can be made between the true Champagne vinified in France and the innumerable sparkling wines that sometimes carry the name of Champagne.

Sherry is believed to have been introduced into what is now the United States of America by the Spanish explorer Álvaro Núñez who discovered Florida in 1528 and who came from a long line of vintners and cellar owners in Jerez. Something is even known of the price of sherry in Spain during those epic days of discovery since there is an account of a certain gentleman paying sixteen golden pesos (8½ dollars, £3.50) for a *botija* or jar of wine.

In conclusion let us move forward a few years to Shakespeare's time and repeat what he had to say in Henry IV Part 2 about the "sherris" drunk in England in the sixteenth and seventeenth centuries: "A good sherris-sack hath a twofold operation in it. It ascends me into the brain; dries me there all the foolish and dull and crudy vapours which environ it; makes it apprehensive, quick, forgetive, full of nimble, fiery and delectable shapes; which delivered o'er to the voice,—the tongue,—which is the birth, becomes excellent wit. The second property of your excellent sherries is,—the warming of the blood; which, before cold and settled, left the liver white and pale, which is the badge of pusillanimity and cowardice; but the sherries warms it and makes it course from the inwards to the parts extreme; it illumineth the face; which, as a beacon, gives warning to all the rest of this little kingdom, man, to arm: and then the vital commoners and inland petty spirits muster me all to their captain, the heart, who great and puffed up with this retinue, doth any deed of courage; and this valour comes of sherries..."

(Act IV, Scene III)

WINES OF SPAIN

NORTH-WESTERN SPAIN

RIBEIRO

Dry white wines . . . . . .   Pazo   Albariño

NORTHERN SPAIN

RIOJA

Dry red wines	Banda Azul	Castillo Ygay	Royal	Viña Tondonia
	Banda Roja	Imperial	Viña Monty	Viña Vial
	Bordon	Marques Riscal	Viña Pomal	Viña Zaco
	Castillo de las Arenas	Reserva Yago	Viña Real	

Dry white wines	Castillo Ygay Reserva	Marques Riscal	Rinsol	Viña Sole
	Corona	Monopole	Viña Paceta	Viña Tondonia
	Etiqueta Blanca			

Medium-sweet white wines . .	Diamante	Monte-Haro	Viña Zaconia

Dry rosé wines	Brillante	Castillo de las Arenas

RIOJA ALTA

Red wines	El Siglo	Monte Real	Viña Ardanza	Viña del Perdon
	Glorioso reserva	Viña Albina Vieja reserva	Viña Ercoyen	

White wines	Canchales	Metropol

Rosé wines . . . .   Viña Ercoyen

NAVARRE

Red wine . . . .   Castillo de Tiebas

CARIÑENA

Dry red wine . . . .   Cariñena

EASTERN SPAIN

ALELLA

Dry red wine . . . .   Marfil

Sweet red wine . . . .   Lacre Violeta

Dry white wines	Lacre Gualda	Marfil	Super Marfil reserva

Red wines	Oro Viejo	Zumilla

Dry rosé wine . . . .   Marfil

PRIORATO

Dry red wines	Falset Garnacha Priorato	High Priorato	Priorato Reserva especial

Sweet red wines	Priorato extra Rancio Solera 1918	Vicosa Generoso Priorato

PANADÉS

Sweet white wines	Malvasia	Moscatel
Red wine	Sumoll	

TARRAGONA

Dry red wines	Spanish Red Wine 1955	Viña Vinlo
Red wines	Aureo	Tarragona-Tawny
Dry white wines	Dry Grand Solera	

JUMILLA

Dry red wine	Solera
White wine	Oro Viejo Solera 1902

CENTRAL SPAIN

NOBLEJAS

Red wine	Noblejas	
White wine	Ocaña	Yepes

VALDEPEÑAS

Red wines	Cencibel (Tinto fino)	Garnacha	Tinto Basto
Dry white wines	Airen (Lairén)	Cirial	Pardillo

SOUTHERN SPAIN

MORILES-MONTILLA

Dry wines	*Amontillado*	Alvear Montilla	
	Amontillado pasado . .	Flor de Montilla	
	Fino	Moriles extra san Joaquin	Los Palcos
	Moriles	Seneca	Tercia
	Oloroso	Oloroso Alvear	
	Oloroso viejo	Diogenes	
	Blanco seco	Solera 1906	

MALAGA

Sweet wines	*Moscatel*	Moscatel Delicioso
	Moscatel dorado	Cariño
	Extra viejo	Pedro Ximenez FP
	Lágrima selecte	Los Frailes
	Dulce	Lacrimae Christi
	Dulce añejo	Malaga
Medium-sweet wine	*Vieja solera*	Pajarete 1908

226

Manzanillas	Aris	Eva	La Piconera	Pochola
	Atalaya	Fina	Macarena	Rayito
	Bertola	Garbosa	Mari-Paz	Rechi
	Bone Dry	Gloria	Merito	Regina
	Caricia	Greta	Montana	Sirena
	Carmelita	Hilda	Olorosa Angelita	Solear
	Carmen	La Ballena	Osborne	Torre Breva
	Carola	La Capitana	Papirusa	Varela
	Clasica	La Especial	Pemartin	Villamarta
	Cochero	La Goya	Petenera	Viva la Pepa
	Deliciosa	La Jaca Andaluza	Piedra	Wisdom & Warter
	Duff Gordon	La Lidia		

Finos	Agustinito	Deportivo	Jardin	Pedro Dry
	Alvaro	Don Algar	La Ina	Pemartin
	Apitiv	Don Zoïlo « Dry	La Condesa	Pinta
	Banquete	Ducal	La Panesa	Preferido
	Barbadillo	Eco	Loredo	Quinta
	Benito	El Catador	Los Compadres	Quisquilla
	Bergantin	Faena	Mantecoso	Redoble
	Betis	Fajardo	Marinero	Rivero
	Bombita	Feria Sherry	Marismeño	Sancho
	Camborio	Finito	Matador Pale Dry	San Patricio
	Campero	Fino F.M.	Menesteo	Tio Mateo
	Canto	Flamenco	Merito	Tio Pepe
	Casanovas	Gaditano	Micalet	Tres Palmas
	Clarita	Hernan Cortés	Olivar	Varela
	Chiquilla	Hidalgo	Palma	Victoria
	Coronel	Inocente	Pando	Viña del Carmen
	Cuesta Alta	Jarana	Pavon	Viña del Cuco

Amontillados	Abolengo	Dry Pale	John Peter	Principe
	Algar	El Botanico	King Alfonso	Rosa
	Amontillado 50	El Cid	La Capilla	Salinera
	Amontillado S.S.S.	El Duque	La Uvita	Salvador
	Anticuario	El Gallo	Lord Sherry	Sancho
	Ataulfo	El Navio	Luque	Santa Cruz
	Barbadillo	El Tresillo	Martial	Siglo de Oro
	Baroness Cocktail	Escogido	Matador	Solito
	Benito	Escuadrilla	Merito	Tio Diego
	Botaina	Fairyland	Millonario	Tio Guillermo
	Buleria	Finest	Miranda	Tito Jaime
	Carta Blanca	Fino Ideal	Nila	Tocayo
	Carta Real	Fino Zuleta	N.P.U.	Tulita
	Casanovas	Florido	Old Dry Classic	Ultra
	Chambergo	Guadalupe	Oñana	Varela
	Club	Guapito	Pemartin	Viejo M.M.M.
	Coquinero	Guerrero	Pizarro	Viña AB
	Del Abuelo	Imperial	Predilecto	Viño del Virrey
	Diestro	Jauna	Primero	Vintners Choice
	Dry Don			

Olorosos	Alfonso	Cacique	Don Quijote	España
	Almirante	Capitan	Don Zoïlo « Medium »	Fandango
	Autumn Leaves	Cartujo	Doña Juana	Favorito
	A Winter's Tale	Casanovas	Double Century	Fenecio
	Bailen	Chambelan	Dry Sack	Galarza
	Barbadillo	Diestro	D.S.	Gran Señor
	B.C. 200	Dique	Duque	Harmony
	Black Tom	Don Gonzalo	El Cesar	La Espuela
	Blazquez	Don Nuño	El Patio	La Infanta

La Merced	Molino	Regio	Solera P.J.
La Novia	Montado	Rio Viejo	Solera Tizon
La Raza	Navigator	Royal Double	Solera Victoria Regina
Long Life	Nina	Sancho	Tercios
Los Flamencos	Nº 10 R.F.	Solariego 1807	Torrecera
Martial Golden	Nº 28	Solera E	Trafalgar Solera 1805
Mayoral	Nutty Solera	Solera Florido	Valdespino
Medium Golden	Ochavico	Solera Granada	Varela
Mercedes	Orrantia	Solera 1842	Viña Isabel
Merito	Pemartin	Solera 1865	Wisdom's Choice
1874	Real	Solera Misa V.O.B.S.	Zuleta

Palos cortados . . . .

Deportivo	Don José	Ojo de Gallo	Superior
Diestro	Eva	Romate	Tres Cortados

Pedro Ximenez . . . .

Bobadilla	El Abuelo	Niños	Solera 1847 (Brown)
Cardenal Cisneros	Gonzalez	Osborne	Solera Superior
Carla	La Goleta	Pemartin	Superior
Cartago (Brown)	Legionario	Procer	Superior
Cob-Nut (Brown)	Martial (Brown)	Reliquia	Valderrama
Consejero	Matador (Brown)	Romate	Venerable
Diestro	M.G.L.	Royal (Brown)	Vintners (Brown)
Diestro (Brown)	1827	Soldado (Brown)	Wisdom
Ducha	1870		

Moscatel . . . .

Ambrosia	Evora	Padre Lerchundi	San Pedro
Atlantida	Fruta	Payaso	Tambora
Baron	Gran Fruta	Pico Plata	Toneles
Duquesa	Laura	Polca	Triunfo
Evangelio	1870	Promesa	Vitoria

Creams . . . .

Abraham	Dalgar	Harmony	Real Tesoro
Armada	Descarado	Infanta	Reverencia
Benito	Diamond Jubilee	Laurel	Romate
Bertola Cream	Diestro	Luque	Royal
Blazquez	Don Zoïlo « Cream »	Matador Cream	Sancho
Carlton House	El Monasterio	Meloso	San Rafael
Carmela	El Tutor	Merito	Sherry Joselito
Casanovas	Eva	Nectar	The Dome
Celebration	Felicita	Orleans 1886	To-Night
Coronation	Flor de Jerez	Osborne	Varela
Cream 201	Gentileza	Palomino	Vintners
Cream Sherry	Grape Cream	Pemartin	Wisdom's Cream
Cristina			

THE WINES OF PORTUGAL

SUZANNE CHANTAL DOS SANTOS

Although in world ranking Portugal stands in only sixth position for the total quantity of wine produced annually—behind Italy, France, Spain, the U.S.S.R. and Argentina—she is in fact the world's number one producer when one relates the density of production to the total area of land (metropolitan and insular) under cultivation. The Portuguese is a great drinker of wine, with an average annual consumption of 20 gallons per head. Despite this, he remains a sober citizen, for he has always known how to drink his wine; also, although flavoursome, it has a low alcohol content and it is rare to see any drunkenness.

Portugal is a country conditioned by the extreme changeableness of its sky and by the great geological variety of its soils. This diversity is reflected in the some 17-20 million gallons of wine that she drinks or exports each year. The country is very much under the influence of the great ocean winds, which favour a climate not unduly dry, except in the plains south of the river Tagus where, in any case, wheat is grown and not vines. Blessed with sunshine, the climate favours viticulture quite outstandingly. One can find traces of the vine in tre very earliest history of the land: for example, on the sarcophagus of Reguengos, dating from two thousand years ago, can be seen the detailed figures of men treading the grape. Much has been said and written on the subject of who first introduced the vine-plant into Portugal, one argument being that it came from Gaul with the Romans, another that it was brought by the Greeks and Phoenicians who, from earliest times, had navigated along the shores of Portugal and had eventually established trading here.

This Lusitania of Roman times was famous for its oil and its wines, since its olive-groves and vineyards made excellent neighbours. So much so that Rome became alarmed at the popularity of the wines, which were competing seriously with those of Italy. The Emperor Domitian decreed severe laws forbidding the cultivation of the vine in the provinces under Roman occupation, often even going as far as having it uprooted and replaced by cereal crops. The vine nevertheless survived this treatment, while both the Barbarians, who drank beer, and the Moors, who tolerantly would allow local customs to be continued in the territories they dominated, left it to prosper and develop. At the time of modern Portugal's birth, in the twelfth century, when young Afonso Henriques was recruiting troops for the Crusades to the Holy Land—as well as to chase the occupying Arab armies out of his future kingdom—we find one of these knight-errants making a prophetic statement: Arnulfo, an Englishman, in a letter which has come down to us, praised highly the merits of the wine from Douro. It was a precursor of what was to be seen, centuries later, as a root of one of the oldest alliances in the world, that of the Portuguese, who make the wine, and the English, who like to drink it. When Afonso Henriques captured Lisbon in 1147, vine-plants were found under the defensive walls of the future capital. As the young kingdom became more populated, the monks planted vineyards in the vast domains which were entrusted to them; and this not merely to obtain their altar wine. The wonderful illustrations of the Apocalypse by Lorvao show the wine harvest and the grape-presses. The Burgundian dynasty, also, was so conscious of the richness that viticulture represented for this country which it dominated for more than two centuries that a decree by Sancho I, at the beginning of the thirteenth century, prescribed that "whomsoever shall destroy a vine-plant shall be brought in judgement as it were for the death of a man".

One of the earliest and the most successful commercial exchanges between Portugal and the northern countries of Europe (England, Germany and The Netherlands) was with wine, which was shipped from Viana do Castelo. The cultivation of the vine, in which the Portuguese excel both by nature and by taste, then took on a new importance. The vineyards spread to the banks of the rivers and into the harshest regions: the sea-shore sands of Colares as well as the rocky ravines of Douro. But of course the day came when wine was over-produced at the expense of its quality, and viticulture, far from nourishing people in Portugal, almost condemned them to die of hunger. Strict measures had again to be taken, as in the days of Rome: wine production was limited, and thousands of inferior-quality vine-stocks were uprooted, to be replaced by more useful crops. In fact, all through its history, the Portuguese vineyard has known a series of crises and successes, and one of the constant factors of its evolution has been the anxiety of the authorities to safeguard

A town renowned throughout the world for the name it has lent to the excellent wines of Douro: Porto. Here in the foreground is a Douro *rabelo*, as this type of boat is called, sailing with its cargo of wine casks.

the quality of the wine used for export. Divergent claims have been made as to whether this policy has been to the detriment or to the benefit of the wines or vineyards considered of secondary importance, since in this sector conditions of production are up to the local growers and there is no outside control.

World events have also had a marked influence on Portuguese viticulture. The sixteenth century seemed almost to be dedicated to the desertion and neglect of the vineyards, as all the fever and ambition of the Portuguese adventurers and explorers was diverted overseas to the newly-discovered foreign lands. Within a very few years, the vines were taken over by heaths and waste-lands. After the wars with Louis XIV of France, England prohibited the importation of the wines of Aquitania and signed, in 1703, the Treaty of Methuen with Portugal which guaranteed a vital exchange—that of a monopoly in Portuguese wines for one in English wools. The wine trade picked up again: from 632 casks (of about 120 gallons each) exported in 1687, it rose spectacularly to 17,000 casks in 1757. England drank mostly the wines from Douro, and a large number of English wine merchants moved to the Continent and established themselves at Porto, where they could buy the standing harvests and closely super-

vise the shipment of the casks. From the very special conditions of this collaboration was to be born the most famous of Portuguese wines: port.

Although the nineteenth century saw improvements in cultivation and in the processes of vinification, successive disasters descended on the unfortunate Portuguese vineyards. In 1832, during the fratricidal warring between the rival kings Pedro and Miguel, Pedro landed in Porto and drew the chaos and horrors of battle into that region. Crops were neglected or pillaged, the winemaking plant in Porto set afire and the wine stocks destroyed.

In 1846, an insidious illness appeared: oïdium. It was necessary to clean out the vineyards, replacing most of the plants with new stock. Then twenty years later came another catastrophe, which was at first attributed to abnormally hot and dry summers and cold and humid winters. Vinegrowers wore themselves out in ineffectual and unorganized battle until it was discovered that this was an epidemic caused by an insect then unknown in Europe: phylloxera. Many growers gave up, discouraged by the terrifying devastation it had wrought. But others persevered, imported American plants to restock and by dint of years of courage, patience and hard work gradually rebuilt the kingdom's vineyards.

230

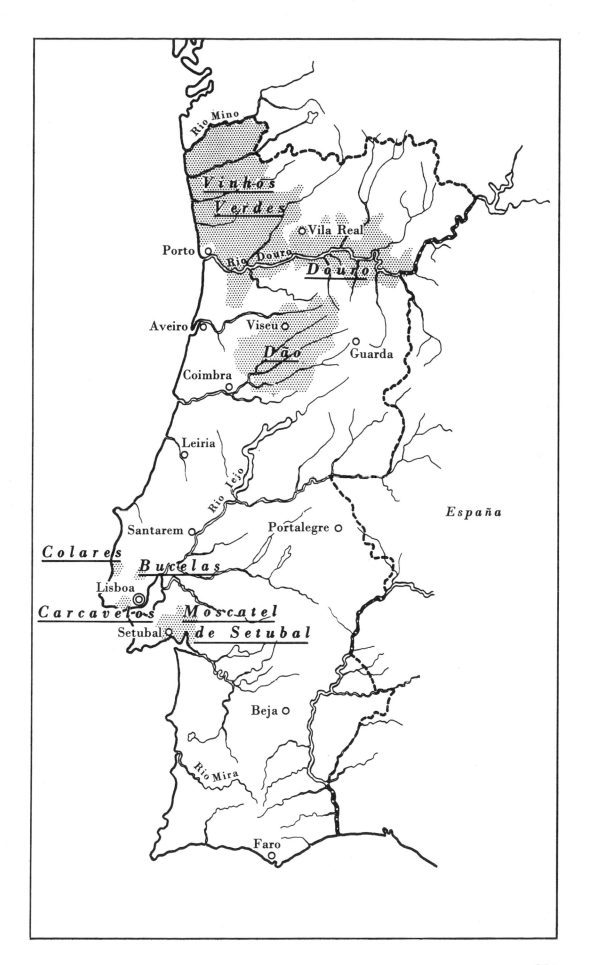

The great majority of the Portuguese vineyards lie to the north of Lisbon. The most important are those of the Upper Douro region, home of the celebrated port wine. Those of the Minho region produce the *vinhos verdes* ("green wines"); then come the vineyards of Dão, Colares and Bucelas. South of the capital, only the vineyards in the region of Setúbal are of any size.

Today, vineyards account for more than 10 per cent of the total agricultural area under cultivation (excepting forestry regions) in Portugal; and the vine, which by its very nature is already diversified, has become even more so under the local methods of cultivation and vinification. But this suits the Portuguese agricultural system, parcelled out as it is into small-holdings, dependant on the family unit, where everyone likes to grow the wheat, rye or maize for his bread, the olives for his oil and the grapes for his wine. This means that many winegrowers drink their own wine—which does not therefore appear in any official production statistics—and have an annual production which is too small to be marketable. Under present conditions, the majority of winegrowers belong to co-operatives, working with the assistance, of special organizations.

THE GREAT WINEGROWING REGIONS OF PORTUGAL

Certain regions have types of wines with such clear-cut characteristics that their zone of cultivation has been legally, and severely, delimited; by the same token, this has given them the right to an *appellation contrôlée*. This is the case with eight of the fourteen great wineproducing regions of Portugal: Bucelas, Carcavelos, Colares, Dão, Douro, Entre-Douro-e-Minho, Madeira and Setúbal.

WINES OF DÃO: Dão is a green and fertile region, both thickly wooded and intensely cultivated, which rises in tiers from the foothills of the two mountainous "spines" of Portugal: the Serra d'Estrela and the Caramulo. The farmer of these parts is stubborn, vigorous, resistant; his wine tends to resemble him, being strong and full-bodied. It ages well, possesses a good and velvety aroma and a deep colour that seems to come from the rolling landscapes with their low-toned tints, pines, purple heather and rocky outcrops.

This wine, long cultivated as a family affair and pressed in the open air, is rightly considered to be Portugal's best table wine. Several varieties exist, as a result of the great diversity of soils (where sometimes shale is mixed with granite) and of the vineyards' varying exposures to the sun. One can find the vine-plant at an altitude of more than 1,600 feet on the heights of Tarouca and Castro Daire, or tumbling along the banks of the Mondego (SANTA COMBA, TABOA, MORTAGUA) and on to the plain (MANGUALDE, VISEU). All these wines are therefore quite distinct, although at the same time related through a common stock: *Tourigo*, a vine which provides a high sugar content and a slightly astringent taste. By mixing red grapes and white grapes, a naturally oily, sweet wine is obtained. The red wines, although having a low alcohol content, are full-bodied, with beautiful deep-ruby reflections, while the whites are light, fresh, clear and very perfumed. In 1979, the area of the vineyard was 49,420 acres, producing 2,507,772 gallons.

WINES OF COLARES: It is really astonishing to see, between Cintra and the coast, within almost a stone's throw of Lisbon, the vine being cultivated along the sea-shore and on sandy lands now left high-and-dry by a retreating sea, particularly in the silted-up-estuary of the old river Galamares. Yet the vineyards of Colares are among the very oldest in Portugal. Stretching to the south of Cabo da Roca, the westernmost point of the European continent, through the regions of Turcifal and Fontanelas and right on to Azenhas do Mar, they have the noteworthy distinction of having survived the terrible phylloxera epidemic, simply because this insect was not able to live in the sand.

The cultivation of these vineyards is extremely difficult and sometimes even dangerous, for the first step entails digging trenches five to ten yards deep in light, running soil in order to get down to the more solid clay layers where the vine-plants can take root. Each plant spreads its roots sideways along the trenches, which are gradually filled in as new shoots appear. The vine-grower carefully layers his stock, enabling each layered shoot, once covered over, to become the basis of still more new shoots. But the extraordinary intricacy of the procedure in encouraging these last shoots means that, in reality, they are still part of the original vine-plant. Sometimes whole rows of vine-plants are thus made up of one solitary vine-plant at the bottom of the original trench, while up above ground, sheltered by heather or leafy screens and cut back very hard to stand up against the strong Atlantic winds, the vines twist and stretch on their way like strange muscular serpents.

With the arrival of summer, the bunches of grapes must be propped up so that they are not dried by the burning sand. The harvest is brief but picturesque and even in these times it is often carried on the backs of donkeys. In present days, too, a local *adega* weighs the grapes on the spot, and they are treated at once. Periods of rest in the cask before and after the press enriches the must in tannin and colouring matter. COLARES wine must be kept in the cask for two years, and attains its best form from the age of five years onwards. The site of the vineyard, the influence of the sea fogs and winds and of course more particularly the *Ramisco* (vine-plant of the sands) all give COLARES a special flavour, full-bodied yet velvety. Event the red wine is extremely light because of its low alcohol content, while the white is highly perfumed. The production of this unsual wine is very small: only 88,000 gallons for a vineyard of 620 acres which, alas, is getting ever smaller as amenities for tourists gradually invade the Lisbon Peninsula.

Vineyards like this one in the region of Torrès Vedras characterize the Portuguese Estramadura district. The predominant planting is the *Ramisco* grape which gives country wines that are pleasant enough to drink and go well with the local food.

WINES OF CARCAVELOS: The Carcavelos region is composed of alluvial deposits on the banks of the Tagus estuary, a soil much less dry and sandy than that of the Colares and producing a different wine.

The vine *Galego Dourado* gives a quick-fermenting must of a clear colour; the wineproducer adds a completely fermented wine called *abafado* which lends a certain velvety texture to this liqueur, dry rather than sweet, with a rather surprising almond flavour and an alcohol content of at least 19° to 20°. Much appreciated in the seventeenth and eighteenth centuries, CARCAVELOS has now become a rare wine (an area of 77 acres produces no more than 5,500 gallons) which is bought up almost entirely by Great Britain and the Scandinavian countries.

WINES OF SETÚBAL: Scarcely 25 miles from the capital but on the southern bank of the Tagus lies the region of Setúbal, with its pines and rice-fields.

A centuries-old reputation enhances MOSCATEL DE SETÚBAL: this was the wine—along with GARNACHE and MALVASIA, both wines from plants of those same names—that was so lauded among the *vins étranges* appreciated in the Paris of the fifteenth century. Rabelais mentions it when describing the *Temple de la Dive*

Bouteille, Louis XIV insisted on having it in his cellars at Versailles and Voltaire had it brought to him at Ferney.

The stalks of the grapes are left in the must, which gives the MOSCATEL its lively perfume, its strong colour and its characteristic taste. The wine is never drunk until it is at least five or six years old, and there are some MOSCATEL, called "museum wines", which are very old indeed and quite unexcelled: the 1920 vintage is perhaps the best of these. This MOSCATEL DE SETÚBAL, particularly appreciated in Canada, has been called by experts "the quintessence of liqueur wines"; it is sweet, light, fruity yet less musk-scented than FRONTIGNAN and lively enough to be excellent when drunk as an aperitif provided it is iced. It goes very well with second courses and desserts or, better still, with cheese, especially Azeitao ewe's cheese with its original flavour and taste of aromatic herbs.

The Estremadura Transtagana (south of the Tagus) produces other good wines: for example, the region of Palmela has light-red clarets and red table wines, notably PIRIQUITA, which is silky, supple yet robust. And Azeitao is the home of FAISCA, a very pleasant rosé which is extremely popular abroad: its delightful colour and thirst-quenching freshness (for it must, of course,

233

Vinhos verdes are made only in Portugal. They can be either white or red, are slightly effervescent and have a low alcohol content (8-10°). Rich in malic and lactic acids, they are now often exported.

be drunk iced) attract the drinker without startling him. Under the trade-name LANCERS, it is one of the best-selling wines in the United States.

WINES OF BUCELAS: The wines of the region of Bucelas, which are produced from the *Arinto* vine of the Tagus estuary, are dry and somewhat acid wines the colour of yellow straw. Much appreciated by Wellington's officers and men during his Peninsula War against Napoleon, they afterwards found a great success in England. Charles Dickens mentions them as among his favourite wines, along with SAUTERNES and sherry, and Lord Byron praises their qualities, to which George III of England adds that of having cured him of a kidney disease.

VINHOS VERDES: While such wines as DÃO, COLARES, BUCELAS, CARCAVELOS and even MOSCATEL have their imitators in other countries, the noted VINHOS VERDES ("green wines") are 100 per cent Portuguese all along the line. Their unusual name does not come from their colour (they are in fact red or white) but from the amount of ripening, for these wines are produced from plants in northern Portugal which are pruned espalier fashion and whose grapes never reach maturity.

These VINHOS VERDES, lively, slightly acid and always extremely young, have a very long history behind them and seem to have been known to Strabo.

Minho, home of VINHOS VERDES, is at the same time Portugal's most densely-populated province and that with perhaps the most difficult land, for its granite-like soil is unforgiving and unrelenting. Centuries-old parcelling of the land has resulted in an infinite number of tiny properties each hardly able to support a family—this is the region of traditional emigration to seek new hope, even though the vineyards hold man close through the unceasing cares which they demand and the joys and benefits they return. Human wisdom over the years has dictated that these vineyards must not be given a soil so dearly needed to feed so many mouths, and by law the vine may be cultivated only on waste ground, along the edges of fields or by paths and roads. So the farmer of Minho plants his vines in espaliers, as high hedges or even, very frequently, on living supports such as chestnuts, sycamores, poplars, cherry-trees or alders. The vine-plant is tied to the tree by fine willow stalks and the vine-shoots are allowed to hang down. These "grape-bearing trees" which delighted Jean Giraudoux, these "hanging vines", these paths of trellis give the landscape a gentle shade and cut up the country roads with a lace-like pattern of chiaroscuro. Their tart grapes come from very old selected vine-stocks: *Vinhão*, *Borracal* and *Espadeira* for the black grapes and *Azal* or *Dourado* for the white grapes.

The vines of the Minho basin remain undisturbed for long years and the plants become almost arborescent. The roots descend deep into a soil dug and fertilized with green heather and animal manure, while above ground, the knotted and muscled stem and the long supple-vine-shoots often reach a height of 15 feet. The humidity of this region encourages plant sickness, which means an unrelenting struggle with long sprays, using special products against the mildew and phylloxera. Harvested in September and racked at the end of the year six weeks after they have been bottled, these VINHOS VERDES are already a sparkling wine—and there is one of their characteristics, even one of their charms. The white wines are thirst-quenching, light and harmless, admirably suited to picnics and summer lunches, with an alcohol content of only 6° to 9°. The red VINHOS VERDES are also of low alcohol content, but these full-bodied wines are of a dark purple colour, with a crimson foam which stains the glass.

The VINHOS VERDES have been long appreciated for their refreshing taste of fruit and their lively youthfulness, but for many years they were drunk only locally, for it was said they travelled badly. Rich in lactic acid and malic acid, they were volatile and lacked body. More recently, it has been possible to stabilize them and they are now exported to Belgium, Africa and Great Britain, not to mention even to France where an equivalent wine does not exist. The price of modern progress has to be paid, however, and today bottles of uniform contents have replaced the attractive little stoneware jugs, the shape and size of which were seldom quite uniform.

There are some 90,000 producers of VINHOS VERDES, of which two-thirds only produce a few hundred gallons each. Production of VINHOS VERDES is falling

234

off, and nowadays only 37,396,600 gallons are made, very little of which is exported.

OTHER WINEPRODUCING REGIONS: Several other regions of Portugal are of quite some interest to viticulture. These are the wines of Pinhel, light and pleasant clarets; the wines of Lafoes, nonsparkling but otherwise similar to the VINHOS VERDES and grown on trellises (these *verdascos* are usually red wines and total about 1,540,000 gallons a year); the wines of Bairrada, semi-sparkling whites or reds which come not far from Dão with its ANADIA wines; the wines of Buçaco, rich and strong yet smooth; wines from the region of Sangalhos with reds which come close to the best of those from Dão, and whites which rival those of Anadia; the wines of Alcobaça, where Cistercian monks in the twelfth century cleared the barren lands to plant the vineyards; the wines of Ribatejo, where the plants stand high to escape the periodical floodings of the Tagus, with notably ALMEIRIM, CARTAXO and several ordinary wines, including the full-flavoured "ordinary" red wine, of a low alcohol content but keeping its quality well, which flows freely during the *festas bravas* that accompany the bullfights and the popular feasting on roast kid; finally, the wines of Torres Vedras, full-bodied tannin-rich ordinary red wines used for blending and also simple wines for café-restaurants and family tables; over

towards Obidos, the GAEIRAS and especially the white type is very worthy.

It is noticeable that, with the exception of MOSCATEL DE SETÚBAL, all these good quality wines are grown north of the Tagus, although the southern provinces do have some of their own. In Alentejo, for example, the names of such places as Cuba, Vidigueira, and so on, would seem to indicate that the vine was once cultivated there, but the region, which is thinly populated, was devoted to other crops—cereals, cork oak and olives, all better adapted to large seasonal monocultures. A few vineyards of Alentejo which escaped the oïdium infection were able to produce, around the end of the nineteenth century, some strong and aromatic wines which were practically unknown outside the region, although one should mention the wine of Borba.

The province of Algarve, in the extreme south, long had the unfair reputation of producing the country's most mediocre wine. It was unfair because here too the vine had to give way to other crops such as almonds, figs and locust-beans, although the local population is considerable and well used to the multiple tasks of small cropping and make good winegrowers. The grapes grown are excellent: the black grapes from *Pauferros* produce a wine with a very good bouquet and the white grapes from *Tamarez* produce a very sweet wine, of

This Portuguese photograph was designed to look like a souvenir of the good old days. Of course, extracting the grape juice was indeed once done by treading, but such work was carried out by big, heavy men wearing next to nothing and covered with grape juice·

which Lagõa is the main producer. The Portuguese government is encouraging viticulture in the province of Algarve and various schemes are in progress for reviving once-popular wines.

Fuzeta and Moncarapacho produce a Malaga-type dessert wine while AFONSO III, a liqueur wine, is a good aperitif with the warmth of sherry.

In the far north of the country, Chaves offers a wine with many connoisseurs called "wine of the dead" because it is sometimes buried to hasten its ageing.

Finally, Portugal produces some natural sparkling wines, notably at Lamego, with also some much appreciated rosés such as the already-mentioned FAISCA. MATEUS ROSÉ is also exported to the whole world—Europe, the United States, Canada, Australia, Hong Kong—and demand for the wine is high.

This abundance (average 222,179,800 gallons in 1973-1979), this diversity, this often exceptional quality, this long and solid reputation mean that wine is a major trump-card for Portugal in the international market-place. Many of these wines are, however, enjoyed less far afield, perhaps particularly by the French, whose country now sets restrictive measures with very limited quotas to protect the French national wine trade against imports of all wines, except those which have no equivalent in France, such as port, Madeira, VINHOS VERDES and some rosés. Portuguese wines exported in the bottle (only 7 per cent of the total, however, because of transport costs) carry a seal of guarantee, but the remainder of the production is exported in casks. In 1979, the total of wine exports to all countries combined exceeded 30,797,200 gallons.

PORT WINES

This famous wine owes to Porto only its name, for the vineyards which produce it are stepped along the ravine sides of the Upper Douro valley, and it is the town of Vila Nova de Gaia (across from Porto itself) where the wine is treated and aged, over many years, in the shade and silence of the great winemaking plants.

But it is from Porto, since time immemorial, and from Porto alone that this famous wine has been shipped to the four corners of the world, and it is the name Porto that one reads today, as one did a hundred years ago, on the casks rolled so gaily along the riverside quays. Some relate the tale that the name *rio douro* means "river of gold" and that this heavy and slow-running water does indeed run over nuggets of gold. The truth, however, is elsewhere and quite different, and one can perhaps remember Jean de La Fontaine: the treasure of the Douro, he maintained, must be wrenched from it with grit, with hard sweat, with faith and with love. For this most generous of wines is born of the most ungenerous and avaricious of lands, and throughout its long life it remains at the mercy of a thousand different perils: drought, wind, frost, fog, storms and all the illnesses of the vine. Just one week, if conditions go wrong at the moment the grape is ripe, can ruin a whole harvest.

The port must is also a fragile substance, which must be observed and handled with loving and knowing care if one is to extract the very best qualities from it. It is sensitive to heat, to air currents, to odours, to any delay in pressing the grapes or in fermentation. It passes long years maturing in large casks where it sheds its skin and absorbs enrichment at the same time, yet this very sojourn reduces also its vitality, for the rate of evaporation can reach as much as 4 per cent a year. Port wine demands a great deal of vigilance and care and costs its producer much. In Douro, from the vinegrower to the consumer, wine is a cult.

Many people claim that the plants which produce port wine came originally from Burgundy. However that may be, it is known that, at the end of the eleventh century, Henry, grandson of Robert I, Duke of Burgundy, had won fame at the side of El Cid in the fighting against the infidels. As a reward, he was given the lands of Douro and Minho and he later married a natural daughter of Alfonso VI, King of Leon and of Castille, receiving also the title of Count of Portugal. As Henry then settled down in his property and seems to have had few other worries than to make the most of his land, it is quite probable that he cultivated the vine and preferred the vine-stock of his home. In any case, it was to be many years before the vineyards of Douro became famous, for their real history begins only after 1700.

The wines at this time were very full-bodied, heavy and loaded with tannin; furthermore, in an effort to heighten their colour, elderberries were added, while various methods of stabilization were attempted so that the wine might survive the voyage to the English shores. It can be admitted outright: the wines were abominable and the English would certainly have preferred the wines of Bordeaux had not their endless quarrels with the French led to a complete ban on the import of the wines of Aquitania. Yet the English soldiers and sailors remembered very well having drunk some very satisfactory local wines in the harbour bars and other places during their campaigns.

The demand for the wines, as a result of the Treaty of Methuen in 1703, encouraged farmers without any experience to try cultivating vine-plants, and the prospect of easy gains had already incited the winegrowers to cut corners on wine production. One must bear in mind, too, that at this time wines were everywhere drunk very young and the secret of ageing the great vintage wines had been lost over the years in the same

The Alto Douro countryside, near Pinhão; terraces of vines are a characteristic of the region. In springtime it looks idyllic but such is not always the case, for Douro is a country of contrasts: the winters are bitterly cold and the summers swelteringly hot.

way as the use of impervious jars. The wine quickly went bad in the barrels and survived no better in the skin containers.

Since they were in any case obliged to drink this unpleasant wine, bought, understandably, at the nearest point to their land, in northern Portugal, the English decided to go and see on the spot how it was made. Merchants established themselves at Porto, although at first they opened only transport offices, later risking their capital by buying the standing harvest. In this way, they discovered the Douro and became winegrowers: they had the necessary capital and made the law of the vineyards, and they could also choose the best musts. But overproduction very rapidly brought the prices down and the valley lived wretchedly.

The REAL COMPANHIA: Bartholomeu Pancorvo, a man richer in ideas than in gold, was the first to understand the vital need to take the whole production of wine in hand in Douro, in order to keep a check on quality and prices. The English, however, caused his plan to fail and the poor man did not survive his ruin. But the idea was now in the air and a monk, Brother Mansilha, in high

favour at Court, developed a scheme to win the game. He had the backing of the great Duke of Pombal. He instigated the founding of the *Real Companhia dos Vinhos do Alto Douro* (Royal Company of the Wines of Upper Douro) in 1756 and took up both the monopoly of trade with England and Brazil and the production of wine-based spirits.

Brother Mansilha began by countering the manoeuvres of the English, who were baulked in their attempted take-over of the vineyard. But, as is often the case, he was opposed even more violently by the very people he hoped to help, for in 1759, three years after the foundation of the Royal Company and at the time of the great popular drinking feasts and carnivals, the price of wine had gone up a few pence in the bars. There was a riot in Porto and the mob, feeding on its own fury, pillaged the premises of the Royal Company and burned all the books. The repression was brutal—people were jailed, hanged, quartered—but when all was said and done order was finally restored.

One of the first jobs for the Royal Company, henceforth sovereign in the field, was to mark out the best

237

region for producing a high quality wine. The exceptional qualities of the wine meant that, with appropriate treatment and ageing, it could become not merely a table wine but a vintage wine. Many mediocre vine-plants were sacrificed and on the confined space remaining, experiments were patiently carried out with more and more rigid methods of vinification.

At the same time, success was achieved in developing mass production of glass vessels in which the wine could rest sheltered from the air. Inaugurated in Portugal, this procedure was to permit the whole world to find again the powerful yet delicate flavour of the ancient wines, while the Upper Douro was to discover the secret of its incomparable port. This wine very rapidly met an immense popularity in England for, warm, comforting, tonic, it brought into the humid mists of the long English winters the living light and the warmth of a beautiful fire in the hearth. Even today port is more popular in colder countries than in its native Portugal, where a lighter wine is preferred.

Porto benefited from the wealth of the vineyards. Always hardworking, thrifty and valiant, the old town had never been very smart. But the gold from port wine now gave her palaces and churches in which one might see, as in San Francisco, vine-shoots and grapeclusters stretching right on to the altars. Roads and bridges were built for transporting the wine, and soon, too, appeared more winemaking plants, official and private offices, and spacious and beautiful houses. English merchants established themselves in a road which was named Street of the English, and built, at great expense, a *factorerie* where they could discuss their business. The Portuguese, for their part, had become aware of their national heritage: proprietors of lands set their estates (called *quintas*) in order and established firms to produce and sell their own wines. Thus two groups, with the same aims, associates yet at the same time competitors, and living even in the heart of a relatively small town two absolutely separate existences, were working side by side—in the vineyards of Douro, in the winemaking plants of Vila Nova de Gaia and in the offices in Porto.

From this comes something of the special physiognomy of Porto. It is certain that its pearly skies, its frequent mists, its freshly cool climate were already making it a "northern capital". And one can understand that the English felt at home, for the natives of Porto were, by nature, hard-working, provident, enemies of waste and false manifestations, to which qualities this contact with the English added efficiency and exactness,

This view of the site of the Cachao de San Salvador da Pesqueira, near Beira, shows us the landscape of the Upper Douro valley as it was in about the middle of the eighteenth century. This is the period that saw, under the impulse of the institute of the *Real Companhia dos Vinhos do Alto Douro*, the restoration of the vineyards and the birth of port wine.

All along the Rio Douro, centuries of winegrowing have left the vines climbing across the steep hillsides and made the landscape look like an enormous staircase fashioned by giants. Even today, springtime still sees the wine moved by boat along the river. The old-fashioned *barcos rabelos* transport the barrels of must to the famous Porto winemaking plants at Vila Nova da Gaia.

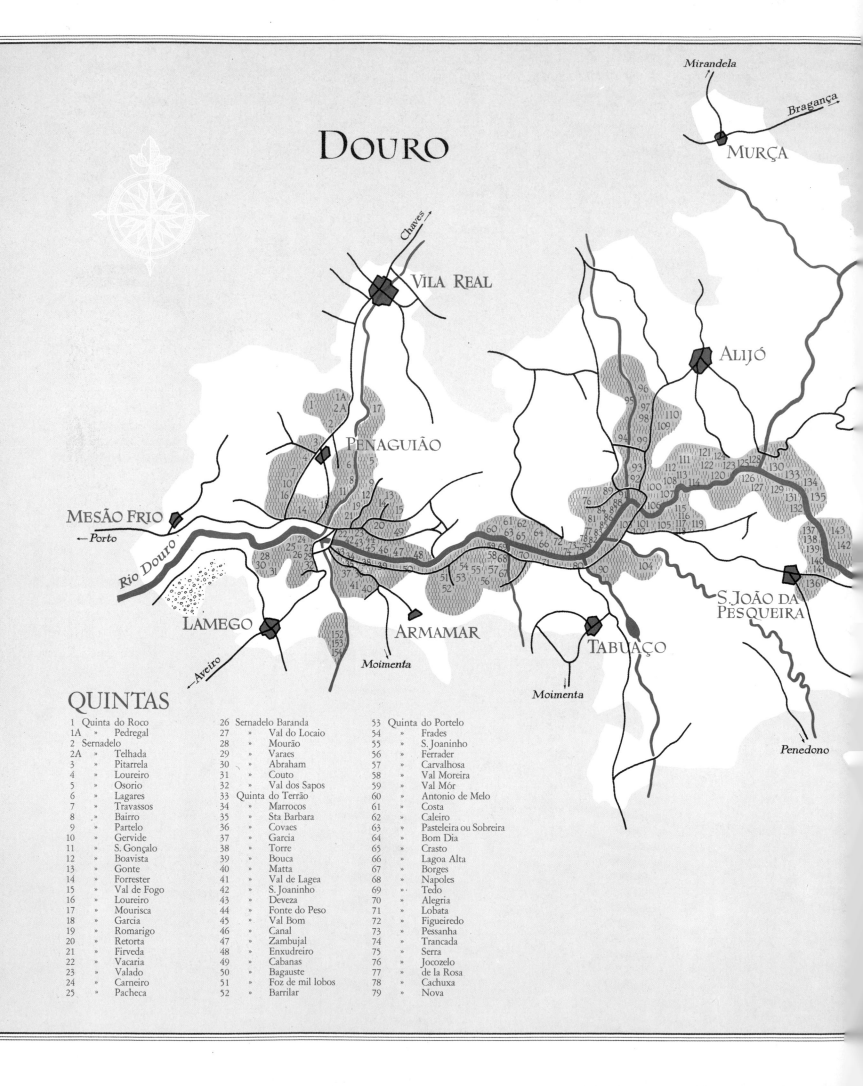

DOURO

Mirandela

Bragança

MURÇA

Chaves

VILA REAL

ALIJÓ

PENAGUIÃO

MESÃO FRIO

← Porto

Rio Douro

LAMEGO

← Aveiro

Moimenta

ARMAMAR

Moimenta

TABUAÇO

S. JOÃO DA PESQUEIRA

Penedono

QUINTAS

1 Quinta do Roco	26 Sernadelo Baranda	53 Quinta do Portelo
1A » Pedregal	27 » Val do Locaio	54 » Frades
2 Sernadelo	28 » Mourão	55 » S. Joaninho
2A » Telhada	29 » Varaes	56 » Ferrader
3 » Pitarrela	30 » Abraham	57 » Carvalhosa
4 » Loureiro	31 » Couto	58 » Val Moreira
5 » Osorio	32 » Val dos Sapos	59 » Val Mór
6 » Lagares	33 Quinta do Terrão	60 » Antonio de Melo
7 » Travassos	34 » Marrocos	61 » Costa
8 » Bairro	35 » Sta Barbara	62 » Caleiro
9 » Partelo	36 » Covaes	63 » Pasteleira ou Sobreira
10 » Gervide	37 » Garcia	64 » Bom Dia
11 » S. Gonçalo	38 » Torre	65 » Crasto
12 » Boavista	39 » Bouca	66 » Lagoa Alta
13 » Gonte	40 » Matta	67 » Borges
14 » Forrester	41 » Val de Lagea	68 » Napoles
15 » Val de Fogo	42 » S. Joaninho	69 » Tedo
16 » Loureiro	43 » Deveza	70 » Alegria
17 » Mourisca	44 » Fonte do Peso	71 » Lobata
18 » Garcia	45 » Val Bom	72 » Figueiredo
19 » Romarigo	46 » Canal	73 » Pessanha
20 » Retorta	47 » Zambujal	74 » Trancada
21 » Firveda	48 » Enxudreiro	75 » Serra
22 » Vacaria	49 » Cabanas	76 » Jocozelo
23 » Valado	50 » Bagauste	77 » de la Rosa
24 » Carneiro	51 » Foz de mil lobos	78 » Cachuxa
25 » Pacheca	52 » Barrilar	79 » Nova

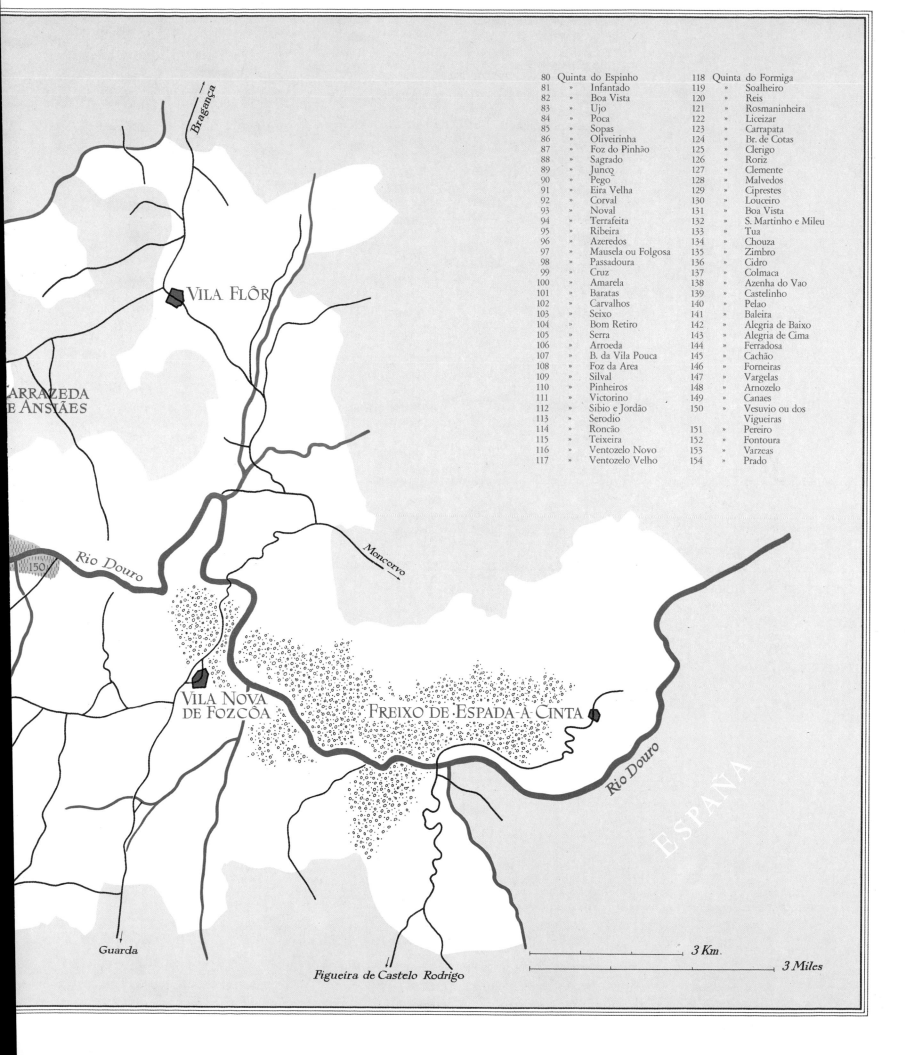

80	Quinta	do Espinho	118	Quinta	do Formiga
81	»	Infantado	119	»	Soalheiro
82	»	Boa Vista	120	»	Reis
83	»	Ujo	121	»	Rosmaninheira
84	»	Poca	122	»	Liceizar
85	»	Sopas	123	»	Carrapata
86	»	Oliveirinha	124	»	Br. de Cotas
87	»	Foz do Pinhão	125	»	Clerigo
88	»	Sagrado	126	»	Roriz
89	»	Junco	127	»	Clemente
90	»	Pego	128	»	Malvedos
91	»	Eira Velha	129	»	Ciprestes
92	»	Corval	130	»	Louceiro
93	»	Noval	131	»	Boa Vista
94	»	Terrafeita	132	»	S. Martinho e Mileu
95	»	Ribeira	133	»	Tua
96	»	Azeredos	134	»	Chouza
97	»	Mausela ou Folgosa	135	»	Zimbro
98	»	Passadoura	136	»	Cidro
99	»	Cruz	137	»	Colmaca
100	»	Amarela	138	»	Azenha do Vao
101	»	Baratas	139	»	Castelinho
102	»	Carvalhos	140	»	Pelao
103	»	Seixo	141	»	Baleira
104	»	Bom Retiro	142	»	Alegria de Baixo
105	»	Serra	143	»	Alegria de Cima
106	»	Arroeda	144	»	Ferradosa
107	»	B. da Vila Pouca	145	»	Cachão
108	»	Foz da Area	146	»	Forneiras
109	»	Silval	147	»	Vargelas
110	»	Pinheiros	148	»	Arnozelo
111	»	Victorino	149	»	Canaes
112	»	Sibio e Jordão	150	»	Vesuvio ou dos
113	»	Serodio			Vigueiras
114	»	Roncão	151	»	Pereiro
115	»	Teixeira	152	»	Fontoura
116	»	Ventozelo Novo	153	»	Varzeas
117	»	Ventozelo Velho	154	»	Prado

Bragança

VILA FLÔR

CARRAZEDA
DE ANSIÃES

Rio Douro

150

Moncorvo

VILA NOVA
DE FOZCÔA

FREIXO DE ESPADA-A-CINTA

Rio Douro

ESPAÑA

Guarda

Figueira de Castelo Rodrigo

3 Km.

3 Miles

as well as a taste for elegance and family comfort. In Porto, behind the austere granite of the house façades, one finds beautiful mahogany, fine carpets, precious silverware, added to the dignity of old port decanted in crystal flasks.

THE VINEYARDS OF DOURO

Any good vine-plant, once acclimatized to Douro, would give port wine, but a vine-plant of Douro transplanted elsewhere would cease to produce port wine. This strange alchemy which, it is believed, presides over the making of this wine is the work of Nature, which has brought together on the banks of the Upper Douro and its tributaries (Corgo, Torto, Tua) conditions which are special, exceptional, mysterious and delicate. Here the vinegrower comes to grips with lava terrains, rugged and rocky. He plants his vine on a chaotic accumulation of eroded, crumbled and broken-up land, the work of the torrents and rivers, for it is true that for a long time there have grown on these ungrateful slopes only scrub brush and aromatic grasses for the mountain goats.

Down in the deep river gorges, the winter air currents are icy and fog collects like thick cottonwool. When summer comes, the storms build up and their effects are felt from valley to valley, until, finally, the sun begins to heat the stone. The valleys become ovens of 40°C. and even 50°, enveloping without a breath of air the whole "land of wine", the region so minutely and strictly laid out in vineyards whose product can be turned into *approveitado* (approved) port wine. The part of the Douro production not used for port will give table wines or wine alcohol.

In 1979, the total production of these vineyards, an area of 64,246 acres, was 47,119,716 gallons.

This goes to show that apart from the position of the lands, their soil composition and their exposure to the sun, one must also count the local conditions, meteorological or otherwise, which increase or reduce the quality of the must each year. And even before the harvest, it was necessary to create the vineyard—with the hand of man and on the back of man. The hard, laminated, slated rock had to be broken up with the hand-pick, crumbled and laid out in terraces, open to the maximum amount of sun and rain. These terraces held by small stone walls, climb the steepest slopes, with the lowest plants at water-level: it is said that the best grapes are picked where they have ripened "listening to the creaking of the river boats' heavy rudders". The plants do not grow above an altitude of 1,000 feet; any higher and ripening cannot take place satisfactorily.

The terraces give the landscape a strange and imposing aspect. As far as the eye can see, the hillsides are striped and patterned as if with giant fingerprints, and everywhere one looks, the plants line up rank on rank, held by vine-props and wires. The shoots hang fairly close to the ground, benefiting from all the emanations of the soil, but care has been taken also to see that the grape-bunches are neither soiled nor damaged by contact with the ground. To conserve the rains of winter and keep a reserve of freshness during the heat of summer, a large ditch is dug and filled with rough stones at the foot of each plant, whose roots go six feet under ground. No secondary crops; the entire vitality of this soil is dedicated to the vine. The leguminous plants between the vine-plants are mulched in as additional fertilizer. The whole winter is spent clearing, cleaning and tidying the vineyard. Working under enormous capes of maize straw for protection against the frequent rain between October and March, the vintners repair the little walls, disinfect and consolidate the vine-props, layer, graft and prune the vine, until along the lines not a dead leaf nor a stone is to be seen. The vine-shoots turn green, the grape-bunches begin to lengthen. It is the perilous time when a morning frost can turn it red and kill it. Throughout the workers must fight parasites, be prepared for storms, watch the sky; and then comes the summer, with its terrible dryness and burning winds. The harvest, in September, is at once a task, a ritual, a feast. It is a final effort, crowning a whole year of hard labour and bringing its reward or, sometimes, withholding it.

THE HARVEST AND THE PRESSING

The ideal moment of ripening of the grapes has to be seized on, a moment that varies for each *quinta* and even for each slope of the hillside. Then the women, with their scissors and baskets, crouch beside the vine-plants, cut the grape-bunches and check each to make sure that not a single spoiled or unripe bunch goes to the press. Under the slight shade of the leaves, the workers suffocate in the heat mirrored by the stones, too hot to rest a hand on them. The baskets are emptied into hods at the end of each row, collected by groups of *barracheiros*, the stalwarts who can carry a load of 165 pounds of grapes well balanced on the nape of the neck with a leather strap and steadied with a steel hook. They walk in a long single file, with a heavy step, in time to the rhythm of the stick of the leader, who guides them down the stone steps and steep paths of the vineyards. The presses are set up as low down the hills as possible, yet high enough to escape the danger of the sudden and violent floods of the often torrential rivers.

In the vastness of the landscape, men trudge onwards like ants, glistening with sweat. The sticky juice glues to their skin the jute sacking with which they protect their backs. These *barracheiros* are irreplaceable, because no other method of transporting the grapes has been found which can be used in these steep vineyards.

At the presses, everything has been made ready. Over the past months, new barrels have been carved and the old ones cleaned. For centuries, the grape was pressed with the feet, because this was believed to be the only way of extracting all the goodness from the pulp and

skin of the grape without crushing the grapepips. Tiring work, in the vats filled with wet and slippery grapes, which had to be pressed till they were crushed and split open and were transformed into a gluey porridge-like mass. The pressers had to bring air down into the mass too, by constantly lifting their knees high, in order to break up the crust that the waste products formed on the surface of the liquid. A team of six men would take twenty hours to extract some 200 gallons of must. But a joyous exaltation seemed to lie over this work, reminiscent of a birth: the pressers, already a little dizzy with the vapours rising from the vat, were encouraged with songs and music, and the womenfolk danced all night long around the stone vats by the light of lanterns. Today, this pressing with the feet has become difficult because of lack of seasonal labour, and is being replaced more and more by a mechanical process, called the Ducellier process, which gives, after a mechanical stoning, excellent results: a system of valves, set in action by the fermentation, simultaneously stirs and aerates the must.

Another critical moment comes with the decision of how much wine alcohol should be added to the must in order to stop the transformation of sugar into the alcohol which results from fermentation. The quantity depends itself on the richness of the must: too much rain, before or during the harvest, swells the grapes but may reduce their sugar content by several degrees, while drought and dry periods give a rich but rarer grape. In Douro, nothing ever seems to be given in quite the right quantities. The measured addition of wine alcohol will therefore give a wine which is more or less dry or sweet.

Suitably "dosed" in this way and allowed to settle, the must is left in the freshness of the cellars of the *quinta*, until in the springtime it is transported to the winemaking plants of the estuary. For many years a curious type of boat was used for this, with a flat bottom and a high poop on which an experienced helmsman ruled. The Douro is treacherous, even impetuous here, seamed with hidden reefs or shoals, and the old-fashioned *barcos rabelos* have given way little by little, first to trains and then to heavy road transport. The valley's charm is the loser, for nothing was more picturesque than this sight of the sailing boats or the *rabelos*, sometimes towed by oxen, beating against the wind.

TYPES OF PORT

Until its arrival at Vila Nova da Gaia, the wine is still young and a little rash, but it will now undergo a long retirement, during which it will learn the best of wisdom. Depending on the characteristics which they show right at the start of their life, that is to say when they leave the presses, the new wines will belong to one or other of the two great port "families": that of the "blends", which are the more numerous, or that of the highly prized "vintages".

The blends, which cover the majority of the port wines, are as their names indicate, blends aged in the wood. Once the must has settled, after two years in the cask, it is again weighed, tasted and appraised. Other types of must are then sought which can be added, bringing with them characteristics of their own which will underline or complement those of the original must. Some of the blending musts may bring strength, others colour, others again bouquet. Any port worthy of the name is made up of at least sixteen varieties of vine-stock. Like a florist making up a display, or a painter mixing the colours on his palette, or a perfumer dosing out the essences, the port experts compose, mix and dose the different port wines.

They work surrounded by retorts, test-tubes, bottle-racks, note-books, in veritable laboratories that the winemaking firms have fitted out.

Listed, their composition carefully analysed, the blends are then put into enormous wooden casks, in order to prevent both their oxydation and too rapid an evaporation. The wines remain there under constant supervision. They are measured, sounded, tasted, and the attentive ear of the master winemaker watches out for and notices the noises, deep or light, which come from the immense *cuvée*. This latter remains alive and moving for, as it takes on greater age, the wine is

Very nearly all of the port wine from Douro is blended and marketed under the names of the famous shippers. This ROYAL OPORTO is an exception in two ways: first, it comes from the Companhia Geral da Agricultura das Vinhas do Alto Douro—the first ever company to market its own Douro wines—and second, it is a vintage, not a blend, from one particular vineyard in the heart of the district, the Quinta das Carvalhas.

PRODUCE OF PORTUGAL

Royal Oporto

Wine Cº.

ROYAL CHARTER A. D. 1756

Quinta das Carvalhas

(A Quinta de maior benefício do Alto Douro)

Vintage 1955

COMPANHIA GERAL DA AGRICULTURA DAS VINHAS DO ALTO DOURO
VILA NOVA DE GAIA (OPORTO) - PORTUGAL

IMPORTED BY:
WINE AGENCIES (LONDON) LTD. - 124 Bolingbroke Grove, LONDON, S. W. 11

COCKBURN'S
REGISTERED TRADE MARK

PORT
"Vintage Character"

ESTABLISHED 1815

SHIPPED BY
COCKBURN SMITHES & CO LTD
OPORTO

PRODUCE OF PORTUGAL

QUINTA DO NOVAL
1963
VINTAGE PORT

This wine has been produced on the **150**th anniversary of the Shipper ANTÓNIO JOSÉ DA SILVA
VINHOS, S. A. R. L.
VILA NOVA DE GAIA — PORTUGAL
and bottled in 1965, **250** years after the first known records of the Quinta do Noval - **1715**

PORT: VINTAGE CHARACTER

1. Name of the wine: "Port". This generic term seems to suffice. – 2. The mention "Port" is here amplified by the expression "Vintage Character". This means that although not vintage nor free from any blending, this port wine has been treated in the manner of a vintage port. i.e. bottled after a few years in the wood and sold while still fairly young. One can therefore expect a good red semi-sweet port. – 3. Name of origin. There is no exact or obligatory formula. – 4. Name of the merchant. The connoisseur will give his preference to a particular firm, or to a particular port from a particular firm and another port from another firm. In this realm, there is nothing to beat experience.

VINTAGE PORT

1. Type of port: "Vintage Port". This is a good red port, from the best growth of a good year. Free of any blending additive, it has been bottled after 2-3 years in the wood. Caution! It is probably necessary to decant it. – 2. Date of vintage. This mention is obligatory for every true vintage port. – 3. This mention indicates the vineyard of origin. – 4. Name of the merchant-producer. – 5. This port was bottled in 1965.

ROYAL OPORTO WINE Cᵒ.
FOUNDED BY ROYAL CHARTER IN 1756

WHITE PORT
EXTRA
(DRY)
PRODUCT OF THE ALTO DOURO

REAL COMPANHIA VELHA

COMPANHIA GERAL DA AGRICULTURA DAS VINHAS DO ALTO DOURO
V. N. DE GAIA — PORTUGAL

O VINHO DO PORTO É UM VINHO NATURAL, SUJEITO A CRIAR DEPÓSITO COM A IDADE RECOMENDA-SE QUE SEJA SERVIDO COM O CUIDADO INDISPENSÁVEL PARA NÃO TURVAR.

WHITE PORT

1. Name of the wine: "White Port". Here again, this mention seems sufficient, particularly as it will be appraised in relation to the name of the merchant. – 2. The mention "extra dry" draws attention to the fact that this white port is very dry; it is in fact an aperitif wine. – 3. Another version of the name of origin. – 4. Name of the merchant. The Real Companhia Velha was, from 1756 onwards, behind the origin of the regulations for port wine.

SIBIO
1. Trade name: "Sibio". – 2. 2a. This name is amplified: dôce = sweet; tinto = deep red; tipo vintage = vintage type (in other words, not aged in the wood). This is therefore a young port, deep-red coloured, with violet reflections. – 3. Name of origin. – 4. Name of the merchant.

PARTNERS' PORT
1. Trade name: "Partners' Port". – 2. In the mention "Finest rich ruby", the word ruby holds the attention and indicates not only its colour but also its age of the wine. "Ruby" also indicates that this port has a beautiful red colour, with reflections as in a precious stone, and an age of 10-15 years. – 3. Name of origin. – 4. Name of the merchant. The connoisseur will appraise the label as a whole when judging the quality of a port, since the name of the merchant cannot be dissociated from the trade name.

EL-REI D. JOSÉ
1. Trade name: "El-Rei D. José". – 2. "Alourado" gives the colour (tawny in English). This type of port will be 15-20 years old. Meio dôce = semi-sweet, this is therefore a dessert wine. – 3. Name of origin. – 4. Name of the merchant.

enlivened and enriched with the careful addition of young and strong musts. No port wine may be drunk before it has aged five to six years in the wood. It reaches its fullness after about thirty years, but one can drink ports of sixty years and more which have remained absolutely marvellous. It is impossible and in fact a vain effort to try to date the different blends; one can merely say that they are *cuvées spéciales*.

For reasons of convenience and economy, the blends are usually exported in barrels and bottled by the importers. The importers of a few large brands, to ensure the unbroken quality of their chosen *cuvée*, insist on bottling in the winemaking plants before the wines are sold, and in this case, the bottle is sealed by the Port Wine Institute. This institute works with two other bodies, the Port Wine Shippers Guild and Douro House, to control and regulate the cultivation, vinification and exporting of port.

Contrary to the blends, the port vintages always have a birth certificate. It is always a *very* good year. When a harvest has been outstandingly good in quality, a vintage year is decided. The must, which is usually treated and kept in the wood for two years, is put straight into bottles without any blending, and the bottle, hermetically sealed, is put in the winemaking plant. There, the wine ages, in austere and silent solitude, for ten, twenty, thirty years or even more. It skins and enriches itself by natural means. It is a *millésimé* port. The vintage ports are more appreciated in England, or at any rate were so in earlier days: the old connoisseurs of Thackeray and Dickens' times valued them more than any other. But the vintage ports, one can well imagine, are fragile: they demand a lot of care in the conservation, transport and even in the drinking. Furthermore, even if their fine uprightness is admirable, they do not have the clever complexity that enchants the connoisseurs of the blended ports. Great vintage years are very rare; one can mention the years 1890, 1900 (still to be found on the market), 1908, 1927, 1931, 1945 and 1947. According to the vine-plant used in their production, vintage ports are more or less light or dark, and with age, darken or lighten, although most vintage ports gradually become "tawny", that is to say, the colour of light mahogany.

In addition to this fundamental difference between blends and vintages, port is divided into extra-dry, dry (usually white port), semi-dry and sweet (red). Ageing, by decanting the colouring matter, touches all with gold, and the shades of colour spread out from light topaz to bronze. The official colours are: deep red, red, ruby (these are the "fulls"), light gold, onion peel (the "tawnies"), pale white, pale straw and golden.

The "fulls" are fairly young port wines, rich, full-bodied, ruby-coloured or deep garnet. The "tawnies" are old wines which have taken on the colour of amber or wild honey. A good port can be recognized first by its aroma, and secondly because it "weeps"; down the sides of the glass slides a long, slow unctuous tear.

PORT IN THE WORLD

England, for some time, has been no longer the world's major importer of port: between 1900 and 1919, the British drank each year 13,200,000 gallons but in 1939 they bought only 6,380,000 gallons.

Up to the war of 1914-1918, port, with Madeira, was intimately linked with the daily life of the upper-class English. It was the sole wine judged worthy of using for the Sovereign's Toast, at the end of a meal. Chosen with the greatest care—and tastes in port could be discussed all night—a bottle was served to the gentlemen, while the ladies "withdrew", going to the drawing-room (or withdrawing-room) for infusions of herbs or tea and light conversation. The men emptied the bottle between them while chatting. Each gentleman's club knew exactly the preferences of its eminent members and kept in reserve a suitable supply of their port and cigars. The great families had their cellars, where reserves were built up, either as a financial investment or for sentimental reasons. A similar custom, still preserved in Douro, established for each child born into a family a stock of bottles which was increased from year to year. The lucky child who came into the world the year of a vintage port could be assured of an outstanding wine with which to celebrate his or her wedding.

But while England began reducing its consumption of port, others, France among them, began to discover it. Or rather, re-discover it, for this wine had been much appreciated long ago, especially after the Napoleonic invasions at the beginning of the nineteenth century. The archives of the region of Douro hold the requisition orders signed by the general occupying Porto, be he the English ally or the French enemy. It is amusing to note that some of these carry the same date: for example, March 29th, 1809 was the day that Wellington, landing unexpectedly, interrupted the lunch of Marshal Soult.

Despite its relatively limited area, the Douro vineyard presents a rich variety of vine-stocks. One remembers, too, that the blends, spread out over ten years or more, obey subtle and supple rules. This is why port wines are so varied and why they suit all tastes.

HOW AND WHEN TO DRINK PORT

One must first know just what one expects of port. If it is a question of serving a refreshing aperitif which at the same time sets an "ambiance", one should choose a dry white port, and serve it chilled, either by chilling the glasses with an ice-cube or by putting the glasses themselves in a chilling recipient. This is the way the French usually drink port wine. For an afternoon refreshment, a five-to-seven reception or the end of a meal, a "tawny" or a "full" is preferable. A semi-dry or a sweet port makes a delightful accompaniment to dessert pastries and to certain fruits, but not citrus varieties.

One should not, moreover, neglect to serve port with the cheese. It is no doubt to enhance the taste of the port

that the English brought into fashion savouries or hot dishes, usually with cheese and spiced and offered right at the end of the meal, when the bottles or decanters are going round. It is also the English who put port into their famous Stilton cheese, cutting into the centre and filling the hole with good port as cutting proceeds, which allows the wine to permeate the creamy mass. All the cheeses in the world—Danish, Dutch or Swiss cheese, Portuguese, Spanish or Italian cheese, and of course the inexhaustible *plateau* of French cheese— have a common denominator: they enhance the port which, in its turn, exalts the cheese.

In Douro and in Portugal in general, port is drunk according to a certain ritual. It must never, even in a public establishment, be served open; the law requires that the bottle be presented. In private homes, the wine is not brought in its bottle; it is considered more elegant, and shows a better knowledge of port itself, to transfer it a few hours beforehand into a decanter, where it may rest and take the air. A vintage port is never uncorked, for in the ten or twenty years of its life, the best of corks would have spoiled and mildewed and thus, inevitably, cork dust would fall in the wine. Real connoisseurs therefore, to open a bottle of a really great port, use a pair of special pliers heated red-hot in a fire, with which they decapitate the bottle.

Although such refinements have largely fallen into disuse, both port wine and the mistress of house who intends to offer it have everything to gain in observing the niceties. There is a wide choice of decanters, some old, engraved, cut, filled gold, others modern, heavy, belted with leather. They usually carry a metal medallion round the neck marked with the word "Port" in more or less fancy letters. The glass, on the other hand, should be very simple, in fine crystal, with a foot, and all in one piece in the shape of a tulip or a balloon. One can thus better appraise the colour of the wine, and the bouquet is more concentrated. Connoisseurs say port should be "chewed" before it is swallowed, after having lengthily held the glass (except in the case of the fresh white ports) in the hollow of the hand. Thus port gratifies all the senses.

These days one can forget the old rule that port is always served in a clockwise direction; but remember that connoisseurs never re-cork a bottle: once opened, it is drunk. If, however, one should wish to keep an opened bottle and not be able to finish it in the following days, it should be decanted into a smaller flask where it will be free from air.

Port for anniversaries and tête-à-tête meals; as a pick-me-up for grandfather or the overworked student; port to warm the hunter after the stalk or the traveller

after the long trip; prelude and conclusion of a large banquet; port in a reducing diet; port drunk with friends informally at a bar or at an important ceremony in an official reception—in brief, port, the truly grand *seigneur*, is at home everywhere.

On the official level, port is also the Portuguese wine which is most carefully watched over by the authorities. Several official organizations watch to ensure that it is cultivated, vinified and marketed according to very strict rules. The *Casa do Douro* supports, advises and sometimes finances the vinegrowers; the *Gremio dos Exportadores*, at Porto, organizes and co-ordinates the trade in wine; and the *Instituto do Vinho do Porto* heads all these other activities, checking and controlling all the wines which will be put on the market and which may not be sold in Portugal without a guarantee seal. This small seal, marked "I.V.P.", seen on a bottle is a sign which does not mislead. Many wines are exported in casks, with a certificate of origin. Some frauds can be carried out when the wine is bottled, but fortunately many countries, including France, have enough respect for great wines, of whatever origin, to punish fraud energetically and effectively. It is therefore possible anywhere to drink a port wine which is just as good as in the cellars of Gaia, where Portugal likes to greet visitors and let them taste these jewel-shaded wines.

THE WINES OF MADEIRA

The equerries of Henry the Navigator landed in Madeira in 1419 after years of searching for the Fortunate Isles. Stranded after a terrible storm on an almost barren island which out of gratitude they had baptized Porto Santo, the voyagers had for months seen a misty silhouette appearing and disappearing on the horizon, a real "enchanted" island. They landed there at last, disembarking in a rocky creek. All around were dense forests, made up of trees whose odour was so strong that men became dizzy when cutting them down. They called the island Madeira, which means wood in Portuguese.

As a result of the travellers' reports men were sent to colonize the islands and they planted both European-

Harvest time on the isle of Madeira. The vinegrower works standing, picking at his own height the bunches of grapes swollen with sugar. These are collected in baskets and sorted on the spot, before being carried down to the presses. As in the Douro region, the must is transported by *borracheiros* carrying goatskins that hold about eleven gallons each.

style and tropical crops. In this way, Madeira grew and side by side flourished cane sugar and grape-vines.

Right from the start, the Madeira wine proved to be excellent. Ca da Mosto, the celebrated Venitian navigator, in 1455 praised the wine drunk in these new isles. The whole of Europe became enthused. The Duke of Clarence, locked up in the Tower of London, chose to drown himself in a barrel of Malmsey wine to escape the vengeance of his brother. Falstaff, as Shakespeare claimed, sold his soul one Friday for a glass of good Madeira and a cold leg of chicken. François I insisted on always having some in his castles in Touraine. Portugal granted special privileges to the English merchants established at Funchal, where trade was brisk, and the wines of the island, which were traded against wheat and dairy produce of Ireland, wood and rice from America, and fish from Newfoundland, provisioned the long-haul sailing ships.

William Bolton, the British Consul at Funchal, a shipowner and banker, played an important role in the development of the Madeira vineyard, and in 1699, complained that the supply could not meet the demand, particularly from the American colonists. The future George IV, the first gentleman of Europe, lent them his prestige in England: nothing else was drunk at Carlton House and 22,000 pipes (a pipe was large-size cask) of wines were exported to Great Britain in 1813. But there was another side to the coin.

In 1852, a terrible disease attacked the island's vineyards: oïdium. Whole plants were decimated. Twenty years later, phylloxera struck. The plants would have been abandoned had it not been for the stubborn work of enlightened winegrowers, who managed to save a part of the vineyard and rebuilt some stocks. Thanks to their patience and devotion, Madeira wine little by little took its place in trade again. Today its role in the country's economy is important: Portugal in 1979 exported 32,997,000 gallons of Madeira out of a total production of 252,977,000 gallons.

THE VINES OF MADEIRA

The island of Madeira is very small—only 30 miles long by 16 miles wide—and one-third of it is hardly suitable for cultivation. It is an old volcano, jutting up out of the ocean, defending itself with high cliffs and caves as deep as 2,400 feet. As in Douro, arable land must be created out of nothing, patiently, tenaciously, by breaking up the lava with the pick. The farmer of Madeira cultivates the smallest patch of ground that can be reached, even if it hangs out into space. The vine is his little luxury, his joy and his pride, so that one sees it growing on trellises along the edges of paths and covering the tiled roofs shadowing the little courtyards where the women sit and embroider. Those grapes are for the family table. But the great wines of Madeira come from the land with the best exposure, in the south-west. The plots are so narrow that the regions are called *estreitos* (straitened). Among the most famous are Campanario, Ponta do Pargo and Madalena.

In order to make use of this area so meagerly awarded, the winegrowers *roll* the vines in numerous tight coils, held up by wires, and strip off the leaves from the vine-shoots so that the grape-bunches may drink in the sun all day long. The sun gilds them, ripens them, gives them their sugar: the grapes must be picked when very ripe, but not one shrunken or spoiled grape must reach the press.

THE HARVEST AND THE TYPES OF WINE

The harvest is a festival. For the same reasons as in Douro, everything must be carried on the backs of men, even the must, which is brought to the winemaking plants in goatskins or in small 80-100 pint barrels.

Even true wine lovers can experience some difficulty in assessing, just by looking at the label, what kind of Madeira the bottle will contain. MALMSEY comes from the *Malvoisie* grape, transplanted from the isle of Crete to that of Madeira in the fifteenth century. This is a dark amber dessert wine with a strong bouquet. At the other end of the scale, SERCIAL is a dry wine.

249

This must is kept in a barrel open to the sun; there, it gradually reduces and caramelizes (the method particularly used for sweet wines). Nowadays, a system of hot-baths heats the must to 50°. The fermented must gives the *vinho claro* which is then left to rest in order to obtain the *vinho trasfugado*.

As with the wine of Porto, Madeira includes two family types: the vintage wine, which is must from an outstanding harvest, aged in closed bottles and with nothing added; and the Madeira *solera* (from the Portuguese for sun), which is a wine aged always in the same barrel. But in the latter, the inevitable evaporation is compensated for each year by filling the barrel to the brim with wine of the same type but one year younger. The date of a vintage *solera* is therefore that of the original must. There still exist on the island a few flasks of a venerable wine called MADÈRE DE NAPOLÉON, produced in 1792. The British Consul at Funchal offered some to Napoleon in 1815 on his way to St. Helena. The exiled emperor was ill and did not touch any of the precious barrels, which were returned after his death to the Consul; the latter sold the Madeira to Charles Blandy, who had it bottled in 1840. One can still sample some of this old Madeira today, although this is indeed an exceptional case. Normally, one is advised to choose from Madeiras aged between twenty and thirty years.

In contrast to port, which demands peace and quiet in its life, Madeira seems all the better for long voyages. This was established in the seventeenth century, on sampling MALVASIAS which had been shipped to America: the rocking of the ships and the heat of the tropics seemed to be so advantageous to the ageing of Madeira that the custom developed of "sending it out on a voyage": so much so that a shipment of wine which had made the round trip to India was very much sought after by connoisseurs. A cargo of MALVASIA was a great prize for pirates and certain shipments are known to have changed the colours under which they were sailing three of four times during the course of a voyage.

The English, during the eighteenth and nineteenth centuries, were great connoisseurs of Madeira. Ladies used it to perfume their handkerchieves and officers on campaigns demanded fifteen bottles a month. The truth is that, in addition to the pleasures it brings, Madeira has great tonic qualities; from 1785 on, it was much recommended for sick or over-worked people and was nicknamed the "milk of the old".

Madeira is also a marvellous wine for cooking, and sets off admirably such dishes as consommés, filet of beef, game, liver and lights, dishes in aspic, punches; and of course it is the essential ingredient of the well-known garnish, Madeira sauce. For cooking, one should use young Madeiras, above all never confusing those used in the kitchen and those drunk in the drawing-room.

A happy and very fashionable innovation consists of giving a reception where only two types of Madeira are served: one very dry, the other sweet and velvety. The first accompanies canapés and salted biscuits, the second, sweets.

There are four great Madeiras, of which the first is MALVASIA or MALMSEY obtained from pressing the ripest of the grapes. This was the very first to be cultivated on the island and was produced from vine-plants which came from Candia. Cultivated in the hottest part of the isle, its grapes are long, conical and very golden. The juice from these grapes is full of the sun's warmth; it is velvety and takes on the appearance of liquid gold, with a smoothness of honey.

MALVASIA has long been the great favourite among the wines of Madeira, for it expresses all the sensual, intoxicating and slightly mysterious charm of this island of perfumes. It is especially suitable as a dessert wine and is drunk at room temperature. On the other hand, SERCIAL, which is produced from vine-plants originating in the Rhine valley, is dry, amber and strong. It evokes quite another aspect of the island: the abysses, the peaks which pierce the clouds, the wild and grandiose landscapes. The best SERCIAL wines come from the vineyard where the soil is the most barren, not far from the abyss above which perches the *Curral das Freiras*, a convent built to escape the pillaging of barbarians. SERCIAL should never be drunk until it has at least eight to ten years of age, and should be served chilled as an aperitif.

VERDELHO, a semi-dry, and BOAL, a semi-sweet, are stronger wines than MALVASIA but do not have its mellowness; on the other hand, if they lack the haughty austerity of SERCIAL, they are more pleasant, more complete and more suitable for every occasion.

Madeira must be served with the same care as port, decanted into a flask before being drunk from fine and transparent glasses.

Finally, one must say a word about the wine of Porto Santo, the neighbouring island of Madeira, and especially the wine of Pico, in the Azores, which also had its moment of glory in the eighteenth and nineteenth centuries at the Russian Court. The vineyards—destroyed by an epidemic and only now just beginning to re-establish themselves—grow on soil which is as black as charcoal. The region is called the Land of Mystery, at the foot of a volcano which is the highest peak in Portugal. Walls of pumice-stone protect the plants, which grow, stunted and clinging to the very stone, never more than a few together. The wine of Pico is dry, lively, a little rough: it could be described as a sort of wild sherry.

In the very strange church of Jesus, at Setúbal, a panel of *azulejos* (Moorish tiles) represents the Tree of Jesse: the tree is a vine-plant which sprouts from the abdomen of the patriarch and then, spreading out, represents the Son of God. Nothing could better express the vital and sacred character of this most noble crop which, in Portugal, reunites the two most precious things: bread and wine. The vine nourishes man, and brings him joy, strength and hope.

WINES OF PORTUGAL

DRY WHITE WINES

Bucelas
Bucelas Velho
Dão Cabido
Dão Caves Império
Dão Grão Vasco
Dão Monástico
Dão Real Vinícola

Dão U. C. B.
Douro Favaios
Vinho Verde Agulha
Vinho Verde Alvarinho-Cepa Velha
Vinho Verde Amarante
Vinho Verde Aveleda — 1 R
Vinho Verde Casa do Landeiro

Vinho Verde Casal Garcia
Vinho Verde Casal de Pejeiros
Vinho Verde Casal da Seara
Vinho Verde Casalinho
Vinho Verde Casal Miranda
Vinho Verde Deu-la-Deu
Vinho Verde Lagosta

Vinho Verde Quinta da Aveleda
Vinho Verde Quinta do Tamariz
Vinho Verde Reserva da Aveleda
Vinho Verde Valverde
Vinho Verde Verdeal
Vinho Verde Lafões
Vinho Verde Sico

SWEET WHITE WINES

Arealva
Borlido

Casalinho
Corveta

Emir
Grandjó

Monte Serves
Murtelas

ROSÉ WINES

Aliança
Dom Silvano

Faísca
Isabel

Mateus
Grandélite

Spiral
Barros

RED WINES

Aliança
Arealva
Carvalho, Ribeiro & Ferreira
Colares M. J. C.
Colares V. S.
Dão Cabido
Dão Caves Aliança
Dão Caves Império
Dão Grão Vasco

Dão Monástico
Dão Real Vinícola
Dão Sóvida
Dão U. C. B.
Dão Vale da Fonte
Evel
J. M. da Fonseca
Lagoa
Lagos

Messias
Palmela-Clarete
Periquita
Quinta do Seminário
Reserva Sogrape
Romeira
Serradayres
Solar
Vinho Verde Casal da Seara

Vinho Verde C. Mendes
Vinho Verde Casal Garcia
Vinho Verde Folgazão
Vinho Verde Moura Basto
Vinho Verde Quinta do Tamariz
Vinho Verde Verdeal
Vinho Verde Lafões
Vinho Verde São Gonçalo
Vinho Verde Valverde

VARIOUS GENEROSOS WINES

Carcavelos-Quinta do Barão
Carcavelos-Quinta da Bela Vista

Estremadura Silveira
Estremadura Lezirão

Moscatel de Setúbal - Setúbal
   superior

Moscatel de Setúbal - Setúbal Roxo
Palmela superior

NATURAL SPARKLING WINES

Assis Brasil
Danúbio

Grande Natal
Monte Crasto

Neto Costa
Principe Real

Raposeira
Companhia Velha

MADEIRA

Sercial   Verdelho   Boal   Malmsey (Malvoisie)   Rainwater   Solera

PORT WINES

VERY DRY WHITE WINES (BRANCOS)

Casino Dry White	D. Fernando Extra Dry White	Porto Aperitivo	Port Dry White Estoril
Dow's Dry White Aperitif Port	Prince Henry	Porto Fino	Carito
Dry Tang	Cocktail Port	Golden Crown White Extra Dry	Dry Tua
Branco Extra Seco	Revisec Extrá Seco	Extra Dry White	Souza Port Dry White
Chip Dry			

DRY WHITE WINES (BRANCOS)

Very Dry, Old	Superior Alto Douro Dry White	Dry Port	Special White Dry
Very Dry White Port	Port	Aperitive	Porto Dry White Estoril
Rainha Santa Dry White	Porto Imperial Dry White	Dry White Port	Dalva's Dry White Port
Top Dry	Argonauta Dry White	Dry Old Port	Dryor
Secco Branco	Dry Finish White Port	Clipper	Porto Triunfal (White Dry Port)
Brig's Port White Dry			

DRY RUBY WINES (ALOIRADOS-CLAROS) DRY TAWNY WINE (ALOIRADO) MEDIUM-DRY WHITE WINE (BRANCO)

D. Velhissimo	Gotas de Ouro (seco)	Velho Seco	Special Pale Dry

MEDIUM-DRY TAWNY WINES (ALOIRADOS)

Directors Reserve	Dow's Boardroom Port	Choco	Commendador	Victória	Dalva's Port

SWEET LIGHT TAWNY WINES (ALOIRADOS-CLAROS)

Fine Royal Choice	Warre's Nimrod Port	Quinta do Bom Retiro	Fine Port	Duque de Bragança

SWEET TAWNY WINES (ALOIRADOS)

Douro Velho	Imperial	Superb Old	Porto Clube
Royal Diamond	Quinta do Junco	Shippers	Very Superior Old Port
Senex	Royal Port No. 3	Old Lodge	Royal Delicate
Medieval Port	Cintra Grand Corona	Lança 2 Coroas	Porto Antonat Tawny
Top Honours	Vintners Choice	Revinor	Porto Nogueira Genuíno
Particular	Emperor	Imperial Tawny Doce	Ultra Tawny
Noval 20 Anos	Boa Vista	Tawny Superior	Porto Cruz
Directorial	His Eminence's Choice	Very Old Superior	Atlantic
Special Reserve	Rodo	Royal Port No. 1	Vasconcellos
54 Port	Acordo Finest Old Tawny Port		

SWEET WHITE WINE   VERY SWEET TAWNY WINES (ALOIRADOS)   WHITE LAGRIMA (BRANCO)

Lacrima Christi	Porto V V	Royal Esmeralda	Lacrima Christi

SWEET RUBY WINES (TINTOS-ALOIRADOS)

Quinta das Quartas	Marquês de Pombal	Crasto V. O. R.	Century Port	Abelha

SWEET RED WINES (TINTOS)

Rainha Santa 840	Imperial Crown

ITALIAN WINES

GIOVANNI DALMASSO

Tracing the origins of winegrowing and winemaking is not an easy undertaking. History from its very beginning often accumulates legends, myths and traditions; reality is distorted by poetry, folklore or fantasy. In Italy this is particularly true. There the cultivation of the vine goes back to very ancient times. Man apparently discovered in the Neolithic age the quasi-magic properties of the fermented grape, which conferred on the moderate drinker the "wise forgetfulness of life" of which Dante speaks. The vine in those times grew freely in its wild state in the forest, winding itself around the trees and climbing to a considerable height. Man learned to cultivate it and produce the still-mysterious process of alcoholic fermentation that the men of science would spend centuries unravelling.

One point remained in dispute for a long time: should our vine, commonly called the European vine (the plant *vitis vinifera*) be considered as a native plant or was it on the other hand imported into Italy on the tide of the great human migrations from Asia Minor or North Africa? Doubtless both theories have a basis in fact. The crossing of the different vine-plants gave birth to the innumerable varieties of vines which led Virgil to exclaim in his *Georgics*: *Quem scire velit, Libyci velit aequoris idem* ("He who would know [the infinite variety of vines] would just as well [count] the grains of sand in the Lybian desert").

Certainly even in Homeric times Sicily was producing abundant quantities of wine. One episode in the *Odyssey* seems to point to this: when, near Etna, the Cyclops Polyphemus, whom Ulysses has blinded, falls stupefied by drink into a deep sleep. The Etruscans, who had settled in Italy perhaps about 1000 B.C., must certainly have contributed to disseminating the vine. They came from the East, where agriculture had already reached a certain stage of evolution, which no doubt included vinegrowing and winemaking. But when the Etruscans landed on the Tyrrhenian sea coast they probably found old and sturdy vines already growing there, since Pliny

had asserted that a statue in Populonia was carved from a single vine plant.

There is no doubt that in the time of Pliny the Elder, Italy already led the world in the quantity and excellence of her wines, outstripping even Greece, whose pupil she had been in winegrowing. In his *Naturalis Historia* Pliny speaks of 195 kinds of wine, of which over half were produced in Italy. What were some of the wines of ancient Italy? The MAMERTINO around Messina, the TAUROMENITANUM from the region of Taormina, the POTULAMUM, the SIRACUSANUM, the wines of Agrigente and Selinote and the BIBLINO in the region of Syracuse. In Calabria the most appreciated were the BRUTIUM and, moving northwards to Lucania, the wines of Consentia, Tempio, Rhegium and Buxentium. Apulia also produced well-reputed wines, notably those of Tarente, Babia, Brindisi, Canosa and Aulon. However the region which in the times of the Empire produced the wines praised most highly by the Latin poets was the area dominated by Naples, Campania, which could boast its FALERNO, its CALENO, its FORMIANO and the wines of Vesuvius.

Latium supplied numerous wines to the capital of the ancient world, but none was of outstanding quality. The same could be said, moving north, of the wines of Umbria, the Marches, and even Tuscany, which today is such an important wineproducing area. It is not until one comes to the Upper Adriatic, around the Gulf of Trieste, that one finds one of the most famous wines of Antiquity: the PUCINUM, produced near the mouth of the Timaro, not far from Aquileia.

The north of Italy produced another great wine, which Virgil himself claimed was only rivalled by the FALERNO. It is nevertheless difficult to know for certain whether it resembled the excellent wines of today from the region of Verona, or those of the Valtelino or even the Trentino.

The fame of Italian wines has in no way diminished over the centuries. Italy today has the world's second largest winegrowing area and is the biggest producer of

wine and dessert grapes. Her average annual production over the decade 1963-1973 was 66 million hectolitres (1450 million gallons). In 1973, it reached 76 million hectolitres (1650 million gallons).

One of the most essential characteristics of Italian winegrowing is its partition into two forms: monoculture and mixed culture. Italy is the only country in the world where the cultivation of vines alongside other plants, either climbing or herbaceous, is still very widespread.

As for the distribution of vineyards according to altitude, the Virgilian precept *Bacchus amat colles* ("Bacchus loves the hills") is still true today in the Italian agricultural economy and continues to give a very typical appearance to the countryside of peninsular Italy. In many regions, for example the Monferrato and the Langhe of Piedmont, or the region of Pavia in Lombardy, the hills which stretch as far as the eye can see are often entirely covered by a mantle of vineyards which seem almost to have been etched there by a calligrapher of olden days.

In many places the way of life and social standards have changed, accompanied inevitably by a progressive reduction in the rural population, which is increasingly attracted by the salary of the urban worker. The labour shortage has brought about a marked change in Italian winegrowing. Mechanization has been introduced almost everywhere. Machines have been tried out for the wine harvests, but sometimes the whole appearance of the vineyards on the plains had to be changed. This is why vines "married" to trees (elms, maples, poplars) are gradually giving way to close-set, regular rows of plants which make possible much more rational methods of cultivation.

The legal decree of 12 July 1963 regulates the production and marketing of wines with the aim of harmonising practices within the European Economic Community. The decree recognises three categories of wine: wines of simple origin (D.O.S.), with about a dozen appellations by the end of 1977; appellation-controlled wines (D.O.C.), about 400 by the same date; while for appellation-controlled and guaranteed wines (D.O.C.G.) no award has yet been made.

The measures for applying the decree have been long in development, and their immediate effect should not be expected. In fact, the ways and means of control seem to be absent for the moment. Nevertheless a clarifying process has been set in motion, which will enable the winelover to rely more on the labels. In this chapter, we have taken into account the new terminology, but we have also noted, as well as the D.O.C. wines, wines and growths that are not included in any official list.

NORTHERN ITALY

Northern Italy, which produces in all nearly half the national production of wine, has a great variety of reds, whites and rosés. They are mainly ordinary, fine or superior wines, but they also include special wines such as sparkling wines and aromatized or *passiti* wines. It would take too long to list them all; better to limit oneself to a few notes on the best ones, on a geographical basis, talking the winegrowing regions in order from west to east.

VALLE D'AOSTA. The motorist who travels through the Grand St. Bernard Tunnel from Switzerland emerges in the Valle d'Aosta, the first agricultural region he comes to in Italy, which boasts two local wines: ENFER D'ARVIER and DONNAZ. The first is produced from *Petit Rouge* grapes, a wine variety that is particular to the Valle d'Aosta, giving a light red, slightly bitter Alpine wine. The DONNAZ is made partly from *Nebbiolo* grapes, and is an aromatic, tasty red wine with a slight scent of almonds which is aged for a legal minimum of three years. Finally, the BLANC DE MORGET should be mentioned, which is made from grapes gathered on the moraines of the Valle d'Aosta at a height of 1000-1100 m (3000 ft).

PIEDMONT. Although other regions of Italy are bigger producers of wine, there is probably not one which surpasses Piedmont in the variety of quality wine yielded by the vineyards which cover its hillsides as far as the eye can see. In general, red table wines predominate, but there is no lack of whites — dry table wines as luxury wines, sparkling, aromatized or not, and there are even some dessert wines.

The most famous red wine of Piedmont is BAROLO; it is referred to as "the king of Italian wines" and "the wine of the kings". The grape which produces this superbwine is the *Nebbiolo*, a vine that was already under cultivation in the Middle Ages. Its delicate bouquet has overtones of violets, mixed with a slight odour of tar. BAROLO is an excellent wine to drink with roasts, game and even truffled *foie gras*. It should be served at a temperature of 20°C and should be opened an hour before drinking, to allow a slight oxydation. In the nineteenth century, it was the favorite wine of the monarchs of the House of Savoy, who even envisaged growing it on their estates.

The name BAROLO can only be given to wines coming from the Communes of Barolo, Castiglione, Falletto and Serralunga, together with certain areas in a few other

In Italy, where the wine is cultivated in each of the twenty administrative districts, the appellation system varies from one region to another, sometimes from one village to the other. The wine's name may be taken from the grape variety, like Barbera, or sometimes from the commune where it is grown, such as Marsala. Other names, for example Sangue di Guida or Lacryma Cristi, are traditional.

255

ITALIA SETTENTRIONALE

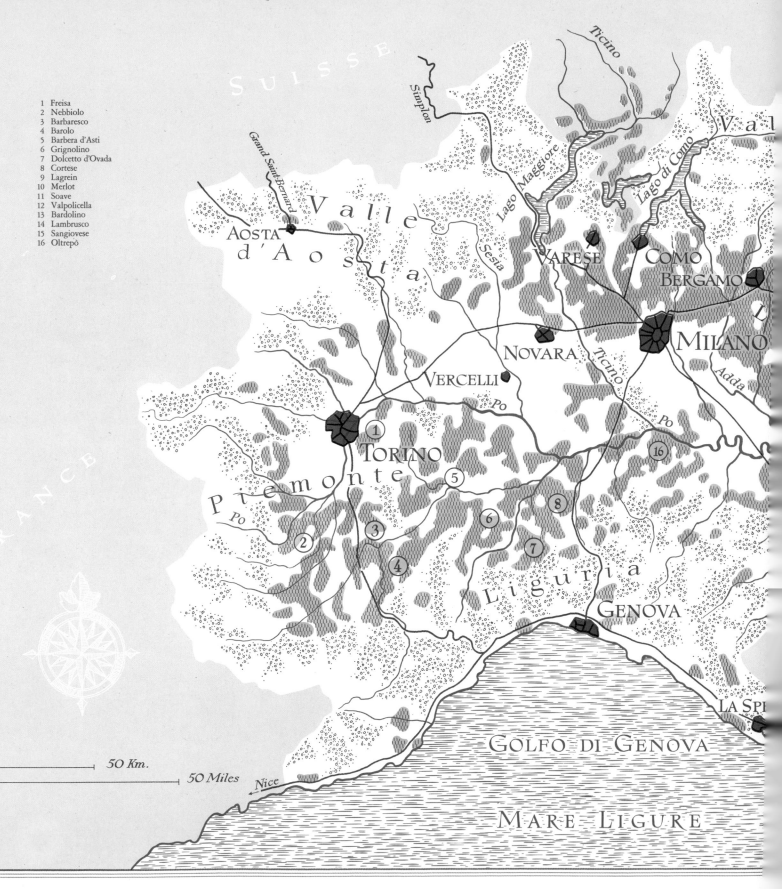

1 Freisa
2 Nebbiolo
3 Barbaresco
4 Barolo
5 Barbera d'Asti
6 Grignolino
7 Dolcetto d'Ovada
8 Cortese
9 Lagrein
10 Merlot
11 Soave
12 Valpolicella
13 Bardolino
14 Lambrusco
15 Sangiovese
16 Oltrepò

SUISSE

Ticino

Simplon

Grand Saint-Bernard

Valle d'Aosta

AOSTA

Lago Maggiore

Lago di Como

Sesia

Val

VARESE

COMO

BERGAMO

Ticino

NOVARA

MILANO

VERCELLI

Adda

Po

Po

TORINO

Piemonte

Po

Po

Liguria

GENOVA

GOLFO DI GENOVA

LA SPE

50 Km.

50 Miles

Nice

MARE LIGURE

FRANCE

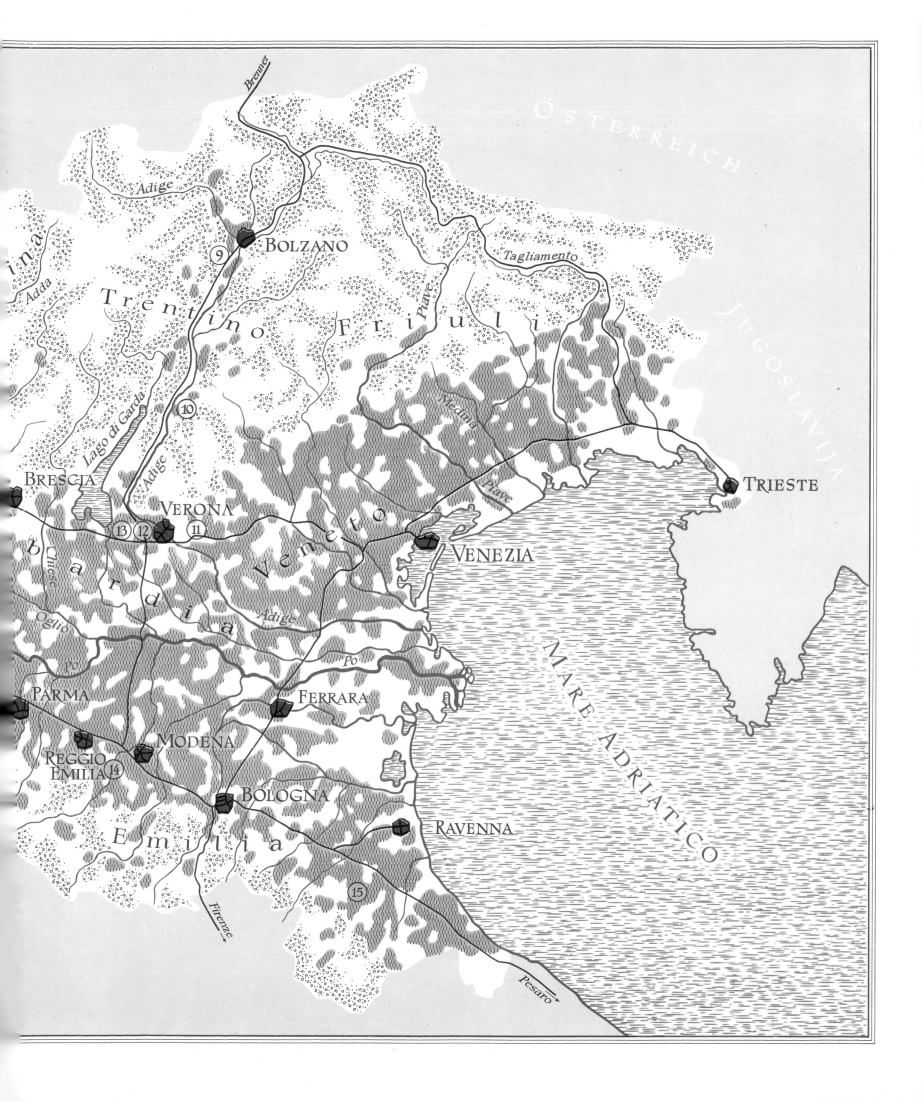

The vines of the Langhe district of Piedmont are grown on chalky, sandy hills which may reach a height of 2000-2500 ft. The commonest grape varieties are *Dolcetto* and *Nebbiolo* which produce wines of the same name.

commures in the province of Cuneo. The law stipulates that BAROLO must pass three years in oak casks before being bottled and sold, and it must have a 12° alcohol content minimum. It has a beautiful orange-red colour, and has a dry, austere yet harmonious and somewhat velvety flavour.

The best vineyeards are: CANNUBIO in the commune of Barolo, ROCCHE in the commune of Castiglione-Falletto, BRUNANTE in La Morra, and VIGNA ROTONDA in the commune of Serralunga d'Alba.

A wine which has much in common with BAROLO is the BARBARESCO, which also comes from the *Nebbiolo* wine. It ages faster, and is lighter yet subtle, and is a good wine to accompany roast meat and game. The best examples come from the communes of BARBARESCO, ASILI, PORA, BRICCO, MONTESTEFANO, or from the commune of Treiso, which produces ROMBONE and GRESY. BARBARESCO may not be sold before it has been aged for two years. Wine that has been aged for three years has the right to the mention "Riserva", and for four years "Riserva speciale".

In Piedmont, the *Nebbiolo* grapes, also called *Spanna*, yield other good quality *da arrosta* (to go with roasts) wines. They are GATTINARA (reputable vineyard: CASTELLI DI PATRIARCA); LESSONA (reputable vineyard: SAN SEBASTIANO ALLO ZOPPA); GHEMME (reputable vineyard: PODERE AI VALLONI). All these wines, which have a sharp taste when young, acquire an admirably harmonious flavour with age.

On the rocky slopes of the hills of the province of Turin, it is once again the *Nebbiolo* grapes — which change their name to *picotener* — which produce a much sought-after wine, CAREMA. The grapes are fermented before pressing, and a clear red wine is produced, which, suitably aged, develops into a wine of rare finesse. Production is strictly limited to the commune of Carema and none is allowed to be sold before four years. The bottles must clearly indicate the vintage.

The size of the area producing it and the quantities in which it is produced make BARBERA the most representative of Piedmont's wines. The name comes from the wine. At an estimation, half the wine production in Piedmont is made up of BARBERA. Young, the wine has strong, flowery bouquet, and is a good accompaniment to local dishes (tripe, salami, stews, etc.); aged, BARBERA has a beautiful ruby colour and a taste and bouquet that recall BAROLO. The best examples are BARBERA D'ASTI (reputable vineyards: BANIN DELL'ANNUNZIATA, DELLA ROCHETTA); BARBERA D'ALBA (reputable vineyards: ARIONE, BUT DI MADONNA COMO, PIAN ROMUALDO, RIVETTI); BARBERA DEL MONTEFERRATO (reputable vineyards: ANNIBALINI, CASTELLO DI GABIANO).

Many of the characteristics of BARBERA may also be attributed to another wine, FREISA, which comes, in part, from the same wine-producing area. Two quite distinct types of FREISA are made, one dry *(tip seco)*. the other semi-sweet *(tipo amabile)*. Notable are the FREISA D'ALBA (reputable vineyards: DEL CIABOT DEL PRETE) and FREISA DI CHIERI. Dry FREISA gains greatly if sufficiently matured (for a shorter time, however, than BARBERA). It develops a delicate violet taste and loses much of its youthful acidity.

Another red table wine, produced in large quantities in Piedmont, is the DOLCETTO, which takes its name from a fast-maturing grape. Despite its name, it is a dry wine, which goes agreeably with white meats (veal, poultry, etc.). Worthy of mention are DOLCETTO D'ALBA (reputable vineyards: BASARIN, BOSCHI DI BERRI, CAGNAST, CAMPETTO DEL COLOMBE, ROCHETTEVINO, SAN CRISTOFORO); DOLCETTO D'ASTI, DOLCETTO D'ACQUI, DOLCETTO DI DIANO D'ALBA, DOLCETTO DI DOGLIANI, DOLCETTO DELLE LANGHE MONREGALESI, and DOLCETTO DI OVADA. The wines have developed all their qualities by the first, or at the latest, the second year. They have body and moderate acidity, with an agreeable, well-rounded aroma, slightly but pleasantly bitter. A slightly sparkling variety, best appreciated outside meal-times, is also produced.

Yet another wine that improves with age is the GRIGNOLINO; many consider it to be among the best of

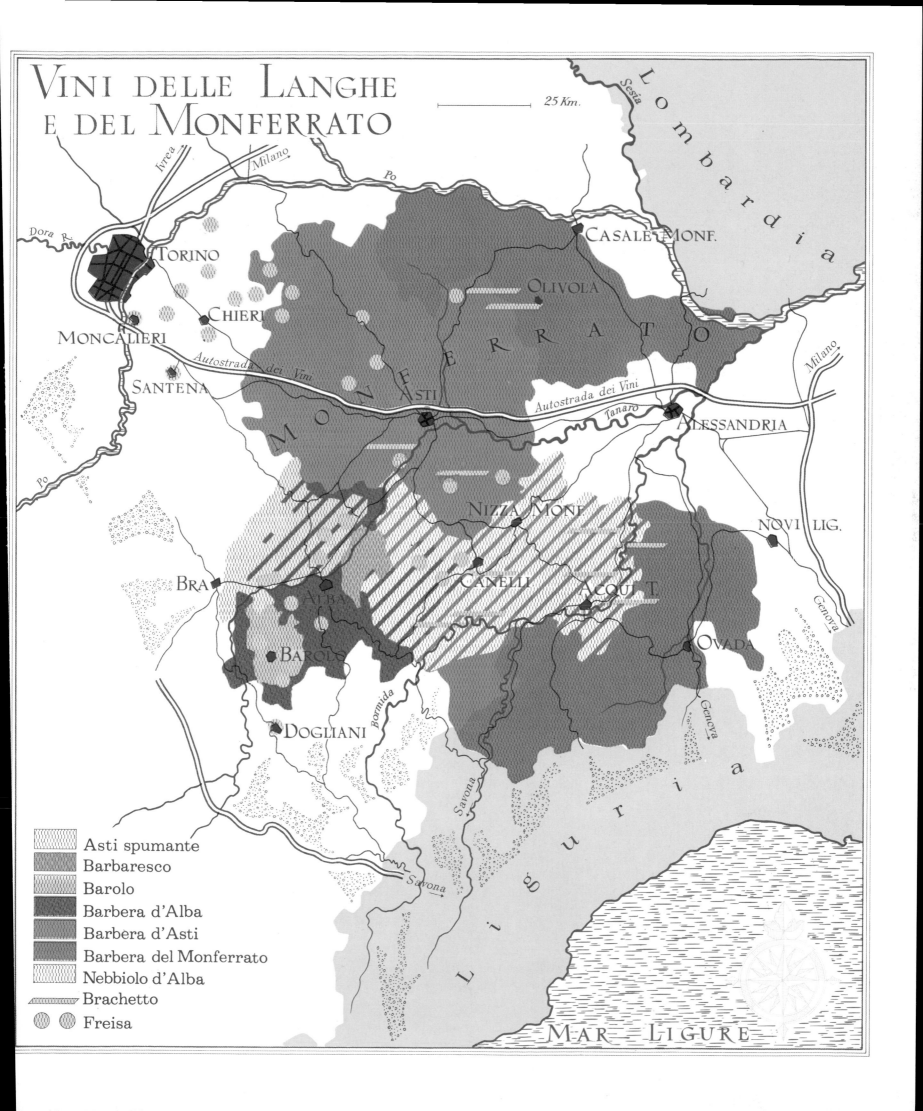

Vini delle Langhe e del Monferrato

25 Km.

Lombardia

Ivrea
Milano
Po
Dora R.
TORINO
CASALE MONF.
MONCALIERI
CHIERI
OLIVOLA
SANTENA
Autostrada dei Vini
M O N F E R R A T O
ASTI
Autostrada dei Vini
Tanaro
ALESSANDRIA
Milano
Po
NIZZA MONF.
NOVI LIG.
BRA
ALBA
CANELLI
ACQUI T.
Genova
BAROLO
OVADA
Genova
Bormida
DOGLIANI
L i g u r i a
Savona
Savona

Asti spumante
Barbaresco
Barolo
Barbera d'Alba
Barbera d'Asti
Barbera del Monferrato
Nebbiolo d'Alba
Brachetto
Freisa

MAR LIGURE

Piedmont's table wines because of its fresh, delicate and harmonious flavour, its fragrant aroma, its fine, light ruby colour, and its moderate alcohol content (11-12°). Notable wines are the GRIGNOLINO D'ASTI (reputable vineyards: CASCINA PRETE, MIGLIANDOLO), and GRIGNOLINO DEL MONFERRATO CASALESE (reputable vineyards: CASCINA, MIGLIAVACCA, TENUTA DE RE).

In the Alba region, *Nebbiolo* grapes give NEBBIOLO D'ALBA, of which there are three types: a dry wine, a sweet wine, and a sparkling wine. NEBBIOLO D'ALBA has a considerable reputation, and may be compared to a lighter BAROLO. Indeed, BAROLOS that fail to reach the legal 12° are sold under this name. Notable vineyards: BERNARDINA, SAN ROCCO, OCHETTI, CARRETTA, LA COLA VALLEMAGGIORE DI LA VEZZA, MONTEU RUERO; VALLEMAGGIORE DI LA VEZZA. Sparkling red NEBBIOLO is served chilled, the sweet wine with dessert, cooled just below room temperature, while the red is served at the same temperature.

Among the other red wines, one should mention BRACHETTO D'ACQUI, a sweet sparkling wine with an

There are three BARBERAS – D'ASTI, D'ALBA and MONTFERRATO. The label shown here clothes a bottle of dry red wine, which takes on garnet highlights with age. It is an excellent wine with roasts.

The vineyards of Monforte d'Alba (left) are planted with *Dolcetto* grapes, which yield the DOLCETTO D'ALBA, a handsome red wine, dry and agreeably balanced.

260

aroma of roses, and one of the rare quality sparkling reds; MALVASIA DI CASORZO D'ASTI, a pretty ruby red wine, sweet and slightly perfumed, MALVASIA DI CASTELNUOVO DON BOSCO, a wine which the special method of interrupted fermentation makes very sweet and perfumed; and RUBINO DI CANTAVENNA, a spirited light red with a dry and vigorous flavour produced by a reputable wine co-operative.

White wines in Piedmont are very much in the minority. The best known are the CORTESE, and among them, the CORTESE DI GAVI, (reputable vineyards: MONTE ROTONDO, ROVERETO); they are delicate, fresh white wines with a light sand colour and a stable perfume, which go very well with fish. There are also sparkling GAVIS. Another fine white wine is ERBALUCE DI CALUSO, a fresh wine for hot days, and CALUSO PASSITO, made from grapes that are partly dried before pressing, producing a sweet, scented dessert wine.

But Piedmont is also proud, and rightly so, of its "special" wines, of which the best examples are MOSCATO DI ASTI and ASTI SPUMANTE. The grapes from which they are made are the *Yellow Muscat*, also called *Muscat di Canelli* after a small town in the centre of the production area and the industrial zone which produces the famous sparkling wines which have won such favour on the national and international markets. These wines are subjected to a complex and detailed treatment, now perfected, and acquire a distinctive personality much prized by the general public.

LIGURIA. Winegrowing plays a modest part in the economy of the region, but Ligurian wines nevertheless deserve a more than honorable mention.

On the western Riviera, between Genoa and Vintimiglia, DOLCEACQUA or ROSSESE DI DOLCEACQUA is grown, a light and fragrant red wine with a touch of bitterness, or a slightly sparkling white, fresh and agreeably scented. In the same region, VERMENTINO is found, a dry white wine of quality, moderate in alcohol, and a pretty pronounced sraw colour, fresh and perfumed.

On the eastern Riviera, the best-known wines are the CINQUE TERRE, a perfumed, fruity white (reputable vineyards: MANAROLA). The Passito is known as CINQUE TERRE SCHIACHETRÀ, and is a dessert wine. The winemaking is unusual here, for the vines traditionally grow on the steep slopes that hang over the sea, clinging to the rocks, and producing a few small bunches of grapes of the white *Rosco*, *Albarola* and *Vermentino* varieties. These wines mature perfectly, giving a juice very rich in sugar, which is converted into dry or dessert wines.

LOMBARDY. Lombardy is certainly not one of the main wineproducing areas of Italy, but it can lay claim to several quality wines. The vineyards are divided into three distinct areas: the Oltrepò of Pavia, the Valteline, and the western shores of Lake Garda.

The first of these would seem to be the prolongation of the hills of Piedmont, or more precisely of the hills of Monferrato. It lies on the province of Pavia and appears to be an endless series of hills, covered by excellent vineyards producing red and white wines. Of the red wines, the majority are produced from the Piedmontese *Barbera* and local vines; *Ovattina* (also called *Bonarda*), *Uva Rara* or "rare grape" and *Ughetta*. The wines are well-known to connoisseurs today: BUTTAFUOCO DELL'OLTREPÒ PAVESE, a deep red, is a much-appreciated table wine, especially from the CASTANA vineyard; the BARBACARLO DELL'OLTREPÒ PAVESE has a delicate perfume of strawberries or violets; the SANGUE DI GIUDA (Judas's blood) DELL'OLTREPÒ PAVESE has a ruby colour; all three wines are dry, well-perfumed, and with a touch of sweetness.

The BONARDA DELL'OLTREPÒ PAVESE, an intense ruby red, has a typical scent of raspberries. Reputable vineyards: SCAZZOLINO DI ROVESCAGLIA and ROVESCAGLIA.

As well as the winegrowing areas of the Valtelline and the Riviera del Garda, Lombardy has a well-known district to the south, the Oltrepò Pavese, which extends along the hills that lie across the River Po. The white and red wines produced there are favourites with connoisseurs.

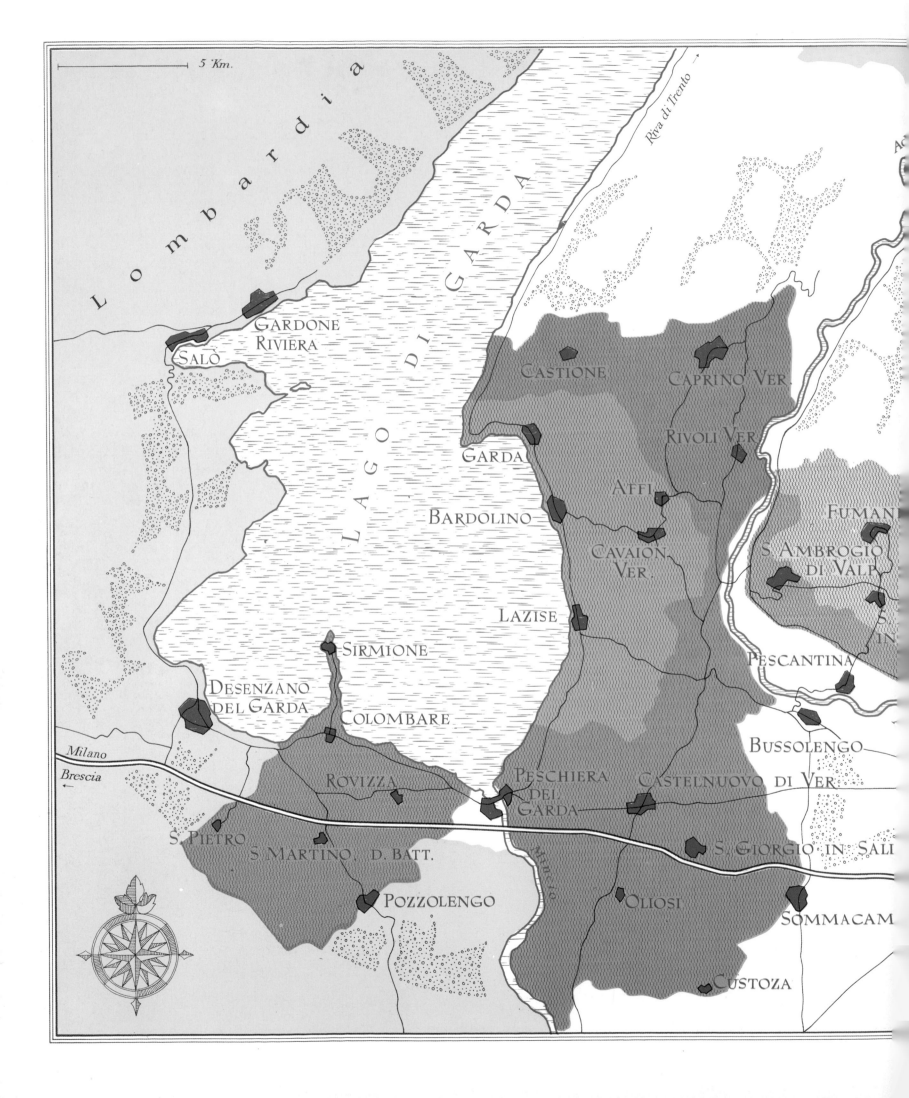

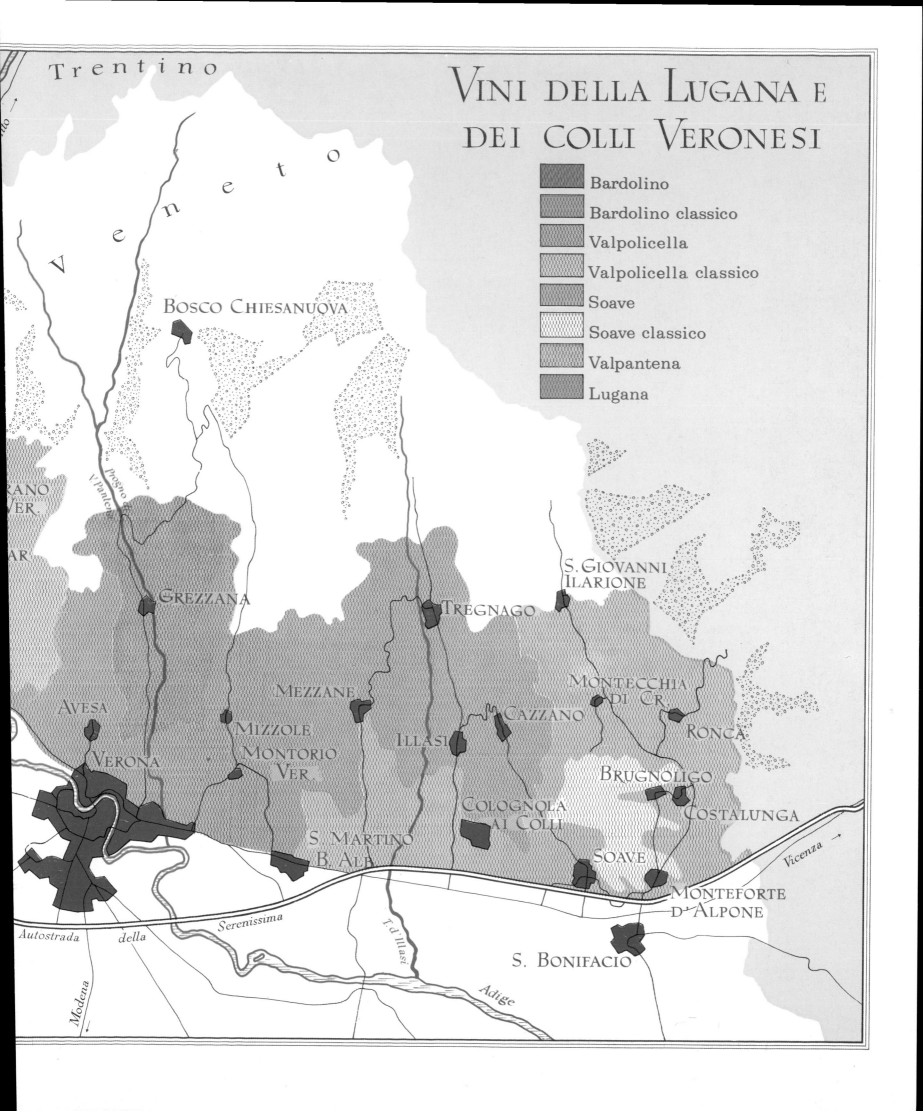

As well as these characteristic wines, the region also produces *Pinots*: PINOT DELL'OLTREPÒ PAVESE (reputable vineyard: MONTECALVO), *Barberas*: BARBERA DELL'OLTREPÒ PAVESE (reputable vineyard: FRACCHION DI ROVESCALA, SCAZZOLINO DI ROVESCALA) and a ROSSO DELL'OLTREPÒ PAVESE.

Of the white wines of the Oltrepò of Pavia, the most outstanding is certainly the RIESLING DELL'OLTREPÒ PAVESE, which is produced by several well-known vineyards: OLIVA, RUGOLON, ROSSELLA, SCAGNO, NAZZANO, and, best of all, CASOLE.

Other white wines produced in the region, such as CLASTIDIO BIANCO, FRECCIAROSSA BIANCO, and CORTESE DELL'OLTREPÒ PAVESE, are dry white wines with a subtle nose. There is also the sweet and aromatic MOSCATO DELL'OLTREPÒ PAVESE for drinking outside meal-times.

The VALTELINO, in the province of Sondrio, is a winegrowing area of Lombardy which is both large and long-established. It has been said that the famous RETICO, which was such a favorite of the Emperor Augustus, is the ancestor of today's Valtelino wines. Most of the wines are made from *Nebbiolo* grapes, which are known locally as *Chavennasca* vines. They produce lively, full, supple and balanced wines, with a sombre

MOSCATO D'ASTI is made solely from the *Muscat Blanc* grapes grown in a limited number of communes in the provinces of Asti and Coni. The vines climb up the hills, surrounding villages, churches and convents, but avoiding the crests which are left to villages or to trees. Above: Around Asti. Right: Near Valdevilla in the late Autumn.

The Poet Virgil, who described so well the daily round of the countryside, would have delighted in this scene, which would have held few surprises for him. Perhaps the sulphate spray might have astonished him as much by its colour as by its works, but he would have found the ox team and the slow rhythm of the work familiar. This traditional method of working is taking place in a vineyard in Venetia.

yet intense colour, subtle perfume, and dry and winey taste. They are known by the name of the places that grow them: SASELLA (reputable vineyard: PARADISO), GRUMELLO, ERACIA, and VALGELLA. In German-speaking countries, the wines are known generally as VELTLINER.

A special wine from the Valtelino is the SFURZAT, which responds to a long maturing process to change into a real dessert wine, rich and sweet, and almost orange in colour.

The work of the winegrowers in the valley of the Adda deserves to be admired. The wines are grown on narrow, vertiginous terraces high above the valley, the plants attached to rocks.

The third well-known winegrowing area of Lombardy lies to the west and south of the Lake Garda. There are grown the following wines: BOTTICINO (reputable vineyard: BETTINA), a red wine with garnet highlights, with a marked taste, slightly tannic, which goes well with country dishes.

CELLATICA, made from various grape varieties (*Schiave*, *Gentile*, *Barbera* and *Cabernet*), is an excellent table wine.

FRANCIACORTA ROSSO is made from *Cabernet*, *Barbera*, *Nebbiolo*, and *Merlot* grapes, and is a red with violet highlights when young, garnet when older. Reputable vineyard: BORGOGNATO.

White wines from the region include FRANCIACORTA PINOT, and VALCALEPIO (there is also a red).

The area to the south of Lake Garda produces red, rosé and white wines under the name of RIVIERA DEL GARDA, rosés and whites as COLLI MORENCICI MANTOVANI DEL GARDA.

LUGANA is a high-quality white wine, a pale straw colour approaching green, and with a delicate, light and fresh taste. Well-known vineyards: LUGANA, LA GHINIDA. The same region also produces PUSTERLA, a delicate wine, made in white, red and rosé. TOCAI DI SAN MARINO DELLA BATTAGLIA has a dry, rounded taste.

VENETIA. This large area of northern Italy competes with Apulia for the first place as the biggest producer of wine. It can also pride itself on possessing an extremely large number of quality wines of all categories.

When the traveller journeys from Milan to Venice, the first wineproducing region of Venetia encountered is in the province of Verona. Within the region, which lies between Lake Garda and Verona, the vines produce above all red wine. The wines are the BARDOLINO

265

The vines of the Alto Adige are grown on terraces along the sides of the river valley. The wines sometimes carry two names, in Italian and German. For example: SANTA MADDALENA or MAGDALENER, CALDERO or KALTERER, TEROLDEGO or TERLANER. This is because the Alto Adige was once administered by Austria, where there is still a large market for the wines.

(reputable vineyard: CALMASINO), one of the most charming of Italian table wines; it has a clear, lively colour, and has a fresh taste and what can best be described as an agreeable bouquet.

VALPOLICELLA-VALPANTENA, an everyday red wine, is a red turning to garnet with age, dry or slightly sweet, and has plenty of body, a balanced velvetyness, and occasionally, a slight taste of bitter almonds. Among the notable vineyards: MAZZUREGA, ARTIZZANA, SAN PERETTO, SAN FLIORANO, PEDEMONTE, SAN GIORGIO, CAMPO FIORIN, LE RAGOSE, MONTE FONTANA.

REGIOTTO DELLA VALPOLICELLA is a strong, slightly sweet red wine, full, warm, soft and seductive. It contains a minimum of 14° alcohol and goes very well with Venetian-style calves' liver (well-known vineyards: LE RAGOSE, MONTE OZMI, TORBE).

South of Verona, BIANCO DI CUSTOZA is produced; it has a soft almost straw colour, with a slightly sweet and bitter perfume.

West of Verona, mostly white wines are made, notably SOAVE (reputable vineyard: CALVARINO). The wine has a straw colour turning to green, a dry taste and

a slight scent of almonds. SOAVE is particularly good served cool with a fish dish. RECIOTO DI SOAVE is a wine made from partly dried grapes, sweet and liquorish, which contains at least 14° alcohol. It has been known a long time in Verona — some say it dates from the time of Theodoric the Great, King of the Ostrogoths (454-526). It is made from the same grapes as VALPOLICELLA.

GAMBELLARA is also a good white table wine, similar to SOAVE, with a typical light and fresh taste.

The wines included under the name COLLI BERICI are white: COLLI BERICI GARGANEGA, COLLI BERICI TOCAI, COLLI BERICI PINOT BIANCO; or red: COLLI BERICI MERLOT, COLLI BERICI TOCAI ROSSO, and COLLI BERICI CABERNET. They are table wines for drinking young.

South of Padua, wine from the COLLI EUGANEI is either red or white. The red comes mostly from *Merlot*, the white from *Garganega*, *Serpina*, and *Tocai Italiano* grapes. COLLI EUGANEI MOSCATO is made from *Muscat Blanc* grapes, it is sometimes made as a sparkling wine. To the north of Padua, between Bassano and the Adriatic lies another of Venetia's wineproducing areas, which is notable for BREGANZE, either white or red; the

266

Italian winegrowers have inherited from the distant past ancient ways of cultivating the vine. According to the quality of the soil and the type of micro-climate, the shoots are trained upwards and supported on trellises, allowing the grapes to mature under the most favourable circumstances. Right: An Emilian vineyard.

Often, the stems are allowed to grow tall, held up by wires, so that the vines look like fruit trees. Sometimes mixed cultivation of vines and vegetables is practised.

white suits the Venetian dish *risi e bisi* (rice and peas) marvellously. PROSECCO DI CONEGLIANO-VALDOBIANE and SUPERIORE DI CARTIZE are dry or sweet ("amabile") white wines which can also be made as sparkling wines.

The province of Treviso produces PIAVE or VINI DEL PIAVE, which are red wines made from *Merlot* grapes (reputable vineyards: CASTELLO DI RONCADE, VALLONTO); *Cabernet* (reputable vineyards: CERTOSA DEL MONTELLO); *Pinot Noir* (reputable vineyard: SAN VENDEMIANO); and whites such as TOCAI (reputable vineyard: SAN LORENZO) and VERDUZZO.

Further east again, CABERNET and MERLOT DI PRAMAGGIORE are found, dry red wines with a slight, although noticeable, taste of herbs.

Finally, the same region produces a white wine called TOCAI DI LISON, which has a light smokey taste, made from *Tocai di Fruili* grapes.

In 1877, Italy's first school specializing in winegrowing and oenology, the School of Conegliano, was founded. It has made a considerable contribution to scientific winemaking throughout Italy.

TRENTINO-UPPER ADIGE. North of Verona, the road leads up to the mountains, first through the Trentino and Upper Adige, and then on to Austria over the Brenner Pass. The winegrowers of the area have made considerable progress in the last few years in the vinification of their wines.

In the Trentino, the most remarkable wine is the TEROLDEGO ROTALIANO, which has a scent of blackberries and a slightly bitter after-taste. Reputable vineyards: MASO SCARI, MASO ISCHIA. There is also a rosé, TEROLEGO ROTALIANO ROSATO. The other D.O.C. ("Denominazione di Origine Controllata") wines are the following: CASTELLER, CALDARO or LAGO DI CALDARO (KALTERERSEE in German) among the reds. TRENTINO is red as TRENTINO CABERNET, TRENTINO LAGREIN, TRENTINO MARZEMINO and TRENTINO MERLOT; white as TRENTINO PINOT, TRENTINO RIESLING; scented or sweet as TRENTINO TRAMINER, TRENTINO MOSCATO and TRENTINO VINO SANTO. There is also a rosé, TRENTINO LAGREIN KRETZER.

North of the Trentino, the Upper Adige region produces both red and white wines, of which the following are the most notable:

Reds: SANTA MADDALENA, sometimes considered the best Tyrolean red, LAGREIN (best vineyard: MURI-GRIES), MERANESE DI COLLINA, COLLI DI BOLZANO, and the various reds named for the grape varieties: (-CABERNET, -LAGREIN, -SCURO, -MALVASIA, -MERLOT, -PINOT NERO, -SCHIAVE). The whites: VALLE ISCARO (-TRAMINER, -PINOT, -PINOT GRIGIO, -SYLVANER, MULLER THURGAU), TERLANO and the various ALTO ADIGE wines (-MOSCATO GIALLO, -PINOT BIANCO, -PINOT GRIGIO, -RIESLING ITALICO, -RIESLING RENNANO [reputable vineyards: KOLBENHOF, TERLANO], -RIESLING SYLVANER, -SYLVANER, -SAUVIGNON, -GEWURZTRAMINER [reputable vineyards: MAZZON, NOVACELLA]). These wines are often known abroad by the German versions of their names: MAGDALENER, LAGREIN-KRETZER, TERLANER, KALTERER.

JULIAN VENETIA – FRIULI. North east of Venice lie two more wineproducing regions, Julian Venetia and Friuli.

Notable wines of Julian Venetia are the LATISANA family (reds: -MERLOT, -CABERNET, -REFOSCO; whites: -TOCAI, -PINOT BIANCO, -PINOT GRIGIO, -VERDUZZO, -TRAMINER, -AROMATICO, -RIESLING RENNANO), the AQUILIEA wines (reds: -MERLOT, -CABERNET, -REFOSCO; whites: -TOCAI, -PINOT BIANCO, -RIESLING) and COLLIO GORIZINAO from the Yugoslav border, sometimes known simply as COLLIO, a dry white wine (reputable vineyards: *Riesling*: CORMONS, DOLEGNA; *Müller-Thurgau*: SPESSA; *Malvasia*: LUCINICO; *Pinot bianco*: RUSSIZ; *Pinot Grigio*: PLESSIVA DI CORMONS; *Sauvignon*: RONCADA RUSSIZA; *Tocai*: PARADIS DI CORMONS, RUSSIZ; *Traminer*: PLESSIVA DI CORMONS.

Friuli has a fewer types of wine; there are the reds and whites of COLLI ORIENTALI DEL FRIULI, better known for the whites, such as *Pinot Gris* (reputable vineyard: GRAMOLIGNO), *Tocai* (reputable vineyard: SAN MARTINI), and *Verduzzo* (reputable vineyard: RONCHI DI ROSAZZO). There are also the wines of the GRAVE DEL FRIULI. There is also a dessert wine made in Friuli, PICCOLIT, the best vineyard being ROCCA BERNARDA.

EMILIA ROMAGNA. In this region, the vines stretch across a plain whose climate is eminently suitable to their growth.

This area is famous for the quality and sumptiousness of its cuisine, which we are more used to hear being called Bolognese (from the town of Bologna).

The red wines grown here belong to the LAMBRUSCHI family and are widely appreciated. But all the wines are not the same quality. The best, no doubt, is the LAMBRUSCO DI SORBARA, an unusual but popular slightly fizzy garnet red wine with a touch of froth. Notable vineyard: VILLANOVA DI LA. One should also mention LAMBRUSCO SALAMINO DI SANTA CROCE (reputable vineyard: CIBERNO), LAMBRUSCO REGGIANO, and LAMBRUSCO GRASPAROSSA DI CASTELVETRO.

LAMBRUSCHI wines all fit perfectly with Emilian cooking, which is highly flavoured and rather greasy, based as it is largely on pork, which demands a slightly acid, bitter wine.

Another red wine from the region is the SAN GIOVESE DI ROMAGNA (reputable vineyard: ROCCA DI RIBANO) which has a red colour with violet highlights, dry and sometimes slightly tannic. There are also GUTTURNIO DEI COLLI PIACENTINA (reputable vineyard: SOLITARIA) and the wines of the COLLI BOLOGNESI DI MONTE SAN PIETRO.

Among the whites should be mentioned LABANA DI ROMAGNA (reputable vineyard: MONTERICCO) and MONTEROSSO VAL D'ARDA, which are each produced in dry and "amabile" or sweet and perfumed versions, known as TREBBIANO DI ROMAGNA (reputable vineyard: BIANCANIGO) and TREBBIANO VAL TREBBIA. There are also white wines produced under the name COLLI BOLOGNESI DI MONTE SAN PIETRO, made from *Sauvignon*, *Pinot blanc*, and *Italian Riesling* grapes.

CENTRAL ITALY

The five regions of Central Italy (Tuscany, Umbria, the Marches, Latium and Abruzzi) produce nearly a sixth of Italy's total, and enjoy a very old reputation as wineproducers.

TUSCANY: Above all, the region is celebrated as the home of CHIANTI, so well known that it is often taken as a synonym of Italian wine. The name is very old, and already appears in thirteenth-century documents. Its name comes from a small area in the centre of Tuscany, between the provinces of Sienna and Florence. The name Chianti appears in very reliable documents as early as 1260, but old texts refer most frequently to a CHIANTI of 1378 when the "CHIANTI League" was instituted (by an official Act of the Republic of Florence), which comprised the present districts of Gaide, Radda and Castellina. The production zone has, however, slowly been extended with the passage of time to include the districts of Poggibonsi, San Sasiano Val di Pesa, Castelnuovo Berardenga and other Tuscan vineyards more or less bordering on it, all of which have produced for a long time a wine which has the same biochemical qualities as the original CHIANTI. The wine is now produced in a zone situated in the centre of Tuscany, and extending over the provinces of Florence, Sienna, Pisa, Pistoia and Arezzo.

The red wines produced in this region go very well with Tuscan cookery, and CHIANTI accompanies particularly well the famous "bistecca alla fiorentina", a steak grilled with pepper, salt and olive oil over a vineroot fire.

CHIANTI is divided into two large classifications: CHIANTI CLASSICO, which is produced in the central, original areas, the hills between Florence and Sienna. Notable among the best vineyards are: CASTELLO DIUZZANO, VIGNAMAGGIO, VIGNA VECCHIO, CAGGIOLO, CASTELLO DI CERETTO, FATTORIA DI TIZZIANO, VILLA D'ARCENO, NOZZOLE, and VERRAZZANO. The other classification is CHIANTI, which is produced in a larger area which surrounds the original area. The wines are allowed to carry, according to their origins, the following appellations: CHIANTI MONTALBANO, CHIANTI DEI COLLI FIORENTINI, CHIANTI DEI COLLI SENESI, CHIANTI DEI COLLI ARETINI, CHIANTI DELLE COLLINI PISANE and CHIANTI RUFINA.

Notable vineyards: ARTIMINO, FATTORIA LA QUERGIA, VILLA DI CAPEZZANA, CASTEL PUGNA, I COLLAZI, I COLLI, and BADIA A COLTIBUONO.

The characteristics of CHIANTI are: a very bright ruby-red colour with tends to garnet as it ages; a dry flavour, slightly impregnated with tannin, which becomes delicate, mild and velvety with age. The regulation on the production of CHIANTI lays down that the basic wines must be 50-80 per cent *Sangiovese*, 10-30 per cent *Canaiolo nero*, 10-30 per cent *Trebbiano*

Toscano and *Malvasia del Chianti*. Among the complementary vines are *Colorino*, *Mammolo* and *Bonannico*.

There is one traditional and characteristic practice in the wine making process of CHIANTI, called the *governo* ("government"). It consists of adding to the new wine during the month of November a small quantity (5 to 10 per cent) of must which has been made from grapes which have been specially conserved on trellises or

The Chianti production zone covers a large area south of Florence. The name CHIANTI CLASSICO is given only to wines coming from the older, original vineyards. CHIANTI VECCHIO should be at least two years old, and CHIANTI RISERVA more than three. The photograph was taken in the cellars of the Villa di Capezzana estate.

hung up on hooks. If the cellar has been kept at the right temperature these grapes ferment and if the casks are hermetically sealed, the carbon dioxide dissolves in the wine, giving it a characteristic tang and adding a surprising but agreeable taste to the young CHIANTI. Tuscans say that it "kisses and bites". CHIANTI can be drunk in its first year, at the latest in late spring. But the best is aged in casks for two or three years. After at least two years, it can be labelled CHIANTI VECCHIO, and after three years of ageing it earns the right to CHIANTI RISERVA.

Other than CHIANTI, Tuscany produces the following red wines: BRUNELLO DI MONTALCINO (reputable vineyard: IL GREPPO DI BARBI), a garnet-red wine with a perfume of violets, excellent with roasts and game, CARMIGNANO, a wine from the two communes of Carmignano and Poggio a Caiano, with a bright ruby colour turning to garnet with age. Notable vineyards: ARTIMO RISERVA DEL GRANDUCA, IL POGGIOLO, VILLA DI CAPEZZANA. Another red wine that deserves an honorable mention is the VINO NOBILE DI MONTEPULCIANO, which, despite a certain coarseness in youth, acquires with maturity style and power, a scent of violets, and a slight taste of cherries. Notable vineyard: SANT'AGNESE, ROSSO DELLE COLLINE LUCCHESI, and PARRINA ROSSO are excellent table wines, balanced and supple.

White wines from the region are fewer and less abundant. One well-known white is the VERNACCIA DI SAN GIMIGNANO (reputable vineyard: FATTORIA DI PETRAFITTA), together with PARRINA BIANCO, MONTECARLO BIANCO, BIANCO DI PITTIGLIANO, BIANCO DELLA VALDINIEVE, and BIANCO VERGINE VAL DI CHIANA. There also some good white CHIANTIS which carry the name CHIANTI BIANCO (reputable vineyard: ABBIA BIANCO, bottled by Ricasoli).

Rosés are also represented in Tuscany, though not in any great number: ROSATELLO COLLI ARETINI, ROSE DI BOLGHERI and VILLA DI CORTE ROSE.

Tuscany today is passing through a slow transformation of cultivation techniques, the traditional mixed cultures giving way to monoculture.

THE MARCHES. In the province, on the Adriatic side of Tuscany, mixed culture still outweighs the specialized methods. It is a region of table wines.

On the whole, the proportion of white wines produced by the Marches is higher than in other regions of Italy. And it is certain that among the whites are found the most characteristic and widely appreciated of the area's wines.

The D.O.C. ("Denominazione di Origine Controllata") white wines are the following: VERDICCHIO DEI CASTELLI DI JESI, dry, balanced, with a pleasant bitter after-taste; VERDICCHIO DI MATELICA; BIANCHELLO DEL METAURO; BIANCO DEI COLLI MACERATESI; FALERIO DEI COLLI ASCOLANI. They are dry wines, pleasant to drink chilled, and which go well with fish.

The red wines from the Marches are good table wines, but few of them can compare with the great Tuscan wines. The best known is ROSSO CONERO (reputable vineyard: VIGNA DEL CURATO); followed by ROSSO PICENO, VERNACCIA DI SERRAPETRONA (reputable vineyard: PIAN DELLE MURA), produced from partially dried grapes, and SANGIOVESE DEI COLLI PESARESI (reputable vineyard: SANGIOVESE DI SANSEVERINO – PIAN DELLE MURA).

UMBRIA. Umbrian wines are above all whites for everyday consumption. There is, however, one wine which on its own earns a well-deserved reputation for the region: ORVIETO, of which there are two types — a dry wine which is the best known nowadays, and a sweet version (abbocato), which is a wine to serve between meals. The sweet wine is produced from the must from withered grapes, which is left to ferment in small vats in deep, cool cellars hollowed out of the volcanic tufa. This encourages the development of the finest bouquets and flavours. ORVIETO ABBOCATO was the favorite wine of Pope Paul III Farnese, in the sixteenth century. Well-known are: CASTELLO DELLA SALA and LEVELETTE.

Other white wines, best consumed locally, may be mentioned: TORGIANO BIANCO, BIANCO DEI COLLI DEL TRASIMENO, BIANCO DI MONTALCINO, MONTEFORCONE BIANCO and TEVERE BIANCO.

Reds, which are less numerous, are also less known: TORGIANO ROSSO (reputable vineyard: RUBESCO RISERVA), MONTEFORCONE ROSSO, PANICALE, ROSSO DI MONTACILNO, SACCIADIAVOLI and SACRAMENTINO.

LATIUM. The fame of the wines of Latium goes back in time to the heyday of the Roman Empire. Latium is today looked on as one of the most important winegrowing regions of Italy, a feature of which is the marked predominance of white wines over the reds. In the provinces of Rieti, Frosinone and Latina some 65 per cent of the wines are white; in Rome and Viterbo, white wines make up 90 per cent of the total.

Among the best known and appreciated wines of the region is FRASCATI, familiar to Romans and to tourists. It is a dry, agreeable wine—there is also a sweet version, known as *canneluio*. In the past, it was a deep yellow colour, for the must was left for a long time to ferment on the skins; nowadays the wine is a pale straw yellow, with touches of gold, and is less strong-tasting than before. Dry FRASCATI goes well with fish. Reputable vineyard: VIGNE DI COLLI MATTIA.

FRASCATI belongs to a group of wines known by the generic name of DEI CASTELLI ("castles"). Others in the group are MARINO and COLLI ALBANI. Both are pleasant, good table wines, appreciated not only locally but also abroad.

Latium also produces another white wine which is often mentioned because of its strange name, EST! EST!! EST!!! DI MONTEFIASCONE, which is a dry or sweet wine perhaps more remarkable for its name than its quality. Other white wines are COLLI LANUVINI, BIANCO CAPENA, MONTECOMPATRI COLONNA and ZAGAROLO. The Aprilia

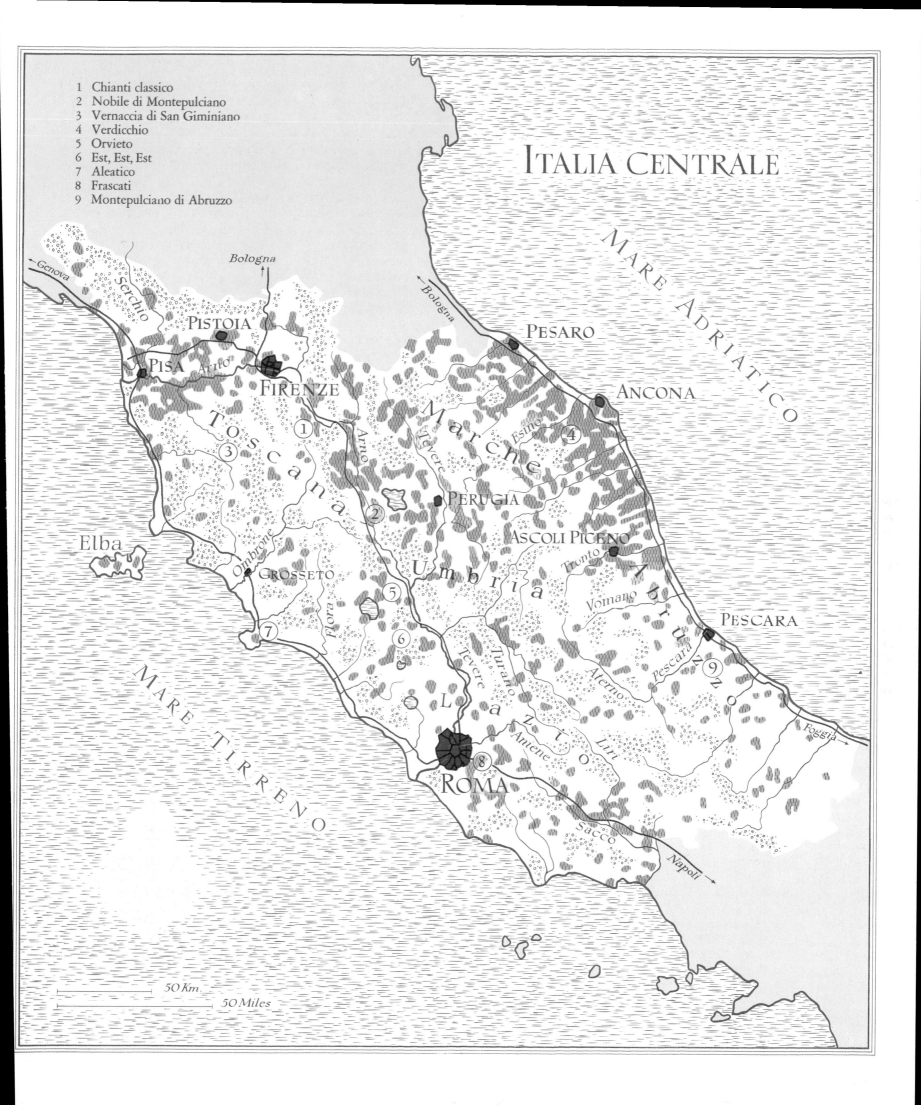

ITALIA CENTRALE

1 Chianti classico
2 Nobile di Montepulciano
3 Vernaccia di San Giminiano
4 Verdicchio
5 Orvieto
6 Est, Est, Est
7 Aleatico
8 Frascati
9 Montepulciano di Abruzzo

MARE ADRIATICO

MARE TIRRENO

Genova →
← Bologna
Bologna ↑

Serchio
Arno
Ombrone
Flora
Tevere
Esino
Tronto
Vomano
Aterno
Pescara
Tevere
Turano
Anione
Sacco
Liri
Foggia →
Napoli →

PISTOIA
PISA
FIRENZE
PESARO
ANCONA
PERUGIA
ASCOLI PICENO
GROSSETO
PESCARA
ROMA

Elba

Toscana
Marche
Umbria
Lazio
Abruzzo

50 Km.
50 Miles

region produces a white, Trebbiano di Aprilia, a rosé, Sangiovese di Aprilia, and a red, Merlot di Aprilia.

Wines from the Aprilia region have a short history compared with many others whose history goes back to pre-Christian times. In fact, the name was given to one of the settlements which followed the draining of the Pontine Marshes a few years before the Second World War. It was a bold venture, for flourishing towns and villages, gentle countryside, orchards and vineyards sprang up where once had only been evil-smelling marshes. The soil there is volcanic in origin, part sand, part clay, and part what is clearly volcanic matter.

Another designated area producing good red and white wines, known by the appellation Cori after the wineproducing centre of the region, is to be found on the hills of Aprilia. The vines here grow in volcanic soil and enjoy a mild climate, thanks to the Lepini hills which shelter them from the cold winds, a combination of natural circumstances particularly conducive to the production of quality wines. The Cori Bianco is made from the grapes of the *Malvasia di Candia, Bellone, Trebbiano Toscano*, and *Trebbiano Giallo* vines; the Cori Rosso from *Montepulciano, Sangiovese* and other local vines. Neither of these table wines is lacking in quality; the white may be dry or sweet, with an alcohol content of about 11°. The red is always dry, but smooth, fresh and with a moderate degree of alcohol.

After the draining of the marshes, a model winegrowing centre was established, the Maccarese estate, which produces highly-reputed red and white wines sold under the name of Castel San Giorgio, as well as other, more ordinary wines.

Cerveteri and Velletri are appellations that cover both red and white wines.

Red wines from the region also deserve a mention here: the Aleatico di Gradoli, a naturally sweet, strong wine; and Cesanese del Piglio, Cesanese di Olevano and Cesanese di Affile, which come in two varieties, dry *(secco, asciutto)* or sweet *(amabile, dolce)*.

Abruzzi and Molise. This a predominantly mountainous region containing the highest peaks of the Appenines (Gran Sasso and Maiella); at the other extreme it is practically at the level of the Adriatic sea. In between stretches a succession of hills, a constantly changing countryside of picturesque villages.

A large proportion of the grapes grown in the province are for eating rather than wine.

The most typical wine is the Cerasuolo d'Abruzzo, so called because of its cherry-red colour, followed by the tasty Montepulciano d'Abruzzo, which is an intense ruby red with violet highlights, maturing to an orange-red. It is a dry wine, slightly tannic, containing 12-13° alcohol.

The principal white wine is Trebbiano d'Abruzzo (notable vineyard: Castellucio-Remartello), dry and with a delicate perfume. Another dry white which deserves a mention is Reginello, produced in the valley of Peligna.

SOUTHERN ITALY

The vine is largely cultivated in Southern Italy, and indeed, most of the lands under viticulture in these vast regions have a very clear "vinegrowing vocation" and could hardly be used for any other crop. There are four winegrowing regions: Campania, Apulia, Calabria and Basilicata.

Campania. The region was known as "Campania felix"—happy Campania—to the Romans, while poets such as Horace, Tibullus and Martial sung the praises of its wines, particularly the well-known Falerno. Another famous wine from Campania is the Lacrima Cristi.

Falerno is produced from *Aglianico* grapes, also called *Ellanico*. Today's Falerno is a heavy, dull-red, full-bodied wine with a slightly bitter taste due to its high tannin content, and a strong (13-16°) alcohol content. There characteristics come from the long fermentation of the musts on the skins.

Lacrima Cristi del Vesuvio originates on the slopes of Mount Vesuvius. The name comes from the tears Christ is supposed to have let fall on Capri, land of sin, after Lucifer, banished by God, stole the island from Paradise and let it fall in the Gulf of Naples. Lacrima Cristi is produced in both red and white versions.

The area around Naples produces other reds, such as Conca and Gragnano, both excellent table wines, the last being slightly bitter; there is also the modest Vesuvio Rosso.

Among the whites, Asprino should be mentioned, a slightly sparkling wine with a slight yellow colour.

Further to the east, but still in Campania, in the Benevento retion, Solopaca is grown, both as red and white wines, both dry and good table wines.

In this painting, Cipriano Cei (1864-1922) celebrated allegorically the beauties and temptations of Italy, amongst which the grape—and therefore wine—were not the least. He hung them around a charming young lady, clad in the traditional Italian costume of the beginning of the century.

Around Avellino, the winegrowers produce AGLIANI-CO, a red wine with a spicy taste, and TAURASI, which becomes a remarkable wine if allowed to age for some years. Italian gourmets recommend it with wild boar. The two regional white wines are FIANO, which has a nutty taste, which goes well with shellfish, and GREGO DI TUFO, a good table wine.

Sorrento only produces local wines (reds, whites and rosés), which are grouped under the generic names of RAVELLO (reputable vineyard: EPISCOPIO) and SORRISO DI SORRENTO.

Further south, in the province of Salerno, there is CORBARA, a beautiful garnet red, and GRAN FUROR DIVINA COSTERIA (ROSSO or BIANCO). The name comes from the place it is grown, rather than its real or imagined effects on the drinker.

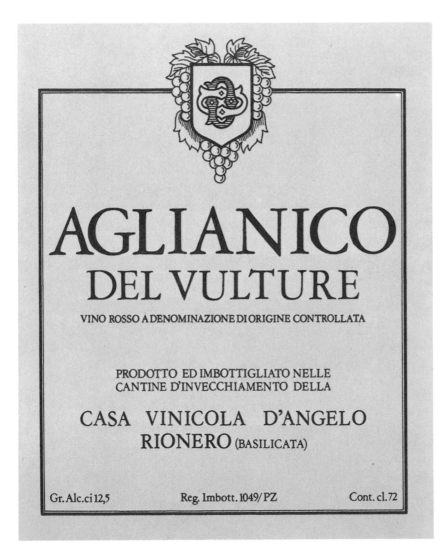

AGLIANICO DEL VULTURE is not greatly known outside Southern Italy. It is a spicy red wine from the region of Potenza, and is a pleasant wine to drink in its own country, especially with a local dish such as *pollo alla lucana*, a meal prepared from chicken stuffed with eggs, goat cheese and chopped liver.

APULIA. The region that extends from Foggia to Tarento, and around Brindisi, in the heel of the Italian boot, is considered here as one region which produces red, white and rosé wines.

Today, the production of quality wines is spreading to a remarkable extent in Apulia, partly because of the introduction of better vine plants, and partly due to change from the traditional methods of pruning the vines (a system of low, heavily pruned bushes recalling the "goblet" shape of the South of France) into the cultivation of taller, more productive plants, introduced wherever the depth, fertility and moisture, either natural or irrigation-produced, of the soil have made it possible. Much better grape harvests are obtained by these methods, and because of their very low sugar content, the grapes can be used to make table wines of every-day quality.

The reds rarely have less then 13° alcoholic strength. They are: ALEATICO DI PUGLIA, a red with a full bouquet and velvety taste; there is also a naturally sweet wine, slightly liquorous. MANDURIA comes from the *Primitivo* vine, hence its official name PRIMITIVO DI MANDURIA, which, like the ALEATICO, is smooth and sweetish; SQUINZANO, dry and rounded, deep garnet red, takes on orange highlights and an agreeable dry and full taste with maturity; SALICE SALENTINO is a dark red wine with a dry, full-bodied flavour. The ROSSO DI CERIGNOLA is a good country wine which goes perfectly with the local cooking, which is flavoury and full of country taste. All of them are D.O.C. wines.

There are also others which deserve mention: BARLETTA, which goes well with pasta and mountain cheeses; FIVE ROSES (sic), a clear red wine with an intense bouquet, excellent with red meat. It should be noted that all these red wines are rarely drunk outside their own province, and almost never outside Italy.

Apulia also produces other D.O.C. wines; reds, whites and rosés carrying names such as CASTEL DEL MONTE, MATINO, and SAN SEVERO ROSSO. ROSATO DEL SALENTO, a rosé wine, is most refreshing.

White wines from Apulia, at least those with D.O.C., are the following: LOCO ROTONDO, dry and pleasant (reputable vineyard: TORRE SUEVA), MARTINA or MARTINA FRANCA, OSTUNI and SAN SEVERO BIANCO, all dry table wines; MOSCATO DI TRANI, sweet or liquorous.

BASILICATA. This region lies between Apulia to the east and Campania to the west. It is mainly mountainous woodland and only a limited area can be used for winegrowing. Most of the wine production of the region is carried out in the district of Vulture, an old volcanic mountain chain in the north of the region. There is grown AGLIANICO DEL VULTURE, one of the best wines of Southern Italy. It has a splendid ruby colour when young, turning to garnet with age. It is a very well-balanced wine after four years maturing, (reputable vineyard: GINESTRA). Its twin brother, though perhaps less appreciated, is AGLIANICO DEI COLLI LUCANI. MALVASIA

In olden days, vines in Italy frequently grew up trees. This made for wine harvests as picturesque as this one painted by Philip Hackert at the end of the eighteenth century in the countryside around Sorrento.

The wines from the Isle of Ischia in the Gulf of Naples are virtually all drunk locally, so much are they appreciated by all who live on or visit the island.

72 cl. F

12 % Vol.
Reg. Imb. NA 22

ISCHIA BIANCO SUPERIORE
V. Q. P. R. D.

DENOMINAZIONE D'ORIGINE CONTROLLATA
IMBOTTIGLIATO IN ISCHIA DA
Perrazzo Srl
CASA FONDATA NEL 1880
Porto D'Ischia
ITALIA

DEL VULTURE is a white wine, generally sparkling, and as such, should be served chilled.

CALABRIA. The region is almost entirely surrounded by the sea, and is essentially mountainous, wooded land. Vines grow in a scattered fashion in only a small part of the region. Calabria's wines were famous even in antiquity and the historian Pliny wrote in praise of the wines of Cosenza, Reggio di Calabria and Tempsa. The best reds are POLLINO (reputable vineyard: EIANINA), CIRÒ and SAVUTO, to which should be added DONNICI. All these wines are dry and have an alcoholic strength of 11.5°, except CIRÒ (there is also a red and a rosé version) which reaches 12.5-13°. All these wines come from the *Gaglioppo* vine, with sometimes some *Greco Nere*. Calabria also produces a rather rare sweet wine, of fine quality, the GRECO DI GERACE.

THE ITALIAN ISLANDS

Along the west coast of Italy are found, from north to south, the Isle of Elba, Sardinia, the Isles of Ischia and Capri, and Sicily, which all produce wines, some of them esteemed among the greatest wines of Italy, be they red or white.

ELBA. The Isle, associated with Napoleon's exile, produces several quality wines from the vineyards which cling in dizzy flights of terraces to its steep and precipitous mountainsides.

Among the reds, there are the ALEATICO DI PORTO-FERRAIO, which is perhaps more a wine to drink between meals, for it is a little sweet. ELBA ROSSO, by contrast, is a good table wine, dry and slightly tannic.

There are more white wines grown: firstly, ELBA BIANCO, dry and balanced, excellent with oysters, crayfish and shellfish; PROCIANICO D'ELBA, dry with a subtle scent of safron, which goes with hors d'œuvre and fish from the sea; and MOSCATO D'ELBA, which is a golden yellow, beautifully perfumed dessert wine, sometimes recommended to convalescents and those suffering from anemia for the iron oxide it contains.

Finally, for those fond of rosé wine or of history, there are the VIEUX ROSÉ DELLA WALEWSKA and the ROSATO DI MADAMA, which honour the memory of the Countess Marie Walewska, Napoleon's "Polish wife" who followed him to Elba during his exile.

SARDINIA. The island is the second largest after Sicily, and winegrowing has been practised there from the earliest times. However, the island was for long outside the commercial mainstream and the tourist track, and the wines are not well known to a large public, even though Sardinia produces some excellent wines (of which the whites in particular have achieved a certain renown, at least in Italy).

Above all, this is true of VERNACCIA DI ORISTANO (reputable vineyard: VERNACCIA IS ARENAS), which has a bouquet with a scent of almond blossom, a dry yet fruity taste, and a strength of 15° minimum. It is a wine to be served with fish, or as an aperitif.

A very characteristic island wine, the NURAGUS DE CAGLIARI, from the *Nuragus* grape, one of the oldest of vines, which dates back to prehistoric times, is an excellent table wine, slightly scented, dry, subtle and fresh (11.5° alcohol). Another dry white wine, the VERMENTINO DI GALLURA (reputable vineyard: AGHILOIA), has an amber colour and a very slightly bitter taste.

The island produces a number of sweet, dessert wines, such as NASCO DI CAGLIARI, of which there are dry versions, a naturally sweet, a sweet liquorous, and a dry liquorous version; MOSCATO DI CAGLIARI, sweet with a strong smell of grapes; MALVASIA DI CAGLIARI, which

leaves in the mouth a characteristic taste of roasted almonds; MALVASIA DI BOSA, sweet or liquorous; and MOSCATO DI SORSO-SENNORI.

From among many red table wines, AMGHELU RUJU, with a cardinal purple colour, and a taste reminiscent of cinnamon; CANNUNAU DI SARDEGNA, a dull ruby colour, dry or slightly sweet; MONICA DI SARDEGNA, grown all over the Sardinia, clear, bright ruby red; TERRALBA from indigenous *Tavale*, *Connanau*, and *Pascale* vines, dry with a slightly bitter aftertaste (13° alcohol minimum) should be noted.

There are also some special red wines: the best known is still OLIENA, which was praised by Gabriele d'Annunzio. It is a strongly alcoholic wine (15-17°), and, without being sweet, is very scented and slightly bitter, and has a reputation for going with the Sardinian game cookery. MONICA DI CAGLIARI is a sweet and liquorous red wine, with a minimum strength of 14.5°, while CIRO DI CAGLIARI, produced in both sweet and dry versions, has a likeness to some of the wines of Malaga in Spain.

ISCHIA. The Isle, magnificently sited at the mouth of the Gulf of Naples, boasts an excellent climate and a volcanic soil very suitable for winegrowing. ISCHIA produces mainly white wines, the most characteristic of which is the CIANCOLELLA D'AMBRA, dry and almond-tasting, which comes from vines grown on the sunniest hills. Those visiting the Isle will find the following vineyards reliable: BUTTAVENTO, CANDIANO, MONTEVETTO, SPARAINO (commune of Barano), MAIO (commune of Casamicciola Terme), BOCCA, FUMARIE, MONTECORBARO, MONTE CORVO, MORTOLA, PANNOCHIA, PENNANOVA (commune of Forio), PIANO LIQUORI (commune of Ischia), CETRANGOLA, FANGO, PANNELLA (commune of Lacco Ameno), CASALE, CIGLIO, COATRO, FASANO, MADONELLA, MARTOFA, and MIGLIACCIO (commune of Serrara Fontana).

ISCHIA BIANCO, produced in the north of the isle, is dry and fresh, with the slightest touch of acidity. It comes from the *Farastera* and *Biancoletta* grapes.

There is only one red, ISCHIA ROSSO, made from *Guarnaccia* and *Pedirosso* grapes. It is a good table wine which goes well with rabbit Ischia-style.

The wines of Ischia are only rarely found outside the district; for the most part, they are table wines which are served to those visiting the Isle.

CAPRI. The Isle of Capri produces a red wine and a white wine, CAPRI. The white is dry and agreeable, with a touch of acidity, and it goes well with seafood. The red is an unpretentions table wine, with less character. As with the wines from neighbouring Ischia, they are best drunk on the spot.

50 Km.
50 Miles

1 Falerno
2 Lacryma Christi
3 Malvasia
4 Etna
5 Corvo
6 Alcamo
7 Pachino
8 Faro
9 Marsala

← Roma

MARE ADRIATICO

Pescara

Candelaro

Celone

Volturno

FOGGIA

Ofanto

Campania

① NAPOLI

② SALERNO

Sele

Calore

Cilento

MARE TIRRENO

Bradano

Basento

MATERA

BARI

Puglia

BRINDISI

TARANTO

③

LECCE

GOLFO DI TARANTO

Agri

Sinni

Basilicata

Platano

Crati

Trionto

Savuto

Calabria

MARE IONIO

Sardegna

Mannu

SASSARI

Tirso

NUORO

Mannu

Flumendosa

Cixerri

CAGLIARI

MESSINA ⑧

REGGIO CALABRIA

PALERMO

TRAPANI

⑥ ⑤

⑨

Sicilia

Simeto

④

Enna

ENNA

CATANIA

CALTANISSETTA

Platani

Salso

AGRIGENTO

Acate

SIRACUSA

⑦

MARE MEDITERRANEO

ITALIA MERIDIONALE E INSULARE

Clearing the ground round the vines in a vineyard near Palermo. In Sicily the vine is not only cultivated along the coasts, but also on the interior plateaux.

SICILY. In the days of Pliny, Sicily could pride itself on possessing several of the most highly-prized wines of Roman Italy such as MAMERTINO, of which Julius Caesar said: "If some one should ever give you... an amphora of MAMERTINO, call it what you like, providing you call it the most famous of wines".

Today Sicily ranks third among the wineproducing regions of Italy. Its expansion has been considerably fostered by aid from the regional Institute of Vines and Wine, set up in Palermo in 1950.

Because of its southerly latitude and the fact that it is an island, Sicily generally has a hotter climate than in other region of Italy. Vines are not only grown all along its splendid beaches with their rich crops of citrus fruits, but are also cultivated inland to quite an altitude, as for instance, on the slopes of Mount Etna. Sicily produces white wines, red wines, and a number of sweet dessert wines.

White wines are more numerous than reds; one should mention ALCAMO, with its straw colour and green highlights, which has a dry, rich, fruity flavour and 11° of alcohol; ETNA BIANCO, straw yellow, dry and fresh; CAPO BIANCO, dry, COMISO, slightly sweet, with a taste of bitter cherries; CORVO BIANCO PRIMA COCCIA and CORVO BIANCO (reputable vineyard: SALLA PARUTA), which are well-bred, dry, fresh wines ; ELORO BIANCO, very typical, dry and fresh, going well with fish; TAORMINA, dry; VAL DI LUPO BIANCO dry and delicate; MAMERTINO, of which there are dry and sweet (amabile) types; ALBANELLO DI

SIRACUSA, dry with a touch of bitterness, an apéritif wine, as is PARTINICO BIANCO.

Among the red wines, are: CERASUOLO DI VITTORIA (reputable vineyard: VILLA FONTANE), which has a cherry colour, a delicate perfume, and is sometimes used to mix with other Italian wines; ETNA ROSSO, with a dry, warm, full and lively taste (12.5° alcohol); CAPO ROSSO, ruby red, dry and good table wine; CORVO ROSSO (reputable vineyard: SALA PARUTA) with a ruby red colour, a strong scent, and a full and balanced taste, which is an excellent table wine which goes well with country dishes and venison, as does ELORO ROSSO; FARO, little known, which has a delicate perfume reminiscent of oranges, and is dry and generous; SAN SALVADOR and VAL DI LUPO ROSSO, which are good table wines.

Sicily also produces special wines, the best known being MARSALA, the most famous and prized of Sicilian wines. Its origins go back to 1773, when an Englishman, John Woodhouse, who exported the produce of western Sicily to England, discovered the quality of the wines of the Marsala vineyards, developed their production and was responsible for their rise in popularity. MARSALA is made from the *Grillo* and *Cataratto* vines and, to a lesser extent from the *Inzolia* and *Catanese*; all bear grapes with a high sugar content and little acidity. The vineyards of Marsala, which jut out into the provinces of Palermo and Agrigente, but otherwise lie almost entirely in the province of Trapano, enjoy a hot climate. MARSALA is made by adding cooked concentrated must to fermented must. The different types of MARSALA, varying in sweetness and alcohol content are the result of variations in the proportions of this mixture. The alcohol content ranges from 17° to 20°, and the sugar content from 5 to 10 per cent. A prerequisite for obtaining the best quality MARSALA is to let it mature in wooden casks. A remarkable thing is that this process takes place in large buildings, even on the ground floor, where the wine is subject to sudden changes in temperature. There are various types of MARSALA: MARSALA FINO, MARSALA SPECIALE, MARSALA SUPERIORE and MARSALA VERGINE. The Lipari Isles produce MARSALA DI LIPARI.

Marsala is more or less universally accredited as being a distinguished wine—at least the better bottles of it—although, as with any drink that has a particularly distinctive taste, not everybody could claim to actually like it. It is used, blended with egg yolks, as the base of a popular Italian sweet, *zabaglione*.

Apart from MARSALA, Sicilian special wines are made from *muscat* and *malvasia* grapes, to which other local grapes are added. There are MOSCATO DI NOTO (also produced as a sparkling wine), MOSCATO DI SIRACUSA, MOSCATO DI PANTELLARIA and MOSCATO PASSITO DI PANTELLARIA; MALVASIA DELLE LIPARI, which despite its name, is not produced on Lipari but on the Isles of SALINA and STROMBOLI. It has a golden yellow or amber colour, and an exceptional taste and perfume (15-16° alcohol). It is produced in sweet and liquorous versions.

WINES OF ITALY

The new Italian wine quality regulations (Denominazione di Origine Controllata) provide for three categories of wines:

1. *Wines of simple origin:* D.O.S. (Denominazione di Origine Semplice). This is applied to all wines produced from traditional vine stocks, cultivated by the local methods, and coming from the classified wineproducing areas.

2. *Wines of controlled origin:* D.O.C. (Denominazione di Origine Controllata). Applies only to wines coming from strictly demarcated winegrowing areas, and which reach a prescribed standard.

3. *Wines of controlled origin and guaranteed:* D.O.C.G. (Denominazione di Origine Controllata e Guarantita). Applied to wines of the highest standard. This category has yet to be applied to any Italian wine produced at present.

VALLE D'AOSTA

D.O.C. wines (see above): Enfer d'Arvier – Donnaz

PIEDMONT

D.O.C. wines: Barbera – Barbera d'Asti – Barbera d'Alba – Barbera del Montferrato – Nebbiolo d'Alba – Barolo – Gattinara – Carema – Barbaresco – Erbaluce di Caluso – Malvasia di Casorzo d'Asti – Brachetto d'Acqui – Fara – Ghemme – Sizzano – Boca – Colli Tortonesi – Dolcetto d'Acqui – Dolcetto d'Alba – Dolcetto d'Asti – Dolcetto di Diano d'Alba – Dolcetto di Dogliani – Dolcetto delle Langhe Monregalesi – Dolcetto d'Ovada – Freisa d'Asti – Freisa di Chieri – Gavi or Cortese di Gavi – Grignolino del Montferrato Casalese – Malvasia di Castelnuovo Don Bosco – Dolceacqua – Rubino di Cantavenna – Grignolino d'Asti

Dry red wines:	Barolo	Boca	Barbera d'Alba
	Nebbiolo d'Alba	Fara	Barbera del Montferrato
	Carema	Ghemme	Dolcetto delle Langhe e d'Ovada
	Gattinara	Sizzano	Freisa di Chieri e d'Asti
	Lessona	Barbera d'Asti	Grignolino d'Asti
Medium-sweet red wines:	Brachetto d'Acqui	Barbera d'Asti	Freisa di Chieri
	Malvasia di Casorzo	Barbera d'Alba	Freisa d'Asti
	Nebbiolo Piemontese	Barbera del Montferrato	Grignolino d'Asti
Dry white wines:	Cortese di Gavi (or dell'Alto Montferrato)	Erbaluce di Caluso	
Sweet white wines:	Moscato d'Asti	Asti spumante	Caluso Passito

LOMBARDY

D.O.C. wines: Barbera dell'Oltrepò Pavese – Bonarda dell'Oltrepò Pavese – Moscato dell'Oltrepò Pavese – Pinot dell'Oltrepò Pavese – Riesling dell'Oltrepò Pavese – Cortese dell'Oltrepò Pavese – Barbacarlo dell'Oltrepò Pavese – Buttafuoco dell'Oltrepò Pavese – Sangue di Giuda dell'Oltrepò Pavese – Valtellina – Valtellina Superiore – Riviera del Garda – Franciacorta Rosso – Franciacorta Pinot – Lugana – Botticino – Cellatica – Colli Morenici Montovani del Garda – Tocai di San Martino della Battaglia – Valcalepio

Dry red wines:	Barbacarlo dell'Oltrepò Pavese	Grumello	Riviera del Garda
	Buttafuoco dell'Oltrepò Pavese	Inferno	Franciacorta
	Sangue di Giudia Oltrepò Pavese	Sassella	Botticino
	Freccia Rossa di Casteggio	Valgella	Cellatica
Medium-sweet red wines:	Barbacarlo dell'Oltrepò Pavese	Canneto	Clastidium
	Sangue di Giuda Oltrepò	Bonardo amabile	Nebbiolo di Retorbido
Dry white wines:	Riesling dell'Oltrepò Pavese	Frecciarossa di Casteggio	Tocai di San Martino della Battaglia
	Cortese dell'Oltrepò Pavese	Lugana	Pusterla
Medium-dry white wine:	Clastidio di Casteggio		
Sweet white wines:	Spumante di S. Maria della Versa	Moscato di Casteggio	
Dry rosé wines:	Chiaretto del Garda	Pusterla	

LIGURIA

D.O.C. wines: Rossese di Dolceaqua – Cinque Terre – Cinque Terre Sciacchetrà

Dry red wine:	Rossese di Dolceaqua		
Dry white wines:	Vermentino	Polcevera	Cinqueterre
	Coronata		
Sweet white wine:	Cinqueterre passito (Sciacchetrà)		

TRENTINO-ALTO ADIGE

D.O.C. wines: Santa Maddalena – Lagrein – Teroldego Rotaliano – Terlano – Marzemino – Merlot – Riesling – Traminer – Cabernet – Meranese di Collina – Valle Isarco – Casteller – Colli di Bolzano – Valdadige – Lago di Caldaro – Alto Adige

Dry red wines:	Lago di Caldaro (or Caldaro)	Marzemino	Cabernet
	Santa Maddalena	Lagrein	Merlot
	Teroldego	Termeno	Pinot
Dry white wines:	Pinot	Traminer	Sylvaner verde
	Ruländer	Riesling renano	Terlano
Sweet white wines:	Moscato trentino	Moscato atesino	
Rosé wines:	Lagarino rosato (Lagrein)	Mazermino d'Isera	

VENETIA

D.O.C. wines: Valpolicella – Recioto della Valpolicella – Soave – Recioto di Soave – Bardolino – Prosecco di Conegliano – Valdobbiadene – Breganze – Gambellara – Colli Euganei – Bianco di Custoza – Cabernet di Pramaggiore – Colli Berici – Tocia di Lison – Vini del Piave – Merlot di Pramaggiore

Dry red wines:	Bardolino	Valpolicella	Merlot delle Venezie
	Valpantena	Cabernet delle Venezie	Rosso dei Colli veronesi
Sweet red wines:	Recioto della Valpolicella	Recioto Veronese	
Dry white wines:	Soave	Bianco dei Colli Berici	Valdobbiadene
	Bianco di Breganze	Bianco dei Colli Eganei	Verduzzo
	Bianco di Gambellare	Prosecco di Conegliano	Pinot
Medium-dry white wines:	Bianco dei Colli Berici	Colli Trevigiani	

FRIULI AND JULIAN VENETIA

D.O.C. wines: Colli Orientali del Friuli – Grave del Friuli – Collio Goriziano – Isonzo – Latisana – Aquileia

Dry red wines:	Rossi dei Colli Friulani	Cabernet friulano	Merlot friulano
	Rossi del Collio Goriziano	Tocai friulano	Refoschi
Dry white wines:	Bianchi dei Colli Friulani	Bianchi del Collio Goriziano	Tocai friulano

EMILIA AND ROMAGNA

D.O.C. wines: Lambrusco Salamino di Santa Croce – Lambrusco Grasparossa di Castelvetro – Lambrusco di Sorbara – Lambrusco Reggiano – Albana di Romagna – Sangiovese di Romagna – Gutturino dei Colli Piacentini – Colli bolognesi di Monte San Pietro – Monterosso Val d'Arda – Trebbiano di Romagna – Trebbiani – no Val Trebbia

Dry red wines:	Lambrusco di Sorbara	Lambrusco grasparossa di Castelve-tro	Sangiovese di Romagna
	Lambrusco Salamino di Sta Croce	Gutturino dei Colli Piacentini	Grasparossa
Dry white wines:	Albana di Romagna	Trebbiano di Romagna	Bertinoro
Sweet white wines:	Albana di Romagna		

TUSCANY

D.O.C. wines: Chianti – Chianti Classico – Chianti Montalbano – Chianti dei Colli Fiorentini – Chianti dei Colli Senesi – Chianti dei Collli Aretini – Chianti delle Colline Pisane – Chianti Rufina – Elba Bianco – Elba Rosso – Vernaccia di San Gimignano – Brunello di Montalcino – Vino Nobile di Montepulciano – Bianco Vergine Val di Chiana – Carmignano – Parrina – Bianco della Valdinievole

Dry red wines:	Chianti	Chianti Rufina	Nipozzano
	Chianti classico	Chianti Colline Pisane	Artimino
	Chianti Colli Aretini	Brunello di Montalcino	Carmignano
	Chianti Colli Fiorentini	Vino Nobile di Montepulciano	Monte-Carlo
	Chianti Colli Senesi	Antinori	Rosso delle Colline Lucchesi
	Chianti Montalbano	Brolio	Elba
Sweet red wine:	Aleatico di Porto-Ferraio		
Dry white wines:	Vernaccia di San Gimignano	Arbia	Bianco dell'Elba
	Bianchi vergini dell'Aretino	Moscadello di Montalcina	Monte-Carlo
Sweet white wines:	Moscato dell'Elba	Vino Santo toscano	

280

THE MARCHES

D.O.C. wines: Bianchello del Metauro – Sangiovese dei Colli Pesaresi – Rosso Piceno – Vernaccia di Serrapetrona – Verdicchio dei Castelli di Jesi – Verdicchio di Matelica – Bianco dei Colli Maceratesi – Rosso Conero – Falerio dei Colli Ascolani

Dry red wines:	Rosso Conero	Rosso Piceno	
Sweet red wine:	Vernaccia di Serrapetrona		
Dry white wines:	Verdicchio dei Castelli di Jesi	Verdicchio di Matelica	Bianchello del Metauro

UMBRIA

D.O.C. wines: Torgiano – Orvieto – Colli del Trasimeno

Red wines:	Torgiano	Sacrantino de Montefalco	
Dry white wines:	Orvieto	Torgiano	Greco di Todi
Sweet white wine:	Orvieto		

LAZIO

D.O.C.: Est! Est!! Est!!! di Montefiascone – Frascati – Colli Albani – Marino – Cerveteri – Trebbiano di Aprilia – Sangiovese di Aprilia – Aleatico di Gradoli – Bianco Capena – Cesanese di Affile – Cesanese del Piglio – Cesanese di Olevano – Montecompatri – Colonna – Velletri – Zagarolo – Merlot di Aprilia

Dry red wines:	Cesanese Cesanese del Piglio	Sangiovese di Aprilia Falerno	Merlot di Aprilia Castel San Giorgio
Medium-sweet red wine:	Cesanese del Piglio		
Sweet red wine:	Aleatico viterbese		
Dry white wines:	Est! Est!! Est!!! Colli Lanuvini Colli Albani Colonna	Frascati Marino Velletri Montecompatri	Cori Trebbiano di Aprilia Falerno
Medium-dry white wines:	Est! Est!! Est!!! Colli Albani Colli Lanuvini	Colonna Frascati Marino	Malvasia di Grotta-ferrata (or Grotta-ferrata) Cori
Sweet white wines:	Moscato di Terracina	Colonna	Frascati

ABRUZZI

D.O.C. wines: Montepulciano d'Abruzzo – Trebbiano d'Abruzzo

Dry red wines:	Cerasuolo di Abruzzo	Montepulciano di Abruzzo
Medium-sweet white wines:	Cerasuolo di Abruzzo	
Medium-dry white wines:	Trebbiano di Abruzzo	Peligno

CAMPANIA

D.O.C. wines: Ischia Bianco Superiore – Greco di Tufo – Taurasi – Solopaca

Dry red wines:	Aglianico Lacryma Christi del Vesuvio Falerno	Taurasi Vesuvio	Ischia Ravello
Medium-sweet red wines:	Conca	Gragnano	Solopaca
Dry white wines:	Capri Ischia Greco di Tufo	Lacryma Christi del Vesuvio Ravello Falerno	Furor divina Costiera Asprinio Bianco d'Avellino
Medium-dry white wines:	Solopaca	Greco di Tufo	
Dry rosé wine:	Ravello		
Medium-dry rosé wine:	Solopaca		

APULIA

D.O.C. wines: Locorotondo – Martina Franca – Ostuni – Primitivo di Manduria – Squinzano – Salice Salentino – Matino – Rosso di Cerignola – Aleatico di Puglia – Castel del Monte – Moscato di Trani – San Severo – Cacc'e Mmitte di Lucera

Dry red wines:	Castel del Monte Santo Stefano di Cerignola	Primitivo di Gioia e Manduria	Barletta
Medium-sweet red wines:	Castel Acquaro	Primitivo di Manduria	
Sweet red wines:	Aleatico di Puglia	Moscato del Salento (or Salento)	Zagarese
Dry white wines:	Sansevero	Martinafranca Locorotondo Ostuni	Torre Giulia di Cerignola
Sweet white wines:	Moscato di Salento (or Salento liquoroso)		Moscato di Trani
Dry rosé wines:	Castel del Monte	Gigliano	

BASILICATA

D.O.C. wine: Aglianico del Vulture

Dry red wine:	Aglianico del Vulture	
Dry white wine:	Provitaro	
Sweet white wines:	Malvasia del Vulture	Moscato del Vulture
Medium-dry rosé wine:	Malvasia di Lucania	

CALABRIA

D.O.C. wine: Donnici-Savuto

Dry red wines:	Ciro di Calabria Savuto di Rogliano	Pollino	Lacryma di Castrovillari
Dry white wines:	Provitaro	Balbino	
Sweet white wines:	Greco di Gerace	Moscato di Cosenza	Malvasia di Cosenza
Rosé wine:	Pellaro		

SICILY

D.O.C. wines: Etna – Marsala – Cerasuolo di Vittoria – Alcamo – Moscato di Pantelleria – Moscato Passito di Pantelleria – Malvasia delle Lipari – Moscato di Siracusa – Moscato di Noto

Dry red wines:	Faro Etna	Eloro Corvo di Casteldaccia	Frappato di Vittoria Cerasuolo di Vittoria
Dry white wines:	Corvo di Casteldaccia Etna	Eloro Lo Zucco	Bianco di Alcamo
Medium-dry white wines:	Mamertino	Marsala vergine	
Sweet white wines:	Malvasia di Lipari Mamertino Marsala	Moscato Lo Zucco Moscato di Siracusa Moscato di Noto	Moscato Passito di Pantelleria Cerasuolo di Vittoria
Dry rosé wines:	Eloro	Etna rosato	

SARDINIA

D.O.C. wines: Vermentino di Gallura – Cannonau di Sardegna – Monica di Sardegna – Vernaccia di Oristano – Campidano di Terralba – Nuragus di Cagliari – Ciro di Cagliari – Moscato di Sorso-Sennori – Malvasia di Cagliari – Moscato di Cagliari – Nasco di Cagliari – Monica di Cagliari – Malvasia di Bosa – Terralba

Dry red wines:	Oliena	Cannonau del Campidano	Campidano di Cagliari
Sweet red wines:	Cirò di Sardegna	Monica di Sardegna	
Dry white wines:	Nuragus Vernaccia di Oristano	Vermentino di Gallura Vernaccia di Sardegna	Malvasia di Bosa
Sweet white wines:	Nasco	Moscato del Campidano	Moscato di Tempio

THE WINES
OF THE RHINE

JOSEPH JOBÉ, JOSEPH DREYER and HELMUT ARNTZ

Had not the Rhine river carried its civilizing influences northward, the vine would have remained confined to the basin of the Rhône. As early as the fourth century B.C. Greek adventurers pushed their way up the Rhône to the Swiss plateau and very probably made contact with the Celts along the Jura as far as Basel long before the Romans arrived. They probably introduced vines which they had acclimatized in Gaul. The process was completed by the gradual Romanization and, later, the Christianization of Central Europe. Once the vine had crossed the barrier of the Alps, it became established in the east wherever the altitude permitted, and permanent vineyards grew up round the veterans' colonies and the earliest monastic establishments on the Rhine until at last a new chain of vineyards stretched from Chur to Bonn.

The source of the Rhine, or at least of the larger of its two branches known as the Upper Rhine, is not very far from the source of the Rhône. The stream issuing from Lake Tuma is only a few miles from the Furka glacier; but the two rivers flow in different directions, turning, as it were, their backs on each other. The Rhine, starting higher up, goes farther and is slower to decide on its final course. The vine in the Grisons grows lower down than the vine in the Valais—not above 1,800 feet—where the Rhine first definitely flows northwards. It favours the red grape, which, indeed, is the predominating variety all along the Upper Rhine. The landscape, with the Alps in the background, often verges on the sublime. The language along the river moves on from Romanche to the various dialects of eastern Switzerland, while the impetuous stream is tamed by man and becomes international. The right bank borders the Austrian Vorarlberg and the tiny Principality of Liechtenstein, where the vine is scanty, but where the inhabitants, looking to Switzerland, have always felt that the Rhine brings them closer to the Swiss rather than separating them.

Now the river comes to Lake Constance, where, like the Rhône in Lake Leman, its waters slow down and disappear in the broad expanse. To the north, the first German vineyards shimmer on the foothills of the Black Forest. Opposite, the red grapes of the Rheintal in St. Gallen and the Untersee in Thurgau counterbalance the whites of Baden. The town of St. Gallen, a far-famed bulwark of medieval culture, is not far away—one more link in the chain of episcopal and university towns of the Middle Rhine, like Constance, Basel, Freiburg-in-Breisgau and Strasbourg.

Flowing through Lake Constance the river makes a deep bend, turning sharply east and west; and it maintains this course as far as Basel. Over a hundred yards wide here, it flows past the vineyards of the Klettgau in the Canton of Schaffhausen and narrows somewhat in the loom of the Swabian Jura just before it makes an impressive leap of over sixty feet that sends it hurtling through the Cantons of Zurich and Aargau. There, as it flows past the vineyards of Baden to the north, its tributary, the Aare, which links it to most of the Swiss lakes, flows in from the left. The vineyards of Zurich, the Bernese Jura, Fribourg and Neuchâtel are thus connected up with the Rhine. Indeed, the connection has always been very close, as is shown by the alliance concluded in the sixteenth century between the people of Strasbourg and the people of Zurich. The good burghers of Zurich, to show how speedily they could come to Strasbourg's aid, rowed down the Limmat, the Aare and the Rhine and reached the city in less than eighteen hours, "before a dish of millet had time to cool". Neuchâtel, it should be noted, was subject to French influence; here the *Riesling*, the traditional variety of the Rhine, yields to a stock brought in from the west, the *Chasselas*.

The Rhine achieves its maturity at Basel. Meeting the buttress of the Jura's eastern end, it turns definitely north along the passage formed by the parallel ranges of the Black Forest and the Vosges. It is still seven hundred and fifty feet above sea-level and it takes it some five hundred miles to descend to the sea. The wine road, continuous on the right bank, does not start again

to the west until Mulhouse, where the famous Alsatian winegrowing region begins. The vineyards on the French bank, carefully terraced on the last outcroppings of the Vosges, exposed to the rising sun and with an extremely favourable climate, are parcelled out in very small lots. Their wines have been distributed for ages throughout Europe by the Rhine itself and, in medieval times, many a boat carried the precious SYLVANER and RIESLING to the courts of Swabia, Bavaria, Sweden and England.

To the east the vineyards of Baden and Württemberg are separated by the Black Forest, joined nowadays in a single *Land* of the Federal Republic of Germany. The wines of the Neckar were as celebrated in feudal Europe as those of the Moselle and the Aare.

Although the vineyards are so densely concentrated, this has in no way detracted from the personality of each region. The Rhine wines are derived from a very few varieties of grape and would seem to be closely akin, but each vineyard has a pronounced character of its own and its neighbour has no wish to imitate it. The Palatinate, to which the river now brings us, is simply a natural extension of Alsace, and yet the soil has changed. Our hearts were won by the GEWÜRZTRAMINER, but now we are enchanted by the celebrated growths of Forst and Deidesheim. It is hard to choose between them, for it is very true that "the sky, the climate and the land are all in every glass" of these delightful wines.

The landscape gradually changes from Karlsruhe to Mainz, becoming less abrupt; the rapids gradually disappear, as do the alluvial deposits between its many branches, and the river spreads in a broad stream over a deep and stable bed, with firm banks: it becomes navigable. The towns, which hitherto seemed to shun the banks, are now situated closer to the river, like Worms, whose lofty Romanesque cathedral surveys the ripening Palatinate wines to the south and the wines of Rheinhesse to the north.

From Mainz the vineyards follow the winding route of the Main, threading eastward through Franconia to successfully invade Bavarian territory, despite its apparent total occupation by the hop. At Bingen, on the other bank, at the very moment when the Rhine at last emerges from the vast curve it had described downstream from Worms, the Nahe takes over the vine and carries it up into Rheinhesse (from where, once it has turned into wine, it will return to the Rhine).

Now we come to the heart of the romantic Germany, the fantastic stage-setting of marauding Burgraves and elves, massacres and sorceries, Fürstenberg, Gutenfels, the Pfalz, that lowering pile jutting out of the waters, the Cat and the Mouse, still defying each other, and Rheinfels—ruined towers, jagged keeps, massive and disturbing shades, and among them on either bank the vineyards of the Lower Rhineland, a miracle of life amidst all this ancient death.

At Koblenz, at the junction with the Moselle, and not far from the junction with the Lahn, the wine road becomes a three-pronged fork, the middle prong going as far as Bonn. Thereafter, reaching the northern limit of the area dictated by nature, the vine becomes scarce. Rotterdam and the sea are too far away for wine to reach them except by import. But, if only along one half of its course, the story of the vines of the Rhine gives us a convincing example of what a natural means of communication can bestow upon man by way of increasing his pleasure and his profit. Despite many bloody episodes, the Rhine has been more than a left and right bank; there has been an upstream and a downstream as well, a flowing route which, as the centuries passed, spread the art of printing, the humanism of Erasmus, the fantasies of Romanticism and, more recently, the European spirit. More celebrated here than anywhere, the vine has, through undisclosed channels, contributed to an awareness of the Rhine's high mission.

THE WINES OF THE UPPER RHINE

The wine districts of eastern and northern Switzerland are all part of the Rhine basin. It seems to suit them less well than the Valais and the shores of Lake Leman, though the winegrowing tradition is quite as ancient. The growers formerly produced mainly white wines, but the reds predominate nowadays, except in the vineyards of the Lakes of Biel and Neuchâtel.

In this part of Switzerland the vine seems more threatened than in the Rhine Valley, for various reasons, including the constant growth of industrialization and urbanization and competition from foreign wines. Some vineyards are now mere fossils, such as those of

Basel-City, Lucerne, Solothurn and Schwyz, none of which exceeds 20 acres.

Of the old white varieties, the *Elbling* has practically disappeared and the *Räuschling* and *Completer* are merely curiosities; they have been replaced by the *Riesling-Sylvaner*, which is as preponderant in these areas as the *Chasselas* in western Switzerland. The *Riesling-Sylvaner* was produced in 1882 from a cross between the *Riesling*, a late-ripening grape with a high acid content, and the green *Sylvaner* (or *Johannisberg*), also a late ripener. In Germany this variety has kept the name of its inventor, *Müller-Thurgau*. After several

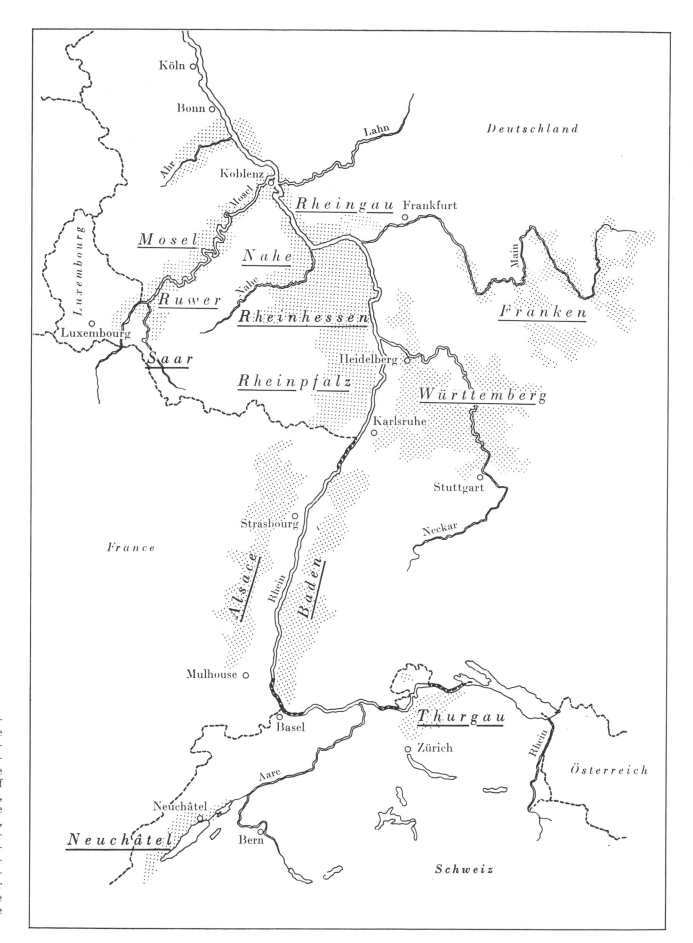

"Wines of the Rhine" covers the wines of the Upper Rhine (the wine-growing cantons of German Switzerland), the wines from the shores of the Lake of Neuchâtel, those of Alsace, and the German wines of Baden, Württemburg, the Palatinate, Rheinhesse, the valley of the Nahe, Franconia, the Rheingau, the valleys of the Moselle, Saar and Ruwer, and of the Ahr, and the Middle Rhine (or Mittelrhein).

285

During their fermentation, the Swiss wines from the Bündner Herrschaft (Grisons) are kept under close scrutiny by wine experts. Here one is sampling a red wine, which, if it yields 85.4° on the Oechsle scale and contains 11 to 13 per cent acidity, is reckoned to be a good vintage.

years of experiment and improvement, he produced a new variety, stable, prolific, rather low in acid and not exacting about soils. It is the variety best suited to the local climatic and soil conditions. The *Riesling-Sylvaner* gives a wine with a fine bouquet, light-bodied and fresh, with a slight muscat flavour.

The commonest red variety is the *Pinot Noir*, called here the *Blauburgunder*, or *Blue Burgundy*. It was introduced into the Grisons between 1630 and 1635 by the Duc de Rohan who was in command of French troops at Maienfeld. The variety became common in other regions later, especially in regions with a good exposure and a deep, rich, loose soil. The *Pinot Noir* wines produced in the Grisons are, together with the wines of Neuchâtel, the best in Switzerland, but do not give the highest yields.

CANTON OF THE GRISONS. Travelling down the Upper Rhine, we come to vineyards downstream from Chur, those of Costamser, Trimmis and Zizers. Here the *Pinot Noir* produces a light red wine and the *Riesling-Sylvaner* a white with a strong bouquet.

After the confluence with the River Landquart, the Lower Rhine Valley seems more suited to the vine, and the vineyards of the Grisons Seigneury—the Bündner Herrschaft—spread over the communes of Malans, Jenins, Maienfeld and Fläsch. By far the commonest variety (99 per cent) is the *Pinot Noir*, which was introduced during the Thirty Years War. This region of the Grisons, less frequented by tourists than the Engadine, enjoys a very pleasant climate, especially in

September and October; fog is virtually unknown and though the *fœhn*, the warm south wind, is unpleasant to man, it is beneficial to the grape, which thus ripens in conditions more favourable than those in many other parts of German-speaking Switzerland.

Most of the vineyards are owned by smallholders who trellis the vine and devote to its care about 400 to 600 hours per acre per year. Though this vine has never been afflicted with the phylloxera, it is being gradually replaced with resistant stocks. A variety of unknown origin, the *Completer*, is still to be found in the commune of Malans; it produces a white wine which is a local speciality. The best Grisons growths are the reds, which are fragrant and well-balanced. They are drunk young and preferably on the spot. The yield is very variable, but averages 132,000 gallons.

CANTON OF ST. GALLEN. Further down the Rhine we enter the Canton of St. Gallen. The area under wine cultivation may be divided into three regions:
— The southern region, with the vineyards lying between the districts of Bad Ragaz, Sargans and Lake Walen. The wines are mainly red, and the best-known growths include the SCHLOSS WERDENBERG and the PORTASER from Pfäfers.
— The northern region comprises the vineyards situated between Hub and the entry of the Rhine into Lake Constance. As in the northern part of the Grisons, the valley of the Rhine is suitable here for vinegrowing, but the area under cultivation has shrunk by three-quarters since the end of the last century. The best red wines bear the names of BALGACHER, SONNENBURGER, REBSTEINER, MARBACHER, PFAUENHALDE, ROSENBERG, EICHHOLZ, MONSTEINER, BERNERKER and BUCHENBERG, the latter known as "the pearl of the Rheintal". The FORSTWEIN from Altstätten fetches remarkable prices. All these wines are from the *Blauburgunder*. The two winegrowing communes of the Canton of Appenzell, Wolfhalden and Lutzenberg, may be added to this region; they produce, half and half, red and white wines for local consumption.
— The small vineyards in the north-west of the Canton, Bronschhofen and Wil, where the WILBERG is highly appreciated. Growers in this region make a wine from red grapes after removing the stalks, known as BEERLIWEIN; it is full-bodied and fragrant and has a heavy bouquet.

CANTON OF THURGAU. The vineyards of Thurgau lie between the lower arm of Lake Constance, the Rhine and the Thur. Most of them (80 per cent) produce a red wine from the *Pinot Noir*, the remainder being a white from the *Riesling-Sylvaner*.

The ARENENBERG DOMANE is worth bearing in mind and tasting locally. Further south, the vineyards of Stettfurt produce the famous SONNENBERG, a growth of admirable consistency.

Almost all the wines in this region are drunk locally. The tourist will certainly drink them with the local dishes—*féra*, a fish from Lake Constance, with a white wine from the Untersee; and slices of liver pâté, Thurgau style, with a red from Warth.

CANTON OF SCHAFFHAUSEN. In the Schaffhausen region, the vine crosses the Rhine to the right bank. The foothills at the end of the Jura form a protecting screen. The *Pinot Noir* is grown on the heavier soils, the *Riesling-Sylvaner* on the chalk regions.

In 1900, the area planted to the vine was 2,710 acres; it has stabilized in recent years at between 890 and 940 acres.

Some 90 per cent of the area produces red wines from the *Pinot Noir*. The whites come from the *Riesling-Sylvaner* and are distinguished by a very strong bouquet. Some other varieties (*Pinot Gris* and *Elbling*) are rarely to be found. Hallau is the largest winegrowing commune, and its most notable wine is the HALLAUER "IM

The winegrowers of the village of Dorf, in the Zürich Unterland, protect their vines from the spring frosts — especially those which commonly arrive in early May — with straw mats, a tried and true local expedient.

The Munot vineyard at Schaffhouse, Switzerland, lies on a very steep slope. So much so that the winegrowers have installed a winch and cables to haul the cultivators up between the rows of wines which overlook the medieval town. The MUNOTLER is a full-bodied red wine, made from *Blauburgunder (Pinot Noir)* grapes.

HINTERE WAATELBUCK", a red of first-rate quality. Passing through Schaffhausen, where the traveller will visit the Zu Allerheiligen Museum or the Falls of the Rhine, according to his taste, he will be able to sample a full-bodied red, the MUNOT, which takes its name from the squat keep which dominates the town.

CANTON OF ZURICH. Further south again, in the Canton of Zurich, residential and industrial areas have gradually encroached upon the winegrowing area, which has shrunk from some 12,400 acres at the beginning of the century to 740 today. The climate is less suited to the vine in this region than on the banks of the Rhine, particularly because of the spring frosts. The vine clings, however, to the most sheltered and sunniest slopes. This winegrowing area may be divided into three regions:
— In the north: the Zurich vineyards—the district is called the *Weinland*, or wine country—follow on from those in Thurgau and, like them, produces red wines from the *Pinot Noir* and whites from the *Riesling-Sylvaner* and the *Räuschling*, full-bodied wines which are suitable for laying down.
— Farther to the west, the Zurich Unterland is still part of the Jura and produces a great variety of wines, mostly reds from the *Pinot Noir* and whites from the *Riesling-Sylvaner*. These are local wines for local consumption.
— In the south: the shores of the Lake of Zurich and the banks of the Limmat, downstream from Zurich,

produce wines which are well reputed. Stäffa, the largest winegrowing commune in the canton, is proud of its STERNENHALDE and its LATTENBERG; Herrliberg produces a CLEVNER SCHIPFGUT, well-reputed among local connoisseurs. Other wines are APPENHALDE, CHORHERRENHALDE, ÄBLETEN and TURMGUT. Weiningen, on the slopes of the Limmat, is the second largest of the winegrowing communes in the canton.

The people of Zurich have many local dishes and it is not hard to find a range of wines worthy to go with them. However, these pleasures of the table are confined to those who can take advantage of an undisturbed sojourn in the canton, since none of the wines grown under what are called "regional agreements" may be exported.

CANTON OF AARGAU. The course of the Limmat takes us quite naturally into the Canton of Aargau. Here the vine spreads along the slopes of the Aare and its tributaries, the Limmat and the Reuss, on the sheltered slopes of the Jura and the north-eastern shore of Lake Hallwil. The area covers no more than 740 acres. The *Riesling-Sylvaner* (27 per cent) and the *Pinot Noir* (55 per cent) are the two main varieties. The wines are light and fragrant, with a low alcohol content. The white wines, such as the SCHINZNACHER RÜHBERG, have a bouquet that is highly appreciated; the reds, especially the NETTELER,

GOLDWAND and BRESTENBERGER, are excellent table wines.

The vineyards in the Canton of Lucerne, an extension of the Aargau vineyards southwards, are certainly more of a curiosity than anything else, since they cover only 4 acres (171 ares).

CANTON OF BASEL. From the border of the Canton of Schaffhausen to Basel there are no vineyards along the

The refractometer, which replaces the good old must balances, is an optical instrument that is used to evaluate the sugar content of the grape juice. By its aid, the wine harvest can be fixed at the moment when the grape reaches its fullest maturity.

Rhine. The twin cantons of Basel-City and Basel-Country each possess some vineyards. That of Basel-City—there is only one—is on the other side of the Rhine at Riehen, is called *Im Schlipf* and is only about 2½ acres in area. Basel-Country is rather better off (about 125 acres), particularly on the end slopes of the Jura and along the Birs. Very little but white wines are produced, from the *Chasselas* and the *Riesling-Sylvaner*, and they are curiosities more for the local fancier than the passing tourist.

Canton of Solothurn. Going up the Aare from Basel we cross the Canton of Solothurn, which produces local wines with an alcoholic content varying from 9 to 11°. The white wines are from the *Chasselas*, locally known as the *Gutedel*, and the reds from the *Burgunder*. The winegrowing area in Solothurn has been greatly reduced in less than a century and today covers only about ten acres.

Canton of Bern. We now come to the Lake of Biel, the north shores of which, backed by the Jura, form a winegrowing district from Vingelz-Biel to La Neuveville, extending westwards into the Canton of Neuchâtel. It is planted almost entirely with *Pinot Noir* and *Chasselas*, the latter greatly predominating. These wines are light, fragrant and sharp, and are best drunk young. The best-known are the Twanner and the Schafiser. A long way upstream, at the very threshold of the Alps, there lie the vineyards of Spiez and Oberhofen, which produce white wines from the *Riesling-Sylvaner* and reds from the *Pinot Noir*.

THE WINES OF NEUCHÂTEL

Although they are part of the Rhine basin, the vineyards along the shores of the Lake of Neuchâtel are in French-speaking Switzerland, a Latin country. That is perhaps why a local poet has asserted that "The land of Neuchâtel is not yet of the South, but is by no means any longer of the North".

In this region, transitional both geographically and historically, the vine seems to have been known even before the coming of the Romans. Winegrowing in this district has been established with certainty by a document dating from A.D. 998; Rodolphe, Lord of Neuchâtel, donated a vineyard at Bevaix to the Abbey of the Benedictines at Cluny. Today, the winegrowing region of the Lake of Neuchâtel extends along the lower foothills of the Jura from the Lake of Biel to the banks of the Orbe; the western part, in fact, lies within the Canton of Vaud. This region takes the form of a long ribbon some 30 miles in length by less than a mile in breadth. Along the lake it is about 1,300 feet above sea-level; the highest vineyards are at 1,800 feet, but most lie between 1,300 and 1,600 feet. These benefit from the lake's heat and stabilizing influence; at Neuchâtel itself the mean winter temperature is 1 to 1.5 degrees higher than at Fribourg or Bern. In summer the vine receives light and heat reflected from the lake, but it is subject to spring frosts despite the range of the Jura which protects it from the cold north winds. The area under vine cultivation is at present 1,560 acres in the Canton of Neuchâtel and 500 acres in Vaud.

The markets for Neuchâtel wine trade have varied greatly. At times the trade was mainly with Bern, at others with Solothurn when that city received the foreign ambassadors accredited to the Federal Diet. There is a story that the boatmen carrying barrels of wine from Neuchâtel to Solothurn sometimes succumbed to the temptation to sample the goods, replenishing the casks with the same volume of water.

The wines of Neuchâtel are well known today far beyond the frontiers of Switzerland. They are now sold under the generic name of Neuchâtel, since the quality of the vineyards is remarkably homogeneous. Some growers and estate-bottlers add a place or growth name. The knowledgeable wine-lover may well choose a Neuchâtel-Saint-Blaise or a Neuchâtel-Cortaillod, denoting communes, or a Neuchâtel-Château d'Auvernier or Neuchâtel-Hôpital de Pourtalès, denoting a growth. Bottlers and shippers undertake to sell only Neuchâtel wines. There is an official inspection for quality and production. For over twenty-five years the State of Neuchâtel has exercised a control over the alcohol content at harvest time, and this induces growers to defer the picking and pay special attention to quality. The inspectors are paid by the State, must hold themselves available to the bottler and inspect every *gerle* (about 22 gallons) as it reaches the vat.

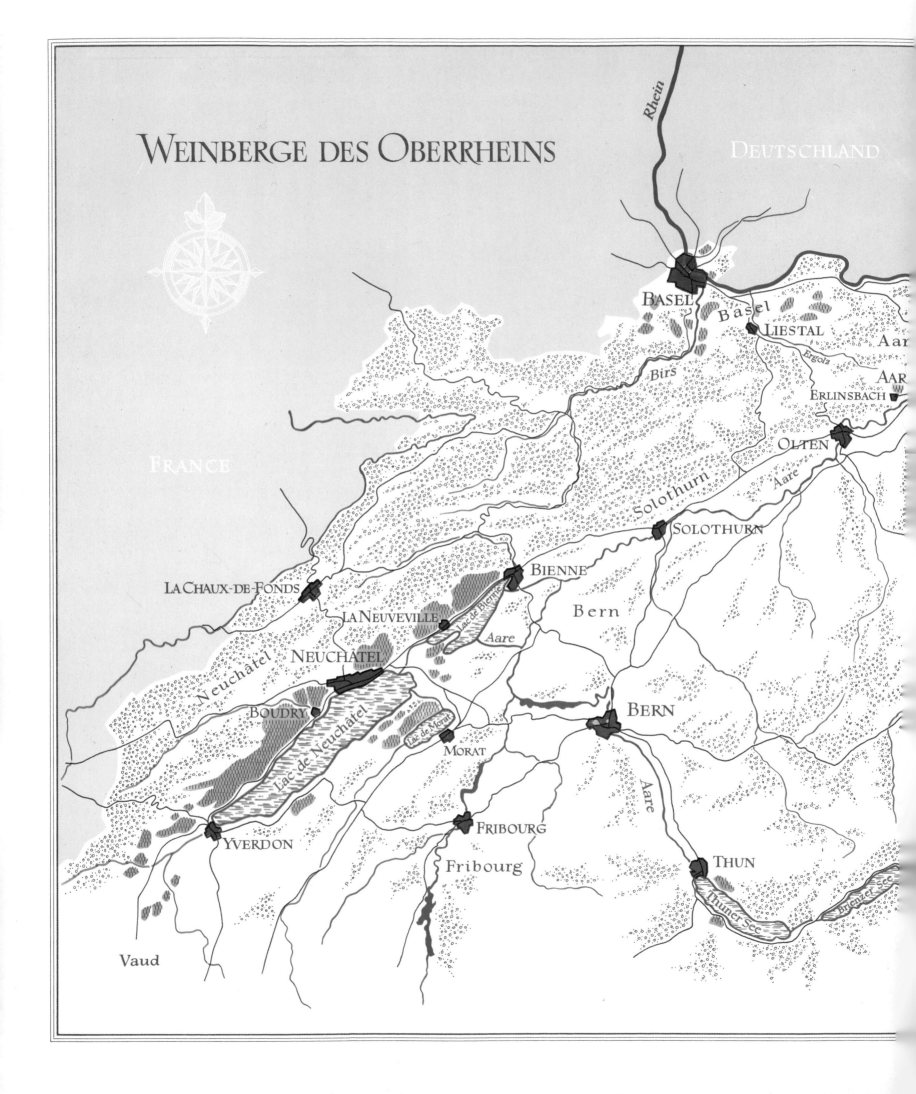

Weinberge des Oberrheins

Deutschland

Rhein

FRANCE

Basel

Basel

Liestal

Aar

Aar

Birs

Ergolz

Erlinsbach

Olten

Aare

Solothurn

Solothurn

Aare

La Chaux-de-Fonds

Bienne

Bern

La Neuveville

Lac de Bienne

Aare

Neuchâtel

Boudry

Neuchâtel

Lac de Neuchâtel

Lac de Morat

Morat

Bern

Yverdon

Fribourg

Aare

Thun

Fribourg

Thuner See

Brienzer See

Vaud

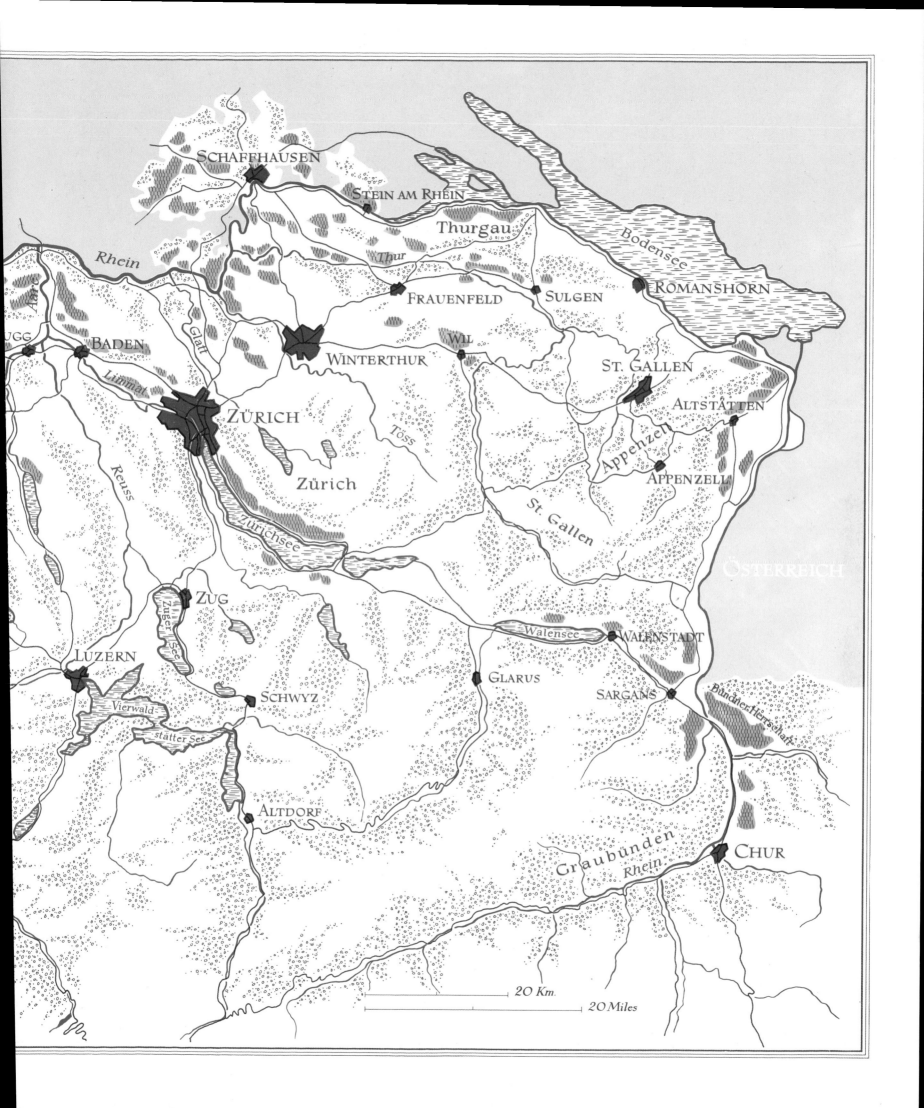

This print of the Romantic period shows the Neuchâtel winegrowing district seen from the south-west near Colombier, looking towards Auvernier and Neuchâtel. The vineyards stretch in a ribbon some 30 miles in length, and an average of less than one mile wide. The lake mitigates the harsh climate and the range of the Jura protects the vineyards from the north winds; but frost can be a problem.

The Neuchâtel red wines are some of the best in Switzerland. They are splendidly rich in colour and have a strong bouquet; they are fragrant and fairly sharp and develop a delicate and well-bred aroma. One of the best is that of Cortaillod. All are derived from the *Pinot Noir*. The ŒIL DE PERDRIX (partridge eye) also comes from the *Pinot Noir*, but is slightly fermented in the vat; it is a light wine of an intriguing shade and one which is drunk young.

All the white wines (about three times as many as the reds) come from the *Chasselas*. Bottled while they are still on the lees, they retain enough carbonic acid gas to make them slightly sparkling. Locally they are said "to make the star"—i.e. they show the sparkle. They are light and fresh, with a very delicate floweriness. Some may find they have a flinty taste. Besides the wines from the *Chasselas* it is possible to find—but in limited quantities only—whites from the green *Sylvaner*, delicate and well-balanced; from the *Riesling-Sylvaner*, with a strong muscat flavour; from the grey *Pinot*, flowery, supple and bland; and from the white *Pinot*, very delicate indeed. Throughout the region the *Chasselas* whites go extremely well with the fish which are characteristic of the Lake of Neuchâtel, notably those called *palée* and *bondelle*. The reds from the *Pinot Noir* go very well with red meat or game. Total production

year in and year out stands at between 1,320,000 and 1,540,000 gallons.

The westernmost part of the region, which is in the Canton of Vaud, is also planted to *Chasselas* and *Pinot Noir*, as well as some special local varieties. Some growers make the wine "Neuchâtel style", i.e. on the lees, and produce wines comparable to the true Neuchâtel. Others vinify "Vaudois style", by racking, and produce a more supple wine, which, however, in the opinion of some people, loses something of its original quality. Most of these wines are sold under the name BONVILLARS. Both the reds and the whites are typical local wines *(vin du pays)*.

Whereas the Vaudois wines of La Côte, Lavaux and the Chablais (see chapter on wines of the Rhône) usually have an alcohol content of 10.5 to 13°, these run from 9.5 to 11°, occasionally to 12°. They are wines which sparkle gaily, but are not treacherous; and they are believed to encourage liveliness and wit.

In the Rhine basin, too, we should mention the winegrowing district on the southern slopes of Mont-Vully, between the Lake of Neuchâtel and the Lake of Morat. The white *Chasselas* wines are light, acid and fresh; the few red wines from the *Pinot Noir* or the *Gamay* have a fine colour and a distinctly agreeable bouquet. These, too, are local wines.

292

THE WINES OF ALSACE

Alsace lies in a rift-valley running north and south, originating in an ancient massif the remains of which form the Vosges on the west and the Black Forest on the east. Shut in by the Jura on the south and the hills of Lower Alsace on the north, it forms a "punchbowl" with a continental climate, cold in winter and hot in summer, with its maximum rainfall in July and August and its minimum in winter.

The Alsatian winegrowing district covers the foothills of the Vosges from Thann in the south to Marlenheim in the north. Here, between the Belfort Gap and the Col de Saverne are the only breaches in the mountain wall through which air flows in from the west, to disturb the thermal and climatic balance of the part of Alsace centring on Colmar. This area is practically on the 48th parallel, the same latitude as Orleans. The prevailing winds are south in winter and north in summer. On an average computed over fifty years there are about sixty days of frost annually at Colmar; they occur even at the beginning of May, on the three days known as the *saints de glace* ("the ice saints"). Serious damage is, however, comparatively rare and remains localized. The reason is that the vineyards are situated at a height between about 550 and 1,200 feet, above the fogs that form in the flatlands, and the exposure to the sun and the geological conditions for heat storage are far more favourable than they are in the flatlands. The mean annual temperature at Colmar is 10.8° C.; on the slopes it is several tenths of a degree higher. Since the Vosges themselves catch most of the rain, the rainfall in the foothills is slight, from 20 to 28 inches annually.

The climatic conditions of the Alsatian winegrowing district are therefore extremely favourable. The annual cycle usually follows the same rhythm: budding in mid-April, flowering in mid-June, ripening in mid-August and harvest about October 10th; this gives the

The village of Kalzenthal, a few miles north-west of Colmar, is surrounded by vines. It is said that here the *Muscat* and *Riesling* grapes have found the soil that suits them best.

293

grapes about 115 days to develop, spread over a spring which is usually fine, a hot and thundery summer and a sunny autumn.

The Alsatian vineyards also benefit from exceptional geological conditions. The foothills of the Vosges are the outcrop of the rift-valley and have a very complex geological structure; triassic, liassic and tertiary jurassic rock lie side-by-side and are blended with modern alluvial deposits, partly covered by older gravelly layers, with scree talus of glacial origin or surface deposits of loess from the flatlands. These climatic and geological conditions are the key to the special characteristics of the wines of Alsace, as compared with other wines, and the key to the principles of Alsatian wine-growing.

CHARACTERISTICS OF THE WINES OF ALSACE

Wine is, of course, produced by the fermentation of the juice of grapes; and grape juice possesses in a latent state all the qualities which the wine may later aspire to. A wine can never be improved; all that can be done is to preserve the qualities it already possesses. The heat stored up during the process of ripening comes out in the sugar concentration and determines the subsequent strength of the wine; the soil forms its body, and the variations in temperature caused by the inflow of continental or oceanic cold air modulate its fragrance. Therefore, as we move from a warm to a cooler region, the sugar content lessens and the strength diminishes; conversely, the acidity increases and reaches the maximum permissible limit near the northerly limit of winegrowing, while the fruity aromas thin out and are finally lost in an acid tartness. This may be demonstrated by following the white wines from south to north and examining the relationship between their two antagonistic components, acidity and sugar. A white wine from the south naturally has an excess of natural sweetness and an inconsistent acidity (Bordeaux wines, Monbazillac, etc.). North of a certain latitude all the sugar can be fermented; this produces a dry wine. If the acidity is comparatively low, the wine takes on fragrance by developing body (Burgundies, Mâcon in particular); as it increases, the aromas of the fruit

Hunawihr, near Ribeauville, is one of the 93 communes that have a right to the appellation Vin d'Alsace. The village possesses, in the midst of the vines, a curious church surrounded by a fortified wall that dates from the sixteenth century.

294

The inhabitants of Alsace are proud of their wines, which come from four noble grape varieties: *Traminer* (or *Gewurtztraminer*), *Riesling, Tokay* and *Muscat*. It should be noted that Alsace wines are always known by their grape variety. The Bergheim vineyards (left) and the Zellenberg (below) lie in the central region of the winegrowing area.

become more prominent and more delicate and the wines become fruity (Alsatian and Austrian wines). Again, if there is a great deal of natural acidity in the grape juice, vinification becomes difficult, for simultaneously to lessen the concentration of acidity and to accentuate the compensating sweetness requires great technical skill and knowledge of vinification.

In Alsace vinification is simple: it is designed purely to keep the wine in its natural state. The alcohol content is usually between 11 and 14°, and in good years many growths retain a few grammes of residual sugar per litre. The tartaric acid content of the matured wines ranges from 5 to 7 grammes per litre. The prerequisites for producing a well-balanced wine are therefore excellent. But to preserve the original and special character of an Alsatian wine it is essential to preserve the taste of the fruit, that is its fruitiness and its youth. Hence oxidation must be prevented at all costs, since that would mean vinifying in the Burgundy manner, and this would completely change the wine's type. This technical detail of winemaking is a very delicate matter and requires constant vigilance, which accounts for the fact that the winegrowers of Alsace refuse to deliver in cask and bottle their own wines in their own cellars as early as the month of May.

To sum up, the wines of Alsace have three basic characteristics: freshness, fruitiness and youth, owing to the triple balance between body, acidity and the taste of the fruit. They therefore give an impression of freshness, delicacy and "race", varying with the variety of the grape and the relation between the three components. People accustomed to the creamy quality called *moelleux* are somewhat startled by their first taste of an Alsatian wine, since the threefold balance typical of it is almost unique among the French wines and even among the German; but they speedily acquire a taste for these attractive and well-bred wines which conceal a relatively luxuriant substance behind a cool approach; they are always natural, frank and genuine.

THE PRINCIPLES OF ALSATIAN WINEGROWING

Alsatian winegrowing is governed by climatic and geological imperatives and by tradition.

Except for a few climatically similar districts in Central Europe, there is no winegrowing district where the vine grows as densely as in Alsace. Mounted on stakes, the vines usually grow to about 7 feet 8 inches (2.4 metres) and consequently bear a high yield. The district, therefore, is naturally propitious to quantity production, and efforts have always been made to push it in that direction, whereas the Alsatian grower in his wisdom, taking advantage of the extreme geological variety of the soil, has always devoted his attention to finding the variety of grape that will enable him to combine satisfaction of the market demand with the essential maintenance of the quality of his wines.

It has been stated in various works on the subject that the Alsatian winegrowing region has been considerably reduced in area. In actual fact it has remained practically the same for centuries, but it must be understood that "the winegrowing district of Alsace" means the traditional winegrowing region on the foothills of the Vosges, about 35,000 acres under production and 5,000 to 7,500 acres fallow or being readied, in accordance with the normal growing cycle. Since 1961 the whole of this region has been officially recognized as a winegrowing district entitled to the so-called *appellation d'origine contrôlée* (A.O.C.). It produces some 24,706,000 gallons annually, 99 per cent of it white wine. This delimitation is the outcome of constant efforts over many years to recover the stability and quality control which was formerly customary in the towns and villages in the district, which did their utmost to reduce or even eliminate winegrowing on the flatlands and to prevent the planting of coarse varieties with their accompanying excessively large yields.

A ministerial decree with force of law issued in 1945 defined the varieties permitted. There are now considerably fewer, only those which furnish the most dependable quality having been retained. A distinction is drawn between the noble varieties—*Riesling, Muscat, Gewürztraminer,* the *Pinots* (white, grey, or Alsatian *Tokay,* and red) and *Sylvaner*—and the ordinary varieties, the *Chasselas, Knipperlé* and *Goldriesling.* All the others listed in the older classifications have disappeared.

These varieties are of very ancient stock; most of them, mentioned from the sixteenth century onward, have been selected by centuries-old tradition and long deliberation. Each requires the appropriate soil, the limestone supplying lightness and elegance and the clay body and solidity. Whereas the *Sylvaner* is fairly indifferent to the type of soil, the *Pinots* prefer chalk and the *Muscat* and the *Gewürztraminer* soil rich in clay; the *Riesling,* on the other hand, does best on primary formations. Given the extreme variety of the soils, each commune is able—some, of course, more successfully than others—to grow most of the varieties.

THE WINES OF ALSACE

The ZWICKER is a light and pleasant wine with no great pretentions, generally served as a carafe wine. It comes from several varieties of grape, usually the *Chasselas,* and legally must be from a noble variety.

The SYLVANER is fruitier and sharper, with an apparent sparkle, and is very pleasing to drink. It is of good quality at Barr; very full-bodied in the Haut-Rhin; and really appetizing at Westhalten.

The PINOT BLANC is a very well-balanced wine which could be described as discreet and distinguished. It is currently very popular.

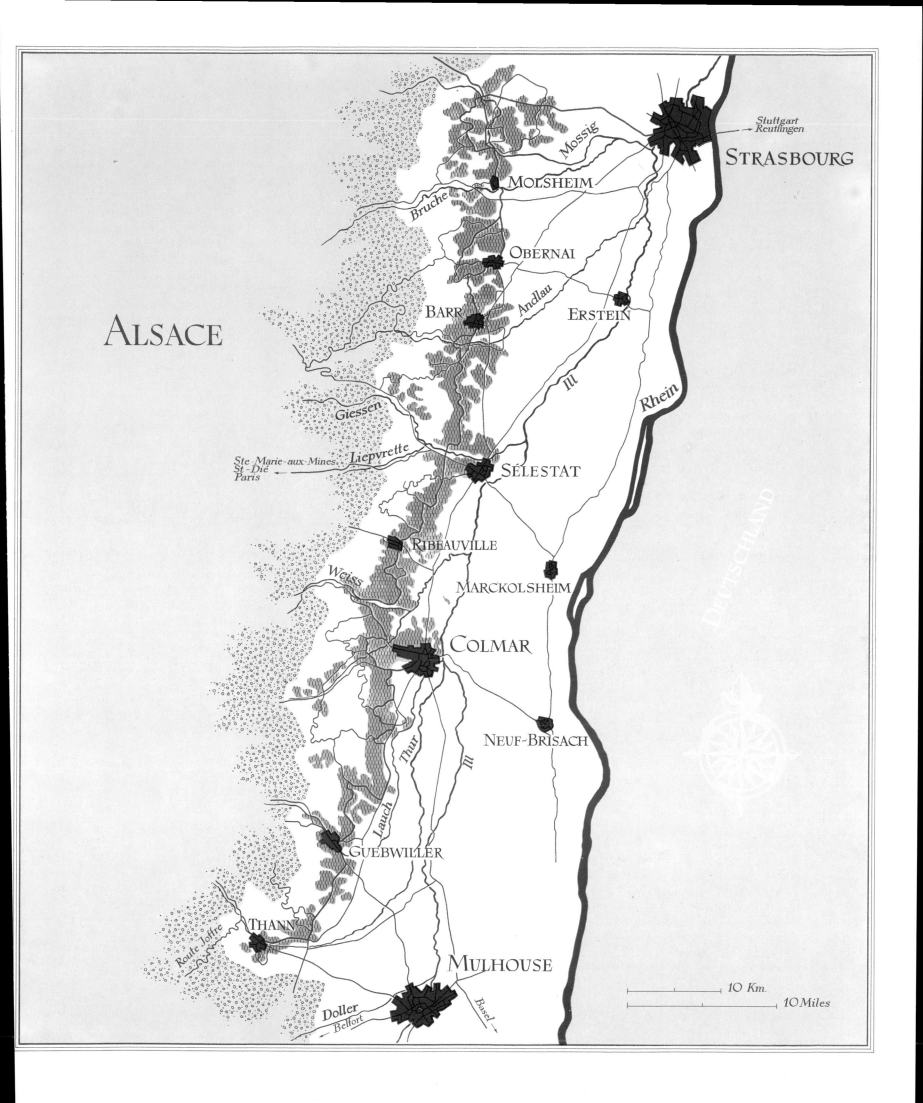

ALSACE
APPELLATION ALSACE CONTROLÉE

DEPUIS 1639

RIESLING "HUGEL"®

700 ml ℮

MISE EN BOUTEILLE PAR HUGEL ET FILS-RIQUEWIHR-ALSACE-FRANCE

PRODUCT OF FRANCE   BOTTLED IN FRANCE

Alsace wines are always denominated by the grape varieties from which they are made. A distinction is made between noble varieties: *Riesling, Gewurztraminer, Muscat, Tokay d'Alsace (Pinot Gris)* and fine varieties: *Sylvaner* and *Pinot Blanc (Clevner)*. The EDELZWICKER wine is a blend of wines from noble plants; ZWICKER is a blend from common varieties *(Chasselas, Kniperlé)* with the addition of at least one noble variety.

The ALSATIAN TOKAY, from the grey *Pinot*, is a wine of rare elegance with a regal build; it is the richest of the Alsatian growths and has a most attractive velvety flavour. It is called Tokay because of the tradition embodied in an ancient legend that General Lazare de Schwendi, warring against the Turks in Hungary around 1560, brought back some roots which he cultivated in his conservatory at Kientzheim. This wine is still grown around Kientzheim in the central district of the Haut-Rhin area, between Eguisheim and Bergheim, where some of the really best-known Alsatian vineyards are situated.

The ALSATIAN MUSCAT is the wine with the strongest but also the freshest bouquet in the whole range of Alsatian wines. Its fruitiness is very characteristic; it faithfully reproduces the savour of the fresh grape.

The GEWÜRZTRAMINER, which is known outside Alsace sometimes simply as "Gewürz" and sometimes as "Traminer", is the great Alsatian speciality. This wine is clothed in velvet, it is perfumed, it is brilliant and it seduces the ladies, for it is potent and enchanting.

The RIESLING is an elegant and distinguished wine, with a great deal of discretion. Delicate and fragrant, it has a fine and subtle bouquet. Many Alsatians call the RIESLING the emperor of Alsatian wines. The RIESLINGS from Turckheim to Bergheim in the Haut-Rhin and Dambach area in the Bas-Rhin are highly spoken of. These wines age extraordinarily well.

FROM PRESS TO TABLE

Until a few years ago the whole grape harvest was pressed by the grower and the wine was sold by the barrel in the grower's own cellar after tasting, comparing and discussing the price with the shipper, innkeeper or private buyer through a local expert broker. Since 1945 the Alsatian wine district has undergone a great, though necessary, change; but a change that is rather to be regretted nevertheless. Formerly all the growers used to keep their own wines in their own cellars and people visited them there, tasted, laughed, spent whole nights among the vats, sang, emptied glasses and ate bacon or smoked ham with the wine.

This atmosphere is now to be found only at the cellars of a few large growers. The handlers, who bring in their own grapes, vinify their wines and sell them direct to the consumer. Many of the growers' cellars are empty and the magnificent oak barrels ring hollow; the grapes are sold to the trade or taken to the co-operative, which does the winemaking and marketing. Some of the poetry is lost, but quality is gained.

Growers, co-operatives and handlers very seldom sell their wines by the barrel, but in bottles known as Alsace *flûtes*, holding 72 centilitres (about 24 fluid ounces) for quality wines or a litre for carafe wines. The ordinary wines are bottled in March and the better wines in May or June. All these bottles bear a label which must state *Appellation Alsace Contrôlée*, usually with the addition of the name of the grape variety and the shipper. Sometimes such qualifications as *grande réserve, grand vin* or *vin fin* are added; these are conventional terms for wines which must by law be over 11° in strength. The consumer thus receives wines which are absolutely reliable and need have no qualms as to whether this year's crate will live up to his expectations.

All that the buyer has to do, therefore, is to lay the bottles down in a cool and slightly damp cellar kept in the dark at a temperature of about 12° C. If this is done, a quality wine will keep from five to ten years depending on whether it is a full-bodied wine, that is to say, of a sunny vintage year, or a lighter wine of a year in which there was not much sun. The Confrérie Saint-Etienne, the main selling and connoisseur organization, even has bottles of the 1834 and 1865 vintages, over a century old but still in perfect condition; actually, 1834 was a fairly difficult year but 1865 was the great year of the century.

Alsace wine is drunk cool, but not iced, at a temperature of about 12° C. If the chill is taken off slightly, it develops its bouquet deliciously, but keeps its youthful flavour. It may, of course, be drunk by itself as a thirst-quencher; the CHASSELAS, ZWICKER and SYLVANER are wines of which one can never grow tired. Even better though, for sipping, are the PINOT BLANC or the EDELZWICKER, while on great occasions one of the Big Four, RIESLING, MUSCAT, TOKAY or GEWÜRZTRAMINER, with a slight preference for a fine MUSCAT.

The Alsatians always take some rather out-of-the-way snack with their wine, such as walnuts and wholemeal bread with a new wine, or unsweetened tarts with cheese puff paste or almonds or olives before they sit down to a board amply stocked, but not as groaning as it was in the old days. Alsace, despite its many misfortunes, has always been a wealthy region and for centuries the granary and cellar of a large part of Europe. It had everything—fish, fowl, meat of all kinds, game, frogs, snails, white bread, cheese, and, above all, splendid wines which were exported in all directions from as early as the seventh century to stock the tables of princes and wealthy merchants.

Alsace has the reputation of always keeping a decent balance from every point of view, and all excess at table is frowned upon. Libations are copious, true, but never to excess; the Alsatian knows by nature how to drink decently, and he never fails to stop before laughter degenerates into imbecility. At table the wines are married to the dishes in accordance with simple rules conforming to the methodical Alsatian nature. An ordinary carafe wine is adequate with a good saverkraut, a *baeckaeffa* or cold meats for a modest meal. Or, if something rather better is wanted, a PINOT BLANC or a modest RIESLING. For a more elaborate meal, with cheese and dessert, a bottle of TRAMINER is opened towards the end of the meal. The number of glasses beside each place increases for a banquet, for each dish calls for its own wine. Thus, a RIESLING is proper—or, going down the scale, a PINOT or a SYLVANER—with dishes which are not highly seasoned, such as asparagus, shell-fish, trout *au bleu* or white meat. The GEWÜRZTRAMINER is essential with a lobster *à l'américaine* or a well-ripened, strong munster or roquefort cheese, for it marries with them inimitably. For rich food, such as Strasbourg foie gras, the TRAMINER, and especially the TOKAY, is essential for the marriage. For the main dish the choice is wide open, though a really good vintage TOKAY is not to be sneezed at on occasion.

Alsatian women are excellents cooks, but a bottle of wine beside the pot is needed, for plenty of wine used in cooking a country dish makes it far more digestible.

The Alsatian philosophy of the table is that you must never eat purely for eating's sake nor drink simply to drink; but you should eat to drink better and drink to eat better. And the Alsatians take great care to stick to this maxim.

The Alsatian vineyards are among the oldest in France; they appeared soon after those around Narbonne. They experienced great prosperity from the seventh century onward, growing with that of Strasbourg, long the largest river port on the Rhine and the most famed wine market in central Europe; and this lasted until the Thirty Years War, which brought endless disturbances in its train. The winegrowing district was rich, but not opulent; it was and still is bourgeois; there are no châteaux, only cities and affluent market towns with a rigid sense of duty.

During the German occupation of Alsace that ended with the Treaty of Versailles in 1919, the authorities had adopted a policy of eradicating all possible trace of French influence. Not surprisingly, then, one of their first targets was the proud Alsatian winegrowing tradition, with its obvious French heritage. It was even forbidden to market the wines as "Alsace wine", with the result that Alsatian wines remained virtually unknown to the rest of the world until the 1920s.

The Alsatian winegrower is a bourgeois; he is his own master; serfdom and share-cropping have never existed. He buys his land, never rents it; he makes his wine and he ensures that it is good enough for himself and his friends. This accounts for his character, and, too, the degree to which in Alsace, a wealthy and generous land, everything is imbued with balance.

Before being delivered to the press, the grapes pass from the picker's basket to the porter's, who in turn empties them into a tub (known locally as a bettig) carried on a cart. The grapes are pressed down with a long-handled pestle (stessel).

THE WINES OF GERMANY

Germany, together with Canada and the U.S.S.R., is the most northerly winegrowing country in the world. Comparatively weak sunlight lasting over a long period creates the ideal conditions for white wines with a low alcohol content, an acid freshness and a bouquet not blurred by a high sugar content.

Winegrowing reached the Celtic area on the left bank of the Rhine before the Roman era, and excavations in the valleys of the Moselle, the Ahr and the Middle Rhine have demonstrated conclusively that the Romans cultivated the vine on the left bank. On the right bank in Roman times there was some trade in wine, and it has been proved that in the Frankish period (about A.D. 800) winegrowing was carried on everywhere where the vine still grows, while during the warm period of the Middle Ages it extended in a most remarkable way throughout the territory of the Germanic Holy Roman Empire. In the twelfth century the vine was grown in East and West Prussia and in Mecklenburg, and even in parts of Schleswig-Holstein and in Denmark.

A regression began in the sixteenth century and has not yet been halted. The deterioration of the climate after 1550 was only one factor. Imports of better quality at moderate prices by the League of Hanseatic towns and the dissolution by the Reformation of the monasteries which had hitherto been the main centres of winegrowing were disastrous to North Germany. In other regions, such as Württemberg, winegrowing never recovered from the Thirty Years War.

In addition, consumers' tastes changed. Wine had conquered regions whose climate was generally unfavourable to the slow ripening of grapes. It would hardly be true to say that the Germans of the Middle Ages preferred bitter drinks as well as having a documented predilection for bitter foods. The wine often produced nothing but alcohol; it was sweetened with honey, spiced and very often heated and drunk as a sort of hot punch. Until the end of the sixteenth century the consumption of wine must have been ten times higher than it is now. Bavaria, nowadays considered to be wholly devoted to beer, grew wine in the fifteenth to seventeenth centuries even in the Upper Bavarian regions.

But around 1500 the art of winning alcohol by distilling other fruits became widespread in Germany, and beer, which was dearer than wine till about 1550, became much cheaper. All these reasons, not to speak of the huge burden of customs duties and excise, account for the fact that the winegrowing area today is considerably less than half what it was around 1550.

In recent years the yield of must has been some 130 to 155 million gallons, 85 per cent of which is white and the remaining 15 per cent, red. The greater proportion of this, some 100 million gallons, is supplied by three adjacent regions: the Palatinate, Rheinhesse and the valleys of the Moselle, Saar and Ruwer. Comparatively insignificant districts such as the Ahr and the Middle Rhine, including Siebenbergen, remind us that the vine was once grown much farther to the north until the competition from wines imported from southern Europe, through Hamburg especially, became so fierce that German wine production fell off steeply, a decline hastened by the devastations of the last of the great religious wars. Present-day consumption amounts to an average of 28 pints per capita; 36.4 per cent of it is met out of imports.

GRAPE VARIETIES. Some of the whites—*Riesling, Sylvaner, Traminer, Ruländer*—do not give of their best except in good years and in very sunny exposures. This is notably the case with *Riesling*. Others, however, like the *Müller-Thurgau*, ripen more quickly and produce an agreeable wine even if there is not much sun. The soil also makes a great deal of difference; indeed, it and the

German wine labels are particularly colourful, and always explicit. The winegrowing region can be seen at a glance (Nahe, Rheinhessen, Rheinpfalz, Mosel-Saar-Ruwer in these examples). But the very large number of growths and vineyards make the rest of the label less easy to decipher for the non-initiated.

variety together determine the wine's character. This particular feature distinguishes Germany sharply from the other winegrowing countries. It is due to the low alcohol and sugar content; since neither of these two components are present in large quantities to affect the wine's smell and taste, the delicate qualities derived from the rocks in the sub-soil which do affect nose and palate come into their own.

Germany leaves the pre-eminence in the red varieties to her neighbour to the west. But the *Spätburgunder*, the German version of the Burgundian *Pinot Noir* grape, grown on red sandstone and schist, gives a ruby wine of a firm ripeness, outstanding in quality, deep burgundy in shade, with a character that yields nothing to wines from other countries. This is true, too, of the garnet-coloured *Frühburgunder*; the wine is first-rate, full-bodied, sometimes velvety; the *Portugieser* produces a paler wine, which has little bouquet and is lighter; it is sensitive to frost and early-ripening, and it is drunk young. In good years it is warm and velvety and its colour becomes dark red.

All these grape varieties are perfectly suited to the peculiarities of their soil and climate.

Total vineyard area is now 1,848,000 acres, of which 1,716,000 acres were planted to the vine before 1971. The following table shows a break-down of varieties grown:

White grapes	Müller-Thurgau	25 %
	Riesling	24 %
	Sylvaner	23 %
	Ruländer (Pinot Gris)	3 %
	Morio-Muskat	3 %
Red grapes	Portugieser	7 %
	Blauer Spätburgunder	4 %
	Trollinger	2 %
Other varieties (including Traminer, Gutedel, Limberger)		9 %
		100 %

The better German wines have a character all their own—fruity acidity, balanced, flowery bouquet, a low alcohol content and lightness—and are thus a type of wine for which there is an ever-growing demand.

A new German law governing wine was passed in 1969, but the creation of a European wine-market commission has resulted in most of the legislative control being handed over to the EEC. It has thus been necessary to modify the new law, which took effect as of 19 July 1971, to meet the new circumstances. The EEC classifies vineyard areas as A, B, CI, CII and CIII, whereunder Germany (with the exception of Baden) and Luxemburg are zone A. Baden, like certain parts of France (Alsace and the Loire valley, for example), is classified as zone B.

The grapes are gathered rather late in the season in the Rheingau. Thus, even on fine days, mists shroud the hills along the Rhine, and shade the shapes of the barges which ceaselessly succeed or pass one another along the river.

This strange machine enables a grape harvester to double his production. He sits on a seat slung from a gantry, and cuts the grapes with secateurs. The grapes are then sucked into the containers through flexible pipes.

ASSMANNSHÄUSER HÖLLENBERG

1. Name of the wine: Assmannshäuser Höllenberg (name of commune plus name of growth). — 2. District appellation: Rheingau. — 3. Proprietor-cellarer. — 4. Indication of grape type (*Spätburgunder*) and type of vintage (*Edelbeerenauslese*, selected grapes). — 5. Without added sugar.

BINGER SCHLOSSBERG-SCHWÄTZERCHEN

1. Name of the wine: Binger Schlossberg-Schwätzerchen (name of commune plus name of growth). — 2. Place of origin (a, Rheinhessen) and statement of first quality (b). — 3. Proprietor-grower. — 4. Grape variety and type of vintage.

BACHARACHER SCHLOSS STAHLECK RIESLING

1. Name of the wine: Bacharacher Schloss Stahleck (name of commune plus name of growth). — 2. District appellation: Mittelrhein. — 3. Proprietor. — 4. Cellarer-merchant.

BADENWEILER RÖMERBERG

1. Name of the wine: Badenweiler Römerberg (name of commune plus name of growth). — 2. District appellation (Baden) and year. — 3. Grape variety (*Ruländer*) and type of vintage (grapes picked when dry and selected). — 4. Proprietor-cellarer.

BEREICH BERNKASTEL

1. Name of the wine: Bernkastel (name of the area). — 2. Statement of ordinary quality (a) and district of origin (Mosel-Saar-Ruwer). — 3. Cellarer-merchant.

DEIDESHEIMER HOHENMORGEN

1. Name of the wine: Deidesheimer Hohenmorgen (name of commune plus name of growth). — 2. Statement of first quality (a) and district of origin (Rheinpfalz). — 3. Proprietor-grower. — 4. Type of wine: Riesling Trockenbeerenauslese.

303

BADEN

The winegrowing region of the Upper Rhine, incorporated by referendum since 1952 in the *Land* of Baden-Württemberg, is divided up into six completely different winegrowing districts. In the south-west, on the shores of Lake Constance—at Meersburg to be exact—there is the SEEWEIN. This sharp and full bodied wine from the *Ruländer, Traminer* and *Burgunder* varieties grown on moraines suffers from the altitude, and this is only partly counterbalanced by the southern climate and the broad stretch of water. Here, as elsewhere in Baden, is the famous WEISSHERBST, derived from a *Burgunder* vinified as a white wine. It is full-bodied with a fine bouquet.

On the deep clayey soils, partly covered with loess, of the Margraviate, between Basel and Freiburg-in-Breisgau, the *Gutedel*, or *Chasselas*, imported from Geneva in 1780, produces a soft, perfumed wine of low acidity. Between Freiburg and Baden-Baden three regions share the warmth of the upper valley of the Rhine and the protection of the range of the Black Forest against the east winds: Breisgau, the vineyards of the Kaiserstuhl and Ortenau. On the Kaiserstuhl the vine grows on volcanic tuff, in Breisgau on loess, in Ortenau on granite, in the valley of the Glotter on gneiss.

The new wine law created two new regions: the Badische Bergstrasse/Kraichgau (an amalgam of the old Bergstrasse, Kraichgau, Pfinzgau and Enzgau regions) and the Badisches Frankenland.

The 25,000 acres of the Baden vineyards are planted with 30 per cent *Müller-Thurgau* and 20 per cent *Blauer Spätburgunder*. The *Gutedel (Chasselas)* makes up 11 per cent, the *Ruländer (Pinot Gris)* 15 per cent, the

Sylvaner 6 per cent and the *Riesling* 7 per cent. The remaining 9 per cent include *Traminer, Portugieser, Weissburgunder* (3.1 per cent), *Auxerrois* (1.1 per cent) and some new crosses such as the *Freisamer*. About 30,800,000 gallons of wine is produced, 25 per cent of which is red.

At Neuweier and in neighbouring areas the MAUERWEIN is bottled in flagons, or *Bocksbeutel*, as in Franconia; elsewhere it comes in long bottles, as in the Moselle. One sixth of the 400,000 farms cultivate the vine as well as other crops. Baden is a *Land* of wine co-operatives; there are about 110 of them and they account for two-thirds of the production. They are managed by an organization called the Central Federation of Wine-Growers' Co-operatives.

Among the Breisgau wines the GLOTTERTÄLER is famed and, indeed, rather feared for its effects.

The best wines come from the Kaiserstuhl, which dominates the plain of the Rhine. The principal places are Achkarren (SCHLOSSBERG), Ihringen (WINKLERBERG, FOHRENBERG, ABTSWEINGARTEN), Bickensohl (STEINFELSEN, EICHBERG, HOCHSTATT), Oberrottweil (HENKENBERG, KIRCHBERG, EICHBERG), Bischoffingen (STEINBRUCK, ROSENKRANZ) and the State domains of Blankenhornsberg. The vine grows everywhere on the eroded basaltic tuff of the old volcano, producing wines of a *Sylvaner* type, full and ripe, the *Riesling*, acid and elegant, the *Spätburgunder*, outstanding, and the *Ruländer*, ardent and impetuous with a soft and exquisite fruity flavour.

In the Ortenau, where the *Riesling* is called *Klingelberger* after the castle around which it was first planted in 1776, there are also some wines of quality at Durbach, Ortenberg, Neuweier and Oberkirch, for instance; the best red wines of the Ortenau are derived from the *Blauer Spätburgunder*. The MAUERBERG at Neuweier and the SONNENBERG, the KLOSTERBERG and the NÄGELSFÖRST at Varnhalt are wines of repute. This district also produces perfumed TRAMINERS reminiscent of the Alsatian wine.

In the Bühlertal red wines predominate, such as WALDULM, KAPPELRODECK, BÜHLERTAL and AFFENTALER, the label of the latter being decorated with a monkey, although the name really comes from the Latin *Ave*.

Northern Baden up to Heidelberg once had extensive vineyards, but in many places they have been reduced to insignificance by industrialization. But on the slopes of the Kraichgau and the Odenwald, BERGSTRASSENWEINE (wines of the mountain road) are still produced, as well as table wines from north of Heidelberg. Lastly, at the north-eastern end, the Taubergrund produces a wine which is almost contiguous at Wertheim-am-Main with the Franconian wines, which it closely resembles.

The Badeners' "wine road" is considerably longer than the Palatines', for Baden extends for 125 miles. A Baden label guarantees the quality of the wine.

The Kaiserstuhl vineyards lie on the right bank of the Rhine, slightly to the north of Freiburg-im-Brisgau. The soil there is volcanic. The village of Achkarren (photograph) is in the region of Kaiserstuhl-Tuniberg, which produces the district's best wines.

In winter, the terraced vines of Mundelsheim on the Neckar form a pattern that pleases the eye.

WÜRTTEMBERG

The vineyards are terraced in the valleys of the Neckar and its tributaries, the Jagst, Kocher, Rems, Enz, Murr, Bottwar and Zaber. The soil is partly triassic and partly conchiferous limestone. The triassic soils are heavy and chalky, especially where they are broken down by deposits of marl. The conchiferous lime is lighter and warmer.

Until the Thirty Years War the Swabian wine district covered 100,000 acres. Today it has only 16,000 acres producing 10,120,000 gallons of wine. The main variety is the *Trolinger* (28.4 per cent), which is found only in Württemberg and produces a brick-red, full-bodied wine; 24.8 per cent is planted to *Riesling* and 13.1 per cent to *Sylvaner*. The remainder is divided between the *Portugieser* (10.6 per cent), the *Müller-Thurgau* (6.3 per cent), the dark red *Limberger* (6 per cent), the *Samtrot* and the *Schwarzriesling*.

Near Reutlingen the vineyards climb to over 1,700 feet. The cultivation is a typical co-operative enterprise. In 1920 the co-operatives took over a district which had gone completely out of cultivation for many years and have brought it to a level which can bear comparison with other districts. The Württemberg wines are hard to find on the market; apparently, the growers drink their wine themselves, usually very young, in the first two years after it has been made.

One of the Württemberg specialities is the SCHILLER-WEIN, something like the French rosé. It is made either by blending red and white grapes in the press or by leaving the skins of red grapes in the must for a short time (which is how the WEISSHERBST is produced in Baden). Another Württemberg speciality is a young wine which has not completed the fermentation process; it is called SUSER and is a very good and easy wine to drink. The communes of Cannstatt, Untertürckheim and Feuerbach produce excellent growths.

Stuttgart, the capital of Baden-Württemberg, is not only a large centre of the wine trade but still has a 2,000-acre vineyard. A French saying of about 1630 claimed that "if the grape of Stuttgart were not picked, the city would drown in wine".

The *Sylvaner* grape produces fresh green wines in the upper valley of the Neckar. There are fragrant, full-bodied Rieslings in the valley of the Rems as well as luscious Sylvaners. The Rems valley produces the famous STETTENER BROTWASSER. The valleys of the Murr and the Bottwar shelter Steinheim, Kirchheim, Murr, Kleinbottwar, Grossbottwar, Lombach and Marbach, the home of the poet Schiller, whose family is said to have given its name to the SCHILLERWEIN.

There is another place with the name of Stetten in the red wine district of Heuchelberg and, farther on, Schwaigen. In the valley of the lower Neckar there is Lauffen, where the vine grows on conchiferous lime, as at Heilbronn and Flein. It is on this soil too that the *Riesling* and *Sylvaner* of Taubergrund ripen. Maulbronn and Gundelsheim, as well as Schnait in the valley of the Rems, produce wines which are well spoken of.

THE PALATINATE

The Palatinate has 48,000 acres of vineyards and produces 39,500,000 gallons of must on an average; it is the largest wine-growing region in Germany. The *Sylvaner* is the principal variety of vine-plant grown in this district, with 31.3 per cent of the total area, followed by the *Müller-Thurgau* with 23.3 per cent, the red *Portugieser* with 15.8. per cent and the *Riesling* with 13.9 per cent. As early as the period of the Holy Roman Empire the Palatinate was known as "the wine-cellar of the Empire". This region is particularly favoured by nature; it gets an average of 1,875 hours of sunshine and the winter lasts less than three months. The vineyards are mostly on the flatlands and are easy to farm mechanically; only in a few places are they situated as high as 900 feet. The Haardt mountain range, which is an extension of the Vosges, protects the Palatinate plain from the bitter north winds and from the rain and snow from the west. The vine stretches in a ribbon 50 miles long by some two to four miles wide from the Alsatian border northwards to the edge of the Rheinhesse along the *Weinstrasse* (wine road) from the Wine Gate at Schweigen to Grünstadt.

The region is rich in archaeological finds which prove that the Romans cultivated the vine here on a large scale. Many of these finds are to be seen in the Wine Museum at Speyer, the largest in Germany. The importance of this winegrowing district at the time of the Frankish kingdoms was due to the fact that by the Treaty of Verdun in A.D. 834, which parcelled out the empire of Charlemagne, the region of Speyer, Worms and the Nahe was given to Germania because of its wealth of wine *(propter vini copiam)*.

The Palatinate comprises two winegrowing regions: the Südliche Weinstrasse (from Schweigen on the Alsatian border to Maikammer, south of Neustadt) and the Mittelhaardt-Deutsche Weinstrasse (from Neustadt-Diedesfeld to Bockenheim and Zellertal). The southern area has fertile loess soils on which the *Sylvaner* produces fresh and generous table wines in some 50 communes between the Alsatian border and Maikammer. The *Müller-Thurgau* (30.4 per cent), *Morio-Muskat* (8.4 per cent) and *Ruländer* (3.1 per cent) prosper there too. Hambach, Maikammer and Edenknoben are noted for their high yields. The best growths are to be found between Gleisweiler and Hasbach; Edenknoben and Diedesfeld are the best-known communes, producing sound and characteristic wines.

Farther north, the transition to the Mittelhaardt-Deutsche Weinstrasse is virtually imperceptible; the best-known communes are Neustadt, Deidesheim, Ruppertsberg, Forst and Wachenheim. The district extends to Dachenheim and Weisenheim-am-Berg. The soils are lighter on the whole, compounded of sand and warm gravel; the rainfall is slight. The Forst and Deidesheim vineyards are improved with powdered basalt, which makes them even warmer.

On the escarpments of the Haardt range there are triassic, red sandstone and schist outcrops, besides granite, gneiss and schist, and chalky and clayey alluvial deposits at the foot of the range. The *Riesling* is not much grown, but produces a vigorous and fruity wine here, with a very prominent tang of the local soil; while the *Sylvaner* is represented by soft and rather sweet wines of a high quality—as, indeed, is the *Traminer*, which produces wines that are at the same time both fiery and round.

The Mittelhaardt produces the heavist must in Germany. In the large vineyards which produce these selected and dried-out grapes, they remain on the stem until as late as mid-November even in average years.

The nearly 3,500 different types of wine are being systematically reduced. Besides the great internationally famous estates (such as Bassemann-Jordan, von Buhl and Bürklin-Wolf) there are co-operatives which own huge vineyards.

A list of the most famous names in the Central Haardt would certainly include the following growths (listed here by commune): at Forst, KIRCHENSTÜCK, FREUNDSTÜCK, JESUITENGARTEN, UNGEHEUER; at Deidesheim,

The winegrowers of Edenkoben, in the Palatinate, work hard, for they know that the vines need constant care. They all hope for favourable weather, since the vineyards are liable to give a poor yield without it.

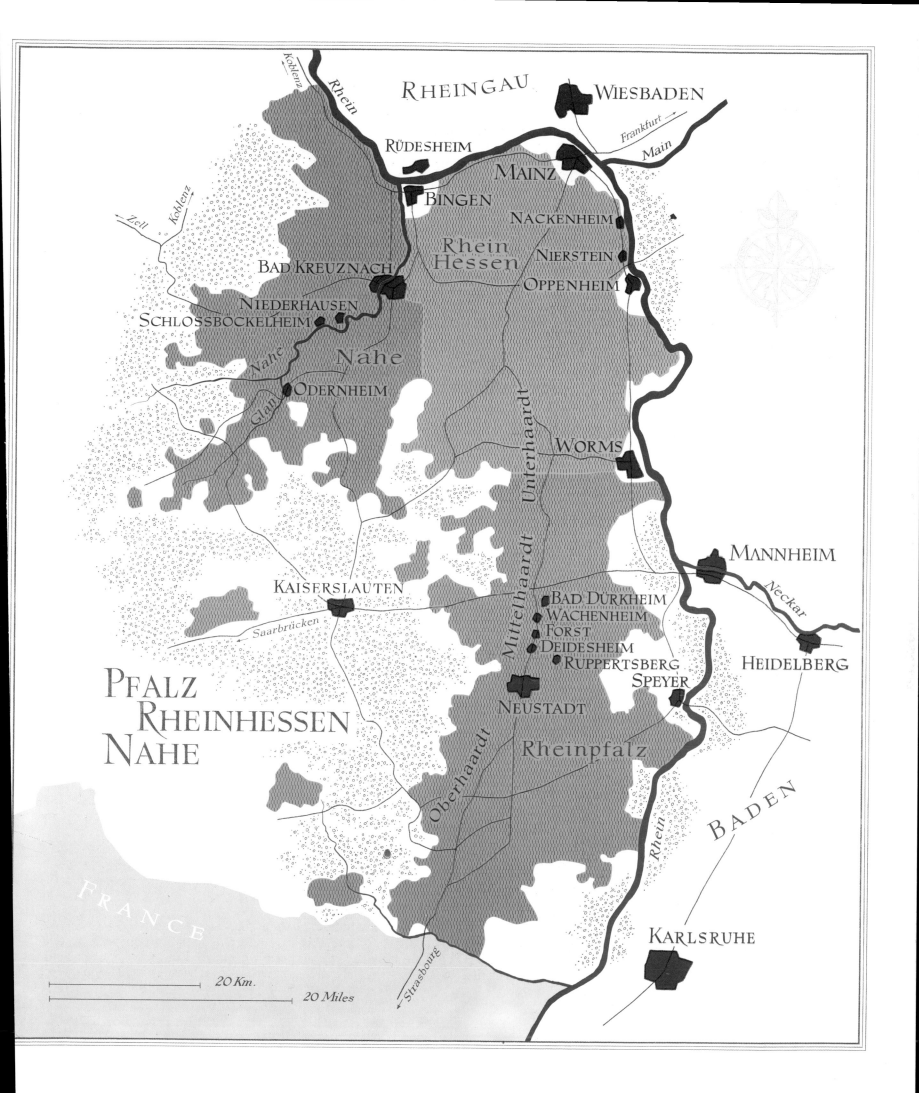

RHEINGAU

WIESBADEN

RÜDESHEIM

Koblenz

Rhein

MAINZ

BINGEN

Zell *Koblenz*

NACKENHEIM

Rhein
Hessen

NIERSTEIN

BAD KREUZNACH

OPPENHEIM

NIEDERHAUSEN

SCHLOSSBÖCKELHEIM

Nahe

Nahe

Glan

ODERNHEIM

Unterhaardt

WORMS

MANNHEIM

Neckar

KAISERSLAUTEN

Saarbrücken

Mittelhaardt

BAD DÜRKHEIM

WACHENHEIM

FORST

DEIDESHEIM

RUPPERTSBERG

SPEYER

HEIDELBERG

PFALZ
RHEINHESSEN
NAHE

Rheinpfalz

NEUSTADT

Oberhaardt

Rhein

BADEN

FRANCE

KARLSRUHE

Strasbourg

20 Km.

20 Miles

GRAINHÜBEL, HOHENMORGEN, KIESELBERG, LEINHÖHLE, MÄUSHÖHLE; at Ruppertsberg, REITERPFAD, HOHEBURG, NUSSBIEN; at Wachenheim, BÖHLIG, GOLDBÄCHEL, GERÜMPEL; at Bad Dürkheim, HOCHBENN, MICHELSBERG, SPIELBERG.

There are also quality wines from Gimmeldingen, Kallstadt (NILL), Ungstein (HERRENBERG), Freinsheim and Herxheim-am-Berg.

The Unterhaardt, or Lower Haardt, which stretches as far as Rheinhesse and the Nahe, supplies *Konsumwein* (everyday wines) and table wines, the ZELLER SCHWARZER HERRGOTT being the best of them. A poet has said of Palatinate wine that in combining maturity with gentleness it is the maternal female among wines, and another has described it thus: "The wine of the Palatinate has the advantage over its two brothers (the Rheingau and the Rheinhesse) of having its own very special temperament, which ranges from the gracious levity of adolescence to the impetuous passion of the grown man, from blooming, perfumed and frivolous youth to noble, polite and dignified maturity."

RHEINHESSE

From the name one would suppose that Rheinhesse was the old *Land* lying between the Imperial Cathedral Cities of Worms and Mainz, but that disappeared from the political map in 1945. Rheinhesse is now a region of the Rhineland-Palatinate, a *Land* of the Federal Republic, with Mainz as its capital. In the south the Palatinate vineyards near Worms merge into the Rheinhesse. In the north and east the border follows the bend of the Rhine from Bingen to Worms, and in the west it extends up the valley of the Nahe. Legend is fond of associating the cultivation of the vine in the Rheinhesse with Charlemagne, but, as in other regions, there is evidence that it existed there as early as A.D. 753.

The Rheinhesse is the second-largest winegrowing district in Germany. Extending over 176 communes, 50,000 acres are planted to vines, 7.5 per cent to red varieties (almost all *Portugieser*). The *Sylvaner* predominates among the whites (with 38 per cent), followed by the *Müller-Thurgau* (37 per cent) and the *Riesling* (6.2 per cent). Only as far back as 1948, the *Müller-Thurgau* represented just 15 per cent; and the *Sylvaner*, 60 per cent. The harvest of must amounts to one quarter of the entire German yield.

The *Sylvaner* grows best on heavy soils, producing a sweet wine with a rich bouquet. This valley country has chalky and marly soils as well as clayey soils which, though none too good in wet years since the water does not drain off easily, are very favourable to the grape in hot summers. Loess and friable sandstone are also common, particularly between Worms, Osthofen and Oppenheim. On the mountain slopes in the southeastern part of the region the vineyards are set on porphyritic quartz with a high potassium content. On the other hand, around Nachenheim and Nierstein there are surface outcrops of red sandstone and sandy clay of the Permian period. Near Bingen the vineyards are set on quartz shales, the soil best suited to the *Riesling*, and produce a light, luscious wine with a natural sweetness smacking of the grape.

The Rheinhesse wine best known abroad does not come from one growth. Large vineyards cultivated by monks stretch round the church of Our Lady of Worms. "Monk" is *minch* in the local dialect and becomes *milch*, and this is the origin of the name LIEBFRAUENMILCH, which has been adopted for all the sweet wines of the Rheinhesse that have the fine qualities of Rhine wine. Even the neighbouring wines of the Palatinate claim the right to sell under the LIEBFRAUENMILCH label.

The quality wines in the strict sense come from the district along the Rhine. The hinterland to Alzey and the valley of the Nahe supplies *Konsumwein*. Mainz and Worms are the capitals of the German wine trade. The vineyards are mostly owned by small-holders, medium-sized holdings and co-operatives, but, for all that, Bingen, Nierstein and Oppenheim have estates which enjoy a world-wide reputation.

Oppenheim, with its chalk and marl, produces *Auslese* (wines from carefully selected bunches of grapes) and *Beerenauslese* (selected berries, i.e. wines made from overripe grapes that have acquired the noble rot—the *Edelfäule*—picked immediately after the harvest and pressed separately). These wines can attain great age. The Oppenheim wines are heavy and ripe, particularly such great growths as KREUZ and SACKTRÄGER, together with the world-renowned HERRENBERG.

On the red sandstone spur which crops out at Nierstein white wines are produced which are indubitably among the best-known in the world; they have a fruity bouquet and great elegance. Thirty years ago an attempt was made to reduce the vast number of names which had led to a great deal of confusion, especially abroad. A single name was selected for each growth to include all the others, but this necessary reform is still only a project. The names of the wines with a worldwide reputation are AUFLANGEN, REHBACH, ORBEL, ÖLBERG, KRANZBERG and PETTENPAL, closely followed by HEILIGENBAUM and GUTES DOMTAL.

But Rheinhesse is, of course, more than the OPPENHEIM, NIERSTEIN and LIEBFRAUENMILCH names combined, although the ROTTENBERG from Nackenheim and the STEIG from Dalsheim are perhaps the only other "internationally reputed growths" besides those already

listed. Above Bingen the Rochusberg—with the SCHLOSSBERG, SCHWÄTZERCHEN and SANKT ROCHUSKAPELLE—and the Scharlachberg produce very high quality wines; and the following are also certainly worth mentioning: HOCH SANKT ALBAN, WESTRUM and SILBERBERG from Bodenheim; ENGELSBERG and FENCHELBERG from Nackenheim; and STEIG and BURG-RODENSTEIN from the Flörsheim-Dalsheim area.

We come at length to Ingelheim, where the *Blauer Burgunder* produces the famous reds of PARES and the various communes of KAISERPFALZ (Jugenheim, Engel-

stadt, Schwabenheim, Wackernheim and Heidesheim all produce this wine).

Shortly after 1800 the Romantic poet Ludwig Tieck described the Rheinhesse wines in the following terms: "These excellent spritely waves which range from the light LAUBENHEIM to the strong NIERSTEINER in whetting your whistle flatter the palate, purifying, refreshing and toning up the senses. To what should they be compared but to the tranquil steadiness of good writers, to generosity and fullness devoid of chimeras and gothick allegory?"

THE NAHE VALLEY

The winegrowing valley of the Nahe stretches from Bingerbrück at the confluence of the Nahe and the Rhine to Martinstein, with the lateral valleys of Krebsbach, Guldenbach, Trollbach, Gräfenbach, Alsenz and Glan. Politically, the Nahe region was part of Rhenish Prussia until 1946; it is now a region of the Rhineland-Palatinate.

The vineyards are protected on the north, west and east sides by the slopes of the Rhine massif. They enjoy warm weather, very little wind and, with only 20 to 24 inches of rainfall per year, one of the driest climates in Germany. This makes the area ideal for winegrowing. The soils are extremely varied here, owing to the numerous tributary streams flowing into the area through the often steep-sided valleys.

Because the valley breaks down into three distinct tiers it is common to talk of the Upper, Middle and Lower Nahe. The wines which come from the banks of the Nahe's three tributaries, the Krebsbach, the Trollbach and the Guldenbach, relate to those of the Rheingau and Middle Rhine and share similar geological and climatic conditions.

The heart of the winegrowing region, the Middle Nahe, lies between Bad Kreuznach and Schlossböckelheim. Apart from heavy, clay soils, there are also some volcanic soils whose wines have contributed much to the reputation of Nahe wine.

The Upper Nahe runs from Sobernheim to Martinsheim, and the wines often recall those of the Moselle and the Saar. Meddersheim and Monzingen, whose wines were once praised by Goethe, are the principal winegrowing communes. The Glan and Alsenz valleys produce quality wines with flavour and characteristics all their own.

Archaeological evidence suggests that the vine has been cultivated in the valley for more than two thousand years; for all that, because the Nahe has never been navigable, the wine was transported down the Rhine and sold as Rhine wine, hence never bearing its own name until the twentieth century.

Despite the 1971 wine law, the most celebrated

growths have remained pretty well unchanged. The Nahe winegrowing region includes the vineyards of Kreuznach, with its up to 9,750 acres of vineyards, and Schlossböckelheim, with up to 7,300 acres. The generic appellation SCHLOSSKAPELLE includes 62 growths and covers nearly half the region; KRONENBERG follows in order of size with 45 growths, including those of Bad Kreuznach. The appellation PFARRGARTEN includes 30 growths while that of SONNENBORN covers a further seven. The Schlossböckelheim area is covered by the generic appellations ROSENGARTEN (with 37 growths), BURGWEG (64), PARADIESGARTEN (43) and LANDSBERG (39).

Growths which have achieved international fame are the KUPFERGRUBE, KÖNIGSFELS and FELSENBERG from Schlossböckelheim, the KAUZENBERG, BRÜCKES, KRÖTENPFUHL and NARRENKAPPE from Bad Kreuznach, the ROTENFELS from Münster-am-Stein, and the HERMANNSBERG, HERMANNSHÖHLE and ROSENHECK from Niederhausen. Nevertheless, the other growths of Schlossböckelheim, Waldböckelheim, der Kreuznach, Münster-am-Stein, Niederhausen and Norheim enjoy a high reputation, and in the Alsenz and Glan valleys Altenbamberg, Ebernburg and Dielkirchen produce wines of equal quality.

The state lands around Schlossböckelheim and Niederhausen originated on land cleared of forest. The area was later extended by taking over abandoned farms and by buying up vineyards near Altenbamberg, which had long lain fallow after the ravages of phylloxera. The wines are fruity and luscious, at times oncoming and vigorous, at times gently mature, but always with a distinct and attractive character. It has often been said that the wines of the Nahe, lying between the vineyards of the Rheinhesse and those of the Moselle, combine the qualities of both these regions.

For centuries the pun was repeated (in German) that the *Weine bei der Nahe* (wines beside the Nahe) were *beinahe Weine* (almost wines). In 1816 only 2,500 acres were planted to the vine; since then the area has grown a great deal and now covers some 11,200 acres (with 31 per cent *Müller-Thurgau*, 24.3 per cent *Sylvaner* and 22.5 per cent *Riesling* growths).

FRANCONIA

At the beginning of the nineteenth century there were still some 27,000 acres planted to vines in Franconia in the Free State of Bavaria; today, there are only 5,700 acres, with an average annual yield of 3 million gallons of must.

The Franconian vineyards stretch from Hanau in the west to Bamberg in the east, and in the north from a line running from Bad Kissingen to Hammelburg to near Ansbach in the south. The climate is oceanic west of the Spessart range and continental east of it. Geologically, Franconia is Triassic marl from Zeil-am-Obermain to the Aichgrund, conchiferous lime from Schweinfurth to Ochsenfurth and variegated sandstone on the western slopes of the Spessart. The pebbly soils are in many places covered with loess and sand. The yield per acre is only 880 to 1,100 gallons, but this means that the wine has all the more body and bouquet. The bouquet and not the alcohol content has given it the reputation of a heady wine. The *Sylvaner* predominates, with 45 per cent. The *Müller-Thurgau* accounts for 40 per cent and the *Riesling* is inconsiderable, with only 4 per cent, though it should be said that the *Riesling* is the variety that produces the best growths from Würzburg, the capital, namely the sweet and round LEISTE and the STEIN, sharp and perfumed, the wine which has lent its name to the typical wine of Franconia, the STEINWEIN. The wines from Eschendorf, Randersacker and Iphofen are equally good. Eschendorf produces the best: LUMP, KIRCHBERG and EULENGRUBE; the vines grow on chalk-and-clay strata here, with loam and silt. Randersacker has the PFÜLBEN, a wine with a world-wide reputation, and the HOHBURG, SPIELBERG and TEUFELSKELLER; Iphofen produces the JULIUS-ECHTERBERG, KRONSBERG KALB and BURGWEG. But Hörstein and Frickenhausen also produce wines of the best quality, as does Klingenberg, where the *Burgunder* grows on variegated sandstone.

Besides such celebrated vineyards as the Juliusspital and Bürgerspital there are several co-operatives. The largest State domain in Germany is in Franconia, covering about 400 acres. The Carolingians bestowed large donations of vineyards upon the monasteries scattered throughout the region. After the separation of Church and State, all the Church property reverted to the Free State of Bavaria. The properties include some of the most famous Franconia wines, especially the STEIN at Würzburg and the ABTSLEITE and the LEISTE on the other bank of the Main; farther upstream, the RANDERSACKER; and downstream, the THÜNGERSHEIM. The Bavarian Wine Institute, of which the former Royal Bavarian Cellars at Würzburg and the State Wine Institute at Veitshochheim are branches, has a great reputation for experimental cultivation. With few exceptions, the wines of Franconia are put up in the special flagon called *Bocksbeutel*.

The wine of Franconia smacks of the soil that produces it. It can be full-bodied and down to earth, but it may also be well-bred and fresh. In any particular year, its quality greatly depends on the weather. This wine, a poet once said, has all the variations of cold steel, from Damascene blade to Turkish scimitar.

THE RHEINGAU

The 7,584 acres of the Rheingau vineyards are divided up among no more than twenty communes and stretch for some 30 miles along the right bank of the Rhine between Wiesbaden and the Wisper valley near Lorch (Hochheim-am-Main also belongs to the Rheingau). The region was part of Rhenish Prussia until 1946, after which it was included in the *Land* of Hessen, the capital being Wiesbaden, itself a winegrowing commune of the Rheingau. The Rhine, which elsewhere flows north and south, here flows east and west. The vineyards in the "elbow of the Rhine" enjoy a full southern exposure, so that they have a truly southern winegrowing climate, especially as the Taunus range of hills protects the Rheingau from the cold north winds, and the river bends enough to cut off most of the wind from the east or the west.

An inland geological sea and its deposits which were covered with a layer of clayey loess in the Diluvian epoch gradually built up the Upper Rheingau in ter-races from Hochheim to Rüdesheim. The southern slopes, which rise to 600 feet, draw additional warmth from the sun's reflection from the Rhine, which is some half a mile wide in this part. The warm summers and the humidity from evaporation make up for the frequently inadequate warmth of the soil.

Upstream from Rüdesheim the river flows between high cliffs and its bed is 100 fathoms deep. The shores are no longer gentle slopes, as in the Upper Rheingau, but sheer drops, terraced with innumerable low walls climbing from the river to the top of the cliffs some 1000 feet above. The Rhine flows through Assmannshausen, which produces from the *Spätburgunder* a red wine with a strong flavour of almonds. But white varieties are grown in the rest of the Rheingau.

In area the Rheingau is only the seventh-largest German winegrowing district, but in quality its wines certainly rank with the best in the world. The Hochheim wines have such a reputation in Britain that all Rhine

The painter Janscha produced this watercolour in 1789; it shows the village of Oestrich beside the Rhine, and, on the far right, Schloss Johannisberg. The Emperor Francis II of Austria presented this property to Prince von Metternich in 1816 in gratitude for his restoration of Austrian power in Europe. Today, Schloss Johannisberg produces the greatest and most famous wines of the Rheingau district.

wines are called hock there. The saying "a good hock keeps the doctor away" was probably coined at the time Queen Victoria visited Germany, but the wines from the Rheingau had been celebrated since the sixteenth and seventeenth centuries, owing particularly to the highly skilled viniculture practised at the Abbeys of Johannisberg and Eberbach. It was here that the first *Spätlese* wines were made, from overripe grapes picked after the ordinary harvest, and especially the *Trockenbeerenauslese*, wines made from overripe grapes which have acquired the "noble rot" and have been left to dry on the vine. Ten people have to work for two whole weeks to gather enough grapes to make 20 bottles of these wines. It is no accident that such wines are found only here, for the autumn mist that rises from the Rhine, known as the *Traubendrücker*, or grape-presser, causes the grapes to become overripe and to acquire the noble rot *(Edelfäule)* and, if the weather is suitable, the grapes may be picked as late as the second fortnight in November. One of the regional specialities is the EISWEIN ("ice wine") which comes from sudden frosts; the frozen water remains in the press and the vat collects only an extract of the ethers of sugared oils and perfume.

All the best growths are produced by the *Riesling*,

which accounts for 77 per cent of the area planted to vines; the remainder is partly *Müller-Thurgau* (17.9 per cent) and partly *Sylvaner* (7.6 per cent). The average yield is about 4,620,000 gallons. The vineyards, because of the inheritance laws, are mostly small-holdings. The large properties, however, are also very productive. There are hardly any co-operatives.

The wines from the *Riesling* combine an elegant fruitiness and sweetness with acidity in a noble harmony which the connoisseur calls *finesse*, meaning something like "supreme delicacy". The bouquet is flowery and elegant. Though made from overripe grapes, the wines of the Rheingau are light, considerably lighter, for instance, than the fine wines of Baden or the Palatinate. This is due in great part to the soils. On the terraces above the Rhine the vine grows on sericite and clayey shale and often, too, on quartz. The eroded rocks have broken down into clayey and loamy soil and the alluvial loess has a high lime content.

It is hard to choose among so many very great wines. Of those with a world-wide reputation Hochheim would undoubtedly be represented primarily by the DOMDECHANEY, KIRCHENSTÜCK and STEIN. Eltville produces the LANGENSTÜCK, SONNENBERG and TAUBENBERG. The wines

311

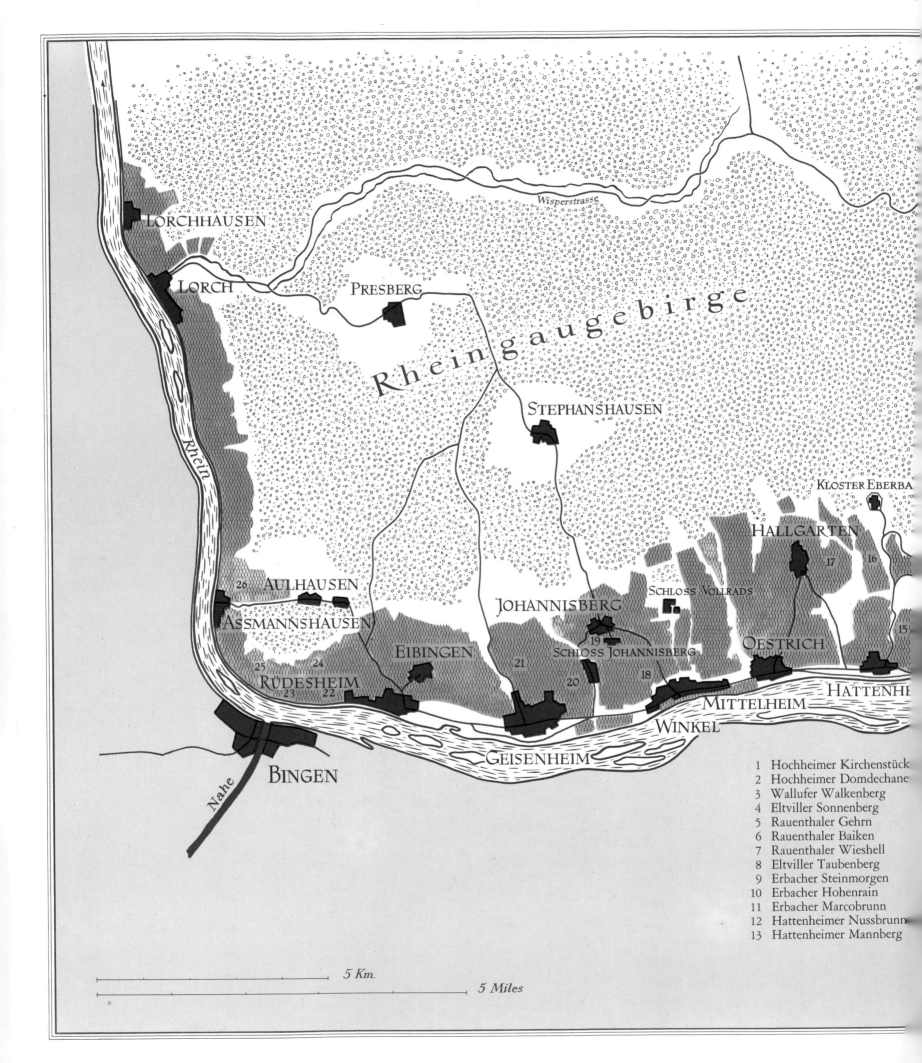

LORCHHAUSEN

LORCH

PRESBERG

Wisperstrasse

Rheingaugebirge

STEPHANSHAUSEN

KLOSTER EBERBA

HALLGARTEN

17   16

26   AULHAUSEN

Schloss Vollrads

ASSMANNSHAUSEN

JOHANNISBERG

15

OESTRICH

EIBINGEN

21   Schloss Johannisberg

19

25   24

20   18

RÜDESHEIM

HATTENHE

23   22

MITTELHEIM

WINKEL

Rhein

GEISENHEIM

Nahe

BINGEN

1 Hochheimer Kirchenstück
2 Hochheimer Domdechane
3 Wallufer Walkenberg
4 Eltviller Sonnenberg
5 Rauenthaler Gehrn
6 Rauenthaler Baiken
7 Rauenthaler Wieshell
8 Eltviller Taubenberg
9 Erbacher Steinmorgen
10 Erbacher Hohenrain
11 Erbacher Marcobrunn
12 Hattenheimer Nussbrunn
13 Hattenheimer Mannberg

5 Km.

5 Miles

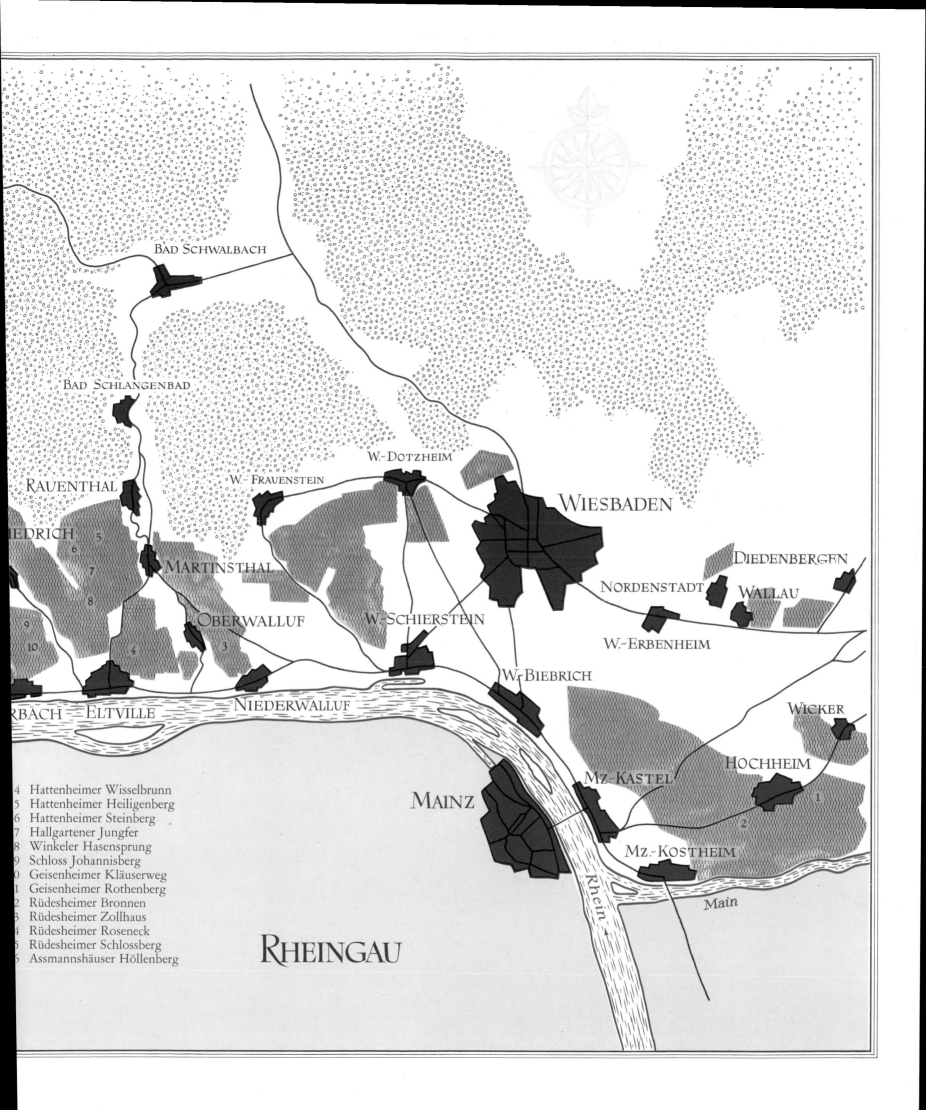

BAD SCHWALBACH

BAD SCHLANGENBAD

RAUENTHAL

W.-DOTZHEIM

W.-FRAUENSTEIN

WIESBADEN

DIEDENBERGEN

IEDRICH

5

6

7

8

9

10

MARTINSTHAL

NORDENSTADT

WALLAU

OBERWALLUF

W.-SCHIERSTEIN

W.-ERBENHEIM

4

3

W.-BIEBRICH

WICKER

RBACH ELTVILLE

NIEDERWALLUF

4   Hattenheimer Wisselbrunn
5   Hattenheimer Heiligenberg
6   Hattenheimer Steinberg
7   Hallgartener Jungfer
8   Winkeler Hasensprung
9   Schloss Johannisberg
0   Geisenheimer Kläuserweg
1   Geisenheimer Rothenberg
2   Rüdesheimer Bronnen
3   Rüdesheimer Zollhaus
4   Rüdesheimer Roseneck
5   Rüdesheimer Schlossberg
6   Assmannshäuser Höllenberg

MAINZ

MZ-KASTEL

HOCHHEIM

1

2

MZ.-KOSTHEIM

Rhein

Main

RHEINGAU

from Eltville, like those from the large vineyards owned by the Graf von Eltz and the Barons Langwerth von Simmern, are of great character.

Erbach too has wines with a world-wide reputation, such as the famous MARKOBRUNN, HOHENRAIN and SIEGELSBERG; Hattenheim can boast of the ENGELMANNSBERG, HASSEL, MANNBERG, NUSSBRUNNEN and WISSELBRUNN; Oestrich the DOOSBERG, KLOSTERBERG and LENCHEN. The EDELMANN and GOLDBERG are the two main growths from Mittelheim, full-bodied with a strong bouquet.

Immediately thereafter comes Winkel; Goethe esteemed its noble wines, such as the DACHSBERG, HASENSPRUNG and JESUITENGARTEN. In the commune of Winkel, too, there is Schloss Vollrads, which has been in the possession of the Greiffenklaus family since the fourteenth century, and nearby is Schloss Johannisberg, presented by the Emperor of Austria to Prince von Metternich in 1816. Some connoisseurs consider the SCHLOSS JOHANNISBERGER the king of German wines, but the HÖLLE and KLAUS are equally magnificent.

Geisenheim produces the ROTHENBERG, KLÄUSERBERG, FUCHSBERG and MÄUERCHEN; and the next down, Rüdesheim, boasts internationally reputed wines: the RÜDESHEIMER BERG, BRONNEN, BURGWEG, KLOSTERLAY, ROSENECK and ROTTLAND and the BISCHOFSBERG and SCHLOSSBERG growths. The Rüdesheim wines are said to be particularly full-bodied.

Assmannshausen is known for its red wines from the *Spätburgunder* grape, the main growths being the HÖLLENBERG and HINTERKIRCH. Some connoisseurs consider that the red wines of Assmannshausen are the best in Germany. Rauenthal produces the BAIKEN, GEHRN, ROTHENBERG and WÜLFEN. These upland wines have a remarkable body and bouquet, and some people say they are for gentlemen only, but their velvety suppleness and delicate perfume recommend them to the ladies too.

Of the wines of Kiedrich we may mention the GRÄFENBERG, WASSEROS and SANDGRUBE. A few miles farther on grows the STEINBERG, the vineyard, like the Abbey of

Lochhausen is the most northerly vineyard of the Rheingau (further north lies the Mittelrhein region). The slopes are steep; the winters, relatively mild, and the warm summers suit the vine. The majority of the vineyard is planted to *Riesling*, which produces a much appreciated wine. However, the great wines come from the area between Wiesbaden and Rüdesheim.

Eberbach, being State property. The name alone has such a reputation that the grower adds only the description of the method used—*Kabinett* (or "special reserve"), *Spätlese* (late picking), *Auslese* (specially selected berries, or grapes), *Beerenauslese* (specially selected berries, or grapes) or *Trockenbeerenauslese* (selected overripe grapes left on the vine till dried in order to achieve the maximum sugar content possible).

There only remains Hallgarten, with its HENDELSBERG, JUNGFER and SCHÖNHELL; its clayey marl produces wines highly esteemed for their great elegance and full-bodied character. The vineyards here rise to a height of some 900 feet in places.

The State domains in the Rheingau date back to 1866, when the Duke of Nassau had to cede his possessions to the King of Prussia. The Steinberg, the largest single vineyard, is 125 acres in extent. The domain also includes vineyards at Rüdesheim, Hattenheim, Rauenthal, Kiedrich and Hochheim, as well as the Assmannshausen vineyards, which produce mainly red wines. The State owns in all over 350 acres, almost all the whites coming from the *Riesling* grape.

The Institute for Tree, Wine and Horticultural Research, founded at Geisenheim in 1872, is in the forefront of wine research in Germany, while the former Cistercian Abbey at Eberbach is a kind of pilgrims' shrine for wine-lovers.

An English poet who compared the German wines to people called the Rheingau wine "a noblewoman". It should be respected accordingly.

MOSELLE – SAAR – RUWER

The three valleys of the Moselle and two of its tributaries, the Saar and the Ruwer, extend for some 190 miles. The winegrowing district of the Moselle stretches from Perl to Koblenz for 125 miles. From the ancient and fairy-tale-like village of Serrig to the confluence with the Moselle near Konz, the Saar district spreads for some 30 miles, and Waldrach-Sommerau is some 75 miles from the confluence of the Moselle with the Ruwer. There are also some good vineyards along such tributaries of the Moselle as the Dhron and the Lieser. Most of the district is in the Rhineland-Palatinate, and only a very small part of it, with 125 acres of vineyards, encroaches upon the Saar.

The three valleys form a unit, though their wines have characteristics all their own. All of them share the typical *Riesling* bouquet and have a fine and fruity acidity. The Saar wines are sparkling and well-bred; the Ruwer wines are noted for their so-called smoky taste and elegant acidity. The Moselles are usually fuller-bodied. The district is divided into the Upper, Middle and Lower Moselle. The vineyards are protected by the cliffs of the Hunsrück and the Eifel mountains. They follow the windings of the river, which wanders so much that, especially in the Middle Moselle, the loops seem to cross their own course and the river triples its length. Hence the exposure keeps changing, so that many sunny slopes facing east and south give way without transition to shady woods and pastures. The canalization of the Moselle has proved advantageous because of the more intense reflection of the sun due to the uniform raising of the water level.

Unlike the vineyards in the Palatinate and the Neckar valley, the vineyards here are situated on the slopes. They are so steep in the Lower Moselle that all work has to be done by hand. As at Bremm, the growers have to carry back in hods the earth washed down by the rains. Here the vineyards can no longer compete within the EEC with vineyards that can be worked by machine.

The banks of the Moselle between the Lorraine border and the junction with the Saar are made of white chalk; thence to the junction with the Ruwer they are the red sandstone of the Trier basin. Only thereafter begin the blueish banks of shale.

Winegrowing in the valley of the Moselle is the oldest in Germany. It may well have been introduced into the Trier region, then Celtic, by Greek colonists from Massilia (Marseilles).

This German wine label gives the following information: 1. the region — Mosel-Saar-Ruwer; 2. the commune — Trittenheim; 3. the vineyard — Altärchen; 4. the type of wine — Riesling + Kabinett, thus a selected Riesling wine; 5. the guarantee of quality — Qualitätswein mit Prädikat.

The old grape variety *Elbling*, which was the only one grown along the Moselle before the Thirty Years War, now covers only 11 per cent of the 25,000 acres of vineyards, which produce only whites. The *Riesling* is ahead with 73 per cent; the remainder is *Müller-Thurgau*. The average yield is 24 million gallons.

The Upper Moselle, stretching from the Luxemburg border to the junction with the Saar near Trier, produces lesser table wines, which are also used for the manufacture of sparkling wines. The Lower Moselle, between Boulay and the confluence with the Rhine, produces ordinary *Konsumwein*, but also in places some very decent table wines, at Bremm, Ediger, Beilstein, Valwig, Pommern and Winningen. Sometimes they have some of the characteristics of Rhine wines. The growers gather them with some difficulty from the parcels of land terraced steeply above each other.

The Middle Moselle is one great vineyard from the old Imperial Roman City of Trier to Alf and Bullay. The most famous villages are Trittenheim with its ALTÄRCHEN, APOTHEKE and LAURENTIUSBERG; then Neumagen (ROSENGÄRTCHEN, ENGELGRUBE and LAUDAMUSBERG), Dhron (HOFBERG, ROTERD and SÄNGEREI) and Piesport (GOLDTRÖPFCHEN, GÜNTERSLAY and FALKENBERG). Piesport is world-famous for the unequalled *finesse* of the perfume of its wines. After Wintrich, with the Ohligsberg and

Geierslay, we very soon come to Brauneberg, which until only fifty years ago was still called Dusemont (from the Latin *in dulce monte*—"on the sweet hill"), a very appropriate name for it, for all the Great Growths, such as the FALKENBERG, HASENLAUFER and JUFFER, have a southern exposure and produce a very delicate bouquet. The following villages produce wines with a world-wide reputation: Lieser (NIEDERBERG), Bernkastel, Kues, Wehlen, Graach, Zeltingen, Erden, Ürzig and Traben-Trarbach. The BERNKASTLER DOKTOR, also sold under the name of DOKTOR UND GRABEN, and, facing it at Bernkastel-Kues, the JOHANNISBRÜNCHEN, KARDINALSBERG and PAULINUSHOFBERG open the way to the culminating point of the Moselle vineyards, Ürzig. The famous wines of Wehlen are the LAY, NONNENBERG and SONNENUHR; at Graach the ABTSBERG, DOMPROBST and HIMMELREICH; at Zeltingen the HIMMELREICH (another one), SONNENUHR and SCHLOSSBERG; at Erden the BUSSLAY, HERRENBERG, PRÄLAT and TREPPCHEN; at Ürzig the WÜRZGARTEN; and at Traben the GAISPFAD, GEIERSLAY, KRÄUTERHAUS, WÜRZGARTEN, ZOLLTURM and KÖNIGSBERG.

The Saar produces wine on its lower stream after emerging from the industrial region. It then becomes a narrow picturesque valley in which the vine roots bristle from the steep and rocky slopes. The vineyards begin near Staadt, and there are decent wines at Serrig,

316

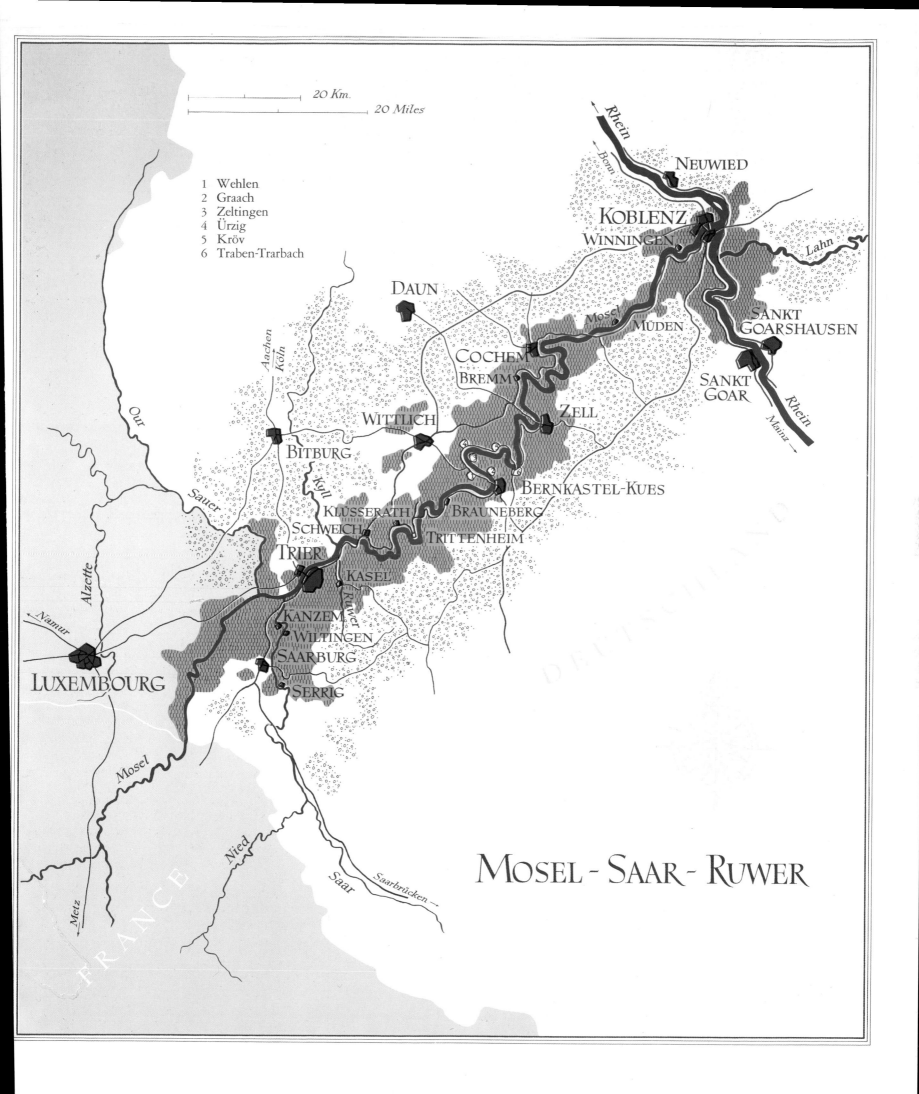

20 Km.

20 Miles

1 Wehlen
2 Graach
3 Zeltingen
4 Ürzig
5 Kröv
6 Traben-Trarbach

Rhein

Bonn

NEUWIED

KOBLENZ

WINNINGEN

Lahn

DAUN

Mosel

MÜDEN

SANKT
GOARSHAUSEN

Aachen
Köln

COCHEM

BREMM

ZELL

SANKT
GOAR

WITTLICH

Rhein

Our

BITBURG

Kyll

BERNKASTEL-KUES

Mainz

Sauer

KLÜSSERATH

BRAUNEBERG

SCHWEICH

TRITTENHEIM

TRIER

KASEL

Ruwer

Namur

KANZEM

Alzette

WILTINGEN

SAARBURG

LUXEMBOURG

SERRIG

DEUTSCHLAND

Mosel

Metz

Nied

Saar

Saarbrücken

MOSEL · SAAR · RUWER

FRANCE

Saarburg and Irsch (Hubertusberg), and especially good ones at Ayl (Kupp), Ockfen (Bockstein, Geisberg and Herrenberg), Wavern (Herrenberg) and Wiltingen (Scharzhofberg, Braune Kupp and Dohr). Wiltingen is the largest viticultural commune in the Saar valley. Its most famous vineyard, the Scharzhofberg, was not planted until 1750.

Some of the best wines from Oberemmel are the Agritiusberg, Scharzberg and Hütte. The Altenberg, Sonnenberg and Hörecker are the best from Kanzem; Altenberg and Euchariusberg are the pride of Krettnach; Filzen produces a Herrenberg; and, lastly, the Falkenstein, from Konz, like the Schartzhofberger from Wiltingen, needs no commune name.

The Ruwer produces great wines at Waldrach (Hahnenberg, Hubertusberg, Jesuitengarten, Jungfernberg and Krone), at Kasel (Nies'gen, Kernagel and Käulchen) and from the two large vineyards at Grünhaus (Maximin Grünhäuser) and Karthäuserhof, which belonged to the Carthusian Order from the fourteenth century on (Eitelsbacher Karthäuser Hofberg). There is also the vineyard at Avelsbach (Altenberg, Herrenberg and Hammerstein). All over the Moselle, Saar and Ruwer districts one is struck by the abundance of ecclesiastical names. The Bishopric of Trier and the monasteries, which have done so much for the cultivation of the vine ever since the establishment of Christianity here, still own the best vineyards, such as the Bernkastel Hospital, founded at Küs by Cardinal Nicolas de Cusa.

Moselle wines cleanse the palate and stimulate the appetite. They go best with fish, hors-d'œuvres and salads. Lively, a soft green in colour, they are of invigorating freshness. When young, Moselle contains a little carbonic acid gas and pricks the tongue; it is slightly sparkling. It is drunk young, for its freshness and character are liable to go off with age. Moselle needs sun; it does not attain its natural sweetness in years when there is not much sun, and has to be improved artificially. "Nowhere else", Baudelaire said, "is so much hard work, so much sweat and so much ardent sun needed to bring the grapes to life and to imbue the wine with soul."

A spectacular bend on the Moselle, slightly exaggerated by the camera lens. The vineyards are those of Kröv on the Middle Moselle. But there are many similar landscapes, for the river winds so much that its course doubles the straightline distance between Koblenz and Trier.

Harvesting *Riesling* grapes in the Ahr valley. The *Riesling* grapes are often picked late (spätlese), or by successive, selected pickings (beerenauslese). These indications are carried on the label if the wine is approved at compulsory official tastings.

The Ahr valley vineyards are amongst the smallest in Germany. There are only 1235 acres along the 15½ miles of valley. The picture shows the Mayschon vineyard. The Ahr reds stand at the forefront of German red wines.

THE VALLEY OF THE AHR

The Ahr virtually follows the northern border of the Rhineland-Palatinate. Winegrowing is restricted to a strip some 15 miles long in the lower valley, where the vine is set on shale. It grows on rocky terraces, very narrow in places, where a thin layer of earth often holds only a few roots. With its 11 winegrowing communes and 1,312 acres, producing 660,000 gallons of wine at most, at the most northerly limit of winegrowing in the world, the Ahr wine district is romantic. Moreover, it is the largest red wine district in Germany, though the 31.1 per cent of *Portugieser* and 25.2 per cent of *Blauer Spätburgunder* are supplemented by 43 per cent of white grapes, 23 per cent *Riesling* and 17 per cent *Müller-Thurgau*. It is to be hoped the region will remain faithful to the *Spätburgunder*, which derives a warmth

and special fineness from the sun-drenched schist. Especially round the State domain, the former monastry of Marienthal, noble, velvety and soft red wines are produced in good years. The winegrowing district begins at Altenahr, where the Ahr finishes its romantic course between the cliffs, continues via Rech, May-schoss and Dernau to Ahrweiler, Marienthal and Wal-portzheim, and ends at Bad Neuenahr and Heimerz-heim well before reaching the Rhine.

The first German wine co-operatives were established in the Ahr district, which formerly experienced great difficulty in marketing its wines; the fact that holdings were only about an acre in extent made it an economic necessity to regroup them if they were to survive as a commercial operation.

319

THE MIDDLE RHINE

All the wines from north of a line running from Bingen to Lochhausen—except the valleys of the Moselle and the Ahr—are designated as coming from the Mittelrhein, or Middle Rhine. The region is part of the Rhineland-Palatinate *Land*, except the northern part, which encroaches upon Rhein-Westfalen. The winegrowing area, stretching for more than 75 miles and containing 104 communes, covers over 2,000 acres. It has constantly diminished over the past few centuries; in 1883 it was still 7,907 acres. As late as 1828 there were 2,903 acres of vineyards in the district of Neuwied; there were no more than 534 acres in 1949. Red wine exists in any quantity only in the Siebenbergen district. The *Riesling* predominates in the Middle Rhine proper (83 per cent). The *Müller-Thurgau* accounts for as much as 37.2 per cent in the Siebenbergen, but elsewhere for only 6.2 per cent. The total yield is some 1,540,000 gallons.

This decline is not due to a falling-off in quality. Industry has drained off labour from winegrowing, and on the flatlands other kinds of fruit are more profitable. The phylloxera, too, was a decisive factor in this reconversion. Faced with such economic risks, most of the Mittelrhein growers decided not to replant vines. On the left bank there are no vineyards north of Koblenz. The main winegrowing districts on the left bank lie south of Koblenz at Steeg, Bachrach, Oberwesel and Boppard, while Kaub and Braubach are on the right bank. On the right bank the vineyards stretch to Königswinter and Niederdollendorf via Leutesdorf, Hammerstein and Leubsdorf. Bachrach was a famous German wine centre until the eighteenth century, mainly because it was the place where the wines from the Palatinate and the Rheinhesse were transhipped because they could not pass the falls upstream from Bingen.

Following the Rheingau, and to the north of it, lie the Mittelrhein vineyards. The river here is at its most romantic, and the vines climb the steep river banks. The famous Pfalz castle is seen in the middle of the Rhine, and perched up on the left, the towers of Gutenfels.

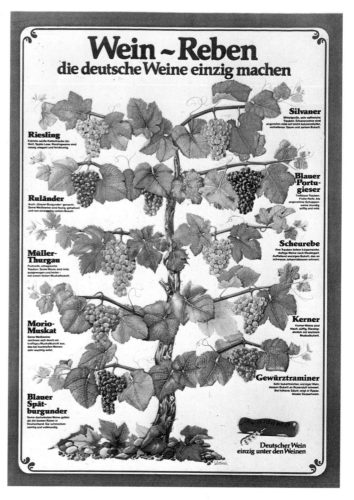

Right: A chart of the usual grape varieties found in West Germany. White wines fill 88 per cent of the winegrowing area, reds 12 per cent. *Müller-Thurgau*, a very resistant variety, takes the lion's share with 27.3 per cent, followed closely by *Riesling*, 20.5 per cent. Then comes *Sylvaner* with 15 per cent. All the other varieties occupy less than 5 per cent each of the land devoted to vinegrowing.

When the *Riesling* is late harvested, the vines have practically their winter aspect. Not only have the leaves turned yellow, but most of them have already fallen.

New German Wine Controls

After the first edition of this book was published, a German law dated 19 July 1971 changed the classification of wines produced in German Federal Republic territory. For several years, old and new labels will co-exist on the market. The principal characteristics of the new legislation are given below. From the date of application of the law, German wines were officially controlled and divided into three categories.

1. German table wines ("Deutsche Tafelweine")

These are ordinary local wines, wines for everyday drinking, and blended wines. After addition of sugar, if necessary, the wines should have a minimum 8.5° alcohol and a maximum of 15°, and an acidity of at least 4.5 g per litre. White wines are considered to be those wines obtained only from white grapes; red wines, wines obtained by the fermentation of red musts made from pressed red grapes; rosé wines, wines made from rosé musts from red grapes. The grape variety may only be indicated if the wine is made from at least 75 per cent of the indicated variety and if the variety gives the wine its character. *Label information:* The mention "deutsch" may only be made if grapes grown in Germany are used. If a table wine comes exclusively from one of the six large winegrowing areas: Oberrhein Römertor, Oberrhein Burgengau, Neckar, Main, Rhein, Mosel, this is also mentioned on the label. The label may also carry the district name ("Bereich") if 75 per cent of the grapes come from the same area, but may never carry the name of a vineyard.

2. Quality wines ("Qualitätsweine")

These are wines meeting certain standards and grown in clearly defined regions. *Label information:* The label, as well as the "Qualitätswein" mention and the identifying test number, must mention the region it came from: Baden, Württemberg, Franken, Hessische Bergstrasse, Rheinpfalz, Rheinhessen, Nahe, Mosel-Saar-Ruwer, Rheingau, Mittelrhein and Ahr, to which is added the name of the vineyard.

3. Superior quality wines with special mention ("Qualitätsweine mit Prädikat")

This category includes all fine wines which contain their own natural sugar. The labels carry the QmP number, and the same general information as category 2, with the addition of one of the following classifications, in ascending order of ripeness: Kabinett (driest of selected, unsugared wine); Spätlese (late gathered); Auslese (late-gathered with high sugar content); Beerenauslese (individual bunches very late-gathered); Trockenbeerenauslese (made from individually selected withered grapes, very luscious wine). Apart from any of these, the label may state "Eiswein", made from grapes frozen on the vine, thus having a strong concentration of flavour and sugar.

The grape variety is indicated if the wine comes from at least 75 per cent of the variety in question, and that it determines the characteristics of the wine. The year may only be indicated if at least 75 per cent of the grapes are harvested in that year.

THE WINES OF THE RHINE

SWISS WINES OF THE UPPER RHINE

CANTON OF THE GRISONS

White wines . . . . . . Malanser Completer, Malanser Tokayer, Tokayer Eigenbau, Churer Tokayer aus dem Lochert

Red wines . . . . Malanser Blauburgunder, Malanser Blauburgunder Fuchsen, Malanser Blauburgunder Rüfiser, Churer Süssdruck Lürlibader, Churer Costamser Beerli, Süssdruck Duc de Rohan, Süssdruck Bündner Rheinwein, Malanser Rüfiwingert, Schloss Freudenberg, Maienfelder Blauburgunder Kuoni-Wii, Maienfelder Schloss Salenegg, Jeninser Chüechler Beerliwein, Malanser Beerli Weisstorkel

CANTON OF ST. GALLEN

White wines . . . . . . Tokayer Hoch Chapf Eichberg, Balgacher Riesling-Sylvaner

Red wines . . . . Altstätter Forst, Altstätter Rebhaldner Blauburgunder, Balgach Beerli Blauburgunder, Rebsteiner Süssdruck Blauburgunder, Hoch Chapf Eichberg, Bernecker Blauburgunder, Sarganser Langstrich Blauburgunder, Bernecker Rosenberger, Balgacher Buggler, Walenstadt Beerli Felixer am Ölberg, Melser Beerli Ritterweg, Portaser Blauburgunder, Baccastieler-Beerli Sevelen, Freudenberger Beerli

CANTON OF THURGAU

White wines . . . . . . Kalchrainer Tokayer, Arenenberg Domaine

Red wines . . . . Nussbaumer, Götighofer, Kalchrainer Blauburgunder, Hüttwiler Stadtschryber

CANTON OF SCHAFFHAUSEN

White wines . . . . . . Löhningen, Munötler Tokayer

Red wines . . . . Buchberger, Gächlinger, Osterfinger, Trasadinger, Steiner, Wilchinger Beerli, Hallauer Blauburgunder, Siblingen Eisenhalder, Osterfinger Blauburgunder, Osterfinger-Beerli Badreben, Hallauer Beerli Graf von Spiegelberg, Blauburgunder Beerli Munötler, Löhninger Clevner Beerli, Chäfer-Steiner Blaurock, Hallauer Süssdruck vom Schälleweg

CANTON OF ZURICH

White wines . . . . . . Riesling-Sylvaner Berg am Irchel, Riesling-Sylvaner Meilen, Meilener Räuschling, Riesling-Sylvaner Stäfner, Tokayer Weiningen, Riesling-Sylvaner Weinigen, Eglisauer Riesling-Sylvaner, Eglisauer Tokayer, Weininger Räuschling, Flurlinger Tokayer, Räuschling Küsnacht, Riesling-Sylvaner Sternenhalde

Red wines . . . . Blauburgunder Oberembach, Blauburgunder Schlosshof Berg am Irchel, Birmenstorfer Klevner, Eglisauer Blauburgunder, Stammheimer Blauburgunder, Eglisauer Stadtberger Beerli, Weiniger Klevner, Worrenberger Blauburgunder Rebhüsli, Blauburgunder Burg Schiterberger, Blauburgunder Schloss Goldenberg, Clävner Sternenhalde, Rudolfinger Beerli Blauburgunder, Stammheimer Beerli Blauburgunder, Clevner Sternhalden Stäfa

CANTON OF AARGAU

White wines . . . . . . Zeininger Riesling-Sylvaner, Bözer Riesling-Sylvaner, Tokayer Schlossberg Villingen, Mandacher Riesling-Sylvaner, Riesling-Sylvaner Würenlingen, Schinznacher Riesling-Sylvaner, Schinznacher Rütiberger

Red wines . . . . Birmenstorfer Klevner, Blauburgunder Klingnauer Kloster Sion, Blauburgunder Schlossberg Villigen, Brestenberger Klevner, Döttinger Clevner Auslese, Döttinger Süssdruck, Elfinger Blauburgunder Schlotterboden, Ennetbadener-Beerli, Goldwändler, Klevner Villiger Steinbrüchler Beerliwein, Rütiberger, Wettinger Herrenberg Blauburgunder, Wettinger Kläfner, Wettinger Scharten, Zeininger Clevner

CANTON OF LUCERNE

White wine . . . . . . Riesling-Sylvaner Schloss Heidegg
Red wine . . . . Schloss Heidegg Clevner

CANTON OF BASEL

White wine . . . . Arlesheimer Schlossberg Gutedel
Red wines . . . . Arlesheimer Blauburgunder, Benkener Blauburgunder, Liestaler Blauburgunder

WINES OF LAKES BIEL AND NEUCHÂTEL

CANTON OF BERN

White wines . . . . . . Ligerzer, Ligerzer Kirchwein, Schafiser, Schafiser Bois de Dieu, Schafiser Engel, Schafiser Stägli-Wy, Schafiser Schlössliwy, Twanner, Twanner Engelwein, Twanner Engelwein pinot gris, Twanner Kapfgut Clos des Merles, Twanner Kapfgut Sous la roche, Twanner Steinächt, Twanner Auslese Johanniter, Der edle Twanner Chroshalde, Twanner Closer, Tschugger, Erlach Chasselas Lamperten, Schlossberg Erlach Gutedel

Red wines . . . . La Neuveville Oeil-de-Perdrix, Twanner Blauburgunder, Schafiser Pinot noir, Tschugger Pinot noir, Schlossberger Erlach Blauburgunder

CANTON OF NEUCHÂTEL

Compulsory generic trade name : Neuchâtel

White wines . . . . . . Pinot gris, Cortaillod, Auvernier, Cressier, Domaine de Champréveyres, Champréveyres de la Ville, Château d'Auvernier, Domaine de Chambleau P.H. Burgat, Goutte d'or, Domaine du Mas des Chaux, Chasse-Peines, Cru des Gravanys, Hôpital Pourtalès, Cressier La Rochette, La Grillette, Clos des Sous-Monthaux, Francœur, Cru des Bourguillards, Cru des Chair d'Ane, Cru des Merloses

Red wines . . . . Pinot noir, la Béroche, Oeil de Perdrix, Cru d'Hauterive, Francarmin, Cru des Gravanys, Hôpital Pourtalès, Pinot noir Cru des Chanez, Cru de la Ville, La Grillette, Clos des Sous-Monthaux, Tour de Pierre

CANTON OF VAUD

Red wines . . . . Salvagnin Clos du Manoir, Salvagnin Grand Nef, Clos Chenevières, Domaine du Château de Valeyres, Pinot noir Clos du Terraillex, Pinot noir Vin des Croisés

WINES OF ALSACE

Zwicker, Edelzwicker, Sylvaner, Pinot blanc-clevner, Riesling, Muscat, Gewürztraminer, Tokay d'Alsace

WINES OF GERMANY

MIDDLE RHINE (Mittelrhein). Two winegrowing districts: Bacharach and Rheinburgengau.

Bacharach district includes vineyards in the communes of Bacharach, Manubach, Oberdiebach, Niederheimbach, Oberheimbach, Trechtingshausen.

Generic name: Schloss Reichenstein

Quality wines: Soonecker Schlossberg – Froher Weingarten – Reifersley – Schloss Hohneck – Klosterberg – Römerberg – Sonne – Wahrheit – Morgenbachtaler.

Generic name: Schloss Stahleck

Quality wines: Kloster Fürstental – Posten – Hahn – Mathias Weingarten – Wolfshöhle – St. Jost – Lennenborn – Schloss Stahlberg – Hambusch – Insel Heylesen Wert – Heilgarten – Mönchwingert – St. Oswald – Langgarten – Rheinberg – Fürstenberg – Kräuterberg – Bischofshub.

The Rheinburgengau district includes the generic names and quality wines from the Rhein-Hunsrück and Rhein-Lahn districts, the Koblenz and Neuwied rural districts, the urban district of Koblenz, as well as Königswinter (Siebengebirge).

Generic name: Herrenberg

Quality wines: Backofen – Rauscheley – Blüchertal – Pfalzgrafenstein – Rossstein – Burg Gutenfels – Kupferflöz – Wolfsnack.

Generic name: Schloss Schönburg

Quality wines: Sieben Jungfrauen – Ölsberg – St. Martinsberg – Bernstein – Goldemund – Römerkrug – Bienenberg – St. Wernerberg – Sonnenstock – Frankenhell – Rosental – Rheingoldberg – Hundert – Beulsberg.

Generic name: Loreleyfelsen

Quality wines: Loreley-Edel – Burg Katz – Burg Maus – Hessern – Rothenack – Teufelstein – Brünnchen – Pilgerfahrt – Liebenstein-Sterrenberg.

Generic name: Burg Rheinfels

Quality wines: Rosenberg – Kuhstall – Ameisenberg – Frohwingert.
The Probsteiberg vineyard (Hirzenach commune) mentions no generic name.

Generic name: Gedeonseck

Quality wines: Elfenley – Fässerlay – Weingrube – Mandelstein – Feuerley – Ohlenberg – Engelstein – Sonnenlay – König Wenzel – Hämmchen.

Generic name: Marksburg

Quality wines: Koppelstein – Marmorberg – Mühlberg – Pfarrgarten – Kreuzberg – Rheinnieder – Liebeneck-Sonnenlay.

Generic name: Burg Hammerstein

Quality wines: Forstberg – Gartenlay – Rosenberg – Römerberg – Monte Jub – Schlossberg – Sonnenberg – Berg – Weisses Kreuz – Stehlerberg – Rheinhöller – Gertrudenberg – In den Layfelsen – Hölle.

Generic name: Drachenfels

Quality wines: Laurentiusberg – Sülzenberg – Rosenberg – Longenberg Berg – Heisterberg – Domley – Ulaneneck – Am Domstein.

AHR Walporzheim/Ahrtal winegrowing district. The generic name Klosterberg covers the whole of the Ahr district.

Eck – Übigberg – Mönchberg – Silberberg – Laacherberg – Schieferlay – Burgberg – Lochmühlerley – Herrenberg – Blume – Hardtberg – Goldkaul – Pfarrwingert – Burggarten – Jesuitengarten – Trotzenberg – Klostergarten – Rosenberg – Stiftsberg – Domlay – Kräuterberg – Gärkammer – Himmlechen – Pfaffenberg – Alte Lay – Rosental – Daubhaus – Silberberg – Iorstberg – Usulinengärtchen – Riegelfeld – Karlskopf – Sonnenschein – Steinkaul – Schieferlay – Sonnenberg – Kirchtürmchen – Landskrone – Burggarten – Kapellenberg.

RHEINGAU. This district includes the winegrowing area of Johannisberg. It extends along the Rhine from Lorchhausen to Wiesbaden, and from there to Flörsheim.

Generic name: Steil

Quality wines: Frankenthal – Höllenberg – Hinterkirch – Berg Kaisersteinfels.

Generic name: Burgweg

Quality wines: Berg Kaisersteinfels – Rothenberg – Kläuserweg – Fuchsberg – Kilzberg – Mäuerchen – Mönchspfad – Schlossgarten – Klaus – Schlossberg – Kapellenberg – KroneP – Bodental-Steinberg – Rosenberg – Seligmacher – Berg Rosenberg – Berg Rottland – Berg – Pfaffenwies – Schlossberg – Bischofsberg – Drachenstein – Kirchenpfad – Klosterberg – Klosterlay – Magdalenenkreuz – Rosengarten.

Generic name: Erntebringer

Quality wines: Kläuserweg – Kilzberg – Klaus – Schwarzenstein – Vogelsang – Hölle – Mittelhölle – Hansenberg – Goldatzel – Klaus – Goldberg – Dachsberg – Schloss Johannisberg.

Generic name: Honigberg

Quality wines: St. Nikolaus – Edelmann – Goldberg – Gutenberg – Schlossberg – Jesuitengarten – Hasensprung – Bienengarten – Schloss Vollrads – Klaus – Dachsberg.

Generic name: Gottesthal

Quality wines: Kosterberg – Lenchen – Doosberg – Schloss Rheinhartshausen.

Generic name: Deutelsberg

Quality wines: Marcobrunn – Schlossberg – Siegelsberg – Honigberg – Michelsmark – Hohenrain – Steinmorgen – Mannberg – Nussbrunnen – Wisselbrunnen – Hassel – Heiligenberg – Schützenhaus – Englemannsberg – Pfaffenberg – Steinberg.

Generic name: Mehrhölzchen

Quality wines: Schönhell – Jungfer – Würzgarten – Hendelberg – Edelmann – Klosterberg.

Generic name: Heilgenstock

Quality wines: Klosterberg – Gräfenberg – Wasserros – Sandgrub – Taubenberg – Langenstück – Sonnenberg – Rheinberg.

Generic name: Steinmächer

Quality wines: Taubenberg – Langenstück – Sonnenberg – Rheinberg – Wildsau – Langenberg – Rödchen – Berg Bildstock – Walkenberg – Oberberg – Fitusberg – Neroberg – Baiken – Gehrn – Wülfen – Rothenberg – Nonnenberg – Dachsberg – Hölle – Marschall – Homberg – Herrnberg – Judenkirch.

Generic name: Daubhaus

Quality wines: Königin Victoriaberg – Hofmeister – Stielweg – Sommerheil – Hölle – Domdechaney – Kirchenstück – Reichesthal – Weiss Erd – Berg – Steig – Herrnberg – Lohrberger Hang – Stein – Goldene Luft – König-Wilhelmsberg – Nonnenberg.

MOSEL-SAAR-RUWER. The area is divided into four winegrowing districts: Zell, Bernkastel, Saar-Ruwer and Obermosel.

Zell district (lower Moselle) which includes the vineyards between Koblenz and Zell.

Generic name: Weinhex

Quality wines: Bleidenberg – Burgberg – Hunnenstein – Bischofstein – Heilgraben – Bienengarten – Königsfels – Marienberg – Röttgen – Burg Bischofsteiner – Bischofstein – Kirchberg – Stolzenberg – Steinchen – Fahrberg – Neuwingert – Fuchshöhle – Gäns – Kehrberg – Schlossberg – Weissenberg – Hamm – Hubertusborn – Ausoniusstein – Klosterberg – Lay – Würzlay – Goldblume – Sonnenring – Fächern – Goldlay – Kahllay – Brauneberg – Rosenberg – Brückstück – Domgarten – Uhlen – Im Röttgen.

Generic name: Goldbäumchen

Quality wines: Götterlay – Bischofstuhl – Herrenberg – Hochlay – Klostergarten – Pinnerkreuzberg – Schlossberg – Sonnenberg – Rüberberger Domherrenberg – Altarberg – Feuerberg – Kirchlay – Brauneberg – Burg Coreidelsteiner – Rosenberg – Sonnengold – Kirchberg – Übereltzer – Funkenberg – Grosslay – Leckmauer – St. Castorhöhle – Sonnenring – Goldberg – Sonnenuhr – Römerberg – Dechantsberg – Juffermauer – Münsterberg – Kurfürst – Zeisel.

Generic name: Rosenhang

Quality wines: Schlossberg – Abtei Kloster Stuben – Herrenberg – Kapellenberg – Römergarten – Servatiusberg – Layenberg – Martinshorn – Rathausberg – Rosenberg – Pfarrgarten – Arzlay – Nikolausberg – Silberberg – Woogberg – Abteiberg – Deuslay – Goldgrübchen – Bienengarten – Vogteiberg – Wahrsager – Greth – Treppchen – Palmberg – Schwarzenberg.

The Lay vineyard (Senheim commune) carries no generic name.

Generic name: Grafschaft

Quality wines: Arrasburg-Schlossberg – Burggraf – Herrenberg-Hölle – Kapellenberg – Katzenkopf – Kronenberg – Pelzerberger – Laurentiusberg – Schlemmertröpfchen – Frauenberg – Brautrock – Graf Beyssel-Herrenberg – Kirchweingarten – Kronenberg – Sonneck – Bienenlay – Calmont – Elzogberg – Engelströpfchen – Feuerberg – Höll – Osterlämmchen – Pfaffenberg – Pfirsichgarten – Schützenlay – Petersberg – Rosenberg – Römerberg – Himmelreich – Klosterkammer – Palmberg Terrassen.

Generic name: Schwarze Katz

Quality wines: Burglay-Felsen – Domherrenberg – Geisberg – Kreuzlay – Nussberg – Petersborn-Kabertchen – Pomerell – Marienburger – Römerquelle – Rosenborn – Adler – Fettgarten – Klosterberg – Königslay Terrassen – Stefansberg – Sonneck.

The Bernkastel district (middle Moselle) which includes the vineyards which lie between Zell, Traben-Trarbach, Erden, Ürzig, Wehlen, Bernkastel, Brauneberg, Drohn, Trittenheim and Ruwer.

Generic name: Vom Heissen Stein

Quality wines: Herzchen – Nonnegarten – Schäferlay – Schelm – Weisserberg – Marienburg – Rosenberg – Falklay – Goldlay – Moullay-Hofberg – Sorentberg.

Generic name: Schwarzlay

Quality wines: Herzlay – Hubertuslay – Falklay – Hahnenschrittchen – Schlossberg – Thomasberg – Wendelstück – Johannisberg – Batterieberg – Edelberg – Ellergrub – Herrenberg – Monteneubel – Steffensberg – Weinkammer – Zeppwingert – Busslay – Prälat – Treppchen – Reichelberg – Rosenberg – Burgberg – Försterlay – Klosterberg – Rotlay – Auf der Heide – Burgweg – Gaispfad – Goldgrube – Hühnerberg – Königsberg – Kräuterhaus – Kreuzberg – Rosengarten – Schatzgarten – Sonnenlay – Tauberhaus – Ungsberg – Würzgarten – Zollturm – Bottchen – Felsentreppchen – Kupp – Lay – Portnersberg.

Generic name: Nacktarsch

Quality wines: Burglay – Herrenberg – Kirchlay – Letterlay – Paradies – Steffensberg.

Generic name: Münzlay

Quality wines: Abtsberg – Domprobst – Himmelreich – Josephshöfer – Nonnenberg – Hofberg – Sonnenuhr – Klosterberg – Abtei – Klosterhofgut – Deutschherrenberg – Schlossberg.

Generic name: Badstube

Quality wines: Bratenhöfchen – Doctor – Graben – Lay – Matheisbildchen.

Generic name: Beerenlay

Quality wines: Niederberg-Helden – Rosenlay – Süssenberg.

Generic name: Kurfürstlay

Quality wines: Schlossberg – Johannisbrünnchen – Kardinalsberg – Rosenberg – Weissenstein – Hasenläufer – Juffer – Juffer-Sonnenuhr – Kammer – Klostergarten – Mandelgraben – Hasenläufer – Kirchberg – Hömerberg – Herrenberg – Paulinsberg – Paulinshofberg – Honigberg – Klosterberg – Römerpfad – Sonnenuhr – Amtsgarten – Elisenberg – Helenenkloster – Sonnenlay – Kätzchen – Kirchlay – Paulinslay – Carlsberg – Eisenberg – Grafschafter Sonnenberg – Mühlberg – Grosser Herrgott – Ohligsberg – Sonnenseite – Stefanslay – Geierslay.

Generic name: Michelsberg

Quality wines: Burglay – Günterslay – Kapellchen – Rosenlay – Engelgrube – Grafenberg – Grosser Hengelberg – Häschen – Hofberger – Nusswingert – Laudamusberg – Rosengärtchen – Roterd – Sonnenuhr – Domherr – Falkenberg – Gärtchen – Goldtröpfchen – Kreuzwingert – Schubertslay – Treppchen – Brauneberg – Geisberg – Niederberg – Rosenberg – Rotlay – Altärchen – Apotheke – Felsenkopf – Leiterchen.

Generic name: St. Michael

Quality wines: Brauneberg – Klostergarten – Schlossberg – Mühlenberg – St. Martin – Sonnelay – Bruderschaft – Köngisberg – Laurentiuslay – Blattenberg – Goldkupp – Zellerberg – Held – Südlay – Klosterberg – Sonnenberg – Enggass – Ritsch – Schiesslay – Würzgarten – Maximiner Klosterlay.

Generic name: Probstberg

Quality wines: Maximiner Burgberg – Held – Maximiner Hofgarten – Hirschlay – Maximiner Herrenberg – Römerberg – Annaberg – Burgmauer.

Saar-Ruwer district which includes the vineyards which lie between Ruwer, Trier, Kanzem, Wiltingen, Saarburg and Serrig.

Generic name: Römerlay

Quality wines: Johannisberg – Dominikanerberg – Herrenberg – Hitzlay – Kehrnagel – Nieschen – Paulinsberg – Timpert – Laykaul – Felslay – Mäuerchen – Abtsberg – Bruderberg – Kuhnchen – Heiligenhäuschen – Schlossberg – Altenberg – Andreasberg – Augenscheiner – Benediktinerberg – Burgberg – Deutschherrenberg – Deutschherrenköpfchen – Domherrenberg – Hammerstein – Jesuitenwingert – Kupp – Kurfürstenhofberg – Marienholz – Maximiner – Rotlay – St. Martiner Hofberg – St. Matheiser – St. Maximiner Kreuzberg – St. Martiner Kreuzberg – St. Petrusberg – Sonnenberg – Thiergarten Unterm Kreuz – Thiergarten Felsköpfchen – Karthäuserhofberg Burgberg – Karthäuserhofberg Kronenberg – Karthäuserhofberg Orthsberg – Karthäuserhofberg Sang – Karthäuserhofberg Stirn – Doktorberg – Ehrenberg – Hubertusberg – Jesuitengarten – Jungfernberg – Krone – Kurfürstenberg – Laurentiusberg – Meisenberg.

Generic name: Scharzberg

Quality wines: Herrenberger – Kupp – Scheidterberger – Herrenberg – Liebfrauenberg – Pulchen – Steinberger – Unterberg – Urbelt – Hubertusberg – Sonnenberg – Vogelsang – Hörecker - Schlossberg – Altenberg – König Johann Berg – Maximin Staadt – Feld – Kirchberg – Auf der Kupp – Brauneberg – Euchariusberg – Falkensteiner – Hofberg – Klosterberg – Sprung – Agritiusberg – Hütte – Karlsberg – Raul – Rosenberg – Bockstein – Zickelgarten – Neuwies – Laurentiusberg – Heppenstein – Jesuitengarten – Antoniusbrunnen – Bergschlösschen – Fuchs – Stirn – Rausch – Saarfelser Marienberg – Brüderberg – Heiligenborn – Hoeppslei – Schloss Saarsteiner – Schloss Saarfelser Schlossberg – Würtzberg – Goldberg – Jesuitenberg – Ritterpfad – Braune Kupp – Braunfels – Gottesfuss – Hölle – Sandberg – Scharzhofberger – Schlangengraben – Herrgottsrock.

Obermosel district (upper Moselle) which includes the vineyards that lie between Liersberg, Fellerich, Onsdorf and Nenning.

Generic name: Königsberg

Quality wines: Dullgärten – Pilgerberg.

Generic name: Gipfel

Quality wines: Schleidberg – Kapellenberg – Schloss Thorner Kupp – Blümchen – Leiterchen – Rochusfels – Hirtengarten – Römerberg – Hubertusberg – Karlsfelsen – Lay – Münstertsatt – St. Georgshof – Albachtaler – Reinig auf der Burg – Rosenberg – Altenberg – Burg Warsberg – Fuchsloch.

Quality vineyards with no generic names: Schlossberg – Römerberg – Klosterberg – Marienberg – Quirinusberg – Hasenberg.

NAHE. The area includes the two districts of Kreuznach and Schloss Böckelheim

Kreuznach district, which includes the vineyards between Bingen-Bingerbrück, Spabrücken, Bad Kreuznach and Langenlonsheim.

Generic name: Schlosskapelle

Quality wines: Felsenberg – Hölle – Schlossgarten – Steyerberg – Rossel – Rothenberg – Schlossberg – Steinköpfchen – Hölle – Johannisberg – Laurenziweg – Klosterpfad – Burgberg – Goldloch – Honigberg – Pittermännchen – Trollberg – Nixenweg – Jungbrunnen Layer Berg – Abtei Ruppertsberg – Hildegardisbrünnchen – Klostergarten – Römerberg – Binderweg – Alteburg – Domberg – Hörnchen – Lieseberg – Otterberg – Saukopf – Sonnenmorgen – Hölle – Preiselberg – Hausgiebel – Schäfchen – Römerberg – Fels – Rosenberg – Honigberg – Apostelberg – St. Martin – Teufelsküche – Hölle – Rosenteich – Hipperich – Sonnenberg – Steinkopf – Königsschloss – Dautenpflänzer – Rheinberg – Trollberg – Pittersberg – Liebehöll – Kapellenberg – Römerberg – Vogelsang – Karthäuser – St. Remigiusberg – Krone – Hörnchen – Junker – Fuchsen.

Generic name: Sonnenborn

Quality wines: St. Antoniusweg – Bergborn – Rothenberg – Königsschild – Lauerweg – Steinchen – Löhrer Berg.

Generic name: Pfarrgarten

Quality wines: Ritterhölle – Sonnenberg – Schlossberg – Herrschaftsgarten – Mönchberg – Hörnchen – Mühlenberg – Felseneck – Laurentiusberg – Sonnenweg – Backöfchen – Pastorenberg – Kirschheck – Johannisberg – Hasensprung – Höllenpfad – Steinrossel – Ratsgrund – Birkenberg – Römerberg – Sonnenlauf – St. Ruppertsberg – Schloss Gutenburg – Schäfersberg – Höll.

Generic name: Kronenberg

Quality wines: Mollenbrunnen – Straussberg – Hofgut – Pastorei – Vogelsang – Schlossgarten – Felsenköpfchen – Osterhöll – Hinkelstein – Forst – Monhard – Narrenkappe – Steinberg – Hungriger Wolf – Mönchberg – Gutental – In den 17 Morgen – Honigberg – Berg – Rosenheck – Hopfgarten – Kahlenberg – Steinweg – Kapellenpfad – Krötenpfuhl – Breitenweg – St. Martin – Brückes – Rodenberg – Tilgesbrunnen – Galgenberg – Höllenbrand – Hirtenhain – Paradies – Nonnengarten – Katzenhölle – Römerhalde – Junker – Himmelgarten – Agnesienberg – Schloss Kauzenberg – In den Mauern – Rosenhügel.

Schloss Böckelheim district, which includes the vineyards that lie between Braunweiler, Martinstein, Meisenheim, Bayerfeld-Steckweiler, Altenbamberg, Bad Münster/Ebernburg and Schloss Böckelheim.

Generic name: Rosengarten

Quality wines: Michaeliskapelle – Helenenpfad – Wetterkreuz – Schlossberg – Steinkreuz – Klostergarten – Fels – Birkenberg – Mühlenberg – Höllenpfad – Hüttenberg – Berg – Sonnenberg – Becherbrunnen – Dellchen – Alte Römerstrasse – Rosengarten – Palmengarten – Goldgrube – Wiesberg – Grafenberg – Mühlberg – Abtei – Pfaffenberg – Im Felseneck – Geisberg – Im Neuberg – Stromberg – Steinkraut – Kellerberg – Kantergrube – Mönchberg – Steuer – Gutenhölle.

Generic name: Paradiesgarten

Quality wines: Goldgrube – Herrenberg – Kastell – Johannisberg – Auf dem Zimmerberg – Heiligenberg – Herrenzehntel – Schlossberg – Frülingsplätzchen – Rosenberg – Halenberg – Rotfeld – Höllenberg – Sonnenberg – Römerstich – Kaulenberg – Marbach – Domberg – Spitalberg – Hunolsteiner – Römerberg –

Vogelsang – Altenberg – Liebfrauenberg – Präsent – Rheingrafenberg – Edelberg – Wildgrafenberg – Lump – Vor der Hölle – Hengstberg – Allenberg – Schwalbennest – Obere Heimbach – Kloster Disibodenberg – Hessweg – Montfort – Kapellenberg – Weinsack – Hahn – Schikanenbuckel – Königsgarten – Feuerberg – Bocksberg – Kahlenberg – Höchstes Kreuz – Liebesbrunnen – Falkenberg – Elkersberg – Pfaffenpfad – Hölle – Graukatz – Rheingasse – Inkelhöll – Rosenberg – Weissenstein – Schloss Randeck – Seidenberg – Layenberg – Hahnhölle – Silberberg – Geissenkopf – Langhölle – Schlossberg – Sonnenplätzchen – Beutelstein – Feuersteinrossel – Römerpfad – Würzhölle – Schloss Stolzenberg – Mittelberg – Aspenberg – Adelsberg.

Generic name: Burgweg

Quality wines: Drachenbrunnen – Kronenfels – Hamm – Römerberg – Kirchberg – Muckerhölle – Mühlberg – Marienpforter Klosterberg – Heimberg – Königsfels – In den Felsen – Kupfergrube – Felsenberg – Pfingstweide – Hermannshöhle – Klamm – Kertz – Rosenheck – Felsensteyer – Pfaffenstein – Stollenberg – Steinberg – Rosenberg – Steinwingert – Hermannsberg – Nonnengarten – Rotenfels – Kickelskopf – Bastei – Kafels – Dellchen – Kirschheck – Oberberg – Sonnenberg – Onkelchen – Klosterberg – Götzenfeld – Rotenfelser im Winkel – Höll – Steigerdell – Königsgarten – Götzenfels – Luisengarten – Feuerberg – Stephansberg – Köhler-Köpfchen – Erzgrube – Felseneck – Rotenberg – Laurentiusberg – Treuenfels – Kehrenberg – Schlossberg – Kaiserberg – Vogelschlag – Kieselberg – Leistenberg.

RHEINHESSEN. Three winegrowing districts: Bingen, Nierstein and Wonnegau.

Bingen district, which includes the vineyards that lie between Bingen, Erbes-Büdesheim, Wörrstadt and Wackernheim.

Generic name: Sankt Rochuskapelle

Quality wines: Johannisberg – Sonnenberg – Bubenstück – Kapellenberg – Kirchberg – Osterberg – Pfarrgarten – Rosengarten – Scharlachberg – Schelmenstück – Schlossberg – Schwätzerchen – Schwarzenberg – Honigberg – Klosterweg – Mainzerweg – Ölberg – Gewürzgärtchen – Goldberg – Hockenmühle – Kreuz – Laberstall – St. Jakobsberg – Schönhölle – Palmenstein – Kirchgärtchen – Klostergarten – Galgenberg – Römerberg – Kieselberg – Hölle – Mandelbaum.

Generic name: Abtei

Quality wines: Daubhaus – Drosselborn – Eselspfad – Hundertgulden – Goldberg – Johannesberg – Rothenberg – St. Laurenzikapelle – Steinert – Honigberg – Steinacker – Mönchpforte – Sankt Georgen – Steinberg – Geyersberg – Klostergarten – Hölle – Sonnenberg – Wissberg – Götzenborn – Osterberg – Sankt Kathrin.

Generic name: Rheingrafenstein

Quality wines: Eselstreiber – Kirchberg – Sonnenköpfchen – Goldenes Horn – Heerkretz – Höllberg – Martinsberg – Äffchen – Haarberg-Katzensteg – Hölle – Ölberg – Sonnenberg – Rheingrafenberg – Fels – Reichskeller – Eichelberg – Kapellenberg – Steige – Klostergarten – Gewürzgarten – Kirchberg – Galgenberg – Eichelberg – Kirschwingert – Kletterberg – Sternberg – Graukatz – Liebfrau – Mönchberg – Alte Römerstrasse.

Generic name: Adelberg

Quality wines: Geiersberg – Goldstückchen – Leckerberg – Hildegardisberg – Hähnchen – Hütte-Terrassen – Kirchenstück – Schönberg – Kachelberg – Geisterberg – Vogelsang – Bingerberg – Klostergarten – La Roche – Pfaffenberg – Rotenpfad – Mandelberg – Ahrenberg – Wingertsberg – Greifenberg – Honigberg – Schildberg – Heiligenpfad – Steigerberg – Rheingrafenberg.

Generic name: Kurfürstenstück

Quality wines: Bockshaut – Kapelle – Saukopf – Geyersberg – Kaisergarten – Wissberg – Schlosshölle – Goldberg – Sonnenberg – Heil – Vogelsang.

Generic name: Kaiserpfalz

Quality wines: Honigberg – Kallenberg – Adelpfad – Römerberg – Bockstein – Heilighäuschen – Klosterbruder – Geissberg – Höllenberg – Steinacker – Burgberg – Höllenweg – Horn – Kirchenstück – Lottenstück – Pares – Rabenkopf – Rheinhöhe – Roten Kreuz – Sonnenberg – Sonnenhang – Schloss-Westernhaus – Täuscherspfad – Goldberg – Hasensprung – Heiligenhäuschen – St. Georgenberg – Klostergarten – Schlossberg – Schwalben – Steinberg.

Nierstein district, which includes the vineyards that lie between Mainz, Gabsheim, Dalheim, Oppenheim, Nierstein and Mettenheim.

Generic name: St. Alban

Quality wines: Burgweg – Ebersberg – Heitersbrünnchen – Hoch – Kapelle – Kreuzberg – Leidhecke – Mönchspfad – Silberberg – Westrum – Reichsritterstift – Glockenberg – Herrnberg – Kellersberg – Pfaffenweg – Börnchen – Lieth – Schlossberg – Hohberg – Ölgild – Edelmann – Hüttberg – Johannisberg – Kirchenstück – Klosterberg – Sand – Weinkeller.

Generic name: Domherr

Quality wines: Römerberg – Teufelspfad – Dornpfad – Kirchberg – Rosengarten – Geiershöll – Herrgottshaus – Villenkeller – Kapellenberg – Haubenberg – Heiligenhaus – Hölle – Pfaffengarten – Probstey – Schlossberg – Mönchspfad – Ritterberg – Sonnenhang – Blume – Bockstein – Lenchen – Spitzberg – Tempelchen – Goldberg – Kirchberg – Sonnenberg.

Generic name: Gutes Domtal

Quality wines: Altdörr – Kranzberg – Steinberg – Doktor – Bergpfad – Knopf – Moosberg – Goldgrube – Königstuhl – Kloppenberg – Silbergrube – Schmittskapellchen – Goldberg – Klosterberg – Sonnenberg – Pfaffenkappe – Gottesgarten – Osterberg – Rheinpforte – Hohberg – Kehr – Dachgewann – Güldenmorgen – Mönchbäumchen – Pilgerweg – Vogelsang.

Generic name: Spiegelberg

Quality wines: Engelsberg – Rothenburg – Bildstock – Brückchen – Ebersberg – Findling – Hölle – Kirchplatte – Klostergarten – Paterberg – Rosenberg – Schloss Hohenrechen.

Generic name: Rehbach

Quality wines: Brudersberg – Goldene Luft – Hipping – Pettenthal.

Generic name: Auflangen

Quality wines: Bergkirche – Glöck – Heiligenbaum – Kranzberg – Ölberg – Orbel – Schloss Schwabsburg – Zehnmorgen.

Generic name: Güldenmorgen

Quality wines: Falkenberg – Höhlchen – Kreuz – Siliusbrunnen – Tafelstein – Daubhaus – Gutleuthaus – Herrenberg – Sackträger – Schützenhütte – Zuckerberg.

Generic name: Krötenbrunnen

Quality wines: Kreuzberg – Schützenhütte – Hexelberg – Römerschanze – Sonnenhang – Liebfrauenthal – Sonnenweg – Eiserne Hand – Sonnenberg – Sankt Julianenbrunnen – Steinberg – Altenberg – Sonnheil – Honigberg – Goldberg – Herrengarten – Paterhof – Schloss – Schlossberg – Aulenberg – Frauengarten.

Generic name: Vogelsgärten

Quality wines: Authental – Bornpfad – Himmelthal – Kreuzkapelle – Steig-Terrassen – Teufelskopf.

Generic name: Petersberg

Quality wines: Homberg – Hundskopf – Schloss Hammerstein – Klosterberg – Sonnenberg – Wingertstor – Pilgerstein – Rosenberg – Hornberg – Kreuzweg – Zechberg – Pfarrgarten – Schlossberg – Fuchsloch – Herrgottspfad – Ölberg – Vogelsang – Osterberg.

Generic name: Rheinblick

Quality wines: Fischerpfad – Frühmesse – Römerberg – Sonnenberg – Hasensprung – Michelsberg – Schlossberg.

Wonnegau district, which includes the vineyards that lie between Mauchenheim, Alzey, Dittelsheim, Worms and Wachenheim.

Generic name: Sybillenstein

Quality wines: Kapellenberg – Pfaffenhalde – Römerberg – Rotenfels – Wartberg – Fröhlich – Himmelacker – Frankenstein – Sonnenberg – Sioner Klosterberg – Mandelberg – Schelmen – Heiliger Blutberg – Hölle – Kirchenstück.

Generic name: Bergkloster

Quality wines: Hasenlauf – Felsen – Goldberg – Feuerberg – Höllenbrand – Königstuhl – Hungerbiene – Mandelbrunnen – Sonnenberg – Sommerwende – Aulerde – Benn – Brunnenhäuschen – Kirchspiel – Morstein – Rotenstein – Steingrube.

Generic name: Pilgerpfad

Quality wines: Hasensprung – Heiligkreuz – Edle Weingärten – Geiersberg – Kloppberg – Leckerberg – Liebfrauenberg – Mönchhube – Mondschein – Pfaffenmütze – Heil – Goldberg – Steinböhl – Kirchberg – Klosterberg – Liebenberg – Rheinberg.

Generic name: Gotteshilfe

Quality wines: Geyersberg – Rosengarten – Stein – Goldberg – Hasenbiss – Neuberg/Leckzapfen.

Generic name: Burg Rodenstein

Quality wines: Seilgarten – Bürgel – Frauenberg – Goldberg – Hubacker – Sauloch – Steig – Katzebuckel – Nonnengarten – Blücherpfad – Deutschherrenberg.

Generic name: Domblick

Quality wines: Kirchenstück – Sonnenberg – Silberberg – Zellerweg am schwarzen Herrgott – Rosengarten – Engelsberg – Schlossgarten – Horn – Rotenberg.

Generic name: Liebfrauenmorgen

Quality wines: Affenberg – Am Heiligen Häuschen – Bildstock – Burgweg – Goldberg – Goldpfad – Hochberg – Kapellenstück – Klausenberg – Kreuzblick – Lerchelsberg – Liebfrauenstift-Kirchenstück – Nonnenwingert – Remeyerhof – Rheinberg – Römersteg – Sankt Annaberg – Sankt Cyriakusstift – Sankt Georgenberg – Schneckenberg.

THE PALATINATE (Rheinpfalz). The area is divided into two winegrowing districts: Mittelhaardt Deutsche Weinstrasse and Südliche Weinstrasse.

Mittelhaardt Deutsche Weinstrasse district, which includes the vineyards that lie between Morschheim, Kirchheimbolanden, Bad Dürkheim, Wachenheim, Forst, Deidesheim and Neustadt.

Generic name: Schnepfenflug vom Zellertal

Quality wines: Heiligenborn – Schlossberg – Hahnenkamm – Goldloch – Sonnenstück – Esper – Im Heubusch – Schlossgarten – Bräunersberg – Am hohen Stein – Breinsberg – Heilighäuschen – Klosterstück – Königsweg – Schwarzer Herrgott.

Generic name: Grafenstück

Quality wines: Burggarten – Heiligenkirche – Klosterschaffnerei – Schlossberg – Goldgrube – Vogelsang – Burgweg – Sonnenberg – Katzenstein – Benn – Hochgericht – Mandelgarten – Rosengarten – Schloss – Hassmannsberg.

Generic name: Höllenpfad

Quality wines: Schlossberg – Bergel – Goldberg – Honigsack – Hütt – Klostergarten – Röth – St. Stephan – Schloss – Frauenländchen – Herrenberg – Herrgottsacker – Kieselberg – Senn – St. Martinskreuz – Feuermännchen – Sonnenberg.

Generic name: Schwarzerde

Quality wines: Goldberg – Held – Orlenberg – Steig – Herrgottsacker – Jesuitenhofgarten – Mandelpfad – Klosterweg – Lerchenspiel – Burgweg – Osterberg – Schafberg – Lange Els – Steinkopf – Geisskopf – Kreuz – Römerstrasse – Steinacker – Schlossgarten – Vorderberg – Kirschgarten – Mandelberg – Schnepp – Kapellenberg.

Generic name: Rosenbühl

Quality wines: Kieselberg – Goldberg – Altenberg – Burgweg – Hahnen – Halde – Hasenzeile.

Generic name: Kobnert

Quality wines: Kapellgarten – Liebesbrunnen – Mandelröth – Kirschgarten – Musikantenbuckel – Oschelskopf – Schwarzes Kreuz – Himmelreich – Honigsack – Kirchenstück – Kronenberg – Steinacker – Herzfeld – Kalkofen – Bettelhaus – Osterberg – Sonnenberg.

Generic name: Feuerberg

Quality wines: Herrenmorgen – Nonnengarten – Steinberg – Kieselberg – Ohligpfad – Bubeneck – Dickkopp – Sonnenberg – Martinshöhe – Annaberg – Kreidekeller – Vogelsang.

Generic name: Saumagen

Quality wines: Horn – Kirchenstück – Nill.

Generic name: Honigsäckel

Quality wines: Herrenberg – Nussriegel – Weilberg.

Generic name: Hochmess

Quality wines: Hochbenn – Rittergarten – Spielberg – Michelsberg.

Generic name: Schenkenböhl

Quality wines: Abtsfronhof – Fronhof – Fuchsmantel – Königswingert – Mandelgarten – Odinstal – Schlossberg.

Generic name: Schnepfendlung an der Weinstrasse

Quality wines: Letten – Stift – Süsskopf – Kreuz – Schlossgarten – Bischofsgarten – Luginsland.

Generic name: Mariengarten

Quality wines: Grainhübel – Hergottsacker – Hohenmorgen – Kalkofen – Kieselberg – Langenmorgen – Leinhöhle – Mäuselhöhle – Paradiesgarten – Elster – Freundstück – Jesuitengarten – Kirschenstück – Musenhang – Pechstein – Ungeheuer – Altenburg – Belz – Böhlig – Gerümpel – Goldbächel – Rechbächel.

Generic name: Hofstück

Quality wines: Nonnenstück – Kirchenstück – Gerümpel – Rosengarten – Klostergarten – Mandelgarten – Sonnenberg – Fuchsloch – Neuberg – Spielberg – Wolfsdarm – Osterbrunnen – Schlossberg – Gaisböhl – Hoheburg – Linsenbusch – Nussbien – Reiterpfad – Spiess.

Generic name: Meerspinne

Quality wines: Biengarten – Kapellenberg – Mandelgarten – Schlössel – Bürgergarten – Herrenletten – Herzog – Mandelring – Idig – Jesuitengarten – Ölberg – Reiterpfad – Bischofsweg – Eselshaut – Glockenzehnt – Johannitergarten – Kurfürst – Spiegel – Mönchgarten.

Generic name: Rebstöckel

Quality wines: Johanniskirchel – Ölgässel – Paradies – Feuer – Kaiserstuhl – Kirchberg – Schlossberg – Grain – Erkenbrecht.

Generic name: Pfaffengrund

Quality wines: Berg – Kalkberg – Kreuzberg – Mandelberg – Gässel – Römerbrunnen – Kroatenpfad – Langenstein – Lerchenböhl.

Südliche Weinstrasse, which includes the vineyards that lie to the south of Neustadt.

Generic name: Mandelhöhe

Quality wines: Mandelberg – Oberschloss – Römerweg – Heiligenberg – Immengarten – Kapellenberg – Kirchenstück.

Generic name: Schloss Ludwigshöhe

Quality wines: Bergel – Blücherhöhe – Heidegarten – Heiligkreuz – Kastaniengarten – Klostergarten – Mühlberg – Schwarzer Letten – Baron – Kirchberg – Zitadelle.

Generic name: Ordensgut

Quality wines: Forst – Mandelhang – Rosengarten – Schloss – Kapelle – Kirchenstück – Letten – Klosterpfad – Schlossberg – Heide – Michelsberg.

Generic name: Trappenberg

Quality wines: Gottesacker – Hochgericht – Gollenberg – Ortelberg – Neuberg – Osterberg – Rossberg – Sonnenberg – Bildberg – Kirchberg – Roterberg – Klostergarten – Kahlenberg – Alter Berg – Narrenberg – Schlittberg – Bründelsberg – Doktor – Schlossberg.

Generic name: Bischofskreuz

Quality wines: Rosenkranz – Altenforst – St. Annaberg – Schäwer – Schlossgarten – Höhe – Herrenbuckel – Vogelsprung – Zechpeter – Hölle – Hohenrain – Herrenberg – Kaiserberg – Kirchenstück – Rosenkränzel – Simonsgarten – Forstweg – Silberberg.

Generic name: Königsgarten

Quality wines: Kirchberg – Latt – Seligmacher – Rosenberg – Kastanienbusch – Mandelberg – Biengarten – Kalkgrube – Klostergarten – Münzberg – Altes Löhl – Im Sonnenschein – Mönchspfad.

Generic name: Herrlich

Quality wines: Hasen – Kaiserberg – Engelsberg – Am Gaisberg – Rittersberg – Abtsberg – Schäfergarten – Sonnenberg – Pfaffenberg – Mütterle.

Generic name: Kloster Liebfrauenberg

Quality wines: Altenberg – Kirchberg – Pfaffenberg – Sauschwänzel – Steingebiss – Venusbuckel – Mandelpfad – Rosenberg – Frühmess – Narrenberg – Herrenpfad – Rosengarten – Maria Magdalena – Silberberg – Frohnwingert – Schlossberg.

Generic name: Guttenberg

Quality wines: Wonneberg – Kirchhöh – Gräfenberg – Galgenberg – Lerchenberg – Herrenberg – Eselsbuckel – Sonnenberg – Wolfsberg – Herrenwingert – Krapfenberg.

HESSISCHE BERGSTRASSE. The wine law of 1971 named the small Hessische Bergstrasse area an independent winegrowing district lying between Zwingenberg and Heppenheim. It includes the districts of Starkenburg and Umstadt.

Starkenburg district.

Generic name: Schlossberg
Quality wines: Eckweg – Guldenzoll – Maiberg – Steinkopf – Centgericht – Stemmler.

Generic name: Wolfsmagen
Quality wines: Paulus – Hemsberg – Streichling – Kirchberg – Kalkgasse.

Generic name: Rott
Quality wines: Herrnwingert – Fürstenlager – Höllberg – Steingeröll – Alte Burg.
The Mundklingen vineyard (Seeheim commune) carries no generic name.

Umstadt district.
Quality wines: Steingerück – Herrnberg – Stachelberg – Rossberg – Wingertsberg.

FRANCONIA (Franken). The Franconian winegrowing area (Bavaria) includes three districts: Mainviereck, Maindreieck and Steigerwald, which are attached for administrative reasons to Lower Franconia. The only Bavarian winegrowing district is the Bayerischer Bodensee (Lake Constance region). It is thus dealt with in this section.

Mainviereck district, which includes the vineyards that lie between Hörstein, Aschaffenburg, Grossostheim, Miltenberg and Kreuzwertheim.

Generic name: Reuschberg

Quality wines: Abtsberg.

Quality wines which carry no generic name: Apostelgarten – Steinberg – Pompejaner – Schlossberg – Sanderberg.

Generic name: Heiligenthal

Quality wines: Reischklingeberg – Harstell.

Quality wines which carry no generic name: Lützelalterberg – Johannisberg – Jesuitenberg – Hochberg – Schlossberg – Bischofsberg – Klostergarten – Steingrübler – Mainhölle – Centgrafenberg – Predigtstuhl – Kaffelstein.

Maindreieck district, which includes the vineyards that lie between Gambach, Homburg, Würzburg, Randersacker and Escherndorf.

Quality wines which carry no generic name: Kallmuth – Edelfrau – Alter Berg – Oberrot – Krähenschnabel.

Generic name: Burg

Quality wines: Trautlestal – Schlossberg – Heroldsberg – St. Klausen – Scheinberg.

Generic name: Rosstal

Quality wines: Arnberg – First – Stein – Kalbenstein – Im Stein – Langenberg – Kelter.

Generic name: Ravensburg

Quality wines: Johannisberg – Scharlachberg – Weinsteig – Wölflein – Sommerstuhl – Benediktusberg.

Quality wines which carry no generic name: Sonnenschein – Kobersberg – Wurmberg – Paffenberg – Stein – Stein/Harfe – Schlossberg – Innere Leiste – Abtsleite – Kirchberg – Dabug.

Generic name: Ewig Leben

Quality wines: Teufelskeller – Sonnenstuhl – Marsberg – Pfülben.

Generic name: Ölspiel

Quality wines: Steinbach – Reifenstein.

Quality wines which carry no generic name: Kapellenberg – Mönchsleite – Königin – Feuerstein – Fischer – Markgraf – Babenberg.

Generic name: Hofrat

Quality wines: Maustal – Cyriakusberg – Wilhelmsberg – Heisser Stein – Sonnenberg – Kaiser Karl – Hofstück – Zobelsberg – Pfaffensteig.

Generic name: Honigberg

Quality wines: Berg-Rondell – Sonnenleite.

Generic name: Kirchberg

Quality wines: Karthäuser – Vögelein – Kreuzberg – Eselsberg – Höll – Sonnenberg – Katzenkopf – Rosenberg – Lump – Fürstenberg – Berg – Landsknecht – Ratsherr – Sonnenleite – Glatzen – Zehntgraf.

Quality wines which carry no generic name: Schlossberg – Rosenberg – Peterstirn – Mainleite.

Steigerwald district, which includes the vineyards that lie between Wipfeld (south of Schweinfurt) and Iphofen.

Generic name: Kapellenberg

Quality wines: Ölschnabel – Nonnenberg – Kronberg – Eulengrund.

Quality wines which carry no generic name: Stollberg – Teufel – Krone – Sonnenwinkel – Vollburg – Herrenberg – Monchshang – Langstein – Schlossleute – Wutschenberg – Burg Hoheneck.

Generic name: Schild

Quality wines: Altenberg – Bastel.

Generic name: Herrenberg

Quality wines: Schlossberg – Hohnart – Bausch – Kirschberg – Kugelspiel – Trautberg – Feuerbach – Reitsteig.

Generic name: Schlossberg

Quality wines: Wachhügel – Storchenbrünnle – Küchenmeister – Schwanleite – Kiliansberg.

Generic name: Burgweg

Quality wines: Vogelsang – Julius-Echter-Berg – Kronsberg – Kalb.

Generic name: Schlossstück

Quality wines: Herrschaftsberg – Paradies – Hohenbühl – Tannenberg.

Bayerischer Bodensee district.

Quality wines which carry no generic name: Seehalde – Sonnenbüschel.

BADEN. The Baden area is subdivided into seven winegrowing districts: Badisches Frankenland, Badische Bergstrasse/Kraichgau, Ortenau, Breisgau, Kaiserstuhl/Tuniberg, Markgräflerland, and Bodensee.

Badisches Frankenland district, which includes the vineyards that lie between Wertheim, Tauberbischofsheim, Lauda, Königshofen, Boxberg and Krautheim (rural districts of Buchen and Tauberbischofsheim).

Generic name: Tauberklinge

Quality wines: Altenberg – Beilberg – Ebenrain – Edelberg – First – Frankenberg – Heiligenberg – Herrenberg – Hirschberg – Hoher Herrgott – Kailberg – Kemelrain – Kirchberg – Mandelberg – Mühlberg – Nonnenberg – Satzenberg – Schlossberg – Silberquell – Sonnenberg – Stahlberg – Steinklinge – Turmberg – Walterstal.

Badische Bergstrasse/Kraichgau district, which includes the vineyards that lie between Laudenbach, Heidelberg, Wiesloch, Bruchsal and Karlsruhe (rural districts of Bruchsaal, Karlsruhe, Heidelberg, Mannheim, Mosbach, Pforzheim and Sinsheim, as well as the urban districts of Heidelberg and Karlsruhe).

Generic name: Rittersberg

Quality wines: Heiligenberg – Herrnwingert – Hubberg – Kahlberg – Kuhberg – Madonnenberg – Olberg – Sandrocken – Schlossberg – Sonnberg – Sonnenseite ob der Bruck – Stephansberg – Staudenberg – Wüstberg.

Ortenau district, which includes the vineyards that lie between Baden-Baden, Bühl, Achern, Offenburg and Niederschopfheim (rural districts of Offenburg, Kehl, Bühl, and Rastatt, together with the urban district of Baden-Baden.

Generic name: Schloss Rodeck

Quality wines: Altenberg – Alter Gott – Althof – Betschgräber – Bienenberg – Burg Windeck – Kastanienhalde – Eckberg – Eichwäldle – Engelsfelsen Frühmessler Gänsberg – Grafensprung – Gut Alsenhof – Heiligenstein – Hex vom Dasenstein – Kestelberg – Klosterbergfelsen – Klostergut – Fremersberger – Feigenwäldchen – Klostergut Schelzberg – Klotzberg – Kreuzberg – Mauerberg – Pfarrberg – Sätzler – Schlossberg – Schloss Neu-Windeck – Sommerhalde – Sonnenberg – Steingrübler – Sternenberg – Stich den Buben – Wolfhag – Yburgberg.

Generic name: Fürsteneck

Quality wines: Abtsberg – Amselberg – Andreasberg – Bergle – Bienengarten – Franzensberger – Freudental – Josephsberg – Kapellenberg – Kasselberg – Kinzigtäler – Kochberg – Kreuzberg – Nollenköpfle – Ölberg – Plauelrain – Renchtäler – Schlossberg – Schloss Grohl – Steinberg.

Breisgau district, which includes the vineyards that lie between Oberschopfheim, near Offenburg, Lahr and Freiburg-im-Bresgau (communes in the rural district of Freiburg north of the Dreisam and east of the Karlsruhe-Bâle autobahn, and part of the urban district of Freiburg north of the Driesam, together with the rural districts of Emmendingen and Lahr).

Generic name: Schutterlindenberg

Quality wines: Haselstaude – Herrentisch – Kirchberg – Kronenbühl.

Generic name: Burg Lichteneck

Quality wines: Alte Burg – Bienenberg – Hummelberg – Herrenberg – Kaiserberg – Roter Berg – Schlossberg – Sommerhalde.

Generic name: Burg Zähringen

Quality wines: Bergle – Eichberg – Halde – Roter Bur – Schlossberg – Sonnenberg – Sonnhalde.

Kaiserstuhl/Tuniberg district, which includes the vineyards that lie between Riegel, Sasbach, Bickensohl, Achkarren, Ihringen and Munzingen (communes to the west of the Karlsruhe-Bâle autobahn forming part of the rural districts of Freiburg-im-Bresgau and Emmendingen).

Generic name: Vulkanfelsen

Quality wines: Augustinerberg – Bassgeige – Castellberg – Doktorgarten – Eckartsberg – Eckberg – Eichberg – Eichert – Engelsberg – Enselberg – Feuerberg – Fohrenberg – Gestühl – Hasenberg – Henkenberg – Herrenstück – Herrenbuck – Hochberg – Käsleberg – Kirchberg – Kreuzhalde – Lasenberg – Lerchenberg – Limburg – Lützelberg – Ölberg – Pulverbuck – Rosenkranz – Rote Halde – Scheibenbuck – Schlossberg – Schlossgarten – Silberberg – Steinbuck – Steinfelsen – Steinhalde – Steingrube – Steingrüble – St. Michaelsberg – Tannacker – Teufelsburg – Winklerberg.

Generic name: Attilafelsen

Quality wines: Bühl – Franziskaner – Kapellenberg – Kirchberg – Rebtal – Rotgrund – Sonnenberg – Steinmauer.

Markgräflerland district, which includes the vineyards that lie between Freiburg-im-Bresgau, Bad Krozingen, Müllheim and Weil (rural districts of Lörrach and Müllheim, the communes in the rural and urban districts of Freiburg-im-Bresgau south of the Dreisam and east of the Karlsruhe-Basel autobahn).

Generic name: Lorettoberg

Quality wines: Alemannenbuck – Altenberg – Batzenberg – Dürrenberg – Höllberg – Höllhagen – Jesuitenschloss – Kapuzinerbuch – Kirchberg – Maltesergarten – Oberdürrenberg – Ölberg – Rosenberg – Sommerberg – Sonnhohle – Schlossberg – Steinberg – Steingrüble – Steinler.

Generic name: Burg Neuenfels

Quality wines: Altenberg – Castellberg – Frauenberg – Gottesacker – Höllberg – Kirchberg – Letten – Paradies – Pfaffenstück – Reggenhag – Römerberg – Röthen – Rosenberg – Schlossgarten – Sonnenstück – Sonnhalde – Sonnhole – Schäf.

Generic name: Vogtei Rötteln

Quality wines: Hornfelsen – Kapellenberg – Kirchberg – Ölberg – Sonnenhohle – Sonnhohle – Schlipf – Steinacker – Steingässle – Stiege – Wolfer.

Bodensee district (Lake Constance), which includes the vineyards that lie between Überlingen, Markdorf, Immenstadt and Constance, and those of the Isle of Reichenau (rural districts of Waldshut, Constance, Stockach and Überlingen).

Generic name: Sonnenufer

Quality wines: Bengel – Burgstall – Chorherrnhalde – Elisabethenberg – Felsengarten – Fohrenberg – Haltnau – Hochwart – Jungfernstieg – Kirchhalde – Königsweingarten – Leopoldsberg – Lerchenberg – Olgaberg – Rieschen – Sängerhalde – Sonnenhalde – Schlossberg – Kapellenberg – Steinler.

WÜRTEMBERG. The area includes three winegrowing districts: Kocher-Jagst-Tauber, Württembergisch Unterland (Lower Würtemberg) and Remstal-Stuttgart.

Kocher-Jagst-Tauber district, which includes the vineyards that lie between Markelsheim (near Bad Mergentheim), Künzelsau and Mockmühl (rural districts of Künzelsau and Mergentheim; communes of Bittelbronn, Jagsthausen, Mockmühl, Olnhausen, Roigheim, Siglingen, Widdern and Züttlingen in the rural district of Heilbronn; communes of Forchtenberg, Ernsbach and Sindringen in the rural district of Öhringen).

Generic name: Tauberberg

Quality wines: Hardt – Karlsberg – Mönchsberg – Probstberg – Röde – Schafsteige – Schmecker.

Generic name: Kocherberg

Quality wines: Altenberg – Ammerlanden – Burgstall – Engweg – Flatterberg – Heiligkreuz – Hofberg – Hoher Berg – Schlüsselberg – Sommerberg.

Württembergisch Unterland (Lower Würtemberg) district, which includes the vineyards which lie between Brettach, Heilbronn, Knittlingen, Lugwigsburg and Rietenau (south-west part of the rural district of Backnang to south-west of the communes of Nassach, Oppenweiler, Sulzbach, Murrhardt and Fornsbach; rural district of Heilbronn excluding communes mentioned under Kocher-Jagst-Tauber; the urban district of Heilbronn, rural district of Öhringen excluding communes mentioned under Kocher-Jagst-Tauber; rural district of Vaihingen/Enz).

Generic name: Staufenberg

Quality wines: Berg – Himmelreich – Kayberg – Scheuerberg – Schön – Stahlbühl – Stiftsberg – Vogelsang – Wartberg.

Generic name: Lindelberg

Quality wines: Dachsteiger – Goldberg – Himmelreich – Margarete – Schlossberg – Schneckenhof – Schwobajörgle – Spielbühl – Verrenberg.

Generic name: Salzberg

Quality wines: Altenberg – Althälde – Dezberg – Dieblesberg – Eberfürst – Frauenzimmer – Hundsberg – Nonnenrain – Paradies – Ranzenberg – Schemelsberg – Schlierbach – Sommerhalde – Steinacker – Wildenberg – Wohlfahrtsberg – Zeilberg.

Generic name: Schozachtal

Quality wines: Burgberg – Burg Wildeck – Rappen – Schlossberg – Sommerberg.

Generic name: Wunnenstein

Quality wines: Forstberg – Götzenberg – Harzberg – Lichtenberg – Oberer Berg – Schlosswengert – Steinberg – Süssmond – Wartberg.

Generic name: Kirchweinberg

Quality wines: Altenberg – Eselsberg – Herrlesberg – Hohe Eiche – Jungfer – Katzenbeisser – Mühlberg – Nonnenberg – Riedersbückele – Roter Berg – Schelmenklinge – Schlossberg – Sonnenberg.

Generic name: Heuchelberg

Quality wines: Altenberg – Dachsberg – Grafenberg – Gräfenberg – Hahnenberg – Hohenberg – Jupiterberg – Kaiserberg – Katzenöhrle – Krähenberg – Leiresberg – Mönchsberg – Michaelsberg – Ochsenberg – Ruthe – Schlossberg – Sonnenberg – Sonntagsberg – Staig – Steingrube – Vogelsang – Wolfsaugen – Zweifelberg.

Generic name: Stromberg

Quality wines: Eichelberg – Eilfingerberg – Klosterstück – Forstgrube – Halde – Heiligenberg – Höllisch Feuer – Kirchberg – Klosterberg – König – Kupferhalde – Lerchenberg – Lichtenberg – Liebenberg – Reichshalde – Sauberg – Schranzreiter – Sonnenberg – Steinbachhof – Wachtkopf.

Generic name: Schalkstein

Quality wines: Alter Berg – Berg – Burgberg – Felsengarten – Güldenkern – Käsberg – Katzenöhrle – Kelterberg – Königsberg – Mühlbächer – Neckarberg – Neckarhälde – Rozenberg – Schlossberg – Sankt Kohännser – Wurmberg.

Remstal-Stuttgart district, including the urban district of Stuttgart, and the rural districts of Esslingen, Leonberg, Nürtingen and Waiblingen, also the town of Metzingen in the rural district of Reutlingen.

Generic name: Weinsteige

Quality wines: Abelsberg – Ailenberg – Altenberg – Berg – Bopser – Gips – Goldberg – Götzenberg – Halde – Herzogenberg – Hinterer Berg – Kirchberg – Kriegsberg – Lämmer – Lenzenberg – Mönchberg – Mönchhalde – Scharrenberg – Schlossberg – Steingrube – Steinhalde – Wetzstein – Zuckerle.

Generic name: Kopf

Quality wines: Berg – Berghalde – Grafenberg – Greiner – Grossmulde – Holzenberg – Hörnle – Hungerberg – Rossberg – Schlossberg – Sommerhalde – Söhrenberg – Wanne.

Generic name: Wartbühl

Quality wines: Altenberg – Brotwasser – Gastenklinge – Häder – Happenhalde – Haselstein – Himmelreich – Käppele – Klingle – Lichtenberg – Lindhälder – Luginsland – Maien – Nonnenberg – Pulvermächer – Sonnenberg – Steingrüble – Wetzstein – Zügernberg.

Generic name: Sonnenbühl

Quality wines: Altenberg – Burghalde – Hintere Klinge – Mönchberg.

Generic name: Hohenneuffen

Quality wines: Hofsteige – Schlosssteige.

THE WINES
OF CENTRAL EUROPE,
THE BALKANS AND
THE USSR

JOSEPH JOBÉ, BORIS POGRMILOVIC and SERGUEI KASKO

At the time of the Roman Empire, the vine was cultivated in Spain, Gaul and Helvetia as well as along the frontiers of the Empire, on the Rhine and on the Danube. In the Middle Ages, all the countries of central Europe produced some wine. However the climate and geological conditions as well as the economic and political fluctuations were less favourable to wine production in these countries than, for example, in France and Italy.

Today Czechoslovakia, of all the central European countries, is the one where the least wine is produced and drunk; just over a gallon per person per year. It is easy to understand this: the vineyards, situated at the farthest point north of the viticultural zone, are only cultivated on a marginal basis. However, at the beginning of the seventeenth century, before the Thirty Years War, even Bohemia, and in particular the area around Prague, was a country of vineyards and rich in wine. Before phylloxera attacked the stock, the Czech vineyards were as important as those of the present republic of Austria. It is true that the last few centuries have seen a slight change in climate which has adversely affected the vine, but there are other reasons for this regression. Czechoslovakia, Austria, Hungary and part of Yugoslavia all once belonged to a single large conglomeration of which Austria was the predominant element. Within this Empire, an increase or a reduction in the amount of land allotted to the cultivation of the vine depended not only on climatic conditions but also on historical events. Moreover, certain provinces, especially Hungary, suffered from the influence and invasion of the Moslem Turks, who were not wine drinkers. As wine was sometimes scarce in the most highly productive areas, a greater effort was required from the winegrowers in other regions of the Empire. At the end

of First World War, each of the new states born of the fall of the Austro-Hungarian Empire had to view the future in a new light.

The Austrian vineyards, more ancient than the name of the country, have made very little progress. The vine here is cultivated on a very small scale and is confined to the eastern part of the country.

In Czechoslovakia, however, the vine covered 42,000 acres in 1917 and 25,000 acres in 1947; today it covers about 98,840 acres. The Hungarian vineyards have developed on quite a different scale. Here, production has always been maintained (1973-1977) at around 495,000 acres and only to fell to 429,954 acres in 1979. Hungarians drink from $5\frac{1}{2}$ to $6\frac{1}{2}$ gallons of wine per person per year, and export 1/5 of their production.

The Greeks as much as the Romans were responsible for the introduction of the vine to Yugoslavia, where its development was further encouraged by the lords of the land and the monasteries. Under Turkish domination, the actual area under cultivation dwindled, but it did not disappear entirely. Since the beginning of this century, the area under vines has doubled. Consumption *per capita* is on a par with the neighbouring countries of Austria, Hungary and Bulgaria.

In Rumania and Bulgaria it would seem the vine was first introduced by the Greeks and later by the Romans. These two countries have better climatic conditions than Czechoslovakia, and in Rumania especially, the influence of the Black Sea does much to temper the excesses of the continental climate. In that country, the vine grows wherever the soil is favourable and the sun shines sufficiently. Despite a long period of submission to the Turkish Empire, the Rumanians continued to grow the vine though their overlords cared little for the fruits of their labour.

In 1913, Rumania had only 178,000 acres of soil under cultivation; today it has about 827,785. It produces more white wine than red, while in Bulgaria the opposite is the case. The increase of production continues under the incentive of co-operatives.

In Bulgaria, the soil planted to vines in 1913 was 131,000 acres; today it is about 494,200 acres and consumption has more than doubled in the last ten years. It is now 3 to 5 gallons per person per year.

A similar situation exists in southern Russia: in 1914 the vineyards were spread over 526 acres, while today they have developed to cover about 2 1/2 million. It is true that the Russians are not great consumers of still wines; they prefer sparkling wines to the extent of about 200 bottles a year per thousand inhabitants.

Throughout the whole area, which stretches from Prague to the Black Sea and the Adriatic, there is only one wine as famous as the "great" wines: TOKAY.

AUSTRIA

Today Austria produces much less wine than it once did. The ebb and flow of history are responsible for this decrease. The Romans most probably introduced the vine to the banks of the Danube 2,000 years ago. After the invasion of the Barbarians who destroyed the Roman colonies, the vines were replanted under Emperor Otto I, from the year 955 onwards. Towards the end of the Middle Ages, the vine covered 200,000 acres in Lower Austria alone. When neighbouring Hungary was occupied by the Turks in 1526, the whole wine trade—and the competition in wines—between the two countries came to an end. As one result, for one and a

This wine label is rather confusing to the non-initiated. It should perhaps be pointed out that Gumpoldskirchen is the commune from which the wine comes, south of Vienna, Stocknarren is the vineyard, and Spätrot-Rotgipfler the grape variety.

WINZERGENOSSENSCHAFT
Gumpoldskirchen
SPÄTROT · ROTGIPFLER
Stocknarren
ECHT NUR MIT KORKBRAND
WIG

half centuries the amount of land under cultivation in Austria increased greatly. The present area under cultivation is only a tenth of what it used to be at its zenith. Today, some 138,376 acres of vineyards produce 57,194,800 gallons of wine. As the country imports 5,499,500 gallons, it may be deduced that every Austrian drinks an average of 3.3 gallons of wine a year, as against 15 gallons of beer. Austria exports 3,959,640 to 5,499,500 gallons of wine a year, nearly all white.

In fact, most of the wine produced (85 per cent) is white wine made from various grape-stocks. The best known are the *Riesling*, the *Traminer*, the *Sylvaner*, as well as the *Grüner Veltliner*. Sometimes the *Sauvignon*, *Rotgipfler* and *Muskat-Ottonel* are also used.

Austrian wines have been much appreciated for many years. Nearly four centuries ago, in 1580, Johannes Rasch wrote an important work on viticulture in this country. At the end of the seventeenth century wines were already classified according to their quality, and the list was ratified by the Imperial Court in 1673.

In 1780, the Empress Maria Theresa promulgated a law on wine which still affects the industry today. Certain provisions of this law stated that every vineyard had the right to sell the wine from its vines without paying taxes. When a wine-merchant had wine in his cellar, he would place a crown of leaves or straw above his cellar-door to indicate to the passer-by that he was welcome within. Here, he might rest himself and partake of some liquid refreshment. This was the origin of the famous *Heurigen*, where every year the Viennese and countless numbers of tourists go to enjoy a few moments of laughter and merry-making. Under the shady bowers, amidst a lovely countryside and preferably in good company, the lover of white wine can savour the best local products such as GRINZING, SIEBE-RING and NUSSDORF, as well as WIENER NUSSBERG, probably the best of all. Let us hasten to add that the vineyards around Vienna are neither the only ones, nor even the best in the country.

The winegrowing area of Burgenland includes the banks of Lake Neusiedel and, farther south, the area around the town of Eisenberg. Usually, local wines are drunk in such places as Oggau, Mörbisch, Rust, St.

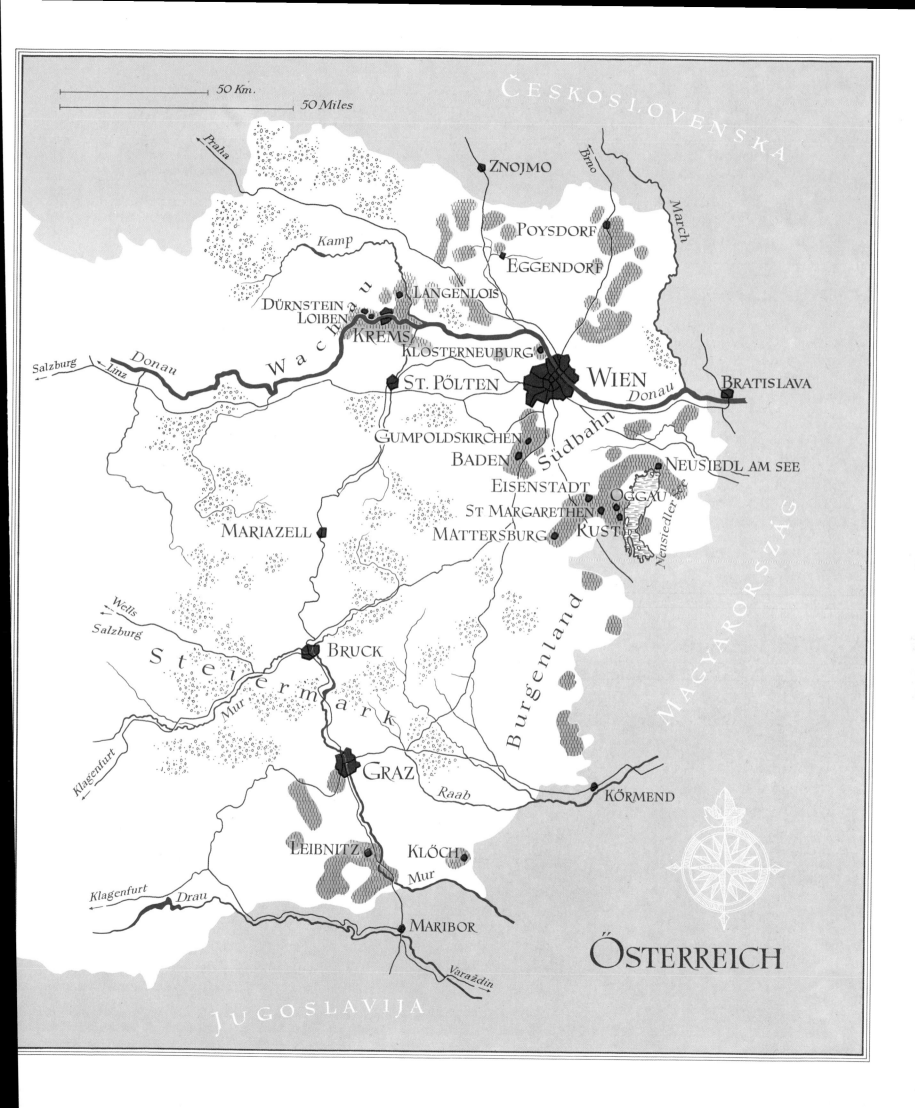

ČESKOSLOVENSKA

Praha

ZNOJMO

Brno

March

POYSDORF

Kamp

EGGENDORF

Wachau

LANGENLOIS

DÜRNSTEIN

LOIBEN

KREMS

KLOSTERNEUBURG

Salzburg   Linz   Donau

WIEN

BRATISLAVA

ST. PÖLTEN

Donau

GUMPOLDSKIRCHEN

Südbahn

BADEN

NEUSIEDL AM SEE

EISENSTADT

OGGAU

St MARGARETHEN

Neusiedler See

MARIAZELL

MATTERSBURG   RUST

MAGYARORSZÁG

Wells

Salzburg

Burgenland

Steiermark

Klagenfurt

BRUCK

Mur

KÖRMEND

GRAZ

Raab

LEIBNITZ

KLÖCH

Klagenfurt   Drau

Mur

MARIBOR

ÖSTERREICH

Varaždin

JUGOSLAVIJA

50 Km.

50 Miles

Margarethen, Eisenstadt, Mattesburg and Oberpullendorf. Some wines, naturally, are better than others: among the white wines these are the RUSTER GREINER, RUSTER SATZ, RUSTER TURNER, while among the red wines there are the RUSTER BAUMGARTEN, RUSTER G'MÄRK, RUSTER MITTELKRÄFTEN, and especially the RUST LIMBERGER, a *Pinot Noir*. Styria, in the Mur valley, near the lower part of Graz and Sulm, mainly produces white wines. The best-known vineyard is situated in the commune of Klöch, and some consider the KLÖCHER BERG one of the best *Traminers* in Europe. Other local wines highly-thought of by the Austrians are the HARTBERGER RING, the HARTBERGER LÖFFELBACH, the GRASSNITZBERG, the OTTENBERGER WITSCHEINBERG and the KOBELBERG.

In the Baden region to the south of Vienna—a region also called Südbahn—the best-known white wines are those of Gumpoldskirchen, in particular the GUMPOLDS-KIRCHNER SPIEGEL, the GUMPOLDSKIRCHNER WIEGE and the GUMPOLDSKIRCHNER SONNBERG. Of the red wines, the VÖSLAUER ROTWEIN deserves particular mention.

The winegrowing areas, which produce local wines, white for the most part, are north of the Danube in the Weinviertel, which along the length and the western side runs from Vienna to Czechoslovakia, as well as along the banks of the Danube from Vienna to the confluence of the river Kamp, including Klosternberg, the Kamp valley and Langenlois.

However, it is especially the region of Krems and of Wachau above Krems that produce the best Austrian wines. In the past, these wines were not so well thought of because of their somewhat high acid content—in fact a well-known saying had it *sauer wie der Wachauer* ("as sour as Wachauer wine"). The winegrowers of Krems, a dynamic and pretty little town, were however able to produce Rieslings with a full-flavoured bouquet. The best of these may be compared to the Moselle Rieslings. KREMSLER KÖGL, KREMSER KREMSLEITEN and KREMSER WACHTBERG are strongly recommended.

Farther up-stream is Dürnstein, a very picturesque place with the ruins of a feudal castle. It is well-known for its DÜRNSTEINER LIERENBERG, and for the DÜRNSTEINER HOLLERIN, which was served in 1955 at the time of the signing of the Austrian State Treaty which proclaimed Austria's independence. Yet farther up-stream, the

The Soos vineyards, near Baden (Austria) are situated in the region known as the Südbahn, which produces white wines—notably the GUMPOLDSKIRCHEN—and red wines, VÖSLAUER, which are among Austria's best.

After leaving Vienna by road in the direction of Brno in Czechoslovakia, the wine-lover may wish to stop at Mistelbach, halfway between the Austrian capital and the Czech frontier. Although the wines there are related to the whites of the Wachau (Krems), they are not quite as good.

Stein vineyards produce the STEINER GOLDBERG, made from the best *Müller-Thurgau* grape in Wachau. The Loiben wines are some of the best white wines to come from the Danube: wines such as the LOIBENER KAISER WEIN and the UNTERLOIBENER BRUGSTALL.

The traveller faced with a list of Austrian wines is often puzzled, as the names by which these wines are known are not always mentioned as fully or as systematically on the wine-list as is the practice elsewhere. For some wines only the place of origin is given—for example, WACHAUER 1959, a wine produced in Wachau in the year 1959. Others are known by the name of the grape used, without mentioning the place of origin, as in the case of VELTLINER 1959; this simply designates a wine produced from the *Grüner Veltliner* grape in the year 1959. Yet others mention the grape used preceded by the name of the commune; for example, the STEINER VELTLINER 1959, produced from the *Grüner Veltliner* grape in the commune of Stein in the year 1959. It should be noted, however, that the best wines, especially those we have referred to, mention the name of the commune or the village, followed by the name of the vineyard. For example: DÜRNSTEINER LIEBENBERG, designating a wine grown in the vineyard of Liebenberg in the commune of Dürnstein. A wine-lover who choses any of these wines will be sure to have chosen from among the best wines of Austria.

Austrian wines are little known abroad; for the most part they must be drunk in the country itself. The white wines are considered the best, but they should not be compared to the German wines made from the same stock. Those drunk in the "Heurigen" near Vienna have a low alcohol content; they are pale-coloured wines, sometimes of a milky white hue.

337

HUNGARY

The most famous Hungarian wine is Tokay. Associated with the names of emperors and kings, lords and poets, it has overshadowed all the other wines of the country. For Hungary is a country rich in vineyards and wines; it has 432,425 acres of vine and produces nearly 87,992,000 to 109,990,000 gallons of wine, which places it in about tenth position among the wineproducing countries of Europe.

The Romans introduced the vine to the Hungarian plains. Since those days, the vine there has undergone many vicissitudes. First cultivated by the Magyars, it was neglected when the Tartars laid the country waste in 1241. Later again, settlers from the west brought with them a new vine-plant, *Furmint*, from which Tokay was produced. Afterwards, when for 173 years (from 1526 to 1699) the country was occupied by Moslem Turks, the vine was once again neglected. In the eighteenth century, however, the Hungarian wine-cellars were among the best-stocked in Europe, thanks to Count István Szecheny.

Today Hungarian production fluctuates around 88 million gallons of wine, a quarter of which, at the most, is for export. Hungary produces mainly white wines (60 per cent). It also produces rosés (25 per cent) and a little red wine (15 per cent). These wines are usually known by a compound name; the first indicates the place of origin, the second the grape. For example, Badacsonyi Keknyelü means that the wine is made rom the *Kéknyelü* ("blue stalk") grape, in the Badacsony region. The white wines of Sopron, Somló, Villány-Pécs, Gyöngyös-Visonta are ordinary wines mainly for local consumption.

Red wine can be found in Sopron, which is near the Austrian border, in particular in the district of Szekszárd, to the south of Lake Balaton. Most of the reds come from an original Balkan grape, the *Kadarka*.

The western bank of Lake Balaton, on the slopes of Mount Badacsony, is particularly favourable to the cultivation of grapes such as *Kéknyelü*, *Furmint*, and *Szürkebarát (Pinot Gris)*. Badacsonyi Keknyelü is a dry white wine with a pleasant bouquet and an attractive colour bordering on green, while Badacsonyi Szürkebarat is a semi-sweet white wine which, when mature, has a rich amber colour. Nevertheless, it does not have the distinction of the *Pinot Gris* wines in other parts of Europe. Rieslings are cheap white wines of Italian origin, very different from those of the Rhine.

The Mór region, farther to the north, is one of Hungary's oldest viticultural areas. The Möri Ezerjo, which means "the one-thousandfold good Mor", is a dry wine with a very lovely light green colour and an agreeably sharp tang.

The Debröi Hárslevelü is another typical Hungarian white wine. The grape *Hárslevelü* ("lime-blossom") is cultivated in the mountainous region of the north; it produces a sweet wine which is on the whole highly thought of by the Hungarians.

The Egri Bikaver, or "Bull's Blood of Eger" is the only Hungarian red wine known abroad, no doubt because of its name. The Eger region is situated between Budapest and the Tokay region. The Egri Bikaver has a dark rich colour and a slightly bitter taste. It is made from a mixture of several vines: the *Kadarka*, *Médoc Noir* and *Bourguignon*. In Hungary it is much recommended during convalescence owing to its tonic properties. The Egri Leanyka is a white wine made from an indigenous grape, the *Leanyka*.

Tokay is by all odds the best-known. The town which gave its name to the wines of this region is situated on the Bodrog, at the foot of the Hégalja, which dominates the Tisza plain. This is an area of orchards and vineyards where only 28 villages have the right to call the wine they produce Tokay. (It should be stated quite clearly that the name Tokay does not cover the whole range of wines produced in this region.) The excellence of this wine springs from a wonderful harmony that exists between the soil and the climate, the grape and the process of vinification. The soil consists of a layer of crumbled lava which covers alluvial mountain deposits on a bed of volcanic rocks. The climate is varied; the summers are very hot and very dry, the autumns long and sunny, but the winters are harsh. The altitude of the vineyard varies from 500 to 650 feet above sea-level. The grape which gives Tokay its special character is the *Furmint*. Students of the vine are divided in their opinions as to its origin, but agree that in this country it has found the soil and the climate most suitable for it. It is believed that settlers coming from the west brought the *Furmint* to prominence. Its name is probably derived from the French *froment* (wheat) which has become *Furmint* in Magyar; no doubt it has to do with the colour of the grapes. To this grape, which is always the predominant one in Tokay, are sometimes added small quantities of *Hárslevelü* and *Muscat Jaune*. The third factor responsible for its success is the process of vinification and the special storage cellars.

First, there is the Tokaji Furmint, or Furmint de Tokay, a wine made according to traditional methods, by pressing the juice of the *Furmint* grape-clusters without using the dry grapes. This is a full-flavoured, fruity wine. Often the year of manufacture is on the label.

The Tokaji Szamarodni or Szamarodni de Tokay is made from the fermentation of grapes which have not been specially selected but picked late and so have clusters which are dry or have reached a stage of *pourriture noble* (noble rot). Its alcohol content is higher than that of the Tokaji Furmint; it can be sweet, as it is in sunny years, but when dry makes an excellent aperitif. The label on the bottle will indicate the year and type of wine.

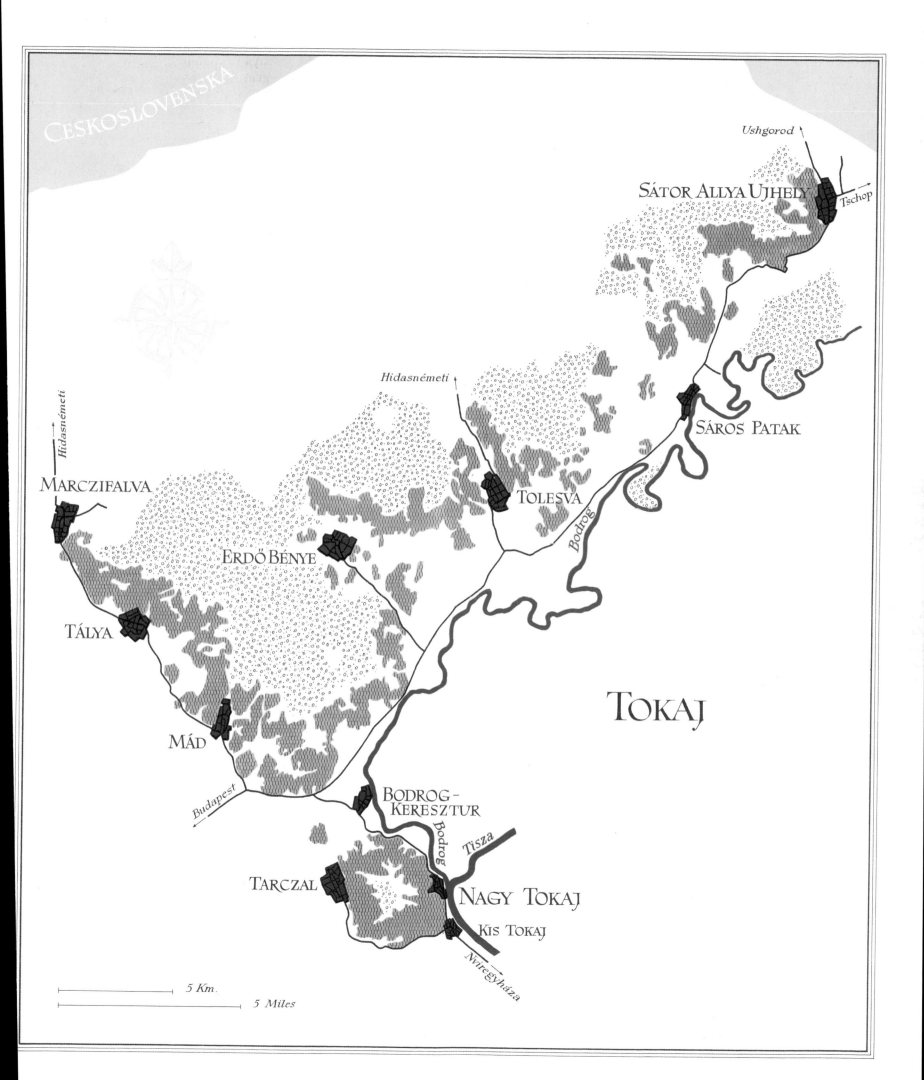

CESKOSLOVENSKA

Ushgorod

SÁTOR ALLYA UJHELY

Tschop

Hidasnémeti

SÁROS PATAK

Hidasnémeti

MARCZIFALVA

Bodrog

TOLESVA

ERDŐ BÉNYE

TÁLYA

TOKAJ

MÁD

Budapest

BODROG-
KERESZTUR

Bodrog

Tisza

TARCZAL

NAGY TOKAJ

Bodrog

KIS TOKAJ

Nyiregyháza

5 Km.

5 Miles

The TOKAJI ASZU or ASZU DE TOKAY is the most famous of all the TOKAYS and is usually the one referred to when speaking simply of TOKAY. It is said to owe its origin to a seventeenth-century local war, which caused a delay in the vine-harvest; the winegrowers thus rediscovered the advantages of a late wineharvest which had already been known to their forefathers. Late in the season, sometimes even after the first snow has fallen, when the grapes are overripe and have reached a *pourriture noble*, the wine-harvesters pick them one by one. The grapes are then crushed and stirred together until they form a kind of crust. When this process has been completed, 2 to 6 basketfuls (*puttonos*) weighing 33 pounds each of the final mixture are added to every hogshead of 30 gallons of must or wine, whether it is young or old, which is produced in the same region.

The sugar and aroma from the pressing of dried grapes dissolves in the must or wine, which after a second slow fermentation produces the world-famous TOKAJI ASZU. The number of basketfuls poured into each hogshead depends on several factors: on the one hand on the quality of the must or wine which is being used—this varies from year to year—on the other hand on the type of TOKAJI ASZU one wishes to produce. For this wine can be sweet or semi-sweet.

The TOKAJI ASZU maintains essentially the same degree of excellence from year to year largely owing to the art of the master winemakers. The TOKAJI FURMINT and the TOKAJI SZAMARODNI, however, vary from year to

year depending on the quality of the wine-harvest. When buying TOKAJI ASZU, one should know that the label on the bottle always mentions how many basketfuls of concentrated grapes have been put into each hogshead. For example: "3 puttonos" means that the wine is sweet, yet not nearly as sweet as a wine with a label reading "6 puttonos". This is the maximum. Moreover, the TOKAJI ASZU bottle has a traditional shape; it is pot-bellied like a Burgundy bottle, with a well-defined neck longer than that of the claret bottle. The wine will keep for a long time, like a sherry.

The TOKAJI MASLAS is produced by fermenting must or wine on the lees of TOKAY, usually on the lees of the ASZU or the SZAMARODNI. In order to produce the desired results the must stands for several months in small barrels called *Gönci*.

The TOKAJI ESZENCIA, or ESSENCE OF TOKAY is made by fermenting a thick must made from overripe grapes or those which have reached a state of *pourriture noble*. It is a very sweet, liqueur-like dessert wine.

TOKAY is produced in several countries (Alsace, northern Italy and eastern Switzerland), but only those wines referred to here come from Hungary and are authentic TOKAYS. They are exported by the Hungarian Board of Foreign Trade (Monimpex). Rarely, one does find a very old bottle of TOKAY, a delight to the connoisseur or anyone nostalgic for the charm of the gay nights in Budapest at the time of the Austro-Hungarian monarchy or between the two wars.

CZECHOSLOVAKIA

Czechoslovakia, of all the countries which were part of the former Austro-Hungarian Empire, is certainly the one which produces the least wine. Its output is about 4,399,600 gallons a year.

Bohemia, in the Melnik region, Roudnice and Litomerice, to the north of Prague, produce an ordinary white wine called LUOMILLA, made from the *Sylvaner* and *Traminer* grapes. The red wines are made from *Bourguignon Bleu*, *Portugais* or *Saint-Laurent* grapes. Because of its geographical position Bohemia produces wines similar to those of certain German wine regions.

Morovia has little wine, and almost all of it comes from the region near the Austrian frontier.

Of the three main regions in the country, Slovakia is the best developed from the point of view of viticulture

and gives about three-quarters of the national yield. Near the Hungarian frontier, to the north of the Tokay region, the Mala Trna and Nove Mestro vineyards also produce so-called TOKAY. Elsewhere, in the Bratislava area, they make VELTLINER, RIESLING or SYLVANER.

Czechoslovakia has to import a certain amount of wine: in 1978 it imported 8,249,250 gallons, and 6,863,376 gallons in 1979. Wine here is by no means a national drink; the average Czech drinks only about ten pints of wine a year. As there are no great wines, the tourist must console himself with the local white wines. These are light, fruity, and of low alcohol content and may be enjoyed in charming surroundings. The Czech wines have much improved since the establishment of a control over their quality.

RUMANIA

The Rumanian winegrowers have for centuries managed to maintain a difficult balance between the soil, the climate and the art of cultivating the vine. Although the country geographically belongs in a temperate zone

considered favourable for the vine, its climate is nevertheless extreme: very hot in the summer, very cold and windy in winter. Yet wine has been produced in this country since before the seventh century B.C. When the

The Tihany vineyards extend along a promontory that juts out into Lake Balaton, Hungary.

The vineyards on the west bank of Lake Balaton lie on the slopes of Mt Badacsony (far side of the lake in the photo). Dry and semi-dry white wines are produced.

341

Greeks founded their Black Sea colonies they cultivated the vine here in order to produce wine which they then stored in huge pot-bellied amphoras and sent throughout the civilized world.

By the development of the nurseries and the application of modern scientific methods of viticulture and viniculture the area of Rumania's winegrowing districts has been greatly enlarged in the past few years. The present Rumanian vineyard covers more than 741,300 acres and produces 153,986,000 to 175,984,000 gallons of wine, most of it white wine.

The principal vineyards are the Cotnari and the Murfatlar, producing dessert wines; the Tirnave; the Dealul-Mare, the Focsain and the Banat, producing both red and white table wines. The best-known and the most renowned of the Rumanian white wines come from the Tirnave Mare and Tirnave Mica valleys, in the centre of the country. The TIRNAVE PEARL, a wine made from a mixture of several grapes which give it a very well-balanced bouquet, is well known outside Rumania. Other white wines are made from a single vine-plant whose name they carry; for example, the FETEASCA DE TIRNAVE, RIESLING DE TIRNAVE, or RIESLING DE DEALUL-MARE, near Ploiesti in Munténie.

The KADARKA is the most common red wine in the Balkans; the wine from Teremia, near the Yugoslav border, is often referred to; and there is also the SEGARCEA CABERNET, made from the *Cabernet* grape. It comes from the vineyards of the Valea Calugaresca (Valley of the Monks) which lies to the east of Ploiesti. The SADOVA is a slightly sweet rosé from the Dragasani region, where the vine is often more than a century old. The white dessert wines from these parts are very highly thought of. In the north, the COTNARI wine is sweet and fruity. The MURFATLAR, from near the Black Sea, has a fine orange-blossom bouquet which is probably unique.

Rumanian wines are exported mainly to Germany, Austria and the Eastern European countries, although the Focsani Fructexport also sells a certain amount of wine to such countries as Switzerland, Belgium, Holland, Sweden, Denmark, France and Great Britain. Rumania has many indigenous stocks, but is making a real effort to improve the quality of its wines through a progressive elimination of hybrids and a selection of vine types. The new co-operatives have also done much to improve the standard in vine culture and turn the country's great wine potential to the best account.

In Eastern European countries, the wine harvests often have an air of the past. Here the grapes are carried in baskets to a cask into which they are emptied before being taken to the press. All the operations take place in the open air.

BULGARIA

Before World War II, the vineyards of Bulgaria spread over an area of 331,200 acres; in 1978 they covered 447,251 acres. This increase is due on the one hand to a major change in the system of ownership, and on the other to a systematic reconstruction of the vineyards so that mechanization could be introduced on a large scale. The country today produces 66,000,000 gallons of wine per year; 52 per cent red wines, 48 per cent white wines. Although it is divided into viticultural regions, it would not be correct to attribute a particular wine to a given region. It might also be practical to mention only the better-known Bulgarian wines.

The *Dimiat* is the best-known grape. It grows near the Black Sea, in the Choumen regions and farther west in the province of Tarnovo. It produces a dry but fruity wine of a rich golden-green colour. Wines are named by their grape or by regional names, and sometimes by a combination of both. (WARNENSKI DIMIAT means a DIMIAT from Warna.) These wines recall the Rieslings, while the wines from the *Misket* grapes, in particular the MISKET KARLOVA or the MISKET DE KARLOVO, bring to mind the Sylvaner, as does the SONGURLARE MISKET which is produced on the coast. Other, more common white wines are the BALGARSKE SLANTSE or BULGARIAN SUN made from the *Furmint* grape; the DOUNAVSKA PERLA or PEARL OF THE DANUBE, and the SLANTCHEV BIRAG or SUNSHINE COAST, made from a Georgian grape, the *Rehaziteli*. The SLAVIANKA is a wine made from the *Muscat* grape; it is

golden and full-flavoured, with the characteristic savour of the grape.

Although there are many more red wines, they are much less varied. Usually they are known by their grape. PAMID is purely for domestic consumption. GAMSA (the Bulgarian name for KADARKA) is an agreeable wine, with a pleasant bouquet, especially when young. Sometimes it is known by a local name such as KRAMOLINSKA, or wine from Kramoline.

MAVROUD, produced in the Assennovgrad region, has a rich dark red colour, and is somewhat acid, with an alcoholic content of 11 to 12 degrees. This wine is often used for blending with lighter red wines.

MELNIK is a wine from the north-west region. It is dark red, somewhat full-bodied, but of good quality. The *Melnik* grape variety has been cultivated in Bulgaria since ancient times and is probably a plant of French origin. The CABERNET is another Bulgarian wine made from the *Cabernet-Sauvignon* grape, which was introduced into the country.

Vines are cultivated on the southern slopes of the Rhodope mountains, above the Marica basin. The regions of Assenovgrad, Plovdiv and Pazardjik produce red wines from *Mavroud* grapes.

The wine harvest near Cirpan, in Bulgaria. Wine producing is on the increase in Bulgaria, but is not the only use for the vine; many tons of table grapes are exported.

In Serbia, as in any other wineproducing region, the vintage is a time for celebrations and festivities. The wines produced here are mostly reds for local consumption and well-bred, elegant whites.

The large Yugoslav vineyards are grouped in co-operatives and winegrowing is increasingly mechanized, a factor which is changing the face of the countryside, as here in Slovenia.

A vineyard in Croatia, the principal wineproducing region in Yugoslavia. The effects of soil type and climate have necessitated some unusual viticultural techniques.

YUGOSLAVIA

The history of Yugoslav vine culture and wines is similar to that of Italy, France and Spain. They all use the same vinification methods and even the same grapes: the *Burgundac* or *Pinot Noir*, the *Cabernet*, the *Merlot* and the *Riesling*. The Yugoslav climate and soil give a particular character to its wines. The vineyards cover 617,750 acres and produce, apart from table grapes, 110 to 132 million gallons of wine. The vine is cultivated throughout the country, from north to south in the following six regions: Slovenia, Istria, Croatia, Dalmatia, Serbia and Macedonia.

Slovenia has a flourishing vineyard situated in the Sava and Drava valleys, including the districts of Ljutomer, Ormoz, Ptuj, Radgona and Maribor, as well as along the Adriatic to the Italian frontier. In this area, most of the white wines are made from the grapes of the *Traminer, Riesling Rhenan, Riesling Laski,* the *Sauvignon, Pinot Blanc* and *Sipon,* the local counterparts of the Hungarian *Furmint.*

Istria is known for its red wines made from the grapes of the *Teran, Bogonja (Gamay), Merlot* and *Cabernet* varieties. Two white wines are also produced here, one made from the *Pinot* grapes, the other from the *Malvasia* or Malmsey grape. The Istrian growers employ the Italian methods of mixed cultivation, so that other plants can be seen growing side by side with the vines.

Croatia is one of the most important winegrowing regions in Yugoslavia. The north produces white wines, light but somewhat acid, or wines with a rich bouquet and very high alcohol content. *Traminer, Riesling, Sauvignon* and *Semillon* grape varieties are greatly cultivated in this area. The coastal wines are red, similar to the full and heady wines from the Mediterranean.

The most famous grape-vine in Dalmatia is the *Plavac,* which produces a red wine of the same name. It is a full-bodied, ruby-red wine with a very special bouquet. Dalmatia also makes some semi-dry red wines known as DINGAC and POSTUP. An unusual type of sweet wine called PROSEK can be found in this area but it rarely appeals to the taste of foreigners.

The Serbian vineyard is the largest of all the Yugoslav vineyards and is responsible for half the wine produced in Yugoslavia. It makes mainly white wines and just a few red wines such as the ZUPA. The area around the town of Smederevo grows a white wine called SMEDEREVKA, similar to CHABLIS from Burgundy. Other celebrated white wines are the FRUSKA GORA, the VRSAC and the SUBOTICA. Elsewhere in Serbia, an indigenous grape, the *Prokupac,* is cultivated. It makes a very good table wine. Macedonia mainly produces ordinary red wines. Yugoslavia also exports wines from Herzegovina, the ZILAVKA, a dry white wine, as well as wines from Kosovo and Metohija, known in West Germany as AMSELFELDER SPÄTBURGUNDER.

Since the end of World War II, the establishment of co-operative underground cellars has done much to improve methods of vinification and wine-storage. Yugoslavian wine (17,598,400 to 21,998,000 gallons per year) is exported mainly to East Germany, Czechoslovakia, Poland and Italy.

THE SOVIET UNION

Wine production made its appearance in the territory of the Soviet Union with prehistoric man. Vestiges of wine cultivation dating back to the Bronze Age have been discovered in Georgia, Azerbaidjan, Armenia and in Turkmenistan. Wine making and drinking have been known in these regions since the dawn of history.

In pre-revolutionary Russia, vinicultural activity was in the hands of small producers. The area planted to vines in 1913 did not exceed 531,265 acres, and production was about 66 million gallons, some 2 per cent of world production. Today, the USSR includes 12.7 per cent of the world's winegrowing area, and produces 11.4 per cent of grapes and 11 per cent of the world total wine production.

Russia holds third place in vineyard area (after Spain and Italy), and fourth in wine production (after Italy, France and Argentina).

The grapes once gathered are processed by large organisations, containing installations for continuous fermentation for the production of red and white wines, ultra-refrigerators, filters, presses and other modern machinery. A large part of production is undertaken by factories with a capacity to process 10,000 tonnes or more of grapes during a season, the result of a series of Five Year Agricultural Plans.

A smaller sector of the wine producing market is taken by factories with a capacity of 440,000 gallons or over per year.

Sparkling wines are produced in 11 republics by the so-called *en continu* method. However, certain concerns use a new means of production by a superconcentration of fermenting agents. The capacity of most enterprises producing sparkling wines is somewhat in excess of 5 million bottles a year.

Today, Russia's wine-production range includes some 604 table and dessert wine appellations and a total of 32 sparkling wines.

Viticulture and the wine industry in the USSR is developing rapidly, thanks to scientific research carried out throughout the country. The National Institute for Scientific Viticultural Research—MAGARATCH—co-ordinates these efforts.

The wine industry in the USSR may be summed up by the following statistics (1980):

RSFSR (Russia): 486,787 acres; 233,618,760 gallons; 65 million bottles of sparkling wine

SSR Ukraine: 635,047 acres; 96,791,200 gallons; 44.9 million bottles of sparkling wine

SSR Moldavia: 635,047 acres; 94,151,440 gallons; 5.2 million bottles of sparkling wine

SSR Georgia: 353,353 acres; 47,515,680 gallons; 13 million bottles of sparkling wine

SSR Armenia: 88,956 acres; 20,238,160 gallons; 5 million bottles of sparkling wine

SSR Azerbaidjan: 593,040 acres; 48,395,600 gallons; 5.8 million bottles of sparkling wine

SSR Kazakhstan: 66,717 acres; 34,096,900 gallons; 9.25 million bottles of sparkling wine

SSR Uzbekistan: 239,687 acres; 7.6 million bottles of sparkling wine

SSR Tadjikistan: 69,188 acres; 2.85 million bottles of sparkling wine

SSR Kirghizia: 19,768 acres; 7,699,300 gallons; 5.7 million bottles of sparkling wine

SSR Turkmenistan: 37,065 acres; 3,299,700 gallons.

The Russian Socialist Federal Soviet Republic holds first place in the USR for wine production. It produces 34.7 per cent of the still wine and 36.7 per cent of all the sparkling wine made in the USSR.

The wine industry is concentrated in the regions of Krasnodar and Stavropol, and the autonomous republics of Daghestan and Checheno-Ingush, near the Rostov province.

The Krasnodar region is known for its excellent wines: REISLING ABRAOU, CABERNET ABRAOU, REISLING

The Massandra winegrowing region in the Crimea is very rugged country, but it produces famous dessert wines, such as MUSCAT NOIR DE MASSANDRA (red) and the MUSCAT BLANC PIERRE ROUGE (white).

ANAPA, CABERNET ANAPA, ALIGOTE GUELENDJIK, MUSCAT AMBRE, PERLE DE RUSSIE, and YEUX NOIRS. The famous sparkling ABRAOUDIOURSSO, known beyond the region, is also produced there. Krasnodar is a centre for Russian wheat, sunflower, rice, tobacco and fruit crops, and there are rich deposits of oil and gas.

The autonomous republics of Daghestan and Checheno-Ingush have grown grapes since time out of mind. Production in these regions is orientated towards table and dessert wines; in Gaghestan RKATSITELI GEDJOUKH, and dessert wines HIZLIARSK and TERSK; in Checheno-Irgush, NAOURSK dessert wine, and SILVANER TERSKI. The Stavropol region produces white wines: REISLING BECHTAOU and SILVANER BECHTAOU; the Rostov region mostly light table wines.

347

The Republic of Moldavia contains land favourable to intensive winegrowing. The vineyards are so large that cultivation is done by means of caterpillar tractors, since it would be impossible to work the enormous (635,040 acre) vineyards by hand.

The Ukraine produces 14.3 per cent of all Russian wines and 25.3 per cent of its sparkling wines. The wine industry is divided between the Crimea, Odessa, Nikolayev, Kherson and the Transcarpathia regions.

The south coast of the Crimea well deserves its name of "the pearl of the Soviet wine industry". It is there that are produced the famous liquorish dessert wines: MUSCAT BLANC "PIERRE ROUGE", MUSCAT LIVADIA, MUSCAT ROSE dessert, MUSCAT NOIR MASSANDRA. The MUSCAT BLANC "PIERRE ROUGE" is unique of its type; it is only made when weather conditions allow the grape to contain at least 30 per cent sugar. The sugar content of the wine is 23 per cent and its alcoholic strength 13 per cent. It can be drunk between 2 and 20 years old, but may be kept for much longer, when it acquires a most original bouquet. No other Muscat keeps its perfume so long; a perfume utterly typical of Muscat blunded with flowers and lemon.

Fortified wines, port, madeira and sherry type, enjoy a great reputation, among them PORTO ROUGE LIVADIA and MADERE MASSANDRA. It is said that the latter is twice-born, once in the grapes, and a second time when it rests for five years in an oak barrel in the sun. The wine closely resembles its Portuguese namesake.

The table wines from the Steppes region of the Crimea are also worthy of attention: they are ALIGOTE ZOLOTAIA BALKA, REISLING DE CRIMÉE, and the red table wine ALOUCHTA, made from a blend of grape varieties.

The Republic of Moldavia produces 14 per cent of all wine and 2.9 per cent of the sparkling wine made in the Soviet Union. The central zone specialises in the production of appellation controlled white wines and musts for sparkling wines. The southern region produces red wines, dessert wines, and some fortified wines.

In times gone by, the weakly alcoholic, poorly made Moldavian wines enjoyed such a bad reputation that the *Encyclopaedia Britannica* felt obliged to describe them as "local wine, sour, and liable to go bad in transport". Happily, this is no longer the case.

Amongst the better-known wines are NEGRU DE PURKAR, ROCHOU DE PURKAR, ROMANECHTI and CABERNET. Dessert wines well worthy of mention include CAHORS TCHOUMAI, NECTAR, and TENDRESSE.

The Republic of Georgia enjoys particularly favourable conditions for wine producing. It makes 6.6 per cent of the wines and 7.1 per cent of the sparkling wine produced in the USSR.

The specialities are red and white table wines—TSINANDALI, GOURDJAANI, TELIANI, MOUKOUZANI, NAPAREOULI, TIBAANI and SAPERAVI. In the eastern region of Georgia, Kakhetia, wines are made according to traditional methods, though equally nowadays industrially, in terracotta vessels containing 330-660 gallons. Among the semi-sweet natural wines of Georgia are KHVANTCHKARA, KINDZMARAOULI, AKHACHENI, TVICHI, TCHHAVERI, TETRA, and others too numerous to list.

The Republic of Armenia makes 3 per cent of all the wines and 2.8 per cent of the sparkling wines that are correctly produced in the USSR.

Wine making is mostly developed in the southern part of the republic, in the plains and foothills of the Ararat valley, which enjoys a warm continental climate. Armenia produces white wines, such as STCMIADZINE, red wines, such as NORACHEN, and dessert wines, AREVCHAT and AREVIK; AIGECHAT is a fortified wine.

The Republic of Azerbaidjan makes 7.1 per cent of all the wine and 3.3 per cent of the sparkling wine produced in the Soviet Union.

The most important wine area is Kirovabadakstafinsk, where, above all, appellation controlled wines are produced.

In the Upper Chirvan region, semi-sweet table wines are made, together with dessert wines such as KIOURDAMIR (red).

In the Nagorno-Karabakh province red table wines and dessert wines are produced. Amongst the better-known ones are: SADILLY (white), MATRASSA (red), AKSTAFA (white port type) MIL (white dessert), CHAMAKHY (red dessert) and KARA-TCHANAKH (white dessert).

The other regions of the Soviet Union where wine production is developed are Kazakhstan, Uzbeckistan, Tadjikistan, Khirghizia and Turkmenistan.

348

WINES OF CENTRAL EUROPE

AUSTRIA

WACHAU

White wines	Loibener Kaiserwein	Dürnsteiner Liebenberg	Weissenkirchner Achleiten	Undhof Wieden Spät- und
	Unterloibener Rotenberg	Kremser Pfaffenberg	Undhof Wieden-	Auslese Grüne Veltliner
	Unterloibener Burgstall	Steiner Pfaffenberg	Weissburgunder	Dürnsteiner Muskat-Ottonel
	Kremser Kögl	Steiner Schreck	Weisser Burgunder	Zöbinger Muskat-Ottonel
	Steiner Goldberg	Dürnsteiner Hollerin	Ruländer	Sonnenkönig
	Kremser Kremsleiten	Dürnsteiner Himmelsstiege	Neuburger	Heiligensteiner Sauvignon
	Kremser Wachtberg	Weissenkirchner Klaus		Undhof Goldberg

Red wines	Alter Knabe - Saint Laurent			

VIENNA-SÜDBAHN

White wines . . .	Wiener Nussberg	Klosterneuburger	Kahlenberger Traminer	Kavalier-Zierfandler
	Gumpoldskirchner Spiegel	Rheinriesling	Sauvignon	Zierfandler Ried Kramer
	Gumpoldskirchner Sonnberg	Nussberger Schwarze Katz	Weisser Burgunder	Gumpoldskirchner
	Gumpoldskirchner	Original Gumpoldskirchner	Klostercabinet	Zierfandler
	Goldknöpfel	Rheinriesling	Franzhauser Kabinett-	Goldknöpferl-Rotgipfler
	Gumpoldskirchner Rasslerin	Neuburger	Neuburger	Rotgipfler Spät- und
	Gumpoldskirchner	Neuburger Spät-	Grüner Veltliner	Auslesen
	Grimmling	und Auslesen	Jungherrn Müller-Thurgau	Kreuzweingarten-Spätlese
	Gumpoldskirchner	Badener Lumpentürl-	Königswein Zierfandler	Zierfandler-Rotgipfler
	Stocknarrn	Neuburger	Zierfandler	Sonnberg
				Spätrot-Rotgipfler

Red wines	Blauburgunder	Saint Laurent		
	Soosser Blauer Burgunder	Sooser Blauer Portugieser	Saint-Laurent-Ausstich	Vöslauer Rotwein

BURGENLAND

White wines	Ruster Greiner	Ruster Ruländer	Original Golser	Ruster Ausbruch
	Ruster Satz	Original Joiser Ruländer	Welschriesling	Müller-Thurgau
	Ruster Turner	Ruster Muskateller	Weisser Storch Ruster	Beerenauslese
	Ruster Vogelsang	Muskat-Ottonel	Welschriesling	Oggauer Ambrosi
	Muskat-Traminer	Welschriesling-Spätlesen		

Red wines	Ruster Baumgarten	Rust Limberger	Oggauer Blaufränkisch	Schützenberger Rotkelch
	Ruster G'märk	Ruster Blauburgunder	Blaufränkisch	Blaufränkisch Spätlesen
	Ruster Mittelkräften	Blauer Burgunder Spätlese	Pöttelsdorfer Bismarckwein	

STEIERMARK

White wines	Klöcher Berg	Köbelberg	Silberberg	Hochbrudersegg
	Hartberger Ring	Sulztal	Hochkittenberg	Muskat-Sylvaner
	Hartberger Löffelbach	Glanzer Berg	Morillon	Sausaler Welschriesling
	Grassnitzberg .	Steinbach	Ruländer	Müller-Thurgau
	Ottenberger Witscheinberg	Schlossberg	Muskateller	

Red wine	Schilcher			

CZECHOSLOVAKIA

Furmint   Harchlevelu   Lipouvina   Muskat de Lunel   Muskat Ztly

HUNGARY

White wines	Tokaji Szamorodni (dry)	Badacsonyi Kéknyelü	Balatonfüredi	Debröi Hárslevelü
	Tokaji Furmint	Badacsonyi Szürkebarát	Móri Ezerjó	Léanyka

Red wines	Egri Bikavér	Soproni Kékfrankos		

Dessert wines	Tokaji Aszu (3-5 puttonos)	Tokaji Szamorodni (sweet)		

WINES OF THE BALKANS

YUGOSLAVIA

White wines	Banatski rizling (Kreaca) — dry Belan — dry Graševina (Italian Riesling) — dry	Grk Malvazija — dry and sweet Maraština — dry and medium-dry Muskat Ottonel — medium-dry and sweet	Pošip — dry Rebula — dry Silvanac — dry and medium-dry Smederevka — dry	Traminac — dry and medium-dry Vugava Žilavka — dry
Rosé wines	Cviček — dry	Opol dalmatinski — dry	Ruzica — dry	
Red wines	Burgundac crni (pinot noir) — dry Dingač — medium-dry Frankovka — dry	Kavčina (Žametna črnica) — dry Kraski teran — dry Kratošija — dry	Muskat ruza (Moscate rosa) — medium-sweet and sweet Plavac — dry Postup — medium-dry	Prokupac — dry and medium-sweet Refošk — dry and medium-sweet Vranac — dry

BULGARIA

White wines	Pomoria Dimiat Preslav Dimiat Tchirpan Dimiat	Varna Dimiat Euxinograd Hemona	Songurlaré Misket Liaskovetz Riesling	Riesling of the Valley of Roses
Red wines	Chipka Novosseltzi Gamza Pavlikeni Gamza	Soukhindol Gamza Kalouger Kramolin	Loud Guidia Assénovgrad Mavroud Melnik	Pamid Pirgovo
Dessert wines	Bisser Hebros	Kadarka "Valley of Roses" Vratza Misket	Pomoria Slavianka	Tarnovo Varna

ROUMANIA

White wines	Dealul Mare Diosig Drâgâsani	Husi Murfatlar Muscel	Nicoresti Teremia-Tomnatic-Comlos Valea lui Mihai	Valea Târnavelor Cotnar
Red wines	Sarica-Niculitel	Cotnar		

WINES OF THE SOVIET UNION

White wines of the Crimea	Aligoté Ay-Danil Riesling Massandra	Riesling Alkadar	Semillon Oreanda
White wines of Krasnodar	Riesling Abraou	Riesling Anapa	
White wines of Georgia	Gurdjurni Manadis Mukuzani	Myshako Riesling Mzvane	Napureouli Tsinandali
Red wines of Azerbaidjan	Chemakha	Kurdamir	Matrassa
Red wines of the Crimea	Bordo Ay-Danil	Cabernet Livadia	Saperavi Massandra
Red wines of Krasnodar	Cabernet Abraou		

350

THE WINES OF THE EASTERN MEDITERRANEAN

JOSEPH JOBÉ

All the countries of the Eastern Mediterranean basin have cultivated the vine since ancient times. The Egypt of the Pharaohs, the Promised Land of the Hebrews, the vast Persian Empire as well as the ancient Greek cities all produced wine. Under the benevolent eyes of the gods, the poets sang its praises, artisans and artists immortalized it on bas-reliefs and frescoes. The aged Homer celebrated "wine that gives us a manly heart"; Archilochus put the following truculent lines into the mouth of a galley-slave:

> One cannot mount guard
> While dying of thirst

The gentle Anachreon had a more melancholy turn of phrase:

> When I drink wine
> My pain is driven away
> And my dark thoughts
> Fly to the ocean winds

Like an echo come the words from the Book of Proverbs (xxxi, 6-7): "Give strong drink unto him that is ready to perish, and wine unto those that be of heavy hearts. Let him drink, and forget his poverty, and remember his misery no more."

When paganism gave way to Christianity the people of the Mediterranean basin continued to cultivate the vine and to produce wine right up to the Moslem era.

The later history of the vine in these regions may be explained in part by the ebb and flow of Christianity and Islam. Even today, Moslem influence is predominant in Egypt and Jordan; it is also felt in Moslem Turkey and, more surprisingly, in Christian Greece through the marketing of a considerable part of the vine-harvest, not as wine but as dried grapes or raisins (more than a hundred thousand tons per year in each country).

After World War I, cultivation of the vine in this part of the world increased at a phenomenal rate. The surface under cultivation in Greece multiplied fifteen-fold and production of wine rose ten times. Cyprus, on the other hand, made somewhat slower progress. But in Turkey, between 1939 and 1966, the number of vineyards doubled and wine production rose by four times. The evolution of the vineyard in Israel shows remarkable variations, but since 1965, the average has been about 22,240 acres. However, despite these fluctuations, the actual production of wine has been constantly on the increase, and averages, good or bad years, some 8,535,224 gallons. Egypt and the Lebanon have also increased their viticultural areas and their production of wine, but to a lesser degree. At present Egypt produces some 1,363,876 gallons yearly, and the Lebanon, 879,920 gallons; these are negligible amounts in comparison with the large viticultural regions of France. The Greeks and the Cypriots are, needless to say, the heaviest wine-drinkers of all these peoples.

GREECE

In Greece, vineyards and wine are as old as the gods, the land and the poets. Dionysus cultivated the vine and Homer sang the praises of wine in the Iliad and the Odyssey. More important still, the Greeks transplanted the vine to their colonies. Thus it is that many famous vineyards like those of Sicily, Malaga, Jerez and the Rhône valley are of Greek origin.

The present viticultural area is 500,000 acres which produce 118,789,200 gallons of wine, 196,840 tons of dessert grapes and nearly as many dried grapes. The Greek likes his wine, and drinks about 50 to 70 pints a year. Exports average 19,798,200 gallons a year.

The Peloponnese is the most important viticultural region. Its wines are mentioned on most wine-lists in hotels. They are dry white wines, such as the DEMESTICA, the SANTA HELENA, the ANTIKA or the SANTA LAOURA. The Peloponnese vineyards may be split into three regions. The central part produces a well-balanced

The LION DE NEMEA wine is a red from the province of Corinth, and is made from a local grape variety, *Agiogitiko*. It is of an intense ruby red colour, dry and full of flavour. It has about 12-13° alcohol. Although it cannot compete with a great French red wine, it makes an excellent Greek table wine.

The CHEVALIER DE RHODES is a red wine from Rhodes, dry, full-bodied and well-balanced, and of a beautiful garnet red colour. It is stronger than the LION DE NEMEA at 14-15°. Frequently found on Rhodes, it is not much exported to the other islands or to the mainland.

white wine, the MANTINEIA, around the ruins of the same name. The Patras region produces excellent dessert wines, such as the MAVRODAPHNE (red) or the MUSCAT DE PATRAS (white). In the third part, along the banks of the Gulf of Corinth and in particular at Nemea, a red full-bodied wine is made, the NEMEA or the HIGH NEMEA, depending on the altitude of the vineyard; these start at sea-level and reach up to about 2,500 feet.

On the mainland, Attica, already a land of wines and olives in ancient times, today produces a whole range of white wines made from the *Saviatiano* grape. Attica is also famous for its RETSINA, which in the opinion of many is the best in the land. The tourist who likes to taste the local wines will find something to satisfy his curiosity almost everywhere. For the benefit of those who visit the beautiful ruins of the site dedicated to Apollo, there is the wine of Arakhova, a village near Delphi. Macedonia offers the best red wine, NAOUSSA, made from the *Popolka* grape which is also known as the *Noir de Naoussa*. Thessalia has two red wines, the RAPSANI and the AMBELAKIA; Epirus makes only one semi-sweet white wine, the ZITSA.

The soil and climate of the Greek islands are usually favourable to the vine, and nearly every island has its own vineyard. Crete, for example, has a very important growth. In the east, there are fortified red table wines, wines of substance though not much spirit, made from the *Leatiko* grape; farther west, the Heraklion region produces red wines made from the *Ketsifali* and *Mandilari* grape varieties; these are full-bodied, rich wines with a heavy bouquet. At the farthest point west, in the region of Canea, only the red grape *Romeikon* is cultivated. On the other hand, the little island of Santonni is very fertile thanks to its volcanic soil, and produces such dry white wines as the NYCHTERI or sweet white wines like the VINO SANTO. The island of Samos offers a whole range of white wines, dry wines, resinated wines and sweet dessert wines, known as MUSCAT DE SAMOS. The islands of Rhodes and Zakinthos also have dry white wines; Leucadia produces reds.

Greece is, of course, the home of RETSINA, a wine which one either loves or hates. It has a bitter taste, acquired by flavouring the wine with resin during the process of fermentation. The resin comes from a pine-tree—the *calitris quadrivalvis*—which grows in that region. As the RETSINA takes on a bitter taste only after it has aged one year, those who are tasting it for the first time are advised to try a youthful RETSINA, preferably one of those from the Attica area.

Well-known and highly thought of are the dessert wines of Greece, starting perhaps with the MUSCAT DE SAMOS already mentioned, and going on to the MAVRODAPHNI, a very sweet red wine, a type of Malaga. We might also mention that the *Malvasia*, or Malmsey grape, originated in Peloponnisos. Today, the grape can be found in many other countries, Italy, France, Spain and Madeira for instance, where it has adapted well to local conditions and gives excellent white wines.

352

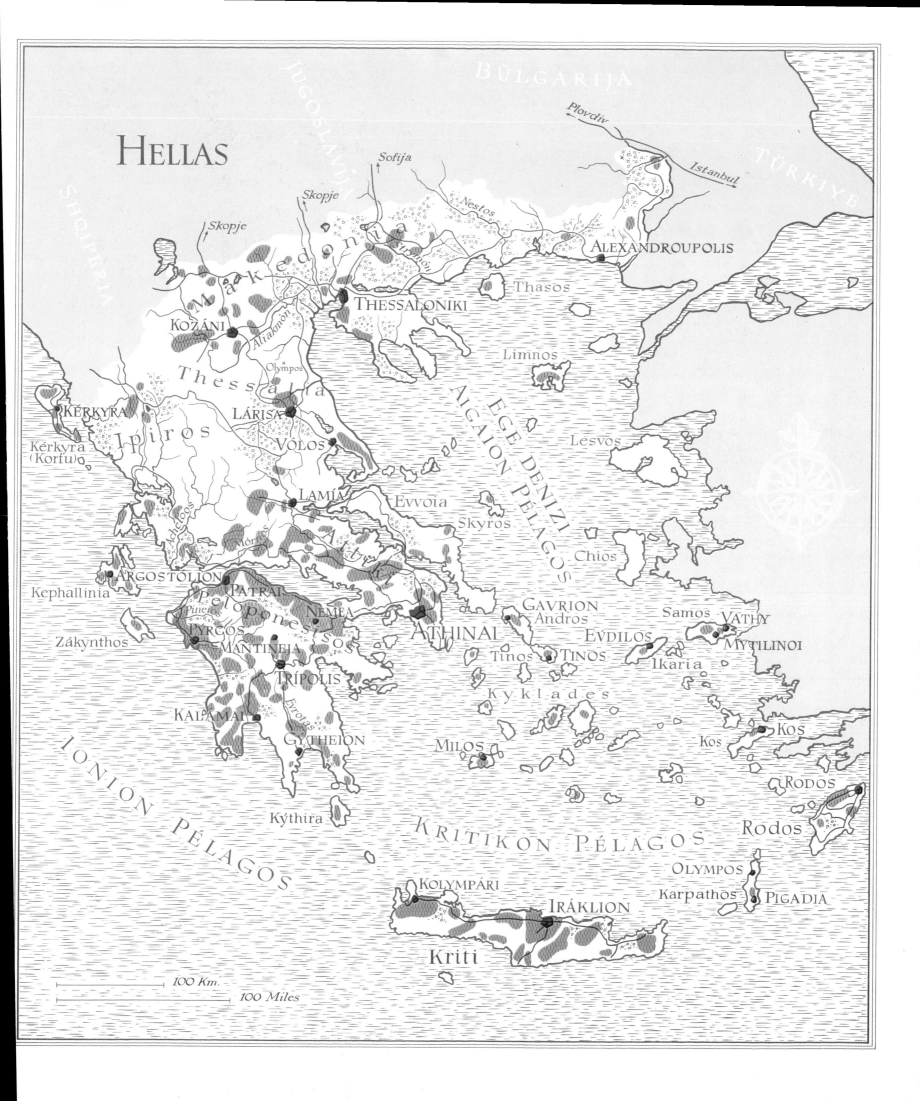

CYPRUS

Thanks to its privileged geographical situation, Cyprus not only cultivated the vine at a very early date but participated throughout ancient times in the flourishing wine trade between Egypt, Greece and Rome. After the fall of the Roman Empire in the west in 476 A.D., there followed a long night of seven centuries for the vine on the island.

The Crusaders and the Knights Templars were responsible for the revival of viniculture in Cyprus. But again, when the Turks arrived in 1571, the vine suffered another period of neglect although it did not disappear completely. It survived in the south-west part of the isle on the sunny slopes of Mounts Troghodhus and Makhera. From the grapes which grow in these parts, the Cypriot winegrowers make mainly ordinary table wines: red full-bodied wines, with a high tannin content, such as AFAMES and OTHELLO. There are fewer white wines. The driest and the best are APHRODITE and ANSINOE. A rosé, KOKKINELLI, is a fresh, semi-sweet wine, although it is somewhat darker in colour than most rosés. The best Cypriot wine is a dessert wine called COMMANDARIA. Named after the Knights Templars who guarded the Temple of Colossus, it is made from white or red grapes, specially dried in order to increase their sugar content. Usually the red grapes are used as they are more abundant. Only about twenty villages (Kalokhono, Zoopiyi, Yerass, Ayias and Mancas are the better known) are authorized to produce COMMANDARIA, and experts can distinguish the qualities which each village gives to the COMMANDARIA just as a connoisseur of Burgundy can tell from which particular vineyard along the Côte de Nuits or Beaune the Burgundy he is tasting has come.

Cyprus exports a good third of its wines, in particular red wines and COMMANDARIA.

As a final point of interest, one should mention that it was vine-shoots from Cyprus that produced, in the fifteenth century, the first Madeira wine.

TURKEY

If one believes, as many do, that Anatolia is the mother-country of the European vine, then Turkey has indeed a long heritage of viticulture. For as long as there were non-Moslem peoples living within the Turkish frontiers in Europe, there were Turkish wines for sale on the domestic and foreign markets. At the beginning of the twentieth century, following a period of political unrest, wine production went into a steep decline, but the whole picture changed with the establishment in 1928 of a Monopolies Board. From its lowest ebb in 1928 of 590,000 gallons, production reached 7,699,300 gallons in 1978. However, only 2 to 3 per cent of the grapes grown are used to make wine. Turkey has white wines *(beyez)* and red wines *(kirmizi)* which are found mainly in Thrace and along the shores of the Sea of Marmara, in Izmir (Smyrna) and in Anatolia. The best of the dry white wines usually come from the *Hasandede*, *Narince* and *Emir* grape varieties. The best red wines are made from the *Oküzgüzö-bogazkere*, *Papaskarasin* and *Kalecikkarasi* grape varieties; these wines have a very dark colour.

Well known on the international market is BUZBAG, a wine from Anatolia made from the *Bogazkere* grape, and TRAKYA, a dry red or white wine from the European part of Turkey.

Sweden imports BEYAZ, a semi-dry white wine, which comes from Tekirdag in Thrace.

Other wines of quality are the red ADABAG and KALEBAG. The Turks like sweet wines and the term "sarap" on a label indicates a very sweet wine, too sweet for the Western palate. Among the best of the dessert wines can be named the TEKEL GAZIANTEP and the TEKEL KALEBAG ANKARA, which are both red wines, and a white wine, the TEKEL MISBAG IZMIR.

There are also some ordinary local wines: for example, in Istanbul there is the GÜZEL MARMARA, either a red or a white dry or semi-dry wine; Ankara has the GÜZELBAG, which is also either a red or white dry or semi-dry wine; Izmir produces the IZMIR, once again a dry red or white wine and from Central Anatolia comes both red and white ÇUBUK. All these wines, when available, are drunk open rather than from bottles.

ISRAEL

The Bible attests that the people of Israel cultivated the vine. If ever a cluster of grapes was famous, it is surely the one brought back by the Hebrew scouts from Canaan. And if there ever was a famous drunkard, albeit an involuntary one, it is certainly Noah.

In the same way that Palestine has a turbulent history, so too was the history of its viticulture, for the vine was destroyed by some, replanted by others; reintroduced by the Crusaders, only to be finally abandoned for many centuries.

This extraordinary vine root was photographed near Bursa, in Turkey in Asia. There mostly table grapes and raisins are produced. It is in European Turkey that the best wines are grown, though in modest quantities.

The wine vine (*Vitis vinifera*) originates from Asia, and may well have come from Armenia. The Armenian vineyards produce table grapes and wine for local consumption.

When the first Zionists started to filter into Palestine around 1882, they planted, on the advice of the Rothschilds, French vine-plants. With time, the surface under cultivation increased, and today it reaches about 25,000 acres. Vineyards which produce grapes for making wine are planted in different regions of the country stretching from the south to the north: in the Negev, along the coast-line and on the foothills of Judea, in the mountains around Jerusalem, in the Sharon valley, on the hills of Samaria as well as in Upper and Lower Galilee. The average rainfall varies from 8 inches a year in the Negev to 27 inches in the mountains of Upper Galilee.

The *Cargnan* (41 per cent) and the *Alicante Grenache* (32 per cent) are the most common grape varieties. The winegrowers and viticultural co-operatives produce every conceivable type of wine, even sparkling Champagne-like wine made by the *méthode champenoise*. To name a few: The AVDAT WHITE (dry) and the CARMEL HOCK (semi-dry) are white wines; the MIKWE ISRAIL (dry) and the ADOM ATIC (semi-dry) are red wines, and the BINAYMINA is a rosé. There are also some white dessert wines (MUSCATEL) or reds (INDEPENDENCE WINE). Annual production reaches a total of about 8,535,224 gallons of which about 307,972 are for export.

An Israeli drinks only seven to nine pints of wine a year but he eats 26 to 28 pounds of table grapes.

The viticultural area in the neighbouring countries of Syria, the Lebanon and Jordan is much larger than in Israel. But as these three countries are of the Moslem faith, the produce of their vineyards is marketed, locally or abroad, in the form of table grapes or dried grapes; very little is made into wine. Jordan produces from 22,000 to 330,000 gallons of wine; Syria, about 1,539,860 gallons, and the Lebanon, 879,920 gallons, while the State of Israel produces more than five times as much from an area which is ten times smaller than that of her three neighbours put together. There is also a small vineyard in Iran, in the Azerbaijan and Teheran regions. Kurdistan is noted for its wine which has the scent of violets. Even in the best years, however, only 88,000 gallons of wine are produced.

It is written in the Bible (Numbers 13, 23) "And they came unto the valley of Eshcol, and cut down from thence a branch with a cluster of grapes, and they bare it upon a staff between two". Which shows that Israel has a very ancient winegrowing tradition that continues today with the production of red and white wines and excellent table grapes. The bunch of grapes comes from the Cathedral of Vienna.

EGYPT

The paintings on the tombs of the Pharaohs bear witness to the antiquity of the vine in this country (see page 10). However, after the arrival of the Arabs on the scene, vine cultivation fell into a decline, and wines became either very rare or very bad. Towards the beginning of this century, however, the vines were replanted, and after thirty years of hard work, Egyptian wines have once again found their qualities of yesteryear. And even if Egypt does not figure in many books on viticulture and wine, nor is usually referred to in statistical data, the country of the Pharaohs nonetheless produces each year an average of about 1,363,876 gallons of wine, and excellent wine at that.

The Maryat region, west of the Nile delta, was already famous for its wine in ancient times: Cleopatra offered Caesar a wine from Mareotide when he came to pay her a visit. This region produces two white wines, the CLOS MARIOUT and the CRUS DES PTOLÉMÉES, as well as a red wine, the CLOS MATAMIR.

As Egypt is a Moslem country, its consumption of wine is very low and its imports are negligible. A third of its production is exported.

WINES OF GREECE

DRY WHITE WINES

Agrylos	Gerania	Lindos de Rhodes	Pallini	Verdes
Arcadia	King Minos	Mantineia	Samos	Votrys
Demesticha	Lefkas	Marco	Santa Helena	Ymettos
Peza				Santa Laoura

MEDIUM-SWEET WHITE WINES

Gerania	Pallini	Samos	Zitsa

SWEET WHITE WINES

Samos	Muscat Rion de Patras	Muscat de Limnos	Paros	Rhodes Kair (or Chevalier
Muscat de Samos	Muscat Achaïa de Patras	Vino Santo de Santorin	Pilion	de Rhodes)
Muscat de Rhodes				Ymettos

DRY RED WINES

Agrylos	Halkidiki	Demesticha	Lefkas	Nadussa
Archanès	Castel Danielis	Peza	Marco	Nemea

SWEET RED WINE

Mavrodaphni

SPARKLING WINE

Zitsa

WINES OF ISRAEL

DRY WHITE WINES

Askalon Blanc 1963	Avdat White	Binyamina Blanc	Ein Guedi White	Mikwe Israel Blanc

MEDIUM-DRY WHITE WINES

Carmel Hock	Doron	Ein Guedi	Hock d'Askalon	Hock Patron

DESSERT WINES

Ashdod	Golden Cream	Muscat Supérieur	Muscatel - 19°	Topaz Ein Guedi

ROSÉ WINES

Binyamina Rosé	Mikwe Israel	Pink (dry)	Rose of Carmel (medium-dry)	Vin Rosé d'Askalon

DRY RED WINES

Arad	Avdat Red	Ben-Ami 1965	Binyamina Red	Mikwe Israel

MEDIUM-DRY RED WINES

Adom Atic	Askalon Rouge 1965	Château Binyamina	Ein Guedi Red	Mont Rouge

DESSERT WINES

Château Richon Red	Hadar	Mikwe Israel-Dessert	Porath Atic	Poria
Ein Guedi Red Wine	Independence Wine			

WINES OF CYPRUS

DRY WHITE WINES	RED WINES	ROSÉ WINES	DESSERT WINES
Aphrodite	Cyprus	Othello	Commandaria
Arsinoe	Afames	Kokkineli	Muscat de Chypre

WINES OF EGYPT

RED WINES

Clos Mariout   Cru des Ptolémées

WHITE WINES

Clos Matamir

WINES OF TURKEY

DRY WHITE WINES

Barbaros	Doluca	Kulüp beyaz	Merih	Tekel ürgüp
Diren	Kalebag	Marmara Incisi	Quakaya yildizi	Trakya

MEDIUM-DRY WHITE WINES

Beyaz   Narbag

SWEET WHITE WINES

Tekez Misbag izmir   Adabag

RED WINES

Buzbag	Kalebag	Kulüp	Merih	Trakya	Yakut Damcasi

THE WINES
OF NORTH AFRICA

DENIS BOUVIER

In the nature of its soil and its climate as much as the affinity of its distant past to Latin antiquity, North Africa resembles much more closely the European shores of the Western Mediterranean than the rest of the African continent. The Africans themselves, in fact, call it *djezira el Maghreb*, meaning "the Western Isle". The vine, like some messenger running ahead to announce the arrival of Mediterranean civilization, first saw life in the south, on the spurs of the mountains of Daïa, at the very doors of the Sahara. On this side, towards the north, begins the outer desert, which girdles the Mediterranean. From east to west, the vine runs along the coastal plains, up the hillsides and on the mountains, up to an altitude of about 3,600 feet, stretching from Kelibia in Tunisia as far as Bou Assida in Atlantic Morocco.

Here, as elsewhere, the vine has periodically appeared and disappeared throughout its history. There are many reasons for this, among them the continuous rivalries of nomadic and non-nomadic peoples, the conflicts between Christianity and Islam, and—nearer to our own times—the compelling demands of changing economics and politics.

No trace remains today to show whether the vine existed before the arrival of the Tyrians, who came to found Carthage. It is more than likely that they planted it themselves, in the valley of Medjerdah, before developing it further in their coastal colonies of Northern Africa. But it was Rome who first undertook to colonize this province of Africa which she had taken over from Carthage. The legions sent by Caesar and later by Augustus put to good use their talents as builders, farmers and winegrowers. From Carthage, restored from its ashes, to Lixus, near today's Larache in Morocco, where legend has situated the Garden of the Hesperides, the very end of their world, Rome turned Mauritania into the cellar of its empire. The vine grew near the ports or, farther inland, on the slopes around Roman farms such as we see, for example, on the mosaics of Tabarka. This wine of Africa, so much appreciated in Rome, was equally appreciated in Byzantium, which gave a new impulse to the vine by converting the Berber tribes to Christianity and so spreading the influence of wine right into the mountainous regions of the Atlas.

This agricultural and vinicultural life, however, had soon to give way to a pastoral existence when the Moslem hordes from Arabia undertook, in the seventh century, to conquer North Africa and convert its people to Islam. The former Roman Empire fell then into total chaos. Winegrowing gave way before the increasing, often forced conversion to Islam of the Christian or Israelite populations, and the vine was almost totally wiped out. It would be a mistake, nevertheless, to believe that as a result of the many conflicts inside the country, and the invasions which followed in waves, all contact ceased between the Maghreb and Christian Europe. There still existed in the Algeria of the tenth century nearly 40 cathedral cities, and there is every reason to believe that cultivation, including that of the vine, was continued around them. In other regions more under Arab influence, as in Tunisia, Christian colonies began to spring up after the Eighth Crusade and, although they were very much spread out, wine trading could be established by Tunis between these colonies and Marseilles. In the *fondouk* of Tunis—the fondouk being the walled area reserved for Europeans outside a Moslem town—wine was sold both wholesale and retail, using hall-marked measures. In this way, the "presence" of wine was maintained, incredible as it may seem in a period when Christianity was finding itself in an almost continuous battle with Islam.

This presence was maintained until the arrival of the Turkish sultan's Janissaries who, in their turn, stained the history of the Maghreb with blood. Winegrowing died out rapidly, to revive only at the beginning of the

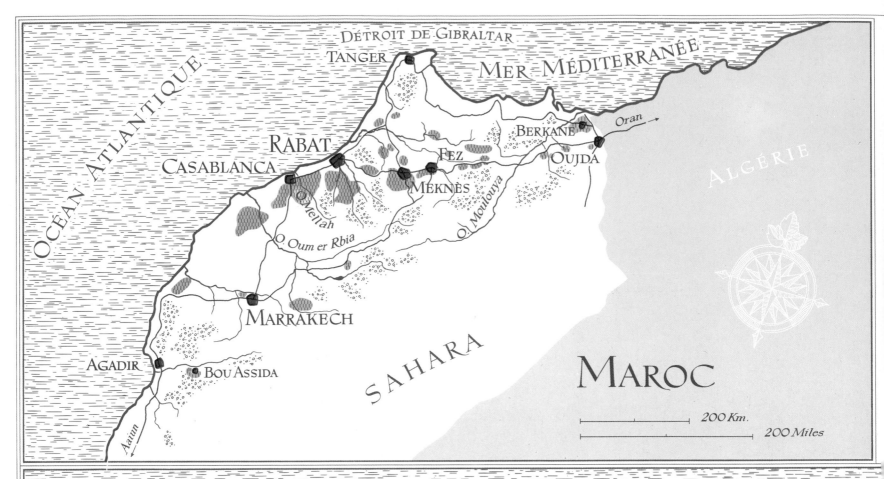

DÉTROIT DE GIBRALTAR

MER MÉDITERRANÉE

OCÉAN ATLANTIQUE

TANGER

RABAT

CASABLANCA

BERKANE

FEZ

OUJDA

ALGÉRIE

MEKNÈS

O. Ouellah

O. Moulouya

O. Oum er Rbia

MARRAKECH

SAHARA

AGADIR

Bou Assida

MAROC

Aaiun

200 Km.

200 Miles

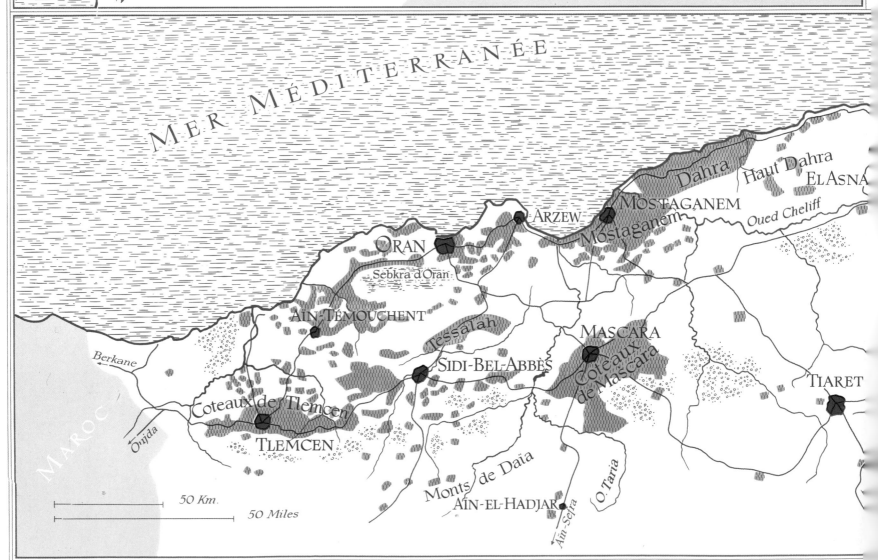

MER MÉDITERRANÉE

Dahra

Haut Dahra

EL ASNA

MOSTAGANEM

ARZEW

Mostaganem

Oued Cheliff

ORAN

Sebkra d'Oran

AÏN-TÉMOUCHENT

Tessalah

MASCARA

MAROC

Berkane

Coteaux de Tlemcen

Oujda

SIDI-BEL-ABBÈS

Coteaux de Mascara

TIARET

TLEMCEN

Monts de Daïa

O. Taria

AÏN-EL-HADJAR

Aïn-Sefra

50 Km.

50 Miles

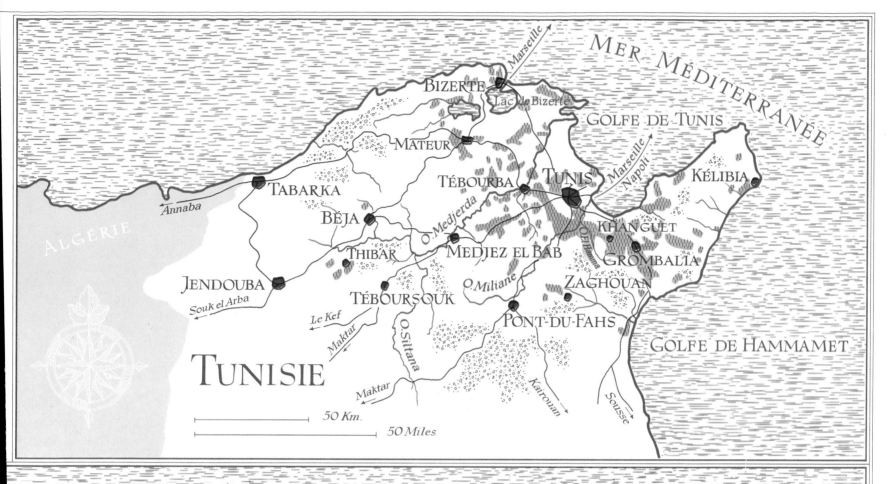

MER MÉDITERRANÉE

Marseille

BIZERTE
Lac de Bizerte
GOLFE DE TUNIS
MATEUR
TÉBOURBA
TUNIS
Marseille
Napoli
KÉLIBIA
TABARKA
Annaba
O. Medjerda
BÉJA
ALGÉRIE
KHANGUET
THIBAR
MEDJEZ EL BAB
O. El Hammil
GROMBALIA
JENDOUBA
TÉBOURSOUK
ZAGHOUAN
Souk el Arba
O. Miliane
Le Kef
O. Siliana
PONT-DU-FAHS
Maktar
GOLFE DE HAMMAMET

TUNISIE

Maktar
Kairouan
Sousse

50 Km.

50 Miles

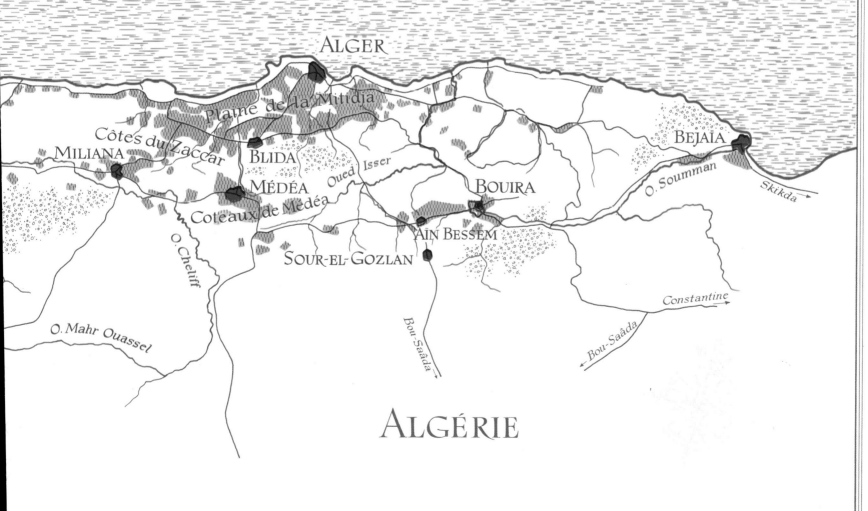

ALGER

MILIANA
Côtes du Zaccar
Plaine de la Mitidja
BLIDA
BEJAÏA
Oued Isser
O. Soumman
Skikda
MÉDÉA
BOUIRA
Coteaux de Médéa
AÏN BESSEM
O. Cheliff
SOUR-EL-GOZLAN
Constantine
Bou-Saâda
O. Mahr Ouassel
Bou-Saâda

ALGÉRIE

eighteenth century. At this time, and notably in Tunisia during the Hussein Dynasty, a more settled way of life developed: the stone-built house reconquered the ground where previously nomads had pitched their tents. A few vineyards were recreated then, chiefly for consumption of the fruit: Tunisia possessed more than 5,000 acres of vines before the French began administrating the land.

The first colonists to follow the conquest into this land cared little about this local cultivation, although a few did take the risk of trying to produce wine in the African climate and with methods not yet adapted to local conditions. They soon ran into the problem of the musts, for in Mediterranean North Africa autumn is still a hot season. The temperature of the winemaking installation is still high, fermentation takes place too rapidly, and the quality of the wine suffers. Several factors, however, contributed later to the development of this winegrowing, notably the arrival from 1871 on of settlers from Alsace and Lorraine, after the Franco-Prussian War. Others followed who had been defeated at home by the phylloxera epidemic of 1880. They came from all the vineyards of France, bringing with them a wide variety of vine-plants which they were able to exploit fully on this immense land, in a climate ideal for viticulture. To this could be added the opportunity of winning the French mainland market, where phylloxera had wiped out entire harvests. These winegrowers seized the chance of increasing the volume of production, both in Algeria and in Tunisia. But soon, the situation changed. In France, the vineyards were replanted with phylloxera-resistant American stock, while North Africa saw the disease reach its own shores, although its spread was quickly stopped. France thus found herself, within a very few years, in possession of two important winegrowing regions, and it became essential to take steps to prevent a dangerous over-production. Vines producing only an ordinary wine were uprooted on a large scale. Fortunately, the Algerian wines—heavy, full-bodied, richly-coloured—harmoniously complemented the lighter and more acid wines of Languedoc-Roussillon of southern France. A permanent organization to export

Algerian blending wines to France could thus be established. The North African vineyard was modernized and developed; the wines improved in quality, thanks also to planting new vines such as *Alicante-Bouschet*, *Cinsault*, *Carignan*, *Clairette* and *Grenache*. Better methods of vinification, more suited to the climate, were also introduced.

From 1919 to 1955, the North African vineyard progressed by leaps and bounds. Cultivation methods were rationalized and winegrowing became an industry, with increased mechanization, new transport and modern distribution methods. Even the actual vinification was now viewed as an industrial operation: the work, from the harvest to the bottling, was simplified to a maximum degree to make up for a lack of qualified labour. Some care was taken, too, to train the local inhabitants as vineyard workers by giving them agricultural instruction in specialized centres. While this effort was only limited in scope, a number of local winegrowers, in Oran especially, began to cultivate the vine for wineproduction, and began selling their produce, either on the open market, or through the numerous agricultural co-operatives.

It is true that troubles due to over-production were never lacking and rivalry never disappeared in the various parts of the Mediterranean. But North Africa had acquired, with its vineyards, a new-found economic dimension of considerable importance.

Can one now look at the future of the North African vineyard more optimistically, after all the political upheavals which Morocco, Tunisia and Algeria have seen in turn? While that question perhaps cannot be answered yet, it would seem that wine production can be kept up provided two main conditions are borne in mind. The first is that the vines must not monopolize land in areas where the government would like to develop food production or industry. The second is that wine exports to foreign markets must be solidly covered by bilateral agreements with European countries and, more particularly, with France. This latter point clearly demonstrates how closely the North African viticultural industry is linked to and indeed controlled by economic and political contingencies.

TUNISIA

When one looks at a map of the Mediterranean around Tunisia, the little port of Kelibia appears like an island, surrounded by the sea on one side and by fields of olives and vines on the other. It is the first vineyard one meets in Tunisia when arriving from the east. Its wine grapes, *Muscat d'Alexandrie*, give a wine full of savour, as if impregnated with the perfumes of the Orient. But one must reach Carthage to be really on the

heart of the great Tunisian vineyard. Here some Punic sculptor of long-ago has cut wine-grapes into the stonework of a monument to the goddess Tanit. In its modern form, this vineyard of 86,485 acres is the work of European colonists. To supplement the few local vines of table grapes spread along the coast, new vineplants were introduced, such as *Grenache*, *Carignan*, *Alicante-Bouschet*, *Mourvèdre*, *Morastel*, *Vocéra*, *Pinot Noir* for

At the time when Tunisia became independent, practically all the vineyards belonged to Europeans. Nowadays, Tunisians themselves cultivate the vine and produce wine, often by traditional methods, for the country is unable to modernise itself as fast as industrialised countries.

red wines, and *Pedro-Ximenez, Sémillon, Sauvignon, Clairette de Provence, Beldi, Ugni, Merseguera, Muscat d'Alexandrie* and *Terracina* for whites.

The Tunisian vineyard, hit by phylloxera only in 1936, faced ten catastrophic years from 1943 to 1953. It managed to make a fresh start with regular expansion of production, despite the departure of many European winegrowers after Tunisia's Declaration of Independence in 1956. Today, 900 small concerns have regrouped themselves into well-equipped co-operatives; the cellars can hold more than ten million gallons of a wine which, thanks to the care given it by qualified workers, can be of a very good quality. But this already considerable stock of wine could be doubled, even tripled, for the French market, which is still the main customer. Home consumption of wine is dropping and new commercial outlets are urgently needed.

Going from west to east, the Tunisian vineyards are located in the regions of Bizerte, Mateur and Raf-Raf in the north; Tebourba, Massicault, Sedjourni and Carthage around Tunis; Khanguet, Grombalia, Bou Arkoub, Bir Drassen and Kelibia on Cape Bon. They thus form a giant crescent around the Gulf of Tunis. Farther south, there are smaller vineyards, those of the Gulf of Hammamet and Zaghouan in the north, and Thibar at the foot of the Teboursouk mountains in the Caidate of the same name.

Tunisian law protects three types of wine. First of all, the VIN SUPÉRIEUR DE TUNISIE, a red, rosé or white wine with an alcohol content of 11 to 13°, depending on the region and the yield, and aged at least one year. Muscat is next, either with a simple *appellation d'origine* MUSCAT DE TUNISIE, or else with an *appellation d'origine contrôlée*, in which case it is sold under the name of the commune where it was produced, such as MUSCAT DE RADÈS or MUSCAT DE THIBAR. Finally, there are the vintage wines, with an *appellation d'origine contrôlée* but where the name of the vine does not appear, such as RADÈS and KELIBIA.

Most Tunisian wines are exported, but one can sample on the spot and with much pleasure a good SAINT-CYPRIEN or a THIBAR from the St. Joseph property.

363

ALGERIA

The colonization of Algeria was certainly responsible for the proper exploitation of its soil, the development of techniques for production, vinification and sale of wines, all of which have placed Algeria among the leading wineproducing countries.

Several years after it gained its independence, the young state has kept alive its viticulture, despite the departure of its qualified European workers and the consequent disappearance of its non-Moslem domestic market. All honour to the nation. It is in any case absolutely essential for Algeria to maintain its viticulture: more than half the agricultural employment comes from the vineyards. The latter are in an even more important position when one realizes that not only do they produce the wine which provides, when sold, half of Algeria's total exports and cargoes for her merchant ships; the vineyards also supply the raw materials for a number of industries born of vinicultural side-products, such as the manufacture of alcohol tartrates, oil, fertilizers and fodder. This trade requires costly and extensive equipment and installations, and the economic and social importance of the vini-viticultural production becomes even clearer. The government thus has not only the first preoccupation of making sure this colonial heritage produces profitably, but they must at the same time increase professional training and put a brake on the exodus from the country side, which has been noticeable since 1962. A certain preference can understandably be seen, however, in favour of the conversion of the viticultural regions to cultivation of some product more independent of the French market, for the shipments of wine are at present only saleable in the former mother country, and the government must remember also that these sales are made thanks largely to commercial agreements which French vintners would be only too happy to see go.

The Algerian vineyards lie between La Calle in the east and Nemours (today called Ghazaouet) in the west, extending also from north to south, from the shores of the Mediterranean to the slopes of the Atlas upper plateau. The total area is about 494,200 acres but their distribution has no uniformity, for Algeria is a very undulating land.

Apart from a few plants of local origin (*Hasseroum*, *Grilla*, *Farhana*), all the vine-plants grown in Algeria come from Europe, and have been grafted with American stocks to combat phylloxera. The red wines are usually wines for blending, full-bodied, with a high alcohol content and a good deal of tannin, although they can also be good vintage wines classified as of superior quality, or given a simple *appellation d'origine*. They come from vine-plants such as *Carignan, Cinsault, Alicante-Bouschet, Morastel, Mourvèdre, Gamay, Pinot Noir* and *Cabernet*. The white wines, which are usually of good quality, full-bodied, rather perfumed, and well alcoholized, come from plants such as *Clairette, Grenache, Ugni Blanc, Faramon, Macabéo* and *Merseguera*, although *Alicante* or *Cinsault* are also used. The climate, the nature of the soil, the exposure to the sun and type of vine-plant all have the usual influence on the wine produced, but here the altitude of the vineyards appears to play a particularly important role. The wines of the plain are usually light and do not keep well; the wines from the mountains are usually full-bodied, rich, heavy and thick, and the wines of the slopes, between the plains and the mountains, are of an intermediate type, fine, lively and with a delicate bouquet. Annual yield is about 198,000,000 gallons.

EASTERN ALGERIA

DEPARTMENT OF ANNABA (BÔNE). Coming in from Tunisia by the Medjerdah Valley, one meets the first mountain vineyards around Souk Ahras, at an altitude of about 2,100 feet. Their wine is supple but full-bodied, with a good colour. Continuing west from Souk Ahras on towards Medjez Sfa, one enters the Wadi Seybouse which leads, northwards, to the Bône plain and, westwards, to the region of Guelma. There are some very fine vineyards here, stretched along the flanks of the valley at an altitude varying between 300 and 900 feet, near Guelma, Heliopolis and Petit. They produce full-bodied but supple wines with a slightly earthy tang. Up towards Bône itself, vines are much rarer and one must edge over to Aïn Mokra, west of Seybouse Valley, to find them again, or else run eastwards along the valley to La Calle, where the wine is clean-tasting, light and with a good body.

DEPARTMENTS OF CONSTANTINE, BATNA AND SÉTIF. Returning from the Wadi Seybouse and following, beyond Guelma, the Wadi Bou Hamdane and the Wadi Zenati, the traveller passes the Kroub to reach Constantine in the north, and Lambèse and Batna in the south. The region just around Constantine produces excellent wines, those of Lambèse and Batna being rather more full-bodied and supple. Beyond Constantine and the Col des Oliviers, the region of Azzaba (Jemmapes) produces very honest table wines. But the palm of victory for the wines of the Constantine region must go, along with those of Souk Ahras, to the wines of BÉNI MELEK, with its vineyards laid out along the Eocene slopes of Skikda (Philippeville). The white wines from here are much sought for their vigour and robustness. Still farther west of Constantine, one meets the vineyards of Petite-Kabylie and their light, lively and almost colourless wines, lacking somewhat in acidity and body; they are to be found around Djidjelli, Chefka, the foothills of Djebel Seddets and in the Wadi Djinedjerre. Finally, there are two vineyards encircling Petite-Kabylie: Sétif, in the south, at an altitude of 3,300 feet, and Akbou-El

Maten-El Kseur in the Wadi Soummam which separates Petite-Kabylie from Grande-Kabylie in the west. The savour and bouquet of these wines is very fine.

CENTRAL ALGERIA

DEPARTMENTS OF ALGIERS AND TIZI OUZOU. The central region of Algeria has immense vineyards and is certainly the second most important of the country's viticultural areas. But here the estates formerly owned by Europeans have passed into the management of the Algerians themselves, and the inexperience of these new winegrowers, who took over from the colonists from one day to the next, shows in the many vines, notably in Mitidja, which were worn out before their time and are now abandoned. Viticulture nevertheless remains one of the primary agricultural activities here, in Mitidja and Sahel d'Alger, from Thénia to Ténès.

Following the Mediterranean shore, one finds east of the capital the vineyards of Thénia, Rouïba, Bou Bérah and Abbo, followed, south-east of Reghaïa, by those of St.-Pierre and Arbatache, then those of Souk el Haad, Chabet-et-Ameur, Isserville-les-Issers and Les Isserts in the Departement of Tizi Ouzou. This region produces very well-balanced wines. Nearer Algiers stretch the vineyards of Aïn Taya, Dar el Baida (Maison-Blanche) and El Harrache (Maison Carrée). In the coastal region are the vinegrowing communes of Boufarik, Hadjout, Sidi Moussa, then Mouzaïa, Blida and El Affroun and, along the slopes, Bouzaréa, Montebello, Beni Mered, Guyotville, Cheragas, Zeralda, Douera, Mahelma, Kolea, Bou Aroun, and so one. Their wines are cool and fruity, with an alcohol content of 10 to 12°.

DEPARTMENT OF EL ASNAM (ORLÉANSVILLE). The vineyards in this Department are in the north, in Sahel; Villebourg, Novi, Gouraya and Ténès; then in Dahra, west of Hadjout, Meurade and Bou Yersen. They produce "wines of the slopes" that are solid, lively and well-coloured. The best-known wines of this Department are, in fact, the Côtes du Zaccar, produced above Miliana and along towards Rouïan and Orléans-ville; they are fairly full-bodied wines, robust and lively and

The vineyards of the Mitidja plain, south of Algiers (photograph) give robust, healthy, well-made wines. Once exported as mixing wines, they are now sold as everyday table wines. However, Algerian wine production has fallen to half that produced in 1963-1973.

365

with an alcohol content of 11 to 13°. Many people do not hesitate to compare them with the French CÔTES DE RHÔNE wines.

DEPARTMENT OF MÉDÉA. There are vineyards at an altitude of 2,100 feet around the towns of Médéa, Damiette, Hassen ben Ali and Lodi, and farther east at an altitude of 1,800 feet, in this region of Sour el Gozlan, Bir Rabalou and Aïn Bessem. The reputation of the MÉDÉA and AIN BESSEM wines is already firmly established and they can be compared to those of Bouïra at the foot of Djurdjura in the Departement of Tizi Ouzou. All are classified as of superior quality.

WESTERN ALGERIA

DEPARTMENT OF MOSTAGANEM. This region still has very many private estates which, up to the time of independence, made up part of the vast Department of Oran, producer of two-thirds of the country's total wine harvest and undoubtedly of the best wines of Algeria.

Going down the right bank of the Wadi Cheliff and leaving behind the vineyards of the Zaccar slopes, one finds not far from the mouth of the watercourse, on the slopes of Dahra, wines which are fine yet fruity and which keep well. South of the Wadi, vineyards of the plains on argillo-siliceous soil, around Mohammédia and Relizane, criss-cross those of the slopes near Mostaganem, Mesra, Rivoli, Mazagran, Aïn Tédelès and so on. Their wines have an alcohol content of only 10 to 12°, but they are honest and robust types, while those of Mostaganem have the right to the appellation V.D.Q.S., as do also those of Mascara, the large viticultural area south of the Beni Chougran mountains. The wines known under the appellation COTEAU DE MASCARA have probably the finest reputation of any in Algeria. The wines called simply MASCARA are not so good.

DEPARTMENT OF ORAN. The vineyard of this Department is divided into four large regions. East of the provincial capital, in a magnificent plain reminiscent of the French landscapes of Languedoc, the vines stretch as far as the eye can see from Sidi Chami to Arzew, past Assi Bou Nif, Fleurus, Gdyel, Renan and Ste. Léonie. Farther south is the little vineyard area of St. Lucien, in the Wadi Tlélat. West of Oran, facing the sea on both sides of Sahel, are the vines of Aïn el Turk and Bou Sfer; then those of Misserghin and Brédéah, turned towards Sebkra d'Oran and the slopes of M'silah. These vines produce lively wines with a pronounced bouquet. South-west of Sahel d'Oran is the area producing the Aïn Témouchent and Aïn Kial wines, while those of Rio Salado and Hammam bou Hadjar come from the Metla plain, at an average altitude of 1,200 feet. Finally, the last viticultural region of this department is that of the Tessalah mountains, which produces excellent reds, whites and rosés deserving the classification of "superior quality". The main centres are Sidi bel Abbès, Sidi Daho, Sidi l'Hassen, Sidi Khaled, Lamtar and Wadi Imbert.

DEPARTMENTS OF TLEMCEN AND SAIDA. Adjoining the frontiers of Morocco, the Department of Tlemcen produces vintage wines of which the best is COTEAUX DE TLEMCEN. Outside of Tlemcen, there are vines in the communes of Bréa, Négrier, Mansourah, Aïn Fezza, Lamoricière and Wadi Chouly. There is a small vineyard at Marnia, north-west of the Tlemcen mountains and near the Moroccan frontier, which produces the same type of wine as the preceding areas.

This tour of the vineyards of Oran and Alger ends in the Department of Saïda, where, backed up against the Daïa mountains and facing the great Sahara, is the vineyard of Saïda, while at the westernmost point of Algeria is Aïn el Hadjar and its excellent wine.

MOROCCO

Tingitan Mauretania, the name given by the Romans to their colony in Morocco, has known the vine since earliest antiquity. Today, the most up-to-date vineyards rub shoulders with the traditional vine which produces grapes for the table. There are in all some 185,000 acres planted to the vine, of which four-fifths produce wine, to the extent of 55,000,000 gallons.

Most Moroccan wines are either reds or rosés, with only a small quantity of whites being produced. The red wines are generous, supple and rich, well-balanced but perhaps lacking a little in spirit, with an alcohol content of 12 to 14°. The rosés are clear, limpid and lively, with an agreeable fruitiness. The whites are distinguished as elegant, warm but a little heavy, with a good bouquet. At Boulaouane, El Jadida (south of Casablanca) and Dem-

nate in the area of Marrakech, there is a production of "grey" wines, which are dry and fruity, and also of table wines made from the *Muscat d'Alexandrie*. The most commonly met vines are *Cinsault, Carignan, Grenache* and *Alicante-Bouschet* for the red wines, and *Pedro Ximenez, Plant X, Clairette* and *Grenache* for the white wines. The main viticultural areas are Oujda, Berkane, Anged El Aioum and Taourirt in the east; around Taza, Fez and Meknès (whose red wines, fairly light, are the best in Morocco) in the centre; and around Rabat and the Chaouïa Plain towards the west. Other vineyards are spread across southern Morocco between Safi and Mogador, and farther east along the Wadi Tensift up to Sidi Addi, and finally at Bou Assida, on the south-west slopes of the High Atlas.

THE WINES
OF SOUTH AFRICA

KENNETH MAXWELL

In the fertile soil of the Cape of Good Hope, the vine has found superb conditions for growth, and it has prospered there for more than three centuries. Today, the vineyards stretch across the hillsides and valleys of the hinterland, from the foot of the mountain which rises above Table Bay to the chain of purple peaks whose imposing stature confers on the Cape such magnificence and such beauty.

Against this backdrop of hills and mountains, the vineyards of the Cape survey one of the most enchanting panoramas in the world. The farms with their gabled-ends and their whitewashed façades are pure history, the history of the first colonists, and they reflect the perseverance and character of the people who conceived this famous Dutch-style Cape architecture.

Three years after the first Dutch settlement was established at the Cape of Good Hope, in February 1655, a ship of the Dutch East India Company sailed into Table Bay, carrying a few European vineplants. Johan van Riebeeck, Governor of the Colony, had these plants set out in the gardens of the Company, at the foot of Table Mountain. Four years later, South Africa's viticulture was born when grapes from those vineplants were pressed to make the first Cape wine. Some twenty years after that, Governor Simon van der Stel himself set out 100,000 roots of vine in a model-farm in Constantia Valley, thus encouraging the colonists to develop cultivation of the vine. And at the end of the seventeenth century, a large number of French Huguenot refugees poured into the Cape, bringing with them the experience and the secrets of winemaking. They settled in the valleys of Stellenbosch, Paarl, Drakenstein and Franschhoek, building up the viticulture there and greatly improving the quality of the region's wines. Some of these farms and workings carry their original French names to this day.

The harvest increased and wine could soon be exported to Batavia. For one must remember that the original reason for the Dutch settlement at the Cape was as a port of call where ships could take in fresh supplies on the voyage from the Netherlands to India. Nevertheless, as the Cape wine became known and appreciated in Europe, considerable quantities were shipped to Great Britain and the Continent of Europe.

Most of the South African wine was at that time being produced in the Constantia Valley by the Groot-Constantia farm, which was then the property of the Cloete family. The Muscat from Constantia was, in fact, described as "undeniably a dessert wine, strong but delicate, and having in its bouquet something singularly agreeable". In 1805, Great Britain, then fighting against Napoleon, occupied the Cape for the second time: her vessels came to take on supplies there, being no longer able to do so in France. The wine-growers were encouraged to produce vintage wines for export, and an official wine taster was appointed to sample the export wines and ensure that they had the required quality and ageing. The British Government wished to stimulate the export of wines still more, and in 1813 introduced a preferential customs tariff for imported colonial wine. The result of this colonial preference was absolutely staggering. The production of wines of all kinds, both natural wines and sweet and liqueur wines, shot up. From 930,000 gallons in 1813, the South African wine production rocketted in 1824 to 2,442,000 gallons, of which very nearly one-half (1,011,000 gallons) was exported. These preferential tariffs were, however, progressively cut back in later years, until they were finally abolished in 1861 by William Gladstone's government.

Phylloxera ravaged the vineyards of the Cape in 1885, leaving the winegrowers in a very poor situation. The disease was finally eliminated in the same way as in Europe, by grafts on American stock resistant to the parasite. But after this cure, the revitalized wines met a fresh problem in the first part of the twentieth century—over-production. Their yield was so generous that in 1916 winegrowers had to be content with a one-penny profit per bottle of good quality wine. To cope with this overabundance and avoid a recurrence of

the crisis, a co-operative organization was formed. The principal vinegrowers had already met several times in 1916 to discuss the advisability of setting up a central organization which would protect their interests. No one who saw this body founded realized that it would become an all-powerful apparatus of control, directing and ruling the activities of vinegrowers and wineproducers alike. A proposal for a central co-operative body was drawn up, and presented at a huge assembly at Paarl. The result was the foundation, in 1918, of the body known as the *Kooperatieve Wijnbouwers van Zuid-Africa* (K.W.V.), or Wine-Growers Co-operative of South Africa. It was then and still is today mainly made up of Afrikaners, and had as its principal aim the conduct, control and regulation of the sale and disposal of its members' production; it also guaranteed or tried to guarantee that their profits would be consistent with their production. Today, nobody can produce wine without the authorization of the K.W.V., which decides the maximum annual production of each vineyard and the minimum prices of good wines and distillation wines, and also calculates the "surplus" factor or proportion of each wineproducer which then has to be delivered free of charge to the K.W.V. No producer may sign a sales contract with a merchant without the prior approval of the K.W.V., which receives the payments due, nor may a producer sell any part of their harvest to individuals without the express consent of this governing body.

WINEGROWING REGIONS

The South African vineyard area is situated in the south-west part of Cape Province, and is divided into two distinct zones. The first part includes the areas around Stellenbosch, Paarl and Wellington, then the area from Malmesbury to Tulbagh, and finally the Cape Peninsula and the famous Constantia Valley. The climate there is temperate: mild in spring, hot and even very hot in summer, either mild or hot in autumn, cold and humid in winter. This comparatively small region—very small, in fact, when one compares it with the regions which produce the many types of European wine—can produce most of the well-known wines thanks to the wide variety of soil and land; most of the South African natural wines of everyday type are to be found there.

The other major wine-producing zone is at a higher altitude. Known as the Little Karoo, it extends from Ladysmith to Outshoorn, between the Drakenstein and the Swartberg, and includes Worcester, Robertson, Bonnievale and Swellendam. The climate here is much more severe than in the coastal region—less rain and more heat, hence the need to irrigate the land—but there is a good production, largely in the domain of dessert wines, sherries or ports.

TYPES OF VINE-PLANT. A wide variety of grapes grow in these two regions, with the vine-plants used for white wines (*Riesling, Stein, Blanc Français, Clairette Blanche*) doing well along the coast. The *Hermitage, Cabernet Sauvignon* and *Shiraz* give light red wines, while the *Pinot, Gamay, Cabernet, Hermitage, Shiraz* and *Pinotage* give full-bodied reds. As far as the wines themselves are concerned, the strongest are produced in the regions close to the coast (Constantia, Sommerset-West and certain parts around Stellenbosch), with the better wines coming from Paarl, Stellenbosch and Tulbagh; the light red wines come from around Paarl and Durbanville. A vine called *Pinotage*, developed by one of K.W.V.'s research workers who crossed *Hermitage* with *Pinot*, is very well known in South Africa and is planted quite extensively. Its wine combines the best qualities of the two separate species: a full-bodied red of good quality, with a fruity and perfumed bouquet which somehow recalls the French Beaujolais. In the Little Karoo region, the *Blanc Français, Hermitage, Hanepoot, Muscat* and *Sultana* vines produce dessert wines.

THE CLIMATE. Although in the southern hemisphere, the whole calendar of vine growth is, naturally, entirely different from that of Europe, the influence of each season is nevertheless very similar. Spring, from September to November, is the busiest time of the year for the vinegrower. In summer, from December to February, the grape ripens; the harvest is carried out in the southern autumn, between March and May.

The South African climate is almost over-generous; in fact, the sun presents some serious problems for the vinegrowers. While in Europe the harvest ripens in the cool of autumn after a relatively short summer, in South Africa it ripens during the heat of midsummer, which creates special problems in the fermentation and ageing. On the other hand, grapes that ripen under a strong sun always contain a high proportion of sugar, which does not always balance out the natural acidity. One can say, too, that the South African winegrower is much less bothered by the capricious moods of the weather than his European counterpart. In the Cape, *every* wine-year is a good year. There is, however, a constant search to profit from what little amount of freshness can be found or engineered during the ripening of the grape, for it facilitates the conservation of the bouquet and aroma in the wine, particularly in the white wines. An interesting difference of opinion is seen in this connection: some farmers use vine-props to lift the vine clear of the ground during the torrid midsummer period, while other farmers take quite the opposite viewpoint and leave the vine close to the ground, claiming that the vine leaves protect the grape from the sun's strength. A great deal of attention is paid to the orientation of the vineyards. It has been proved that the vines which are grown on the cooler southern slopes (remembering that this is the southern hemisphere) produce better white wines, while for good red wines the winegrowers prefer the sites facing north, towards the prevailing sun.

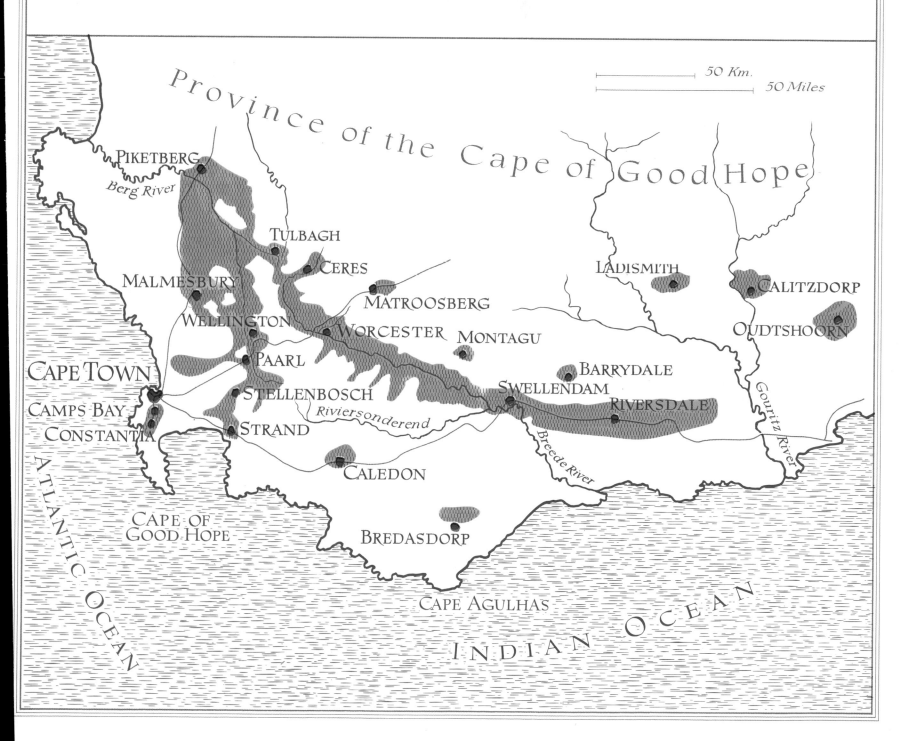

REPUBLIC OF
SOUTH AFRICA

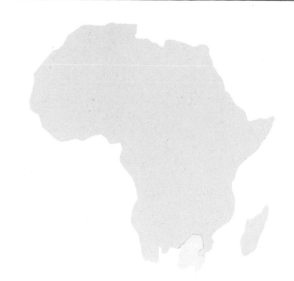

50 Km.

50 Miles

Province of the Cape of Good Hope

PIKETBERG

Berg River

TULBAGH

CERES

MALMESBURY

MATROOSBERG

LADISMITH

CALITZDORP

WELLINGTON

WORCESTER

MONTAGU

OUDTSHOORN

CAPE TOWN

PAARL

CAMPS BAY

STELLENBOSCH

Riviersonderend

BARRYDALE

SWELLENDAM

RIVERSDALE

CONSTANTIA

STRAND

Breede River

Gouritz River

CALEDON

CAPE OF
GOOD HOPE

BREDASDORP

ATLANTIC OCEAN

CAPE AGULHAS

INDIAN OCEAN

GENERAL CHARACTERISTICS OF THE WINES

The products of the Cape vineyards can never be the same as the European wines of similar type, however much the South African growers may simulate European production methods by using modern refrigeration and modern control systems during the fermentation and ageing processes. And even were the vine and the soil identical to those in Europe, the sheer heat of the Cape climate raises the sugar content, reduces the acidity, and consequently gives an entirely different wine. In this respect, wine-lovers who attempted to find in the Cape wines the exact replicas of the European wines they know would be depriving themselves of a rare chance for enjoyment: the Cape wines possess their own aroma and characteristics, despite their apparent resemblance to European wines.

The production of Cape vintage wines has been made possible by the introduction of temperature control in the cellars. By using great stainless-steel or steel containers, the winegrower can now control the speed of fermentation at a low temperature, and can thus re-create the fresh European climate which is needed if the wine is to retain its delicate perfume and its taste. This can be achieved in one of three ways. The required low temperature can be maintained by pumping cold water through pipes which pass through the must, or the must itself can be circulated through a refrigerating circuit, or the temperature of the air in the cellar itself can be lowered by air-conditioning.

The slightly-sweet wines so popular in South Africa are obtained by cutting short the fermentation, either by using a sulphureous gas, or else by compressing or chilling the must so that the wine, which already contains the authorized 2 per cent of sugar, keeps in addition a part of its natural sweetness. After ageing in cool cellars, the wine is clarified by being racked and filtered. In South Africa, white wines are bottled and drunk while they are still very young, sometimes after a mere six months, and while they are still fresh, sparkling and deliciously fruity.

RIESLING is probably the best Cape white wine, followed closely by STEIN. The RIESLING wine tends to be the drier of the two; yet it is not, as the Cape climate might lead one to suppose, as dry as the German RIESLING. The STEIN wine is usually semi-sweet but it can be dry on occasion, in much the same way that the RIESLING can be semi-dry or semi-sweet. These wines, which have such an agreeable taste, fruitiness and aroma, tend, however, to be more full-bodied than the semi-sweet European wines. The wines made from *Clairette Blanche* vines are more delicate, and when drunk young, have an admirably mordant freshness and perfumed aroma.

The alcohol content of the Cape white wines, at 11 to 12° by volume, is slightly higher than the European white wines. The growers now also produce a SPÄT-LESE, a white *mi-flétri*, which by virtue of letting the grapes dry longer before pressing them has a distinctly higher alcohol content. Good wines of a deep yellow colour, they are made from *Steen, Riesling*, or even *Hanepoot* vines.

As for the Cape red wines, they are usually aged for two or three years before being bottled, at which stage they are very drinkable, since most of them are dry and have a very pleasant perfume. To improve their quality still more, connoisseurs keep them yet another two or three years. There are, unfortunately, only a very few wineproducers who take the trouble to indicate the harvest-year on the bottle labels, and even then, these are wines from small winegrowers whose vines are renowned for their quality. A few experienced *restaurateurs* are careful to cellar the wine for two years or so, to avoid the possibility of any disagreeable surprises and to allow it to assert its best qualities.

It is the red wines of the Cape which come closest to European wines. The full-bodied reds, made from *Cabernet, Pinot Noir, Gamay* and *Hermitage* vines in the regions of Paarl, Stellenbosch and Durbanville, are of a Burgundy type, with all the qualities which that can imply. The light reds tend more towards the Bordeaux type and come from vines in Constantia Valley, around Stellenbosch and Somerset-West. The *Shiraz* vine does very well in the Cape climate, producing a red wine with a rich bouquet; blended with *Hermitage* or *Cabernet*, it gives a full-bodied wine of a certain distinction if it has been allowed to age. The red wine made from the crossed vine *Pinotage*, with its bright colour, its fruitiness and its pronounced bouquet, is one of the best full-bodied reds in the country.

The rosé wines, which are much lighter, are finding increasing approval, their freshness being particularly welcome in the South African heat. They have the colour of red wines but the main characteristics of whites; they tend to be astringent and to lack body.

APPELLATIONS. There are no provisions in South African law covering the use of the term *appellation d'origine contrôlée*. In point of fact, such a definition is not suitable for the wines of South Africa. Very many wines are described as "bottled" on such-and-such an estate, but most often they certainly do not come from vines harvested on one single estate; they may even come from a mixture of wines of quite different origins. One can also add that any mention on the label of the A.O.C. would probably not interest the South African consumer, who has more confidence in the guarantee of a standard quality offered in wine coming from the big estates. The name of the vine is sometimes given on the label, an advantage for the lover of good wine who is able to take his choice between wines from *Riesling* or *Cabernet* or *Pinotage*. As so many wines carry only the name of a winegrower, the only really reliable method of investigating their quality is by the tried and trusted one of tasting them. Some labels, however, carry the word "selected", which is usually an indication either that the grape was carefully selected before pressing, or the wine, while still young and before being treated and

aged, was picked out as being of excellent quality. This solitary one-word mention is by no means negligible when it comes to judging the quality of the bottle's contents. The year of the wine-harvest is, as already pointed out, very rarely given: the South African consumer seldom pays any attention to it and the winegrowers claim that since the climatic conditions are always constant and perfect the quality of the wine is equally so!

On this ticklish point of appreciation of the quality of wines, one can mention that the foreign consumer might consider as too sweet or too heavy certain wines which are highly appreciated by the South Africans. Conversely, of course, the connoisseur of European wines might very well find happiness in a wine considered very "so-so" by the South African standards. More than 90 per cent of the wines which have some *appellation d'origine* are produced and sold by only four firms. These establishments, which are both wineproducers and merchants and are equipped with enormous cellars and the latest modern machinery, obtain their grapes either in their own vineyards or from neighbouring estates, and their wine either from their own production or from other wineproducers or co-operatives, in which case they buy young wine.

The Stellenbosch Farmer's Winery (S.F.W.), which also includes the Monis group, has the largest choice of wines. Those from Zonnebloem are its first line and are excellent white wines made from *Riesling*, with a dry and full-bodied CABERNET of delightful bouquet. There is also a semi-sweet, well-ripened ZONNEBLOEM *mi-flétri*.

Another branch of the S.F.W.'s activities concerns the so-called Lanzerac, whose origins date back to 1692. A magnificent and well-preserved Dutch-style farmhouse has been converted into a hotel which today has an international reputation. Here the wines of Lanzerac may be enjoyed, sold in bottles shaped like a dew-drop. They comprise two whites, a dry wine made from *Riesling* called RIESENSCHON and a semi-sweet made from *Stein* called GRÜNMÄDCHEN; while the red wines of Lanzerac are a full-bodied CABERNET and a good specimen of PINOTAGE, lighter than the CABERNET but still fairly full-bodied. There is also a light and semi-sweet rosé.

From the "Oude Libertas" cellars of the S.F.W., dating back to 1707, come very popular moderate-priced wines: GRATITUDE, a type of dry Chablis, and TASHEIMER GOLDTRÖPFCHEN, which is like a semi-sweet Rhine wine. Their CHÂTEAU LIBERTAS, carrying the name of these famous cellars, is a very well-known Burgundy-type wine.

The Stellenbosch Farmer's Winery also produces a whole series of ordinary wines which are very widely distributed. These include a Burgundy-type, TASSENBERG, and a semi-sweet wine called ZONNHEIMER which has a taste of *Hanepoot*. Probably the most popular of their wines is LIEBERSTEIN, a semi-sweet white wine which has been highly publicized.

The Nederburg property, which has recently linked up with the S.F.W., was the first concern in the Cape to experiment with German methods of vinification for fermentation and low-temperature ageing. Furthermore, this property will only plant and develop vines of pure stock. A very nice choice of white wines comes from their cellars. HOCHHEIMER, a Rhine riesling type, and MI-FLÉTRI, for those who prefer the rather sweeter *Spätlesen*, are both outstanding. SYLVANER-NEDERBURG is a pleasant and fairly dry white, but SELECTED RIESLING and RIESLING are the best-selling moderate-priced white wines. The CABERNET from this cellar is full-bodied with a nutty taste. One should note that the Nederburg winery does not produce any ordinary wines.

Gilbey-Santhagens, at Stellenbosch, offer wine drinkers several wines labelled TWEE JONGEZELLENS ("the two young bachelors")—for example, RIESLING "39", a dry Rhine-type wine with a very pleasant bouquet, and the semi-dry STEIN SUPERIOR. The cheapest wines in this series are the dry RIESLING, the semi-dry STEIN, the semi-sweet LIEBFRAUENMILCH, and a sweet rosé.

The Distillers Corporation of South Africa markets two medium quality wines which come from the Clos de la Résidence and which are much appreciated by those

In South African vineyards, it is the northern slopes that receive the greatest amount of sun; and the southern hemisphere vintage time is between March and May. Below: the famous Constantia Valley.

who seek inexpensive refreshment. THEUNISKRAAL, pleasantly dry and with a good taste, is a *Riesling*, while ALTO ROUGE is a tasty dry wine made from *Cabernet*. GRÜNBERGER, a semi-dry stein-type wine contained in bottles of a special shape, VILLA BIANCA and VILLA ROSA, both semi-dry, all come from these same cellars. The Corporation also offers ordinary wines from the well-known WITZENBERG series.

The Castle Wine and Brandy Company of Capetown offers a range of white wines under the name VLOTTENHEIM ESTATES OF VLOTTENBERG. One finds a very pleasant semi-dry SYLVANER, a SCHLOSSBERG, a good quality dry RIESLING KABINETT and a semi-sweet HONIGBERG. Apart from these wines, the best known is ROUGEMONT, a very popular mellow Burgundy. For the rest, the firm's products are mostly very ordinary kinds of wines.

There are a certain number of private vineyards whose wines are worth searching for, although their combined production is very small compared with that of the big concerns. One can find these wines only in their home region, for their producers do not need to find other markets. Taking them in alphabetical order, the list begins with Alphen, the two-centuries old property in Constantia Valley. Alphen produces an ALPHEN RIESLING SELECTED and two light Burgundies, as well as good sherries and good dessert wines. The Bellingham property (Groot-Drakenstein) is trying to match European A.O.C. wines with a balanced range of high quality products, and offers a remarkable BLANC SEC PREMIER GRAND CRU, a semi-dry JOHANNISBERG, a delicious SHIRAZ, a STEIN and a rosé. The Delheim vineyard at Koelenhof produces a *mi-flétri* SPATZENDRECK for those who like a rather sweeter wine, and very worthy red wines which include a full-bodied PINOTAGE and a Burgundy-type wine, CABERNET-SAUVIGNON.

From Muratie, also at Koelenhof, come some very attractive red table wines: their CABERNET-SAUVIGNON is a light and perfumed Burgundy, the full-bodied GAMAY PINOT-NOIR has Burgundy-like qualities and their BORDEAUX brings a light taste of *Hermitage*. The Schoongezicht property, near Stellenbosch, produces two wines much sought after by wine-lovers, particularly the RUSTENBERG, a dry and full-bodied wine made from *Cabernet* which has many of the characteristics of a Médoc and has crowned many a harvest with excellent success. The other is a SCHOONGEZICHT white wine full of taste and with a rich bouquet which takes it name from the property where it is harvested; *Clairette Blanche* grapes are also used for this wine. The Uitkyk vineyard, at Mulders in Vlei, produces two wines which should be better known: the first is a dry white wine sold under the name of CARLSHEIM, the other is CARLONET CABERNET, a full-bodied and very fresh red wine.

In sparkling wines, GRAND MOUSSEUX from the Stellenbosch Farmer's Winery, ranging from extra-dry to sweet, is by far the most popular. These wines have a very fruity taste and are just a little sweeter than European sparkling wines.

South Africa has without any doubt some really excellent products in the field of *liquoreux* wines. The range of dessert wines is simply immense, and covers all types. As examples one might mention MOOIUITSIG WYNKELDERS, from Bonnievale; MONIS MARSALA an excellent product from the S.F.W., and the same firm's delicious MUSCADINE. Two firms offer from their cellars wines which, it seems, are identical to that famous eighteenth-century wine of Constantia: CONSTANTIABERG from Bertrams and the SCHOONGEZICHT FRONTIGNAC.

The range of ports to be found in the Cape is also very large. The *topazes ambrés* are the lightest, going from very light reds to deep reds; the rubies are of a richer colour and more full-bodied. The vintage ports, which are produced only in limited quantities, are a deep red and full-bodied, their mellowness coming from ten to fifteen years of ageing in the bottle.

The best South African ports are made in the coastal region around Paarl and Stellenbosch. Most of the vines come originally from the Portuguese district of Douro, where port wine itself originated. *Pontac, Mataro* and *Shiraz* vines are used in order to be able to blend better, and care is taken to age the port sufficiently, even though the length of time needed in the South African climate is shorter than in Europe.

South African sherries come from authentic *xérès flor* vines, and the South African sherry vineyards are in the same southern latitude as the Spanish sherry vineyards are in the northern hemisphere. Furthermore, the principally used vine is *Palomino*, the "foundation stone" of Spanish sherries. The vines giving light sherries grow at Paarl, Stellenbosch, Tulbagh and Goudini in the south-western part of the Cape, while the more full-bodied sherries come from Worcester, Robertson, Mongatu and Bonnievale. The K.W.V. organization is quite certainly the largest producer and exporter of Cape sherries; many millions of gallons of stock are in the process of ageing.

Although the very dry and pale sherry sought in Europe is unknown in South Africa, there are nevertheless other very excellent sherries. The driest sherries—although even these are much less dry than their Spanish cousins—are the *finos* and the *amontillados*, fairly pale in colour and of a delicate flavour. The *olorosos* are darker, much sweeter and more full-bodied. As for the sherries aged by the *solera* system, they have a much darker colour and a much sweeter taste than the European varieties.

WINES OF AFRICA

ALGERIA

Aïn Bessem-Bouira	Coteaux de Médéa	Côtes du Zaccar	Miliana
Aïn El Hadjar	Coteaux de M'Silah	Haut-Dahra	Monts du Tessalah
Coteaux de Mascara	Coteaux de Tlemcen	Mascara	Mostaganem-Dahra

TUNISIA

Cap Bon	Kélibia	Muscat de Thibar	Sidi-Tabet
Carthage	Muscat de Kélibia	Radès	Thibar
Coteaux de Khanguet	Muscat de Radès	Saint Cyprien	Tébourba

SOUTH AFRICA

SUPERIOR QUALITY WINES

Dry white wines . . . .
Bellingham Premier Grand Cru
Carlsheim 8
Lanzerac Riesenschön
Nederburg Riesling
Nederburg Selected Riesling
Twee Jongegezellen Riesling « 39 »

Medium-dry white wines . . .
Bellingham Late Vintage
Bellingham Vintage Johannisberger
Nederburg Sylvaner
Twee Jongegezellen Stein
Twee Jongegezellen Stein Superior
Vlottenheimer Sylvaner

Medium-sweet white wines . . .
Bellingham Selected Steinwein
Blumberger Late Harvest
Charantelle
Delheim Late-Harvest
« Spatzendreck »
Delheim Selected Stein Goldspatz
Kupferberger Auslese
Lanzerac Grünmädchen
Nederburg Hochheimer
Nederburg Late Harvest
Nederburg Stein
Tulbagher
Twee Jongegezellen Spätlese
Vlottenheimer Schlossberg
Zonneblœm Late Harvest

Dry red wines . . . .
Lanzerac Pinotage
Lanzerac Cabernet
Nederburg Selected Cabernet
Stellenrood
Zonneblœm Cabernet
Alphen Special Old Vintage

Medium-dry red wines . . . .
Bellingham Shiraz
Carlonet Cabernet

Dry rosé wines . . . .
Bellingham Rosé
Nederburg Rosé Sec

Medium-dry rosé wine . . . .
Bellingham Almeida

Medium-sweet rosé wines . . .
Lanzerac Rose
Nederburg Rose

VERY GOOD QUALITY WINES

Dry white wines . . . .
Alphen Dry White
Alphen Selected Riesling
Bellingham Riesling
Constantia Riesling
Culemborg Selected Riesling
Delheim Riesling
Delheim White-French
De Rust Riesling
Huguenot Riesling
La Gratitude
La Residence Theuniskraal
J.C. le Roux Mont Pellier
Molenburg Riesling
Muratie Riesling
Muratie Stein
Paarl Valley Old Riesling
Prestige Selected Riesling
Prestige Selected Stellenblanche
Schoongezicht
Stellenvale Selected Riesling
Stellenvale Selected Stellenblanche
Theuniskraal
Twee Jongegezellen Liebfraumilch
Twee Jongegezellen Riesling
Vlottenheimer Riesling Kabinet
White Leipzig
Witzenberg

Medium-dry white wines . . .
Delheim Selected Riesling
De Rust Stein
Grunberger Stein
Tafelheim
Villa Bianca
Vlottenheimer Selected Riesling
Witzenberg Grand

Medium-sweet white wines . . .	Amaliensteimer	Liebfrauborg	Stellenvale Estate Riesling
	Bruderberg Na Œs (late harvest)	Lombards Liebfraumilch	Tasheimer Goldtröpfchen
	Capinella	Molenberg Stein	Vlottenheimer Honigberg
	Constantia Valley Stein	Molenhof Stein	Volson
	Culemborg Selected Stein	Monis Steinheimer	Winterhock Stein
	Gezellen Liebfraumilch	Stellenvale Hochheimer	Witzenberg Spatlese
	Kloosterberg		
Slightly sparkling white wines .	Culemborg Perlé	La Provence	Nauheimer
Dry red wines	Bodenheim	Delheim Pinotage	Rustenburg
	Bruderberg Selected Cabernet	La Résidence Alto Rouge	St. Augustine
	Château Alphen	Muratie Claret	Valais Rouge
	Château Constantia	Muratie Pinot noir-Gamay	Vredenburg
	Château Le Roux	Nederburg Cabernet	Alphen Red
	Château Libertas	Province Red	Muratie Cabernet Sauvignon
	Château Monis	Rougemont	Vlakkenberg
	Delheim Cabernet-Sauvignon		
Medium-sweet red wines . . .	Back's Claret (light-bodied)	Stellenvale Cabernet (light-bodied)	
Dry rosé wine	Valrosé		
Medium-dry rosé wine	Villa Rose		
Medium-sweet rosé wines . . .	Culemborg Rose	Rosala	Witzenberg Grand Rose
	La Provence	Twee Jongegezellen Rose	

DESSERT AND APERITIF WINES

Dessert wines	Amarella	Malvasia	Mooiuitsig White Muscadel
	Consanto	Miranda	Liqueur Wine
	Constantia Berg	Monis Barbola	Morilos Marsala
	Golden Bonwin	Monis Marsala	Muscadine
	Golden Mantilla	Monis Moscato	Ruby Bonwin
	Kloovendal	Mooiuitsig Red Muscadel Liqueur	Rynilla
	La Rhone	Wine	Stellenvale Marsala
	Malaga Red		
Port wines	Castelo Port	Government House Port	Mooiuitsig Fine Old Port
	Devonvale Port	Libertas	Muratie Port
	D.C. Vintage Port	Monis Cardinal Port	Santyis Old Ruby Vintage Port
Very dry sherries	Gonzales Byass Dry		
D.G. Flor No. 1 sherries . . .	Harvey's Extra Dry	Old Master Amontillado	Libertas
	Karroo Sherry	Devonvale Solera Dry « Flor »	Monis Palido Sherry
	Mattersons Fine Dry	Harvey's Dry Sherry	Tayler's Pale Dry Sherry
Medium-dry sherries	Bertrams Biscuit Sherry	Monis Dry Cream Sherry	Tudor Medium Cream Sherry
	D.G. Flor No. 2	Tayler's Mmooth Medium Sherry	
Medium-sweet sherries	Bertrams Oloroso Sherry	Gonzales Byass Medium	Sedgwick's Medium Cream
	Devon Cream Sherry	Roodezand Sherry	Vlei Sherry
Sweet sherries	D.G. Olorose	Harvey's Full Cream Sherry	Tayler's Full Cream Sherry
	Gonzales Byass Sweet	Libertas	Tayler's Rich Brown Sherry

THE WINES OF
NORTH AMERICA

LEON D. ADAMS

A mention of the wines of North America usually brings connoisseur praise for the varietally-labeled vintages from California, but scorn for most wines grown east of the Rocky Mountains. This is because California wines are produced exclusively from the delicately-flavored *Vitis vinifera* grapes of Europe, whereas the foxy-tasting *Vitis labrusca* grapes which predominate in the eastern United States and Canada have begun only since the 1960s to be replaced by the *vinifera* and French-American hybrid grapes which are now yielding eastern wines of Old World types.

North American wines have had a tumultuous four-century history. *Vinifera* vines were introduced from Spain to Mexico by the *conquistadores* beginning in 1524. To placate the jealous vintners of Spain, Philip II in 1595 ordered a stop to winegrowing in the New World, an order that was only partially obeyed. From Mexico, Franciscan missionaries brought the *vinifera* to Alta California after the founding of San Diego Mission in 1769. These first European vines were of an inferior variety called the *criolla* or Mission. In the 1830s French winegrower Jean Louis Vignes introduced French vines from Bordeaux to Los Angeles. Winegrowing then spread from southern California to the central and northern parts of the state, spurred by the introduction of more European grape varieties and by population growth following the 1849 gold rush. California soon was boomed abroad as a new paradise discovered for the vine, a land of mild winters and long, rainless summers where grapes easily reach full ripe-

ness every year. Viticulturists came from France to investigate the reports, and in 1862 they published their findings: that indeed, California was one American region "capable of entering competition with the wines of Europe, of becoming a serious competitor to France... in the distant future". California's balmy climate is the reason why this single state now produces nine-tenths of the grapes grown in the United States.

In the eastern states there were attempts for three centuries to grow grapes imported from Europe, but the delicate *vinifera* vines invariably withered and died. Cold winters were blamed, but what killed the Old World vines were plant diseases and such pests as phylloxera, to which wild vines that grow in the East are immune. The colonists made wine only from wild grapes until the 1800s, when they began to use domesticated varieties of the wild *labrusca* grapes. An important eastern wine industry then developed, based on such foxy grapes as the Isabella, Catawba, Elvira, Niagara, Delaware, and Dutchess, which are believed to be chance crosses with *vinifera*. By 1859 Ohio, producing Catawba still and sparkling wines, had become the leading wine state of the nation. It was overtaken in 1866 by Missouri and finally in 1870, on completion of the transcontinental railroad, by California, which already was exporting its wines in barrels to Europe, Australia, and the Orient. Meanwhile the foxy Concord, used equally for unfermented grape juice and for wine, became the most widely-grown grape in the East and Midwest. New York by then had become the second

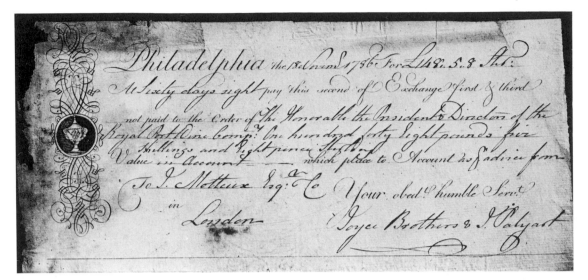

The vineyards of the Beringer winery—a nineteenth century view of which is shown here—have had a continuous history since the firm was first established in Napa Valley in 1876. During Prohibition, the winery turned to making altar wines.

largest winegrowing state, with sparkling wines from its Finger Lakes district being sold throughout the East and winning medals abroad.

But while the American wine industry was approaching maturity during the nineteenth century, the temperance movement, which was to destroy it, was spreading through the eastern states. By the 1840s scores of towns and counties were voting to prohibit the sale of all alcoholic beverages, and during the 1880s whole states began voting dry. Much of the nation had already become legally dry when prohibition became the national law in 1919 and 1920. Although the sale of wine as a beverage was unlawful, more than a hundred wineries survived by making legal sacramental, medicinal, and cooking wines. A few vineyards were uprooted at first,

but then vineyard-planting suddenly increased. A nationwide demand for fresh grapes and concentrated grape juice had been created by one provision of the dry law, which permitted heads of households to ferment up to 200 gallons of "nonintoxicating" fruit juices yearly for home use.

Thus, repeal of national prohibition in 1933 found California growing more grapes than ever before, but of the wrong kinds. Thin-skinned wine grapes had been replaced by tough varieties that withstood cross-country shipment during the fourteen dry years. The wineries, except the few that had continued making altar wines for the clergy, were in ruins. Table wines available for purchase in the United States were mostly undrinkable, oxidized or spoiled. The only palatable

wines were dessert types such as ports and sherries, preserved by the addition of spirits. Dessert-wine consumption in the United States at the time of repeal exceeded that of table wine by four and three gallons to one. Prohibition-generation Americans, accustomed to bootlegged whisky and gin, were unfamiliar with dry table wines, which to them tasted sour, as many were. Much of the nation remained legally dry, and most of the wet states imposed intolerable taxes and restrictions on wine, which their laws treated as merely a minor form of liquor. There was so little demand for table wine that of some 800 wineries in California in 1934, only 212 were left by 1938.

During the 1930s the California and federal governments adopted standards that prohibited the sale of unsound or mislabeled wine, but also approved the continued use of European wine-type names such as burgundy, rhine, chablis, champagne, port and sherry, which American vintners had adopted two centuries

earlier. In the late 1930s journalist-importer Frank Schoonmaker began to popularize varietal labeling, naming wines for such grape varieties as *Johannisberg Riesling*, *Cabernet Sauvignon*, *Catawba*, *Dutchess* and *Delaware*, to which scores of other grape-variety names were added in subsequent years.

Meanwhile the University of California revived its vinicultural research program, first undertaken in 1880, and resumed the teaching of viticulture and enology. During the 1950s and 1960s the vineyard and laboratory at Davis became the world's leading center of wine research, advancing the knowledge of the chemistry of grapes and wines more in those two decades than it had advanced in the preceding two thousand years. Vintners in other countries began sending their sons to Davis to be trained. Foreign governments invited Davis experts to come and advise them on ways to improve their wines. A new breed of university-trained viticulturists and enologists in California applied new scien-

Thirty-five states cultivate the vine, from Florida in the south as far as Washington in the north, as can be seen on this map representing the principal winegrowing regions of the USA.

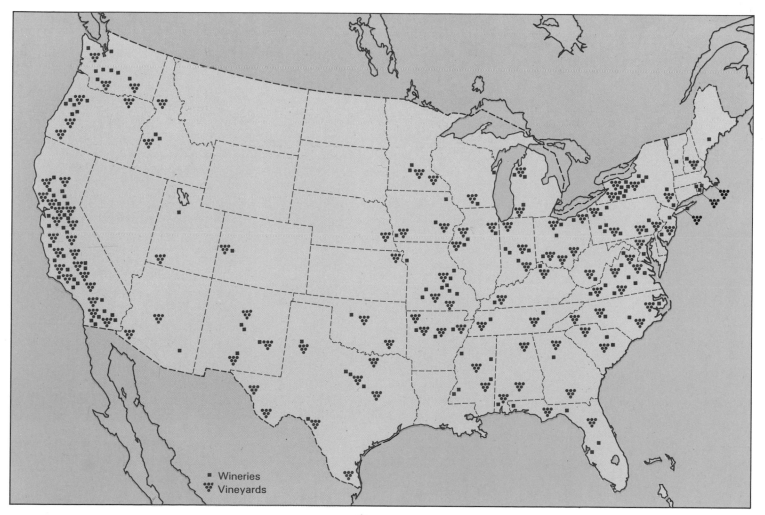

■ Wineries
🍇 Vineyards

VINTAGE 1978

CALIFORNIA
CHARDONNAY

PRODUCED AND BOTTLED BY THE MONTEREY VINEYARD • B.W. 4674
GONZALES, MONTEREY COUNTY, CA. USA • ALCOHOL 13.4% BY VOL.

American wines often bear the name of the vine-plant from which they derive, the so-called "varietal" label. Here the grape is the *Chardonnay*, which gives a white Burgundy-style wine. Quality is guaranteed by the producer's reputation.

tific technology to the ancient art of winegrowing. In vineyards they introduced virus-free vine propagation, new vine-training and pruning methods, sugar-acid ratios, early harvesting and field-crushing of grapes for wine; in wineries, stainless steel tanks in place of concrete and wood, temperature-controlled fermentation, new wine-clarifying methods, micropore filtration, and computerized wine analysis and quality control.

Table wines in the United States then became reliably palatable for the first time anywhere; unpalatable wines virtually disappeared. In 1968 the quantity of table wines consumed nationally exceeded that of dessert wines for the first time since before prohibition. Wine consumption in the United States approached two gallons per capita in 1970, three times the pre-prohibition rate. These developments, and the advances in production technology which caused them, set off a table-wine revolution with reverberations across the continent and in winegrowing countries around the world. It also caused a nationwide wave of vineyard-planting unparalleled in history, a quarter-million acres

of new vineyards set out from coast to coast. New areas suitable for winegrowing were discovered in California, in eastern Washington and western Oregon, and many old vineyard regions were revived in California and in some thirty-five other states. Twenty-two state legislatures enacted laws to encourage the establishment of farm wineries. From a total of 271 wineries in the United States in 1947, the number shot up to almost 900 in 1981, of which 500 were in California alone.

New kinds of American wines made their appearance: the first botrytized German- and Bordeaux-style whites ever produced in North America; *nouveau* and *primeur* reds produced by the carbonic maceration method of Burgundy, and a wide variety of effervescent "pop" wines with added natural flavors. By the end of the 1970s some American wineries also began offering "light," "soft," and "low-calorie" table wine types ranging from 7 to 10 per cent in alcoholic strength instead of the previous average of 12 percent. In 1980, for the first time in history, wine consumption in the United States exceeded the consumption of distilled spirits. Almost nine-tenths of the wine was table wine.

In a series of comparative blind tastings held in France during the late 1970s, a few CHARDONNAYS and CABERNET SAUVIGNONS from California outscored their counterparts from Burgundy and Bordeaux. California wines began appearing on prestigious wine lists in Europe and the Orient. Export demand for American wines also began to revive. These developments brought some of Europe's major vintners with millions to invest in American vineyards. French, Swiss, and German companies bought or acquired partnerships in more than a dozen Napa and Sonoma wineries. Moët et Chandon led the rest, planting its own California vineyards and building a Chandon champagnery in the Napa Valley. Other French champagne houses such as Piper Heidsieck contracted with California wineries for joint production of their sparkling wine cuvées. Large Canadian and European firms planted vineyards and acquired wineries in New York and Virginia. In 1981 American vineyard districts began acquiring government-delimited appellations of origin for their wines, comparable to the *appellation contrôlée* names that distinguish the best wines of France, and a symbol of the growing prestige of individual vineyard areas.

In 1981, the United States ranked sixth among the winegrowing nations, with an average annual wine production of 423 million gallons, nine-tenths of which is produced in California. This compared to 1.8 billion gallons in Italy, 1.7 billion in France, 900 million in Spain, 800 million in the USSR, and 600 million in Argentina. Exceeded were the 234 million-gallon average in Portugal, the 230 million in Germany, and the 200 million in Romania.

Future wine histories will record that the last four decades of the twentieth century saw North American wines finally achieving prominence among the wines of the world.

THE WINES OF CALIFORNIA

WINE DISTRICTS

California grape-growing districts are classed by the University into five climatic regions, numbered I to V according to the average number of days of sunshine recorded during their grape-growing seasons. The counties near the Pacific coast, cooled by ocean breezes and fogs, have mostly Regions I to III climates, roughly equivalent to those of northern Germany, Italy, and France. The Sierra foothill counties have Region III and IV temperatures in various years; the northern San Joaquin Valley is considered Region IV, and the rest of the valley is mostly region V, comparable in summer temperatures to Naples and Algiers. Shy-bearing grape varieties whose wines bring the highest prices, such as *Johannisberg* or *White Riesling, Chardonnay, Cabernet Sauvignon* and *Pinot Noir*, are grown mainly in the coast counties, where they attain the most favorable sugar-acid ratios for premium wines. Less costly grapes such as *Chenin Blanc* and *Colombard* grow both in the coastal districts and to some extent in Regions IV and V. Only the coast counties have thus far produced botrytized white wines. The San Joaquin Valley, where vines yield more tons per acre than in cooler climates, supplies most of the California wines that fit into average family budgets for everyday consumption.

The location of a winery in a particular district does not necessarily mean that all of its wines originate there, not unless the label states that a wine is estate-bottled, which means it was grown in the winery's nearby vineyard. Grapes and wines are regularly transported throughout the state, enabling California to produce virtually every wine type grown anywhere else in the world. Some large wineries bottle dozens of different wines under their various brands, but some of the smaller ones offer only two or three types.

In most California districts, vines grow on resistant rootstocks. The phylloxera vine louse, which devastated European vineyards in the late nineteenth century by killing their *vinifera* roots, was soon carried to California and wrought similar destruction there. It eventually was controlled in the same way as in Europe, by grafting the vines onto wild-grape roots. The Salinas Valley of Monterey County, where the soil is sandy and inhospitable to phylloxera, is the only important California district where all the vineyards are on their own roots.

"NORTH COAST"

"North Coast" as a wine-district appellation means wines grown north of San Francisco—in Napa, Sonoma, Mendocino, and in portions of Solano and Lake Counties. Napa and Sonoma are publicized as "the wine country" because they are close to San Francisco and receive the most visitors. Region I to III climates are shared by Marin, Alameda, and Contra Costa counties, which also border San Francisco Bay, and equally by all of the counties near the coast as far south as the Mexican border, a distance of 600 miles.

The weather in the Californian vineyards along the Pacific coast is heavily influenced by the effects of ocean winds and mists. Climatologists relate the California weather-patterns to those of Germany, northern Italy and France.

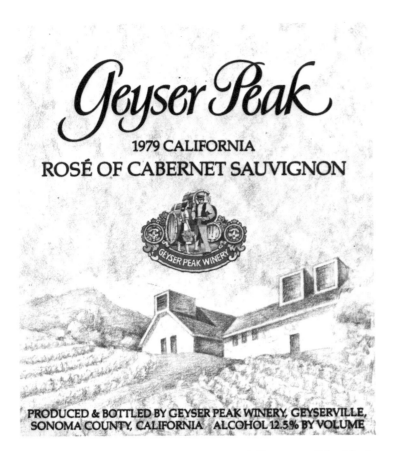

Geyser Peak
1979 CALIFORNIA
ROSÉ OF CABERNET SAUVIGNON

PRODUCED & BOTTLED BY GEYSER PEAK WINERY, GEYSERVILLE, SONOMA COUNTY, CALIFORNIA   ALCOHOL 12.5% BY VOLUME

Californian winegrowers have been especially successful with the *Cabernet Sauvignon*. The grape gives light red or rosé wines, often called clarets, that meet with widespread approval. The Geyser Peak Winery was founded as far back as 1880.

SONOMA

Southernmost Sonoma and Napa counties, close to the Bay, comprise the Carneros ("sheep" in Spanish) district, which many consider one of the best California climates for such burgundian grapes as Chardonnay and Pinot Noir. In Sonoma Valley, which the novelist Jack London named the Valley of the Moon, are fourteen wineries, the oldest of which are Buena Vista, founded in 1856 by the famous Hungarian emigré Agoston Haraszthy; Gundlach-Bundschu, which is two years younger, and Sebastiani, which first opened in 1904. The town of Sonoma is where winegrowing north of San Francisco began. The Franciscans established twenty-one missions in Alta California, planting grapes and making wine at each, between 1769 and 1823. Northernmost and last of the chain was Mission San Francisco Solano de Sonoma, which borders the town square. When the Mission was abandoned by order of the Mexican government in 1834, the provincial *comandante*, General Mariano Guadalupe Vallejo, took over its vineyard, planted more vines on his own extensive lands, and became the first commercial winegrower north of the Bay. It was in the town plaza thirteen years later that the Bear Flag Revolt took place, in which California declared its independence from Mexico.

The rest of Sonoma County's ninety wineries are mostly north of Sonoma Valley, in the Santa Rosa and Russian River Valleys. There the oldest are the Italian Swiss Colony at Asti, the Simi Winery at Healdsburg, and Geyser Peak at Geyserville, all of which date from 1880, and Korbel, which began making "champagne" near Guerneville in 1886. Healdsburg is the wine capital of Sonoma County; thirty wineries list the town as their address. Some of them are in the Alexander Valley east of the town, several are in the Dry Creek Valley to the east, and more are along the west shore of the Russian River. Four of the California viticultural district appellations awaiting government approval in 1981 were "North Coast," "Russian River," "Alexander Valley," and "Dry Creek."

MENDOCINO

Immediately north of Sonoma County is Mendocino, where lumbering is still the county's principal industry. Originally northern Sonoma and Mendocino produced mainly bulk table wines, but with the planting of superior grape varieties during the 1970s, Mendocino became one of the premium wine districts of the state. There were 10,000 acres of vines in the county in 1980, a third more than a decade before. Most of the vineyards are in the Ukiah, Redwood, McDowell, Feliz Creek, and Potter Valleys, where the climate is mostly Region III, but there are newer plantings in the Anderson Valley, twelve miles from the Pacific and classed as Region I. Of seventeen Mendocino wineries producing in 1981, fourteen were less than a decade old. The best-known are Fetzer in Redwood Valley and Parducci and Cresta Blanca at Ukiah. The latter is a former growers'-cooperative cellar that in 1971 was renamed for a century-old Livermore Valley winery.

LAKE COUNTY

East of Mendocino and north of Napa is Lake County, which began awakening during the 1970s to its glamorous but long-forgotten winegrowing past. Before prohibition Lake County had thirty-three wineries, some of whose wines won awards at the Paris Exposition in 1900. In 1887 the internationally famous English actress Lily Langtry, "the Jersey Lily," acquired a Lake County vineyard and winery near Middletown, known as the Guenoc Ranch. Prohibition came before her wine reached the market, but some of the county's vineyards lasted through the dry era, supplying Lake County *Zinfandel* grapes, which were popular among home winemakers in the East. Six hundred acres were still

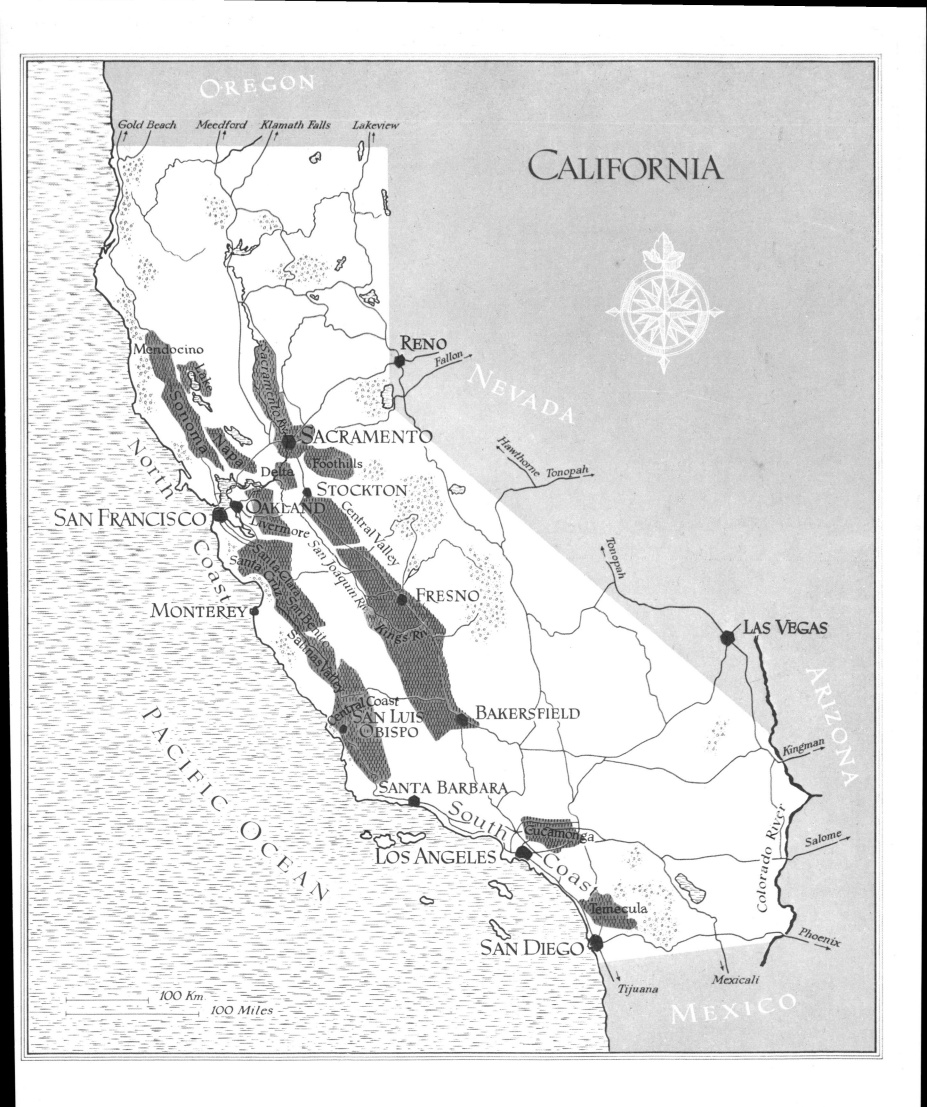

CALIFORNIA

OREGON

Gold Beach Meedford Klamath Falls Lakeview

Mendocino

Lake

Sonoma

Napa

Sacramento Riv.

RENO

Fallon

NEVADA

Hawthorne Tonopah

SACRAMENTO

Delta Foothills

STOCKTON

Central Valley

OAKLAND

Livermore

SAN FRANCISCO

Santa Clara

Santa Cruz

San Benito

San Joaquin Riv.

Tonopah

North Coast

MONTEREY

Salinas Valley

FRESNO

Kings Riv.

LAS VEGAS

ARIZONA

Central Coast

SAN LUIS
OBISPO

BAKERSFIELD

Kingman

PACIFIC OCEAN

SANTA BARBARA

South Coast

Cucamonga

Colorado River

Salome

LOS ANGELES

Temecula

Phoenix

SAN DIEGO

Mexicali

Tijuana

MEXICO

100 Km
100 Miles

1979

Napa Valley
FUMÉ BLANC
Dry Sauvignon Blanc
ALCOHOL 13% BY VOLUME
PRODUCED AND BOTTLED BY
ROBERT MONDAVI WINERY
OAKVILLE, CALIFORNIA

This FUMÉ BLANC is a dry white wine made from *Sauvignon Blanc* grapes adapted for Californian vineyards and renamed *Fumé Blanc*. The Robert Moldavi vineyards (below), in the Napa Valley, have a Region II climate as classified by California University workers.

producing at repeal in 1933 and were bought by wineries in neighboring counties, some of whom identified their products as Lake County wines. In the 1970s came a rebirth of grape-growing, in which the area's vineyard acreage increased sixfold. The vineyards are mainly at 1,300-foot levels around nineteen-mile-long Clear Lake and lofty Mt. Konocti. The climate ranges from Region II to above Region III. Three new wineries were built in the county, the latest a modern cellar erected in 1981 among the revived vineyards on Lily Langtry's Guenoc Ranch. At the same time "Guenoc Valley" was granted government recognition as a distinct viticultural area.

NAPA

Across a spur of the Mayacamas Mountains from Sonoma County is the Napa Valley, the most famous wine district in North America. The expanse of Napa County vineyards has doubled since the 1960s to 26,000 acres, almost as many as in Sonoma, which is twice as

large. In 1981 Napa County counted 114 wineries, more than in any other county on the continent. The Napa Valley is small, only thirty-five miles long and one to five miles wide, but encompasses many different climatic regions. The Carneros district in the south is rated as "low Region I"; northward to Oakville the weather warms to Region II, and St. Helena and Calistoga at the head of the valley are Region III. Vineyards in the mountains west and east of the valley have different growing seasons that are reflected in their wines. A bitter struggle is constantly waged to protect the valley from urban sprawl, which has wiped out many fine vineyards in the other counties neighboring San Francisco Bay. The oldest active winery in the valley is Charles Krug of St. Helena; a stone wall of its original cellar dates from 1861. The younger, nearby Beringer winery has a rival claim to great age, having remained open since it was built in 1876, including the prohibition years when it produced altar wines. Nearly a hundred pre-prohibition stone wineries dot the valley, some now back in operation, some converted to residences, but others only skeletons, reminders of the last century when Napa wines were already becoming famous until the dry law forced them to close. Among the other old Napa wineries are Schramsberg, first opened in 1862; Château Montelena, 1882; Mayacamas, 1889; The Christian Brothers' Greystone cellar, 1889, and Beaulieu Vineyard, 1904. Also famous though

The Christian Brothers Greystone cellar was founded in 1889 and so counts among the oldest in California.

RUTHERFORD HILL

1977
Napa Valley

ZINFANDEL
MEAD RANCH — ATLAS PEAK

PRODUCED AND BOTTLED BY
RUTHERFORD HILL WINERY, RUTHERFORD, CALIFORNIA
Alcohol 15.7% by volume

ZINFANDEL is a wine found only in California. The origins of the *Zinfandel* grape variety are still obscure, but it is believed today to be related to the *Primitivo di Gioia* which grows in the Bari region in Italy.

much younger are Martini, which first located in the valley in the 1930s, and such relatively recent arrivals as Joseph Heitz, Freemark Abbey, Joseph Phelps, Robert Mondavi, Domaine Chandon, and Sterling Vineyard with its showplace hilltop winery that is reached by an aerial tramway. Winiest town in the United States is St. Helena, in the center of the valley; forty wineries list St. Helena as their address. It is the first city in the United States to have established a public wine library, which is supported by the Napa Valley Wine Library Association. Adjoining the library is the Silverado Museum with memorabilia of Robert Louis Stevenson, who while honeymooning in the valley in 1880 wrote his *Silverado Squatters*. Stevenson described the early Napa winegrowers' search for the best vineyard sites: "One corner of land after another is tried with one kind of grape after another... so bit by bit, they grope about for their Clos Vougeot and Lafite... and the wine is bottled poetry." NAPA VALLEY was the first appellation of origin officially recognized by the United States Government (in 1980) to appear on wine labels, but the approved boundaries include most of Napa County, including the warmer Pope Valley across the mountains to the east. Eventually, if the delimitation of American vineyard

384

areas continues, the winegrowers in such Napa viticultural districts as Mount Veeder, Spring Mountain, Diamond Mountain, Oakville, and Rutherford may seek government approval for appellations of their own.

ALAMEDA, CONTRA COSTA AND SOLANO

California's land conservation law, enacted in 1965 to protect farmlands from urbanization, has helped to preserve some of the historic vineyards in Alameda County, which still has 2,000 acres of vines. Most of the preserved vineyards are in the Livermore Valley, which has six wineries. Oldest are the Concannon Vineyard and the nearby Wente Brothers winery at Livermore. Both date from 1883 and both survived prohibition by producing altar wines for the clergy. Equally ancient, near Pleasanton, is the Ruby Hill vineyard and winery, subsequently renamed Stony Ridge. Villa Armando, whose winery at Pleasanton dates from 1904, has 300 acres on the City of San Francisco's water department property at Suñol, safe from urban sprawl. Contra Costa and Solano counties, which had scores of wineries before prohibition, still have 2,000 acres of vineyards, mostly in the latter county, and six wineries. Two of those in Solano are new since the 1970s.

SANTA CLARA, SAN MATEO AND SANTA CRUZ

Santa Clara, San Mateo, and Santa Cruz counties, immediately south of San Francisco, produced some of the best California wines both before and after prohibition. However, exploding population with subdivisions and shopping centers displaced most of the upper Santa Clara Valley vineyards following the end of the Second World War. The valley's most famous wineries with their nineteenth-century founding dates (1852 for Paul Masson and Almadén, Mirassou 1852, Novitiate of Los Gatos 1888) were left with tiny patches of vines to be viewed by the thousands of visitors who crowd their tasting halls. Their vineyards were moved south to less populous areas. Only one new winery, Turgeon & Lohr, has been built in San José since repeal, producing and bottling wines from the grapes it grows near Monterey. But in the western mountain areas of these three counties, where the climate is Regions I and II, there are a dozen small wineries, many of them new, producing some wines finer than any in the past. They have petitioned the government to grant "Santa Cruz Mountains" as an appellation for their viticultural area. There still is a total of 1600 acres of vineyards in the three counties, but most of the crops go to the sixteen old and new wineries in southernmost Santa Clara, between Morgan Hill and Gilroy. The latter town is the capital of the nation's garlic industry and holds an annual garlic festival that brings thousands to sample and buy the local wines.

This Californian vineyard is still cultivated in the "traditional" way; the vines, being allowed to fully develop, are covered in foliage. Note the contrast between this and the completely mechanized vineyards like the one below.

Under the guidance of the Davis Campus workers at the University of California, the winegrowers in the state are among the most conscious of the painstaking care vine cultivation necessitates. Here, a technician is studying the grapes in the Beaulieu vineyards (Napa Valley).

385

Harvest time on a California vineyard. Experienced vintagers come to the wine country each season; here, they are working on the 3750-acre Paicines vineyard, which belongs to the Almaden winery. Founded in 1852 in neighbouring Santa Clara County, the firm had to move as a result of population growth.

SAN BENITO

From Mission San Juan Bautista, a half hour's drive south of Gilroy, the San Benito Valley extends southeastward between the Diablo and Gavilán mountain ranges for some sixty miles. In this valley, outside the surge of population, are nearly 5,000 acres of vineyards, much of them planted to replace those Almadén formerly had in Santa Clara County, and eight wineries, including one making only sake and wines from fruits other than grapes. Almadén owns two of the wineries. Its old cellar in the Cienega district is famous for being built astride the San Andreas earthquake fault. Frequent earth tremors cause the halves of the cellar to move a half-inch farther apart each year. The county's vineyards have applied to the government for "Cienega" and "Lime Kiln Valley" as appellations of origin.

MONTEREY

Across the Gavilán range from the San Benito Valley is the eighty-mile-long Salinas Valley in Monterey County. Here in 1962 Mirassou and Paul Masson, their Santa Clara vineyards threatened by subdivisions, started a vine-planting explosion that within a decade made Monterey the largest coastal winegrowing county in the state with 32,000 acres, more than either Sonoma or Napa. There already was one Salinas Valley vineyard growing premium wine-grape varieties on the Chalone bench of the Gaviláns 2,000 feet above the valley where moisture is so scarce that water was hauled up the mountain in tank trucks to water the vines. The entire valley has scant rainfall, only ten inches annually, half of the minimum required to produce grape crops. But this was no problem because through the valley flows

the Salinas River, the greatest underground stream in America. Water pumped from below the surface to overhead sprinklers supplies plentiful artificial rain. The northern part of the valley, between Chualar and Gonzales, is Region I and II, one of the coolest vineyard areas in the state. After Mirassou and Masson came plantings by Wente Brothers of Livermore, Almadén and many others, from Soledad and Greenfield to as far south as King City and San Lucas, where the climate is Region III. Masson built a winery at Soledad, but Mirassou and the Wentes, with their vineyards almost a hundred miles distant from their wineries, faced the problem of protecting the grapes. They solved it by adding grape-crusher-stemmers to mechanical-harvesting machines and tanks of carbon dioxide gas which blanket the must while it travels in cool, pressurized tank trucks to their wineries. Six more wineries were built in the valley during the 1970s. Largest was The Monterey Vineyard, owned by Coca-Cola of Atlanta, Georgia. Nearby is a still newer cellar which blends and bottles the Taylor California Cellars blends with San Joaquin Valley wines. Vineyards and wineries have spread to the Carmel River Valley and to the Monterey Peninsula area, the locale of John Steinbeck's "Cannery Row." The transformation of the Salinas Valley from

The Almaden ZINFANDEL producers are confident enough in their reputation and the very high quality of their wines not to have to use the more general, regional CALIFORNIAN WINE appellation.

Lack of information isn't something you could criticize on this wine label. From vintage year, grape type, vineyard area, winery, grape sugar content, final acidity, alcohol content and bottling details you get everything you could want to know about the wine, except that these facts and figures actually spell "excellent".

"the nation's salad bowl," when lettuce was its principal crop, to the largest premium winegrowing area in the nation, is celebrated each September at Soledad Mission, which the Franciscans established in 1791.

SAN LUIS OBISPO

San Luis Obispo County, a pre-Prohibition central coast winegrowing region, has become important again. Since the 1960s, when Americans began developing a taste for table wines, its vineyard acreage has jumped from 700 to nearly 5,000 acres. The county's several vineyard districts have climates ranging from Region I to Region IV. There are fourteen wineries: three at Templeton, where one of the vineyards dates from 1856; six in the foothills of the Santa Lucia Mountains west of Paso Robles, where the York Mountain winery boasts a founding date of 1882; a spectacular new cellar near the Estrella River east of Paso Robles; one in the Rancharita Canyon east of Mission San Miguel; two new ones in the Edna Valley south of San Luis Obispo, and another in Corbit Canyon nearby.

ESTATE BOTTLED

Buena Vista

HARASZTHY ZINFANDEL

ESTATE GROWN AND BOTTLED BY
HARASZTHY CELLARS
BUENA VISTA VINEYARDS, SONOMA, CALIF

ALCOHOL 12½% BY VOLUME

HARASZTHY ZINFANDEL
1. Name of the wine and of the grapevine. This grape is rumoured to have been introduced into California from Europe around the middle of the nineteenth century by Count Agoston Haraszthy, but the true place of origin remains to be definitely established. The grape gives a fragrant and fruity red wine characteristic of California. – 2. Name of the vineyard. – 3. Address and registered name of the vineyard. – 4. Indication of place of original bottling. – 5. Statement of alcohol content.

CABERNET SAUVIGNON
1. Name of the wine and of the grapevine. This grape, the same as that which gives Bordeaux clarets, was imported into California. It gives a red wine of a beautiful deep ruby color and with a most agreable flavor. – 2. Name of the vineyard. – 3. Geographical origin of the wine and registered name of the vineyard. – 4. Indication of place or original bottling. – 5. Statement of alcohol content.

Beaulieu Vineyard

BV

ESTATE BOTTLED

NAPA VALLEY

CABERNET SAUVIGNON

PRODUCED & BOTTLED BY BEAULIEU VINEYARD
AT RUTHERFORD, NAPA COUNTY, CALIFORNIA

ALCOHOL 12.5% BY VOLUME

Vineyards Established 1852

ALMADÉN

California Mountain
PINOT NOIR

A distinguished, authentic Pinot Noir, velvety and fine, made entirely from grapes of this illustrious Burgundian variety, grown in Mountain Vineyards at Paicines, California

PRODUCED AND BOTTLED BY
Almadén Vineyards, Los Gatos, California

Alcohol 12½% by volume   0 - 67

PINOT NOIR
1. Name of the wine and of the grapevine. The grape is the same as that grown in Burgundy and which gives those famous red wines. – 2. Name of the vineyard and of the region. – 3. Name and address of the vineyards. – 4. Date of the foundation of the vineyard. – 5. Statement of alcohol content.

PINOT CHARDONNAY

1. Name of the wine and of the grapevine. This grape is very widespread in Champagne and Burgundy and gives a white wine resembling the dry white wine of Champagne that is so much appreciated throughout the world. – 2. Name of the region. – 3. Name of the proprietor. – 4. Vintage date. – 5. Statement of alcohol content.

4

2

1

3

5

4

GEWÜRZ TRAMINER

1. Name of the wine and of the grapevine. This grape, which gives a white wine with a spicy scent and flavor, was imported from Alsace. – 2. Name of the region. – 3. Name of the proprietor. – 4. Date of the foundation of the vineyard. – 5. Statement of alcohol content.

2

1

3

5

SAUTERNE

1. Name of the wine. The name does not indicate the grapevine but the type of wine, which is a sweet white variety similar to many of the French ones whose name it borrows. This wine can be made from grapes coming from several different regions of California. – 2. Name of the wine merchant. – 3. Statement of alcohol content.

1

2
3

Santa Ynez Valley Winery *1979*

CALIFORNIA

CHARDONNAY
RESERVE DE CAVE

PRODUCED AND BOTTLED BY THE SANTA YNEZ VALLEY WINERY
SANTA YNEZ, CALIFORNIA

ALCOHOL 13.1% BY VOLUME

By Californian standards, Santa Barbara County has a cool climate, with little sun, being classified as only Region I on the University scale. Still, this doesn't detract in the least from the fine CHARDONNAY RESERVE DE CAVE produced in the Santa Ynez Valley Winery.

SANTA BARBARA

"Central Coast" as a wine-region name links San Luis Obispo with Santa Barbara County, its neighbor on the south. Santa Barbara has 7,000 of the 12,000-acre regional total. That both counties, and also nearby Ventura, were important wine districts in the past century is evidenced by the various "Vineyard Roads" on their maps. What is now the city of Santa Barbara once was dotted with vineyards, as was Santa Cruz Island, thirty miles off the coast. There are thirteen wineries in the county, one in the city of Santa Barbara, one each in the Santa Ynez, Los Alamos, and Lompoc Valleys, and several around Buellton and the tourist center of Solvang, the latter a onetime Danish colony that has preserved its Danish decor. The best-known is The Firestone Vineyard at Los Olivos, established during the 1970s by Brooks Firestone of the family whose name is associated with automobile tires, in a tripartite partnership with his father Leonard and with Suntory, Japan's largest producer of wines and spirits. But the largest Santa Barbara County vineyard district is farther north in the Santa Maria Valley, a twenty-mile-long belt of foothill land where, until the first vines were planted in 1964, there had never been vineyards before. The climate, cooled by the Santa Maria wind and ocean fogs, is Region I. Newest winery in the county is the Los Viñeros cellar, built in Santa Maria city in 1981.

TEMECULA

Southern California, where the state's vineyard industry was born two centuries ago, has seen most of its old vineyard districts overwhelmed by population, industry and smog, but a new district called Temecula, outside the path of urbanization, is growing wines far superior to those of the past. The principal southern California vineyards during the nineteenth century were in the Los Angeles basin. At San Gabriel Mission the adobe building where Indians trod the grapes is still preserved. Vineyards gradually disappeared from Los Angeles after the late nineteenth century, and wine-growing became centered in the Cucamonga Valley to the east, which before 1947, with 20,000 acres of wine grapes, was the third largest winegrowing district in the state. Since World War II, two thirds of the Cucamonga vineyards have also disappeared, victims of smog from industrial and population growth. Of eight wineries remaining around Cucamonga in 1981, only Brookside at the old winery village of Guasti and Filippi at Mira Loma were still actively producing wine. There are two old wineries at Escondido in San Diego County, and a new one was built in nearby San Pasqual Valley in 1974 because its hundred-acre vineyard is situated on protected San Diego city water property. Temecula, the new district, consists of nearly 3,000 acres of superior wine-grape varieties planted since the 1960s around a planned community of ranches called Rancho California in the southwestern corner of Riverside County to which irrigation water was supplied by a new system of wells. Temecula's climate, cooled by winds from the Pacific twenty-three miles to the west, is Region II or III, compared to that of Cucamonga, which is Region IV. A unique part of Temecula's climate pattern is the morning mist, which favors the production of wines from grapes affected by *Botrytis cinerea*, the *Edelfäule* or noble mould. Seven wineries have been built in the Temecula district since Ely Callaway opened the first one on his estate there in 1974. Petitions are pending with the government to grant the Temecula district recognition as an appellation of origin for wines. ("San Pasqual Valley" was established as a viticultural area in 1981.)

THE FOOTHILL DISTRICTS

Scores of new vineyards and two dozen new wineries sprang up during the 1970s in the Sierra foothills counties, known as the Mother Lode for their gold-mining history which is as old as the state. In gold rush days, as the precious metal became scarce, miners planted vines around their diggings and began making wine. More than a hundred wineries operated before prohibition at 2,000 foot and higher elevations in Eldorado, Amador, Calaveras, Nevada, and Placer counties. There were more in Eldorado than in Napa or

390

Sonoma. During the prohibition years grape-growing was less profitable in the foothills because vineyards in the valleys yielded heavier crops. For three decades after repeal there was only one winery in Amador County, the D'Agostini cellar at Plymouth, originally founded in 1856. During the 1960s, wineries seeking new grape-growing areas rejected the foothills because although days of sunshine average mostly as Region III, at foothills elevations only sites with air-drainage are safe from crop injury by frosts. Then in the 1970s, connoisseurs made a discovery: that the *Zinfandel* grape grown in the Shenandoah Valley of Amador county makes a wine of more intense flavor and higher alcoholic content than wine from that grape grown elsewhere in the state. Some of the wineries in Napa County began making wines of *Amador Zinfandel* grapes. Soon new vineyards of *Zinfandel* and many premium wine grape varieties were being planted at such gold rush locations as Plymouth, Fiddletown, and Sutter Creek, and the plantings spread to the other foothill counties, which have climates and volcanic soils similar to Amador's. In 1980 the government received two petitions to establish "Shenandoah Valley" as a viticultural district appellation for wine—one from the valley in Amador county, which has several wineries and has had the name since 1851, the other from the valley in Virginia which has two wineries and has been called Shenandoah since colonial times. Each demanded that the rival petition be denied. At last reports, public opinion favored granting them both.

LODI, THE DELTA, AND SACRAMENTO VALLEY

The Lodi district in northern San Joaquin county is viticulturally unique. Grapevines in the district grow to enormous size, their trunks as large around as trees, in its deep sandy-loam soil. Summer days in most of this county are less torrid than in the main San Joaquin Valley; the climate is Region IV. But at Lodi the vines are further cooled at night by moist winds from the nearby Sacramento-San Joaquin Delta region with its thousand miles of tidewater rivers, bays, and sloughs. During the 1970s some premium white wine varieties such as CHENIN BLANC and SEMILLON were planted around Lodi, where the principal wine grapes grown were such blacks as *Zinfandel* and *Carignane*. But the grape for which Lodi was principally famous is the *Flame Tokay*, a table grape which has no connection whatever with the Tokai wine of Hungary. Only in the Lodi district and in its suburbs of Acampo and Wood-bridge does the *Flame Tokay* develop its flaming red color which attracts fresh-fruit buyers; virtually all *Flame Tokays* in the nation are grown there. The district's pride in its Tokay and its principal table wines is expressed in the mid-September Lodi Grape Festival and National Wine Show, the most elaborate annual vintage celebration held in any grape district in the

nation. Of the dozen wineries in the district, five are large grower-owned cellars producing only bulk wine; five other plants are also bottlers, and have tasting rooms. There are two small farmer wineries, established in the late 1970s.

Along the Sacramento River twenty-five miles northwest of Lodi, and on some of the islands of the Delta region, a new winegrowing district with a "low Region IV" climate was planted during the 1970s. It is between Clarksburg in Yolo county and Courtland across the river in Sacramento county. When famous north coast wineries won prizes for wines they made of grapes they bought from the Delta district vineyardists, two wineries were built at Clarksburg at the end of the decade.

The Sacramento Valley, which stretches northwest from Lodi and the Delta for almost 200 miles, had scores of wineries and nearly 40,000 acres of vineyards before prohibition. Climates on the valley floor are mainly Region V. During the dry era, some of grapes were sun-dried for raisins, but most of the area's vineyards were soon abandoned, because raisin-growing became concentrated around Fresno in the San Joaquin Valley, where in most years grapes can be sun-dried before the first autumn rains. By 1970, only four wineries and less than 500 acres of vines were left in the nine counties from Shasta south. Then came the wine revolution with new demand for table wines, and by 1980 there were 6,000 acres of vineyards in the

Many Californian vineyards rely on a large number of seasonal and permanent agricultural laborers. Considered unqualified workmen, they do the jobs that can't be done by machines.

391

Sacramento Valley again. Wineries in the coast counties were buying the Sacramento Valley grapes but were expressing a preference for those grown in the hills to the east and west. Sacramento, Glenn, and Yolo counties had most of the new plantings. There are several small wineries and one large one in the Sacramento Valley, but most of them are using grapes grown elsewhere

THE MAIN SAN JOAQUIN VALLEY

The more than a dozen California winegrowing districts thus far described represent only a third of the state's wine production. The other two-thirds comes from the nine counties of the 200-mile-long main San Joaquin Valley, an agricultural empire where grapes compete with cotton as the leading income crop. Much of the valley was desert until a century ago, when dams

About only a century ago, the valley of San Joaquin was more or less a desert. Today, thanks to extensive irrigation (below), the vines there produce some two-thirds of all Californian wines currently on the market.

were built in the Sierra Nevada mountains to the east and men began digging the irrigation canals that have transformed the once-parched wasteland into farms more productive than the delta of the Nile. The valley is hot, mainly Region IV at the northern end, and becomes hotter—Region V—in the south. Vines in the valley normally yield eight to twelve tons of grapes per acre, much more than in the cool coastal districts, and seventeen tons is not unusual for an acre of over-cropped raisin grapes. From this valley come all of the raisins produced in the United States, two-thirds of the California table grapes that are eaten fresh, nearly all of the port, sherry, and muscatel dessert wine types, virtually all of the brandy, and more than half of the state's table and sparkling wines. Fleets of tank trucks carry valley wines to other parts of the state, and railroad tank cars take them to other parts of the nation, some to be blended with eastern wines. The planting of superior wine-grape varieties during the 1970s, plus modern technology, has enabled some of the valley wineries to produce table wines that only professionally trained tasters can distinguish from those grown in cooler regions. Wine grape varieties predominate in the Manteca and Escalon districts of San Joaquin, Stanislaus and Merced counties in the northern part of the valley. *Grenache* grapes grown in the Escalon and Manteca areas have long been the basis of many California rosés. At Modesto in Stanislaus county are the headquarters and central cellar of Gallo, one of the largest wineries in the world. Gallo has three other cellars, including a vineyard and winery in Sonoma county, and also uses grapes from other coast counries. *Modesto* means "modest". When the site of its railroad station was chosen in 1870, the first name proposed was that of railroad magnate William Ralston. When he declined the honor, a Mexican companion exclaimed *El senor es muy modesto!*, which promptly was marked on the map. Only eight of the forty-five valley wineries have tasting rooms, and few wines are advertised as valley-grown. Almost the only ones entirely locally-grown that bring premium prices in the market are ports from the little Ficklin Vineyard and Andy Quady winery of Madera and the table and sparkling wines from the nearby Papagni winery, some of which have won prizes in competitions with those from other parts of the state. Fresno county, south of Madera, had 205,000 acres of vineyards in 1980, three-fourths of which were *Thompson Seedless*. This grape, of uncertain origin, is the most widely planted variety in California. Although classified as a raisin variety, it is also one of the principal table grapes, is valued for distillation into brandy, and is part of many white table and "champagne" blends. Tulare county is second to Fresno in the extent of its vineyards with 80,000 acres in 1980, of which a fifth were wine grapes. Kern county, where the San Joaquin valley ends in the foothills of the Tehachapi mountains, had 79,000 acres of vineyards in 1980, more than half of them wine grapes planted since 1972.

CALIFORNIA GRAPES AND WINES

More than one hundred varieties of wine grapes grow commercially in California, and scores of their names appear on the state's varietally-labeled wines. Actually, the bulk of California wine reaches the market under names classed as generic, including "champagne". Use of the latter name has declined since French champagne makers acquired California properties and called their products "sparkling wine" instead.

WHITE VARIETALS

The Charente grape *Colombard* leads all other white wine varieties in California acreage because it ripens with favorable acidity-sugar balance in the warmer as well as the cooler districts of the state and makes full-bodied, aromatic, flavorful dry and off-dry white table wines. Second in acreage is the noble Loire Valley grape, *Chenin Blanc* (also called *Pineau de la Loire*), which is at home in many climates and makes soft, fruity, often slightly sweet wines. Those grown in the coastal climates can gain bouquet with a year or two of bottle-age. Third in white-wine acreage is *Chardonnay*, the noble variety of the great white burgundies of France and the principal white grape of Champagne. In California it is mainly grown in Regions I to III climates and produces the state's finest white wines, lush and velvety and capable of improving in flavor and bouquet with two to five or six years of bottle-age. It also makes the best *blanc de blancs* California "champagnes." The noble German *Johannisberg* or *White Riesling* reached fourth rank during the 1970s among California's white-wine grapes. It makes flowery, fragrant, refreshing table wines and "champagnes". When made sweet, especially from botrytized grapes, the best California Johannisberg Rieslings have retained and enhanced their flavor and bouquet with several years of bottle-age. Fifth in planted acres is the noble *Sauvignon Blanc* of Bordeaux and the Loire. Its spicy but somewhat austere wines are as flavorful and capable of aging as CHARDONNAY. In California, SAUVIGNON BLANC wines are often called FUMÉ BLANC. Ranked next among white grapes is *Palomino*, which has no value for table wine. Because it oxidizes rapidly it is the premier variety for the production of sherry types. The fragrant, flowery, spicy *Gewürztraminer* of Austria, Germany, and Alsace is seventh among whites in California, and its wines, when sweet, have shown great ability to age. Eighth is the noble *Sémillon* of Bordeaux, which makes elegant dry wine when grown in the coast counties, but in the dry summers of California is not often attacked by the noble mould *Botrytis cinerea* which makes Sémillon in France the principal grape for sauternes. California whites with botrytized character have been *Rieslings, Sauvignon Blanc*, and *Chenin Blanc*. Ninth in white acreage is

Emerald Riesling, a *Riesling-Muscadelle* cross developed at the University of California for the warmer districts of the state. Although its wines have Riesling character, its name is unfortunate because it contributes to the confusion in California about wines with "Riesling" as part of their names. The Austrian grape *Sylvaner* makes light, refreshing white wines in the coastal counties, but most of them are sold as *Franken Riesling*, the grape's name in Franconia, and also as *California Riesling*, which is regrettable because the grape is unrelated to the true Riesling. The same applies to *Grey Riesling*, a grape of uncertain parentage, which makes a popular dry white wine in California's Regions I to III climates. Other white varieties whose names appear on California labels include *St-Emilion* and its Italian and French synonyms, *Trebbiano* and *Ugni Blanc*; *Flora*, a university cross between *Gewürztraminer* and *Sémillon*; the Russian variety *Rkatsiteli*, and *Pinot Blanc*. The latter may include some acreages of the grape known in France as *Melon* or *Muscadet*. Some sparkling-wine producers prefer *Pinot Blanc* over *Chardonnay* because when grown in California sunshine, *Chardonnay* contributes more flavor than they require in their cuvées.

MUSCATS

Five *Muscat* grapes are grown commercially in California. The most delicate is the ancient Greek variety grown throughout Europe, best known as *Muscat Blanc* but also as *Muscat Frontignan* in southern France and as *Moscato Canelli* in the Italian Piedmont. California wines of this grape use any of these names. The larger, less delicate *Muscat of Alexandria* is far more widely grown because it serves also as a raisin and as a table grape. California muscat wines are made of either variety, the sparkling versions variously called MOSCATO AMABILE and SPUMANTE, the Italian word for sparkling. *Malvasia Bianca* is a muscat-flavored grape with still another name. MUSCAT table wines are made semi-dry or sweet because they have a bitter aftertaste if made dry. The University has developed a new *symphony* grape with muscat flavor, not yet released for planting, whose wine is not bitter when fermented dry. Two red or black muscats are also grown: *Muscat Hamburgh*, which makes the black muscat dessert wine, and the *Aleatico* of Tuscany, which in California makes a red muscatel.

RED VARIETALS

The most widely-grown red wine grape in California is the round, thin-skinned, juicy *Zinfandel*. Its origin has long been a mystery, but University scientists during

the 1970s found it identical with the *Primitivo di Gioia* variety that grows near Bari in the Apulia region of southeastern Italy. In California's coast-counties climates, *Zinfandel* makes a fresh, bright-ruby wine with a berry-like or "bramble" aroma that is especially delicious when drunk young, like BEAUJOLAIS. But if aged in wood and in the bottle for several years, these ZINFANDEL wines develop a bouquet as fine as that of the noble CABERNETS. Yet few vintners age their ZINFANDEL wines more than a year or two, because old ZINFANDELS do not command the market prices that aged CABERNETS do. ZINFANDELS grown in California foothills districts, as already mentioned, may make wines of fifteen to seventeen percent in alcoholic strength, approaching that of dry ports. In the Lodi, Manteca, and Escalon districts, early-harvested *Zinfandel* makes fruity table wines and is useful, blended with other grapes, in making rosés and red ports. In the main San Joaquin Valley, however, *Zinfandel* is subject to bunch rot unless sprayed with the giberellin plant hormone, which enlarges the berries and loosens the bunch. The versatility of the variety is evident from the number of ZINFANDEL rosés on the market, and the white ZINFANDELS, called ZINFANDEL BLANC, made from the colorless juice.

Second in acreage among reds is the Spanish *Carignane*. In Region IV climates it makes everyday-quality reds, but when grown with low yields on slopes in the coast counties, *Carignane* makes a wine that overcomes early harshness and develops good body and flavor.

Third in red grape acreage is the noble *Cabernet Sauvignon* of the Médoc. Tannic, deep in color, with a bouquet reminiscent of violets, *Cabernet Sauvignon* makes the best of all California wines. Before prohibition and for a few decades after repeal, the best CABERNET wines in the coast counties were allowed to ferment to dryness in contact with the grape skins, and many were almost undrinkable until they had aged in wood and bottle for at least four years. But eventually, as in Bordeaux, California makers of CABERNET learned to shorten the time of contact with the skins, with the result that their CABERNET SAUVIGNONS became delicious after only one or two years of age. During the 1960s and 1970s, wineries in the coast counties began planting increased acreages of *Merlot Noir*, the lesser Bordeaux variety which makes a softer, more quickly-aged wine, and blending it with their *Cabernet Sauvignon*. Not only did the blend make it possible again to ferment *Cabernets* to dryness on the skins, but the vintners discovered that unblended *Merlot* in the coast counties makes one of the best hundred-percent varietal red wines.

Fourth in acreage among the state's reds is *Barbera*, which in the Italian Piedmont competes in distinction with *Nebbiolo*. Grown in California's coast-counties climates, *Barbera* has made some excellent wines. But few coast-counties growers are willing to grow the grape because it is the principal red of the main San Joaquin Valley. Its special virtue in the valley is the high acidity it retains when grown in hot climates, and this is why valley-grown *Barberas* are soft, pleasantly flavorful red table wines. Much the same is true of the *Ruby Cabernet* grape, a cross of *Cabernet Sauvignon* with *Grenache* developed by the University in the 1940s for planting in Region IV and V climates. Some Lodi RUBY CABERNET wines have so much character that they are difficult to distinguish from coast-counties CABERNET SAUVIGNONS. The University more recently has developed two more *Cabernet-Grenache* crosses named *Carnelian* and *Centurion*, both of which have improved some of the main San Joaquin Valley table wines. There is another recent University cross named *Carmine*, intended for Region I to III climates, which makes wine with more *Cabernet* character than the noble *Cabernet*; but it is not widely planted because its name lacks the glamor associated with "Cabernet." Some coast-counties growers during the 1970s began planting the other Bordeaux Cabernet variety, the aromatic *Cabernet Franc*. In that decade also came the nationwide boom in white table wine sales, and the growers discovered they had more *Cabernet Sauvignon* grapes than they could use. This inspired some of the wineries to begin making CABERNET SAUVIGNON rosés and also some very acceptable CABERNET BLANCS.

Sixth in acreage among California red grapes is *Grenache*, the Spanish grape important in the blended wines of southern France. In California as in France, there are no red wines with Grenache as a varietal label. The only wine labels that mention the variety are the GRENACHE ROSÉS.

Wines of *Petite Sirah*, seventh among the state's reds, bring premium prices when grown in Region I to IV climates because this grape contributes to wines a peppery flavor that harmonizes with many foods. The variety resembles and may be a relative of the *Syrah* (*Sirah* or *Shiraz*) grape of Persia, which is responsible for the piquant flavor of the best red wines of Tain l'Hermitage in the Rhône Valley of France. However, the *Petite Sirah* of California more closely resembles another Rhône variety the French call *Durif* or *Duriff*. Its wines, grown in the coast counties, have the ability to age and to develop bouquet for several years. During the 1970s, the true French *Syrah* was planted in many California vineyards. Whether it will replace the *Petite Sirah* or *Duriff* remains to be seen.

Eighth red in California acreage is the noble *Pinot Noir*, which makes the great red wines of Burgundy and a part of the sparkling white wines of Champagne. For more than a century California winegrowers wondered why some of their *Pinot Noir* plantings yielded wines with the velvety, subtle, but pepperminty flavor and great bouquet of the great red burgundies of the Côte d'Or, but why vines with the same name, cultivated with equal care, gave them wines which, while pleasant, had none of the burgundy appeal. During the 1960s and 1970s the Californians learned some of the answers to the puzzle. One was that the noble *Pinot Noir* through the centuries has divided itself into some two hundred

sub-varieties or clones. Another was that the perfect clone required planting only in certain soils and cool climates to yield wines of Côte d'Or red burgundy character. A third was that the juice required warmer temperatures during fermentation than required for CABERNETS; and a fourth was that apparently some of the desired flavor came from the inclusion of various proportions of grape stems in the must. Region I temperatures for slow ripening of the grapes appeared to be the most important, and the Carneros district of southern Sonoma and Napa counties began to produce the most successful wines of *Pinot Noir*, which in recent double-blind comparative tastings have outscored many red burgundies of France. Meanwhile, the identification of *Pinot Noir* clones became entangled with the puzzle about Gamay grapes and wines.

For a century, California has grown a grape called Napa Gamay and has produced wines so named, which differ from those made in Burgundy from a grape called *Gamay Noir à jus blanc*. At the same time, some California winegrowers were producing wines of markedly different character from a grape called *Gamay Beaujolais*. During the past decade the confusion has been dispelled: the Napa *Gamay* grape has been identified by French ampelographer Pierre Galet as the Valdiguié of the French department of Lot; and the *Gamay Beaujolais* grape of California has been identified by California ampelographer Dr. Harold P. Olmo, confirmed by Dr. Galet, as one of the many clones of *Pinot Noir*. California nurserymen now call it "Pinot Noir Number Two". The result is that only *Pinot Noir* Number One is now used to produce most PINOT NOIR wines, and that the wines of Number Two are called GAMAY BEAUJOLAIS. During the 1970s California wineries have learned to use the *macération carbonique* method (fermentation of whole, uncrushed bunches of grapes) to make *nouveau* or *primeur* wines resembling young Beaujolais. They are introduced to the American market weeks after the harvest, competing with the Beaujolais of France. Also during the same decade, California "champagne" producers began using *Pinot Noir* Number One in their sparkling-wine cuvées, labeling the products BLANC DE NOIR. Then, when red grapes were in surplus during the white wine boom, there appeared many whites called PINOT NOIR BLANC, and also some PINOT NOIR ROSÉS.

The original Mission or *criolla* grape is still grown extensively in California, but almost entirely for use in making sherries. There are also two coast-counties red table wines of grapes whose European origins are not yet known. One is CHARBONO, also spelled Charbonneau, but no one is certain whether or not it is the same variety so named in Switzerland or called *Douce Noire* in Savoie. The other is PINOT ST-GEORGE, which Dr. Galet thinks is the Negrette of southern France. The best California ports are now made from three Portuguese varieties: TOURIGA, SOUZÃO and TINTA MADEIRA.

Californian wines always carry their names and distinctions on the bottle label, but cannot be readily identified as Californian purely by bottle shape, as for instance can the French Bordeaux or Burgundy wines. Still, the Californian labels are generally a good deal more informative than their often cryptic French counterparts. The "Fresh, Dry and Fruity" on Sebastiani's label (below) is a real boon to wine enthusiasts who know what they like but don't have an encyclopedic memory for names.

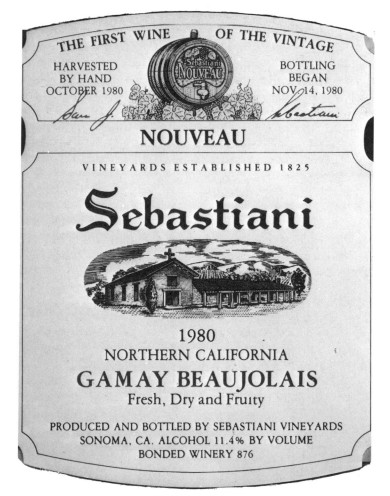

THE FIRST WINE   OF THE VINTAGE

HARVESTED
BY HAND
OCTOBER 1980

BOTTLING
BEGAN
NOV. 14, 1980

NOUVEAU

VINEYARDS ESTABLISHED 1825

Sebastiani

1980
NORTHERN CALIFORNIA
GAMAY BEAUJOLAIS
Fresh, Dry and Fruity

PRODUCED AND BOTTLED BY SEBASTIANI VINEYARDS
SONOMA, CA. ALCOHOL 11.4% BY VOLUME
BONDED WINERY 876

WINES OF OTHER WESTERN STATES

Three Pacific Northwest states—Washington, Oregon, and Idaho—have begun producing premium *vinifera* table wines since the late 1960s. Their wines, still available in limited quantities, have been judged equal and in some cases superior to those from California.

Washington, the northernmost state, has grown grapes commercially since the 1870s, when a *Vitis labrusca* variety called *Island Belle* was first planted around Puget Sound in the cool, rainy western part of the state. Eastern Washington, with less than eight inches of annual rainfall, was a virtual desert until irrigation projects after 1906 transformed the desert into a lush fruit-growing region. There, in the Yakima Valley and Columbia Basin, the *Concord* grape of the East was planted to produce fresh grape juice. Washington became the nation's third largest grape-growing state, after California and New York. Twoscore Washington wineries opened at the repeal of prohibition, making *labrusca* wines for sale in taverns; out-of-state wines then were available only in the state monopoly liquor stores. A Yakima Valley winery owner named William Bridgman made a study of California and European winegrowing climates and noted that Yakima, at 46 degrees north latitude, is midway between the latitudes of Burgundy and Bordeaux. He concluded that with more days of sunshine than in the French districts, the Yakima Valley should have the best winegrowing climate in the world. He planted *vinifera* grapes, but nobody paid much attention until a group of amateur winemakers on the state university's faculty at Seattle began making wines of Bridgman's grapes. In 1967 noted California enologist André Tchelistcheff visited Washington, tasted the professors' homemade wines, and pronounced them of excellent quality. Tchelistcheff advised American Wine Growers, the state's largest vintner, to devote part of its winery near Seattle as an experimental cellar for *vinifera* wines. The results were tasted by connoisseurs in California and highly praised. American Wine Growers, renamed Chateau Ste. Michelle, planted 5,000 more acres of *vinifera*, built two new wineries and modernized a third, and by 1974 was producing the first northwestern *méthode champenoise* sparkling wines of *Pinot Noir*. Meanwhile, the college-professor winemakers at Seattle opened a bonded winery, named it Associated Vintners, and since have had to enlarge it twice to keep up with the demand for their wines. A dozen more wineries opened in Washington State, *vinifera* plantings reached 5,000 acres, and were expanding at a fifth more per year. Annual judgings of northwestern states' wines are now held in Seattle by the Enological Society of the Pacific Northwest. The best Washington wines thus far have been Rieslings, Gewürztraminers, Chardonnays, Muscats, Cabernets, Merlots, and Grenache.

What may be most important about the emergence of Washington as a winegrowing state is that land is available east of the Cascade Mountains for as much as 100,000 acres of additional *vinifera* vineyards, which will be needed if the table-wine revolution in the United States continues at the same rate as in recent years. The only limiting factor is that severe winters have frequently caused serious crop losses.

OREGON

Winegrowing is older in Oregon than in Washington, its northern neighbor. Among the first settlers who came to the territory in wagon trains over the Oregon Trail were some who brought *labrusca* vine cuttings and began producing wine in the Willamette Valley south of Portland. *Vinifera* vines were introduced from California to the Rogue River Valley in southern Oregon as early as 1854. There were dozens of Oregon wineries before prohibition began in 1920, but only two continued long in business after the dry law was repealed in the 1930s. Prohibitionist zeal continued among state agricultural authorities, who as late as 1965 recommended the planting of *Vitis labrusca* vines as the only kind "suited to Oregon climates." Four years earlier,

The Hillcrest Vineyard, in Oregon, was planted in 1963. The region's climate is particularly suitable for the *Riesling* grape, which gives here a dry fruity wine similar to that of the Rhine in Germany.

1979

Hillcrest Vineyard

Oregon's Umpqua Valley

WHITE RIESLING

Alcohol 10% by Volume

Produced and Bottled by Hillcrest Vineyard
Roseburg, Oregon — Bonded Winery OR-44

young Richard Sommer, who had learned in his introductory viticulture course at the University of California that the best wines are grown in the coolest climates, went to Oregon, where it is still cooler, to plant a *vinifera* vineyard. He chose a site near Roseburg in the Umpqua Valley of western Oregon, where he bonded his Hillcrest Vineyard winery in 1963. During the next several years four more seekers after cool climates came from California and established wineries on their vineyards in western Oregon. Their wines sold well in Portland gourmet shops and began winning customers in California. More estate wineries were established. In 1977 they persuaded state officials to restrict Oregon *vinifera* wine labels to varietal names and to require at least ninety per cent varietal content. By 1981, Oregon wineries had multiplied to three dozen, *vinifera* vineyards in the state approached a thousand acres, and one winery had already made the state's first sparkling wine. Thus far, Oregon wines have been of the same varieties as in California and Washington, with the addition of one of *Pinot Gris*. There has been special interest in *Pinot Noir* since the Eyrie Vineyards' 1975 *Pinot Noir*, grown in the Dundee Hills of the Willamette Valley, scored second in a 1980 tasting at Paris against six French burgundies and five other wines from the United States, Switzerland, Australia, and Greece.

IDAHO

Idaho, like Oregon, had vineyards and wineries before prohibition. At repeal, wine sales in Idaho were restricted to state monopoly liquor stores. When the law was changed in 1971 to permit wine sales in private stores, vineyard planting increased in several districts but was limited by Idaho wheat growers' use of herbicide sprays which kill grapevines. The first successful winery in Idaho since prohibition is the Ste. Chapelle cellar at Sunny Slope in the Snake River Valley west of Boise, the state capital. Its first four vintages of RIESLINGS and CHARDONNAYS won gold medals in the northwest judging at Seattle, and another at Bristol in England in 1980. A second Idaho winery opened near Caldwell in 1981.

ARIZONA, COLORADO AND UTAH

Premium wine grape varieties have been planted at mountain elevations in Arizona, and farm wineries are planned when these grapes mature. The state already has a small winery, opened in 1980, but it thus far uses only California grapes. Colorado has a small winery producing local *vinifera* wines in the fruit-growing area near Grand Junction in the western part of the state. Utah, too, has a winery opened in 1981 by a church group in Salt Lake City which plans to plant a vineyard

Prizewinner at a multi-national wine tasting held in Paris, France, in 1980, the Eyrie Vineyards' 1975 PINOT NOIR has cultivated a marked increase of interest in that grape as an Oregon vinestock.

but brings its grapes from California for the present. *Vinifera* grapes already grow in southwestern Utah. There, at Toquerville, Mormon prophet Brigham Young had his disciples build a winery during the late nineteenth century, but he ordered it closed about 1900 because its wines could not compete with those from California. A research project undertaken about 1970 by the federally-financed Four Corners Regional Commission aims to develop winegrowing industries in Arizona, Colorado, Utah, and New Mexico.

NEW MEXICO

In New Mexico, winegrowing began in the seventeenth century when Franciscan priests established vineyards at their missions to provide wine for the Mass. Many wineries later were established in the Rio Grande Valley and continued until prohibition, and several were revived after repeal. Unable to compete with California wines, their number dwindled until only two were left by 1976. In that year, at the old Rico winery near Albuquerque, a California-trained enolo-

gist produced the first premium New Mexico wines from a *vinifera* vineyard 6,000 feet high in the mountains. Since then, two new small modern wineries have produced premium New Mexico wines. One winery is on the Pecos River south of Roswell, the other west of Anthony in the southern part of the state. The western-most American vineyard is at the little Tedeschi winery two thousand feet high on the Hawaiian island of Maui. Its first wine of the red *Carnelian* grape was excellent, but until the vineyard begins to produce adequate crops, the winery's only commercial product is a pineapple wine.

WINES OF THE EASTERN AND MIDWESTERN STATES

Commercial winegrowing began during the seventeenth, eighteenth, and nineteenth centuries in the eastern and midwestern United States. The wines were mainly of foxy *Vitis labrusca* grape varieties, but in some cases nonfoxy grapes of *Vitis riparia* parentage were used. In the southeastern states wines were also made of the native wild *Scuppernong*. In 1849 the blue *Concord*, a hardy *labrusca* variety, was introduced by Ephraim Bull of Massachusetts. Pasteurized sweet Concord juice, introduced by prohibitionist dentist Dr. Thomas Welch in 1870 as "unfermented wine", became the basis of a nationwide fresh grape juice industry, and *Concord* became the most widely grown grape in the eastern half of the country. *Concord* wines are sweet; if fermented dry they have a harsh taste. There were other less-foxy *labrusca* varieties than *Concord*, notably the white *Dutchess* and *Delaware* and the pink *Catawba*, which by the 1870s were making popular white table wines and "champagnes". There were wineries in thirty eastern and midwestern states by 1880, when Kansas passed a state prohibition law. In the wave of dry legislation that followed, wineries were forced to close in state after state, but some were still operating in four eastern states when national prohibition came in 1919 and 1920. During the dry era, a Maryland journalist and home winemaker named Philip Wagner, who disliked *labrusca* wines, introduced to the East the nonfoxy French hybrid wine grapes which are widely grown in France. There were many small plantings of the hybrids during the 1940s and 1950s. In 1957 Russian-born German emigré Dr. Konstantin Frank, at his vineyard near Hammondsport in the Finger Lakes district of New York, proved that the noble *Vitis vinifera* grapes of Europe can also be grown successfully in the East when they are carefully cultivated and protected by modern chemical sprays. When the boom in consumption of table wines in the United States began in the late 1960s, hundreds of new vineyards, some of hybrids and others of *vinifera*, were planted in the East and Midwest. During the 1970s and early 1980s more than two hundred new farm wineries were established in twenty states, where laws were changed to encourage farmers to grow and sell their own table wines.

Ever since French hybrids were first introduced into New York State as an alternative to the native foxy-tasting grapes, the winegrowers have produced wine with names borrowed from the vinestock's country of origin, like this AMERICAN CHABLIS.

GOLD SEAL
American
Chablis

MADE AND BOTTLED AT THE WINERY BY GOLD SEAL VINEYARDS HAMMONDSPORT, NEW YORK *Charles Fournier* ALCOHOL 12% BY VOLUME

NEW YORK

Grapes have been grown for wine in New York State since the mid-seventeenth century, when the cultivation of vineyards began on Manhattan and Long Islands. (Grapes were grown in New York City as late as 1846.) Winegrowing spread to the Hudson Valley by 1677, to Chautauqua County on Lake Erie by 1818, to the Finger Lakes region by 1829, and to the Niagara Peninsula by 1860. New York still was growing only *labrusca* grapes when the first scattered plantings of Wagner's hybrids and Dr. Frank's *vinifera* appeared in the state. During the 1970s, *vinifera* plantings began in a fifth New York district—northeastern Long Island—where studies showed the climate is moderated sufficiently by neigh-

New York State's vineyards (above) spread over some 53,000 acres. As local consumers have shown a strong preference for sparkling wines, the producers are duty bound to play into this market with wines like GOLD DUCK.

boring bodies of water to enable the delicate European vines to survive New York's severe winters. In 1976, the New York legislature passed laws to encourage grape growers to establish wineries on their farms. Until then, most New York table wines still tasted of *labrusca*. By 1981, three dozen new farm wineries had opened in all five of the state's vineyard districts, and most of them had planted French hybrids or *vinifera* and specialized in selling nonfoxy wines. Almost two thirds of the state's 43,000 acres of vineyards in 1978 still were *Concords*, but 5,000 acres of French hybrids and *vinifera* had been added in the few preceding years. New stars appeared among New York table wines offered for sale and entered for judging in eastern competitions: Among the whites were *Johannisberg Rieslings*, *Chardonnays*, *Gewürztraminers*, and *Cayuga*, a new nonfoxy grape bred at the Geneva Experiment Station and introduced in 1973. The leading whites of French hybrids were *Seyval Blanc* (described as "the Chardonnay of the East"), *Vidal, Ravat, Verdelet*, and *Rayon d'Or*. Among *vinifera* reds, a few New York farm wineries competed with Dr. Frank in producing *Cabernet Sauvignons* and *Pinot Noirs*. New York red table wines of such hybrids as *Maréchal Foch, Chancellor*, and *Baco Noir* began appear-

399

For centuries, the wines produced in New York State have originated from the *Vitis labrusca* species, which gives a strong foxy taste. Today, using the *Concord* variety, this taste is no more and the wines now resemble ports or sherries.

ing on prestigious winelists, and some were being shipped to buyers in neighboring states. New York also produces some much-admired aged wines of port and sherry types, making the latter of *Concords* from which the *labrusca* taste has been removed. Many eastern consumers prefer New York "champagnes" and medium-sweet table wines that have the slight *labrusca* fragrance supplied by Dutchess and Delaware, the least-foxy native grapes. These are exclusively New York products because California has not been successful in growing these grapes.

PENNSYLVANIA

William Penn, the founder of Pennsylvania, attempted to establish a wine industry at Philadelphia in 1683, planting vines from France and Spain, but they failed to grow. In 1793, more than a century later, a Frenchman named Pierre Legaux established near Philadelphia the first commercial winery in the United States. He introduced a grape variety which he named "Cape of Constantia," the planting of which soon spread to several other states. It eventually turned out to be a *labrusca* seedling or perhaps a chance *labrusca-vinifera* cross. Legaux's Pennsylvania Vine Company produced wine until his death in 1827. Other wineries started near Philadelphia and in other parts of Pennsylvania, and some continued operating until the beginning of national prohibition. But at repeal, when wineries reopened in some of the other eastern states, none started in Pennsylvania because wine was subject to the state's new liquor monopoly and could only be sold in its state-operated liquor stores. Grape-growing languished, except that there were Concord vineyards supplying a grape-juice plant in northwestern Erie County, which is an extension of New York's Chautauqua Grape Belt. In the 1960s, a group of amateur winemakers among the Erie Concord growers planted some French hybrids and *vinifera*, found they made good wines, and launched a movement to revive the state's wine industry. They got the state law amended in 1968 to permit farm wineries to make wines and to sell them at the cellar doors. Some thirty such wineries were opened across the state during the next dozen years. Vineyards of hybrids and *vinifera* were established west of Philadelphia, the area pioneered by William Penn and Pierre Legaux. Although the reborn Pennsylvania wine industry is still young, its wines are meeting with public favor. The best thus far have been SEYVAL, VIDAL, RIESLING, and CABERNET SAUVIGNON.

NEW JERSEY

Neighboring New Jersey has had a local wine industry for more than a century. It was based on a *labrusca* grape called Noah, which during the phylloxera epidemic of the 1870s was planted in several parts of France. The Renault winery at Egg Harbor City dates from 1864 and operated through the prohibition era under a government permit, making a wine tonic that sold in drugstores across the nation. Renault still makes a full line of wines, including bulk-process "champagnes". In 1981, when the New Jersey legislature adopted a farm winery law to encourage the planting of more vineyards, there were ten wineries in the state, and it appeared certain that there soon would be more.

THE NEW ENGLAND STATES

There are records of grape-growing and winemaking from colonial times through the nineteenth century in the New England states, which are east of New York. A few wine-grape vineyards were planted in Connecticut after prohibition was repealed in 1933, but no wine was made commercially because the laws of these states required the payment of exorbitant license fees for its sale. During the 1960s, vineyards planted by hobbyists produced crops that proved the region is as climatically suited for winegrowing as are most other parts of the East. During the 1970s, the legislatures of four New England states changed their laws to reduce the license fees for farm wineries and to allow the retail and wholesale sale of their home-grown wines. There already was a farm winery in central New Hampshire, opened in the 1960s. By 1981, five new wineries were operating in Rhode Island, four in Connecticut, and three in Massachusetts, including one on Martha's Vineyard, the island in the Atlantic Ocean ten miles off the southern tip of Cape Cod. New England wines, some of *vinifera*, others of French hybrids and *labrusca* types, are beginning to win favor in these states.

OTHER MIDDLE ATLANTIC STATES

The most rapid spread of winegrowing in the East is occurring in Virginia, which is one of the states that border the national capital at Washington, D.C. Seventeen wine estates have been planted in Virginia since 1970, including two by European investors (Zonin of Italy and Dr. Wilhelm Guth of Germany), and one by Paul Masson of California, a subsidiary of the giant Seagram liquor empire. Factors that have attracted this remarkable growth are evidence that the state's climate is milder than that of New York, where *vinifera* suffer damage in extreme winters; a law passed by the Virginia legislature in 1980 to encourage farm wineries, and the high quality of the first several vintages of Virginia *vinifera* wines. The state has an impressive wine history, for Virginia was the first American colony to plant grapes for wine. In 1619, Lord Delaware brought vines and vignerons from France, and the colonial assembly passed a law requiring every householder to plant at least ten vines. But this was before the development of modern sprays that control vine pests, and all the vines failed to grow. The Virginian Thomas Jefferson, the third president of the United States, also tried unsuccessfully to grow vines he imported from Château d'Yquem to his Monticello estate at Charlottesville. Jefferson's dream came temporarily true a century later when an important Virginia wine industry developed, based on the Norton grape, a nonfoxy *Vitis riparia* or *aestivalis* variety discovered in 1835 at Richmond. By 1880, Virginia had become the eleventh largest wine-producing state in the Union. But this was just when the prohibitionist movement was shrinking the eastern markets for wine, and by 1900 most of the Virginia wineries had been closed. When the state passed a prohibition law in 1914, few Virginia vineyards of any size remained. In 1970, when the present table-wine revolution in America was reaching its height, the planting of vineyards in Virginia began again. By 1981, wine-grape vineyards in the state totaled 500 acres, a third of them of *vinifera* varieties. The new Virginia wineries already were turning out wines of world-class quality: RIESLINGS, CHARDONNAYS, SAUVIGNON BLANCS, CABERNET SAUVIGNONS, and MERLOTS, as well as such French hybrid types as SEYVAL BLANC and MARÉCHAL FOCH.

The neighboring state of West Virginia, too, once had a wine industry, which began before the Civil War that raged from 1861 to 1865. In 1981, the West Virginia legislature passed a farm winery law, and two wineries soon opened in the state, while more were being built.

Maryland, to the north and east of the Virginias, also has a history of early winegrowing. Lord Baltimore attempted to start vineyards there in the seventeenth century, and in 1828 the state created a Maryland Society for Promoting the Culture of the Vine—but to

North America's first vineyard was planted in Virginia back in Colonial times—in 1619—but it was only recently that Virginian wine first made its appearance on the market. Even now, the state can boast no more than 625 acres of vines.

no avail. Maryland now has six wineries using locally-grown French hybrid and *vinifera* grapes. All were established after Philip Wagner introduced the hybrids to America, and after Wagner bonded his little Boordy Vineyard winery in 1954. Future expansion of Maryland vineyards is deterred, however, by a state law which prevents wineries, except in two counties, from selling their products at retail.

OHIO

By 1859, when Ohio was the premier wine state, its white and sparkling CATAWBA wines were sold throughout America and even in London, where the white was praised by one writer as "a finer wine of the hock species and flavour than any hock that comes from the Rhine." The *Catawbas* grown along the Ohio River inspired the connoisseur-poet Henry Wadsworth Longfellow to write in 1854 what may have been the first poem ever dedicated to a grape, his *Ode to Catawba Wine*. But soon afterward, the Ohio River vineyards began to die from black rot and oïdium, for this was still an era when modern preventive sprays were unknown. Then, new vineyards were planted along the Lake Erie shore west of Sandusky and on the cluster of islands which extend across the lake toward Canada. The lake influence gives these islands the longest grape-growing season in the East and Midwest. Prohibition closed the Ohio wineries, but some of those which reopened in the 1930s began planting some of the French hybrids to make wines of European types. During the 1960s, the introduction of modern sprays caused a revival of the Ohio River vineyards. Dozens of new wineries then opened in both the southern and northern parts of the state. Of the forty-two Ohio wineries counted at this writing, half have been established since 1971. Some of the vineyards west of Cleveland and those on North Bass Island in Lake Erie are being replanted with *vinifera* and French hybrids. As their wines reach the market, they are winning new favor for Ohio wines. Examples of the best are those which were awarded prizes in the 1981 judging of eastern wines held in New York State: the ROSÉ from Chalet Debonné at Madison, the BACO NOIR from the Vinterra Vineyard at Houston, the CHELOIS from Meiers Wine Cellars at Silverton, the RIESLINGS and CHARDONNAYS from Arnulf Esterer's Markko Vineyard at Conneaut, and the CHARDONNAY and *méthode champenoise* sparkling wine from the tiny Cedar Hill winery in Dr. Thomas Wykoff's restaurant at Cleveland Heights.

MISSOURI

A revival of winegrowing is under way in Missouri, which was the most important midwestern wine-

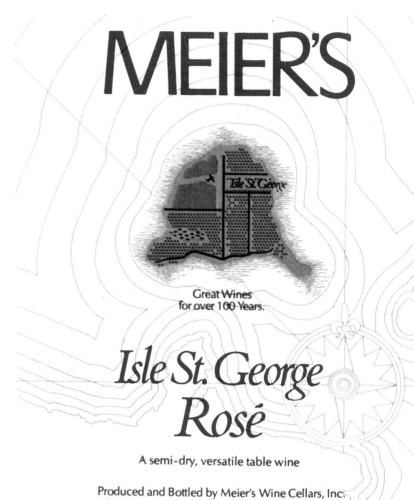

MEIER'S

Great Wines for over 100 Years.

Isle St. George Rosé

A semi-dry, versatile table wine

Produced and Bottled by Meier's Wine Cellars, Inc.
Silverton, Ohio   Alcohol 12% by Volume

Most of the new Ohio wineries are very new indeed—half of them date only from the 1970s—but the state once known world-wide for its Catawba wines has a reputation to be proud of. Meier's vineyard on Isle St. George (Lake Erie) produces a wide range of versatile wines.

producing state a century ago. It began with the reopening in the 1960s of Missouri's two oldest pre-prohibition wineries, Stone Hill at Hermann and Mount Pleasant at Augusta. Within a decade, eighteen more wineries were established on new vineyards in the old wine districts along the Missouri River, in the Ozark Plateau counties, and as far west as the Kansas City area. Vinicultural experts were brought to the state university from California and New York to guide the grape growers and winemakers. The new Missouri wines include such *vinifera* types as RIESLINGS and CHARDONNAYS, but the majority thus far are of French hybrid and *labrusca* grapes. Three Missouri wineries are already making "champagnes." One at St. James makes a red wine of the rare Neva Munson grape, one of the varieties bred in Texas before the turn of the century by famed horticulturist Thomas Volney Munson. It was from Missouri and Texas that France during the 1870s obtained the

millions of phylloxera-resistant vine roots that saved the vineyards of Europe and later those of California. The French Government in 1888 acknowledged this by decorating Munson and Hermann Jaeger of Missouri with the Legion of Honor Cross of *Mérite Agricole*.

KENTUCKY AND INDIANA

The first attempt to grow wine in Kentucky began after 1798, when Jean Jacques Dufour left his father's vineyard at Vevey in Switzerland to found a Swiss winegrowing colony in America. He planted *labrusca* vines along the Kentucky River south of Lexington in Kentucky, but they failed to grow; so he moved them to the Ohio River in Indiana, where they succeeded in producing grapes. Dufour named the Indiana site for his home in Switzerland, spelling it as Americans pronounce the name—Vevay. Vineyards and wineries prospered in both Indiana and Kentucky during the nineteenth century, but they died with the onset of prohibition. Almost a century and a half after Dufour's death, winegrowing returned to Indiana when the state legislature in 1971 adopted a farm-winery law. Nine Indiana wineries were established within a few years, including one at Vevay in Switzerland County, where a Swiss Wine Festival is now held annually to honor the memory of Dufour. Indiana produces some very acceptable wines of French hybrid grapes, and *vinifera* varieties have also been grown in some parts of the state. Vineyards have also revived in Kentucky. There now are two Kentucky wineries making good hybrid vines, but the state law restricts the sale of wines at their cellars. In 1981, the Kentucky Vineyard Society came back to life, organized by grape growers who want their state to adopt a farm-winery law like Indiana's.

MICHIGAN

Michigan is the fifth state in the nation in wine production and has 15,000 acres of vineyards, more than any other in the Midwest. But four-fifths of Michigan grapes are *Concords*, planted during the prohibition era for juice and jelly or to be sold fresh for table use. Four large Michigan wineries which opened at the repeal of prohibition specialized in *labrusca*-type wines, but when the French hybrids and *vinifera* grape varieties began to be planted extensively during the 1970s, they began producing much better wines. The large wineries are located in southwestern Michigan around Paw Paw, where there is a grape and wine festival each September. Newer vineyards and wineries are at Fennville (which in 1971 became the first Michigan viticultural area to be recognized by the federal government) and farther north around the Leelanau Peninsula,

which is bordered by Lake Michigan and Grand Traverse Bay. There have been some excellent MICHIGAN RIESLINGS (including an ice wine produced in 1980), CHARDONNAYS, BACO NOIRS, and VIDALS. The latter is the best Michigan white wine thus far made of any French hybrid grape. Four Michigan wineries make "champagnes", including one by the *méthode champenoise*.

WISCONSIN AND MINNESOTA

At Prairie du Sac in southern Wisconsin is the Wollersheim winery, established in 1973 on the site of a nineteenth-century winery with hillside caves. Excellent table wines of French hybrids are made there, and also a few of *Riesling* and *Chardonnay*. Seven other Wisconsin wineries mainly make wines of cherries and other fruits. In neighboring Minnesota, there are many small vineyards and two wineries which opened during the 1970s. Minnesota winters are so severe that vines need to be taken down from the trellises and covered, as they are in parts of Russia, until the weather warms in

The European trend for fresh, light wines of the "nouveau" or "primeur" types was taken up for the first time in the USA by St Julian, Michigan, in 1980.

St Julian

Southwestern Michigan
1980 Cascade
Nouveau

Cascade is a shy bearing European hybrid variety which produces very distinctive fruit. These, the first grapes crushed at our winery in 1980, were harvested on Sept. 16th. Nouveau, meaning new in French, is traditionally the first wine to be released from each years vintage and is waited for with anticipation as this new wine brings with it the promise of what is to come. We hope you enjoy the unique freshness of this limited release — 550 cases.

Alcohol 11% by volume

**Proudly Produced and Bottled by St. Julian Wine Co.
Paw Paw, Michigan 49079   Bonded Winery - 23**

403

spring. Despite this problem, the Alexis Bailly Vineyard at Hastings, south of Minneapolis, grows the best wine of the red French hybrid grape *Léon Millot* thus far produced in the United States.

ILLINOIS, KANSAS, OKLAHOMA, NEBRASKA AND IOWA

Illinois has three small wineries, and many vineyards of wine grapes were planted during the 1970s there and in such other midwestern states as Kansas, Nebraska, Iowa, and Oklahoma. But the revival of their once-important winegrowing industries awaits the enactment of new laws to protect the vineyards from the herbicides used by grain growers and the correction of archaic state laws which impose high license fees on small wineries and restrict the sales of their wines.

TEXAS

Texas, the largest midcontinent state, produced wine at the Spanish missions in the El Paso Valley as early as the seventeenth century, and scores of wineries operated there and along the Red River near the Oklahoma border until the prohibition era. Only one Texas winery, the Val Verde cellar, established in 1881 at Del Rio on the Rio Grande, reopened at repeal. In 1974, a university feasibility study showed that Texas might someday become one of the nation's important wine-producing states if solutions could be found for its problems of soil, water, and climate, such as cold winters and hailstorms in which golfball-sized hailstones have been known to strip a vine of grapes in the western part of the state. During a few years after the study was released, hundreds of new vineyards and five new wineries sprang up in parts of Texas where wine had not been grown before. Two of the wineries are in the "hill country" north of San Antonio, and two are west of Fort Worth. One of the latter, the Buena Vida Vineyard at Springtown, is already known for its table wines of French hybrids, which it calls ESTRELLA DE VIDA and VIDA DEL SOL. In 1976, the largest winery thus far built in the state opened at Lubbock in west Texas to make wine of French-hybrid and *vinifera* grapes. It is the 15,000 gallon Staked Plain or Llano Estacado winery. (The high plains of Texas were so named by the explorer Coronado for the wooden stakes he drove in the giant grass to guide him back from his trip to New Mexico in 1542.) *Vinifera* vineyards have been planted in two more new Texas areas. One is the extensive lands owned by the state university around Bakersfield in west Texas, where summer temperatures are like those of California's Central Valley—Region V. The other is high in the Davis Mountains, where the climate is Region III like the central Napa Valley; and one vineyard in this new district has already produced very satisfactory SAUVIGNON and CHENIN BLANC and RIESLING wines.

ARKANSAS

Between 1879 and 1900, many Swiss, German, and Italian immigrants settled in north western Arkansas, where the Ozark Plateau extends south from Missouri and slopes toward the Arkansas River Valley. They first made wine of wild grapes called Muscadines, then brought *labrusca* vines from Missouri and also used a grape of *Vitis riparia* or *aestivalis* parentage, called *Cynthiana*. When prohibition closed the early Arkansas wineries, a grape-juice plant was built at Springdale and a boom in the planting of Concord vines ensued. At repeal, Arkansas had more than a hundred wineries, but their number gradually dwindled to nine, of which one at Fayetteville is new. Four are near the Swiss-German village of Altus in the Ozark Plateau region. Largest is the two-million-gallon Wiederkehr cellars, which has an Alpine inn, gift shop, and a Swiss restaurant, around which a grape festival is held in August of each year. Next largest is the half-million gallon winery of the Wiederkehrs' cousins, the Post family. Both claim founding dates of 1880. Their vineyards total 600 acres, mostly of *labrusca*, *Muscadine*, and French hybrid varieties, but Wiederkehr devotes a hundred acres to such *vinifera* as *Riesling*, *Gewürztraminer*, and *Cabernet Sauvignon*. One of the most interesting *Wiederkehr* red table wines is of the *Cynthiana* grape, which some ampelographers say is identical with the *Norton* of Virginia.

WINES OF THE DEEP SOUTH

In the southeastern United States, and no where else in the world, there grows a family of grapes so fragrant that the crews of ships approaching the coast in September detect its rich scent while they are still many miles from shore. The grapes are the *Muscadines*, *Vitis rotundifolia*, of which the best known is the greenish-bronze *Scuppernong*. They grow not in bunches but in clusters, each berry as large and rotund as a cherry or a marble. Their musky aroma is so powerful that when the juice is blended with that of *labrusca* grapes, it

overwhelms and hides the latters' foxy taste. *Scuppernongs* and other *Muscadine* varieties make most of the wines produced commercially in North Carolina, Mississippi, and Alabama, and some are also made in Arkansas, South Carolina, and Georgia. Unblended *Muscadine* wines seem to be preferred by people who are native to the localities where the vines grow; but for consumers of other wines a small percentage of *Muscadine* adds a pleasing flavor to blends with less-flavorful grapes. It was such a blend of *Scuppernong* with New York *labrusca* and California *vinifera* juices that made white and red GARRETT'S VIRGINIA DARE the best-selling wines in the United States for two decades before prohibition. *Muscadines* long were the only grapes grown at low elevations in the Southeast because they are tolerant of a disease there which kills most vines of bunch-grape varieties. At higher elevations, however, bunch-grapes grow successfully. The Biltmore Estate at Asheville, N.C., has been producing commercial wines

of French hybrids since 1977. But *Muscadine* wines are the only products of North Carolina's two young wineries at Edenton and Rose Hill; also of the six wineries that started during the 1970s in Mississippi, and of Alabama's only winery, Perdido Vineyards, which opened in 1979. Grape breeders have bred dozens of new white, red, and black *Muscadine* grapes with such names as *Magnolia, Carlos, Higgins,* and *Noble,* which appear on many varietal labels, but *Scuppernong* is still the best-known. Breeders in Florida and California have crossed Muscadines with *labrusca* and *vinifera* and produced bunch-grapes without *Muscadine* flavor that grow successfully in areas where only *Muscadines* could grow before. New wine industries using these new grapes are starting in Florida and in coastal Tennessee. Two wineries which opened in 1980 at Piedmont elevations in Tennessee are expected to specialize in hybrid and *vinifera* wines.

THE WINES OF CANADA

The history of Canadian wines parallels in many ways that of wines in the United States, but there are some important differences. One is that wine until now has been grown in only two Canadian vineyard districts. The eastern district consists of some 25,000 acres of vineyards on the Niagara Peninsula in southernmost Ontario province, bordered by Lakes Erie, Ontario, and Huron and across from Michigan and New York State. The western district is also limited, some 3,000 acres in the Okanagan and Similkameen Valleys of south-central British Columbia, extending to the border of Washington State. Although there have been grape-growing trials in the Fraser River Valley of south-central B.C., and a promising new vineyard of hybrids and *vinifera* at Kentville in western Nova Scotia released its first *Chardonnay* in 1982, the rest of Canada is too far north to offer suitable climates for the cultivation of wine grapes.

Winegrowing in Ontario dates from 1811, when former German army corporal Johann Schiller began fermenting Niagara Peninsula grapes at Cooksville, which is now a suburb of Toronto. His wines were judged "pure and of excellent quality" at the Paris Exposition in 1867. By the 1890s, there were 5,000 acres of vines and thirteen flourishing wineries in Ontario, including Barnes Wines, founded at St. Catharines in 1873, and Brights, which started a year later at the city of Niagara Falls. The Ontario wineries prospered until the crusade against drinking in the United States spread northward across the border and Canadian towns began voting themselves dry. Then in 1916

and 1917, while Canadian solders were away fighting in Europe, the Canadian provinces (except Québec, with its French heritage) adopted prohibition laws. In Ontario wine was not wholly prohibited, but a buyer had to travel to a winery and buy at least a five-gallon keg or a case; and few did. The Ontario wineries then resorted to smuggling their wines across the lakes to the dry American states, disguising the shipments as exports to Cuba or Central America. This proved so profitable that more wineries started; there were fifty-one when the province repealed its prohibition law in 1927. Ontario wineries made only dessert port and sherry types until the end of U.S. prohibition in 1933, when French enologist Adhemar de Chaunac started the Brights winery producing table wines. He introduced French hybrid and *vinifera* grapes from France and made the first Canadian sparkling wine, which won a medal at the 1949 California State Fair. A replanting of Ontario vineyards with hybrids and *vinifera* grapes began, and it progressed more rapidly than in the eastern United States. By 1980, almost half of Ontario grape production was of European vines, and the government sped the conversion by having surplus *labrusca* grapes distilled into beverage brandy. Niagara Peninsula farmers with quality vineyards were encouraged to open "cottage wineries," and seven were already welcoming visitors to their tasting rooms by 1981. How much Ontario wines have improved in recent years was evidenced by the 1981 judging of eastern wines in New York State. Twenty-one of the several dozen awards, ranging from gold, silver, and bronze medals to "best of class," went

to Ontario-grown wines, including "champagnes" and such table-wine types as Seyval, Vidal, Chelois, Baco Noir, Millot-Chambourcin, Gamay Beaujolais, and Merlot.

British Columbia's Okanagan Valley, 2,000 miles west of Ontario, was inhabited only by Indians, for traders, and missionaries until the introduction of placer mining brought gold prospectors after 1860. The first few grapevines were planted by the Oblate Fathers at a mission they established near Kelowna about 1864. During the 1920s, the first two B.C. wineries opened at Victoria on Vancouver Island to make wine of loganberries grown on the nearby Saanich Peninsula. About the same time, Hungarian winemaker Dr. Eugene Rittich made experimental plantings in the Okanagan Valley of a strangely-flavored grape he called *Okanagan Riesling*. In 1932, the Calona Winery was started at Kelowna to make wine of surplus apples. It soon supplemented them with grapes trucked from California, and the wineries at Victoria began doing the same. More vineyards were planted in the Okanagan, mainly of *labrusca* varieties, supplying Calona and the Andrés winery, which opened in 1961 at Port Moody, near Vancouver. Andrés originated a carbonated light sweet *labrusca* wine named Baby Duck, which enjoys a low tax rate because it is less than seven percent in alcoholic strength. Baby Duck now sells throughout Canada and has even been exported to England. British Columbia wines still were made mostly of California grapes until 1961, when the provincial government established a limit on how much out-of-state grapes could be used. This set off a stampede to plant more vineyards, and the new plantings included some hybrids and *vinifera* varieties. During the 1970s, there were new experimental plantings of German white varieties, including new clones of *Riesling*, *Ehrenfelser*, and *Scheurebe*. These proved successful, and some world-class quality wines were made. Between 1979 and 1981, several small winegrowing estates opened wineries in the Okanagan Valley, all of them specializing in *vinifera* wines. There now are eleven wineries in British Columbia, seven of them new since 1979.

THE WINES OF MEXICO

Although Mexico's wine industry is the oldest in the western hemisphere, it is really very new. In 1524, the conqueror Cortez ordered the planting of grapes for wine, but seventy years later Philip II, to please the jealous vintners of Spain, ordered the vines destroyed. During the wars and revolutions of the seventeenth to nineteenth centuries, Mexican vineyards were neglected. Most of their history had been forgotten by 1950, when the planting of new vineyards and the building of modern wineries began. There was a great increase in vine-planting through the 1970s, raising the national total to 110,000 acres. But this was mostly in the state of Sonora, intended partly for the production of table grapes to supply the American fresh-fruit market, and even more for the distillation of brandy, which is the prestige spirits drink of Mexico, much more popular than tequila. The main winegrowing districts are northern Baja California, Aguascalientes, Parras, and parts of Durango, Coahuila, and Querétaro. The most unusual district is between San Juan del Río and Tequisquiapan in Querétaro, only a hundred miles north of Mexico City. Vines there are within the Torrid Zone, but the climate at the altitude of 6,000 feet is cool enough for premium European wine-grape varieties. Newer vineyards for table wines have lately been planted at altitudes as high as 7,000 feet in the state of Zacatecas. The best Mexican table and *espumosos* (sparkling) wines have come in recent years from several Baja California valleys between San Vicente, Ensenada, and Tecate, within a few hours of the American border. The climate there resembles that of Alta California's coastal valleys because the vineyards are only ten to fifty miles from the Pacific. The best-known Mexican table wines are those of Pedro Domecq of Mexico, Hidalgo of San Juan del Río, and Bodegas de Santo Tomás of Ensenada. There are some sixty wineries in the republic, but the majority specialize in brandy. Mexican table and sparkling wines have become reliably palatable in recent years and are becoming steadily better.

WINES OF CALIFORNIA

Red wines	Claret types	Cabernet Sauvignon	Almadén, Beaulieu, Inglenook, Charles Krug, Louis Martini, Mirassou, Robert Mondavi, Sebastiani, Souverain
		Zinfandel	Buena Vista, Charles Krug, The Christian Bros., Louis Martini, Mirassou, Robert Mondavi, Pedroncelli
		Ruby Cabernet	East-Side
	Burgundy types	Pinot Noir	Almadén, Beaulieu, Hanzell, Heitz Cellar, Inglenook, Louis Martini, Paul Masson, Martin Ray, Wente Bros.
	Italian types	Barbera	Louis Martini, Sebastiani
		Grignolino	Beringer, Heitz Cellar
		Chianti	Gallo, Italian Swiss Colony
White wines	Sauternes types	Sauvignon Blanc	Almadén, Concannon, Robert Mondavi, Wente Bros.
		Semillon	Concannon, Charles Krug, Louis Martini, Wente Bros.
	Burgundy types	Pinot Chardonnay	Almadén, Beaulieu, Hanzell, Heitz Cellar, Paul Masson, Mayacamas, Robert Mondavi, Souverain, Stony Hill, Weibel, Wente Bros.
		Pinot Blanc	Heitz Cellar, Paul Masson, Mirassou, Wente Bros.
		Chenin Blanc	Charles Krug, Souverain
		Folle Blanche	Louis Martini
		Chablis	Beaulieu, The Christian Bros.
	Rhine types	Johannisberger Riesling	Almadén, Beaulieu, Charles Krug, Louis Martini, Souverain
		Grey Riesling	Almadén, Charles Krug, Wente Bros.
		Traminer	Charles Krug, Louis Martini, Mirassou, Stony Hill
		Sylvaner	Buena Vista, Inglenook, Louis Martini
Aperitif and dessert wines	Sherry types	dry	Solera Cocktail (Almadén) Pale dry (Beaulieu, Louis Martini) Ultra Dry (Buena Vista) Dry Watch (Cresta Blanca)
		medium dry	Solera Golden (Almadén) Flor Sherry (Novitiate of Los Gatos, Weibel)
		Sweet and Cream Sherry	Solera Cream (Beaulieu) Triple Cream (Cresta Blanca) Rare Cream (Paul Masson) Cream Flor (Weibel)
	Port types	Solera Ruby	Almadén
		Solera Tawny	Almadén
		Vintage Port	Buena Vista
		Tawny Port	Louis Martini
		Rare Tawny	Paul Masson
		Tinta Port	Ficklin
	Champagne types	Champagne	Almadén, Korbel, Hanns Kornell, Paul Masson, Weibel
		Pink Champagne	Almadén, Korbel, Paul Masson, Weibel
		Sparkling Burgundy	Almadén, Korbel, Hanns Kornell, Paul Masson, Weibel
		Sparkling Muscat	Hanns Kornell
Rosé wines		Grenache rosé	Almadén, Beaulieu, Novitiate of Los Gatos
		Gamay rosé	Louis Martini, Robert Mondavi
		Grignolino rosé	Heitz Cellar

WINES OF NEW YORK STATE

Red wines	Burgundy Claret	Delaware Isabella	Lake Country Red Niagara
White wines	Catawba Delaware Gewürztraminer	Johannisberger Riesling Spätlese Lake Niagara Muscat Ottonel	Pinot Chardonnay Rhine Wine White Tokay

THE WINES
OF SOUTH AMERICA

DENIS BOUVIER

Within hours of their first landings on the coast of South America, the galleons flying the flags of Spain discharged upon the beaches two very disparate cargoes: barrels of gunpowder for their arms, and barrels of wine for the altar set up in the name of Their Very Catholic Majesties. But the supply of wine soon grew short, and the missionaries who landed with the *conquistadores* found themselves obliged to become winegrowers. In this way wine came to South America.

The aim of the emissaries sent out by Ferdinand of Spain and Manuel the Fortunate of Portugal was to conquer the "Western Indies". The sole purpose of the conquest was to appropriate for themselves the gold and wealth of these new countries which stretched from the Atlantic across the Andes to the "Great Ocean" beyond. But neither the cross, nor the royal standard, nor even the quantities of glass beads they brought could persuade the natives to let invaders plunder the riches of their land. The *conquistadores* then used more summary methods, which the Indians answered in their own way: they tortured their prisoners in original fashion, quenching their thirst by giving them molten gold to drink as a reprisal for the wine which the Franciscan and Jesuit Fathers had forced them to drink with the Host. And what remains today of this immense Empire after it was split up into the separate nations of Chile, Argentina, Brazil and Peru? The gold mines are long since empty, the art treasures shamelessly melted down into bullion; the people, decimated by war and bled dry by taxation, are reduced to poverty. The only living thing remaining of what the conquerors brought to

South America is, here and there, a vineplant, a thriving symbol of eternity.

This vine-plant gave birth to the immense South American vineyard area of today, which spreads along the coastline, in the valleys of the Andes right at the foot of the Great Cordillera, and then up on the high plains into the Pampas region and to Uruguay. Wine, which at the heroic time of the *Conquista* was considered to be the perquisite of the new Crusaders, grew to be more appreciated as the Spanish influence came to dominate the people. Viticulture was further intensified when settlers flocked from across the seas; they came from France, Italy and Germany, often bringing with them as their sole possession the love of vineyards and wine as well as the knowledge acquired from centuries of winemaking in Burgundy, the Basque provinces, Tuscany or the banks of the Rhine. Thus viniculture spread through the new land of South America, which previously had only seemed capable of harbouring the sisal plant, or maté, maize and coffee. True, it was first necessary to make the soil suitable for cultivation, for it had been allowed to lie fallow for centuries. Canals were dug to irrigate the land, and experiments made to find the vine-plant best suited to the varied and often capricious climate of the area. Then it was necessary to develop new methods of vinification and culture. Here, the vinegrowers drew on their experiences in the African vineyards.

The South American vineyard area has developed well, and it is today of respectable dimensions. The quality of its produce continues to improve, even though the wine it exports (at competitive prices) cannot hope to rival in quality the great wines of Western Europe. These are wines which compare more favourably with those of North Africa.

Not all countries cultivate the vine: Ecuador, Venezuela, Guiana and Paraguay do not. Of those that do, the

This scene of work on the vineyards was photographed in Chile. Apart from the horse's harness, the photograph may just have well have been taken in Spain or in Italy. Chilean vineyards produce nearly a hundred million gallons of wine per annum.

following are listed in order of importance both as regards the area under cultivation and the production of wine: Argentina, Chile, Brazil, Uruguay, Peru, Bolivia and Columbia. It is interesting to note that until now no South American Government has introduced any official system of classification or control of the proprietary name. In South America there is no *appellation d'origine contrôlée* as there is in France.

ARGENTINA

The vine was introduced into Argentina in the sixteenth century, when the Spaniards first conquered the Pampas. Coming down from the high plains and mineral regions of Bolivia, they searched for new treasures in the foothills of the Andes. By contrast with the gold that the followers of Don Pedro de Castillo and Juan Jupe, the founders of the towns of Mendoza and San Juan sought, the humble vine planted by the Franciscans and the Jesuits did not seem to promise a great future. However, despite the obstacles that the Kings of Spain brought to the development of viticulture in their American possessions, the Cuyo region grew rich thanks to the patience and industry of its winegrowers. Meanwhile, Phillip II's coffers filled with precious metals—and the Spanish economy, mortally paralysed, came to a standstill. The first scattered vineyards planted in the provinces of Mendoza and San Juan probably could not have been extended into the fallow plains without irrigation. Italian immigrants were the first to be able to capture the water, rich in lime, which came down in torrents from the Andes. Thus the vine was extended into regions previously desert, and the famous "viticultural oases" were created. Later, however, the water carried the dreaded phylloxera disease which nearly destroyed the wine-harvests, and while the dense system of irrigation ditches favoured the spread of the disease, it also provided the remedy. It was in fact found possible to dam the channels and flood the vines, drowing the pests that infested them.

The first French vine stocks were introduced in 1855; later, Italian and Spanish varieties were planted. The oldest vine-plant is the *Criollo*, introduced from Mexico and Peru, but which can be considered an indigenous grape. Today it produces white wines.

Little by little, wine, originally produced for local consumption, spread to new markets thanks to the opening up of new communications between the east and west of the country, while at the same time, the nineteenth century, an impulsion was given to viticultural techniques by the European immigrants. Today Argentinian wine production is in full expansion and matches the increasing population of the country. Wine-growers are emphasising the quality of their wines, despite a vinification that often takes place on a very large scale.

Argentina is the largest wine-producer in Latin America—and fifth largest world-wide—making some 440 to 480 million gallons.

The Argentinian wine-growing zone has a continental climate, semi-desert with slight summer rainfall. The soils, alluvial or deposited, are sandy or clayish, but predominately light yet deep. The vines, espaliered or on trellises, are irrigated by channels that carry the meltwater from the Andes; there are also regions irrigated by artesian wells. Average production is 578 gallons per acre, one of the highest in the world.

In 1977 wine exports reached 11 million gallons. Principal customers for wines in bulk (mostly white) are: USSR, Chile, Yugoslavia, Bulgaria, while bottled wines (mostly red) are exported to Paraguay, Venezuela, Brazil, Ecuador and the USA.

VINICULTURAL PROVINCES. In order of importance the chief wine-producing regions are Mendoza, San Juan, Rio Negro and Neuquen, which produce about 95 per cent of Argentina's wine. Then come the regions of Rioja, Catamarca, Cordoba, Slata and Buenos Aires.

MENDOZA. This province is by far the most important. It alone produced 298,817,150 gallons in 1978. In 1977, the area planted to vines was 624,540 acres (an expansion of some 135,905 acres since 1966): which represents 71.07 per cent of the viticultural area of the country. Some 65 per cent of the vines are cultivated in high or low espaliers, the rest on trellises.

Red wines (31 per cent) are made from: *Malbec, Bonarda, Merlot, Barbera, Tempranilla, Lambrusco, Pinot* and *Cabernet* grapes.

White wine (18 per cent) varieties: *Pedro Ximenez, Chenin, Semillon, Palomino, Muscat, Riesling* and *Chardonnay.*

While the province of Mendoza contains thousands of producers, it is nevertheless a country of large, sometimes very large, estates, which are extremely well equipped.

SAN JUAN. A prolongation along the foot of the Andes of the province of Mendoza, the province of San Juan has a wine-growing area of 156,224 acres, which amounts to 18.83 per cent of the grape-growing area of the country.

Some 86 per cent of the vines are grown on trellises. This method is preferred because it keeps the grapes at a distance from the soil, which is generally too hot.

The region principally produces white wines (80 per cent) from *Ceresa, Muscat blanc, Criolla grande, Torrentes* and *Pedro Ximenez* grapes; red wines come from *Barbera, Malbec, Nebbiolo* and *Rabosco del Piave* varieties.

410

Thanks to irrigation, the vines in the San Juan province of Argentina have prospered and now form real "viticultural oases" in an otherwise desert area. The vines above are not more than three years old.

An Argentinian wine label. The trade name is CANCILLER (Chancellor); the wine was made from *Cabernet* stock and bottled by the producer. It comes from Mendoza, far and away the most important wineproducing province in Argentina.

Table grapes and raisins account for about 50 per cent of the harvest.

RIO NEGRO and NEUQUEN. The regions of Rio Negro and Neuquen are the most southerly of the wine-growing areas. The vineyards extend over 42,340 acres, 3 per cent of the Argentinian viticultural surface.

Red wines are produced from: *Malbec*, *Barbera*, *Syrah*, *Pinot*, *Merlot* and *Cabernet* grapes; whites from *Torrontes*, *Pedro Ximenez*, *Semillon*, *Chenin* and *Malvoisie*.

OTHER REGIONS. The rest of the wine producing areas are found in the provinces of Rioja, Catamarca, Jujuy and Buenos Aires.

WINE TYPES. The International Institute of Viti-Viniculture *(El Instituto Internacional de la Viti-vinicultura)* has classified Argentinian wines into two groups: *comunes* (ordinary wines) and *no comunes* (the better grades). The *comunes* wines, which account for 90 per cent of the local production, are those sold as *vinos de mesa* or table wines. They are mostly red, very full-bodied wines, with an alcohol content ranging from

VINO FINO TINTO

CANCILLER

CABERNET

CONT. NETO

700
C.C.

SELECCION DE CEPAS DE UVAS FINAS

Bodega "LA COLINA DE ORO" Maipú - Sótano N°. 6 - Nave N°. 6 - Toneles N°. 451 al 478 Elaborado y Embotellado por sus productores Bodegas y Viñedos GIOL E. E. I. C. en Carril Gómez 265 - General Gutiérrez - Maipú - Mendoza - Inscripto I.N.V. N° A 70941 - D. I. N° 116

ENVASADO EN ORIGEN   INDUSTRIA ARGENTINA

ARGENTINA

11° to 12.5°. The whites are ordinary wines with a higher alcohol content. Ordinary wine from the provinces of La Rioja, San Juan, Catamarca, Córdoba, Jujuy and Salta enjoys a form of regional appellation. These are unblended wines *envasado en origen* (bottled by the producer), or mixed with other wines (provided that the other wine used was made from grapes grown on the territory of the corresponding regional vineyard); these are known as *vinos de corte* (blended wines). The third category of wine known as *comunes* is that of special wines labelled *vinos de postre* (dessert wines) or *moscato*. *Vinos de mesa* and *vinos de postre* can be *seco* (dry), *dulce* (sweet) or *abocado* (a mild wine). The *vino de postre abocado* is made by adding a concentrated must to the wine whilst it is fermenting, and is very highly thought of by Argentinians.

The best Argentinian wines are the *vinos no comunes*. They come in four different categories: *finos* (fine wines), *reservas* (wines in reserve), *reservados* (reserved) and *especiales* (special wines). The fine wines are made mainly from the *Semillon, Pedro Ximenez, Cabernet, Barbera, Malbec* and *Torrontes* grapes. According to their colour they are known as: *tinto, blanco, clarete, rosado* or *criollo*. The reds are well-balanced, dry, strong and full-bodied wines, with an alcohol content from 12° to 13°. The white wines, whose alcohol content is slightly lower than the red, have a rich bouquet; they are well-balanced and have a very pleasant taste. The rosés are also well-balanced, with an alcohol content of from 12° to 13°. The well-known EL TRAPICHE (white, red and rosé) is one of the best wines of Argentina.

Argentina also produces sparkling wines of the Champagne or Asti type as well as aerated wine, as mediocre here as anywhere else in the world. There are also vermouths and quinine waters.

A few Argentinian wines have adopted foreign names, such as Porto, Jerez, Champagne, Marsala, Médoc and Burgundy. It is interesting to note that although in Argentina there is a strict control on the production and quality of wine, there is none on the brand names.

CHILE

Chilean wines are by far the best in South America, and have established the highest reputation on the continent. However, Chile exports very little wine to the world market: only 1.25 per cent from an annual production of about 99,000,000 gallons. Most of the wines for export are honest table wines, and one must visit Chile, or more particularly the Santiago region, to taste the best the country has to offer.

As elsewhere in South America, the Europeans implanted the *vitis vinifera* in Chile, whose climate proved to be very favourable to the cultivation of the vine. The vineyard was modernized in the nineteenth century by Italian, French and German immigrants. The French techniques in viniculture and vinification were the most successful, hence French methods came to be generally accepted and practised in all the *haciendas* and these techniques are still employed today.

An attempt was made to extend viticulture to the drier and less suitable regions, but irrigation proved to be an inseparable problem. A Chilean, Silvestre Ochagavia, imported and planted French vines, and brought the *Cabernet, Sauvignon* and *Pinot* grapes into the

412

central valley in Chile; then, following his example, the Government took measures to encourage the development of viticulture in that area.

Chile has three large viticultural regions. The biggest is the southern vineyard area. Herein are contained the regions of Linares, the banks of the Maule river, Nuble, Conception and the Bio-Bio valley, where the production is mainly red wines (70 per cent), with a small quantity of white wines (30 per cent). These wines, originating for the most part from humid and cold areas, are light, with a low alcohol content; they are practically all made from *Malbec, Cabernet, Semillon* and *Riesling* grape varieties.

The second largest viticultural region—Curico, Talca, Santiago, O'Higgins and Colchaga—has a dry, warm climate, but thanks to irrigation produces excellent wines. Red wines are made from the *Cabernet Franc, Cabernet Sauvignon, Merlot, Malbec* and *Petit Verdot* grapes; the white wines, from the *Semillon* and *Sauvignon* grapes. A few *Pinot Blanc* and *Pinot Noir* grapes can be found here and there, as well as the *País* or *Uva*

del País, the national grape, one of the first vines to be planted on Chilean soil.

The third principal vineyard is farther north, near Coquimbo in the Aconcaga valleys and along the banks of the Maipo river, as well as up to the fringes of the Atacama desert. Here the *Muscat* grape flourishes and gives wines of a very high alcohol content: rich and full-bodied, similar to Madeira, ports or sherry. They are often blended with the southern varieties. The climate here in the northern part of the country does not favour viniculture, for it is either too dry or too humid, depending on the season.

Chilean wines are classified into four different categories according to their age. The first category is for ordinary table wines of one year; the second is the *especiales*, which are two-year-old wines; the third, the *reservados*, have been in the bottle for four years, and are often high quality wines; and finally, the *gran vino* wines are recognized as being the best. Their quality is guaranteed by the State, and they are left to mature in barrels for at least six years.

BRAZIL

Brazil is the third largest wineproducer in South America, with vineyards covering 148,260 acres and producing about 54,995,000 gallons. Planted at the time of the Portuguese conquest, the vine came into its own only at the beginning of the last century. It made some progress between the two wars and is still being developed today: within rather less than fifty years, the area under cultivation increased sevenfold. This development was above all the work of Italian immigrants, who knew how to bring the best out of a soil which until then had been neglected. However, as the average Brazilian only drinks about four pints a year, the rest is sold on the international market, where the main customers are the U.S.A., Argentina and Germany.

THE GRAPE VARIETIES. The *Isabella* is the grape most frequently used; it is an American hybrid which produces an ordinary table wine. The other grapes used are the *Duchesse, Merlot, Cabernet, Barbera, Niagara, Folha de Figos, Black July, Siebel* and such varieties as the *Delaware, Jacques Gaillard, Concord, Gothe, Trebbiano,* and *Moscatel*.

WINES. The Brazilian wine industry is controlled by a series of very simple regulations, which merely distinguish between table, dessert and blended wines. These wines can be called by their grape—BARBERA, MOSCATEL, TREBBIANO, MALVASIA, RIESLING and MERLOT—provided they consist of these varieties in an authorized proportion. As a result, one can find good quality ordinary wines, but never great wines. The ordinary table wines are of a red Burgundy or claret type, rosés, or dry, semi-dry and sweet white wines. Good table wines include those of the *Barbera, Cabernet* and *Merlot*

grapes, which produce reds; or those of the *Trebbiano, Poverella, Malvasia* and *Riesling* grapes, which produce whites. Other good wines have their own trade names. Brazil also produces sparkling wines, made in the bottle or in any of several types of closed containers. These *espumante* (effervescent) wines are from the juice of the *Moscatel* and *Malvasia* grapes.

The Rio Grande do Sul represents the biggest viticultural area, for its climate is the most favourable to vine cultivation. Other wineproducing areas are São Paulo, Santa Caterina, Rio de Janeiro and Minas Gerias, with vineyard altitudes varying from 2,100 to 5,400 feet; surely a record.

Caxias do Sul and Bento-Concalves are the main areas of production in Rio Grande do Sul. Having abandoned the *Lambrusca* grape, which produced a very mediocre growth, the winegrowers here turned mainly to the *Concord, Isabella, Tercy* and *Herbemont* grapes, and to hybrids of the *Seibel* grape. The best alternative grapes used to make red wines are the *Sangiovesi, Barbera* and *Cabernet*; while for white wines, there are the *Merlot, Riesling, Malvasia* and *Trebbiano* grapes. The wines produced in this State, especially the reds, are usually of a very high quality.

In the State of São Paulo, the vine is concentrated around the regions of Jundiai and São Roque, but the best wine comes from Pardo, São José de Rio, Serra Negra, Salto de Itu, Ararquara, Campinas and Guararema. These vines are more or less the same varieties as those in the Rio Grande do Sul.

There are other viticultural centres in Brazil, notably Videira in Santa Catarina and Recife in Pernambuco.

URUGUAY

Viniculture was first introduced into Uruguay towards the end of the last century from the Montevideo region. Smallest of all South American countries (apart from French and Dutch Guiana), it produces 18,700,000 gallons of wine per annum, which puts it fourth among the viticultural countries on this continent. But wine stocks are insignificant and almost exclusively for domestic consumption. Production just about meets the demand, which is nevertheless eight times greater than in the United States, while production is about one-tenth! This underlines the importance of viticulture which, despite competition from *maté*, the national drink, almost doubled in the years 1958 to 1963. Wine is drunk more and more frequently with meals, especially with lamb roasted on the spit, a choice dish in Uruguay.

Because of the delicate balance here between supply and demand for wine, very little of the local production, except what might seep, as it were, into Brazil, can ever be found outside Uruguay itself.

A country with a temperate climate and heavy rainfall, Uruguay has several winegrowing regions, mainly in the south. The Canelones region is the most important; there the vines cover more than 24,500 acres, divided into small-holdings. Montevideo follows, with 13,400 acres shared between 1,874 winegrowers; then San José, Colonia, Paysandu, Florida, and Maldonado in order of production. Although there are quite a few vintners—some 7,300 for the whole country—there are also many large co-operatives, or *bodégueros*, which have their own underground cellars with all the most modern equipment for pressing and vinification. The most common vine in Uruguay is one which is rarely met anywhere else in the world; here it is called *Harriague*. In the Hautes-Pyrénées of France, where it comes from, it is better known as *Tannat*. It gives a good quality red wine. The best wines however, are made from grapes such as *Alicante*, *Carignan*, *Grenache* and *Cinsault*. Other grapes used are *Vidiella*, whose origin is unknown; *Cabernet*, here used to make an ordinary wine; *Barbera* and *Niebbiolo*. Often the quality of the wine is improved through judicious blending. Most white wines are made from *Semillon* and *Pinot Blanc* grapes as well as the American *Isabella*, while some hybrids also produce a very poor quality wine.

Uruguay thus produces the usual variety of wines: *tinto*, *rosado* and *blanco*, of both ordinary and better quality. But there is no methodical classification of wines which would guarantee its quality for the consumer. It seems clear that the wines of the *gran reserva* are better than others, so that an *appellation d'origine* shown on the label might help to distinguish between the local wines and the blended wines. The latter may be blended from a mixture of grapes or with foreign wines. There are also a great many wines which state the name of the grape from which they are made. Finally, Uruguay also produces special wines such a *sherry-quinquina*, dessert wines and sparkling wines.

PERU, BOLIVIA AND COLOMBIA

PERU. Francisco Carabantes, the Spanish conqueror of Peru, introduced the vine here about the middle of the sixteenth century. Peru today has a vineyard area of 24,710 acres producing 1,759,840 gallons of wine, making it the fifth wineproducing country on the Latin-American continent. The main wine areas are Lima, Ica, Chincha, Moquegua, Tacana and Lacumba.

The climate here is not at all favourable to the production of great wines and some regions are completely unable to support vine cultivation. The Andes are for the most part too cold and rugged and other regions are too hot and arid for good wine culture.

The white Peruvian wines are, nevertheless, pleasant, light, and have an agreeable bouquet. The red wines, however, are more ordinary, heavy with tannin and of a very poor quality. All the wine in Peru is produced for domestic consumption. Besides wine and *chicha*, a national drink made from sweet maize, some sweet wine such as Madeira or sherry is also drunk. The wines here are usually known by their place of origin: LOCUMBA, MOQUEGUA, CHINCHA, ICA, and so on.

BOLIVIA. The vine was probably brought to Bolivia from varieties originating in the Canaries. Today, the Bolivian vineyard covers some 5,000 acres and produces about 132,000 gallons a year, concentrated in the province of La Paz. There are also an additional 4,000 acres on which table grapes are cultivated. The wines produced are reds or whites, with an alcohol content from 13° to 15°; they are usually heavy. The country also produces some wines similar to sherry.

COLOMBIA. Colombia is the smallest wineproducer in South America, with a mere two thousand or so gallons. The vinicultural conditions here are exceptional owing to the torrid climate of the country, which allows the grape to mature several times a year, thus upsetting the usual wine-harvest cycle. Colombia produces mainly white sherry, port-type wines and light table wines which are decidedly sweet.

THE WINES OF AUSTRALIA AND NEW ZEALAND

JOHN STANFORD

AUSTRALIA

Australia is one of the youngest and most rapidly developed producers of high quality wines around the world. Wines closely relate in flavour patterns to classic European wines, and use the same grape varieties and general winemaking methods. Despite only 200 years of wine-producing history, Australian table wines such as Cabernet Sauvignons, Pinot Noirs and Chardonnays, and the rich liqueur Muscats, frequently win high awards in European exhibitions.

The large island continent of Australia has many regions ideal for winegrowing, with most of the wine being made in the cooler southeastern corner of the continent between 45 and 28 degrees south. All the older established vineyards are on the mainland. They are contained in a coastal arc 125-250 miles deep stretching around 1200 miles from Adelaide in the south to the border of Queensland in the warmer north, incorporating the principal wine-producing states of South Australia, Victoria and New South Wales. A smaller but significant proportion of prime vinyards is established on the southwestern tip of the continent, between Perth and Albany in Western Australia.

All the southern coastal regions are influenced by cool air and ocean currents from the Southern and Antarctic Oceans. They have maritime climates relating to Mediterranean regions of France, Spain and Italy, or to California and Chile. The southernmost region is the island state of Tasmania; its climate is colder and relates to the Danube or the warmer southern Rhine regions. The low-lying inland vine areas are different. They are hotter, with low rainfall, all of winter incidence. Most vineyards there are grown under irrigation and are highly productive.

Most Australian vine regions have low summer humidity and ample sunshine, and vines have few problems with summer fungus diseases or adequate ripening. Their wines are characterized by aromatic ripe grape flavours; must enrichment with added sugar is neither necessary nor permitted by law.

There being no grape species native to Australia, all present-day production is with *Vitis vinifera* grape vines, first selected and introduced from Europe at the end of the 18th century. Hybrid species exist only as cultured or experimental rootstocks. Many vineyards have been developed with or grafted to superior grape varieties since 1970, with cuttings being drawn from vine research stations in Europe and California.

Approximately half the total wine production comes from superior red varieties such as *Cabernet Sauvignon and Shiraz* or *Malbec*, and white varieties such as (Rhine) *Riesling, Chardonnay, Traminer, Muscat, Semillon, Trebbiano* and *Sauvignon Blanc*. More recent plantings of such classic grapes as *Merlot* and *Pinot Noir* are being expanded nationally.

With an annual wine production of around 87 million gallons, Australia's total vineyard area in 1980 for grapes of all types was 168,000 acres, though there are many areas suitable for winegrowing still being developed or yet to be planted. Total production was 860,000 tons of grapes of which 500,000 were used for winemaking (including distillation for grape spirit and brandy). The majority of grapes used for table wine came from dry-farmed vineyards at yields between 2 and 4 tons per acre. The rest, under irrigation, averaged 8 tons per acre. Of the four major wine-producing States, South Australia produced approximately 308,000 tons, New South Wales 114,000, Victoria 72,000 and Western Australia 7,000 tons of grapes for wine in 1980.

Australia's winemaking industry is technically very advanced by world standards. One major import is French and American oak for maturation (an important feature of the Australian winemaking technique). There are no indigenous cask oaks of this type grown in Australia.

The majority of winemakers are tertiary graduates of œnology schools, trained locally or overseas, or both. Two main graduate colleges of viticultural and œnological training and research are at Roseworthy in South Australia and Wagga Wagga in New South Wales.

The national wine organization is the Australian Wine and Brandy Corporation, with headquarters in Adelaide. It administers internal and overseas matters of industry co-ordination, wine research, regulation, national promotion, market research and statistics in support of all Australian winemakers and grape-growers, and it maintains and administers the internationally accredited Australian Wine Research Institute in Adelaide for pure research in œnology. It also coordinates advanced research into vine breeding, phytology, clonal selection, virology and grafting with the Horticultural Research Division of Australia's major scientific research body, the Commonwealth Scientific and Industrial Research Organization (CSIRO). Their clonal selection programs have resulted in improved local strains of classic European varieties.

The majority of wine production is white and red table wine. Australia is also traditionally a world style leader in making rich aromatic sweet red and white fortified and oak-aged dessert wines similar to Ports, Madeiras and Sherries. Until 1960 the latter were the principal wine types produced, representing 80 per cent of all Australian wine consumption.

Between 1960 and 1980, local production and consumption of wine more than trebled. In the process, the styles of wine being consumed completely reversed their pattern. White and red tables wines are now established as 80 per cent of Australian wine production, with present total annual consumption level around 4 gallons per head of total population. The wine comes from more than 300 privately owned wineries and 6 co-operative ones. There are no state-owned wineries or distilleries.

Comparatively few districts have yet adopted formal appellation classifications, although they make superior and distinctive wines.

The principal vineyard regions with a wine identity are described below (from west to east).

WESTERN AUSTRALIA

SWAN VALLEY. The State's oldest vineyard region, close to the city of Perth along the banks of the Swan River. It was first planted during the early 19th century. Its soils are sandy clay over a red clay base. The climate is warm and dry and occasionally very hot. Rain rarely falls after early spring in the growing season. Present production is mostly soft, full-bodied white wine, from *Semillon, Verdelho* and *Riesling*, along with rosé and soft rich red wines from *Shiraz, Malbec, Cabernet* or *Grenache* varieties. Some rich sweet dessert wines are still produced. Of more than 70 small specialist vignerons in Western Australia, most are in the Swan Valley.

MOONDAH BROOK. A small isolated sub-region 50 miles north of Perth on similar sandy clay soil. It is marginally cooler than the Swan Valley and its dry red and white wines are a little more delicate with the same broad pattern of flavours.

MARGARET RIVER. 150-200 miles south of Perth on the Leeuwin Peninsula. The soils are heavier clay mixtures over limestone subsoils. The rainfall—still only in winter—is higher, and the average temperature is significantly lower than in the Swan Valley. The area produces distinctive, full-flavoured red wines from *Cabernet Sauvignon* and aromatic dry white wines from *Riesling, Semillon, Verdelho* and *Chardonnay.*

FRANKLAND RIVER and MOUNT BARKER. Like Margaret River, these districts are new in viticultural terms. They have been developed only since 1969-1970. They are located 60-120 miles further southwest, are distinctly colder and produce similar but more crisp and slow-maturing dry white wines from *Riesling* and *Chardonnay.* Their dry reds from *Cabernet Sauvignon, Pinot Noir* and *Shiraz* are distinctive aromatic styles that relate to those of central Victoria on the eastern seaboard.

SOUTH AUSTRALIA

BAROSSA VALLEY. 40-60 miles north of the State capital of Adelaide, this is one of Australia's best known older-style vine regions and the headquarters of many of the bigger corporate groups or family wine companies such as Penfolds-Kaiser Stuhl, Orlando, Seppelts, Yalumba, Seagrams-Saltram, Tollana, Leo Buring, Wolf Blass and Masterson.

Its soils are either alkaline duplex types over limestone and clay subsoils or clay loams. Production is varied—from fine light-bodied and aromatic dry whites on the highlands, and fullbodied rich dry reds on lower foothills and river flats, to rich dessert wines in warmer low-lying areas. Winemaking is centred on the four main towns of Tanunda, Nuriootpa, Angaston and Lyndoch.

The characteristically soft and aromatic dry reds come mainly from *Shiraz, Cabernet Sauvignon* and *Grenache* varieties. Dry or semi-sweet white table wines and sparkling wines derive from *Riesling, Crouchen, Chardonnay, Chenin Blanc* and *Muscat* grapes. Sweet fortified types are from *Shiraz* and *Grenache* for red or *Muscadelle, Pedro Ximenes* and *Muscat* for white wines.

EDEN VALLEY and SPRINGTON. A smaller cool highland region adjacent to the main Barossa Valley to the east. The vines have lower production rates, but make finer and more delicate dry white wines, mainly from *Riesling* and, more recently, *Chardonnay.* The region produces long-maturing fresh and deep-flavoured dry reds from *Shiraz* and *Cabernet Sauvignon.*

CLARE and WATERVALE. A cool, highland plateau 35-40 miles northwest of the Barossa Valley around the towns of Clare, Watervale and Auburn. The soils are rich deep clay loams, the rainfall is marginally higher and the climate cooler than in the Barossa Valley. The area is best known for its distinctive *Rieslings* and fullbodied, aromatic and crisp *Cabernet* and *Shiraz* dry

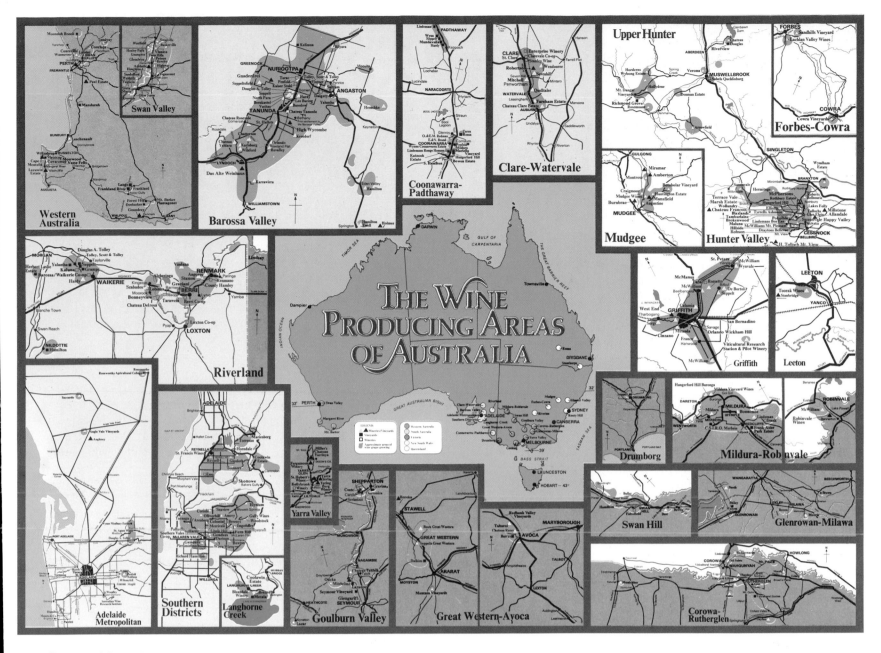

THE WINE PRODUCING AREAS OF AUSTRALIA

Western Australia

Swan Valley

Barossa Valley

Coonawarra-Padthaway

Clare-Watervale

Upper Hunter

Forbes-Cowra

Mudgee

Hunter Valley

Riverland

Griffith

Leeton

Drumborg

Mildura-Robinvale

Swan Hill

Glenrowan-Milawa

Adelaide Metropolitan

Southern Districts

Langhorne Creek

Yarra Valley

Goulburn Valley

Great Western-Ayoca

Corowa-Rutherglen

Centres of Australian wine production. With only a few exceptions, they are concentrated in the (colder) southeast of the island continent.

In this Clare Valley vineyard (South Australia) the vines are planted as if following the contour-lines of the terrain — a cultivation method that helps prevent erosion. Here, white wines are produced from RIESLING grapes.

reds—like the Barossa, in the style of superior Rhône Valley red wines of France.

SOUTHERN VALES. A temperate maritime strip running south from the city of Adelaide between the sea and the low coastal range of the Adelaide Hills, this is one of this State's first vine regions, originally planted around 1840. Most of the vineyards are between the towns of Reynella and McLaren Vale 15-30 miles from Adelaide and eastward through the cooler foothills between Clarendon and Langhorne Creek.

The soils are light sandy loams, clay loams, or red ironstone soils over limestone subsoils. The wines range from aromatic and elegant dry reds mainly from *Shiraz, Cabernet Sauvignon* and *Grenache* to distinctive *Rieslings* and similar dry white types. Some excellent sweet reds related to rich vintage ports and brandies relating to the French Armagnac style are made in smaller volumes.

COONAWARRA. A unique, high-quality vineyard region 225 miles southeast of Adelaide in the coldest, southern corner of South Australia. The terrain is relatively flat and low-lying. The prime vineyards are grown selectively on strips of red ironstone and clay loams, or sandy-clay loams with a moist limestone base, around the towns of Coonawarra, Keppoch and Padthaway. Outside of these delimited zones the soils are very deep black volcanic loams, generally too rich for production of the finer wines.

This is one of Australia's fastest-growing cool high-quality table-wine regions. Crisp deep-flavoured dry red wines are made from *Cabernet Sauvignon, Shiraz* and *Pinot Noir*. Dry whites from *Riesling, Chardonnay, Sauvignon Blanc* and *Chenin Blanc* varieties develop delicate and spiced flavours.

MURRAY VALLEY. A large and extensive string of irrigation settlements is spaced along the banks of the Murray River from northeastern Victoria to the south of South Australia. This large river system runs inland from the alpine regions of the east coast of Australia. It turns down to its mouth on the southern continental coast through the hot and dry eastern half of South Australia 1600 miles away. It exceeds the combined lengths of the Loire and the Rhine.

The main concentrations of vineyards, wineries and distilleries are along its central inland reaches. The large Riverland region (Berri, Renmark, Loxton and Waikerie) is on the South Australian side. Eastwards across the State border is the equally large Sunraysia area (Mildura, Merbein, Karadoc and Buronga), then Robinvale and Swan Hill. Isolated smaller irrigation districts are located both up and down river from these main centres.

Grape types common to all of them are either dual-purpose, drying or wine-making varieties such as *Sultana, Waltham Cross, Muscat* and *Gordo*, or single-purpose wine grapes, such as *Semillon Riesling, Traminer, Sauvignon Blanc, Pedro Ximenes, Cabernet, Grenache* or *Shiraz*.

Soils are deep sands and open sandy loams. Natural rainfall is sparse. Vines, along with many other Mediterranean fruits, are grown under irrigation. They are highly productive due to the consistent hot and sunny climate. All these districts combined produce the majority of Australia's bulk-marketed lower-priced wines. In addition to large quantities of light-bodied, fast-maturing dry red, dry white and rosé table wine, they also make most of Australia's brandy and lower-priced sweet fortified wines. The vineyards are owned mainly by members of grapegrower cooperatives or the largest Barossa Valley winemakers.

ADELAIDE DISTRICT. A decreasing historic cool foothills area being overrun by suburbs and the city of Adelaide. Remaining small vineyards are owned by Penfolds (Grange vineyard) Tolleys, Angoves (St Agnes) and the Wynn (Seaview) group. Fifteen miles north is the warmer Adelaide Plains district, which makes rich, full-bodied Barossa-type wines.

VICTORIA

GREAT WESTERN. A cool, elevated region in the southern Foothills of the Grampian Mountains in central Western Victoria, first planted by a Swiss migrant, Enid Blampied, and her brother, in the mid-19th century. The vines grow on undulating foothills between the former gold-mining of Stawell and Ararat.

This is the centre for the Seppelt Great Western sparkling wine production, with extensive underground cave cellars. The other major winemaker there is Bests, owned by the Thomson family. The region makes distinctive, fine, long-maturing dry reds from *Cabernet Sauvignon, Shiraz, Pinot Meunier* and *Pinot Noir* varieties and delicate dry whites from *Riesling, Traminer, Ondenc* and *Chardonnay* in addition to a selection of sparkling wines.

AVOCA and MOONAMBEL. A cool region 60 miles north of Great Western on the northeastern slopes of the adjacent Pyrennees Range. Recently replanted as a high-quality district it also makes sparkling and dry white wines from *Semillon* and *Chardonnay*, but mostly distinctive rich aromatic dry reds in the Bordeaux style, mainly from *Cabernet Sauvignon* and *Shiraz* grapes.

Apart from a number of small red-wine specialists such as Mount Avoca, Robb and Anderson, production is dominated by French-owned groups. Château Remy—owned by Remy Martin of Cognac—and Taltarni, managed by the Portet family of Bordeaux and California, are the largest producers.

The vine was brought to Australia in 1788 by Captain Arthur Phillip as he came to take formal possession of the new land. His first vineyard was planted in Sydney, in what are now the Botanic Gardens. Later, Sydney was also to be the base of James Busby, the man who has been called the "father of viticulture in Australia". New South Wales vineyards, such as the one photographed here, have a heritage to be proud of.

NORTHEAST VICTORIA. This region incorporates the three related subdistricts of Rutherglen and Corowa, Glenrowan, and Milawa—150-200 miles to the northeast of Melbourne.

BUTHERGLEN and COROWA. An old-established district adjacent to the upper reaches or the Murray River below Albury, the area developed as one of Australia's major sweet dessert wine districts at the same time as the gold rush there, between 1860 and 1890, when the rine was wiped out by phylloxera. The soils are deep clay loams. The climate is cool in spring, but warm to hot in summer.

The region produces two of the finest rich and distinctive sweet white fortified wines in the world. They are made from the *Muscadelle* and the *Red Frontignan Muscat* varieties which ripen to very high sugar levels there. They relate to superior Malmsey Madeiras and the richest *Muscat Frontignan* styles of Europe. Full-bodied sweet red wines of port style are made from *Shiraz* grapes.

There are also distinctive full-bodied dry red and dry white wines. The main vine varieties of many used are *Cabernet Sauvignon, Malbec, Shiraz* and *Durif* for red wines, and *Semillon, Marsanne, Riesling, Traminer* and *Chardonnay* for white wines.

GLENROWAN. A small district 30 miles south of Rutherglen making very similar rich liqueur muscats, and fine full-bodied dry reds of great vigour from *Cabernet* and *Shiraz* grapes. The district was the home territoriy of a notorious bushranger, Ned Kelly.

The Hunter Valley in New South Wales is an area that has won wide acclaim for its red and white table wines. Most of them are produced from highly mechanized vineyards such as that illustrated here: Australia has become a world leader in the application of science and technology to winegrowing.

MILAWA. The coldest and most elevated of the three districts, in the King River Valley on the lower foothills of the Australian Alps east of Glenrowan. The wines are light, crisp and delicate whites from *Riesling, Semillon, Tokay, Chenin Blanc* and *Chardonnay*, and light-bodied dry reds from *Shiraz, Cabernet Sauvignon* and *Mondeuse* varieties.

YARRA VALLEY and LILYDALE. A group of small-scale vineyards in the cool hills close to Melbourne make distinctive, deep-coloured and crisp dry reds from *Cabernet Sauvignon, Pinot Noir* and *Shiraz*, and delicate dry whites from *Riesling* and *Chardonnay*. Replanting since 1970 is around the former sites of famous small vineyards originally planted by the Swiss de Castella and de Pury families in the mid-19th century. Their wines won international awards in London and Paris 80-100 years ago.

GOULBURN VALLEY. The twin centres of Shepparton and Seymour/Mitchelton/Tahbilk in central Victoria represent two different wine styles. Shepparton is highly productive, irrigated, and has a warm climate. Its wines relate to those of the cooler Upper Murray Valley districts.

The Seymour/Mitchelton/Tahbilk and nearby Kyneton districts make distinctive crisp dry white wines from *Riesling, Semillon, Marsanne* and *Chardonnay* grapes, and deep-coloured aromatic dry reds, mainly from *Cabernet Sauvignon* and *Shiraz*. These wines show the influence of the much cooler climate there, and relate to wines of Great Western, Avoca or the Margaret River region of Western Australia.

NEW SOUTH WALES

RIVERINA. The largest production area for wine in New South Wales, making over 80 per cent of that state's total volume. It is 400 miles southwest of Sydney. Like the Murray Valley, the average rainfall is low, at around 12 inches per year, but it is a highly productive irrigated fruit-growing region. It is also Australia's main rice-growing area. Water is pumped through 60 miles of canals from the Murrumbidgee River to the south. Vineyards are centred on the two main wine towns of Griffith and Yenda, and nearby Leeton.

There are 15 wineries, some very large. They produce mainly light-bodied soft dry reds and dry whites, as well as sweet fortified wines and brandy. McWilliams are the largest winemakers there. Winemaking technology is highly sophisticated and advanced. The region supports several viticultural research and training establishments.

Riverina soils are heavier than the Murray Valley and nearly all its vines are planted for winemaking only. Most of them are superior grape strains such as *Cabernet Sauvignon, Malbec, Shiraz* and *Grenache* for red wine, and *Riesling, Semillon, Traminer* along with

varieties like *Muskat* and *Pedro Ximenes* fot white.

THE HAWKESBURY VALLEY. Close to the outskirts of the Greater Sydney urban area, only a few vineyards, near Camden, south of the city, still remain. Along with vineyards in the adjacent Parramatta Valley, these were the first vine areas planted in Australia between 1790 and 1820 by Marsden, Macarthur and Busby.

FORBES and COWRA. Small districts 200-250 miles west of Sydney on the Upper Lachlan River. Cowra grapes have produced high quality *Chardonnay, Riesling* and *Traminer* white wines in recent years, as well as full-bodied *Cabernet Sauvignon* dry reds.

THE HUNTER VALLEY. One of Australia's oldest and best known table-wine regions. The vineyards range from 200 to 300 miles north of Sydney. The climate is warm, but is one of the few areas with equal summer and winter rainfall. Its wines are distinctive aromatic styles relating to the French Mâcon and Rhône wines.

It has two different subregions. The Lower Hunter around Pokolbin and Cessnock is closer to the city of Sydney. This is Australia's largest wine market and population centre. Soils are clay-based basaltic loams over an ancient sandstone sea bed. Production rate is low but there are some distinctive red wines from *Shiraz* and *Cabernet*, and more recently *Pinot Noir*. The area is best known for rich, full-flavoured *Semillon* and *Chardonnay* dry whites.

The Upper Hunter has a similar but cooler climate, and more productive, deeper clay loam and silted clay soils. It makes high-quality lighter-bodied aromatic dry whites from *Chardonnay, Traminer Semillon* and *Riesling*, and deep-coloured, full-flavoured dry reds from *Cabernet Sauvignon* and *Shiraz*. The region has extensive coal deposits and its wine production is threatened by industrial and coal-mining expansion, just as the German Saar and Ruhr vineyards once were.

MUDGEE. A unique, high cool region close to the Upper Hunter and only 75 miles to the west, but completely different in climate. It is on the western highlands of the Australian Alps, and makes distinctively-flavoured full-bodied and aromatic dry reds of high quality from *Shiraz* and *Cabernet Sauvignon*, and dry whites from *Chardonnay, Semillon* and *Riesling*. Rainfall is mainly in winter and spring. Wine styles relate to the Clare region of South Australia. Mudgee has established a regional classification and appellation for its wines.

QUEENSLAND

There are two small vineyard districts in this State, with widely contrasting climates.

STANTHORPE. On a high plateau, 2500-3000 feet above sea level, this unique district has a cool climate influenced by summer rainfall. It makes deep-coloured wines from *Shiraz, Cabernet Sauvignon* and *Pinot Noir*. White wines are from *Chardonnay, Semillon* or dual-purpose grapes in small volume. The soils are mineral-rich granite sands over silted acid clay subsoils. The climate is much cooler than the Hunter Valley, 300 miles to the south, because of the altitude.

ROMA. This is Australia's northernmost commercial wine region, over 250 miles inland and northwest of Stanthorpe. The climate is warm to hot, often humid, and approaches the limit of the temperate zone suited to *Vitis vinifera* grapes. It makes small volumes of rich sweet fortified and table wines which use the rare hybrid variety *Solverino, Semillon* and *Muscat*. Red wines are made from *Shiraz* and *Grenache*. Soils are leached clay mixtures.

TASMANIA

Australia's coldest vine region is on this large island state just south of Victoria. The climate is cool with a long dry autumn for slow ripening and relates to the French Loire Valley. Early 19th century vineyards there died out before the 20th century. Replanting by the Alcorso Moorilla Estate at Hobart and Heemskirk near Launceston recommenced between 1965 and 1970.

PIPERS BROOK. On the northeast coast near Launceston. Soils are deep red and grey loams. Its wines are fresh deep-coloured aromatic *Cabernet Sauvignon, Merlot* and *Shiraz* dry reds of Bordeaux style and aromatic *Pinot Noir* wines. Fine delicate dry whites are mainly from *Riesling*, and *Semillon. Müller-Thurgau* and *Sauvignon Blanc* styles are being developed.

BREAM CREEK. East of Hobart on the southeast coast, these new vineyards make delicate and spiced, light-bodied *Rieslings* and are developing *Chardonnay, Müller-Thurgau* and *Sauvignon Blanc* styles. Red wines are crisp, fresh deep-coloured *Cabernet Sauvignon, Pinot Noir* and *Merlot* types.

NEW ZEALAND

The twin islands of New Zealand in the southern Pacific lie between 47 and 34 degrees south, 1250 miles southeast of Australia. Both islands are long and narrow—around 500 by 125 miles—and are influenced by cold, moist south and west winds from the Southern and Antarctic Oceans. Their climates are colder and wetter than those of Australia or California. Geologically the North Island's soils are of very recent volcanic origin, whereas Australia's are the oldest in the world under viticulture.

Most vineyards and wineries are in the central and east coast areas of the North Island, where annual

rainfall varies from 62 inches around Auckland to 33-40 inches further south around Hawkes Bay and Gisborne. Half of this falls in the autumn ripening period. As a result, grape production rates are high, and wines are light in body and low in alcohol. Must enrichment with added cane sugar is permitted by law, and sometimes necessary.

The South Island has a colder and drier climate. There are permanent snowfields and glaciers along its high central and southern mountain ridge. Sixteen per cent of New Zealand's vines grow in the warmer northeastern corner in Marlborough province and nearby Nelson. They produce crisp, delicate styles relating to Austrian, German or Swiss wines.

New Zealand's historical wine development has followed that of Australia. Both were first settled as British colonies early in the 19th century, and no wine grapes were native to either country. The first vines were planted by Samuel Marsden in 1819 with cuttings from Australia; the first wines were made 15 years later by James Busby, another Australian wine pioneer. French migrants, followed by Spanish, Italian and later Dalmatian and Lebanese, joined English growers during the 19th and early 20th centuries, mostly around Auckland. By 1908 there were 670 acres planted, but population was also small. Around 1895 phylloxera had appeared, just as it had 10 years before in Australia.

The growers were further plagued by a Prohibition lobby seeking to outlaw alcoholic drinks. Vine plantings fell into a low point of only 180 acres in 1923. It was 1935 before legal restraints on wine sales were relaxed and 1950 before vine planting recommenced. As in Australia, most wines then made were fortified sherries, and sweet whites and sweet reds for English tastes and markets. Most of the grapes were North American hybrid strains. These are heavy producers and more resistant to both phylloxera and fungus diseases, but make indifferent wine.

Gradual replanting with superior grafted European vine types began between 1960 and 1970. After the formation, in 1975, of the official wine organization, the Wine Institute of New Zealand, more of these vines were introduced and promoted. Standards of wine quality have since risen dramatically as a result.

By 1970 vineyards had multiplied to 3700 acres and in 1975 to 5800 acres. In 1980 there were some 12,000 acres—6000 of mature bearing vines and a further 6000 of young vines. Ninety per cent of all vines grown now are the higher quality *Vitis vinifera* strains; only 10 per cent are hybrids such as the American *Baco* and *Seibel* which formerly dominated production.

White grapes represent more than 80 per cent of all plantings. *Müller-Thurgau*—locally named *Riesling-Sylvaner*—is the commonest, with almost 40 per cent of the total. Other white grapes are *Chenin Blanc, Chardonnay, Riesling, Gewürztraminer* and *Palomino*. Less than 5 per cent are hybrids. Red varieties including *Cabernet-Sauvignon, Pinotage, Gamay-Beaujolais* and *Pinot Noir*

comprise 12 per cent of all vineyards; red hybrids account for another 6 per cent.

Gisborne and Hawkes Bay, each with 32-33 per cent of the country's vineyards, Marlborough and Nelson on South Island with 16 per cent and Auckland and Henderson with 13 per cent are the four major wine-producing regions.

AUCKLAND and HENDERSON. The oldest planted and wettest region with 62 inches annual rainfall and production rates up to 14-16 tons per acre of vigorous hybrid grapes, which represent the majority of production there. Along with similar smaller areas to the north (Kumeu and Northlands), to the south (The Kauwhata and Waikato) and the east (Thames), the broad area incorporates 2225-2500 acres.

Hybrid types make fortified sweet wines or indifferent bulk table wines. European grapes make delicate low-alcohol dry white and light dry red, and often have problems in ripening completely. Many of these wines relate to the table wines of wet maritime regions of northern Portugal.

GISBORNE and POVERTY BAY. A cooler, drier coastal region 250 miles southeast on the central east coast. Rainfall is around 40 inches, half in summer and autumn. The area has rich deep loamy soils. With almost 4000 acres of vines, mostly of European stock, *Müller-Thurgau* is the largest planting, along with *Palomino, Chasselas* and *Chardonnay*. They make delicate dry whites. *Shiraz, Gamay, Pinotage* and *Cabernet* make light-bodied dry red types.

HAWKES BAY, NAPIER and HASTINGS. A further 125 miles south with 3750 acres of vines, this region's climate is drier, with 29.5-31.5 inches of rainfall, and warmer. It makes most of New Zealand's best dry reds from *Cabernet, Shiraz, Pinotage, Gamay, Malbec* and *Pinot Noir*. It also produces aromatic dry whites and sparkling wines from *Müller-Thurgau, Riesling, Traminer, Chardonnay, Palomino* and hybrid varieties.

MARLBOROUGH and NELSON. One of New Zealand's most important newer vineyard regions with 1850 acres of superior vine varieties. They are on the warmest northeastern corner of the South Island, inland from Blenheim. The area has a cold European-type climate with 24.5-25.5 inches of rain, 25 per cent in autumn and late summer.

The large and sophisticated Seagram-Montana winery there processes most of the grapes. It makes delicate dry whites, of Austrian or southern-German style from *Müller-Thurgau, Riesling, Gewürztraminer* and *Sauvignon Blanc*. Light-bodied reds are from *Cabernet Sauvignon, Pinotage* and *Pinot Noir*.

OTHER REGIONS. Small west coast vineyards north of Wellington relate to Gisborne and Hawkes Bay styles.

South of Marlborough, around Christchurch and Otago, in even colder conditions, some experimental vineyards are being tested for German Rhine styles. Elsewhere on South Island conditions are generally too cold for vines.

THE WINES OF CHAMPAGNE

JEAN ARNABOLDI

It may be said, without fear of contradiction, that Champagne is one of the most celebrated wines in the world. But if man in his wisdom has raised it to such eminence, he must also admit that its origins have been lost in the mists of time. It is perhaps not an exaggeration to speak of predestination. For when the inland sea which in pre-history covered the Champagne region disappeared, it left in its place a chalky subsoil which was gradually covered by a layer of fertile soil wherein plants might prosper. Recent discoveries made near Sézanne have shown that the vine must have existed there as far back as the tertiary period. Fossilized leaves which were excavated have been judged to be very close to the *vitis rotunda folia*, also known as the *plant américain*. What an extraordinary coincidence this proved to be was seen thousands of years later, when this very same grape was to save the Champagne vineyard from the devastations of phylloxera.

The first real facts about Champagne wine to emerge from history date from the Roman conquest, for when the legions reached the banks of the Marne, they found a flourishing viticulture already in existence. Bringing fresh knowledge and new methods, these legions were to contribute to the development of the vine here as they had previously done in the other provinces of Gaul. The Romans already knew arboriculture as it was then practised in Italy, but they were quick to appreciate the advantages of the methods used by the Gauls. On the other hand, they introduced a new concept, the idea of stock selection. They even imported from Narbonne·a quick-growing variety of vine. The reputation of Champagne wines travelled quickly to Rome, as Pliny himself bears witness: "Other wines from Gaul which have been recommended as fit for kings are those from the land of Rheims, known as Ay."

The decree passed by Domitian in A.D. 92 was to prove almost fatal to the future expansion of the vineyards of Gaul and in particular to those around Champagne. The Emperor decreed that all the vines were to be pulled out. Fortunately for posterity, his orders were not obeyed everywhere. It is clear, of course, that occupying troops must live off local produce, and that an army has

greater need of cereals and dairy produce than of liquids whose consumption does not always favour military discipline or heroic behaviour. Perhaps other, more worldly commercial reasons crept in too, for the wines of Gaul competed with those of the Mediterranean shores. Be that as it may, the fact remains that for two hundred years the vine had to be cultivated in secret, until that day when another, better-inspired emperor, Probus, raised the ban, and, furthermore, required his troops to help in the reconstruction of the vineyards, a task which the Gauls themselves undertook with much enthusiasm. From Rheims down south to Chalons, the work was quickly done, and memories of Domitian were forgotten.

The advent and spread of Christianity had a marked influence on viticulture, for the monks were obliged to procure locally the wine they used to celebrate Mass. Monasteries also served as inns where travellers sought food, shelter and a welcoming table. The quality of Champagne was noteworthy from this period.

The soil of Champagne has delivered up many proofs of the importance of its vineyard: earthenware jars, coins imprinted with symbols taken from the vine, and even glasses whose elongated shape foreshadows the flute-shaped Champagne glasses of today.

In the fifth and sixth centuries, Champagne became part of the history of France and perhaps even of Heaven, for Clovis was crowned King of France at Rheims by St. Remi, the apostle to the Franks. The chronicles of the time recount the miracles the good saint accomplished: how he caused wine to flow from a barrel of water, and how he gave Clovis, when the latter was warring with Alaric, "a flask filled with holy wine, and recommended him to continue the war for as long as the flask supplied wine for him and others of his train to whom he wished to offer it. The King as well as several of his officers drank the wine, but the jug remained full." From a more practical point of view, the testament of St. Remi is an irrefutable document which portrays faithfully the economic situation and morals of his time. For example, it relates how wine was often offered by the winegrowers as a gift to the king or to the

archbishop of Rheims. Other chronicles speak of the growing expansion of the Champagne vineyard, and enlighten us as to the quality of its wines and how they were used. In those days, Champagne was a still wine *de qualité, pur et fruité* (fine, pure and fruity), excellent for the sick. The decorations and sculptures on monuments, notably those of Rheims Cathedral and Ay Church, have been inspired directly by the wine and depict some part of the life of those who have given their lives to viniculture.

Flodoard, in his history of the church of Rheims, tells us that the wine harvest of 929 was completed by the month of August, which shows that in those days the grapes ripened much earlier. In the eleventh century, Pope Urbain II, who preached in favour of the Second Crusade, was born at Châtillon-sur-Marne, where a huge statue perpetuates his memory. A kind of redistribution of land took place then, when the lords leaving for the Holy Land entrusted their property to the Church. During their absence, which sometimes became permanent, the monks reorganized and nationalized viniculture, and it is in fact from this period onwards that their influence on the destiny of the Champagne wines became decisive.

Later invasions and battles only served to increase the fame of these wines. It is said that the Emperor of Germany, Wenceslas, when he met the King of France, Charles VI at Rheims in 1398, indulged in such libations that he was ready to sign "whatsoever was desired".

The consecration of the King of France at Rheims heightened the prestige of the wines of Champagne still further. On February 13th, 1575, for the first time, Champagne was the only wine to be served on the occasion of the coronation of Henry III. Its power of seduction seemed so great that emperors and monarchs, Charles V, François I, Henry VIII and a Pope, Jean de Medicis who later became Leon, all had to own a house in Ay. Henry IV was pleased to think of himself as "Sire of Ay" and valued very highly this *vin de Dieu*, light, fruity, and sacred to boot.

Favoured by kings, Champagne soon captured the Court. Poets sang its praises. Winegrowers multiplied their efforts to satisfy the demand and noticed that for some obscure reason the wine would from time to time become effervescent. But they were never able to fathom the mystery. Louis XIV was a great lover of the wine of Ay, but even more fervent admirers were the Marechal de Bois-Dauphin, the Marquis Charles de Saint-Evremond and the Count of Olonne, who would drink no other wine with their meals. In 1672, St. Evremond wrote to Count Olonne: "Don't spare yourself any cost to have the wine of Champagne, be you so far as two hundred leagues from Paris. No other province can produce such excellent wines for all seasons as Champagne. It offers us the wines of Ay, Avenet and Auville until the spring; and Tessy, Sillery and Verzenay for the rest of the year. Were you to ask me which of these wines I prefer, without having

recourse to tastes in fashion which introduce false delicacies, I would tell you that the good wine of Ay is the most natural of all wines. It is by far the healthiest, and is purged of any objectionable tang of the soil. The peach flavour, which characterizes it, gives one a most exquisite feeling."

This analysis and this delicacy of palate shows that already in those times Champagne had attained a position of eminence. It is said that St. Evremond, having fallen into disgrace with the king in 1661, had to flee to Holland, and later to England where he introduced the Court of Charles II to the delicacies of the table and to fine wine. He easily convinced the court, which soon gave Champagne the place of honour.

At this point in time, one should look more closely into the details of the production of Champagne wines and more particularly into a fundamental change that came about, and which can be said to have ensured their place in history, forever distinctive from other wines. These already famous wines had until this time been still—or almost-still—wines. The black grapes, placed in vats for only a short time or even not vatted at all, produced a grey wine, and were dominated by the red wines, even though it was not possible to conserve the latter for more than a short time and their transportation was somewhat hazardous. In the middle of the seventeenth century (1640 or 1660, the date is disputed) the Champagne winegrowers increased their efforts to "produce wines of a finer quality than anywhere else in the kingdom". They succeeded in making pale wines which, in some years, produced in the bottle a certain effervescence which was most agreeable and enhanced their bouquet. This effervescence seemed to occur more often in white wines made from *Pinot* grapes, when the must was fermented separately from the marc, and thus the idea evolved to let this fermentation take place in the bottle. The *vin de Dieu* became *vin Diable* or *saute-bouchon* without, however, losing any of its original qualities or appeal. On the contrary, it has stood the test of time and change, as history has shown.

Dom Perignon was its man of destiny. It is common knowledge that though the wine's merits are acknowledged, its originator is sometimes disputed. It seems a shame to demolish idols, the more so as every inventor always owes something to his predecessors.

Born in the same year as Louis XIV, Dom Perignon (1638-1715) was also to die in the same year. Brought up in a bourgeois family from St. Menehould, he took his vows in the Benedictine Order and entered the Royal Abbey of Saint-Vanne at Verdun, where he distinguished himself by his great knowledge and devout charity. In 1668 he became cellarer of the Benedictine Abbey at Hautvillers, in the diocese of Rheims. His duties were to supervise the supplies of food and other goods, to check the sources of revenue, the running expenses and generally to keep the accounts. The cellars were therefore also in his care.

420

Dom Perignon, a Benedictine monk from the Abbey of Hautvillers, had the brilliant idea of blending the produce of different vineyards in the Champagne region so as to obtain a stock whose quality would be superior to any of the elements from which it was composed. José Frappa has painted him here, old and blind, tasting grapes with the sensitivity and knowledge that enabled him to distinguish each of the varieties brought in the baskets. There never was a man, said one of his contemporaries, more gifted than he in the secrets of winemaking. Although Dom Perignon died over two centuries ago his name is still honoured and will ever be associated with Champagne.

The village of Hautvillers lies on slopes above the Marne valley, and its situation is therefore particularly favourable for the cultivation of the vine. The domain belonging to the Abbey was quite considerable and several other vineyards were adjacent to it. For these reasons, Dom Perignon concentrated his intelligence on winemaking, in which capacity he was well served by his extraordinary gifts as a wine-taster. His first great idea was to bring together the vines in such a way that by intermarrying they would benefit from each other's better qualities, harmoniously, without any one dominating the others. He had such a delicate palate that by tasting a grape he was able to tell which variety it came from. He decided which grapes to use early in the year, and this procedure came to be acknowledged as essen-

tial to the production of sparkling wines. Dom Perignon was also the first in Champagne to seal bottles with cork, which soon replaced the old wooden pegs.

He organized wine production and studied the phenomenon of the rise of foam in the bottle by the rule-of-thumb means at his disposal. No one really knows, however, whether he obtained fermentation in the bottle as a result of the natural sugar content in the wine, that is to say not yet transformed into alcohol, or if he was the first to add cane sugar.

His body lies at rest in the church at Hautvillers and this epitaph is engraved on his tombstone. "Here lies Dom Perignon, for 47 years cellarer of this Monastery who, after administering the property of our community with a care and dignity that merits praise, blessed with

many virtues, the greatest of which was his paternal love for the poor, died in the 77th year of his life, in 1715." His name is remembered to this day.

Henceforth all the humble force of the Benedictine brothers was bent towards the making of Champagne. From this time on, the foam process was "controlled", the wine gained in popularity, and the beginning of the eighteenth century witnessed a great increase in demand. The still wines were neglected for the benefit of the sparkling wines. At the Court, the Marquis of Sillery, well known for his good taste, was an ardent protagonist of the new sparkling wine. The Regent was also convinced of the excellence of Champagne, as were later Louis XV and Louis XVI, though somewhat less flamboyantly. Madame de Pompadour paid it the highest of feminine compliments by declaring "it is the only wine that leaves a woman beautiful after drinking", and the Comtesse de Parabère was accused of drinking like a *lansquenet* (a German mercenary soldier)! In 1739 the city of Paris gave a brilliant ball at which 1,800 bottles of Champagne wine were drunk.

At about this time wine-merchants set up the first wine-shops in Champagne, some of which still exist today. Their wine cellars were built on the chalky soil which favours the preservation of wine, but there remained two problems which had to be solved: the study of the fermentation process and the breakage of bottles. The latter was solved before the former by an apothecary from Châlons known as François and whose name merits eternal fame. The breakage of bottles affected some 40 per cent of the production, but François learned through his research work to control excessive fermentation by fixing the correct sugar dosage. At the same time, the glass-works made great progress in the quality of their glass. Between the two, the distressing problem of breakage was very considerably decreased. In 1858, Maumené, a professor at Rheims, seems to have been the first to study the action of the yeasts which influence fermentation, but it was not until Pasteur's work in this field became known that Champagne was produced scientifically.

Since then, the history of Champagne has been one of victory and success, if still sometimes acquired the hard way, through a disease of the wine or folly of man. The new techniques and the progress achieved, allied to the tenacity, the skill and the knowledge of the winegrowers and wine-merchants of the Champagne area, found their just recompense in a constant expansion of demand throughout the world.

THE CHAMPAGNE VINEYARDS

The Champagne country, whose origins are founded on the same chalky subsoil as the Ile de France, a region which carries through to the Ardennes, forms the eastern part of the Parisian basin. Its landscapes have the same peacefulness, the same harmony born of gently undulating plains, dipping sometimes towards shallow valleys. The slopes dominate by a few hundred feet the rivers whose waters flow peacefully on, and their average altitude is never more than 600 feet.

Geological make-up and geographical position have always given the Champagne region a single identity. At the time of the *Ancien Régime*, the region covered 6,177,500 acres, or almost one-twentieth of the whole of France. Under the Revolution, it was divided into four separate *départements*—Aube, Marne, Haute-Marne, Ardennes—while the remainder of its land was given to Yonne and Aisne.

Its subsoil consists of a chalky sediment from which, in thicker or thinner layers, calcareous, clay and flint sands detach themselves.

The viticultural zone was clearly defined by the law of July 22nd, 1927, which marked it out in accordance with its natural boundaries: only those vineyards which come within its confines are able to use the appellation CHAMPAGNE.

The viticultural area is not all in one block. It covers 778,365 acres, which were planted to the wine in their entirety by the last century. The invasion of phylloxera, however, destroyed a great number of the vines; at the present time, 61,280 acres are fully productive. They are divided up in the following manner: 47,443 acres in Marne, 9,389 in Aube and 14,447 in Aisne. This whole represents about two-hundredths of the entire area given over to viticulture in France.

There are four distinct zones within the Champagne vineyard: the Montagne de Rheims, the Vallée de la Marne, the Côte des Blancs and the vineyards of Aube. The first three are situated in the districts of Rheims and Epernay, and constitute the most important vineyards, the very heart of the Champagne region. It is they that produce the most illustrious growths. The vines, planted in rows along the sides of the slopes, form a ribbon about 75 miles long, but whose width varies from only about 300 yards in some parts to little more than a mile.

Apart from still wines which have their own very specific *appellation d'origine*, Champagne wines do not mention their vineyard of origin in the general classification, for Champagne is, by its very nature, a combination of musts from several varieties of grapes. The particular growth referred to here is therefore called a *cru de raisin*.

THE MONTAGNE DE REIMS. The Montagne de Reims forms the southern side of the Vesle valley, whilst its eastern tip joins up with the Marne valley, which it dominates at Epernay. The Great Growths of the main Champagne vineyard were classified according to very old usage. Verzenay, Mailly, Sillery and Beaumont-sur-Visle are the Great Growths of Montagne de Reims, which is situated to the north at the very edge of Rheims forest. Ludes, Chigny-les-Roses, Rilly-la-Montagne, Villers-Marmery, Verzy, Villers-Allerand and Trépail are some of the best growths.

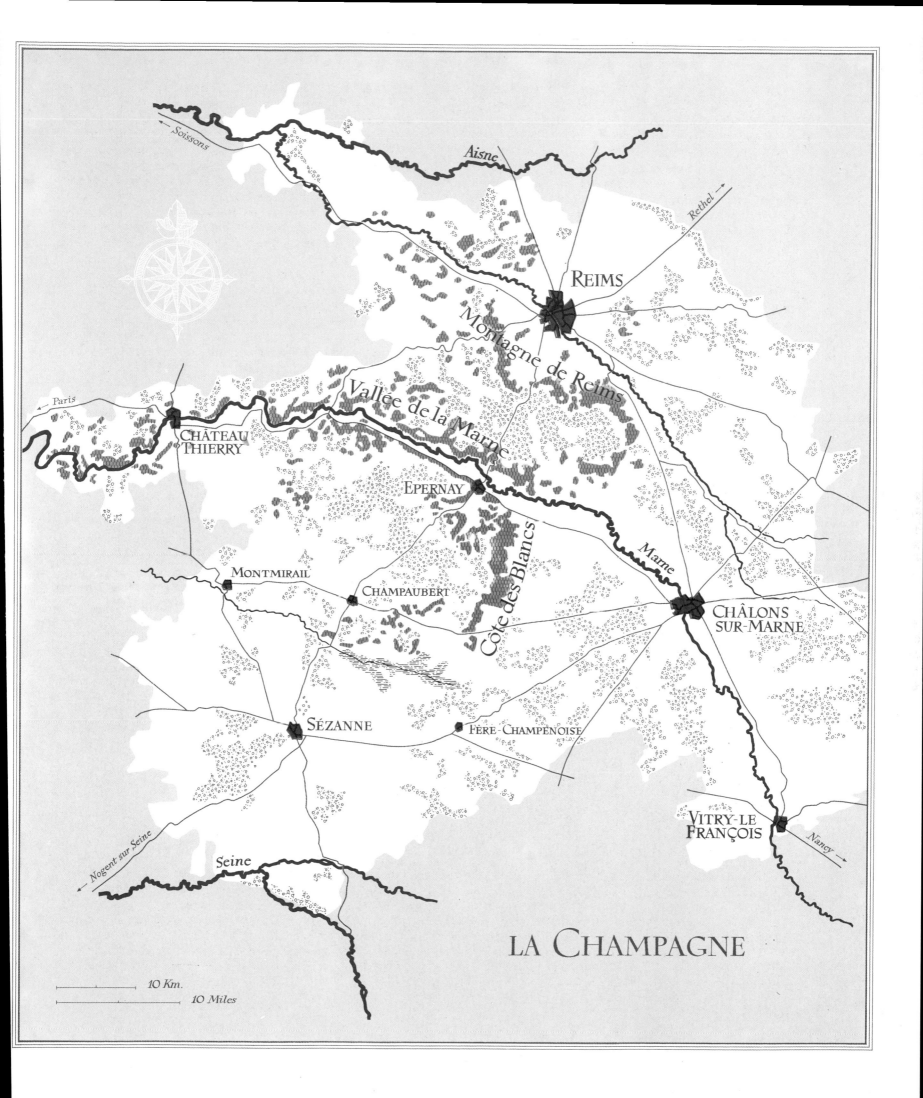

LA CHAMPAGNE

To the south of the town, Petite Montagne also has some good growths, such as Ville-Dommange, Ecueil, Sacy, Pargny-sur-Saulx, Jouy-lès-Reims.

THE MARNE VALLEY. The slopes of the Marne valley stretch the length of the river between Tours-sur-Marne and Dormans, extending towards Château-Thierry and beyond to the borders of the department. Its leading vineyard is Ay, framed by Mareuil-sur-Ay and Dizy, followed in a less elevated rank in the classification of vineyards by Cumières and Hautvillers, the region in which Dom Perignon earned his fame.

On the right bank of the river, the vineyards of Damery, Venteuil, Châtillon-sur-Marne, Vandières, Verneuil and Vincelles deserve mention. For quite a different reason, however, the name of the little hamlet of Tréloup is linked with the history of the Champagne area, for it was here that the first sign of phylloxera was seen in 1890. On the left bank, the valley of Cubry, which ends at Epernay, offers a number of interesting varieties made from the *Pinot Fin* grape, in the vineyards of Epernay and Pierry. Other localities such as Moussy, Vinay and Saint-Martin-d'Ablois grow the *Pinot Meunier* grape, which produces wines noted for their fruitiness. Other well-known vineyards are those in the regions of Mardeuil, Boursault, Leuvrigny, Festigny, Troissy and Dormans.

THE CÔTE DES BLANCS AND OTHER VINEYARDS. The Côte des Blancs is situated directly to the south of the Marne. Its great names ring melodiously in the minds of all connoisseurs of Champagne: Cramant, Avize, Oger and Le-Mesnil-sur-Oger. Chouilly, at the junction of two zones, also recalls happy memories, and its vineyards produce very fine quality white grapes, of which the *Chardonnay* is king.

The Côte des Blancs stretches south to the outskirts of Petit Morin, where it gains an extra slope of black and white grapes, considered to be some of its best. The Petit Morin valley is flanked by several vineyards growing the *Meunier* grape, which produces very fruity wines.

These zones, here rapidly reviewed, make up practically the whole of the Champagne area. There is, however, one other zone of a transitional nature whose geological characteristics are no longer quite as well-defined, but which nevertheless produces wine still entitled to be known by the same appellation. From amongst its vineyards, one can mention these of Côte de Château-Thierry, the Sézanne region and those in the vicinity of Vitry-le-François.

Between the region of Sézanne and the Aube vineyard there is quite a large gap, as it is not until Bar-sur-Aube and Bar-sur-Seine that one finds slopes which form a part of the same viticultural zone.

THE SOIL. The soil, as already indicated, has a chalky subsoil—an essential element. The great vineyards are usually planted halfway up the slopes on a fine layer of loose earth left over from slopes of the tertiary period, rich in chalk of the Senonian stratum, a single block of which can be more than 600 feet thick.

The chalky subsoil assures perfect drainage, stabilizes the infiltration of water and so maintains the ideal amount of humidity. Moreover, this geological composition offers another great advantage; it retains the heat from the sun and emits it again in a regular and constant manner. Finally, the light, which plays a very important role in the ripening of the grapes, is stronger here than the climate would lead one to believe, owing to the reflected whiteness of the chalky soil.

THE CLIMATE. The climate of the Champagne area is practically identical to that of the Parisian basin. Usually it is moderate, and the winters are seldom severe. In spring the weather is uncertain but mild, the summers are hot and the autumns are often good, all of which is of great importance to vine culture. The winds blowing from the sea soften the continental climate characteristics, which at their harshest are often too harsh for the vine, and the average annual temperature is about 50°F.

The wine, moreover, benefits from the surrounding forests and groves, which not only shield it from harsh weather but also provide a most desirable humidity. The altitude at which the vineyard is planted, from about 500 to 600 feet, also serves to protect it to a certain extent from spring frosts and cold early morning mists, which are naturally much worse in the valleys below. The vintner has learned to protect himself from these natural enemies of viticulture, and the modern methods at his disposal have enabled him practically to eliminate their often disastrous effects. This, of course, is equally applicable to hail.

GRAPE VARIETIES. Very strict legal provisions define which grapes may be used to produce Champagne. The varieties permitted are the *Pinot Noir* and the *Pinot Meunier*, both black grapes, and the *Chardonnay*, a white grape. Apart from these, the law permits the use of a few local stocks such as the *Petit Meslier* and the *Arbanne*; these, however, are slowly becoming extinct. It should be noted that following the invasion of phylloxera, the indigenous long-rooted plants were naturally replaced by grafted stock.

This law has but sanctioned centuries-old methods of vinification which winegrowers had practised, by confirming the perfect harmony of these plants with the soil and the climate. The influence of these grapes on the quality of the wine is, needless to say, considerable. Each brings its own quality, and the dosage, the intermarriage, the perfect harmonizing of all these qualities give to Champagne its essential character. Its delicate quality, its bouquet and its mellow warmth are derived from the various grapes, and the different proportions in which they are used decided by the dictates of sensitive palates. This forms a highly complicated and delicate process which will be examined in more detail, although it can be said here that no explanation can take the place of human experience.

The *Pinot Noir* grape (with its varieties) is widespread in Champagne (it is also used, more than any others, to

produce the great red wines of Burgundy). It makes a wine with a full bouquet, generous, powerful and robust. It produces a white wine by a process which we will study later.

The *Pinot Meunier* is a variety of the *Pinot Noir* grape. More hardy, it plays an important role in second quality Champagnes. The *Chardonnay*, which is a white grape, is found mainly on the Côte des Blancs. When blended, it gives forth its essential finesse and elegance.

All these grapes have certain common characteristics: they are precocious, vigorous, quick to mature, produce very sweet musts rich in sugar and have unrivalled finesse and bouquet.

After the phylloxera invasion, all the vineyards of the area were replanted with traditional varieties, grafted to American stocks or hybrids resistant to the attacks of the insect.

A vine lives for about thirty years, and only begins to produce fruit four years after it has been planted. The density in the Champagne vineyards reaches a closely-packed and regular thickness of 3,000 to 4,000 plants per acre, the yield (usually about 6,500 pounds per acre) is kept down in order to maintain the quality. This legal requirement is administered by a body called the Institut National des Appellations d'Origine (I.N.A.O.), which sees to it that the law is strictly carried out.

The countryside around the Champagne vineyards undulates gently, the hilltops, crowned with woods, sloping down to shallow valleys. The summits are rarely higher than 600 ft.

The pruning of the vine is also rigidly regulated by law: all the vines of Champagne must be pruned short, according to the accepted methods of the systems of "Royat", "Chablis", "Guyot" or "Vallée de la Marne".

A WINE-HARVEST TO CONQUER THE WORLD

After a long year of labour, care, anxiety, and hope, harvest-time arrives at last. This penultimate act of the great annual spectacle is performed with extraordinary care and concern, especially in the Champagne region. One might even venture to say that nowhere else in the world are the grapes picked with so much attention paid to each and every detail.

The fruit will have blossomed some hundred days before the date of picking is officially proclaimed by Prefectorial order. Laboratories have carried out tests to establish the exact sugar and acid content of the grapes now attaining their full maturity in the gentle rays of a mid-September sun. Work begins, and it is clear that the local labour is not sufficient. The wine-growers get help from all regions of France, especially miners from the North and from Lorraine. From one year to the next the growers try to find the "flying squads" of temporary workers who are already familiar

The Domaine de la Marguetterie is situated at Pierry, south of Epernay, in the Marne valley, one of the four important Champagne vineyard regions.

with the delicate work of fruit picking and well versed in the habits of the Champagne winegrowers. Split up into small groups called *hordes* or *hordons*, they work methodically and conscientiously, their bright clothes forming multi-coloured patches which bob and weave among the tightly packed green vines. The wine-harvesters receive free board and lodging. Their wages are fixed by the joint committee of the C.I.V.C. according to their age and qualifications. This is to distinguish the pickers (aged from 12, 13, 14 years and up), the carriers of small baskets, the unloaders of big baskets, the general labourers, the group leaders—all these people making up the "foreign" workers.

Then come the press-men, who are also classified by jobs: hydraulic press, and dryer, hydraulic dryer and so on. Every army, even a peaceful one, requires a rear-echelon staff, and the kitchen staff must be added too. The grape pickers, men, women and children, pick the clusters from the root of vines with great care, using shears, make a preliminary sorting of the grapes (if necessary); and they place the grape-bunches in small baskets, each of which holds about eleven pounds.

Then it is the turn of the carriers. They collect the baskets and pour their contents on to large wicker-work hurdles under the watchful eye of the "sorters", who are responsible for a final careful sorting. It is necessary to take out the green grapes or those not sufficiently ripe, as otherwise they would reduce the alcohol content of the wine, as well as the bad and overripe grapes which would spoil the quality of the wine. This work is very burdensome, and some argue as to its necessity. The Champagne winegrowers certainly believe in it.

Those grapes considered good enough for vinification are *placed*—not poured—in large wicker-work baskets, quaintly named *mannequins*, or in similar receptacles, often made of plastic, which can hold some 110 to 180 pounds, and which are then placed with great care by the carriers in vehicles with springs—a peculiarity of this region for a long time—which are driven very carefully to the press-house, with care to avoid bumps that might damage the grapes.

The vine-presses are in *vendangeoirs* which belong either to wine-merchants, local co-operatives, vineyard-owners or to wine-brokers. Except in the case of the *récoltant-manipulant*, the work of the vineyard is now completed. This is a special characteristic of viticultural Champagne. The grapes are weighed and then paid for, according to the price fixed each year by the C.I.V.C., after bargaining between winegrowers and wine-merchants. The sale is completed when the buyer has the grapes poured into the wine-press.

PRESSING THE GRAPES. The grapes are pressed as soon as possible. Champagne vintners use special presses, low and squat, so the must can flow out quickly without dissolving the colouring matter from the stalks, and without any risk of the flavour being spoiled by the wood. Some 9,000 pounds of grapes are placed on the floor of the press. The CHAMPAGNE appellation is given

The Côte d'Hautvillers is a famous vineyard in the Marne valley (above). Here, in harvest time, *cueilleurs* put the grapes they have gathered into small baskets which the *porteurs* carry to the sorters, who carefully sort the grapes into larger baskets. Time is precious, and the grape-pickers—most of them seasonal workers—eat their midday meal among the vines (below).

427

only to those wines whose must has been obtained by pressing not more than a hectolitre of juice per 150 kilos of grapes or about 20 gallons from 300 pounds. For this reason, the limit is fixed at 2,666 litres of must per marc which makes 13 barrels of 45 gallons each.

Then the first pressing takes place, or better, the first *serre* (squeeze). Usually electrically-controlled, the *plancher* (ceiling) held by a *mouton* (stock) is lowered on to the grapes, with a pressure attaining as much as 40 tons per square metre.

The must filters through the mass of grapes being pressed and flows through a spout with a filter into a 220-gallon vat called a *bélon*. The operation is repeated. The grapes must be pressed in one and a half hours, or two hours at the most.

The first ten barrels or 450 gallons are the cuvée from which the great Champagnes will be made. The next three pressings are known as *tailles* (cuts), so-called because it is necessary to cut up the compressed marc with a spade before it is squeezed again. One thus has a first and second pressing of poorer quality.

The must remains for only a short time in the graduated vats, of oak or cement, in which it was first collected. It is very quickly transferred to other types of vats known as *débourbage* (settling) vats where it stays for 10 to 12 hours, time enough for it to settle out all the foreign bodies it still contains: pips, skin and any other impurities.

When the wine has fully settled, the must is drawn off in barrels which hold 45 gallons each and is labelled according to origin. This operation is often carried out with mobile vats. Whatever the method, the wine is then transferred to the cellars where the delicate process of vinification commences.

VINIFICATION. Champagne is the product of two successive fermentations, whose essential elements are yeasts. These micro-organisms appear on the skin of the grape just before it ripens, and they are what changes the must into wine.

THE FIRST FERMENTATION. The first fermentation is also known by the evocative name of *bouillage* (boiling). It takes place either in oaken barrels, or in vats made of glazed cement, enamelled steel or stainless steel. The ambient temperature is maintained at 20° or 22°C., and the must seethes. For several days, fermentation is tumultuous, then its violence slackens and calm follows. Three weeks pass before the first clarifying racking takes place. The wine is next left cold in order to let its deposits settle and the liquid become limpid clear. Then it is drawn off for the second time.

Formerly, Christmas would find the cellar doors wide open to the chill air. Alas, the poetry has gone, giving way to sheer efficiency, and today, in many cellars, modern air-conditioning plants turn this part of the vinification process into an example of precision which is at the same time a guarantee of quality and consistency. For it is now that preparations for making Champagne differ from those for other wines.

LA CUVÉE. This operation is also known as *cuvée de tirage* (draught cuvée), and both its preparation and its carrying out require a careful combination of talent and technical know-how.

At the first racking or drawing-off, usually wines from the same growth are assembled in order to produce a homogeneous vatful which can then be used for later blending operations.

Right from the beginning of the year, specialists from each house taste the harvested wines, for they will be obliged to produce a wine, whatever the variations of that particular harvest may have been, which carries on the qualities and is faithful to the character that has made it known. It is therefore only after the second racking that the different growths are blended.

The vintner is now faced with two possibilities. If he wishes to produce a *millésime* (a wine showing the year of manufacture) it is clear that only wines of the same year may be blended. If he does not wish to produce a *millésime*, the shortcomings in the vintage of a particular year may be compensated for by adding wines from previous years which have been specially kept for this purpose. Needless to say, a successful blending requires several trials before the formula is applied to whole casks. The essential characteristics one must bear in mind in order to achieve an ideal result are: vinosity (flavour and strength), bouquet, aroma, elegance, delicacy, spirit and conservation ability. The latter characteristic will have been confirmed by a complex analysis.

The different wines are mixed in huge casks or in vats equipped with mixers which permit a perfect blending. Traditionally, Champagne is made from a blend of both black and white grapes. There are some varieties, however, made from white grapes alone: these are known as *Blanc de Blancs*. There is also a rosé Champagne, usually made by adding to the original mixture red wine from the Champagne vineyards, although sometimes the rosé Champagne is prepared as a rosé from the time it first goes to the press.

By the beginning of March, the exact composition of the *cuvée* must be ready, so that the producer can start clarifying by filtering or by thinning down.

RACKING. At this stage, the wine in the vat is a still wine, but with the coming of spring, when it is racked, its whole destiny will change. To get the wine into the condition to become frothy, it is now transferred into special clearing vats, at the same time adding natural ferments and a liqueur. This liqueur is in fact a solution of pure cane sugar dissolved in wine. The wine is then stirred so that all the ingredients are well blended.

If one is trying to produce a *crémant* type of Champagne, one adds a smaller quantity of the sweet solution to the wine. The next step is to draw off the wine into bottles, where the mysterious transformation will take place. What seems to happen is that the sugar solution changes into alcohol and carbonic acid gas, which provokes the effervescence. Imprisoned within the

Once selected, the best grapes are placed in baskets called *mannequins* containing from 150 to 180 lbs of grapes. The *débardeurs* (unloaders) then transport them to the winepress.

The foreman of the vineyard (above) keeps a beady eye on all the stages of the harvest, from picking to the presses. In all their various handlings, it is vital that the grapes should never be crushed or even bruised.

Deep in the cellar, a skilled workman performs the delicate task of *remuage*—a slight daily shake and a twist to every bottle so that the sediment will gradually work its way down and settle near the cork (below).

429

bottle, which is now firmly corked and wired, the carbonic acid gas remains dissolved in the liquid and only starts to bubble when the bottle is uncorked.

THE SECOND FERMENTATION. This is the slow continuation of the process just outlined above. Taken immediately into cellars dug out of the chalk subsoil, the bottles are laid carefully on special wooden battens. They are constantly under close surveillance, as there is still a risk of bottle-breakage, despite the great improvements made in glass manufacture: the pressure of the gas can sometimes rise to 5 or 6 atmospheres. The corks also might be faulty and let some wine leak.

When the second fermentation is completed, the wine is clear, with all the deposits at the neck of the bottle, and its alcohol content is about 12°. It is now necessary to remove the deposit and extract the sediment-coated cork.

REMUAGE, OR SETTLING THE DEPOSIT. The bottles are stacked *sur pointe* (with the cork pointing downwards) in wooden frames designed in such a way that the bottle can be inclined in different positions whilst the deposit is working its way down on to the cork. Every day, skilled cellarists give the bottle a sharp turn whilst also shaking it. At the same time, they rotate it one-eighth of a turn to the right or to the left, according to a guide mark painted at the bottom of the bottle, while the frames are tilted a little more downward. This process needs not only a dexterous hand but a rapid one; a good worker can *passer* 30,000 bottles a day.

Finally, the deposit will have all collected at the neck of the bottle, which reaches a vertical position in from six weeks to three months. By then, all the bottles are in the same position.

DEGORGEMENT, OR REMOVAL OF THE CORK. It is now necessary to remove the deposit whilst at the same time allowing the minimum amount of gas and wine to escape. Disgorging, which is entrusted only to experts, is a manœuvre which used to depend on great speed to avoid spillage. Today, this delicate operation is more and more frequently being carried out by freezing the neck of the bottle. The necks of the bottles are inserted in a brine freezing solution at a temperature of minus 20°; very rapidly, ice forms near the cork, trapping the impurities. When the cork is removed, the ice is immediately blown out, along with a small quantity of froth and wine. The bottle is then examined, and a dosage, liqueur consisting of pure cane sugar dissolved in old and high-class Champagne, is added to make up the lost wine. The strength of the liqueur depends on the type of Champagne desired: *brut, sec* (dry), *demi-sec* (semi-dry) or *doux* (sweet). *Extra-brut* means that the Champagne has no sugar content at all.

CORKING. After such a lengthy and delicate operation, it is understandable that corking is very important. The bottles must be hermetically sealed so only the finest quality cork is chosen for this purpose. The cork is 1¾ to 2¼ inches long and 1¼ to 1½ inches wide, and must, by law, have certain information printed on it. Once the cork is in place, a metal capsule is put over it and the whole is encircled by a wire-mesh, so that the pressure of gas in the bottle does not blow the cork out again. The bottles are then put back in the cool cellars to age, some for as long as six or seven years, before they set out to conquer the world.

RANGE OF CHAMPAGNE WINES

Champagne, as has been seen, is obtained by blending wines from three different grapes: the *Pinot Noir* and the *Pinot Meunier*, both black grapes, and the *Chardonnay*, a white grape. Many people are surprised to learn that this wine, so pure and clear, is made to a large extent from black grapes.

As in other vineyards, grapes from the same stocks do not necessarily have the same flavour or qualities, since these are influenced by the soil and place where they are grown. A connoisseur can easily tell the difference between the varieties. But with Champagne it is more difficult to distinguish the range of wines and their varieties because of the grape marriages which initiated the fame of Champagne and contributed so much to its glory. The different firms possess their own particular characteristics, and long experience is needed to distinguish between them.

The soil and a favourable location are so important and make for such a difference in the final variety of the grapes that certain coefficients have been granted to the producing regions, by commune and according to the quality of their produce. It is true that these basic coefficients are liable to change every year, depending on the results of the wine-harvests.

The coefficients range from 77 per cent to 100 per cent; those of 100 per cent are traditionally known as "*grands crus*", while those of 90 to 99 per cent are entitled "*premiers crus*". These titles are rarely carried on the label, because the guarantee of quality is, in most cases, given by the great names of the firms who absorb 80 per cent of the production. The opposite is true for most other wines, which normally are only too pleased to be able to announce "grand cru".

Before examining the various types of Champagne, it is useful to recall the legal protection of the *appellation d'origine contrôlée*, which benefits producers and consumers alike.

Only the following is recognized as Champagne:

1. wine produced from vines planted from authorized stocks, within the limits of the viticultural Champagne region, pruned to the required height, of a limited yield per acre;

2. wine of an assured quality guaranteed by a limited yield in must and by a minimum alcohol content;

3. wine prepared in accordance with the natural procedure known as *méthode champenoise*, in premises within the Champagne region where only wines from this region may be stored;

4. wine stored in bottles prior to shipping for at least one year (but for three years after the harvesting, in the case of wines with a *millésime*).

These principles, which have been progressively sanctioned by French law, are applied and controlled, to avoid any fraud, by the C.I.V.C. in the name of the public authority, vinegrowers and wine-merchants.

After the final stage, the dosing of the wine, the various types of Champagne can then be classified under one of the designations that follows:

Brut without mention of year. This is a wine that is usually light and lively, very suitable as an aperitif as it prepares both the mind and the palate.

Brut millésimé. This is a very good wine which comes from a good vintage year, since only wines of the same year may be blended together in order to produce a first-grade bottle. In some years it might even be a collector's bottle. This type of wine is often more full-bodied and more generous; it deserves to be savoured with particular care. To mention a few of the old vintage wines very difficult to find nowadays: 1928, 1933, 1934, 1937, 1943, 1945, 1949, 1953, 1966, 1969, 1971, and 1973. Their merits vary, but one should be wary of those which have been aged too long. Here again, one might ask: should Champagne be drunk young or old? Several things must be considered. First, although the carbonic acid gas in the Champagne gives it a certain resistance to bacteria and assures its conservation, it does not mean that the wine is impervious to everything and can remain in optimum condition forever. It is as much alive as any other wine and must receive the same attention and care. It ages and may change. After ten years or so, it may take on a slight colour and begin to maderize; this will continue with the years. It is then said to have become a *renarde* (a vixen). It remains drinkable, of course, but its essential qualities fade, just as a beautiful flower fades. Moreover, the pressure of the gas decreases and little by little the wine loses its life. There is no point, therefore—except as an experiment and perhaps in the case of a particularly good vintage year—in keeping Champagne for a long time. It is put on the market at the time in its life when it is suitable for consumption; this is one of the rules which control the quality of Champagne.

Dry and semi-dry Champagne. The present trend is towards the *brut* or extra dry variety, and the sweeter type of Champagne, possessing perhaps a little less character, is certainly much less in demand today. There are wines which are very pleasant with desserts; they must, however, be served at a cooler temperature than the others.

Rosé. This remains an amusing exception, but does not lack attraction nor admirers. A very fruity wine with an excellent colour, it is coming more and more into favour and the big firms have no hesitation in offering it. Its bouquet varies according to the way it has been made. Some are produced by adding a small amount of red wine from Champagne; others—and this is prefer-

In Champagne, the grape-pickers, armed with secateurs, cut the grapes from the stems, and make a first selection before putting the grapes into small baskets which are collected by the *porteurs*. The grapes are then taken to be sorted.

able—are produced as a rosé from the start. It cannot compete with great classical Champagnes.

It should be added that the shippers also prepare wines for specific foreign markets, to meet specific preferences of their clients. The fruitiness and sweetness of these vary according to their destination.

There remain two other effervescent wines of Champagne which should be mentioned, both of which are very pleasant to drink:

The *crémant*, whose gas content is lower than that of Champagne. This is done by reducing the amount of liqueur added to the wine before the second fermentation. These lithe, light, fruity wines go down very well, but they can never match their superiors. They have, nevertheless, their own place in the Champagne family.

The *Blanc de Blancs* is made solely from white grapes, using the *Chardonnay* variety. It is a very elegant, light wine, with a particularly fine bouquet.

Finally, the Champagne region also produces noneffervescent, so-called "still" wines, so that some of the traditions which first made the area famous live on.

THE STILL WINES OF CHAMPAGNE

The still white wines of Champagne are an excellent introduction to a better knowledge of Champagne. There is a *Blanc de Blancs* which has not been *champagnisé* (given a Champagne sparkle), and also a *Blanc de*

431

1

2

3

PERRIER-JOUET
1. Trade name "Champagne Perrier-Jouet". –
2. Type of Champagne: *Extra Brut*. This indicates that no liqueur was added to this wine, which is therefore a very dry Champagne. Bottles marked "Finest Quality" and "Reserve cuvée" mean that the *négociant-manipulant* attributes particular importance to this type of Champagne. In other words, the quality of this Champagne may be judged by the reputation of its *négociant-manipulant* or by one's own experience. – 3. In the reference N.M. 3.624.332, the letters N.M. indicate that this is a vintage of first importance produced by a *négociant-manipulant*. The letters M.A. would signify a wine of secondary quality. The number that follows is the index number of the vintage on the register of the *Comité Interprofessionnel du Vin de Champagne* (C.I.V.C.).

2

1

3

MERCIER
1. Trade name: "Champagne Mercier". – 2. Type of Champagne: *Brut*. This indicates that only a small amount (about 1.5 per cent) of liqueur was added to the wine, or possibly none at all. – 3. The initials N.M. indicate that this is a primary vintage wine produced by a *négociant-manipulant*.

1

2

3

MUMM DOUBLE CORDON
1. Trade name: "Double Cordon de G.H. Mumm", commonly known as "Mumm Double Cordon". – 2. Type of Champagne: *Sec*. This indicates that between 2.5 per cent and 5 per cent of liqueur was added to the wine. This Champagne is therefore not as dry as the *Brut* and *Extra-Brut* Champagnes. – 3. The initials N.M. indicate that this is a primary vintage wine produced by a *négociant-manipulant*.

TAITTINGER

1. Trade name: "Champagne Taittinger". – 2. Type of Champagne: *Demi-sec*. This is a wine to which between 5 per cent and 8 per cent of liqueur has been added. It is therefore a slightly sweet wine. – 3. Here the initials N.M. again indicate a primary vintage wine produced by a *négociant-manipulant*.

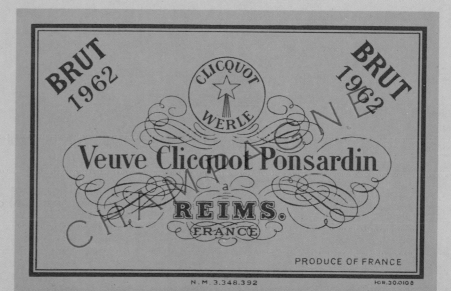

CLICQUOT-PONSARDIN

1. Trade name: "Champagne Veuve Clicquot Ponsardin". – 2. Type of Champagne: *Brut* 1962. This is a *Brut* vintage Champagne. Only the very best years are indicated on Champagne labels. – 3. This is also a primary vintage Champagne produced by a *négociant-manipulant*.

DOM PÉRIGNON

1. Trade name: "Dom Pérignon". This is one of the rare occasions where the name of the wine itself has replaced the name of the *négociant-manipulant*. Dom Pérignon is always a vintage *(millésimé)* Champagne, but conversely not every harvest produces a Dom Pérignon. It is always made from the juice of the first pressings of selected grapes, using white grapes only; it is therefore a *Blanc de Blancs*. – 2. Name of the *négociant-manipulant*. – 3. Primary vintage wine of a *négociant-manipulant*.

Noirs, this latter a much more full-bodied wine. The big firms market it. It offers the dominant characteristics of the Champagne vineyards, with its own particular spirit, colour and charm. The still red wines are simple and excellent, but somewhat fragile. Their flavour and strength remind one of the wines of Burgundy, whilst their tannin content recalls those of Bordeaux. The best known among them is the incomparable Bouzy, but Cumières, Ambonnay, Verzenay, Sillery, Mailly, Saint-Thierry, Vertus also have excellent wines. The appearance of a red wine from Champagne on the table is always greeted with surprise and interest. These amazing red wines have a very special fruity flavour, while their mischievousness is more apparent than real. They are great wines produced with care and should not be drunk at room temperature; they are at their best when cooled. In great vintage years, they are very full-bodied and may be kept for a long time. There is a limit, however: wine of the year 1959, for example, is of a very different order, far removed from the lightheartedness of other years. These red wines at a certain age would seem to become almost too robust and to lose much of their original appeal.

Bouzy is marketed independently of the large Champagne producers by the individual growers since it is not a wine requiring the skilled blending of the sparkling Champagnes.

THE MARKETING OF CHAMPAGNE

The grape has ripened, the Champagne is born. Now it must be marketed—and it has long been known that the people of Champagne are as prudent as they are smart. The whole structure of commercialization and marketing in the Champagne area is as special as the wines. The marketing structure includes:

– *Négociants-manipulants* who themselves vinify the wines from their own vines, or from the must which they buy from individual vinegrowers. They blend and marry, bottle and market the wine themselves.

– *Négociants non manipulants*: companies or individuals marketing Champagne but not making it.

– *Récoltants-manipulants*: vintners who produce and then market their own wine.

– *Co-operatives de manipulation* who press, vinify and blend wines brought to them by member growers. The co-operatives also market the wine themselves.

In the English-speaking countries these terms are rarely met since almost all Champagne is exported by the *grande marque* houses such as Moët et Chandon, Heidsick, G.H. Mumm and Veuve Clicquot, who belong to the first category, the *négociants-manipulants*.

Certain indications must figure on Champagne labels in order to protect the consumer against the danger of possible fraud:

N.M. for a first-quality Champagne belonging to a *négociant-manipulant*.

M.A. (B.O.B.—buyer's own brand—in English) for a lesser Champagne belonging to a *négociant-manipulant* or a *négociant non manipulant* and which he can market under his own chosen name, changing his supplier but not his label should he so wish.

R.M. for a brand from a *récoltant-manipulant*.

C.M. for a brand from a *co-operative-manipulante*.

Another requirement for Champagne labels is for the number accorded to the product by the C.I.V.C. to be indicated after the category initials.

An extraordinary network of cellars dug out of the limestone rock twists and turns its way through the subsoil of Champagne. Some of these chalk cellars can be traced back to Gallo-Roman times, but their continued development required—and still requires—continual maintenance. Today, there are about 125 miles of underground tunnels, sheltering millions of bottles, at a constant temperature of 10° to 11°. Some cellars are up to 45 yards deep, and many of the large Champagne firms feel it a duty, as well as a pleasure, to show people around them. Without these cellars, their wine could not be what it is. In 1980, a total of 176,466,231 bottles left the cellars of Champagne. The record was established in 1978 with 185,922,892 bottles.

The increase in the sales by the growers can be explained by the fact that they can step up production as much as they wish, while the wine-merchants must set a limit to their trade ambitions. Being directly responsible for their own production, the growers can increase direct sales to clients. The wine-merchants, on the other hand, must rely on purchases from vineyards and on the state of the grape market, the latter being directly influenced by the vintage. The wine-merchant must constantly bear in mind that the vines he owns directly meet only one-fifth of his needs; he thus has to buy the remaining four-fifths. The amount of capital he must invest may be judged by the fact that in 1980 a kilogramme (about 2 lb) of grapes was selling for around 20 French francs.

Sales abroad are increasing, which is attracting great interest. Nevertheless, the domestic French market remains far and away the most important: 121,436,120 bottles sold there as against 55,030,111 for export (1980). In 1977-1980, the twelve main markets, in decreasing size, were: Italy, Great Britain, United States, Belgium, Germany, Switzerland, Venezuela, Holland, Canada, Denmark, Mexico and Australia.

WHAT ONE SHOULD KNOW IN ORDER TO BUY WELL. When buying Champagne, first of all, look carefully at the label on the bottle that is the object of your heart's desire, unless it is a particularly well-known name in which you know you can have full confidence. There is practically no fraud in Champagne, but that is not to say that all Champagnes are equally good.

The word "Champagne", as well perhaps as the *millésime* or year of production, should be written either on the main label or on the neck of the bottle, in clearly legible letters. This information is also printed

on the side of the cork, which is of course inside the bottle's neck. Note next the signs just described above in detail, bearing in mind the different categories of merchants in the Champagne trade, the C.I.V.C. index number and the initials indicating the category.

Most people know a good wine-merchant whom they feel they can trust. But never allow him to sell a bottle which has been on display, for it has naturally suffered from this. The bottle must be brought up from the cellar, or at least from a bottle-rack in which it was lying flat, for the cork must always be moistened.

There is no point in building up large stocks of Champagne, and in any case, everything depends of course on how much one consumes. One should set up a Champagne cellar with various types of bottles, going from the ordinary to the best vintage Champagne, and including full-bodied vintage Champagne.

The following selection is given as an example:

Fresh wines: Laurent-Perrier, Lanson, Piper Heidsieck, Mercier, Canard Duchêne, Jeanmaire, etc.

Better-balanced wines with more character: Mumm, Perrier-Jouet, Pommery, Ruinart, Taittinger, etc.

Older and stronger wines: Bollinger, Krug, Pal Roger, Veuve Clicquot, Roederer, etc.

It must be stressed that this list is given purely as an indication, not as a recommendation for buying.

THE PRESTIGE WINES. In recent years, a number of the large firms have tended to establish *cuvées spéciales*, or very special selections of Champagnes. This has been done in a move to meet the requirements for an even higher quality, which would satisfy the taste of the most demanding of connoisseurs, and also from a desire to establish still more solidly the renown of their names. These wines are usually presented with a luxurious refinement, albeit inspired by the simple and seductive shapes of old flasks which thus find a new youth. These are growths of great character. Some of the most famous are : DOM PERIGNON, by Moët et Chandon, which started this trend; the CUVÉE GRAND SIÈCLE by Laurent-Perrier; the COMTES DE CHAMPAGNE by Taittinger; the FLORENS LOUIS by Piper-Heidsieck; the CUVÉE CHARLES VII by Canard Duchêne; the CUVÉE ELYSÉE by Jeanmaire; the CUVÉE DE L'EMPEREUR by Mercier, and the Roederer sold in crystal bottles. Bollinger presented a 1961 vintage Champagne, which was not uncorked until 1971, as the top-quality product of their firm.

Still on the subject of bottles, one can use this opportunity to detail their great variety. Their names are: split (half-pint), pint (1/10 gallon), quart (1/5 gallon), magnum (2 quarts), jeroboam (4 quarts), rehoboam (6 quarts), methuselah (8 quarts), salmanasar (12 quarts), balthazar (16 quarts) and nebuchadnezzar (20 quarts).

It should be said at once that the bottles with resounding biblical names, from magnum on, are only show pieces, derived from folklore. On the other hand, for some inexplicable reason, Champagne in magnums is always first-rate.

As a general rule, it is a good idea to furnish one's cellar with bottles of various sizes, suitable for different occasions, bearing in mind that one bottle is usually adequate to serve six or seven guests, unless they are real lovers and connoisseurs of Champagne. The half-pint bottles, or "splits" should be avoided, as they are rather too small to warrant cellar-space.

CHAMPAGNE AND SPARKLING WINES

Champagne is so very special that, of all the effervescent wines, it is the only one not to be known as a "sparkling wine" or *mousseux*. Here, usage and time have gone against etymology. Yet the term "sparkling wine" is applied to all wines which, after a second artificial fermentation, froth when poured into a glass. Depending on the amount of froth, they are called *perlants* (pearly), *pétillants* (effervescent), or *mousseux* (sparkling). *Crémant* is not reserved exclusively for Champagne.

Sparkling wines are made in three different ways: the rural or natural method; the *méthode champenoise*, and the method known as *cuve close*.

THE RURAL OR NATURAL METHOD. The wine is vinified by its natural fermentation without anything being added to it. It is its natural sugar, which has not been turned into alcohol during the first fermentation, which activates the second fermentation. The wine having been bottled after the first fermentation, a second fermentation now takes place in the bottle which gives the wine its effervescence. Modern processes of analysis and vinification enable the vintner to control the effervescence throughout the whole procedure, and thus to produce at his pleasure either a pearly or an effervescent wine.

This method is used in France, especially in Gaillac, Limoux (BLANQUETTE) and in Die, whose yellowish-gold CLAIRETTE is reputed.

"METHODE CHAMPENOISE". This method has been described already in detail, but the main principles are recalled here.

The first fermentation, aptly called "tumultuous", in former times took place in wooden casks. Nowadays, through modern progress, it usually takes place in vats. The process becomes calmer after three weeks, and up to that point, vinification is more or less the same as in all vineyards. The preparation of the *cuvée* (contents of the vat), however, is characteristic of Champagne, for in this region the blending of grapes is far more subtle than anywhere else. Racking follows, then the natural ferments, plus a liqueur made from a mixture of older wine and sugar, bring about the conditions that lead the wine's becoming frothy in the bottle during the second fermentation.

It is in fact this second, very precisely controlled fermentation which brings that fine quality to the wine, for its sparkle and froth must be enduring as well as

Champagnes are not named after vineyards, as in other winegrowing regions of France, but are known by commercial names. The good name and fame of the Champagne houses—here the Moët et Chandon estate near Epernay—guarantees the quality of the champagne they sell at home and abroad. There are some 140 Champagne houses, of which the 12 most important sell about 65 per cent of the production.

light. The work of the vintners is not ended when the bottles are cellared, for there remain all those intricate steps which are peculiar to the Champagne vineyards and the *méthode champenoise*: *remuage* (moving the deposit towards the cork), uncorking or *dégorgement* (removing the cork with its wad of sediment), *dosage* (addition of more liqueur) and so on.

THE "CUVE CLOSE" METHOD. This differs from the two previous ones in that the second fermentation does not take place in bottles but in enormous vats. The wine is inferior when produced by this method and is certainly no substitute for the *méthode champenoise*. French law forbids Champagne made in *cuve close* to be sold as an A.O.C. wine.

These methods are the only ones used in France, and are followed more or less closely, in other countries producing sparkling wines. In Italy, for example, ASTI SPUMANTE is made by the *méthode champenoise* up to a certain stage of its development; that is, until the second fermentation in the bottle has taken place. To avoid the *remuage* and the operation of uncorking, the wines are transferred from the bottles into enormous closed vats where they are clarified and filtered before being subsequently rebottled.

Finally, and purely for the record, sparkling wine can also be produced by simply adding carbonic acid gas. It need hardly be said that such wines are of a very inferior quality.

436

LIFE IN THE CHAMPAGNE REGION

Life in the Champagne region follows the rhythm of the work in the vineyards. Although the history of the province is particularly rich in facts and fables, its folklore today has fallen into disuse. One must not be too harsh in blaming the people of Champagne; rather, it should be recognized that the nature of their soil and climate is less propitious to popular festivities than that of the large vineyards to the south. This is the land, moreover, that has been rocked and torn by cruel wars over the centuries, tragedies which have contributed to the disappearance of pleasant customs and joyous occasions which are very difficult to keep up when the heart has gone out of them.

On the other hand, one should not conclude that the vinegrowers of Champagne are a sad people. Everywhere that wine is to be found, the people are warmhearted and generous.

In former days, when the winegrower poured the grapes into the vat or wooden barrel, he never failed to pronounce a revered formula which expressed all hopes : *Saint Martin, bon vin* ("Saint Martin, make the wine good"). Having thus satisfied his religious beliefs, he did not hesitate to turn to other practices in which piety had no part! A case of "better safe than sorry", no doubt. To take care of superstitions, he also placed a steel knife between the wood of the barrel and the first metal ring.

The Feast of St. Vincent is celebrated on January 22nd here as in all vineyards. Once the simple religious ceremonies have been concluded, including blessing the vines, a propitiatory bottle of good wine is enjoyed.

On the patron saint's day, as well as at all other festivities, whether religious or secular, the sole joy comes from the wine, and the festival of Mardi Gras or *Feux de la Saint-Jean*, in summer, with their maypoles, dances and chorus-singing, are now of the past. The hard work at harvest time does not prevent the workers from enjoying themselves, but workers brought in from other places to help in the harvest are not the ones to bring back the habits and customs of long ago.

If the *Vigneronne* is no longer danced around the wine-press, the last day of harvesting is still celebrated by the *Cochelet*. This consists mainly of a sumptuous meal, with plenty of Champagne, followed by a local ball and *farandole* dances born from the imaginations of the participants.

Modern times have also killed off the friendly *cavées*, or cellar parties, when each vinegrower brought a log to help keep the fire going and joined in the hearty singing before sharing the *queugnots* (a type of biscuit), united with all his friends under the sign of the vine.

THE COMMANDERY OF THE CHAMPAGNE SLOPES. As in other wine regions, an influential brotherhood has pledged itself to spread the fame of Champagne wines. Its origins date back to the seventeenth century when the founders, the Count of Olonne, the Marquis of Saint-Evremond and the Marquis of Mortemart, practising what they preached, formed a group of famed epicures. In those days they were called les *marquis friands* ("the sweet-toothed marquises"), but the irreverant found them another title wherein could be detected some envy: *les fins débauchés* ("the first-class rakes"). In fact, they shared a common love for a good life and had a predilection for the wines of Champagne, which surely absolves them from any sin. Years passed, and it was only after the war that the brotherhood was brought back from its deep sleep by a winegrower from Champillon, Roger Gaucher, and François Taittinger.

The brotherhood is headed by a Commander (at present, Georges Prade, former vice-president of the Municipal Council of Paris) who is helped by a *Conseil Magistral*. The most prominent members of this Council are the *Capitaine Chambellan* (Captain Chamberlain), the *Connétable Premier officier* (High Constable First Officer), the *Grand Chancelier* (Great Chancellor), the *Gardien de la Constitution* (Guardian of the Constitution), and others of lesser mark.

The objectives of the brotherhood are to propagate the noble wine, to defend its prestige and its quality, and to battle relentlessly against malpractice and fraud.

Caps on their heads and swords at their sides, the high dignitaries often go from place to place, organizing or attending important national and international occasions. They insist strictly on remaining an independent group, and though in close contact and on excellent terms with the firms and wine-merchants, they will not accept any protection, nor admit any exclusive rights.

The ancient house of the Counts of Champagne, built in the thirteenth century, has been bought and restored by Taittinger, and is used today for the firm's receptions. Their quality champagne carries the name "Comte de Champagne".

SPARKLING WINES THROUGHOUT THE WORLD

Sparkling wines are produced in nearly all the large viticultural regions in the world, and can be either white, red or rosé, with a very wide range of quality.

THE SPARKLING WINES OF FRANCE

France is the largest producer of sparkling wines in the world, with 428,961,000 gallons in 1973, including 19,798,200 gallons of Champagne.

Burgundy and Bordelais also produce sparkling wines of the *appellation contrôlée* category, but which cannot pretend to compete with the celebrated growths of the Champagne region. The Rhône basin produces the following sparkling wines: ARBOIS MOUSSEUX, L'ETOILE MOUSSEUX or CÔTES DU JURA MOUSSEUX; and farther south there are the sparkling wines of SAVOIE AYSE (Ayse is the name of the growth), the SEYSSEL MOUSSEUX, the SAINT-PERAY MOUSSEUX and the CLAIRETTE DE DIE MOUSSEUX which carry an A.O.C. In the Loire valley, almost every viticultural region has its own sparkling wine: MONT-LOUIS MOUSSEUX, VOUVRAY MOUSSEUX, TOURAINE MOUSSEUX, SAUMUR MOUSSEUX, ANJOU MOUSSEUX, all of which are popular. BLANQUETTE DE LIMOUX and GAILLAC MOUSSEUX, produced in the southwest, deserve more than passing mention.

All French sparkling wines are obliged by law to state on their labels how they have been made, whether by the *méthode champenoise*, *vin mousseux produit en cuve close*, or *vin mousseux gazéifié*.

THE SPARKLING WINES OF GERMANY

After France, Germany is the next largest producer of sparkling wines. They are known either as *Sekt* or *Schaumwein*, the latter being generally inferior to the *Sekt*. The wines sell at a wide range of prices; the best *Sekt* can cost up to ten times more than an ordinary *Schaumwein*. Most German sparkling wines are not made from German but from imported wines, and purchases of foreign wines can sometimes reach as high as three-quarters of the whole German production of sparkling wines. In 1967, only 23.4 per cent of the country's sparkling wines were of German origin.

There are two types of sparkling wine: "Riesling", which retains the fruity bouquet and the original flavour of the grape, and "Champagne" which is more like a traditional aperitif or dessert wine. Both types have the usual range of tastes, varying from the driest to the sweetest, with the same terms being used as those of Champagne. The law obliges the producer to specify on the label in which country the wine was first bottled. Thus a label which says *Französischer Schaumwein* indicates that it is a French sparkling wine, produced in France, while a label *Deutscher Schaumwein* signifies that the wine was prepared and bottled in Germany. However, the origin of the wine used might be German or foreign. The German equivalent for the French *vin mousseux gazéifié* is *mit Zusatz von Kohlensäure*, indicating that CO_2 has been injected. In order to avoid any misunderstandings, one should note that labels with the name *Beeren-Schaumwein* have nothing in common with labels such as *Trockenbeerenauslese* or *Beerenauslese*; "Beeren-Schaumwein" or "Obst-Schaumwein" simply means "sparkling wine made from currants", or "sparkling wine made from fruit". These are therefore not sparkling wines, but aerated fruit juices.

Most producers of German sparkling wines are in the central viticultural region of Hesse in the Rhineland or the Palatinate. The largest producer, Henkell, is at Wiesbaden. Some of the best and oldest producers are Söhnlein at Wiesbaden-Schierstein, Mattheus Müller (MM) at Eltville, Kupferberg at Mainz, Kessler at Esslingen, Burgeff at Hochheim, and Deinhard at Koblenz. Some German sparkling wines carry the name of their growths and a year. The production of sparkling wines has greatly increased in the last few years.

THE SPARKLING WINES OF THE SOVIET UNION

The Russians seem to have a partiality for sparkling wines: in 1973, they produced 17,818,380 gallons. The SOWJETSKOJE SCHAMPANSKOJE is produced by a second fermentation either in the bottle in *cuve close* or in double vats. If it is kept for three years before being marketed, the qualification "old" is added. This spark-

German sparkling wines are made from musts from Germany, or even from France.

ling wine, when made from red wines, is known as "Soviet Red Champagne". However, if it is made with red wines from Tzymlyansk, it is distinguished by the label ZYMLJANSKSJE. A wine which is artificially injected with carbonic acid gas is known as "aerated wine", and must be so described on the label. The Soviet sparkling wines offer the whole range of varieties, from *brut* to sweet wines with a 10 per cent to 10.5 per cent sugar content. The best Soviet Champagnes are probably KAFFIA in the Crimea, and that produced by Abraou Dursso in the Kouban valley.

THE SPARKLING WINES
OF THE UNITED STATES OF AMERICA

The United States produces various types of sparkling wines. There is the wine commonly known as Champagne: it is a light, sparkling wine whose second fermentation takes place in glass containers holding not more than one gallon (about 3.8 litres), and whose appearance and taste tends to resemble true Champagne as closely as possible. French Champagne producers have always fought against the use of the name of their province and of their product by the producers of American sparkling wines. A certain amount of control does, however, exist, since by Californian law the word "Californian" or "American" must appear on the label as well as a statement defining the vinification method used and the place of production.

There is also the "sparkling grape wine" which is made by the *cuve close* method. If this wine has a Champagne-like taste, it is then called "sparkling wine—Champagne type". "Crackling wine" is an effervescent wine, and "carbonated wine" is an aerated sparkling wine. The total United States production of sparkling wine is about 17,114,444 gallons.

There is not room in these few brief comments on American sparkling wines to permit a fair judgement of their quality. Here, as in many other regions, all the different varieties in all the various prices ranges may be found.

In California the best Champagne-type wines are produced from the *Pinot Noir* and *Pinot Chardonnay* grapes. The *Semillon, Sauvignon Blanc, White Riesling, Pinot Blanc* and *Folle Blanche* also give good results. The Californian Champagnes go through the same *dosage* process as do their French models and have the dry to sweet range, although a really dry Champagne is not often found in this country.

The American connoisseurs of true Champagne are quite numerous: in 1980, 7,095,480 bottles of Champagne were imported.

THE SPARKLING WINES OF OTHER COUNTRIES

Sparkling wine is called *spumante* in Italy, *espumoso* in Spain and *espumante* in Portugal. Italy has only a

Unlike the German "sekt", Asti Spumante benefits from a D.O.C. label; it is a very popular sparkling wine in Italy.

small variety of sparkling wines: ASTI SPUMANTE is very well known even outside of Italy's frontiers, but there are also its cousins BARBERA D'ASTI SPUMANTE, GRIGNOLINO D'ASTI SPUMANTE and MOSCATO D'ASTI SPUMANTE. ASTI SPUMANTE is made by the *méthode champenoise* from a muscat wine. It is a sweet wine but the bubbles prevent the sweetness from being disagreeable and if served very cold this drink is even refreshing. The sweetness is not produced by the addition of sugar or by overripening of the grapes but from the natural sweetness of the grape itself. In Lombardy, MOSCATO DI CASTEGGIO SPUMANTE is also drunk, and PROSECCO DI CONEGLIANO SPUMENTE in Venetia; both of these wines, however, are less well known than the ASTI.

Spain's centre of production of sparkling wines is San Sandurni de Noya, near Villafranca del Panadès. These wines are clear with a bouquet which savours of honey. Spanish wines are made quite often by the classic Champagne method and the phonetic equivalent, Xampan, often appears on the labels. One of the Catalonian Champagne-type wines once lost a High Court case in London and thenceforth Spanish sparkling wines were not allowed to be sold in England as Spanish Champagnes. The fact that the defendant firm was not one that used the traditional *méthode champenoise* did not help their case.

In Portugal, sparkling wines are made in the regions of Bairrada and Lamego, and are often named after the viticultural company which produced them.

Other countries, such as Argentina, Brazil, Israel, South Africa, Switzerland and Uruguay produce some sparkling wines by one or the other of the established methods. Throughout the world, at all latitudes, sparkling wine is a drink for festive occasions, synonymous with happiness, gaiety and joy.

TABLE OF COMPARATIVE FRENCH WINE QUALITIES
BY REGIONS AND YEARS, TAKING INTO ACCOUNT THE EVOLUTION OF THE WINES
compiled by La Compagnie des Courtiers-Gourmets Piqueurs de Vins de Paris

YEARS	Red Bordeaux	White Bordeaux	Red Burgundy	White Burgundy	Côtes du Rhône	Alsace	Pouilly-s./Loire Sancerre	Anjou Touraine
1928	★	••••	••••					
1929	••••	★	★					
1934	••••	•••	★					
1937	•••	★	•••					
1945	★	★	••••		••••			
1947	★	★	••••		••••			★
1949	★	••••	★		••••			••••
1952	•••	•••	•••		••••			•••
1953	••••	•••	•••					•••
1955	••••	••••	••••	•••	••••			••••
1959	•••	••••	★	•••	•••	★		★
1961	★	★	★	•••	•••	••••		•••
1962	••••	••••	•••	•••	•••	••		•••
1964	••••	•	••••	•••	•••	•••		
1966	★	•••	••••	•••	•••	••••		
1967	••••	★	•••	•••	••••	••••		••
1969	••	•	••••	••••	•••	•••		•••
1970	★	•••	•••	••••	••••	••••		•••
1971	••••	•••	••••	••••	•••	★		•••
1972	••	••	•••		••	•		••
1973	•••	••	•••	••••	•	••••	••••	••
1974	•••	•••	••	•••	•	••	•••	••
1975	★	••••		•••	••	•••	•••	•••
1976	••••	•••	••••	••••	•	★	••••	•••
1977	••	•••	••	••	•••	••	•••	••
1978	••••	•••	★	••••	★	•••	••••	••••
1979	••••	•••	•••	•••	•••	•••	•••	•••
1980	Uneven year. Late vintages. Already successes.							

• Medium year   •• Good year   ••• Very good year   •••• Great year   ★ Exceptional year

CHAMPAGNE
Vintages: vary according to brands; notable years at present, 1971 and 1973. Non-vintages (blends): vary according to brands, which are generally consistent.

These appreciations are on an average basis, the exception confirming the rule.

THE WAYS
OF WINE AND MAN

WINE AND HEALTH
A DOCTOR'S GUIDE

GÉRARD DEBUIGNE

Wine has for a very long time been considered as one of the basic elements of human nourishment. In fact, Olivier de Serres, the French agronomist, was only confirming an already widely held opinion when he wrote, in his famous *Théâtre de l'Agriculture* published in 1600: "After bread comes wine, the second nutriment given by the Creator to sustain life and the first to be famed for its excellence." Long before him, the famous words in Ecclesiastes (IX, 7), "Go thy way, eat thy bread with joy, and drink thy wine with a merry heart" proved that even a thousand years before the dawn of Christianity wine was held to be as essential an item of human sustenance as bread.

All this apart, water was actually considered to be unhealthy to drink during the seventeenth and eighteenth centuries. Sydenham, the English doctor who discovered laudanum, claimed that the poor people who drank water managed to remain in good health only because their organisms were adapted to wretched conditions. Buffon, the French naturalist, expressed a similar opinion when he declared: "Pure water is not sufficient to keep up the strength of working men." From time immemorial, man has sought more in his food than the mere satisfaction of a physical need. He has always looked also for a combination of physical and spiritual gratifications, a means to combat worry and fatigue and a mild and pleasant stimulant.

In addition to its hygienic and dietetic properties, wine is the only source of nourishment that ideally fulfils this inherent desire of the human species. No other earth-grown product occupies its singular place of honour; none other speaks more eloquently to our hearts, tastes, memories and dreams. Neither grain, which makes the allegorical "daily bread" a nourishing reality for millions, nor rice, which forms the staple diet of an entire continent, nor coffee, nor tea, both much-loved in some countries, can replace it.

This is why wine, whose history is inseparable from that of mankind and even civilization itself, will undoubtedly always retain its special, privileged place in our minds and on our tables.

THE PROPERTIES OF WINE

Wine's qualities are invaluable, innumerable, irreplaceable. It goes without saying, however, that in order to benefit from wine's wonderful virtues, the maximum daily quantities advocated by authorities on the subject, and confirmed by laboratory experiments, should not be exceeded.

Professor Trémolières provided a good guide during the last European Congress on alcoholism: "For healthy adults whose diet is sufficient and well-balanced, the organism can normally oxidise a maximum of one litre of wine in the case of men, and three quarters of a litre in the case of women. If these measures are exceeded, and if one of the above conditions is not met, as for example in cases of insufficient nourishment, the alcohol is oxidized by toxic processes, and thereby produces a pernicious effect." To which it may be added that, providing reasonable care is taken to distribute the daily intake over the two main meals, wine will not inebriate but contribute its tonic and beneficial properties to the diet of the consumer.

It is worth pointing out that the amount of wine consumed by the average, healthy individual usually falls quite naturally within the specified limits. Alcoholism, so long regarded as a deadly passion and a vice, is increasingly coming to be considered in medical pathology as an illness. The theory of the "alcoholic disease", championed by Jellinek, was introduced into French medical circles around 1956. According to this theory, alcoholism is a "physical compulsion complicated by a mental obsession", its victims being those who suffer from a particular kind of emotional disorder. Only specific types of people, therefore, become alcoholics and there is no reason whatever to stigmatize wine, nor to spoil the pleasure of worthy, decent folk who drink it in moderation by instilling in them a fear that they may become alcoholics.

It is moreover a surprising but accepted fact that the ravages of alcoholism are most marked in those unfortunate regions where no vines are grown. This is not to

442

say that hearty wine drinkers are exempt from the consequences of over-indulgence. But it is primarily those who, already suffering from various nervous or emotional derangements, habitually swallow aperitifs, cocktails, manufactured spirits or anything, good or bad, containing alcohol who are most prone to alcoholism and who have to be treated in the psychiatric wards of hospitals, and rarely those congenial and reasonable imbibers of good wine.

The Nutritional Value of Wine

Since wine is almost 90 per cent water, it is an old and gleeful joke that "any wine drinker is an unwitting drinker of water". Be that as it may, wine also contains many other valuable elements making it a real liquid food with incomparable qualities. But although the most advanced methods of quantitative analysis have succeeded in determining the various proportions of the different constituents of wine, they have yet to reveal the mysterious ingredient which gives wine its reputation of a symbolic and sacred sustenance. The sense of well-being and pleasant euphoria that pervades body and soul while downing a good wine can hardly be expressed in milligrams of one element or another.

We must therefore content ourselves with what information wine itself chooses to divulge as to its own properties and ingredients which, in any case, vary from one wine to another, depending on the kind of soil, the species of grape, the year of harvesting, the length of time the wine has been bottled and, above all, the care and attention it receives during the time it is growing to maturity.

Wine's Calorific Value

This depends on two factors: alcoholic strength and sugar content. Even ignoring all its other ingredients and assuming that wine is merely a dilution of alcohol in water, it would still be a food or, at the very least, a dietary supplement.

As the research carried out by Atwater in 1902 has proved, alcohol is immediately utilized by the body—unlike sugar, fats and amino acids—and it thereby supplements to a certain extent the other energizing foods. However, the work of Schaeffer, Le Breton and Dontcheff has shown that wine can only supply 50 per cent of the body's basic requirements, in other words 600 to 800 calories.

But it cannot be stressed enough that the ten cubic centimetres of alcohol contained in one litre of wine have no relation to the same quantity of alcohol absorbed neat. Wine is not merely and simply a solution of one per cent ethylic alcohol! Intimately blended with a multitude of other living elements, alcohol, an inert substance, enhances the entire complex of wine with its valuable qualities.

The number of calories contained in a litre of wine varies between 600 and 1,000, with an average of 600 to 700 in the case of red wine. Sweet, soft white wines of the Sauternes type with their high sugar content contain more calories than dry white wines. Naturally sweet wines and dessert wines, rich in both sugar and alcohol, contain the most calories of all. In countries enjoying a high standard of living, the calorie content of a wine may seem of trifling importance, and most people are more concerned with reducing an already excessive general intake. Nevertheless, where the source of this body fuel is wine, it certainly seems to possess quite remarkable powers to generate well-being, enthusiasm and intellectual activity.

Vitamins

Wine supplies the body with all the vitamins in the grape. Even on the basis of its wealth of vitamins, wine can be described without exaggeration as a "living drink".

Wine contains the following vitamins:

Vitamin C. This has well-known effects on general physical tone, physical fitness, resistance to cold and fatigue. Athletes need two to three times as much Vitamin C as persons with sedentary occupations.

Vitamin P (or C_2). In association with Vitamin C, this vitamin increases physical resistance and has a very definite effect in certain cases of debility with low blood pressure. Lavollay and Sevestre attribute wine's tonic effect to its Vitamin P content.

Vitamin B_2 or riboflavine. Considered by some to be of nutritive value, this vitamin is active in the metabolism of the glucides, proteins, irons, vitamins A, B_1, PP and the adrenocorticotrophic hormones.

Vitamin B_3 or PP. This is a powerful stimulant of the cell functions. Andross has demonstrated that productivity increased when substantial amounts of this vitamin were included in the diet of a group of workmen.

Mineral Salts and Trace Elements

Without certain minerals, the human system cannot survive. Sulphur, phosphorus, chlorine, sodium, potassium, magnesium, calcium and iron are all essential to life. The system can assimilate these substances only in the form of organic salts, in other words combined with vegetable or animal matter. It cannot assimilate them in their natural state or in the form of mineral salts, except for a few substances such as kitchen salt. In wine, the mineral salts are incorporated with other substances and can be assimilated readily. Although, fortunately, total deficiency in mineral salts is rare, relative deficiency is quite common and wine therefore constitutes a far from negligible source of these valuable substances.

BIOCHEMICAL EFFECTS OF WINE
ON THE SYSTEM

If only on account of the calories, vitamins and mineral salts which it supplies in a highly palatable and easily assimilated form, wine can be considered one of the most valuable foods. Yet these are only a few of the virtues which were proved by our ancestors' instinctive physical need, though it might not have been until the twentieth century that all the mechanisms at work were fully understood and scientifically explained.

Wine Aids Digestion

St. Paul needed no converting to this virtue. He exhorted Timothy: "Stop drinking only water. Take a little wine for your stomach's sake and for your frequent discomforts." Even at that time it was recognized that wine's natural acidity increased the secretions of saliva. Wine thus makes an excellent aperitif, the first few sips preparing the organs for digestion. Furthermore, it is the only good, natural and healthy aperitif which does not "whet the appetite the way that the wrong key opens a lock, by breaking it," as a famous doctor once wittily remarked.

The secretion of gastric juices is also stimulated and increased. Furthermore, wine also contains enzymes similar to those present in the digestive juices, thus facilitating the work of tired or deficient stomachs. Its tannin stimulates the fibres of the entire alimentary canal. The regular use of good wine also stimulates intestinal secretions and thus helps to combat the constipation with which so many people nowadays seem to be plagued.

But, first and foremost, wine has been found to greatly facilitate the digestion of proteins contained in meat, fish, oysters and cheese. Genevois even went so far as to say that it was the only drink which, because of its ionic acidity and low osmotic pressure, allowed proteins to be easily digested. With today's increased standard of living, the modern diet is particularly rich in proteins of animal origin, formerly luxuries in which only the well-to-do could regularly indulge. Wine, combining excellently with these proteins, achieves a perfect gastronomic harmony and subsequently facilitates their digestion. Thus the well-planned marriage of meats, fish, shellfish or cheese with an eligible wine is not only an epicurean refinement but a sensible and scientifically proven aid to healthy digestion.

Wine as an Antiseptic

The bactericidal power of wine has long been recognized. Even the Sumerians used balms and ointments with a wine base, and our forbears instinctively reached for wine to cleanse and asepticize wounds. The bactericidal action of wine is due not only to the alcohol it contains but also to its acids, tannin, sulphurous acid and ethers.

It has been proved that one cubic centimetre of white wine, mixed with one cubic centimetre of culture medium, kills 99 per cent of the colon bacilli and the bacilli of cholera and typhoid. So it is not surprising that armies were sometimes issued with wine during epidemics of dysentery, as we learn from the *Journal* written by a certain Percy during the Prussian campaign in 1807: "The dysentery is improving. The army is only slightly the worse for it now. Wine is being distributed to the troops: it is the best preventative."

Similarly, the custom of sprinkling oysters or other shellfish with white wine not only adds to their delectability but is a prudent health precaution into the bargain. The wine that children can be seen drinking in restaurants in Europe, albeit well diluted, also serves, at least in part, a hygienic purpose.

The Antitoxic Properties of Wine

Wine has proved an effective therapeutic agent in the prevention of infectious and feverish diseases and in certain toxic infections such as influenza. Despite the ever-widening range of modern medicines, a glass of good mulled wine is still a sovereign remedy for incipient 'flu' and one that it would be foolish to relegate to the store of "old wives' tales". The antitoxic action of wine has even prevented certain cases of alkaloid poisoning, such as sparteine and strychnine.

In the same way, marinading and cooking game in wine has shown itself to be a wise precaution. Obviously, wine is primarily used to tenderize rather tough meat and to bring out its flavour. But in the case of beasts or fowl whose bodies may have accumulated a considerable amount of toxins, due to fatigue, or whose wounds may be unclean, wine safeguards against possible food poisoning.

The Anti-Allergic Properties of Wine

These have been demonstrated by Weissenbach who advises crushing strawberries in red wine fifteen minutes before serving, to safeguard against the risk of an allergic reaction to which some people are prone.

WINE AND MODERN MAN

Naturally, wine is no longer the indispensable nutriment of those days when nourishment was very much less rich and varied than today. Nevertheless, is still plays a useful role and remains an ideal drink.

Not only does wine provide stimulating sensations to jaded palates, it also gives our frequently abused systems the necessary tonic to resist the stresses of

modern life. Wine meets a pressing contemporary need: to keep the mind alert and the body in top physical condition. The vitamins it contains happen to be those best suited to combat the fatigue and weariness of a world and age increasingly dominated by the rhythm of machines.

Tannin contributes still further to the bracing properties of wine. Red wines, richer in tannin, are more tonic than white and have a more marked stimulant effect. Red wine is therefore preferable to white when energy flags and the organism had need of a fillip. The habit of drinking a "stirrup-cup" before vaulting into the saddle, so popular in times past, proves the value of this tonic to mind and muscles, the cheering qualities of a stimulant so ideally suited to sustain the horseman on his tiring rides. As long as it is taken in moderate quantities, wine never produces depressing after-effects, the penalty of so many modern drugs.

But although it is an ideal tonic, wine is also the best and healthiest promoter of relaxed well-being. More than ever before, modern man needs "tranquillizers" to help him shoulder his cares, resolve the problems that beset him and cope with the discouraging aura of anxiety about him. Wine promotes optimism and *joie de vivre* and even produces a marked mental improvement in cases of anxiety.

Natural, harmless and nearly as old as the world itself, good wine in reasonable quantities is infinitely better than all the "pep pills" with their dangerous artificial happiness. The sense of well-being that comes from good food and wine naturally and spontaneously produces the state of relaxation with which modern man is so obsessed but which our ancestors had much less need to seek. Furthermore, this method calls for no tiresome procedures, no special equipment—all that is needed is a wine list!

Finally, the infectious euphoria created by good wine gives human relations a friendliness and gaiety which are often all too lacking in the modern world. In an age when worries, overwork and jangled irritation beset the world with strangers and enemies, a quiet glass of wine between friends helps to restore those forgotten qualities of comradeship and human warmth.

WINE AND THE SPORTSMAN

Sport = no alcohol. This is the unequivocal equation advocated by sportsmen and their trainers who believe in rigorous self-denial and who even go so far as to include wine in their uncompromising verdict. However, the latest studies on the subject, far from extolling the special diets formerly in fashion agree that the ideal diet for an athlete is quite simply the ideal, healthy and well-balanced diet of an ordinary man engaged in a strenuous physical occupation. Spirit-based or manufactured aperitifs and liqueurs, except for special occasions, should indeed be excluded from the athlete's menu and forbidden during training, but to condemn wine would be a sad exaggeration.

Wine, which Pasteur described as "the healthiest and most hygienic of drinks" has shown itself to be ideal for sportsmen, even more so than for those with sedentary occupations.

All drinks other than wine have various disadvantages. Fruit juices, especially those of citrus fruits, are not always well tolerated. Although pleasant enough to drink between meals, they hardly make good gastronomic partners with a well-cooked meal. Beer dulls the mind, burdens the stomach and produces unwelcome belching and flatulence. Cider can provoke gastric troubles and has an irritant, laxative effect on the

The Parisian Nicolas Larmessin (born 1640, died 1725) is primarily famous for his album entitled *Grotesques*, a collection of portraits of people clad in and bearing the attributes of their profession. This is the *Habit du Cabaretier* ("The inn-keeper's costume") and grotesque might be the best way to describe it in English, too.

445

intestine. Too much coffee or tea lead to insomnia and excitability, and athletes are already quite nervous enough. Milk, usually badly tolerated by most adults, is a food not a drink. Continual consumption of waters with a high mineral or soda content is not recommended for athletes. What else remains, save slightly aerated mineral water or plain tap water?

More than anyone else, the sportsman, dependent on top physical and mental condition to put out his best effort, needs wine, a valuable mixture which stimulates cell functions and whose beneficial and soothing properties can hardly be denied.

Particularly during training, and when the sport in question involves considerable muscular effort, the athlete is advised to adopt a diet very rich in proteins, such as meats, fish, eggs and cheese. Wine, it will be remembered, is a powerful aid to the digestion of these substances. Its vitamins help to counter muscular and nervous fatigue and keep the athlete in good shape.

The mineral salts contained in wine help to prevent deficiencies which may seriously upset the delicate balance of the athlete's physical form. Iron is an essential element in training, increasing the volume of blood and aiding in its aeration. Similarly, sulphur is needed to eliminate the toxins produced by fatigue from intensive training. Both sulphur and iron are found in wine.

Finally, the tonic and calming properties of wine are most beneficial to the general morale of the athlete, whose strict discipline, often fanatically intensive training and obsession with optimum performances often result in a delicate and even precarious mental state. In these conditions, it is in the athlete's interest to drink a reasonable amount of wine. When he is exerting considerable muscular effort, his pulmonary activity speeds up and he can eliminate alcohol more easily than persons leading a sedentary life.

In fact, authorities on sport are by no means against a reasonable consumption of good wine. Doctor Mathieu, medical adviser to Olympic teams, decalres: "For a normal subject, if the quantity of wine does not exceed half a litre a meal, or one litre a day, the alcohol is entirely burned up by the organism and wine then becomes an excellent nutritional drink." Boigey, whose work on exercise as a form of therapy is now universally recognized, considers that "natural wine is the most commendable of alcoholic drinks. It contains a wonderful range of useful and well-balanced substances which nothing else can replace."

Doctor Encausse, medical officer of the High Commission for Youth and Sport in France, advocates that consumption of wine should be limited to three-quarters of a litre per day for a healthy adult weighing approximately 150 pounds, wisely concluding that the medical profession should recommend temperance rather than abstinence.

Nevertheless, allowing for a certain flexibility of interpretation, not all wines can be recommended for athletic activities. This applies to robust or fortified wines, rich in bouquet and highly coloured. Burgundies and wines from the Côtes du Rhône should, alas, be reserved for Sundays and holidays and forgotten during training. The same applies to white wine which has the unfortunate reputation, especially among mountain guides, of going straight to the legs. However, the athlete still has an entire range of light, attractive red and rosé wines to choose from. He needs no commiseration.

WINE AND YOUTH

Obviously, nobody would think of giving a young child undiluted wine. However, in the traditional Italian family, children do drink very limited quantities of wine at the table, wine being considered as an integral part of the Italian meal. And it is interesting to note that Italy has a lower rate of alcoholism *per capita*, for example, than the United States.

In France, too, well-diluted wine is served with school meals and this is, in fact, far healthier than the fizzy drinks so liberally dispensed to their offspring by English and American parents.

During adolescence, a small quantity of good, undiluted wine, drunk with meals, can do no harm. It should be remembered that many tonics recommended for "the awkward age" have a wine base, yet nobody worries about the dangers of alcoholism in prescribing them. A healthy respect for wine, moderation in its use and discernment for its quality, instilled at an early age, will do much to prevent livers and mental processes from being damaged in later life by the imbibing of dubious or indifferent mixed drinks based on spirits.

WINE AND THE ELDERLY

The virtues of wine for older people are well known. The Médoc, famous as a wineproducing and winedrinking region, is justly proud of its record for the longevity of its inhabitants.

Diminishing digestive secretions often result in old people having poor appetites. Lack of nourishment and vitamin deficiency may result, aggravated by additional factors such as ill-fitting dentures, sometimes mistaken dietary fads or, quite simply, a restricted budget. Good wine, being easily assimilated and pleasant to drink, stimulates old people's appetites and facilitates digestion. Its stimulant and tonic properties are valuable at an age when there is increasing debility. Especially in the case of dessert wines or naturally sweet wines, it also contributes valuable calories and comforting warmth to the system. Attention should also be drawn to the fact that there are many good but quite modestly priced wines. Despite all the care taken in its production, wine is still fairly reasonable in price when compared to the other alcoholic drinks on the market.

WINE AND ILLNESS

Old Hippocrates, the Father of Medecine, who lived from 460 to 377 B. C., taught that "wine is wonderfully suitable for man if, in sickness as in health, it is administered in proper and fair measure".

As long ago as the Carolingian era, the ordinary diet that the sick and elderly received in the monasteries included strengthening and savoury wine soups. In later history, Joan of Arc was also said to be very partial to them.

The bactericidal and antitoxic properties of wine that make it an excellent agent in the prevention of infection have already been mentioned. And Nature, generously providing man with the remedies for the ills she herself inflicts, has foreseen all eventualities by providing different wines for different ailments.

Thus naturally sweet or dessert wines, those delicacies of the vine, are particularly recommended for convalescents, the emaciated and those suffering from debility. On the other hand, diabetics should on no account be given these wines because their diet does not permit food with a high sugar content.

Light, dry white wines, pleasantly sharp and with their low sugar and alcohol content, stimulate the appetite and digestive processes. They are eminently suitable for dyspeptic subjects. They are also recommended in cases of obesity, their calorific value being very modest and their diuretic properties well known: the white wines of Savoy sustain the morale of those heroes who submit to the cure at Bride-les-Bains.

Sparkling wines are recommended for some kinds of dyspepsia, their carbonic acid being an effective remedy for vomiting. Champagne is the prerogative of convalescents, raising the morale as well as helping the system to recover. It is a wonderful "steadier" after a shock and is even useful in cases of low blood pressure.

Wines light in body and alcoholic strength, whatever their colour, are suitable for all invalids and should be chosen for everyday use. Full-bodied wines with rich bouquets should be kept in the cellar to celebrate the time of recovery.

The last word on the subject could very well be left to Sir Alexander Fleming, who once so wisely remarked: "Penicillin may cure human beings, but it is wine that makes them happy."

"And Noah began to be an husbandman, and he planted a vineyard: and he drank of the wine, and was drunken... and Noah lived after the flood three hundred and fifty years. And all the days of Noah were nine hundred and fifty years..." So the wine, other than leading to Canaan's curse, seems to have had no lasting ill effects on the health of the world's first winegrower.

DOCTOR'S ORDERS

Wines that may be drunk— and those that may not be—
by persons suffering from certain bodily disorders:

Ailment	Wines Permitted	Wines Prohibited
Hyperchlorhydria (excess hydrochloric acid in the gastric juices)	Light red wines in small quantities.	Full-bodied red wines, very dry white wines, young and acid wines (beware of white and rosé wines in general), dessert wines.
Hypochlorhydria (inadequate secretion of hydrochloric acid in the stomach)	Light red wines or slightly acid dry white wines of low alcoholic content, young wines, Muscadet, Crépy, Fendant, Champagne, Beaujolais.	Wines of high alcoholic strength, dessert wines.
Various gastric disorders	Light red wines in small quantities, old Médoc.	White and rosé wines, sparkling and semi-sparkling wines.
Ulcers	No wine.	All wines.
Between attacks	No limitation.	None.
Intestinal troubles	All red wines when not acute.	White wines, sparkling wines and those of high alcoholic content, Burgundy, Côtes-du-Rhône. Never drink iced wines.
Constipation	All light wines, white, red or rosé.	Wines of high alcoholic strength, Burgundies, Côtes-du-Rhône.
Serious hepatic deficiencies (alcoholism, precirrhosis, cirrhosis resulting from hepatitis and jaundice)	No alcoholic drinks whatever, not even diluted wine.	
Vesicular lithiasis (biliary dyskinesia, abdominal migraine)	Red or white wine diluted with water (no more than ¼ litre per day).	Neat wine, dessert wines.
Hypercholesterolemy (excess cholesterol) and arteriosclerosis	All wines but in limited quantities.	
Cardiac deficiency	All wines allowed: white, red, rosé dry or sweet.	Avoid very full-bodied wines of high alcoholic strength.
Hepatobiliary disease (biliary lithiasis, family cholemia)	Light wine, particularly red, in small quantities or preferably diluted with water, very little white wine.	Full-bodied, fortified wines rich in mineral extracts, dessert wines, Champagne and sparkling wines, iced wines.
High blood pressure (salt-free and soda-free diets)	Use wine and spirits for flavouring in cooking.	Limit the quantity in cases of inadequate blood circulation.
Renal deficiency (acute nephritis and Bright's disease)	All wines but in small quantities.	
Bladder stones	White, red and rosé wines, dry or sweet.	Avoid Bordeaux rich in mineral extracts, Burgundies and full-bodied wines.

Nutritional disorders (arthritis, gout, uric lithiasis, excess of uric acid in the blood, isolated albuminuria)	Young or old red Bordeaux in limited quantities, very little light white wine, local wines of low alcoholic strength.	Burgundies, Côtes-du-Rhône, Saint-Emilion, Champagnes and sparkling wines, ports, Madeira, dessert wines, all full-bodied, highly coloured, noble wines.
Obesity (crash diet)	No wine.	All wines are forbidden, the food intake being insufficient and unbalanced, the alcohol will be oxidized in the body by toxic processes. In addition, wine would add undesirable extra calories.
Obesity (continuous treatment)	Very dry white wines, young and of low alcohol content, Muscadet, Savoy and Alsace wines, light Bordeaux, local red and rosé wines. $\frac{1}{4}$ to $\frac{1}{2}$ litre per day at the maximum. Remember that the calories contained in wine should be counted in the daily calorie allowance.	Sweet white wines, full-bodied and strong wines, naturally sweet and dessert wines.
Diabetes	Very dry white wine, extra-dry Champagne, red wines of low alcohol content.	Liqueur-like white wines, white Bordeaux, Vouvray, wines of high alcoholic content, Burgundy, Saint-Emilion, dessert wines, naturally sweet wines and fortified French and other wines (muscat, port, Malaga, Madeira and Samos).
Dermatitis	Dry, young and light wines, local red and rosé wines of low alcoholic content.	Full-bodied wines of high alcoholic content, sweet white wines, naturally sweet and liqueur wines.
Emaciation	Sweet white wines, wines made from grapes with "noble rot", dessert wines, naturally sweet and liqueur wines. Médoc, generous Burgundy, Côtes-du-Rhône, old Cahors; a little at frequent intervals through the day, drunk with meals.	Drink as little as possible while eating. Attractive, light wines should thus be avoided.
Convalescence	Champagne, sweet white wines, wines made from grapes with "noble rot", Médoc, old red Burgundy, high-class white Burgundy.	
Low blood pressure	Champagne, full-bodied and aromatic red wines, high-class white wines from Burgundy.	
Nervous breakdown	Champagne, red wines rich in tannin, Bourgueil, Madiran, old Médoc.	Wines with high alcoholic content. Avoid white wines.
Pregnancy	Dry white wines, red Bordeaux (particularly Médoc), Champagne and sparkling wines.	Absolutely no strong wines whatever, particularly fortified wines such as sherry and vermouth.

Should children drink wine?

It is certainly not advisable to give children alcoholic drinks. As far as wines are concerned, heavy or fortified wines should be particularly avoided. At the end of the meal, children may safely be given a little young or light wine, diluted with four times its volume of water, the quantity of wine depending on the child's age. As a rough guide, children between 5 and 7 years could be given a quarter to half a wine-glassful, those between 7 and 10 half a glassful, 10 to 12 year olds two-thirds to three-quarters of a glass, while from the age of 13 onwards a child can quite safely be given a full glass of wine.

These two venerable bottles are witnesses to an age that has practically passed, for it is increasingly rare nowadays that people have cellars that allow them to keep wine for more than ten to fifteen years.

450

TASTING WINE

AND STOCKING YOUR OWN CELLAR

BERNARD GRENOUILLEAU

Without some kind of basic plan and a few tips from the experts it is difficult to envisage stocking up a cellar, however humble the outlay may be. Beginners should not let themselves be daunted by the prospect for, although in terms of commercial investment the buying price will not grow very quickly, the pleasure of drinking a wine which has been bought and nurtured until it is ready and fully matured is beyond price.

Despite the work of oenologists and the studies of renowned scientists on the inherent properties of wines, particularly great wines, and notwithstanding the results of intensive research by eminent biologists and even mathematicians, wine still retains a good part of its mystery and wine-tasting has not yet been elevated to the level of a science or even a technique. It is still essentially an art.

Nonetheless, the professional wine-taster is guided by certain established and accepted rules and codes. He is ethically bound to subdue his own personal tastes and preferences and endeavour to be as objective as is humanly possible, for his is the duty of pronouncing judgements which could have far-reaching consequences, and for which he will be held personally and professionally responsible. Such strict measures of quality and criticism are the only means by which a norm or standard can be made acceptable to producers and tasters alike.

All the considerations taken into account by the professional, exaggerated as they may appear to the uninitiated, are distilled here into simple, practical hints. The professional aids to wine selection are interesting to know but not absolutely necessary to someone who merely wishes to discover a good wine to his liking. This chapter only aims to guide the amateur through the maze of intricate but infinitely evocative and pleasurable paths that lead to familiarity with wine. As Boileau, Provost of Paris in the thirteenth century,

observed, "He who knows not how to drink knows nothing."

TOUCH AND HEARING

It has been argued that the effects of touch and hearing are due more to imagination than anything else, although the pleasant feeling of a fine crystal glass or a silver goblet held between the fingers, and the sound of its delicate ring in the half-light of an echoing cellar, undoubtedly enhance the drinker's pleasure. Actually, touch does in fact play a very real part in the appreciation of wine. It is neither pretentious nor exaggerated to talk of "tactile tasting" in describing the sensations perceived by the various parts of the mouth which are capable of judging the wine's consistency, its fluidity or viscosity, both valuable clues to quality described as the "architectural relief of wine". And as a certain Monsieur Orizet, well known for his appreciation of the elixirs of the grape and of his own eloquence, once remarked "To what else but our sensations of touch can we attribute our reactions when we describe a wine as harsh, round, supple, tender, thin or velvety?" In a more modest way, hearing also contributes to determining the quality of wine, if only in detecting latent fermentation by holding the glass up to the ear.

SIGHT TEST

The first gesture the wine-taster makes is to raise his filled glass to the light of day. This inspection yields valuable insight into the quality of the wine.

White wine, which should be bottled young and not have been exposed to coloration from a prolonged sojourn in wood, should appear clear and gleam with a whiteness tinted slightly green. There are exceptions to the rule, of course, such as the yellow wines from Arbois and the pale amber of Sauternes. It is also

The tastevin, in silver or silver plated, is the essential tool of the wine taster. Although the eighteenth-century examples shown here have been chosen from among the most elaborate and decorative, it should not be assumed that the *tate-vin*, as it is also known in France, is a thing of the distant past; on the contrary, it is still very much in use today by wine connoisseurs and has lent its name to the famous *Confrérie des Chevaliers du Tastevin* of Burgundy, that noble organization that has devoted so much time and effort towards maintaining the high standards of Burgundy wine. Some of the more modern tastevins have two series of ridges, of different heights, which help a comprehensive examination of the wine.

recognized that all the great white wines assume a delicate golden hue over the years. As far as young wines are concerned, an indefinite or murky colour always denotes the presence of some disease or defect while a yellowish tint betrays oxidization, resulting in a sweet, pervasive flavour which only very few people consider as a virtue. But the taster should not attach too much importance to clarity alone: a non-filtered wine can still be of excellent quality.

Sight as well as hearing can detect the tiny gas bubbles which, if they cloud the wine to any appreciable extent, are probably due to a second fermentation. On the other hand, there are some naturally slightly sparkling wines, known as such, whose mild effervescence does not affect their clarity. Many Swiss white wines have this slight effervescence, often depending on how long they have been bottled, as do some of the wines from France and neighbouring countries. Agreeable though it may be, this sparkle can sometimes conceal a certain mediocrity. In the case of red wines, it is rarer and less highly esteemed, although it certainly gives some wines, such as the delicious Valpolicella, a very special charm.

As far as rosé is concerned, the appearance of the wine is very important. From the rose-pink Tavel to the pale red of Côtes de Toul, the colour range is infinite, the more so because with the growing fashion for this wine, many vineyards are now beginning to produce rosé. It should not be too pale in colour as this is both unattractive and often indicates dubious production methods.

None of these observations applies to very new wines which are naturally clouded by a large quantity of lees. Even at this stage, however, a great deal can be learned by visual examination. Moreover, any healthy wine will clear rapidly if allowed to do so.

As far as red wines are concerned, visual inspection is very important and provides valuable hints to quality, age and even origin. The depth of colour, dependent on the species of grape and the length of time the grapes were left to ferment, decreases with time. But whether it be muted, as in the case of Beaujolais, or deep ruby as in Châteauneuf-du-Pape, or even richer in colour for a young Bordeaux, the colour should be pure and true. A good bright red, tending towards cherry-red, usually denotes good quality. Tints of purplish blue, on the other hand, can be a sign of hybrid or mixed wine. The "robe" of a red wine, to use the expert's term for colour, is of the greatest significance. Visual examination also enables the trained eye to detect various diseases, such as casse, and even to differentiate between the various kinds of the disease—brown, blue, ferrous and so on. An experienced taster will be able to diagnose the grease disease, which makes wine oily and ropy, or the *tourne* which betrays its presence by silky ripples when the liquid is agitated. Especially in the case of red wines, a sight test also gives a good indication of whether or not a wine is mature or on the decline.

Lifting his tastevin, the wine taster prepares to pass judgement. Many of the world's leading wine connoisseurs make a point of always carrying their own tastevin to a tasting, since even though the glasses may be washed with the utmost care, there is always the danger of a taste of detergent remaining.

A GOOD NOSE

"A good nose for wine" should not always be interpreted as a derogatory expression. One of the classic gestures of the wine-taster is to swirl the wine around the glass before raising it to his nostrils. There is good reason for this ritual. The wine, gently swirling, spreads a thin coating of liquid over the upper walls of the glass so that a greater surface of the wine is exposed to the air, resulting in maximum evaporation of the odoriferous substances. This procedure is of paramount importance for, as everyone knows, a wine's "bouquet" determines its character.

At this stage, great powers of discernment and a good memory are required by the taster to recall the characteristics of all the wines he has ever tasted before and all the aromas that have ever been encountered by his nasal passages. It is by smell that he can recognize native tangs and the approximate region of the vineyard, the aroma being closely linked to the type of grape planted in a specific soil.

The primary aroma of a must before aromatic fermentation is essentially a product of the type of grape: it is particularly distinctive, for instance, in the juice from

453

muscat grapes. After fermentation is complete, good new wines exude a multitude of scents constituting the secondary aromas, some flowery, some fruity. These fragrances of iris, violet, rose, lime, black-currant, apple, cherry, strawberry and raspberry have led to the designation of new wines as "fruity". Subsequently, through the slow and mysterious alchemy that nature brings to bear, first in the casks and later in the bottle, the wine gradually becomes transformed, the primary and secondary perfumes dwindling, becoming less identifiable, and mingling at last into the final "bouquet", more discreetly floral in character and exuding a whole new range of aromas whose synthesis enables the connoisseur to recognize the wine, its origin and its year. In this final bouquet, which lingers on until the wine begins to deteriorate, the wine-lover will recall many familiar odours such as coffee, Russian leather, amber, truffles and even fowl droppings, as described by vinegrowers of the Médoc.

It is sometimes as well to reserve judgement on those wines which seem to flatter the palate at the first sip but which may, like new-found friends, reveal a lack of sincerity on deeper acquaintance. Most of the great wines only slowly and gradually divulge their true characters as the bottle empties, which explains why producers of red Graves used to declare that their wines should only be judged after the third glass. Although perhaps exaggerated, this sentiment was the sincere distillation of long years of experience.

THE TASTE

Tasting is actually the last and most important stage in judging a wine. The most logical one of all, indeed, since wine is intended to be consumed. After the

One of the more purposeful of the splendid wine taps in the Musée des arts et traditions populaires, Paris, photographic archives.

454

wine-taster has examined the wine and explored its aromas, he sips and rolls the wine around his mouth.

Strictly speaking, the tongue plays the leading rôle in tasting, but the tongue can only distinguish between the four basic tastes, namely acidity, bitterness, saltiness and sweetness, all other nuances of tastes being but variations of these primary four. Schools of wine-tasting test their trainees' natural aptitudes by presenting them with these four basic tastes.

Bitterness is detected at the back of the tongue; saltiness and sweetness by the tongue's tip and sides. Acidity is recognized by the centre and the sides of the tongue. Simultaneously, fragrance and the subtleties of flavour are discerned by the olfactory cells and swell the harmonic symphony of sensations experienced by the taster who should, by now, be ready to pronounce judgement. If he is a well-trained expert, he will be able to determine the alcoholic strength of the wine, define the amount of reducing sugars, the total acidity and the volatile acidity, if this is present to any marked degree, with only a small margin of error. He should be able to express his opinion as to the wine's quality although subjective factors will inevitably colour his judgement, however objective he may strive to be.

Many are the tales extolling the extraordinary tasting powers of certain palates. Paul Mounet, member of the Comédie-Française, brother of Mounet-Sully and a native of Bergerac, the Dordogne town famed for its wine and truffles, was said to be capable of telling the age and vineyard of any great wine even when blind-folded. It is a pity to debunk such stories but this one is scarcely credible. The worthy gentleman may well have successfully performed such a feat once, or even on several occasions, but the wines in question were very likely those of a distinctive type and ones with which Mounet was already reasonably familiar. Furthermore, probably only one or two wines were submitted to him at any one time, thus husbanding the sensitivity of his palate.

Correct and unerring recognition of the origin and year of a wine is really only possible on a local or, at the most, a regional scale by an inhabitant of the region. Obviously a wineproducer in Beaujolais, accustomed to sampling all the different local wines each season is able to recognize wines from the various vineyards in his area and even to distinguish between those of individual producers which, although made from the same type of grape, can differ to a considerable extent. Although identification of new wines is relatively simple, the process becomes very much more difficult in the case of fully matured ones.

In any case, as a certain Monsieur de la Palice once so rightly remarked, a wine must be tasted to be known. And who can possibly have tasted every wine? Hence the necessity for the professional taster to specialize in only various types of wines.

PRACTICAL ADVICE

A few words are in order concerning the physical and material circumstances surrounding the ritual of tasting. It has been established beyond doubt that the taster's state of health, the time of day and even the general ambiance will all affect his reactions. His state of health is particularly important and even so slight an indisposition as a cold can seriously impair the judgement. In my early days, I remember that I would often seek the advice of an old wine merchant whose sureness of palate I had always admired. After several years it seemed to me that the old man's judgements were less accurate, until one day we found ourselves in complete contradiction on certain points. Extremely awed by the old gentleman and not daring to contradict him outright, I solicited the opinions of his acquaintances and learned that for some time he had had diabetes, undoubtedly the cause of his failing acumen.

The best time for tasting is usually at the end of the morning, just before the midday meal, when most people begin to feel the first stirrings of appetite. The mental state as well as the general surroundings are of great importance. Some interesting experiments have been made on the effects of external influences such as light, temperature and even ambient noise and it has been found that the same taster can experience different reactions depending on the colour of the light, the temperature of the room and whether tasting took place in silence or to the accompaniment of music.

As far as the amateur is concerned, the essential requirement for serious tasting is total concentration and any noise should be discouraged. Tasting should take place in daylight or, if this is not possible, the light should be white and non-fluorescent. In a cellar, the clarity and brilliance of the wine is best judged by candlelight. If the wine-lower is seriously interested in determining the wine's quality for future reference, he should abstain from eating all those tempting titbits such as cheese, nuts and canapés which are habitually offered round on such occasions. The least of all evils is a small piece of dry bread.

The importance of the type of glass cannot be over-estimated. It should preferably be of crystal with a very fine rim, barrel-shaped or in the form of a chalice. The washing of the glasses is a very important factor and one that gives rise to many difficulties. The increasing habit of putting everything into dishwashing machines which use detergents can result in a pervasive taste clinging to the glass which can fundamentally affect the taste of the wine. Certain tasters insist on their glasses being rinsed in distilled water while professionals always carry their own silver tasting cup, although this is definitely less acceptable than a fine crystal glass, especially for white wines.

Wine should not be tasted in an over-heated or a very cold room. The ideal temperature is between 20° and 22° centigrade (around 68° to 70°F.). Naturally, any manufactured or natural perfumes must be avoided and even vases of flowers should be abandoned on the day of the tasting. A strongly flavoured toothpaste or tobacco smoke can be ruinous.

Tasting may be a complicated art but it is also much more pleasant and rewarding than is generally thought. As Paul Claudel, French diplomat and writer, so clo quently proclaimed, "...wine is the professor of taste, the liberator of the spirit, and the light of intelligence..."

USEFUL TERMS FOR DESCRIBING WINE

	Qualities	Defects
General Character	Robust, well-built, rich, full, fleshy, velvety, clean, well-knit, dainty, rugged.	Thin, harsh, ill-balanced, acid, sour, austere, short, mediocre.
Colour	Sumptuous, ruby, amber-coloured, clear, lively, brilliant.	Faded, cloudy, over-strong.
Flavour and Strength	Lively, sinuous, noble, massive, full, heady, stout, robust.	Flabby, flat, light, cold.
Sugar Content	Dry, sweet, mellow, liqueurish.	Ill-balanced, flat, raw, rugged, insipid.
Bouquet	Fruity, fine, flowery, scented.	Short, dull, corked, fading.

GLOSSARY OF WINE-TASTING TERMS

Acid	excessively sharp taste	*Harsh*	rough, astringent, catches the tongue
Aromatic	smooth, subtle and pleasant aroma, usually "grapey"	*Heady*	fiery and aromatic, high alcohol content
Astringent	excessive tannin, harsh on the palate	*Heavy*	unctuous and full-bodied, containing much "extract"
Attractive	light, fresh, easy to drink	*Light*	pale in colour, moderate strength, well-balanced
Austere	under-developed; often applicable to bouquet of a fine wine expected to develop	*Lively*	vigorous, acid, pleasantly pungent effect on nose and palate
Bitter	flavour sometimes met in the aftertaste; usually a sign of ill health in the wine	*Long*	descriptive of a great wine, well-sustained flavour and aroma
Body	the weight of a wine in the mouth	*Madérisé*	having acquired the yellowish-brown tint and smoky, burnt taste of Madeira, due to heat and oxygen
Bouquet	scent or smell of good wine; often characteristic		
Clean	fresh, unalloyed taste	*Massive*	full-bodied, powerful, spirited, rich
Complete	well-built and balanced, fragant and agreeable	*Mellow*	soft and smooth, mature
Corked	tasting of cork, unpleasantly musty	*Noble*	with the distinctive characteristics of its origin
Dainty	fresh and fruity	*Nose*	term applied to a wine with a fine bouquet
Delicate	of good quality; just short of distinguished	*Ordinary*	undistinguished, of indefinite origin
Distinguished	of the highest quality in all respects	*Perfumed*	powerfully scented
Dumb	under-developed as yet	*Rich*	silky, smooth, well rounded
Fading	deteriorating in quality but still drinkable	*Robust*	rich, full, good consistency and alcoholic strength
Fiery	goes to the head quickly, often a sign of too much alcohol for true balance	*Round*	full-bodied, well balanced and mellow
Fine	elegant, distinguished, with a delicate bouquet	*Sharp*	slightly over acid with a tartness that stings the palate
Firm	rather hard and pungent but well-built	*Short*	ephemeral taste, lacking in persistence
Flabby	unattractive, lacking in body and natural acidity	*Sinuous*	lively, fresh, vigorous, promising to mature well
Flat	dull, lifeless, insipid flavour	*Sound*	a healthy wine with good lasting qualities
Fleshy	full-bodied, rich with good general consistency	*Sweet*	very sugary, full, noticeable glycerine quality but pleasant in taste
Fresh	having the fruitiness and qualities of young wine	*Thin*	lacking in body and strength (usually wines from poor years)
Fruity	mellow, fragrant; fleshy quality derived from, but not generally tasting of, ripe grapes	*Unbalanced*	lack of harmony between physical constituents and aesthetic elements
Full	rich, fleshy, well-knit with a clean taste	*Velvety*	fine, full, silky and particularly soft in texture
Generous	strong, robust, invigorating, full of flavour	*Vinous*	full-bodied, good alcoholic strength, plenty of grip, fruit and strength of character
Goût de terroir	a characteristic earthy taste of wine from specific vineyards	*Well-knit*	balanced, robust and harmonious in all respects
Green	young, sharp and acid (not vinegary)	*Young*	raw, harsh and under-developed (not a fault)
Hard	excessive tannin, lacking in smoothness and fruit		

YOUR OWN CELLAR

The first essentials for a good wine cellar are constant temperature, darkness and adequate ventilation. The temperature should be about 11°C., or 52°F. The cellar should be neither too dry nor too humid; ideally it should be cut out of rock or vaulted in mortared stone and always facing north. In certain wineproducing regions, as elsewhere, houses are naturally built with underground cellars. These days, however, in the provinces as well as in metropolitan areas, those who have a good, large cellar under the house can consider themselves as very fortunate.

If the cellar already meets these basic requirements, all that remains is to equip and arrange it to the best possible advantage. If, on the other hand, it is over-dry or over-humid, these disadvantages can be partly remedied by modern materials. An effective and traditional touch is achieved by spreading river-bed sand over the floor and watering it when the weather becomes too hot. If the cellar is equipped with air-shafts or other means of ventilation these should always be kept closed during periods of extreme cold or heat. Condensation should be guarded against as variations in temperature can result in streaming walls and dripping ceilings. Any cellar should be as free as possible from vibrations, something not always easy to achieve for those who live in the city.

Naturally, the cellar must be clean, tidy and well kept and perishables should be prohibited. This can be a delicate problem when the housewife sees this attractive, clean, cool place which is so ideal for storing things. Nevertheless, no fruit or vegetables which might decay should be allowed in the cellar, nor any old clothes, papers and the like as, with time, they can give off a musty smell which is likely eventually to permeate and spoil the wine.

THE APARTMENT CELLAR

From the traditional interpretation of the word, a cellar in an apartment seems a paradox. Yet with a reasonable amount of skill and imagination, what could be called an "apartment cellar" can be easily arranged. Even in a smallish flat, a closet or wall cupboard can serve, providing this is sufficiently far away from the kitchen or a heat source of any kind. If needs be, one can use the recess of a blocked-up-door. Ventilation is necessary but this is quite simply achieved with wire mesh at the top and bottom and a lining of fibre glass, necessary for good thermal insulation. Obviously a small cellar of the kind in question cannot contain a large stock of wine, but it should easily hold between fifty and a hundred bottles. If these are choice wines, that is a fair number and also represents a substantial cash investment.

Whatever the size, shape or location of the cellar, once it is ready it is just a matter of filling it. Racks for bottles can be of wood, cement, brick or iron, depending on individual tastes and means. If small barrels of wine are to be stored, then stands of wood, stone or cement must be installed.

CHOOSING WINE

Not surprisingly, the most difficult part of setting up a private cellar is knowing what wine to buy and this, precisely, is the most difficult advice to give. It depends primarily on how much money is available, but also, of course, on personal tastes and preferences and whether or not a wineproducing region is near at hand. In this chapter, some general guidelines will be given as to how cost, personal preference and availability may best be combined.

For private individuals, buying in barrels is recommended only for local wines. For those fortunate enough to have access to such wines, it is often a very good idea to buy a barrel, or even a hogshead, depending on the size of the family and the amount of entertaining that is done. Before ordering wine in barrel, it is most important to find out whether it is ready for bottling or if it requires special attention beforehand. Such a wine will probably be a standard type and the attention needed very simple and straightforward. The most important thing is for the wine to be allowed time to settle. If it has not previously been treated, it is perhaps even advisable to clarify it. There is no need for professional filtering equipment or procedures. The old method of clarifying with white of egg is perfectly adequate and is still practised by reputable wineries producing high-class wines. For a cask containing approximately 50 gallons, two or three egg whites are whisked with a pinch of coarse salt, using an earthenware—but never a metal—bowl. The mixture is then poured into the cask through the bung-hole in the top, stirred with a special whisk or a clean stick and left to settle for a few days. The albumin draws all impurities down to the bottom of the cask. If it is a sound and well-constituted wine, it can be bottled several days later, after ensuring that the tap is placed high enough off the bottom of the barrel so that only perfectly clear wine pours out. If it is considered preferable to siphon the wine out with a rubber tube, a stick should be attached whose end projects about an inch below the end of the tube, so that the tube will not touch the bottom.

If the wine is stored in the cask for any length of time, the cask should be lying down on its stand with the bung on the top; otherwise, when the level of the wine drops, it will be necessary to ullage it frequently to ensure a

good wine when bottled. Normally, the cask is not kept in this way until the wine is at least a year old. Should ullage prove absolutely necessary, the traditional method can be used. This consists of putting enough carefully washed and dried pebbles into the liquid to bring the surface of the wine flush with the bung-hole. Obviously, if the wine is very young it must be racked periodically to draw off the clear wine from the lees, but this requires special kinds of vessels. It should be borne in mind that casks are very difficult to keep in good condition. An empty cask quickly spoils and filling it later can be disastrous.

Bottles should be very carefully washed so that not the slightest trace of smell can be transferred to the wine. They must be drained thoroughly on a proper rack, protected from dust. As for corks it is a mistake to economise, particularly in the case of wines which will be kept for a considerable time. For ordinary wines to be drunk in the course of the year, or the following one at the latest, conical corks are available which can be inserted by hand. However, whether conical or any other shape, they must be of good quality. Nothing is more disagreeable than to find that a good wine has been spoilt by a bad cork. Corks should be dipped in boiling water, seasoned in wine or, better still, moistened with a neutral alcohol of the brandy spirit type.

Once the bottles are filled and corked it only remains to lay them carefully in their racks. In some countries, when the bottles are to be kept for a long time, they are buried in sand, temperamental white wines being buried standing up.

As for sealing the wine, it is better to use sealing wax rather than the familiar metal foil for bottles which are to be stored for a long time. Apart from its efficiency, this lends the bottle a good seal, if the pun may be excused, with a touch of old-fashioned charm and craftsmanship. The wax is melted with a spoonful of oil in any kind of small, deep pot, over a gentle heat just sufficient to keep the sealing wax liquid. The necks of the bottles should first be carefully wiped free of any moisture to prevent cracking, then dipped into the wax and removed with a quick turn.

For those people who insist on foil caps, these can actually be applied without a machine, but there is a knack to it. A piece of string should be attached to a hook or some point on the wall, the other end being held in one hand. The capsule is firmly pressed on to the neck of the bottle and the string is then looped round it. The string is pulled as tight as possible and the neck of the bottle twirled up and down the entire length of the string. With a bit of practice the caps are firmly fixed in place.

Bottling and maturing wine is not recommended for amateurs. If a good, clear, filtered local wine can be found and they wish to bottle it themselves, this can be an amusing pastime providing they have enough patience and time. It can also be an economic proposition as bulk wine costs less. But whether the wine is in cask or bottle it is well worth while purchasing it at least several months before drinking. And having said that, another reminder is due that by no means all wine should be kept much *longer* than several months, either.

Examples of rustic manufacture, in wood and in metal, of the *entonnoir*, or funnel, used for filling the barrels up to the brim, and the *broc à vin* (also known as the *ouillette*) or wine pitcher. The photographs appear courtesy of the Musée des arts et traditions populaires, Paris.

In a real cellar intended to hold several hundred bottles the most rational method is to have one compartment for each wine. There are many ways of arranging the bottles; by region and by *cru*, the reds on the left (diagram); chronologically, the oldest on the left; for lovers of wines of a particular region, one compartment to the wine of each sub-region; in adjoining compartments wines from regions or countries with nothing in common. The important thing is to have an orderly and logical system that facilitates periodic sampling and stock-taking and the replenishing of stocks when necessary. The name and vintage of the wine should be specified on each compartment.

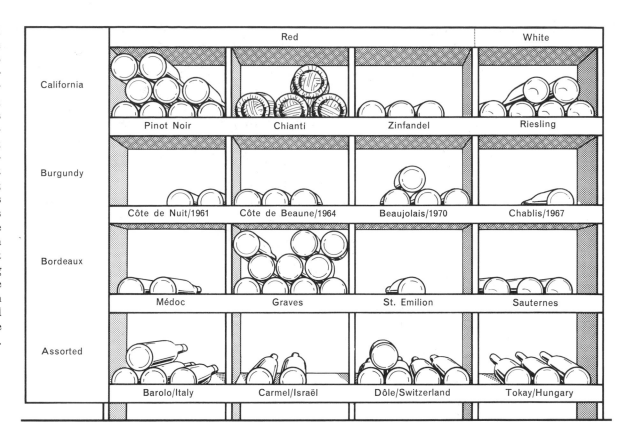

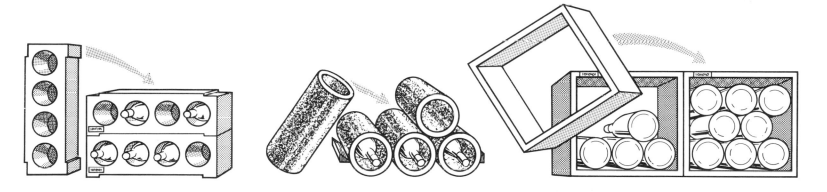

Arranging a stock of fine wines is not necessarily a complicated undertaking. Here are a few suggestions, although there are many other equally good solutions: *(left to right, top)* racks placed one on top of the other; lengths of clay piping; wooden or plastic packing cases; *(bottom)* a gaily painted box divided diagonally; a ready-made bottle holder (available on the market); a converted set of small, deep shelves.

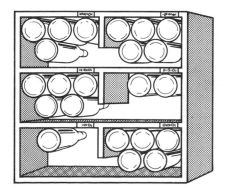

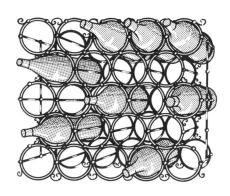

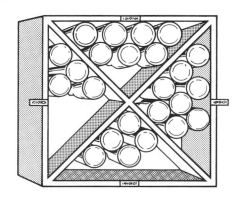

460

A CELLAR TO BE ENVIED

Even with the humblest of cellars, the average wine-lover should take good care to have at least 50 bottles of *vin ordinaire* in stock for everyday use, and to replenish his supplies before they run really low. This practice makes it easier for purchaser and merchant alike to maintain the same quality. It is a wise and well-known French saying that "it is always a pleasure to change bread, but never the wine". The quantity of 50 bottles only serves as an example for those with limited cellar space, although even the amateur aspires to greater things. Apart from all the pleasure and satisfaction derived from owning a private cellar, laying down a stock of choice wines can also be a financial investment, inasmuch as prices increase as wines age. There is ample proof of this in the astronomical prices fetched by bottles auctioned from private cellars.

A cellar of fine wines with any pretension to being well-stocked should contain, on the average, a thousand bottles covering a variety of wines. The following suggestions give some idea of how the stock would be divided up.

– 25 to 50 bottles of Champagne, to be renewed at least every two years. 50 bottles of SAUTERNES or vintage sweet wines, bought during a good year and laid down for future use.

– 200 bottles, at least, of good red Bordeaux such as MÉDOC, GRAVES, SAINT-EMILION, as many as possible of good vintages, which should be replaced from time to time so that stocks are never exhausted.

– 200 bottles of red and white Burgundy for drinking within three, four or five years.

– 50 bottles of special aperitif or dessert wines such as port, Madeira, SAMOS, BANYULS, MALVASIA, MARSALA and MAVRODAPHNI.

– 100 bottles of assorted whites from such districts as the Rhine and Moselle, from Hungary, Alsace, Switzerland, Italy and Central Europe, including CHABLIS, POUILLY, MUSCADET, GRAVES, HUELVA.

The remainder, about a third of the total, can be made up from miscellaneous or informal red wines, suitable for drinking at any time of day and not necessarily with meals. They will almost certainly include Beaujolais, except for the best vintages which should be laid down for future use; CÔTES-DU-RHÔNE, rosé wines from Provence and elsewhere in France, notably Anjou, fruity red wines from Spain, VALPOLICELLA from Italy, and so on.

This fulfils the basic requirement for a good cellar stock: a good selection of important French wines for drinking with special meals; a range of aperitif and dessert wines; a range of local or unusual foreign wines, depending on the owner's taste; young, delicate white wines of any origin and a good light table wine with a low alcohol content and a clean, fresh taste.

SUGGESTIONS FOR A CELLAR OF MODERATE SIZE

The proportion of white wines to red is obviously a matter of personal preference. Perhaps a good balance would be 12 different kinds of red wine and 10 different white wines, allowing for twelve bottles of each as the minimum. The suggestions below merely provide a guide to constituting a well-balanced cellar, a theme for endless, individual variations.

CHOICE OF WHITE WINES

4 dry white wines to serve with fish and seafood and, occasionally, to drink as an aperitif.

2 medium-dry, mellow white wines for rice dishes, various entrées and vegetable dishes.

2 sweet wines to accompany desserts.

2 Champagnes or, failing this, 2 first-class sparkling wines.

CHOICE OF RED WINES

2 light red wines to serve with roast fowl, veal and lamb.

4 full-bodied red wines to accompany red meat, roast meat of any kind and cheese.

6 good vintage red wines kept in reserve for special occasions and banquets.

Dry white wines

Germany:	Riesling from the Moselle, Rheingau or Palatinate. These should be tasted before ordering.
Alsace:	Riesling, Pinot Gris, Tokay.

Light red wines

Burgundy:	Beaujolais.
Côtes du Rhône:	Châteauneuf-du-Pape, Crozes, Hermitage.

Those of us who live on the eighteenth floor of modern apartment blocks are not likely to be considering setting up a cellar quite as grandiose as this one in Saumur-Anjou, on the Loire, France.

WHITE WINES

Italy:	Orvieto, Vino del garda, Frascati, Vernaccia, Est! Est!! Est!!!, Trevigiani, Garganega di Ganbellara.
Loire:	Sancerre, Anjou, Muscadet.
Portugal:	Vinho verde (branco).
Savoy:	Roussette de Savoie.
Switzerland:	Neuchâtel, Dorin, Fendant.
Yugoslavia:	Smederevka, Zilavka.
U.S.A.:	Chablis, Riesling and Sylvaner from California.

All these wines should be gradually restocked at the rate they are consumed. On the average they can only be kept for four years.

Mellow or medium-dry white wines

Alsace:	Gewürztraminer.
Germany:	Riesling Spätlese from the Moselle or Rhine, also Sylvaner Spätlese from Franconia and the Rheinhesse.
Bordeaux:	Graves de Vayres, Premières Côtes de Bordeaux, Saint-Foy, Saint-Macaire.
Touraine:	Vouvray.
Italy:	Castelli Romani, Frascati, Orvieto, Verdicchio with the mention abbocato or semi-seccho.
Switzerland:	Malvoisie, Petite Arvine.
Austria:	Riesling, Zierfandler and Rotgipfler "Spätlese".
Hungary :	Badacsonyi Kéknyelu, Badacsonyi Szurkebarat.

These wines should be gradually restocked at the rate they are consumed. They will not keep in prime condition longer than an average of four years.

Sweet white wines and dessert wines

Bordeaux:	Sauternes, Cérons, Loupiac, Barsac, Montbazillac.
Anjou:	Vouvray.
Hungary:	Tokay aszu (3 to 6 puttonyos).
Spain:	Malaga or Priorato extra rancio, sweet sherry.
Italy:	Cinqueterre (sweet), Malvasia di Lipari, Moscato, Vino santo, Caluso passito.
Greece:	Mavrodaphni, Samos.
Portugal:	Port.
Germany:	Moselle or Rhine wines with the mention "Trockenbeerenauslese".
Yugoslavia:	Spalato prosecco, Stolacer Ausbruch.
Roumania:	Cotnari Grase, Murfatlar-Muskat.
America:	Tokay from California.

These wines can usually keep for five years or more and some of them for about ten years. Their conditions can best be judged by periodic tasting.

Champagnes

Champagne brut, dry or demi-sec.

A high-class sparkling wine can replace Champagne if preferred. Champagne can usually be kept for four to five years.

462

RED WINES

Bordeaux:	Light Médoc or Graves.
Italy:	Chianti, Bardolino, Barbusco, Grignolino Valpolicella.
Spain:	Priorato tinto.
Portugal:	Vinho verde (tinto).
Switzerland:	Salvagnin.
Austria:	Blauburgunder (Pinot Noir).
Germany:	Spätburgunder (Pinot Noir).
California:	Zinfandel.
Bulgaria:	Kramolin.

There is no reason why really good local wines, if available, should not replace the wines in the above list. As in the case of medium-dry or dry white wines, these should gradually be replaced as stocks are depleted. On average, these wines should be drunk within five years.

Full-bodied red wines

Burgundy:	From known regional vineyards or Premiers Crus from the Côtes de Nuits and Côtes de Beaune.
Côtes du Rhône:	Hermitage, Côte Rôtie.
Switzerland:	Dôle from the Valais.
Italy:	Barbera, Nebbiolo, Reciotto, Veronese, Falerno.
Bordeaux:	From the best vineyards in the Médoc, Saint-Emilion and Pomerol.
Algeria:	Wines from Médéa and Tlemcen.
Spain:	The best Rioja (Rioja Imperial, Rioja Marqués de Riscal), Viña Pomal.
Chile:	Wines from Curico and Talca.
Portugal:	Dão or Colares wines.
Yugoslavia:	Plavac.
Hungary:	Egri Bikaver.

These wines can be kept six to eight years; certain Bordeaux and Burgundies keep even longer. Only tasting can determine the condition and maturity of the wine.

Great red wines

This list is limited to wines from the best vineyards. They are generally quite costly but have the advantage of keeping longer.

Burgundy:	Chambertin or one of the other great wines from the Gevrey-Chambertin region; Bonnes Mares (Côte de Nuits); Corton (Côte de Beaune); Musigny; Clos-de-Vougeot; Romanée Conti or one of the other great wines from Vosné-Romanée.
Bordeaux:	Château Margaux or one of the great classified wines from Margaux; Château Lafitte or one of the great classified wines from Pauillac; Château Montrose or one of the great classified wines from Saint-Estèphe; Château Ausone or another superior Saint-Emilion; Château Haut-Brion or another superior red Graves.
Italy:	Barolo, Vino Nobile de Montepulciano.
Austria:	Oggauer Blaufränkisch Alte Reserve.
Germany:	Ihringer Blankenhornsberg.

The great red wines can be kept for over ten years but, apart from very exceptional wines, not longer than fifteen. The best vintages should be chosen, bearing in mind that these vary from one wineproducing region to another.

SAMPLE CELLAR STOCKS

1. Those who like vin rosé should choose from the following list

Germany:	Assmannhäuser Höllenberg, Durbacher Schlossberg Weissherbst Auslese, Ihringer Jesuitengarten, Burgunder Weissherbst Auslese.
Austria:	Schloss Kirchberg.
France:	Tavel (rosé), Sancerre (rosé), Cabernet d'Anjou, Brégançon (Provence).
Italy:	Chiareto del Garda, Cagarino, Ravello.
Switzerland:	Œil-de-Perdrix (Neuchâtel).

All these wines should be drunk young as they rarely keep longer than three years.

2. For those who like Pinot

Here is a selection of wines made from the famous Pinot grape which is cultivated throughout Europe as well as in South Africa and California.

a) Pinot Noir (Blauburgunder, Spätburgunder)

Germany:	Oberingelheimer Sonnenberg Spätburgunder (Rheinhesse), Ihringer Winklerberg (Baden), Assmannshäuser Höllenberg (Rheingau).
Switzerland:	Dôle (Valais), Duc de Rohan Pinot Noir (Bündner Herrschaft), Auvernier Pinot Noir (Neuchâtel).
France:	All the red Burgundies from Côte de Nuits and Côte de Beaune.
Italy:	Pinot Nero (Trentino).
Roumania:	Dealne Mare.
Yugoslavia:	Burgundac crni.
California:	Pinot Noir or Red Pinot.

b) Pinot Gris (Ruländer in Germany and Austria), Tokay in Alsace and eastern Switzerland, Szürkebarat in Hungary, Malvoisie in Valais.

Germany:	Durbacher Herrenberg (Baden), Bickensohler Steinfelsen (Kaiserstuhl).
Austria:	Ruster Ruländer (Burgenland).
Switzerland:	Malvoisie (Valais), Malauser Tokajer (Grisons).
Italy:	Pinot grigio (Trentino).
Hungary:	Badacsonyi Szürkebarat (Lake Balaton).
Yugoslavia:	Ljutomer Rulendac sivi (Slovenia).

c) Pinot Blanc — Weisser Burgunder in Germany) or Pinot Chardonnay.

Germany:	Blankenhornsberger Weissburgunder (Kaiserstuhl), Ihringer Winklerberg (Ihringen).
Austria:	Undhof Wieden Weissburgunder (Wachau), Kloster-Cabinet Weissburgunder (Klosterneuburg).
France:	Montrachet, Meursault, Chablis and Pouilly-Fuissé.
Italy:	Pinot bianco (Trentin).
Yugoslavia:	Collio, Burgundac Bijeli (Slovenia).
South Africa:	White Pinot.

3. A cellar for Riesling enthusiasts

Germany:	Rüdesheimer Schlossberg (Rheingau), Wehlener Sonnenuhr (Moselle), Diedesheimer Leinhöhle (Rheinpfalz), Oppenheimer Sackträger (Rheinhesse), Durbacher Schlossberg (Baden).
Austria:	Kremser Kögl, Dürnsteiner Hollerin.
Switzerland:	Goût du Conseil (Valais).
France:	Riesling d'Alsace.
California:	Johannisberg-Riesling.
South Africa:	Paarl-Riesling.
Chile:	Coquinto-Riesling.
Australia:	Quelltaler Hock.

4. A cellar for those specializing in rare or unusual wines

Each wineproducing area has its specialities whose fame sometimes never crosses local boundaries. Travellers and gourmets often appreciate these rarities, choosing them according to the countries they visit and the discoveries made.

Some of these delightful and little-known wines are listed below as a starting point for those who will doubtless add discoveries of their own.

Germany:	Wines with the mention "Trockenbeerenauslese" or "Eiswein", Durbacher Herrenberg (Baden), Assmannshäuser Höllenberg Rotwein Edelbeerenauslese (Rheingau).
Austria:	Ruster Ausbruch (Burgenland): very sweet.
Switzerland:	Réze (*vin de glacier*, Valais), Malanser Completer (Grisons), Païen (Traminer de Visperterminen, Valais).
France:	Château-Chalon (young wine from the Jura). Romanée (the rarest of the great red wines from Burgundy, only 2,500 litres produced each year). White Musigny (the rarest of the great white wines from Burgundy, only 800 litres produced each year).
Italy:	Falerno (red), the wine extolled by Horace. Cinqueterre (white), praised by Pliny, Petrarch and D'Annunzio. Marsala vergini.
Spain:	A wine from Los Moriles (sherry type with a nutty flavour).
Portugal:	An authentic vintage port of 1921, 1927, 1931, 1935, 1943, 1945 or 1947.
Cyprus:	Commandaria (a sweet wine).

5. Other Suggestions

Some people favour specializing in wines from a certain geographical region. A cellar can be stocked with Rhône wines, ranging from the Canton of Valais to the Côtes du Rhône, or Rhine wines coming from the Swiss Canton of Grisons to the Rheingau. Some people concentrate on wines from Italy, as they are readily available in most places.

Apart from a conventional basic stock, it is a good idea to lay in a few bottles of some wine that is relatively unknown locally. It makes a good conversation piece as well as a pleasant change for visitors to have something different from the well-known bottles seen every day in the main street windows or the supermarket.

463

FOR DRINKING

PIERRE ANDRIEU

The drinking glass appears only relatively late in the history of mankind. It was certainly known by the Egyptians and Phoenicians; the glass-works of Sidon and Alexandria were famous. The origin of glass itself is obscure. A French authority on the subject, J. Girardin, once wrote, "Chance played a considerable rôle in the invention of glass. However it is difficult to believe the writing of Pliny the Elder in this connection. According to him, the Phoenician soda merchants, having landed on the banks of the River Balus, there prepared their meals. For lack of anything better, they used slabs of natron with which to steady the cooking pots. But during the cooking process the slabs melted and the sand underneath was turned into glass. Obviously, considering the high temperatures required, glass as we know it today could never have been produced in the circumstances reported by Pliny."

Whatever its origins, the Persians were already using glass receptacles during the reign of Alexander the Great, and archaeologists have discovered ancient Egyptian flasks containing evidence of their use for wine. It was probably around 1800 B.C. that the Phoenicians started to make the glassware that graced Roman tables during the reign of Nero, and in the first century A.D. glass-works were established in Gaul and Spain. Egypt, especially the region around Alexandria, supplied most of the very expensive and sometimes coloured crystal glass during this period. It is very surprising to discover in ancient writings that these crystal glasses and goblets did not break when they were dropped. François Carnot, a noted glass expert, has drawn attention to the fact that these were probably the first blow-moulded glass articles. "They were very slowly cooled in the mould," he wrote, "thereby producing a toughened glass." Manufacture developed rapidly and, all over the territory occupied during the Roman Conquest, small cups, flasks and other glass vessels are found interred in graves with the ashes of their one-time owners or keepers.

Apart from the jewel-encrusted goblets or wine cups in gold and silver, served at the palace tables of emperors and kings, the first tableware made for a prosperous clientele was in copper. The designs on the Greek and Roman vessels were admirably wrought and featured heads of contemporary gods such as Bacchus, vine leaves, bunches of grapes and similar appropriate designs in relief.

On the other hand, the metal specimens remaining from the pre-Roman era in Gaul, such as bronze and pottery vessels, are much simpler in design although their shape is not without elegance. At Celtic feasts, beer, mead or wine were served in horns. Wild ox horns, often richly ornamented with gold and silver trimmings, were particularly favoured and continued in use throughout the Merovingian era; they are even mentioned up to the fifteenth century. Another somewhat macabre drinking vessel was made from a human skull, either, so the historians claim, that of an enemy killed in battle or of some ancestor. It was considered a great honour for a guest to be invited to drink from a skull, and in order to qualify for such a privilege he had to have killed an enemy in battle.

For less ceremonial, family gatherings, earthenware cups or bowls were used, each guest serving himself by dipping his cup into an earthenware pot placed on the table or on the ground, a custom not far removed from our punch bowl.

From King Dagobert's solid gold wine cup to the gilded silver ostrich egg facsimile belonging to Charles V, many bizarre, opulent or unusual drinking vessels were created according to the fashion of the day or to satisfy the whims and wit of those who ordered these personal expressions of their eccentricities. Among these memorable historic vessels was the richly decorated goblet encrusted with diamonds belonging to Good King René of Anjou. It held three pints, a fair draught of wine in any age. As curios or merely specimens of extremely fine craftsmanship, these exam-

Forms and materials for wine receptacles were very varied. In the background, right, a Syro-roman "bubble" flagon; on the left, a Turkish jug (fifteenth to sixteenth century) and, below it, a Persian earthenware bottle (twelfth to thirteenth century). In the foreground are two examples of twelfth-century Persian pottery.

465

Glass-making was already flourishing in Roman times, as witness this carafe, goblet and drinking glass, all made for wine.

ples of early glass now fetch very high prices as collector's pieces on the world's markets, on those rare occasions when they change hands.

During the Middle Ages, glass drinking vessels, oddly enough, disappeared for several centuries from some regions, becoming so rare that two guests often shared one glass. At this period, the window-glass makers, producers of a coarse green glass, occasionally turned out a few small goblets with inverted conical bases, but these were rather rare. The outside surfaces carried ornamental tracery and arabesque patterns made by sticking coarse glass threads on to the blown shape.

Glassware certainly proliferated during the Renaissance, when the craft attained its peak under the Italian influence. Glass-makers established themselves over all the wooded regions of France such as Normandy, Lorraine, Nevers, Orleans, Poitou, Dauphiné and Provence. Although recognized as Guilds of Gentlemen,

they were inclined to be nomadic, moving on when their local fuel supply of wood or bracken ran out. From the sixteenth century onwards, they often intermarried with glass-making families from Murano and Altare brought from Italy by the French nobility. The glass they made differed markedly from region to region. Amber glass came from Provence; a bluish variety from the Margeride region, marbled in appearance and lined with white, pale blue or dark red enamel; and rose-coloured glasses from Burgundy and Nevers, although these unfortunately often "threw out their salt and spoilt the wine". From each place came glasses of different shape, colour and design with simple or elaborate decoration in jewels or multi-coloured enamels. "Bell-shaped goblets" and the hanaps made in the forests of Chamborant around 1340 by a certain Guionet are no longer to be found, and rare indeed are examples of pre-Renaissance glassware.

Renewed interest in the use of glass drinking vessels stemmed from the Arabs and, to a great degree, the glass-makers of Damascus who produced very fine enamelled glasses from the thirteenth to the fifteenth century. Contrary to the generally accepted belief, the Venetians copied the delightfully designed glasses which their seafarers brought from the far coasts. Famous as shrewd merchants and shippers, the burghers of Venice traded in this glassware and established the celebrated Venetian glass industry. They had greater success than their counterparts in other countries, since they were able to improve in the original production methods. They were also more skilled in applying gold, and their enamelling was more delicate. The Venetian pearl-workers, accustomed to working with minute pearls, wielded the sticks of enamel with a light and delicate touch. The beautiful Venetian goblets or decanters are superb works of art and were reserved for the tables of sovereigns and high dignitaries.

By the sixteenth century the Venetians' skill in making glass had progressed to the point of producing white glass so pure and clear that it was called "crystalline" or "Venetian crystal". During the same period they manufactured a more ordinary "fern glass", so called because of the engraved design on its sides. It is only fair to mention that the famous works of Murano were founded by Greek workers who took refuge in Venice, after the fall of Constantinople.

Silver drinking mugs were very practical when travelling, hunting or eating out of doors, a whole set easily nesting one inside the other. These were German cups personalized with engravings of the owners' names and with various decorative motifs.

Two specimens of seventeenth-century glasses from the Lower Rhine. The one on the left is reminiscent of the *Römer* in general shape and by the superposition of two elements, in this example a cone and a cylinder, moulded separately. The drinking vessel on the right is made of green glass in the form of a small barrel.

467

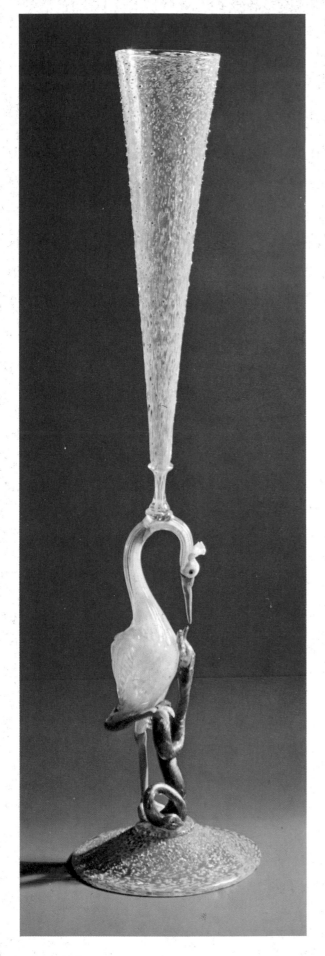

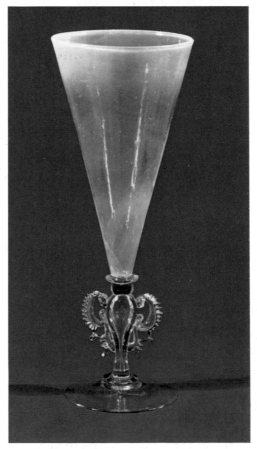

From the sixteenth century on, the Venetians were past masters in the art of glass-making, enamelling and relief ornamentation. The oval drinking cup, above, in engraved agate dates from the late sixteenth century. Emeralds set in enamelled gold and silver give it a regal air. The seventeenth-century Venetian flute glasses (left) are worthy of any collector's pride— or envy.

The two nautilus cups on the facing page bear witness to the consumate artistry of the German goldsmiths and silversmiths of the seventeenth century. Splendid show pieces as they may be, they are scarcely suitable as vessels for drinking wine.

To reduce the measures of wine staked during card games, these glasses were divided into sections, each corresponding to one game.

The numerous fiefs that split Germany during the seventeenth century gave rise to endless disputes over inheritances. On these emblazoned glasses, the feudal lord asserted his properties, his territorial claims and even the territory he hoped to acquire.

These ordinary glasses were not always highly esteemed and pedlars, heedless of possible breakages, hawked their wares through town and countryside, the streets echoing to the refrain,

Lovely glasses, pretty glasses,
Beer glasses, a penny a pair.

In the sixteenth century the influence of the Venetian glass-makers spread to Holland. Here, as in most other countries, the glass-works were installed by natives from the City of the Doges. In Holland, already recognized as the home of the diamond cutter, glassware was decorated with fine engravings of arms and other heraldry, cut into the glass with a diamond point. During the eighteenth century some of these engravers perfected a new type of stippling.

Across the Channel, glasses were designed with a very heavy cap-shaped base, but the stem became finer as time went on. Small bubbles of air were sometimes purposely trapped inside the crystal, resulting in an original effect in the play of light. Some of the glasses were also ornamented with filigree work. Towards the end of the seventeenth century the English discovered their own special type of crystal by adding barium and lead to the glass. Compared to Venetian glass, crystal produced in Britain was heavy, but fickle fashion, perennial follower of the newly created or novel, developed a taste for the heavy, pure glass, with dire effects on the Venetian glass-making industry. The English shipped their glass to Holland for engraving, not by the diamond method but with a small wheel, a delicate and intricate technique demanding considerable solidity in the glass.

Jacobean engraved glasses, glasses for religious ceremonies and those used on board sailing vessels were particularly conspicuous because of their short stem and their solid, heavy base.

In Silesia, as in Bohemia, crystal with a potash base was generally used, while engraving was replaced by mouldings on the outside of glasses which were lavishly ornamented in gold and often delicately etched. Occasionally landscapes were painted in black, and all over Germany examples of enamelled glassware, not without artistic merit, could be found. In Bohemia the method of tinting glass with purple by means of gold salts was discovered and these glasses were often further enhanced by designs interwoven with purple and gold.

At the invitation of Catherine the Great, the Silesian glass-makers set up a factory near Moscow, bringing with them experience and skill acquired in Bohemia, which could again be traced back to the Venetians.

Spanish glass was not unnaturally first influenced by that from the Arab countries resulting in glassware with garish, ill-assorted colours. Venetian craftsmen subsequently transformed the yellow Spanish glass by giving it a delicate crackle finish and enlarging the coloured scrolls favoured by their predecessors.

During the sixteenth century, Venetian glass-makers installed their first works at Antwerp, in Flanders. Early in the seventeenth century they opened another in the Principality of Liége. These yellowish glasses were usually tall, decorated with masks and blue beaded designs. The enamelled varieties always bore the distinctive sign of a lily of the valley.

Although Louis XIV owned five magnificent goblets in rock crystal, this noble material fell from favour during the eighteenth century and was replaced on royal and lordly tables by Bohemian glass which was also produced in France. At Tourlaville in the region of Cherbourg, at Saint-Louis, Montcenis, Baccarat and Sèvres, still renowned today for its fine table-ware, crystal-works sprang up and thrived. Cafés and *bistros* had also to be supplied and so bar or counter glasses for serving spirits were produced—"trick" glasses, really, as their shape and thickness gave the impression of holding much more than they actually did.

These two elegant glasses are made in a shape that was popular throughout Germany in the eighteenth century. Their fine engraving and delicate lines are in striking contrast to the glasses on p. 467. Admirable though they are as collector's items, all the drinking vessels shown on these pages are ill suited to modern requirements.

The well-known "hock" glasses with their graceful long stems surmounted by a bulbous cup, the *Römer* as they are called in German, were manufactured at Cologne. Here, the other typical glasses were also made with scrolls and enamelled serpents' heads.

Bavarian enamelled glasses were well suited to the renowned capacity of their users. They provided ample space for portraying the full Imperial Eagle as well as the armorial bearings of all the states under the Emperor. In celebration of the Augsburg peace treaty, glasses were designed bearing the portraits of the French, German and Swedish monarchs, Catholics on one side of the glass and Protestants on the other, all receiving the Lord's blessing and embrace. All such occasions gave rise to commemorative glassware and the family arms or those of the great dynasties were often used together with a host of other heraldic devices to decorate these expansive surfaces.

No discussion of European glassware is complete without mention of Saint-Louis crystal. Reported in print as long ago as 1673, the Saint-Louis glass-works were in existence under the name of Münsthal as far back as 1586. During the Thirty Years' War they were destroyed, then reborn as the "Royal Glass Works of Saint-Louis" when Lorraine came once more under French rule. "The Company of Crystal Makers of Saint-Louis", as it has been known since 1829, is the birthplace of the first crystal in France.

A bottle of wine, a glass of wine... Although as far as wine historians can tell there has been little change in the basic nature of the contents for the last two millenia, there has been an enormous outward change in the receptacles themselves. The stone bottle and wooden drinking cup shown here are reproduced courtesy of the Musée des arts et traditions populaires, Paris.

472

BOTTLES AND DECANTERS

Wine bottles are taken so much for granted today that scarcely a thought is given to their history. Actually, the custom of storing wine in glass bottles only goes back to the fifteenth century.

Glass vessels were certainly known earlier, as far back as Alexandria, Athens and Rome, but they were usually reserved for perfumes. If glass was employed at all to hold wine the vessels had an intermediate use—similar to that of our decanters—and brought the wine from wherever it was stored for serving.

Before glass bottles came into general use, ceramic or metal pots and jugs of varying artistic merit were provided by the potters or metal workers, and archaeologists have uncovered proof of their existence in Gallo-Roman time. A silver pot dating back to the first century B.C., glass goblets and bottles together with medals and coins bearing the effigy of the Emperor Trajan, a wine cup in red clay with the words *Reims Feliciter* and dating from the second or third century, a clay carafe, the lower part of its handle ornamented with a bunch of grapes, have all been excavated in the province of Champagne.

In homes in Gaul, servants brought wine to the table in earthenware or silver receptacles which resembled cooking pots. Each guest helped himself in turn with a small cup called a *cyathe*.

Froissart, the French chronicler, records that when the Earl of Douglas carried the heart of the King of Scotland to the Holy Sepulchure in 1328, there was little else in his baggage save gold bottles—though posterity is not informed as to the contents of these opulent flasks. Two silver bottles are listed in the inventory of the personal belongings of Charles V after his death. In the Louvre Museum in Paris are two beautiful gilt silver bottles bearing the arms of Henry III, exquisite in their simplicity of form and decoration, their general shape seemingly inspired by the gourd. Even King John of England used bottles in 1360, as shown by the following entry in a list of the royal expenses: "To Jehan Petit Fay, the sum of sixty sous minted at Tours for four leather bottles in which to carry water and wine for the said Sire when he is going to the country." When travelling, wine was also carried in metal flasks, usually made in silver.

In many ways, the silversmith made a considerable contribution to the development of the common wine bottle's illustrious ancestors. During the ninth century their powerful guild was granted a charter by King Charles the Bald. Previous to this, silver work appears to have been almost entirely confined to the monastery workshops. Fourteenth-century records show that glass receptacles were beginning to compete for favour with those in precious metals. The last will and testament of a certain Jehanne of Burgundy in 1352 mentions "two small bottles in glass mounted with silver".

From the sixteenth century onwards, glass receptacles began to appear in well-to-do homes and the word "bottle" began to assume the bacchic implications which it has enjoyed ever since. Pierre de l'Estoile, in his "Diary of a Parisian Bourgeois", dubbed the Cardinal of Guise "Cardinal of the Bottles", remarking that "...he loved them so dearly and hardly concerned himself with anything but the delights of the kitchen of which he had so much greater knowledge and understanding than affairs of Church and State." It is better to gloss over the unhappy end of this epicurean prelate whose afflictions were so prolonged as to allow him ample time to reflect on his self-indulgent past and to be scourged with pain.

During this period, glass-making was the only manual craft to which a gentleman could turn his hand without any loss of dignity. In the glass-works, strange to relate, only the nobility had the right to blow bottles. When the glass was melted, the nobleman took the iron blow-pipe

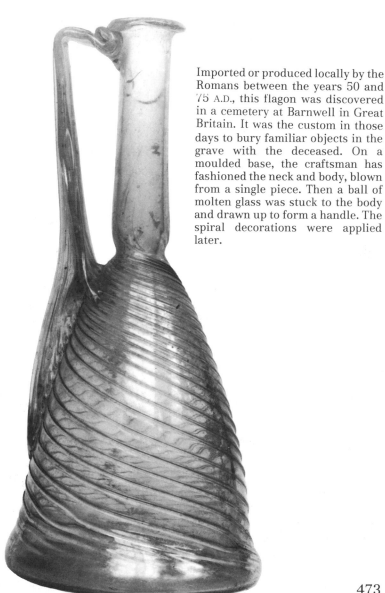

Imported or produced locally by the Romans between the years 50 and 75 A.D., this flagon was discovered in a cemetery at Barnwell in Great Britain. It was the custom in those days to bury familiar objects in the grave with the deceased. On a moulded base, the craftsman has fashioned the neck and body, blown from a single piece. Then a ball of molten glass was stuck to the body and drawn up to form a handle. The spiral decorations were applied later.

Despite the gradual appearance of glass, earthenware containers for wine have never altogether disappeared. Light wine regains the freshness of the cellar when reposing in a cool earthenware pitcher. Shapes have altered little since ancient times. Above can be seen a small Roman jug dating from the third century. On the left, a rustic German pot, turned on a wheel sometime at the beginning of the sixteenth century.

spelling during the gradual but wider adoption of the English language in the British Isles gave rise to that comforting form of the well-worn word, bottle. While the bottle was emerging as a form of practical packaging, most farmers and agricultural workers used earthenware receptacles or those made from other forms of fired clay. These shapes, too, were probably inspired by the gourd. Others carried their wine ration in small barrels of the same materials, decorated with pastoral or allegorical scenes.

It was only around the fifteenth century that the bottle began to assume a more elegant and practical shape, similar to that of today; but glass bottles had not yet supplanted those in metal or leather used until then. Silver bottles, engraved with the arms of the owner, were still being made in the sixteenth century.

Towards the seventeenth century, glass containers came into everyday use. They were called flagons, carafes, decanters, flasks and so on, the word *bouteille* being strictly reserved for receptacles containing wine. Although other forms of containers abounded, bearing heraldic devices or decorative emblems, in the wine cellar and the church the bottle reigned supreme. Such bottles were designed with a broad base and, in order to minimize the effect of sediment on the contents, the bottom of the bottle was recessed inwardly, a device that had already been employed by goldsmiths and silversmiths in the Middle Ages.

Until the end of the eighteenth century, goblets and drinking glasses did not form part of the table setting, but remained on the sideboard together with whatever contained the wine. It was customary to signal to a servant who filled the glass, brought it to the table on a small tray, waited while it was drunk and then returned it to the sideboard. In surroundings of great luxury, two servants performed this service, standing on the left of the diner, one holding the glass while the other filled it from a decanter of carafe. The unconventional Marquis de Rouillac, who died in 1662, was the first member of high society to have the idea of dismissing the servants and eating in peace. Few dared to imitate him, so bottles and glasses did not cross the hallowed gap between sideboard and dining table until about 1760.

In the region of Montreuil-Bellay in Anjou, a certain number of highly interesting old bottles have been collected, such as a seventeenth century half-bottle, called a *fillette*, and others dating from the same period in dark glass, varying in capacity and irregular in shape with the shoulder sometimes wider than the base. There are also some amusing specimens such as the "priest's bottle". These ecclesiastical gentlemen were entitled to levy a tithe in kind on the year's wine harvest, and with this in mind of course took good care to select bottles of generous cubic capacity.

In the eighteenth century, bottle shapes began to assume more slender, graceful lines, similar to those we recognize and accept today. About this time, too, French crystal began to face serious competition from England,

and started the operation. Savary, a duke, general and high functionary under the French First Empire, noted "It behoves only a gentleman glassmaker to blow glass." This tradition can be traced back to the fourteenth century and there is evidence to prove that even the haughty Louis XIV blew glass on December 19th, 1655, the historians tell us.

Very often, when someone wanted to drink something, they would simply draw wine from the barrel as and when they wanted it. This was the case not only with trades-people and in the inns and taverns, but even in the regal surroundings of the great lords' *châteaux*. It had the disadvantage of leaving the barrel part-empty. In the province of Anjou, mounted travellers used a kind of leather bottle, placed beside them on the saddle, containing a small quantity of wine for the journey. This receptacle was called a *boutille*, an early form of the French word *bouteille*. Changes in pronunciation and

the popularity of whose lead-glass was fast spreading, and French glass-makers were obliged to turn their production over to other products, including bottles and flagons. Owners of estates ordered their heraldic arms to be emblazoned on bottles especially blown for them, and various vintners, notably those from Liége, had their coats-of-arms represented on the bottles coming from their own cellars. By 1775, the fame of the glass-works in Ingrandes-sur-Loire, in the province of Anjou, was widespread. Its bottles were exported as far afield as America and the Indies.

In the seventeenth century it had already been discovered that the inverted conical recess in the bottom of the bottle facilitated precipitation of the sediment which forms after bottling. Being heavier than the liquid, it remained at the lowest level with little risk of it contaminating the wine if care is taken in handling the bottle. The bottle's neck gradually tapered up, to a certain point, leaving very little surface exposed to the air and thus helping to prevent evaporation. So the evolution of the bottle's shape was not arbitrary, but determined by good sense and experience.

In the extremely rare *Treatise on the Cultivation of Vines and the Art of Making Wine*, many notes are found relating to bottles, whose shape varied from country to country. "In England," it is noted, "the neck is short and flattened out, the body practically the same width all the way down. In France, its capacity varies, thus encouraging knavery. Some bottles have a very elongated neck, short body and deeply recessed base. All these bottles are more or less in the shape of a pear. It would be desirable that the regulations drawn up for Champagne were enforced throughout France; one would thus be sure of the quantity of wine one orders, for the buyer often sees only the shape of the bottle and is misled as to its contents. For example, the ordinary bottle does not even hold three-quarters of a pint whereas, according to the law of equity, it should contain a pint. Therefore the buyer is always cheated to a greater or lesser extent, as he cannot be in Champagne."

During the eighteenth century the bottle came into general use. While Louis XV was on the throne, one thousand one hundred and four bottles, large and small, with or without coats-of-arms, were counted at the house of Mlle Desmares, evidence that the bottle had, at last, been granted the "freedom of the city" on the tables of the world, in the homes of rich and poor alike.

During the greater part of the nineteenth century, the

At the beginning of the eighteenth century, flagons still lacked grace and slenderness. The silhouette of the English bottle on the right is still similar to that of the twelfth century. The shape of the Dutch bottle (left) was popular at the end of the seventeenth century.

shrewder wine merchants turned topical events and personalities to good account by having special bottles designed in unexpected shapes. Among the more popular were a cockerel, an umbrella, a grenadier, the Eiffel Tower, a pipe, a lantern, a dwarf holding a pistol, the heads of eminent French politicans such as Gambetta and General Boulanger and a beatified Joan of Arc.

The famous Belgian wine connoisseur, Maurice des Ombiaux, however, seemed to care little what shape the bottle might be when he wrote, "I like to see a bottle of Médoc or Pauillac with its stamped cork, a dusty bottle of old Vougeot over which several generations of spiders have spun their gossamer, or the bottle covered with tide-marks from the winter's floods. But, also, I like to contemplate the ruby of a St. Emilion, the purplish-brown of a Nuits, the sea-green of a Pouilly, the corn yellow of a Sauternes, the gold of a Meursault or the straw yellow of an Arbois through the faceted crystal of a decanter. What greater pleasure for the eyes can there be than the tints which Bacchus has bestowed on his nectars?"

Up until the last century, merchants did not always supply the exact quantity of wine for which they charged and the buyer was often tricked by the shape of the bottle.

The bottles of times past were heavier yet more fragile than those of today and perhaps more handsome and attractive.

LABELS

In the first century, during the time when Gaius Petronius was proconsul in Bethany, wine was kept in two-handled jugs called amphoras. Corks being as yet unknown, the neck was closed with a plaster stopped or a plug of oil-soaked cloth. But even these primitive amphoras bore a mention not only of the vineyard but also of the consul in office at the time of filling.

So far, extensive research has failed to reveal any examples of labels, even handwritten ones, prior to the eighteenth century. The earliest specimens were very plain. Bereft of coats of arms or any kind of decorative design, they were simply bordered with a thin line, often drawn with pen and ruler, and stated their contents with matter-of-fact succinctness: "Vins Mousseux—1741—Claude Moët" or "Rozé—Claude et J.-R. Moët—Epernay", or "Vins vieux—1743—Claude Moët—Epernay", and seldom or never anything more enlightening than that.

This selection of lables from the last century demonstrates how little importance producer and merchant alike attached to the appearance of the bottle, even in the case of great wines. The label of CHÂTEAU D'YSSAN, the oldest of the three, is very reticent as to the origin of its contents. The MARGAUX label is slightly more forthcoming, but the label below suggests that the innkeeper was the only guarantor for the wine.

Later in the eighteenth century, the form of the label became more elaborate. A certain Commander Quenaidit supplies the following description: "Generally in the shape of a vertical rectangle, or trapezoid with the shorter side at the base, some with the tops rounded to a lesser or greater degree. They were very ordinary and nondescript with floral borders, like most chemists' labels of the same era. This type is still used to label samples of wine, the year and the name of the vineyard being written in the centre by hand."

The art of labelling reached its prime in the nineteenth century. Such was the proliferation of rich and luxurious symbols that they have been described as "the orchestration of a triumphant hymn to the glory of the vineyards of the world". Up until the twentieth century, liqueur labels of the same period reflected changing tastes and fashions, whereas wine labels never busied themselves, one might say, with such trivia, loftily contenting themselves, with very few exceptions, to indicating the year, the vineyard and its owner, and occasionally the wine's name.

A full study of wine labels is an immense undertaking requiring far greater space than is available here and so those used on Champagne bottles over the ages must serve as representatives of the gradual evolution.

Researchers are universally grateful to an anonymous municipal employee, long since unmindful of such earthly things, who collected Champagne labels in his youth, sticking them into an old school exercise book. Together with other collections, the fruits of his youthful zeal give us a good idea of the type of labels in use during the first half on the nineteenth century. The earliest appears to date from about 1820 and carries the name of the Chanoine brothers who decorated this label according to contemporary taste with silver lettering on a black ground. Shortly afterwards, Moët and Chandon followed suit with a similar design featuring blue lettering on white. Although this was designed for their Ay rosé wine by the painter J.-B. Isabey, it was to be the forerunner of their famous *carte bleue*. All these labels were lithographed. Early in the nineteenth century, Moët and Chandon also used a shield-shaped label which was later redesigned for their famous 1928 vintage which has been so widely acclaimed.

In certain wineproducing areas, where vineyards were owned by individuals rather than syndicates, little attempt was made for a very long time to distinguish the produce of one vineyard from another, hence those labels so uniform and alike in appearance.

Towards 1835, the sparkling wines from Champagne were decked with labels having a coloured ground with a white or gold ornamental border composed of parallel hatchings which gradually developed into ornamental foliage, garlands and Renaissance-style fleurons. In

By associating their wines with famous names, the winegrowers of the last century hoped to increase their sales. Top left: Pabstman dedicated his wine to Queen Victoria; above right, a label with the Emperors Franz-Josef, William I and the Tsar Alexander II. Above and right: The artists who designed these labels in the art nouveau style drew attention to the virtues of the wines: one was called Fontaine de Jouvence (fountain of youth), the other Source de Fraîcheur (cool spring).

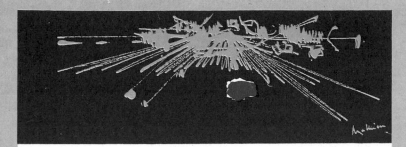

Nowadays, great care is taken over the presentation of great wines. Noblesse obligé. If not every label has the distinction of the CHÂTEAU MOUTON-ROTHSCHILD label designed by the painter Georges Mathieu, they each in their way show evidence of the efforts made to make them attractive.

Dessin inédit   *de Mathieu*

1961   *1961*

Cette récolte a produit :
76.732 Bordelaises et 1/2 B.ᵉˢ de 1 à 76.732
900 Magnums de M 1 à M 900
72 Grands Formats de GF 1 à GF 72
double-magnums, jéroboams, impériales
2.000 "Réserve du Château" marquées R.C.
Ci,

Philippe de Rothschild

Château
Mouton Rothschild

BARON PHILIPPE DE ROTHSCHILD PROPRIÉTAIRE A PAUILLAC

APPELLATION PAUILLAC CONTRÔLÉE

TOUTE LA RÉCOLTE MISE EN BOUTEILLES AU CHÂTEAU

Incisione del XVIII Secolo

Fattorie dei Marchesi   *Lodovico e Piero Antinori*
Firenze   *Italy*

VILLA ANTINORI

Chianti Classico

Imbottigliato alle Cantine Antinori in S. Casciano Val di Pesa - Vino a gradi 12,5 - Cont. Litri 0,720
Si raccomanda di servire chambrè

EPESSES

PREMIER CHOIX

A L'ENSEIGNE DU

VIEUX CHÊNE

SVP

SOCIÉTÉ VINICOLE DE PERROY S.A.

VINTAGE
1966

LIVERMORE

PINOT CHARDONNAY

A LIGHT WINE OF PINOT CHARDONNAY GRAPES

PRODUCED AND BOTTLED AT THE WINERY BY

ESTATE
BOTTLED

WENTE BROS.

ALCOHOL 12% BY VOLUME   LIVERMORE, CALIFORNIA, U.S.A.

EAST OF THE ROCKY MTS.		WEST OF THE ROCKY MTS.
"21" Brands Inc.	Distributed By	PARROTT & Co.
NEW YORK, N. Y.		SAN FRANCISCO, CALIF.

Rheims, around 1830, the first labels for Pommery and Greno appeared. These were extremely simple, featuring only the name in black on a white ground. Roederer bordered their labels with wine leaves while Clicquot-Ponsardin favoured beautiful ornamental script. Some wineproducers believed in small labels, such as those used by Ruinart Père et Fils for their sparkling Œil de Perdrix or that chosen by Jacquesson & Fils for the sparkling Ay at about the same time. Apart from surmounting their name with a crown they seemed to think their wine needed no further introduction.

Most wine merchants at this time considered that the function of the label was merely to indicate the nature of the contents. In consequence, labels simply and unceremoniously read: "Sparkling Burgundy", "Volnay", "Vosne", "Beaune", "Romanée" with the renowned Chambertin which was spelt as "Chambetin". The name Meursault was boxed in with vine leaves or occasionally appeared, like those of Volnay and Pommard (spelt at that time with only one "m"), below a small oval picture showing the imposing gateway to a château in Burgundy.

With the Second Empire came a great variety of decorative labels, but copper-plate engraving and lithography were often abandoned in favour of rather carelessly produced glossy lithographs in colour.

Since the laws and other special legislation concerning *appellations d'origine* came into force in the 1930s the wording on most labels has been strictly controlled. However, this by no means prevented printers and designers from giving free rein to their imagination; landscapes, scenes from the grape harvest, costumes or symbolic emblems resulted in a colourful fresco, gay as the bubbles in wine, blending pictorial skills and the needs of sales promotion. Some printers specializing in labels produced what can legitimately be considered works of art. Perhaps this progress in label design was responsible for the expression that a bottle was *bien habillée*, or "well-dressed".

In Burgundy, various viticulturists and wine merchants now vie with one another to produce labels in the old-fashioned style, while taking advantage of modern techniques. In the region around Bordeaux the great number of vineyards has given rose to a plethora of labels, most of which have "the château" represented in varying degrees of importance.

Baron Philippe de Rothschild is to be commended for his initiative in approaching the greatest artists of the day to design labels for his famous vintages. Artists like Jean Cocteau (1947), Marie Laurencin (1948), Dignimont (1949), Vertès (1951), Leonor Fini (1952), Carzou (1954), Georges Braque (1955), Salvador Dali (1958), Jacques Villon (1960) and Georges Mathieu (1961) contributed to the value of the Rothschild vintages. The labels on wines from Alsace, Provence, Roussillon, the Côtes du Rhône, the Jura and the province of Béarn also deserve honourable mentions while those from Champagne maintain a lordly grandeur. The label serves as a visiting card for the bottle's contents. It is both an advertisement and a pedigree, an indication of statuts, and an invitation to better acquaintance. It should attract yet impress, reflect the quality within and provide a visual foretaste of the gastronomic delights that lie in store. But, above all, it must be in keeping with the type of wine inside. It would scarcely be appropriate for a modest red wine to bear the glowing label of a vintage port, nor would a costly Chambertin be fittingly attired with the rough-and-ready label of a *vin ordinaire* to wash down a simple snack.

Labels also reflect national characteristics. The Swiss dress their bottles with typical reserve and delicacy. In France, character varies from one region to another. Alsace labels are restrained in colour, Champagne labels shine with gold, a splash of colours lights up those from Provence and Roussillon. Pouilly-Fumé, Muscadet and wines from the Loire reflect the clear sky above their homes and are circumspect in their attire. The labels of Côtes-du-Rhône shimmer with the sunshine of their birthplace, while Burgundies and Bordeaux maintain a non-committal dignity.

Spanish labels with their bright colours and bold lettering display a flamboyant nobility and Moorish richness. Rich as the wine from Oporto and sparkling as the "green wines" of their country, the Portuguese labels are as illuminated as old manuscripts. They feature saints and holy figures on stained glass windows, conquistadores portrayed in flame, blood-red and gold, as if to remind one of the accumulated riches in the treasure houses of Villanova de Gaya.

Italy surrounds its vermouths and chiantis in bright but less subtle colours. Sometimes its labels are unexpectedly quiet and subdued but this is more the exception than the rule. Those from Naples and Piedmont, Venice and Florence exude an extrovert, meridional flavour. Luxembourg labels are similar to those from Alsace and share, with the Rhine wines, the soft tints of their local skies.

Around the world, similar relationships exist between each country, its national characteristics, its wine and its labels to which, one hopes, artists will continue to contribute all their skills and imagination. They need have no fear of belittling their reputation.

WINE AND FOOD

FLAVIEN MONOD

Few housewives who pride themselves in the appearance of their home will leave it without flowers, however modest the bouquet. For very similar reasons, the master of the house will see to the proper care and stocking of his wine cellar. In both cases, it is knowledge and skill in selecting that makes the difference between an ordinary home and one brightened by a touch of colour and harmony—and the reward is the pleasure of sharing one of the joys of life.

A man's home may be his castle, as is frequently heard in Britain, but a house anywhere is a meeting place where friends and relations gather. The inside as well as the outside aspect reflects the taste of those who live there, reveals their personalities and shows to what extent they have acquired the art of living. A quick glance at the books on the shelves or the wines on the racks in the cellar can divulge many secrets. One meal may not reveal all, but it will serve to show whether the guest is made the object of special attention, with spontaneous gaiety and warmth, or whether he is merely the object of dutiful obligation.

Quite often, a posy of wild flowers or, as on the European Continent, a bunch of dried aromatic herbs is more appreciated than a sumptious basket of flowers arranged by strange, impersonal hands, or an overflowing store-bought cornucopia. Better often the warm, lively embrace of unsophisticated family repartee and sincere cordiality than the strained conventional social conversations. In the same way, a friendly little wine with its clean, simple taste and fresh colour in a humble bottle is sometimes better received than a famous vintage, heavily labelled and pretentious, decorated with the arms of some distant nobility.

THE DAILY TABLE WINE

How would you choose an "everyday" wine to drink with the family or share with an intimate friend? What is "a wine for everyday"? And what kind of wine is suitable for drinking with meals, every day, and to offer occasionally to those friends who don't need to be impressed with a showy label? Such a wine should quench the thirst, be light enough to drink deeply from brimming glasses and have a consistently reliable quality. Above all, it should be friendly and unpretentious. There is no need here to flatter a creation from the kitchen, or raise a meal to olympian heights; but at the same time, the wine should not quarrel with a dish. It should be accommodating, jovial, sympathetic and, above all, without after effects. Therefore it will not suffice to choose just any little *vin rosé* or red wine for this purpose without prior trial or testimonial. That innocent pink blush often conceals unpleasant surprises: drowsiness, heavy heads, and confused thoughts.

A light wine does not always mean a mediocre wine, just as simplicity does not always mean foolishness. A wine without frills can be a good companion to a quick meal. It can help work go smoothly, inspire goodwill and a genial disposition, all important qualities in our age of frenzied activity.

For everyday wines, we shall consider only light young red wines here. White wines and those of famous vintages are for other occasions. Naturally, personal taste plays its part here as in everything else. Anyone who lives a wine-producing region does not have far to look for suitable, often even excellent wines. Nor should hybrid wines be spurned. If they are chosen carefully they can reveal many attractive qualities. As a rough guide to local taste an Italian would probably opt for a light wine from Piedmont, the Spaniard for one from Galicia, while the favourite with a Portuguese would be a Colares, although it would be very difficult indeed to make a similar generalization for the French.

SOME SUGGESTIONS

From the wines of France, one would choose a light MÉDOC, POMEROL, a Beaujolais of the current year, a CÔTES DU VENTOUX, a CHÂTILLON EN DIOIS, a BOURGUEIL or a CHINON. From Italy, CHIANTI or VALPOLICELLA would fit the bill. From Spain, the choice would be one of the light reds of Galicia. If you know where to find a Swiss wine you cannot do better than ask for a SALVAGNIN.

FEASTS, FRIENDS AND FAMILY

Wine is the best of friends on any occasion. All over the world, the gathering of friends and family around the table on Sundays is synonymous with relaxation of body and freedom of the spirit. A family table is a friendly table and its preparation is inspired more by love, affection and friendship than by respect for form or etiquette. And to choose a wine for friends and relatives is one of those truly unselfish pleasures; pleasurable in itself, it gives pleasure to others.

In discussing the choice of wines, a few words on food are necessary. The passing years have happily eroded the habit of confusing quantity with quality, which often left guests so overstuffed as to be apoplectic and weak at the knees. A well-planned meal with a properly chosen wine should leave the wits clear and the shanks firm. Consider, for instance, a meal of hors-d'œuvres, a light entrée, a meat dish, vegetables, cheese and dessert. If the main dish is rich and heavy—a meat with a rich cream sauce, or game—then one of the other courses can be left out. Some people may also appreciate a light salad, and there is no need to fear the truism that salad does not go well with wine—this is the moment to serve a glass of fresh (but not iced) water. It is refreshing to the palate and makes a "taste interval" between the main wine and the wine served with the cheese. The dessert does not have to be a heavy dish but can be a pastry or, possibly, fresh fruit.

A simply chosen menu will influence the choice of wines. On the other hand, a very good way of choosing a menu is to plan it around some well-known wine which has reached its full and glorious maturity and thus becomes the focal point for the whole meal. The main dish is decided upon first and from this point one can go backwards and forwards through the menu. The wine can be from Burgundy, Bordeaux, Tuscany, Douro, Rioja or of even more exotic origins such as the Romanian Kadarka, the Yugoslavian Plavac, Naonassa from Greece or one of many others from all over the old and new worlds.

The most generally accepted and popular choice for the main wine is a red and if this be so then the main course should be red meat, a meat with rich sauce or a fowl. But this does not mean that a classic dry white wine cannot be served beforehand as a piquant overture. The tried and true belief that such a wine goes with such-and-such a dish still holds good. A more comprehensive guide to compatible wines and dishes can be gleaned from the lists which follow.

FAMILY REUNIONS

Family reunions usually fall into two main classifications; those with religious overtones and those which are simply social get-togethers. In the Anglo-Saxon world families naturally gravitate together at Christmas, for New Year celebrations, wedding anniversaries, birthdays and on other traditional occasions, but in Continental Europe families meet on any pretext, even if only to enjoy a good old unrestrained gossip. Wedding breakfasts and lunches, the receptions which follow, christenings and similar celebrations are traditionally formal, restrained and discreet. Although they should not be the occasion for gastronomic over-indulgence, the food may nevertheless be excellent and the wines of top quality. In such solemn circumstances the wines should be limited to three, a white wine and two reds. The classic rule still applies: progression in strength and richness throughout the meal.

Many changes can be rung on these three basic choices. If, for example, all the wines are to be from Burgundy then a dry white and two reds, the second being of greater body, can be chosen. All the wines can be from Bordeaux or from one cellar, in which case the host's pocket and knowledge guide his choice.

MENU BASED ON BURGUNDY

Concentrating on Côtes de Beaune

White	MEURSAULT, MONTRACHET
First red	POMMARD, SAVIGNY
Second red	PERNAND-VERGELESSE, ALOXE-CORTON

Concentrating on Côtes de Nuits

White	CLOS VOUGEOT BLANC
First red	CHAMBOLLE-MUSIGNY, FIXIN
Second red	ROMANÉE-CONTI, CLOS-VOUGEOT

MENU BASED ON BORDEAUX

White	DRY GRAVES
First red	MÉDOC, POMEROL
Second red	PAUILLAC, ST-ESTÈPHE, ST-EMILION

It is always pleasant to sit down to a well-laid table, which gives a foretaste of the joys to come: the bottle of Barbera Bersano goes very well with the prime ribs of beef, new potatoes and green beans.

A MENU FROM YOUR OWN CELLAR

Balancing three wines from your own stock depends on the size and variety of your cellar. At times like these one wishes one had been more courageous by investing in a few more bottles! But one should not be afraid to mix the vintages. There is no reason why a Swiss or German white cannot be followed by, say, a red Italian and then a Portuguese or Spanish red.

For special occasions when an unexpected meal with wine is required (and these can occur quite frequently), the meal may well be preceded by a good *brut* Champagne; but, it must be repeated, this should be served before the meal. In exceptional circumstances, Champagne could possibly be drunk before the coffee, but to serve it immediately afterwards would be bad taste and one of the few deadly sins left in this permissive age.

FORMAL DINNERS OR RECEPTIONS

Wine can make or break a formal dinner. Without its noble presence the whole affair would be much less memorable or spectacular. Its inherent prestige, the way it is handled, the care with which it is chosen, sets the seal on the dignity and the importance of the occasion. The most valuable wines play their regal part in a setting of good taste, impeccable manners and a relaxed if formal atmosphere. The house is a stage set to impress the guests and establish the mood. Serving plates, dishes, and glasses, silver and linen are all proudly on view. The food has been chosen and cooked with patience and care and now the guests have assembled. When they have had time enough to make or renew aquaintanceships they proceed to their places at the table. The memory of the predinner drinks fades from the fickle mind as the first wine makes its impressive entrance.

Bottles, opened beforehand, are brought from a cool store; the reds that have been breathing in the *chambré* atmosphere are brought to the fore. The term *chambré* can, as a reminder, bear some explanation here. It was adopted by our forbears and is somewhat of an anachronism today. Inside the thick stone walls of ancient and unheated houses, dining-rooms were much cooler in olden times. Today, with very rare exceptions, no wine can bear the temperature of a room where men may be wearing tropical weight suits or women can sit comfortably in low-cut evening or dinner dresses. It is as unthinkable to put a lump of ice into a glass of white wine as it is to serve an over-warm red wine.

It is taken for granted that most of the guests, if not experts, will be at least reasonably knowledgeable about wine. Their comments or even criticisms will not be judged out of place. Pertinent remarks will be appreciated by the host who will gladly reveal the wine's origin and pedigree as far as he knows it.

Professional tasting terms should be used with caution and accuracy. The technical vocabulary should simplify conversation and not complicate it. One can say, for example, that a great red wine has a beautiful colour, a strong bouquet of well-blended aromas, that it leaves a clean taste on the palate, that it is long with a lingering flavour. Never say that it is well-dressed (that means the label), that it has an agreeable perfume or a delicious taste. Say, if you must, that it has body and bouquet and that it will age well. Best of all, say that it has been selected by a true connoisseur and that little as you profess to know about the subject, you can appreciate its qualities. Everyone will then marvel at your modesty!

Returning to the first bottle on the menu, a white wine makes a good introduction to most meals. The quality must be carefully taken into account observing the golden rule which demands that no wine must ever make the palate regret the wine which precedes it. Thus the triumphant entry of a great white wine should not make the first red wine that follows it appear too modest in comparison. Wine, in all its nobility, has an inborn courtesy and should never intrude or attract attention to itself. A dinner should never be allowed to turn into a tiresome wine-tasting; there is a time and place for both. Like a well-mannered friend the wine's presence should not compete with, but should complement the subtle tastes produced with such care in the kitchen, or even ennoble them.

When four wines complement a meal they should progress from lightest to fullest in body, from humblest to noblest, from youngest to most mature, from first to last or, in other words, from better to better.

WHEN FRIENDS DROP BY

There is no doubt that the very appearance of a bottle of wine creates an atmosphere of relaxation. It creates a level on which people of like tastes can meet and informally pass the time. If the weatherman permits, then eating and drinking in the open air, having a picnic or a barbecue adds to the informality. Here all pretence is abandoned and a simple friendly meal is as enjoyable as something cooked with great care after many hours of preparation. Wine can even be served at a sausage party, preferably with the Vienna variety, as the grease on fried or grilled sausages does not combine well with wine.

Wines on these occasions should be able to stand up to unwonted extremes of temperature. There is no reason why such a party cannot be held with snow on the ground providing there is shelter from the wind. If one lives near or by a vineyard it is only a matter of buying what the local producers drink themselves in the same circumstances. These wines only need to be attractive, lively, gay, young and pleasant. Light whites, light reds, authentic *vin rosé* but not *pelure d'oignon*,

fruity or "flinty" wines, and dry white wines are good choices. Highly alcoholic wines should be avoided.

Popular wines for drinking in this open atmosphere are French white wines from the Loire or those from the Swiss canton of Vaud, the light SYLVANERS and the RIESLINGS from Alsace, or wines from the Rhine and Moselle districts. A *rosé* from Provence in France might be chosen, as would the pinkish wines of the Balearic Islands, the MAVROD from Bulgaria, or the CVICEK from Slovenia. There are innumerable reds of almost every nationality to choose from. They should be light in colour, fruity, and clean on the palate. They can come from places as far apart as Beaujolais and Austria, Périgord and California, where SANTA ROSA is a good example. Slightly sparkling natural wines are ideal at such times, whether they come from Anjou, Saumur, Touraine, Seyssel or Neuchâtel. The RIESLING ITALICA or LAMBRUSCO would be excellent.

Modern technology has come to the aid of the wine-lover: the portable ice-box or insulated container should be used whenever possible to carry the wines and to store them while they are being served. The wine warms up only too quickly in glasses held between the fingers, or in the sun. Of course, if you can lay hands on one, a small cask is a worthy centre-piece for any meal in the open, even if covered with old wet sacks soaked in brine to keep it cool or nestling on a bed of crushed ice. There is nothing like the sensation of drawing off a glass of wine from a wooden barrel.

WINE IN RESTAURANTS

A business lunch or a restaurant meal with friends is an important part of the eating-out habits of the modern male. For business lunches, most people want to order a contradiction in terms; a good meal, a light meal, and a quick meal. Accordingly, the special delights of the kitchen must sometimes be sacrificed. To make up for this, the wine may be carefully selected. The golden rule is, the simpler the better. Work in the afternoon prohibits the choice of wines that are too rich. Most wine waiters now appreciate this and have a good light wine which does not tend to put a client or an associate to sleep over his desk during the afternoon. Such after-effects are inclined to make the guest think twice before accepting another invitation.

It is just as well, however, to know how to read the wine list and not only the right-hand column! Those "little white wines" which "go down just like milk" can sometimes have a treacherous delayed action, whilst light red wines, for instance those with a high tannin content, are often more open and less insidious.

Dining with friends or entertaining a guest who is just passing through is quite a different matter. There is usually more time, and the whole night following for the constitution to recover. In these circumstances that favourite showplace of a restaurant or popular country inn can be just as important as the local architecture or the natural scenic beauty. Fewer limitations are imposed and a wide choice of carefully selected wines can show the guest he is not only welcome but appreciated. Of course, knowing the guest's tastes beforehand makes everything simpler. Knowing the restaurant and its cellar is a great help, too, as it is not always the most expensive or most well-known shipper's or château label which is best suited to the guest's palate or the host's pocket.

TALKING OVER WINE

When a friend drops in for a gossip, to put the world to rights or just to renew old aquaintance, wine can be a splendid change from the old, tired, spirit-based concoction of the cocktail era. As a matter of fact, some hosts, especially when dining out or even at business lunches, have taken to seating their guests at the table instead of standing by the bar, and serving them a light wine instead of an aperitif. The wine blends better with whatever is to follow and is less of a shock to the system than a potent iced mixture.

With a private cellar, following the habit of the continental European, it is a delightful practice to invite visitors to make their own choice of wine guided by a few words of expertise. The welcome offering of a bottle of wine, too, is always a compliment to the caller who brings it. For the casual visitor, the wine should be chosen for its personal history, such as one brought back from an interesting journey, or a particularly good year which is maturing in a bin; but whatever it is, it should be something special.

To talk over a bottle of wine is an experience. Conversation flows, stimulated by the quiet genie in the bottle which relaxes the mind and soothes the way to near-forgotten conversational delights. Choose wines

For high days and holidays, the menu will be longer and more elaborate, the wines carefully chosen. They are occasions to bring out one or ▷ another treasure from the cellar. On the following pages, the seafood dish is accompanied by a Rheingau wine, the leg of lamb with a superb Mouton-Rothschild, and the meal finished by pastries and vintage champagne.

485

that bring mental pictures of grapes harvested in distant places. Serve wines that have been bought for the cellar and not yet tasted. A new wine on a strange palate is a good opening for conversation.

This is the time to find out if the year fulfils its expected promise. These are the times to try the wines from Israel or Turkey, from Yugoslavia and Hungary. Their names sing an invitation to taste; TEKIGRAD, BOZCAADA, MÜREFTE, ELAZIG, and KOKINELLI from Cyprus, KOONAWARA from Southern Australia, STELLENBOSCH from South Africa, and EL TRAPICHE from the Argentine. It is the time when you can test out your guests' knowledge, their recognition of the wine regions, and their tastes for future occasions. You might even imbue them with your own enthusiasm for this fascinating subject, wine.

CHEESE AND WINE

It is well known that the taste of wine is at its most glorious with cheese. There are so many cheeses and so many wines that it would require an encyclopaedic work to marry them all. However, there is a general rule that certain cheeses go with certain wines, just as with other dishes, and classic partners are cited in this chapter, well-established after long aquaintance. Roquefort with a great red wine? Most certainly, but there are esoteric connoisseurs who sing the praises of Roquefort combined with MONTBAZILLAC. Who is to say? There is ample choice and the field is open for all tastes. Here is a general guide to the marriage of wines and cheeses:

Great, strong, robust and well-knit red wines from all regions: Danish blue, Gorgonzola, Roquefort, and Stilton.

Red wines of high to medium strength from all regions: Brie and Camembert.

Red wines of medium body and bouquet from Dalmatia, Médoc, Morgon, The Palatinate, and Tuscany: Maroilles, Livarot and Munster.

White wines and robust red wines from Bordeaux, Burgundy, Andalusia, Piedmont and Tunisia: Cheddar and Gruyère.

White wines, rosés, dry or fruity red wines from Beaujolais, Galicia, the Loire, Umbria, Savoy and Serbia: Cantal, Gouda, Hervé and Port-Salut.

Light and dry wines, local wines from the cheese-producing regions: goat cheese and dry cheese made from ewes' milk.

Apart from these, there are those cream and curd cheeses like Petits-Suisse which are served sprinkled with salt or sugar. Sweetened cheeses come to the table as desserts or with salads. White wines, rosé or light red wines on the dry side should be drunk with such world-famous cheese dishes as *fondue* or *raclette*.

There is little complication with cheese soufflés as the wine is chosen to suit the cheese on which the dish is based. Cheese savouries, most common on the Anglo-Saxon table and usually eaten at the end of the meal, can be accompanied by a sherry or a dry port.

The main wine served with the meat or game can equally well accompany the cheese, bearing in mind that it should not interfere with the good order of the hierarchy of the wines as the meal progresses.

SWEETS, DESSERTS AND WINES

As a general rule, wines are not desirable with sweet dishes. There are exceptions which are listed here, and they should be studied to complete a knowledge of wines and food. Under no circumstances should wine be served with aciduous fruits or any desserts containing chocolate in any form. Although this law should really not be transgressed, a little cheating is forgivable in some cases and authorities on the subject reluctantly admit there may be something to be said for the following combinations:

Soft and sweet wines: ALICANTE, BARSAC, LACHRYMA CHRISTI, MOSCATI DI PANTELLERIA, MARSALA ALEATICO, SAUTERNES, VINO SANTA.

Slightly sparkling sweet wines: ASTI SPUMANTE, BLANQUETTE DE LIMOUX, medium-dry CHAMPAGNE, CLAIRETTE DE DIE, may be drunk with cakes, biscuits, petits fours and tarts.

Red wines of medium body with a fruity bouquet with strawberries, raspberries and peaches.

Sweet, unfortified wines: FRONTIGNAN, MALVOISIE, MAVRODAPHI DE PATRAS, MOSCATEL with pastries without much cream.

It is not always possible to prevent someone from finishing their wine with the dessert, but with careful management the meal can be arranged so that the glass can be finished earlier. A good way around the problem is to provide a cool, but noticed, glass of fresh water and then, immediately after the sweet course, serve a dessert wine when the palate has been cleared. Frequently, those delicious dessert wines are forgotten: the good ports, Madeiras, Malaga and oloroso sherry, while the taste of a great MONTBAZILLAC is a pleasure and an experience not to be missed.

WINE IN FOOD

Countless recipes prescribe wine in making a sauce or for including in the cooking, as in casseroles or marinades. If a cheap *vin ordinaire* is not obtainable it always seems a pity to raid the cellar, but the accepted rule demands that the wine used in the cooking should be the same as that served on the table. However, here too a little cheating is permissible, and normally, a Riesling, a cheap Burgundy or a simple Côtes-du-Rhône will do well enough.

GREAT MENUS AND GREAT WINES

Old menus have more value as comparative history than as practical hints for the modern kitchen. Many explanations have been put forward for the continued decrease in the quantity of food consumed by guests at table. It may not be necessary but perhaps just as well to point out that in the days of the great banquets guests were only helped to a choice of the fifty or so courses served and were not obliged to eat their way through them all. However, it must be understood that social class structures were totally different from those of today and such menus were only served in baronial castles, in the palaces of royalty and the clergy, and the mansions of the rich leisured classes whose pleasures were mainly active and out of doors and entailed quite a lot more physical exercise and expenditure of energy than most of us know today.

Modern society has produced different pressures and the demands of work and hygiene have developed a more balanced, simplified and cleaner diet gradually to replace the gluttonies of yesteryear. However, it is to be hoped that our modern physical condition still allows us to do justice to the menu of a banquet.

ANCIENT MENUS

In the year 1656, a certain Madame la Chancelière invited Louis XIV to dinner at her château at Pontchartrain. The first course was composed of twenty-four dishes, including sixteen warm hors-d'œuvre, and eight rich soups. This was followed by eight plates bearing the meat that had been cooked in the soup and sixteen dishes of lean meat. The third course was made up of eight platters of roasts and sixteen dishes of vegetables prepared in the meat gravy. The fourth course offered the choice of eight pies, cold meat or fish and sixteen kinds of salads with oil, cream and butter. Last of all, twenty-four different pastries, twenty-four dishes of fresh fruit, twenty-four dishes of sweetmeats, preserves and sweet sauces. In all, 168 dishes or prepared plates were served, without counting the vas number of different desserts.

In this account by Prosper Montagné no mention is made of the wines served with the dinner. It does, however, give an indication of the abundance of the food served at the time of the Sun King, who was himself reputed to have an extraordinarily large appetite. The following menu, served to three great nineteenth-century figures, is nearer our subject and less shocking to our modern tastes:

Menu for the dinner of the "Three Emperors"
served to Alexander II, the Tsar and the King of Prussia
at the Café Anglais, Paris, June 7, 1867

Soups
Imperatrice, Fontanges

Removes
Soufflé à la Reine
Sole filets à la vénitienne
Turbot steaks au gratin
Saddle of mutton

Entrées
Poulets à la portugaise
Hot quail pie
Lobster à la parisienne
Champagne sorbet

Roasts
Duck à la rouennaise
Canapés of bunting

Wines
MADEIRA, RETURN FROM INDIA 1846
XÉRÈS 1821
CHÂTEAU YQUEM 1847
CHAMBERTIN 1846
CHÂTEAU MARGAUX 1847
CHÂTEAU LATOUR 1847
CHÂTEAU LAFITE 1848

Desserts
Aubergines à l'espagnole
Asparagus
Cassolettes princesse
Bombe glacée

Wines and cheese go very well together, and several possibilities are shown on the following pages: Beaujolais with soft cheese, a Swiss white wine with a hard, cooked cheese, a chianti with uncooked hard cheese, a white Rhine wine with a fresh young cheese, and a tasty claret with a cheese with herbs.

489

In this example the wines are mentioned, but the question arises as to what dish was served with which wine. Was the Château Yquem served with the soufflé, the buntings or the *bombe glacée*? One can guess or, better still, try them out. In the next menu there are still no details but the combinations are easier to guess.

Banquet held in the honour of
Emile Loubet, President of the French Republic,
on his return from Russia,
May 27, 1902,
at the invitation of the Conseil général du Nord, at Dunkirk.

Hors-d'œuvre à la Russe
Dunkirk salmon à la Flamande
Filet de Bœuf à la Parisienne
Jellied duck
Poularde du Mans à l'Estragon
Salade Jean-Bart
Suprêmes de Pêches and Greengage plums
à la Montmorency
Desserts

Wines
BARSAC
MÉDOC
CHÂTEAU GRUAND-LAROSE
MONTEBELLO FRAPPÉ
LIQUEURS

GREAT MENUS OF TODAY

WITH BURGUNDY

A meal based on Burgundy wines alone can combine all possible and imaginable variations. The choice of food can, as previously suggested, be guided by the wines. The MONTRACHET goes just as well with another fish entrée, while the Côte de Beaune wines, because of their good colour and reputation, marry well with strongly flavoured meats.

Salmon mousse
CHEVALIER-MONTRACHET

Ham à la Villandry
SAVIGNY-LÈS-BEAUNE

Fowl stuffed with truffles
Timbales Agnès Sorel
Mimosa Salad
RICHEBOURG

Sabayon au Madère
MADEIRA

WITH BORDEAUX

The great white wines of Bordeaux are not very well known but similar wines can be found outside France and have been mentioned in this book. In the following menu salmon mousse has been included for Bordeaux as well as, previously, for Burgundy. As for drinking a soft and sweet wine with *foie gras*, just try it and you will be convinced that it is an excellent combination.

Salmon mousse
CÔTES-DE-BLAYE

Crawfish tails au gratin
SAINTE-CROIX-DU-MONT SEC

Saddle of lamb
CHÂTEAU LAFITE

Parfait au foie gras
Crêpes fourrées
CHÂTEAU YQUEM

On special occasions, either official or private, dinners will follow the best traditions of gastronomy. An elegant and reputable restaurant may be able to provide a special room and service, together with all the resources of its kitchens and cellars, leaving you to create, as opposite, a symphony of wine and food that will delight your guests.

492

For an official or intimate dinner it is sometimes preferable to order according to the established gastronomic rules. A first-class and reputable restaurant can always provide a small separate room with service, and will supply all the needs from its kitchens and cellars. A good head waiter will be able to guide you in creating a symphony of wine and food which will enchant the guests so do not hesitate to consult him.

MENU WITH CHAMPAGNE

Champagne wines are either liked or disliked—it is a simple as that. If they are enjoyed then there is no further comment to be made and the following dishes are well-married to the wine.

Jellied filets of sole
AVIZE
Truffles in pastry
CRAMANT
Pheasant à la Bohémienne
MAREUIL-SUR-AY
Cardons à la moelle
Salade Aïda
BOUZY
Biscuit glacé Lyrique
MAILLY-CHAMPAGNE

MENUS WITH DIFFERENT WINES

Before dinner: CHAMPAGNE BRUT
Foie gras en croûte
CHAMPAGNE NATURE
Soufflé de truites Beauvilliers
ENTRE-DEUX-MERS-HAUT-BENAUGE
Prague Ham à la Chablisienne
POMMARD
Nest of Quails
Pommes Bonne-femme
Salades Béatrix
NUITS-SAINT-GEORGES
Nut cake
CHÂTEAU-CHALON

Médaillons de jambon Polignac
BLANC DE L'ETOILE
Crawfish tails à la mode du couvent de Chorin
MEURSAULT
Poulet de grain Jaqueline garniture Marie-Louise
Salade Orloff
POMEROL
Charlotte Royale
QUART-DE-CHAUME

Lobster and coconut salad
MÂCON BLANC
Timballe Sully
MARGAUX
Filets de bœuf Wellington
Samade Rachel
CHAMBOLLE-MUSIGNY
Diplomate chaud
VIN DE PAILLE

Langouste en Bellevue
PALETTE
Selle de chevreuil Grand Veneur
Timbales Maréchale
Salade Belle Hélène
GEVREY-CHAMBERTIN
Croûte à l'ananas
PINEAU DES CHARENTES

494

WINE AND TRAVEL

Unfortunately, not many people nowadays have the time, the means or the inclination to set off on a purely gastronomic journey. However, it may just be possible to arrange a business trip, a cultural or educational tour or even a relaxing holiday which takes in places famous for their blend of cellar and kitchen, whether they be towns, provinces or countries.

The itineraries suggested here are based on personal experiences and include some memorable possibilities. The choice of localities has been dictated more by the wines than food. If French provinces predominate, this is because France is the mother of wines, and there are many different regions which have their own typical vintages. All in all the names represent an imaginary journey across the Continent of Europe and a sampling of regional delicacies and specialities encountered all too rarely elsewhere.

Many of these specialities and wines, listed alphabetically to spare regional and national jealousies, are not widely known or acclaimed. Simple and exquisite, each dish is accompanied by a special wine and they are minor poems in casseroles and carafes.

ALSACE	Tokay from Alsace	White	Braised ham and apple crumble
	Gewürztraminer	White	Pheasant *à la Strasbourg*
ANJOU	Champigny	Red	*Bouilleture* (fish stewed in red wine and herbs)
AUSTRIA	Prälatenwein	White	Quetsche plums with almonds in pastry
AUVERGNE	Chanturgue	Red	Besse-en-Chandesse *coq au vin*
BEARN	Irouléguy	Red	Wild goat with mushrooms
BERRY	Châteaumeillant	Red	Pancakes with pork cracklings
BORDEAUX	Pomerol or Lalande de Pomerol	Red	Lamprey *à la bordelaise*
BOURBONNAIS	Saint-Pourçain	Red	*Truffat* (potato pie)
BURGUNDY	Passe-tout-grain	Red	Pigeon stew
	Beaujolais	Red	*Pot-au-feu* or *Bœuf-gros-sel*
BRITTANY	Muscadet	White	Rabbit cooked in Muscadet wine
BUGEY	Charveyron	Red	Bernardine ragout of woodcock
CORSICA	Sciaccarello	Red	*Coppa, figatello, lonzo* (cold meat specialities)
DAUPHINÉ	Jarjayes	White	*Poulet roussille*
FRANCHE-COMTÉ	Hypocras	Red	Baume-les-Dames quince cheese
GASCONY	Madiran	Red	*Sanguète de poulet*
GERMANY	Schloss Böckelsheimer Kupfergrube	White	Goose breasts grilled over vine shoots, sautéed potatoes and cranberry sauce
ITALY	Rocca-di-papa	White	Mozzarella in carrozza (toasted cheese and ham sandwich)
	Chianti	Red	Beefsteak *alla Fiorentina*
	Vino Nobile di Montepulciano	Red	*Osso buco*
LANGUEDOC	Minervois	Red	Mourtayrol (boiled beef, chicken and ham with saffron)
LORRAINE	Gris de Pagny-sur-Moselle	White	Boulay frogs *au gratin*
LYONS	Beaujolais of the year	Red	Stuffed veal
ORLEANS	Cour Cheverny	White	Montargis mushrooms on toast
PÉRIGORD	Côtes de Duras	Red	Goat's cheese
PORTUGAL	Moscatel de Setubal	White	*Doce d'ovos* (dessert made from egg yolks)
PROVENCE	Taradeau	White	Snails *à la suçarelle*
SAVOY	Princess-Rocheray	Red	Pork cooked in wine with a cream sauce
SPAIN	Ribeiro	White	Octopus stewed in its own ink
SWITZERLAND	Dézaley	White	Liver sausage
	Abbaye de Mont	White	Filet of perch

WINE MUSEUMS

PHOTOGRAPHIC CREDITS

ACKNOWLEDGEMENTS

The Publisher extends his warmest thanks to the Curators of Museums and libraries,
the Directors and Administrators of official organizations or private societies and the collectors who have
helped in the preparation of this work. Special thanks are due to:

Israelian Embassy, Bern; Pierre Androuët, Paris; Piero Antinori, Florence; François des Aulnoyes, Centre National de Coordination, Paris; Dr von Bassermann-Jordan'sches Weingut, Deidesheim; Ferdinando de Bianchi, Madeira Wine Association Ltd., Funchal; Bouchard Père & Fils, Beaune; Louis Philippe Bovard, Office de propagande pour les vins vaudois, Lausanne; Carlos Cavero Beyart, Presidente del Sindicato Nacional de la Vid, Madrid; Champagne Mercier, Epernay; Champagne Perrier-Jouët, Epernay; Champagne Taittinger, Reims; Jacques Chevignard, Grand Chambellan de la Confrérie des Chevaliers du Tastevin, Nuits-Saint-Georges; Cockburn Smithes & Co. Lda, Vila Nova de Gaia; Comité Interprofessionnel du Vin d'Alsace, Colmar; Comité Interprofessionnel des Vins à Appellation Contrôlée de Touraine, Tours; Companhia Geral da Agricultura das Vinhas do Alto Douro "Real Companhia Velha", Vila Nova de Gaia; Confrérie Saint-Etienne d'Alsace, Colmar; Confrérie des Vignerons de Saint Vincent, Mâcon; Confrérie des Vignerons Vevey; Conseil Interprofessionnel des Vins d'Anjou et de Saumur, Angers; Consejo Regulador de la Denominación de Origen Jerez, Jerez de la Frontera; Consejo Regulador de la Denominación de Origen Panadés, Vilafranca del Panadés; Consejo Regulador de la Denominación de Origen Rioja, Logroño; Il Corriere Vinicolo, Rome; J.M. Courteau, Conseil Interprofessionnel du Vin de Bordeaux, Bordeaux; J. Dargent, Comité Interprofessionnel du Vin de Champagne, Epernay; Kemalettin Demirer, Turkish Embassy, Bern; Manuel Cotta Dias, Junta Nacional lo Vinho, Lisbon; Pedro Domecq S.A., Jerez; Joseph Drouhin, Beaune; H. Dubosq, Saint-Estèphe; J. Faiveley, Nuit-Saint-Georges; F.A.O., Rome; Héritiers Fourcaud-Laussac, Saint-Emilion; P. Fridas, sous-directeur Office International de la Vigne et du Vin, Paris; Pierre Galet, Ecole Nationale Supérieure Agronomique de Montpellier, Montpellier; Garvey S.A., Jerez Gonzalez, Byass & Co. Ltd., Jerez; Dr Heger, Ihringen; Juliusspital-Weingut, Würzburg; A.S. Hogg, Peter Dominic Limited, London; Dr. Harry Kühnel, Archivdirektor, Krems a.d. Donau; Restaurant Ledoyen, Paris; Henri Leyvraz, Station fédérale d'essais agricoles, section de viticulture, Lausanne/Pully; Madame Edmond Loubat, Pomerol; Henri Maire, Arbois; Manuel & Cie S.A., Lausanne; Dr A. Miederbacher, Unione Italiani Vini, Milan; Moët & Chandon, Epernay; Jean Mommessin, Mâcon; Monimpex, Budapest; G.H. Mumm & Co., Reims; New Zealand High Commission, London; H.F.M. Palmer, Adelaide; Dr Adolf Paulus, Museum für die Geschichte des Weines, Rüdesheim; Americo Pedrosa Piros de Lima, Instituto do Vinho do Porto, Porto; Porcelaine Limoges-Unic, Paris; R. Protin, Directeur de l'Office International de la Vigne et du Vin, Paris; Joh. Jos. Prüm, Wehlen; C. Quittanson, Inspecteur Divisionnaire du Service de la Répression des Fraudes et du Contrôle de la Qualité, Ministère de l'Agriculture, Dijon; Real Companhia Vinicola do Norte de Portugal, Vila Nova de Gaia;

Représentation Commerciale de l'U.R.S.S. en Suisse, Bern; Gilbert Rohrer, Lausanne; Roth & Sauter, Lausanne; Baron Philippe de Rothschild, Mouton-Rothschild; Fritz Salomon, Präsident des Österreichischen Weininstituts, Vienna; Sandeman Bros. & Co., Jerez; José Augusto dos Santos, Casa de Portugal, Paris; Francisco Sanz Carnero, Dirección General de Agricultura, Madrid; Antonio Carlos Sarmento de Vasconcellos, Instituto do Vinho do Porto, Porto; Dr Karl Schultz, Konservator, Historisches Museum der Pfalz, Speyer; Antonio José da Silva Vinhos, S.A.R.L., Vila Nova de Gaia; Jean-Louis Simon, Station fédérale d'essais agricoles, section de viticulture, Lausanne/Pully; Société Civile du Domaine de la Romanée-Conti, Vosne-Romanée; Société Vinicole Perroy S.A., Epesses; Société des Domaines Woltner, Bordeaux; Staatliche Lehr- und Versuchsanstalt für Wein- und Obstbau, Weinsberg; Staatsweingut, Weinbaulehranstalt, Bad Kreuznach; Syndicat régional des Vins de Savoie, Chambéry; Szende László, Orszagos Borminösitö Intézet, Budapest; J. Thorin, Pontanevaux; E. Tomov, Embassy of the Republic of Bulgaria, Bern; Johann Traxler, Österreichisches Weininstitut, Vienna; Verwaltung der Staatsweingüter im Rheingau, Eltville; Veuve Clicquot-Ponsardin, Reims; Wente Bros., Livermore, California; Fred Wick, Vevey; Dr Robert Wildhaber, Basel; Williams & Humbert Ltd., Jerez; Terence McInnes, The Wine Institute, San Francisco; Leo Wunderle, Lucerne; Zoilo Ruiz-Mateos S.A., Jerez.

The colour maps were drawn by Robert Flach, from documents and information provided by:

Pierre Forgeot, Beaune; Office International de la Vigne et du Vin, Paris; Office de propagande pour les vins vaudois, Lausanne; Fédération des Vins de Savoie, Chambéry; Comité Interprofessionnel des Vins des Côtes du Rhône, Avignon; Comité Interprofessionnel des Vins à Appellation Contrôlée de Touraine, Tours; Conseil Interprofessionnel des Vins d'Anjou et de Saumur, Angers; Conseil Interprofessionnel des Vins de Bordeaux; Comité Interprofessionnel du Vin d'Alsace, Colmar; Consejo Regulador de la Denominación de Origen Jerez, Jerez de la Frontera; Consejo Regulador de la Denominación de Origen Rioja, Logroño; Dirección General de Agricultura, Madrid; Instituto do Vinho do Porto, Porto; Verkehrsverein Rüdesheim; Österreichisches Weininstitut, Vienna; Wine Institute, San Francisco; Comité Interprofessionnel du Vin de Champagne, Epernay.

English translations by Michael and Angela Kelly, Pully, Switzerland, Peter Dewhirst, I.T.E.S., Geneva, Tim Chilvers and Simon Fear, Edita Lausanne.

LIST OF COLOUR MAPS

WINE INDEX

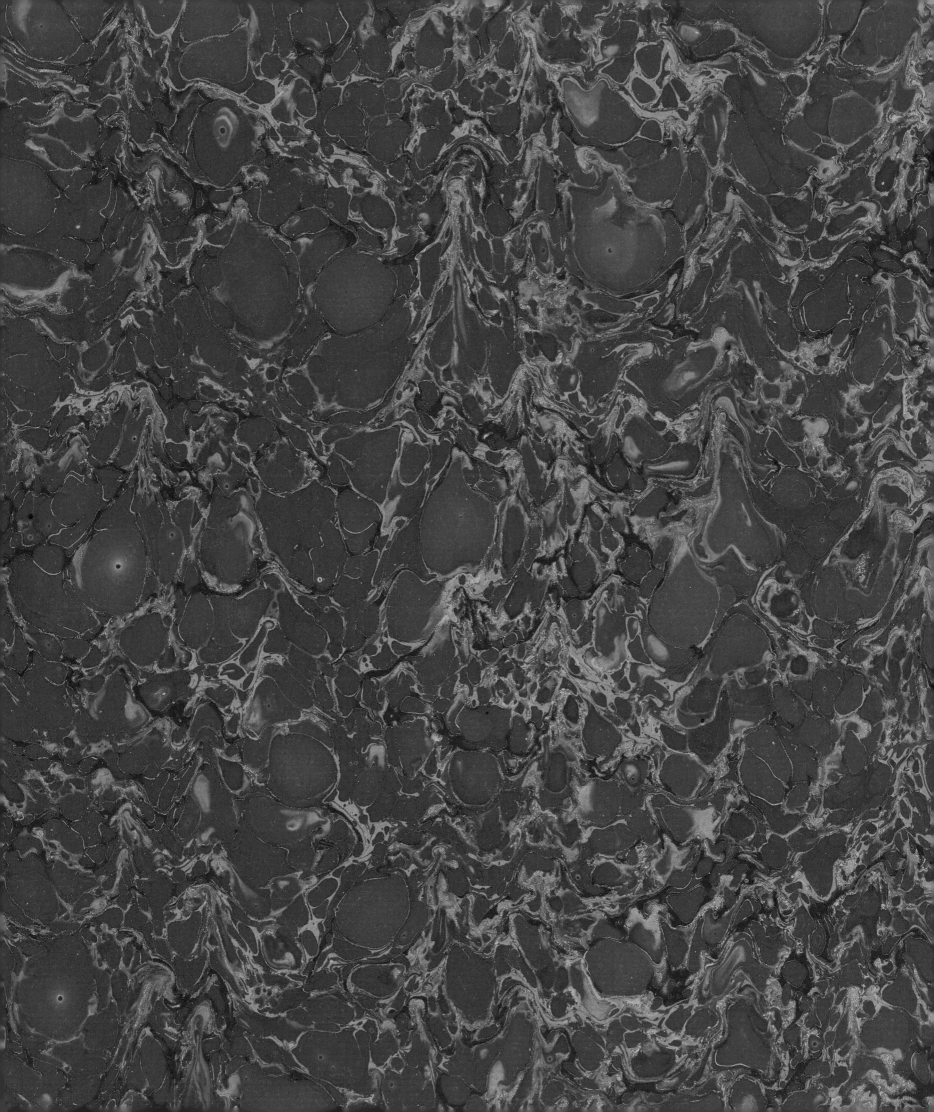